ART
THROUGH THE AGES

AN INTRODUCTION TO ITS
HISTORY AND SIGNIFICANCE

BY

HELEN GARDNER, A·M

IN CHARGE OF INSTRUCTION
IN HISTORY OF ART IN
THE SCHOOL OF THE ART INSTITUTE
OF CHICAGO

NEW YORK
HARCOURT, BRACE & COMPANY

PREFACE

THE purpose of this book is to introduce the reader to certain phases of art — architecture, painting, sculpture, and the minor arts — from the remote days of the glacial age in Europe, through the successive civilizations of the Near East, Europe, America, and the Orient, to the twentieth century. The material as here presented has been developed from the History of Art course given in the School of Art of the Art Institute of Chicago; and while the book has been written primarily for an introductory course in educational institutions, it is hoped that it will prove useful also for the general reader and traveler.

The organization of the material is somewhat different from that usually found in works on this subject. Hence one purpose of the book is to serve as a method of study and of teaching. This organization is based first on the chronological order (FIG. 132). Each civilization contains so many elements from the preceding age that it is incomprehensible without a knowledge of that age. The only exception to this is the ancient American and Oriental art, in which the influences from Europe are so uncertain, and so essentially minor as far as the significant quality of the best art is concerned, that the chapters devoted to these subjects have been placed by themselves at the end of the book.

Each era is studied as a unit of culture. A brief historical survey suggests the most important conditions that have influenced the art — geography, climate, nature of material; social, economic, and political conditions; and religious beliefs. Following this introductory matter is a discussion and analysis of a few typical examples of architecture, sculpture, painting, and the minor arts, in varying order and occasionally with omission of some member in the classification, for not every age produced equally in all, and in so restricted a volume only the highest points can be touched. A brief summary then presents the aesthetic significance of the period as a whole.

In regard to the classification outlined above, a word is necessary both of caution and of explanation. A classification is a convenient way of outlining work, but, in the case of art especially, should be used only with the understanding that works of art cannot be classified dogmatically; they are too closely inter related for that. The statue may be a decoration of a building, an integral part of the structure and determined by it. The painting frequently decorates a great wall surface or the page of a manu script and much of its composition and color is determined by its use and its technique. The stained-glass window plays it part in the whole interior ensemble and is not merely an example of the minor arts. Until within the last two hundred year artists were craftsmen and frequently one man pursued several crafts equally well. Pheidias was painter as well as sculptor Leonardo was engineer, musician, painter, and sculptor; Piero della Francesca was a mathematician; in fact, in the Renaissance it was the rule and not the exception that a man could, for example, build a palace, carve a statue, paint a ceiling, and design and execute a piece of jewelry. Individualism and speciali zation are modern. Until recent times the differentiation so frequently heard of "major" and "minor" did not exist.

By the term minor arts we designate jewelry, books and manu scripts, textiles, furniture, ceramics, the work of the goldsmith and ivory carver — all that world of smaller objects, minor only in size, through which creative ability has found abundant ex pression and for which there seems to be no adequately inclusive term.[1]

With these qualifications, the method here followed, it has been found, enables the student to develop a broader and deeper capacity of appreciation and understanding and also to make a more vital correlation among all fine arts: to read Homer in the light of Minoan art; to feel the music and the dance of India in Rajput painting and in the Khmer reliefs; to read the thoughts and aspirations of the Middle Ages in the Gothic cathedral; the Romantic movement of the nineteenth century in Delacroix; and the poetry of China in Chinese landscape painting.

In order to cover so vast a field in one volume, unsparing elim ination has been necessary; each age must be treated as a whole, and only significant movements considered. For this reason bio graphical details and amusing but irrelevant anecdotes have been almost entirely omitted and even well-known artists left unmen tioned, as this kind of material can easily be found in most libra ries. Controversial questions of attribution and influences have also been omitted as belonging properly to specialized books.

---

[1] "Allied arts," "crafts" or "handicrafts," "derivative arts," and "industrial arts" have also been used.

The space thus gained has been used for a fuller analysis than is usual of the few works discussed, in the belief that the thorough study of a few works is more helpful than the recital of many names and dates.

In a general survey of the arts of all ages, the accomplishment of the last two decades hardly finds a place. Any attempt to evaluate it is bound to be tentative, as the great difference of opinion has already proved, especially in view of the fact that these decades have been an age of restlessness and transition in all aspects of life. Hence this survey has been brought only to about the beginning of the twentieth century. A final chapter, however, has been added, suggesting some of the conditions that underlie the general art movements of the period, together with a bibliography of current literature, in order that each may judge and evaluate for himself.

An indispensable part of the study of art is illustration. No work, therefore, is seriously discussed for which there is no illustration for reference; and a list is appended of sources where inexpensive reproductions of supplementary illustrative material, often in color, may be obtained.

The bibliography at the end of each chapter and the list of periodicals have been compiled with a well equipped but not specialized art library in mind. Hence rare and costly books have been omitted, and among the works in foreign languages only a few which are inexpensive and particularly desirable for their illustrations have been included.

The writing of a book of so general a nature and the gathering and sifting of the large amount of material necessary in the process, is impossible for one person working alone. Hence it is with a sense of genuine appreciation that the author wishes to extend her thanks to the many friends, colleagues, students, museums, and publishers who have made the undertaking possible: for suggestions and criticism on the manuscript to Dr. T. G. Allen, Dr. J. H. Breasted, Dr. W. E. Clark, Dr. Edith Rickert, Prof. Walter Sargent, and Dr. E. H. Wilkins, of the University of Chicago; Mr. Robert B. Harshe, Mr. Charles F. Kelley of the Art Institute, Miss S. Louise Mitchell of the Ryerson Library, and Mr. Ernst Detterer of the Printing Arts Department of the School of the Art Institute. The serious problem of procuring suitable material for the illustrations was appreciably lightened by the special courtesies on the part of the Art Institute of Chicago, Boston Museum of Fine Arts, Dr. Jean Capart, Dr. Ananda K. Coomaraswamy, the India Office, Dr. Clarence Kennedy, Dr.

Berthold Laufer, Metropolitan Museum of New York, Musé
de Cluny, Musée Indo-Chinois, Mr. Parish-Watson, Mr. C. L
Ricketts, Mr. Martin A. Ryerson, Victoria and Albert Museum
and Miss Carolyn Wicker. To Haskell Oriental Museum of th
University of Chicago the author wishes to express thanks fo
the most helpful assistance with the illustrations of Egyptia
subjects; and to the Ryerson Library of the Art Institute of Chi
cago for its unlimited generosity in the use of its photograph col
lection. Specific mention of photographic sources is indicate
with the illustrations.

As the sources of illustrations reproduced from publication
could be but briefly indicated on the plates, full acknowledgmen
is here recorded and appreciation for courtesies extended:

To the American Museum of Natural History and Dr. H. J. Spinden for Figs. 10
and 114 from *Ancient Civilizations of Mexico and Central America;* to Karl Baedeker fo
Fig. 32 from *Egypt;* to B. T. Batsford Ltd. for Pls. 25C and 52B from Anderson an
Spiers, *Architecture of Greece and Rome,* Pl. 140B from Swarbrick, *Lives and Work o
Robert and James Adam,* Fig. 100 from Anderson, *Architecture of the Renaissance i
Italy,* Fig. 105 from Garner and Stratton, *Domestic Architecture of England Durin
the Tudor Period;* to G. Bell and Sons Ltd. for Pl. 139B from Blomfield, *History o
Renaissance Architecture in England;* to Ernest Benn Ltd. and Messrs Kendrick an
Tattersall for Fig. 86 from Kendrick and Tattersall, *Handwoven Carpets;* to the
British Museum for Pl. 24D from Dalton, *Treasure of the Oxus,* Pls. 40A and 41A
from Smith, *Sculptures of the Parthenon,* Pl. 77D from Millar, *Lindisfarne Gospels*
and Fig. 64 from Smith, *Catalogue of Greek and Etruscan Vases in the British Museum,*
to the British School at Athens for Pl. 25A and Figs. 43, 44, and 45 from the
British School Annual; to F. Bruckmann for Pls. 30, 31, and 43 from Furtwängler-
Reichhold, *Griechische Vasenmalerei;* to Cambridge University Press for Pl. 49C from
Minns, *Scythians and Greeks;* to Bruno Cassirer for Pl. 8B from Fechheimer, *Die
Plastik der Aegypter,* Pls. 24C and 70B from Sarre, *Die Kunst der alten Persien;* to
Chapman and Hall for Pl. 24A from Perrot and Chipiez, *History of Art in Persia,*
and Fig. 17 from Perrot and Chipiez, *History of Art in Ancient Egypt;* to the Clarendon
Press for Fig. 55 from Percy Gardner, *Catalogue of Greek Vases in the Ashmolean
Museum;* to the Cleveland Museum of Art and the Yale University Press for Pl. 172;
to the Egypt Exploration Society for Pls. 4B and 12C, from the *Journal of Egyptian
Archaeology,* Pl.9C and Figs. 29 and 30 from Naville, *Temple of Deir el Bahari,* Pl. 13A
and Figs. 35 and 36 from Newberry, *Beni Hasan;* to the Field Museum of Natural
History for Figs. 109, 110, and 111 from Holmes, *Archaeological Studies Among the
Ancient Cities in Mexico,* and Fig. 129 from Laufer, *Jade;* to Hachette et Cie. for
Figs. 47 and 48 from Perrot and Chipiez, *Histoire de l'art dans l'antiquité;* to J. C. Hin-
richs for Pl. 3A and B from Hoelscher, *Das Grabdenkmal des Königs Chephren,* Pl. 4A
from Borchardt, *Das Grabdenkmal des Königs Sahure,* Pl. 6B from Steindorff, *Das
Grab des Ti,* Fig. 39 from Andrae, *Der Anu-Adad Tempel,* and Fig. 42 from Koldewey,
Das Ishtar-Tor in Babylon; to U. Hoepli for Pl. 26C from *Monumenti Antichi* and
Pl. 60B from Muñoz, *Il Rotulo di Giosué;* to E. Houvet for Pls. 81 and 82B–D from
Cathédral de Chartres and *Monographie de la Cathédral de Chartres;* to the India Society
for Pl. 163B and C from Herringham, *Ajanta Frescoes;* to the Japanese Government
for Pls. 170C, 171, 173A and C, and Fig. 131; to *Kokka* for Pl. 173B; to John Lane for
Pl. 126C from Calvert, *Goya;* to H. Laurens for Fig. 28 from Benoit, *L'Architecture. Antiquité,* and Fig. 62 from Morin-Jean, *Le Dessin des animaux en Grèce;*

E. Leroux for Pl. 82A from *Monuments Piot;* to the Macmillan Company for
. 49B; to Masson et Cie. for Pl. 1C and Fig. 3 from Piette, *L'Art pendant l'age du
nne;* to Methuen and Company Ltd. for Pl. 77C from Herbert, *Illuminated Manu-
ripts;* to the Morgan Library and the Burlington Fine Arts Club for Pl. 48C from
n Exhibition of Ancient Greek Art; to John Murray for Pl. 102B from Berenson,
Drawings of the Florentine Painters and Figs. 122 and 123 from Fergusson, *History
* *Indian and Eastern Architecture;* to R. Oldenbourg for Figs. 46 and 74B from
.uckenbach, *Kunst und Geschichte;* to *Ostasiatische Zeitschrift* for Fig. 128; to the
British School of Archaeology in Egypt and Sir W. M. Flinders Petrie for Pl. 14B
:om *Tell el Amarna;* to A. Picard et Fils for Figs. 4 and 14 from Déchelette, *Manuel
'archéologie préhistorique* and Figs. 126 and 127 from Paléologue, *L'Art Chinois;* to
3. P. Putnam's Sons and the Medici Society Ltd. for Fig. 113; to B. Quaritch for
°l. 174A from Taki, *Three Essays on Oriental Painting;* to D. Reimer for Pl. 70A
:om Sarre und Hertzfeld, *Archäologische Reise im Euphrat-u. Tigris-Gebiet;* to the
Society for the Promotion of Hellenic Studies for Fig. 50; to the University Museum
of Philadelphia for Pl. 28B and Fig. 52 from Seager, *Excavations on the Island of
Pseira, Crete;* to Ernst Wasmuth for Pls. 64B and 71A from Lessing, *Die Gewebe-
Sammlung des K. Kunstgewerbe-Museums,* and Figs. 33 and 34 from Borchardt, *Die
Aegyptische Pflanzensäule;* to Yale University Press and Dr. G. G. MacCurdy for
Figs. 115 and 116; to Yale University Press and Prof. A. K. Porter for Fig. 87.

For the drawings in the text the author is indebted to her students: Marjorie H. Batchelder, Edward Gressendorf, Electra
Papadopoulos, and Edith Sternfeld; for the drawing of the
chronological chart, to her colleague, Mr. Lloyd Cowan; and for
assistance upon the bibliographies, proof, and index, to Marion F.
Williams.

By no means the least source of genuine appreciation, especially
in the light of the difficult problems involved in handling so large
a scheme of illustration, have been the unfailing patience and
generous coöperation of the publishers.

                                                    HELEN GARDNER

CONTENTS

CONTENTS

LIST OF COLOR PLATES

ART THROUGH THE AGES

CHAPTER I

PREHISTORIC PERIOD IN EUROPE

From Earliest Times to c. 2000 B.C.

A. PALEOLITHIC AGE

From Earliest Times to c. 10,000 B.C.

HISTORICAL BACKGROUND

In the long development of man's life upon earth, when did art first appear? What was the character of man's earliest effort? Was it childishly crude, or was it in any way comparable to those accomplishments which the world has looked upon as its greatest? Until recently, the story of human life upon earth was thought to have been short, perhaps a few thousand years at the most. But the researches of the last half-century have shown that instead of those few thousand years, vastly remote ages lie behind us, along which man by amazingly slow evolution has reached the stage of culture at which we now see him.

In 1879 a Spaniard who was interested in this problem was exploring in a cave on his estate at Altamira in northern Spain, searching for further examples of flint and carved bone, for already he had found such relics in this cavern. With him was his little daughter. As the cave was dark, he was working by the light of a lamp, while the child was scrambling over the rough rocks. Suddenly she called out, "Bulls! Bulls!" pointing to the ceiling, so low that he could touch it with his hand. To satisfy the child, he lifted his lamp and there saw on the uneven surface numbers of bison and other animals drawn with great realism and painted in bright colors. When the discovery was published and the painting declared to be the work of men who lived ages ago, people shook their heads; and, for a while, the skeptics had their way. "Impossible," they said. "The work is too good and the color too fresh; some erratic person of recent years has done this for some unknown purpose." Slowly, however, the belief began to grow among a few people that all these things were revealing ages of far greater antiquity than man had ever dreamed of. Slowly skepticism broke down and further great discoveries have yielded enough evidence for us to catch a glimpse of man and his activities in this remote age.

Europe, at the time of earliest man, was quite different from what it is today.[1] This continent, like America, has experienced four glacial epochs, with periods of subsidence of the land in glacial times and elevation in interglacial, when England, Ireland, Scandinavia, and Africa were connected with it; the North Sea and the English Channel were river valleys; and the Mediterranean Sea was broken into two inland lakes. The climate during the interglacial periods was warm and moist. In the tropical jungles roamed the elephant, rhinoceros, and hippopotamus, and on the high plateaus the wild horse, boar, and ibex. As the glacier approached and the climate changed, the animals migrated or adapted themselves; and we find in the cold periods the shaggy mammoth and the reindeer. These changes, we must remember, came about very slowly, hundreds of thousands of years elapsing during one transition only from warm to cool.

Earliest man in Europe was a creature without clothing and without fire, and had only a wooden implement to protect himself and to secure food. With such a weapon it was the smaller animals only that he could combat. This food he ate raw, until he discovered fire, perhaps as the lightning cleft a tree and started flames in the dry leaves of the forest; or as the red-hot lava burst from the crater of

a volcano. This was one of his important discoveries. Another was the use of stone to take the place of his wooden implement. Now he was equipped to protect himself better, to obtain his food more easily, and to live more comfortably. This epoch we call the Early Stone or Paleolithic Age. The earliest successful weapon that he fashioned was a fist-hatchet (FIG. 1), which is so shaped that he could grasp it securely at the smaller end and use the larger for striking or crude cutting. It was probably only after long ages of experimentation in chipping stone that he evolved this implement.[2]

Fig. 1. Flint Fist-Hatchet. L. 7½ in. British Museum, London.

As the ice descended for the fourth and last time, perhaps about

[1] For maps to illustrate this chapter, see Osborn, *Men of the Old Stone Age*, and Breasted, *Ancient Times*.

[2] The best authorities differ widely on the dates for this period. Osborn puts the date of the first hatchet 125,000 years ago; other authorities, not less than 50,000 years.

thirty thousand years ago, the climate became chilly. Reindeer were abundant, a fact that suggests the name sometimes given to the period — the Reindeer Age. Man, like the animals, migrated or adapted himself to the change, finding shelter in caves or under shelving rocks, and clothing himself with the skins of the larger animals that he now could more easily overcome with his stone weapons. For in the long ages since he first evolved his fist-hatchet he had made a

Fig. 2. Flint Implements of the Chase, Fishing, and Industry. L. 2–4 in.

great advance in the number and quality of his tools (FIG. 2). He had learned how to make knives with stems for attaching a wooden handle, spear-heads, awls, drills, and fine points for engraving, all of which were carefully shaped with a feeling for symmetry. The fine edges and points were made by pressing against the stone with a piece of bone, rather than by chipping it with stone, the method used in making the fist-hatchet. These tools were sharp enough to cut bone, ivory, and horn, from which men now fashioned implements and weapons of the chase, for they were primarily hunters in this last cold period.

MINOR ARTS

Fig. 3. Dart-Thrower. Of reindeer horn. L. 10½ in. (Piette)

One of the important implements of this early age was the dart-thrower (FIGS. 3 and 4), into which the hunter inserted the spear so as to increase the power of his arm in hurling the weapon. The noticeable thing about the dart-thrower is its decoration: the bone has been carved into the shape of an antelope, and very skillfully the animal form has been adapted to the cylindrical surface of the implement, the curved horns encircling the shape snugly and the whole forming an appropriate and effective piece of decoration.

It is in these implements of the Reindeer Age that we find o
first works of art; and we notice that they are the everyda
things of life, embellished.

The purpose of the *Head of a Whinnying Horse* (PL. 1C) is ur

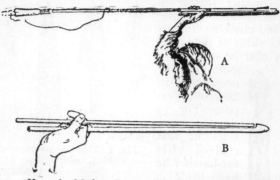

Fig. 4. How the Modern Eskimo (*A*) and the Australian (*B*)
Use the Dart-Thrower. (Déchelette)

known, for it is a fragment. This tiny work well expresses the
spirit of the wild horse, a few firm lines revealing all the essentia
features of form and spirit. And this was done, we must remember, with only a piece of flint for an instrument. In the *Chargin*

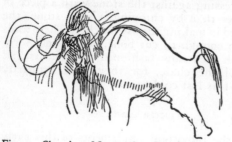

Fig. 5. Charging Mammoth. Engraved on a
piece of ivory tusk. (De Mortillet)

Mammoth (FIG. 5) we
have the entire figure
in silhouette, with no
indication of perspec-
tive, and with two legs
only. The huge
monster is infuriated,
with head and tail
raised in anger. Yet
only a few essential
lines have been used to
indicate the form, both
as a structure and as an

expression of the angry passion that dominates it. There is no
shading, no unnecessary detail, no background.

In contrast to the vigorous movement of the wild horse and
the raging mammoth, we find in the *Grazing Reindeer* (FIG. 6) a
quiet aspect of animal life. How truthfully is expressed the weight
of the head, heavy with the great antlers, as the animal lowers

it to browse. There is an advance over the mammoth in the drawing, for here the four legs are indicated and very naturalistically too. Keenly the hunter had watched the reindeer, observing the position of each part of the body as the animal bent its head, retaining all the essential lines in his memory until, with his flint point, he could express the image on the piece of horn. The sketchy suggestion of landscape in the foreground is unique in this art. In the *Herd of Reindeer* (FIG. 7), at the right the artist has sketched the complete figures of three animals and, at the left, one. To indicate the remainder of the herd he has selected the most characteristic feature, the antlers, exaggerating their size, to be sure, and has indicated the bodies by short strokes. By

Fig. 6. Grazing Reindeer. Engraved around a piece of reindeer antler. L. 5 in. (Heim)

means of these few significant lines he has given us an amazingly naturalistic impression of the whole herd.

PAINTING

In the examples at which we have been looking, the subject matter has been restricted to animal life used in the decoration of small implements and personal belongings. To see examples of painting, we must go to the caves of southern France and northern Spain, where the hunters of the Reindeer Age sought shelter from the cold. These caverns are subterranean water channels varying in length from a few hundred to four thousand feet and are now choked in many places by deposits, rubbish, and stalactites, and hence difficult to explore.

FIG. 8 reproduces an early work, the picture of an elephant drawn with red crayon on the walls of a cave. It is the simplest outline possible, with only two legs shown, no details, no light and shade, no perspective. Yet there is no doubt in our minds as to what animal is represented, so convincingly does the line indi-

Fig. 7. Herd of Reindeer. Engraved on the wing bone of an eagle.
L. 8 in. (Capitan and Breuil)

cate the essential characteristics. The question as to whether this work is childlike can perhaps be answered by placing the drawing of an average child beside this elephant. Many similarities will be found — the profile outline with no accessories such as a background, and with great economy of line. But this economy of line in the drawing of the Reindeer Age artist reveals a maturity of observation, a marvelous power of memory, and a grasp of essentials quite lacking in the child's drawing.

Fig. 8. Elephant. H. 18 in. Pindal Cave, Spain. (Alcalde del Río)

Gradually the hunters became more facile in the rendering of these animal forms. Sometimes they incised them on the stone walls with a piece of sharp flint, sometimes they drew them with pieces of red or yellow chalk, the used stubs of which have been discovered on the cave floors; and sometimes they painted them, mixing their pigment with animal fat and using the shoulder-blade of a reindeer for a palette. An example of this last method is the *Bison* (PL. 1 A), in which we discern the heavy bulkiness and stolidity so characteristic of the animal. Compare this with a modern painting of a bison that expresses more detail and a landscape background. If the purpose of the artist is to give expression to the significant aspect of "his bisonship," has not the hunter-artist been marvelously successful? How much do detail and landscape add to this expression? Such a comparison will reveal the fact that these cave paintings equal if they do not surpass the best animal representations of any other age.

To paint one of these animals, the artist first with a piece of finely pointed flint incised on the wall the outline of the figure and such details as hair, eye, horns, and mouth (FIG. 9). He then painted a strong black contour line around the edge and finally filled in with his other colors, using altogether four — black, brown, red, and yellow — indicating the roundness of the form by shading.

The ceiling of the cave at Altamira is not smooth, but has convex bosses from four to five feet long and three to four feet wide. On these oval surfaces the artist painted bison lying down in such a way that only the horns and the tail project beyond the surface of the boss. Yet the pose is very lifelike, the drawing and modeling accurate, and such details as the bottom of the hoofs most carefully done. Such a painting is only another manifestation of the boldness of these hunter-artists in handling a difficult situation and of their sensitiveness to the decorative possibility of the animal form.

A constant characteristic that we have noticed in this art of the Reindeer Age is the keen observation of animal life and the ability to represent it in its most significant aspect with the greatest economy of line. But the artist who painted the *Reindeer* (PL. 1B) on the cave wall not only observed and recorded accurately, but showed

Fig. 9. Preliminary Engraving of a Bison. H. 2 ft. Cave of Marsoulas, France. (*L'Anthropologie*)

furthermore that he was sensitive to the beauty to be found in the animal world. In the instantaneous pose that he has caught as the reindeer is about to bend his head, he has seen the beauty of the curve of the back; and in the wide sweeping line with which he has painted the antlers he has given expression to his innate feeling for the beauty of line itself.

In the *Procession of Mammoth, Bison, Reindeer, and Horses* (FIG. 10) all moving in one direction we have one of the few examples in which the figures appear arranged in some order and in some relation to each other. This is the nearest approach, in Paleolithic art, to what we understand as composition. It is a solemn procession as it moves slowly on; and we feel that we are looking at a work of art created with a serious purpose. In fact, all these drawings and paintings are clearly free of triviality. What then was the purpose of the artists of the Reindeer Age? Why did they penetrate these caverns, so far into the hillside that not a ray of light can reach them, and by the help of a little stone lamp in which they burned animal fat, engrave and paint these animal figures upon the walls and ceilings? Surely not for

Fig. 10. Procession of Mammoth and Other Animals. L. c. 14 ft. Cave of Font-de-Gaume, France. (Capitan and Breuil)

pleasure alone. The people did not live in the caverns, but at the entrance or under the shelving cliffs near by.

If we turn for a moment to investigate the customs of the most primitive people living today, we find that the Australians draw a picture of the animal that they intend to hunt, and perform

Fig. 11. Hunters. H. c. 4 in. Caves of Eastern Spain. (Obermaier and Wernert)

rites around it; the Eskimos paint a seal in the belief that the magical influence of the picture will bring success. So we may infer that the men of the Reindeer Age, who were primarily hunters, looked upon these caverns as sacred places and there painted pictures that had a magical purpose. The bison painted in the cave would bring success in the hunt, while the antelope carved on the dart-thrower would make the arm sure for bringing down the game.

So far, the subject matter has been narrowly restricted to animals. The human figure has been found, but is expressed very crudely in comparison with the ability to depict animal form. An exception to this statement appears in some wall paintings found in the caves of one locality only, eastern Spain (FIG. 11). These appear to belong to the late Paleolithic Age, but they are very different from anything that we have seen; first, because many represent human figures, hunters armed with bows and arrows; and second, because they exhibit not only great vigor but an exaggeration of movement quite unlike the reserve and serenity of the animal paintings. They show little regard for proportion and natural appearance, but express with amazing power the essence of movement. In the archer, for example, we do not realize the figure of the hunter nearly so much as the powerful draw upon the bowstring.

SCULPTURE

Few examples of sculpture were found up to the outbreak of the War, but important discoveries have recently been reported.[3] They all reveal the same general characteristics that we saw in the cave paintings — a clear mental picture of the animal form, gained from keen observation, and the ability to express it in its simplest, most significant aspects. Human figures are formed as well as animals; but they are crude and ungainly.

SUMMARY

Finally the fourth or last ice age came to an end, probably not less than ten thousand years ago. The ice melted, the reindeer migrated north and the Reindeer Age, with its art, disappeared. Its hunter-artists Mr. Osborn calls "Paleolithic Greeks"; and closely akin they surely were to this later gifted race in their feeling for form and symmetry, their sense of design seen in the ability to adapt the subject matter to the space and medium, their appreciation of the beauty of form and line, and particularly in their ability to select the essential characteristics and express them with a few significant lines entirely free from irrelevant detail.

[3] For an interesting account of a recent discovery of sculpture and also a vivid picture of the perilous undertakings incident to the exploration of subterranean caves, see Casteret, "Discovering the Oldest Statues in the World," *National Geographic Magazine*, XLVI (1924), p. 123.

B. NEOLITHIC AGE

c. 10,000–*c.* 2,000 B.C.

HISTORICAL BACKGROUND AND THE MINOR ARTS

With the passing of the Reindeer Age, the geography and climate of Europe became approximately what they are today; and a new race appeared, many features of whose life, such as domesti-

cated animals and grain, indicate its independence of the preceding age. Life advanced in many respects. With the cultivation of grain, a more settled life replaced the nomadic type. Home life developed; for protection, villages were built on piles in lakes, and homes were equipped with a considerable number of comforts. Pottery, for example, the earliest known, now appears, as a result of man's effort to obtain hot water. Formerly he had smeared clay over a basket to protect the basket and hold the water. Soon he observed how the clay, when subjected to the fire, hardened. Hence he omitted the basket, shaping the clay alone for this purpose. Skin clothing gave way to woven, for the discovery of spinning whorls indicates that the weaving of

Fig. 12. Polished Stone Implement. Originally mounted in a handle. L. 8¾ in. British Museum, London.

textiles was now understood. Stone, however, still continued to furnish the material out of which were fashioned tools; hence the period is called the Late Stone or Neolithic Age. Many new varieties of implements were added because of the demands of agriculture, and of the building and furnishing of permanent homes. They were still made, in great numbers, by the old method of chipping and flaking. Such a knife as that shown in PL. 8 c, in the beauty of its shape, and in the precision and rhythm of its flakings, constitutes a real work of art. But a new method was used in the production of polished stone implements (FIG. 12). Man had now

Fig. 13. Neolithic Jar. H. c. 9 in.

learned how to obtain a smooth surface and a fine cutting edge by grinding; and by attaching a wooden handle he supplied himself with a tool very comparable, in effectiveness, to those used in modern times.

The earliest pottery (FIG. 13) was made by hand, without the

use of the potter's wheel. In shape it is crude. But its decoration
frequently follows and thus strengthens the structural lines of the
object. The motifs used were concentric circles, broken zigzag,
spirals, all of which have been basic elements
of decoration through man's entire career.
The spiral particularly (FIG. 14) we find not
only in a number of variations, but with a
surprisingly vigorous quality.

BUILDING

With more settled conditions of life, resulting in the growth of communities and the rise
of trades and industries, monumental work
appears in the tombs of the chieftains. One
form of these tombs consisted of two or three
great stones with a covering slab which, be-

Fig. 14. Fragments
of Neolithic Pottery.
(Déchelette)

cause of its resemblance to a table, is called a dolmen (FIG. 15),
meaning table-stone. Single monoliths called menhirs, sometimes
seventy feet high, were set up, occasionally decorated with a

Fig. 15. Dolmen. Normandy.

crude relief, or arranged in long rows the purpose of which is not
clear. But the most pretentious consist of a circle of stones,
known as cromlechs, as *Stonehenge* (FIG. 16). This circle consists
of an outer ring of huge monoliths, capped with lintels, roughly
cut just as they came from the quarry and laid without mortar.
Inside this is a line of smaller stones; then a broken ring of five
pairs of huge monoliths, each with its lintel; and again an inner
broken circle of smaller stones, inside of which is a large slab
that may have served as an altar. In the arrangement there is
a feeling for order and symmetry, and a rhythm that is varied by
alternating the large and small concentric circles. Such a structure

is not, properly speaking, architecture. But it is the nearest approach that we find to it in western Europe until Roman times.

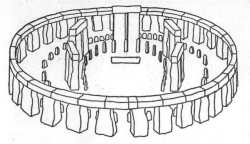

Fig. 16. Stonehenge, Restored.   Salisbury Plain, England. D. c. 100 ft.

SUMMARY

On the whole, in comparison with that of the earlier Reindeer Age, the art impulse of Neolithic man was crude. To be sure, life had advanced in many respects. But there were lacking as yet at least two vital elements without which further progress seemed impossible — metal and writing. In the meantime, while Neolithic man was cutting the monoliths for *Stonehenge* with his stone tools and was without means of recording his deeds by a system of writing, the Egyptian in the Nile valley was shaping the wonderfully cut stones of the pyramids with his copper chisel and was advancing along all lines because, with his writing, he was not dependent for the management of his affairs upon word of mouth alone. From the Near East,[4] Europe eventually obtained both metal and a system of writing.

BIBLIOGRAPHY

AVEBURY, J. L., Prehistoric Times. N.Y., Holt, 1913.
BREASTED, J. H., Ancient Times. Boston, Ginn, 1916.
BRITISH MUSEUM, Pictorial postcards. Set XV: Antiquities of the Stone Age.
KIMBALL, FISKE, AND EDGELL, G. H., History of Architecture. N.Y., Harper, 1918.
KÜHN, HERBERT, Malerei der Eiszeit. Munich, Delphin Verlag, 1922.
MUNRO, ROBERT, Palaeolithic Man and the Terramara Settlements in Europe. N.Y., Macmillan, 1912.
——— ———, Lake Dwellings of Europe. London, Cassell, 1890.
OSBORN, H. E., Men of the Old Stone Age, Their Environment, Life, and Art. N.Y., Scribner, 1921.
PARKYN, E. A., Introduction to the Study of Prehistoric Art. N.Y., Longmans, 1915.
PIETTE, EDOUARD, L'Art pendant l'âge du renne. Paris, Masson, 1907.
REINACH, SALOMON, Apollo (tr. Simmonds). N.Y., Scribner, 1924.
SOLLAS, W. J., Ancient Hunters and Their Modern Representatives. N.Y., Macmillan, 1924.
SPEARING, H. G., Childhood of Art. N.Y., Putnam, 1913.
WELLS, H. G., Outline of History. N.Y., Macmillan, 1922.

[4] In this book "Near East" is used to include Egypt and that part of Asia that lies west of India; "Orient" is applied to eastern Asia, chiefly India, China, and Japan.

PLATE I

(*A*) Bison. Painted on the ceiling of the cave of Altamira, Spain. c. 15,000 B.C. (Cartaillac and Breuil)

(*B*) Reindeer. Painted on the wall of the cave of Font-de-Gaume, France. c. 15,000 B.C. (Cartaillac and Breuil)

(*C*) Head of a Whinnying Horse. Carved in reindeer horn. L. c. 3 in. Saint Germain-en-Laye. (Piette)

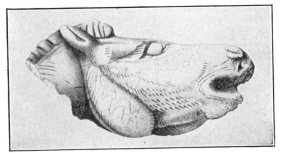

PLATE 2

(*A*) Egypt at Low Nile. At the top of the steep bank is the cultivated area, with palm trees; in the background rise the cliffs of the desert plateau. (Author)

(*B*) Tomb Model of a Nobleman Inspecting Cattle. Cairo Museum. (Metropolitan Museum)

(*C*) Pyramids of Gizeh. IV Dynasty (2900–2750 B.C.). (Gaddis and Seif)

PLATE 3

(*A*) Pyramids of Khufu and Khafre, Restored. Gizeh. (Hoelscher)

(*B*) Valley-Temple of the Pyramid of Khafre, Restored. c. 2850 B.C. (Hoelscher)

(*C*) Ranofer. V Dynasty (2750–2625 B.C.). Cairo Museum.

PLATE 4

(*A*) Pyramid of Sahure, Restored. Abusir. Colonnaded hall of the chapel.
c. 2735 B.C. (Borchardt)

(*B*) Statue of a Lady, Probably a Princess. H. c. 10 in. IV Dynasty (2900–2750 B.C.). Coll. of the late Earl of Carnarvon. (*Journal of Egyptian Archaeology*)

(*C*) Khafre. Of diorite, life size. IV Dynasty (2900–2750 B.C.). Cairo Museum. (Stoedtner)

CHAPTER II

EGYPTIAN PERIOD (1)

Early Egypt and the Old Kingdom, c. 4500–2475 B.C.[1]

HISTORICAL BACKGROUND

From the top of the great pyramid we look out on long horizontals, as far as the eye can reach; a narrow valley through which meanders a glistening river, with a narrow fringe of green fields and palm groves, bordered on either side by low barren cliffs from which extend vast undulating deserts; a glorious sun in a cloudless sky — this is Egypt (PL. 2 A and c).

Of this environment, two outstanding facts always confronted the Egyptian — the brilliant sun and the Nile River; and so insistently did they impress themselves on his mind that they early became dominating forces in his religious belief. The daily spectacle of the radiant sun in an almost rainless sky soon led him to personify this great natural force in the sun-god Re; while the Nile River, through whose annual rise comes the productive soil, found its counterpart in Osiris. This god, once a king upon earth, according to the legend, was craftily killed by his wicked brother Set, but through the powerful incantations of his wife Isis was brought to life. As existence upon earth was impossible, Osiris went to the spirit world to become the god of the dead. And just as Osiris, after an earthly death, entered upon a new existence in another world and just as nature with the rise of the Nile burst into new life, so to every Egyptian lay open the opportunity for a similar experience of reviving life hereafter. This hope constituted one of the most powerful influences in Egyptian civilization.

While these legends were slowly shaping themselves into a religious system, other forces were working toward the evolution of the Egyptian state, which was the first to emerge from vastly remote prehistoric ages and to develop what we may term a civilization. The trench cut by the Nile River through the

[1] There is considerable difference of opinion among scholars on the question of Egyptian chronology and of the spelling of Egyptian names. In Chapters II and III of this book, the chronology is that of J. H. Breasted; the spelling follows the system adopted by the Oriental Institute of the University of Chicago.

Sahara plateau was a thick morass until men of the Stone Age coming in from the plateau, reclaimed the valley and built their hamlets along the stream. By 4241 B.C. they had invented calendar; by 4000 had discovered metal, perhaps accidentally as the molten drops of copper separated from the rock in their camp fires in the Sinai peninsula; and long before 3000, they had evolved a system of picture writing. Tiny states began to emerge along the river, and slowly coalesced into two kingdoms, Upper and Lower Egypt, which were finally united about 3400 by a king called Menes. At the head of the political and social system we see a supreme pharaoh, who probably owned all the land; a group of nobles suppressed, receiving their appointments from him; the mass of the people, with possible exceptions, slaves. The chief economic basis was agriculture, though the industries of the potter, stone-cutter, and goldsmith were highly developed and commerce was carried on with the Bedouins of Sinai, and

Fig. 17. Villa of a Nobleman, Restored.
(Perrot and Chipiez)

with the Ægean lands. The government became highly efficient and thoroughly organized with different administrative departments. Toward the end of the period, however, a change can be discerned. As the nobles gained in power, the strength of the pharaoh weakened while the official class became hereditary, laying the foundation of a feudal state.

The Egyptian noble we see living in a villa (FIG. 17) set in a garden with trees and pools of water, all surrounded by a high wall. His life was spent for the most part in the out-of-doors, in which he found many of his pleasures, too. For we see him in his reed boat, accompanied by his family, hunting fowl in

he papyrus swamp (PL. 15 B); or out on the desert after game.
He loved the out-of-doors, observed keenly all the plants, animals, and birds which he found there, and then painted and
carved them on his walls and patterned his decorations and
shaped his useful things of everyday life after them. Again we
see him and his wife watching the work in the fields (FIG. 18).
In the two upper rows the harvesters are cutting the grain, leav-
ng a high stubble just as they do in Egypt today; below, men
with staves are driving the donkeys back and forth over the

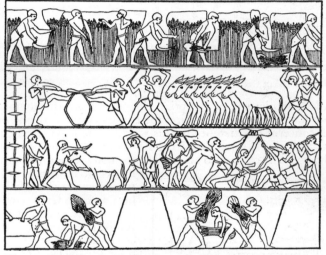

Fig. 18. Work in the Fields: Reaping, Threshing, and Stacking.
From the mastaba of Ti, Saqquara.

threshing floor, tying the grain in great bags and loading it on
the donkeys' backs or tossing the bundles into the granaries.
Stock-raising played a large part in the life of the Egyptian.
In PL. 2 B we see the lord sitting on his veranda, inspecting the
cattle as they are driven past him. His son squats on the floor
beside him, just as the Arabs do today, while four clerks with
scrolls on their laps take down the count. In driving the cattle
to pasture, frequent canals must be crossed (FIG. 19), and the
cowboy with a kindly heart carries on his back the young calf
that is anxiously looking back toward the cow.

To provide the noble with clothing, ornaments, and household
equipment, the craftsmen drill out stone vases (FIG. 20); the

goldsmiths hammer the metal and with their long blowpipe
keep the furnaces hot and fashion collar-necklaces such as Nof
retete wears (COLOR PL. I). Others carve ivory feet for the noble'
chairs and beds while the women weave the linen for his kilt

Fig. 19. Herd of Cattle Fording a Canal. From the mastaba of Ti, Saqquara.

All these pictures of Egyptian life come from the tombs; for
as we have said, the provision for life hereafter was one of the
chief concerns of existence in this world. The Egyptian believed
that there was a force called the Ka which was the counterpar
of the body. It came into being with the body, continued through
life with it, was in all fea
tures like it, though invisi
ble, and at death accompa
nied it into the next world
As the Ka and the body wer
coexistent, the body mus
be carefully preserve
through mummification, and
the Ka, through offerings of
all kinds. Thus to secure for
the spirit land, which wa
but a reflection of this world
both necessities and luxuries

Fig. 20. Drilling Stone Vases. One
worker remarks, "This is a beautiful vase
that I am making"; the other replies,
"Indeed it is."

it was necessary to paint or carve all these scenes upon the tomb
walls or to place small models in the burial chambers each of
which, with the proper incantation, would function normally
in the hereafter.

For building these enduring monuments, for carving relief
and statues and for his handicraft, the natural resources of
Egypt greatly aided the artist by providing an abundanc
of excellent material. Great quarries of limestone, sandstone

labaster, and granite were readily accessible; harder stones, :equently valuable for their beauty of color — diorite, porphyry, reen and yellow breccia — though found more sparingly and in ·laces difficult of access because of desert conditions, furnished hoice material for the sculptor and maker of vases.

ARCHITECTURE

In view of the religious beliefs of the Egyptian, it is not sur-prising to find his architecture strongly influenced by a desire o create a permanent abiding place for the dead, for he could not conceive of a future existence without the body. Hence one of he most characteristic structures of Egypt and one which tands out as the chief accomplishment of this period in architec-ure is the royal tomb, which culminates in the great *Pyramids f Gizeh*. Before studying these monuments in detail let us stop it a distant view (PL. 2 C) and notice first, that they stand on the plateau which forms the brink of the Nile valley, safe from the ughest level of the river; second, they gradually rise in un-

broken line from the long
horizontal plateau up
against a cloudless sky to
in apex pointing to the
un which they symbo-
ize, affording a shape of
great simplicity and
lignity entirely fitting
or a tomb. Contrast for
a moment the façade of a
Gothic cathedral (PL. 84)
with its multiplicity of
vertical lines, each pointed arch, statue, pinnacle,
buttress, and tower con-
tributing to the soaring
quality and to the broken
light and shade; and no-

Fig. 21. Pyramid of Khufu. Gizeh. H. originally 481 ft.; 755 ft. square; covering an area of 13 acres; c. 2900 B.C.

tice how different is the feeling of unrest and exaltation there experienced from the quiet repose that comes from the unity of the unbroken line and surface of the pyramid.

Approaching the *Pyramid of Khufu* (FIG. 21), the northern one of the group at Gizeh, as we wander about or sit down in the sand, let us think back over the long development that led up to

the building of this tomb. As far back as we can trace the Egyp
tian, he buried his dead in a pit over which he heaped up the sand
holding it in place with stones and twigs. By slow process thi
pit and sand heap grew; the actual chamber below the groun

became rectangular and wa
faced with wood, brick, and
finally stone. At the sam
time the mound above wa
covered with brick or stone
which followed in a genera
way the lines of the san
heap and thus attained
shape that looks like a low
truncated pyramid, called
mastaba (FIG. 22). Finally
some king ambitious to erec

Fig. 22. Group of Mastabas. *Mastaba*
is an Arabic word meaning a bench or terrace.

a still mightier tomb began to pile mastaba upon mastaba
forming a step-pyramid; and then, by filling in the steps
attained the pure pyramidal form.[2]

At first the mastaba was simple (FIG. 23), built of solid material
except for the small chapel that served as a reception room of the
Ka, where the family and priests gathered to place the offerings
before the false door facing the east, through which the Ka

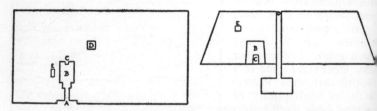

Fig. 23. Typical Mastaba. *A*, entrance; *B*, chapel; *C*, false door; *D*, shaft down
which the sarcophagus was let into the burial chamber below; *E*, serdab for the
statue. L. 40–50 ft.

came from the spirit land of the west. A tiny secret chamber
known as the *serdab*, or cellar, was built in the heart of the
structure to contain a statue of the deceased that could represent
him in the spirit world, should anything happen to the actual
body. This chapel became quite complex, as time went on, with
additional rooms and corridors which were covered with reliefs

[2] For a graphic illustration of this development, see Breasted, *Ancient Times*, p. 54.

hat vividly picture the everyday life of the Egyptian, for the
benefit, as we have said, of the Ka.

The ragged condition of Khufu's pyramid is due to the fact
that when the builders of the city of Cairo needed stone, it was
far easier to take it, all cut, from the pyramids than to quarry
it even from the near-by cliffs. In the time of Khufu (2900 B.C.)
the pyramid was entirely covered with casing blocks of fine,
early white limestone, and so presented a perfectly smooth
surface from foundation to tip. Some of these casing stones can
still be seen at the base, and so perfect are the joinings of the
blocks that the eye can scarcely detect them. With the exception
of the burial chamber and galleries, the structure is of solid
masonry. In considering its huge size, one comes to a realization
of the niceties of engineering on the part of the pharaoh's architects; for even the most delicate modern surveying instrument
can detect only about one-half inch error in the measurement of
one side. Likewise in the burial chamber within the pyramid, the
technical skill shown in forming the angles of the blocks, and
in joining the blocks, has scarcely ever been equaled. As each
of these blocks weighs, on the average, two and one-half tons,
we wonder how such a piece of engineering was possible in the
days when there were no surveying instruments and no machinery. This is fairly clear, however. The stones were roughly cut
in the quarries of the eastern Nile cliffs, directly across from
Gizeh; then during the short period of high Nile they were
floated across to the base of the plateau where the pyramid was
building. The Greek traveler Herodotus, who visited Egypt
about 450 B.C., describes the great stone ramp, or inclined passage, which led from the valley to the plateau, up which the
great stones were dragged by human labor. There the masons
finished them off and marked them with red ink to indicate the
place of each in the structure, tossing the great piles of chips
over the edge of the plateau into the valley. Then great gangs of
men dragged them up temporary ramps which were erected
alongside the permanent structure as it rose layer upon layer.[3]
This same Herodotus tells us of a tradition that a hundred
thousand men were working twenty years in the building of this
pyramid. A small city in itself the stone yards and living quarters must have made, the maintenance of which was no small
drain on the royal exchequer. In fact we shall see that, as the
power of the pharaoh waned and the funds at his disposal decreased, the pyramids too decreased in size. Yet it is not merely

[3] An unfinished pyramid in the foreground of PL. 3 A shows these ramps.

because of its tremendous size and its engineering that the *Pyra-mid of Khufu* is deservedly ranked as a great work of art, bu chiefly because of the marvelous accuracy of its workmanshi and because through its simple dignity and strength it perform its function fittingly as a tomb and through its shape and pro portions is adapted to its physiographical environment.

On the east side of the great pyramid are three small pyramid belonging to members of the royal family, while clustered abou are rows of mastabas of the great nobles who, having bee associated with the pharaoh in life, wished to continue in thi place of honor even in the tomb. The pyramid of the pharaoh however, is the dominating structure of the whole cemeter (PL. 3 A), just as he himself had been the dominating power o Egyptian life.

The middle pyramid of the triple group at Gizeh, the *Pyrami of Khafre*, is somewhat smaller than that of Khufu, indicating as we have said, the declining power of the pharaoh. It is ver important for our purpose, however, because from the remain surrounding this pyramid we can study all the additional struc tures, which, together with the pyramid itself, comprise th pyramid complex. To do this let us look first at the mastaba shaped structure in the right foreground of PL. 3 A. Notic that the building is in the valley, that the *Sphinx* is immediatel at the side, and that above on the plateau looms the pyramid itself What is the relation between the pyramid and this structure, s long misunderstood and still frequently called the *Temple of th Sphinx?* Notice once more how the pyramid stands up on th plateau above the valley in which lay the town. In order t provide for the spirit of the dead, offerings must be placed at th tomb frequently. The hot climb up over the sandy hill led to th erection of a covered causeway from the valley up to the littl chapel adjoining the eastern side of the pyramid. For, as th spirit land lay in the west, the spirit must come toward the eas to receive the offerings. Hence tombs were built on the wester bank, and the chapel was on the eastern side of the pyramid. Th beginning of the causeway presupposed some kind of entrance o vestibule. And that is the function which our so-called *Templ of the Sphinx* performs.

Looking at the ground plan (FIG. 24), we see that a pyrami complex consists of (*a*) the pyramid itself, within or below which was the burial chamber; (*b*) the chapel adjoining the pyramid o the eastern side, where the offerings were made and ceremonie performed, and where the linen, grain, honey, oil, and othe

ferings of food and drink were kept in store-chambers, and also
the rich ceremonial vessels (PL. 7 B) for use in the daily rites;
) the covered causeway leading over the cliffs; and (*d*) the
alley-temple, or vestibule of the causeway, down in the valley.
Let us look more closely at the valley-temple (PL. 3 B). It is

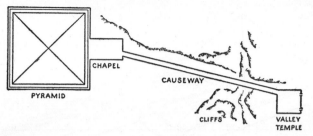

Fig. 24. Plan of a Pyramid Complex.

built on the lintel system, that is, the upright supports are
ridged over with horizontal beams, just as a child would build
a house with rectangular blocks. Here the supports are huge red
granite pillars, each a monolith, finely proportioned, skilfully cut
and polished, and entirely devoid of decoration. The lintels are
of the same material and finish. Alabaster slabs cover the floor,
while seated statues are ranged alongside, the only embellishment. This interior, protected from the hot sun by the great
blocks, must have been cool and dim. It is lighted by a few
rays filtering in from above, slantwise. This is because the
pillars of the central aisle are higher than the side walls, and the
roof over the central part, therefore, at a higher level than
over the sides. In the vertical
space left between these two
levels are slits in the stone,
through which the light comes,
forming an embryonic clerestory
(FIG. 25), a structural feature
that became so characteristic of
early Christian churches. With

Fig. 25. Valley-Temple of Khafre.
Section showing the clerestory.
(After Hoelscher)

its plain, simple dignity, it is a remarkably impressive room,
harmonizing with the simple massive tomb to which it led.

In the limestone cliffs over which the covered causeway led was
a rocky projection which prevented the architect from building
the passage at right angles with the pyramids. Perhaps unsightly
too, this cliff had proved to be nothing but an obstacle, until it

occurred to some one that a use could be made of it by carving
it into a likeness of the pharaoh whose tomb was near by. As a
result we have the great *Sphinx*, a portrait statue of Khafre,
which represents a colossal recumbent lion, with outstretched
paws, bearing the head of a man who wears a linen headdress

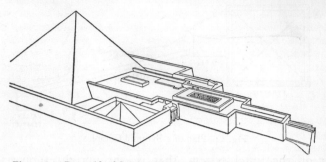

Fig. 26 A. Pyramid of Sahure, Restored. Abusir. Pyramid, chapel,
and upper end of the causeway; c. 2735 B.C. (After Borchardt)

and a ceremonial beard, now broken off. This form of representation of the pharaoh was not uncommon with the Egyptians,
as the lion's body symbolized the royal power.

Leaving Gizeh and traveling up the river to Abusir, let us look
at the *Pyramid of Sahure* (FIG. 26), built about one hundred years
after that of Khafre. In looking at the valley-temple here and

Fig. 26 B. Pyramid of Sahure, Restored.
Valley-temple.

into the open court of
the chapel (PL. 4 A) we
see at once something not
found in the pyramids at
Gizeh, and that is rows
of columns, the origin
of which is the row of
rectangular pillars in
Khafre's valley-temple.
Observing nature round
about him the Egyptian selected the palm tree with its round
trunk and spreading leaves to support his roof. Brightly colored
wall decorations also appear, which soften and enrich the
effect, producing a refinement and elegance which contrasts
sharply with the austerity and simplicity of the valley-temple
of Khafre.

SCULPTURE

As architecture in early Egypt was employed largely to protect the dead, so sculpture was bound up with the desire either to perpetuate or to serve the dead. Should the body, though carefully mummified, by any chance perish, then a statue as near as near the original as possible might represent the body in the world to come. Hence we are not surprised to find portraiture early developed. In the statue of *Ranofer* (PL. 3 c) we see that the figure is standing rigidly erect, facing directly to the front, with the left foot advanced and the arms held close to the side of the body. All these features are conventions in Egyptian standing figures. He wears a linen kilt and a large wig, both characteristic of the dress of the time. Notice the finely developed muscular chest and arm and the modeling of the knees. We feel that this man is every inch a noble, and that the sculptor, in order to emphasize his social class, has suppressed his individual traits and imbued him with a serious, almost hieratic dignity.

The statue of the *Princess* (PL. 4 b), though fragmentary, shows the same rigid frontal pose as that of *Ranofer*, even though it may have been a seated figure. She wears a tightly fitting garment of white linen, with two straps over the shoulders; a broad collarlike necklace and the usual ceremonial wig, held by a decorated band, beneath which appears the natural hair, smoothly parted over the forehead. The vivacity of the *Princess* is due very largely to the fact that the statue is painted in lifelike colors. The necklace, eyebrows, and ornaments of the headband are painted on, not carved in the stone; the flesh is a warm yellowish tone because the Egyptian woman led a more secluded life than the man, whose skin, tanned by his outdoor life, is usually but not invariably indicated by a dark reddish color; the lips are red; the necklace red and blue; the hair and brows black. The eyes are made of rock crystal set into the stone and add not a little to the lifelike expression. The figure is well modeled, and particularly noteworthy is the feeling for the form as it is suggested under the almost transparent linen. The brightness of the color adds a note of gayety to the charming *Princess*.

In PL. 4 c we see the profile view of the upper part of the statue of *Khafre*, which was found in his valley-temple where it stood in the row of statues ranged along the side of the hall (PL. 3 b). It is carved from diorite, a stone so hard that it will resist a steel tool. The character of the material has to a large extent determined the modeling, which, though surprisingly accurate, indicates only the essential characteristics. The streaked surfac of the stone, now so disconcerting to the eye, was originall covered with fine stucco and painted, like the statue of th *Princess*. On his head Khafre wears a linen headdress, whic smoothly covers the forehead and falls in plaited folds dow each side of the breast. The false ceremonial beard is partl broken off. The sacred hawk, with wings spread protectingl about the head, symbolizes the semi-divine station of the pha raoh, who is here looking out over his domain with the perfec calm of a divinity far removed from the turmoil and tragedy c everyday life. While the statue is a generalized portrait c Khafre, still the individual man is hidden beneath his office, an the inherent significance of the statue is its magnificent expressio of the abstract quality of sovereignty.

In the *Sheikh el-Beled* (PL. 5 A) we see a fat, self-satisfied ap proachable fellow, standing in the same frontal position a *Ranofer*, with the left foot advanced and right arm outstretched Originally the wood was probably covered with linen, glued o to furnish a better surface for painting. The crystal eyes are stil in place and add greatly to the vivacious individuality of th man, who is probably a middle-class overseer. In fact, so lifelik is the statue that the natives who were helping in the excavation where it was found, struck by its close resemblance to thei village chief, called out immediately, "*Sheikh el-Beled*," whic means "Chief of the Village," a name it has borne eve since.

The figure of the *Seated Scribe* (PL. 5 B) shows us a keen, aler man sitting cross-legged on the ground with his book resting o his kilt, his pen in hand, as is indicated by the position of th fingers, ready in an instant to take down what his master i dictating. The figure, though squatting, still maintains the rigic frontal position; the head is highly individualized, showin that this scribe, with his spare face, square jaw, and thin lips is a shrewd man with a sense of humor. The body is not so wel modeled as the head. In fact, the legs are but roughly blockec out. Yet the whole figure is expressive of expectancy.

More freedom of pose is found in the small statues of servant placed in the tombs, the brewer, baker, butcher, carpenter, o goldsmith who, as we have said, were able through the prope magic to perform their respective services for the master in th spirit world.[4] They are realistic sketches quite free from the con

[4] For an interesting group of these tomb models, see the Metropolitan Museum o Art, "Egyptian Expedition, 1918-20," in *Bulletin of the Metropolitan Museum*, Dec., 1920, Part II

entions that control the representations of the pharaohs and nobles.

Thus, sculpture in the round[5] appears to fall into two classes. Ranofer, the *Princess*, and *Khafre* represent the aristocratic, formal class of work in which, while there are distinct individual traits, yet the social class or the abstract quality is preëminent; the *Sheikh el-Beled*, the *Seated Scribe*, and the tomb models typify the friendly, intimate, informal class.

As we turn to the reliefs we find that the figures are carved so low that they approach drawing and painting more closely than sculpture. Among examples of early work is the *Palette of King Narmer* (PL. 5 c), which was dedicated in the temple by this king, in commemoration of some victory. It is carved on both sides; on one, Narmer stands clutching his fallen enemy by the hair and with lifted mace is about to smite him; below, two running figures represent the fleeing army. The other side is divided into four zones, the upper one of which bears the name of the king in the center, balanced on each side by the head of the goddess Hathor; in the second the king, large of stature, followed by a sandal bearer and preceded by his prime minister and four standard bearers, is looking at his enemies, whose bodies, with their decapitated heads carefully placed between their legs, lie on the ground before him in two rows. The next zone is occupied by two curious animals whose long necks intertwine to form a circular depression, their angry lion heads kept apart by two men who pull vigorously on ropes attached to their necks. In the lowest zone is a bull, symbolic of the king, battering down the walls of the enemy's town and trampling his foes underfoot. In this early relief we can discern several characteristics of Egyptian work: first, the conventional way in which the human figure is drawn — the head and legs in profile, the torso and the eye in front view; second, the lack of perspective. For example, the artist wished to show two rows of bodies lying on the ground; unable to do this he placed one body above another, as a child would do — the usual way of expressing distance in Egyptian drawing; third, sensitiveness to good design in the adaptation of the figures to the space. The two animals with intertwined necks balance each other even to their tails, which curl up over their backs to form an almost complete circle, echoing the motive of

---

5 *In the round* and *relief* are technical terms applied to sculpture. The first means that the statue is fully modeled in three dimensions so that it is possible to walk around it; relief means that the figures are but partly modeled, projecting beyond the background to which they are attached, sometimes very little (known as *bas relief*) and sometimes so far that they are nearly in the round but still attached (known as *high relief*). There is no sharp line of demarcation between bas and high relief and both are frequently combined in the same work.

the central circle, which is again repeated in the horns of th
Hathor heads above. From this repetition unity of design re
sults; cover up the smaller circles and see what a difference i
makes in the design. The two little figures pulling so vigorousl
on the ropes well fill the space left on each side of the animals
This means that the artist, in thinking out his design, pai
particular attention to adapting his figures to the space they wer
to fill. Furthermore, the figures were carved by a man who wa
very sure-handed in the use of his chisel. The firm, unfalterin
lines that express essentials only are discernible in all the figure
of the palette and are indicative of a climax in a long develop
ment that had begun centuries before 3000 B.C., the process o
which is lost to us.

The great mass of Egyptian reliefs come from the tomb chapels
the walls of which were covered with scenes from everyday lif
— the production of grain, the raising of cattle, the making o
boats, jewelry, vases, hunting on the desert or in the papyru
swamp; and this all for the utilitarian purpose, as we have said
of providing the dead with the necessities and the pleasures o
life. The scenes are arranged in horizontal zones (FIG. 18) and
the figures are drawn mostly in profile with very little grouping
that necessitates overlapping, except in the case of the animals
where depth is shown by repeating the silhouette. Though the
figures are drawn with the conventions that we observed in
studying the *Palette of Narmer*, conventions that had now become fixed in Egyptian art, still they are filled with vigor and
movement, while the animals show great naturalism based upon
a careful observation of the animal form and also the animal
characteristics — the calm placidity of the oxen and the pathetic
gloom of the donkeys. A frank acceptance of two points of view
is again seen in the oxen, where the front view of the horns is
placed upon a profile view of the head. All the figures are
painted in bright flat colors that are not only lifelike but
carefully planned so as to form a scheme of color-harmony, so
that the wall, apart from the subject interest, is primarily decorative.

How the artists went about his work we have been able to
see in some of the tombs where the walls have been left unfinished. Here we learn that he planned his decoration with the
help of guide lines to proportion the spaces and also the individual figures; he sketched the latter in, made an incision along the
lines of the preliminary sketch with a chisel, and then cut away
the background, leaving his design in relief. If the stone was

too uneven to offer a good foundation for painting, he covered it with a thin coating of fine plaster. His pigment he mixed with some binding medium, probably a gum, and applied it to the dry stone or plaster with brushes made of reeds, in flat even tones, using no light and shade. Whatever modeling was done, was done by the contour line made in the preliminary sketch and by the chisel.

The never failing sense of design that characterizes Egyptian art reveals itself in the relief of *Ti Hunting in the Papyrus Marsh* (PL. 6 B). Ti, large of stature as usual, is in his reed boat; from the river, filled with hippopotami and fish, rise the stems of papyrus plants, conventionalized to form a background for the figures. As the straight lines approach the top of the panel, however, some of them bend under the weight of the weasel that is stealing up to the nest with its young birds while the parents fly anxiously about — a very happy combination of the conventional and the naturalistic. The scene among the flowers and buds above balances that on the river below; yet both are connected and emphasized by the background of the vertical stems.

A tomb relief that embodies the same characteristics in another medium is the panel of *Hesire*, carved in wood (PL. 7 A). Though a single figure is represented, it is not placed in the center of the panel; yet the balance is maintained by the staff and the writing utensils which Hesire holds in his left hand; the horizontals of the feet, baton, girdle, and shoulders happily balance the otherwise insistent verticals. Let us look more closely at the figure itself. To appreciate its high quality we must frankly accept the conventional way in which different parts of the body are drawn from different points of view. This was not because the Egyptian could not execute a profile, as we shall see, but simply because this conventional method of drawing the figure, established early in Egypt, held a more powerful grip upon the artist than a naturalistic rendering. Possibly actual rather than visual truth appealed more strongly. For example, the artist knew that a man had two arms although in a profile he could see but one; and his instinct bade him indicate the fact rather than record the visual image. In the case of *Hesire*, the feeling of distortion is not so disconcerting as usual, for the artist here has united the parts skillfully. In this relief, we feel the proud bearing of a noble and also the strength of a man of determination. Note the individualized face, with its high cheek bones and firm mouth; the careful modeling about the neck, shoulders, and knees; and the firmness and strength of all the lines.

PAINTING

The painting of early Egypt is best represented by the *Geese of Meidum* (PL. 6 A). On a panel are two pairs of waddling ducks and geese feeding; small clumps of herbage are scantily suggested. The artist who painted this panel had observed ducks and geese closely enough to be familiar with the clumsy gait and the "grave self-sufficiency" of the ducks, with the curves of the neck of the goose as it bends for food and with the characteristic markings of the plumage. The significant aspects alone he has reproduced in his painting, using essential lines only and flat tones, with no light and shade and no perspective. Furthermore, he has arranged his birds in such a way that they form a composition balanced but free from monotony because of the variety in the plumage. The result is a work of superbly decorative design.

MINOR ARTS

But it was not in the fields of architecture, sculpture, and painting alone that early Egyptian art excelled. Supplementing these were the products of various craftsmen; and if we would understand aright the art of Egypt we must not disregard the creations of the goldsmith, stone-cutter, the weaver, and other craftsmen. In neolithic times man had developed stone-cutting until he flaked knives that were beautiful in shape and precise in technique (PL. 8 c). Thus the stone-cutter in historic times had an inherited tradition; and with the invention, before 3000 B.C., of the stone-pointed drill with a shaft, fly-wheel, and crank for turning (FIG. 20) and, somewhat after 3000 B.C., of the tubular drill of metal, he was enabled to produce vessels of astonishing quality for various household purposes — for the table, for storage, and for the toilet. Such hard stones as porphyry, diorite, and hematite were used, as is seen in PL. 8 D, where the variegated color of the stone adds a decorative quality. A bowl like this was first shaped from the block of stone; then the inside was drilled out. If it had a wide mouth, it might be put on a wheel and ground while revolving, just as the potter molded his vase by keeping it moving with treadles. Finally, the exterior was ground to a polish. Among the softer stones alabaster was widely used (PL. 8 E), for not only was its creamy white color attractive but the veining could be utilized by a skilled craftsman as a decorative element. The shape and size vary greatly; from the tiny jar for unguent to the great storage jars, bowls, and plates a foot in diameter. Some of these stone

(*A*) Sheikh el-Beled. Of wood. IV Dynasty (2900–2750 B.C.). Cairo Museum. (Haskell Oriental Museum)

(*B*) Seated Scribe. H. c. 2 ft. Louvre, Paris. (Giraudon)

(*C*) Palette of King Narmer. Slate. H. c. 20 in. Cairo Museum.

PLATE 6

(A) Geese of Meidum. So called because the panel was found in a tomb chapel near

(B) Ti Hunting in the Papyrus Marsh. From the mastaba of Ti, Saqquara. V Dynasty (2750–2625 B.C.). (Steindorff)

PLATE 7

Meidum. IV Dynasty (2900–2750 B.C.). Cairo Museum.

(A) Panel of Hesire. Wood. H. c. 4 ft.
c. 2800 B.C. Cairo Museum.

(B) Ceremonial Vase, Restored. Of gold and lapis
lazuli. H. c. 2 ft. c. 2750 B.C. (Stoedtner)

PLATE 8

(A) Bracelet. Gold, turquoise, and amethyst.
c. 3400 B.C. Cairo Museum.

(B) Head of a Hawk. Gold. H. 4 in.
Cairo Museum. (Fechheimer)

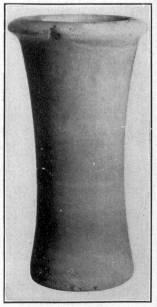

(C) Ripple-Flaked Knife. L. c. 10 in.
Brussels Museum. (Brussels Museum)

(D) Bowl, Engraved with the Name of Menes. Por-
phyry. D. 8 in. c. 3400 B.C. Haskell Oriental
Museum, University of Chicago. (Haskell Oriental
Museum)

(E) Alabaster Ointment Vase. H. 7 in.
Art Institute, Chicago. (Art Institute)

vessels, especially the alabaster plates and wide-mouthed bowls, are worked to a translucent thinness. Ornamentation is rarely found on the stone vases, for the varied color and the mottling and veining of the stone furnished sufficient decoration.

Closely allied with the work of the stone-cutter was that of the goldsmith, as is seen in a bracelet (Pl. 8 a), composed of two groups of beads joined by twisted bands. The materials used are gold, amethyst, and turquoise. In the center of the large group of beads is a gold rosette, one of the earliest examples of this motif, which is derived from the lotus flower; joined to this are groups of turquoise and gold beads graduating in size and alternating in color until they meet the large balls of deep amethyst; the smaller group of beads corresponds with the larger, except for the rosette, and the two are connected by a twisted band of hair and gold, the metal drawn out to the same diameter as the hair. The soldering of the gold is so skillfully done that it can scarcely be detected with the magnifying glass. The dignity and fine taste displayed in the design of this bracelet, together with the technical skill shown, only manifest in another way the same sound judgment and lofty restraint in artistic matters that we have seen in the *Pyramids of Gizeh*, the statue of *Khafre*, and the panel of *Hesire*.

Another example of the goldsmith's work is a hawk's head (Pl. 8 b) that was originally attached to a bronze body by rivets still left just below the neck. With his hammer and sheet of gold the craftsman beat out of the metal the different parts, soldered them together, and inserted the eyes cut from red jasper. Like the painter of the *Geese of Meidum*, this goldsmith had observed his bird form and knew it well; and with an amazing economy of modeling and of line he has shown both the great vivacity of the hawk and also the significant characteristics of its physiognomy.

The same astonishing ability in craftsmanship is again seen in a ceremonial vase (Pl. 7 b) found in one of the pyramids at Abusir. In making this vase the artist first cut out a wooden core which he covered with gold, and then inlaid the metal with blue lapis lazuli. The design on the neck and the band just below the shoulder, derived from the iridescent peacock plumage, unifies the composition and also emphasizes the hieroglyphs that are arranged so decoratively on the shoulder of the vase. The elegance of the shape the artist has enhanced by making his design follow the structural lines, at the same time obtaining a balance of vertical and horizontal line by a zonal arrangement.

SUMMARY

In early Egypt up to the end of the Old Kingdom, we have seen an art which, though restricted by certain conventions, gives evidence of keen powers of observation and orderly thinking which discerned essentials in structure and design, and recognized the purpose for which the idea was to be adapted and the material through which it was to be expressed. This led to a clarity and directness of expression in which there was no need for covering defects by unnecessary detail or superficial prettiness. And whether we take as examples of this art the *Pyramid of Khufu*, the statue of *Khafre*, the *Geese of Meidum*, or the bracelet, we find each conceived with vigor and dignity, and executed with amazing craftsmanship.

BIBLIOGRAPHY

BAEDEKER, KARL, Egypt. Leipzig, 1914.

BAIKIE, JAMES, Life in the Ancient East. N.Y., Macmillan, 1923.

BREASTED, J. H., Ancient Times. Boston, Ginn, 1916.

—— ——, History of Egypt from the Earliest Times to the Persian Conquest. N.Y., Scribner, 1909.

—— ——, Development of Religion and Thought in Ancient Egypt. N.Y., Scribner, 1912.

BRITISH MUSEUM, Wall Decorations of Egyptian Tombs. London, 1914.

—— ——, Pictorial postcards. Set XXXIII: Portrait Statues of the Kings and Queens of Egypt; XXXIV: Egyptian Sculptures, B.C. 4000–100; XXXV: Egyptian Mummies; XXXVI: Egyptian Coffins; C1: Egyptian Book of the Dead; C2: Egyptian Mummies and Coffins.

CAPART, JEAN, L'Art égyptien. 2 v. Brussels, Vromant, 1909–11.

—— ——, Egyptian Art (tr. Dawson). London, Allen, 1923.

CARTER, HOWARD, AND MACE, A. C., Tomb of Tut-ankh-Amen. London, Cassell, 1923.

CHICAGO ART INSTITUTE, Handbook of the Egyptian Collection, by T. G. Allen. Chicago, University of Chicago Press, 1923.

FECHHEIMER, HEDWIG, Kleinplastik der Aegypter. Berlin, Cassirer, 1921.

—— ——, Plastik der Aegypter. Berlin, Cassirer, 1923.

FLETCHER, SIR BANISTER, History of Architecture on the Comparative Method. N.Y., Scribner, 1924.

HAMLIN, A. D. F., History of Ornament, Ancient and Medieval. N.Y., Century, 1921.

KIMBALL, FISKE, AND EDGELL, G. H., History of Architecture. N.Y., Harper, 1918.

LAURIE, A. P., Materials of the Painter's Craft in Europe and Egypt. Philadelphia, Lippincott, 1911.

MASPERO, G. C. C., Art in Egypt. N.Y., Scribner, 1912.

—— ——, Manual of Egyptian Archæology. N.Y., Putnam, 1914.

—— ——, Popular Stories of Ancient Egypt (tr. Johns). N.Y., Putnam, 1915.

METROPOLITAN MUSEUM OF ART, Tomb of Nakht at Thebes (by N. de G. Davies). N.Y. 1917.

—— ——, Tomb of Perneb. N.Y., 1916.

—— ——, "Treasure of Lahun." Bulletin XIV, Pt. II.   N.Y., Dec., 1919.

Petrie, Sir W. M. F., Arts and Crafts of Ancient Egypt. London, Foulis, 1923.
—— ——, Social Life in Ancient Egypt. London, Constable, 1923.
Weigall, A. E. P., Life and Times of Akhnaton. N.Y., Putnam, 1922.
Winlock, H. E., "Bas-Reliefs from the Temple of Rameses I at Abydos." Metropolitan Museum of Art Papers, v. I, Pt. I. N.Y., 1921.
Winter, Franz, ed., Kunstgeschichte in Bildern: v. I, Das Altertum. Leipzig, Seemann, 1913.

CHAPTER III
EGYPTIAN PERIOD (2)
The Middle Kingdom and Empire, 2160–1090 B.C.

HISTORICAL BACKGROUND

The tendency toward weakening the power of the pharaoh to the advantage of the nobles had plunged the country into a period of struggle and disorder out of which eventually arose a feudal state at the head of which still stood the pharaoh; but he maintained his power by balancing the nobles one against another. Economically it was a period of great prosperity. Agriculture was developed by building canals and reclaiming the land; commerce was carried on not only in the south but also with Asia and the Ægean islands. And now Egypt became a military power. Athirst for conquests, she extended her boundaries not only far south into Nubia but east to the Euphrates. So on the monuments we see military subjects, weapons, chariots, and the horse, which, coming with the pre-Indo-Europeans from the grasslands of central Asia, finally reached the Nile valley about 1700 B.C. The wealth that came from the booty taken in these wars made possible the development of the capital city, Thebes, into a great metropolis with magnificent palaces, tombs, and temples ranged along both banks of the river (FIG. 27).

A considerable advance had been made in thought and religion. The Egyptian could now look back over his own history for centuries. The fresh and vital faith of the pyramid age, in the light of the futility of man's greatest efforts, changed to pessimism which is reflected in the portraits of the age (PL. 12 c) and also in the literature.

> I have heard the words of Imhotep and Harzozef,
> Whose utterances are of much reputation;
> Yet how are the places thereof?
> Their walls are in ruin,
> Their places are no more, —
> As if they had never been.
> None cometh from thence,
> That he might tell us of their state;
> That he might restore our hearts,
> Until we too depart to the place,

Whither they have gone.
Encourage thy heart to forget it,
And let the heart dwell upon that which is profitable for thee.
Follow thy desire while thou livest,

. . . .
Celebrate the glad day!
Rest not therein!
For lo, none taketh his goods with him,
Yea, no man returneth again, that is gone thither.[1]

At the same time we discern a new note in reference to the future life; for to the earlier faith in the possibility of a hereafter was added a conception of a day of judgment when the final weighing of the deeds of this life would condition the next. Hence, on the tombs we find inscriptions of this kind: "I gave bread to the hungry, water to the thirsty, clothing to the naked, and a ferryboat to the boatless." "I was father to the orphan, husband to the widow, and a shelter to the shelterless." Magic formulæ were written on papyrus and buried with the dead to assist him on the judgment day as he stood before Osiris for the weighing of his deeds. This practice, however, led to great corruption on the part of the priests, from whom it was possible to purchase formulæ by which evil deeds would not testify against a man.

It was an age also of the development of folk tales, when stories of adventures and of animals took shape, forming the basis of the tales of Sinbad the Sailor, and Brer Fox and Brer Rabbit.

This broadening horizon of thought and the growth of the idea of world empire fired the imagination of a young king (1375–1358 B.C.), who, applying the principle of political power to the realm of religion, conceived the idea of one god and creator, whom he called Aton, an old name of the sun-god Re. He then broke both politically and religiously with the powerful though corrupt régime at Thebes, took for himself the name Ikhnaton, which means "spirit of Aton," and set up a new capitol at a place that he called Akhetaton (now known as Amarna) meaning "horizon of Aton." Something of the spirit of the new faith we feel in the hymns that Ikhnaton wrote:

The Splendor of Aton

Thy dawning is beautiful in the horizon of heaven,
O living Aton, Beginning of life!
When thou risest in the eastern horizon of heaven,
Thou fillest every land with thy beauty;
For thou art beautiful, great, glittering, high over the earth;
Thy rays, they encompass the lands, even all thou hast made.

. . . .

[1] Breasted, *History of Egypt*, p. 206.

How manifold are all thy works!
They are hidden from before us,
O thou sole god, whose powers no other possesseth.
Thou didst create the earth according to thy desire,
While thou wast alone:
Men, all cattle large and small,
All that are upon the earth,
That fly with their wings,
The countries of Syria and Nubia,
The land of Egypt.
Thou settest every man in his place,
Thou suppliest their necessities.[2]

Egypt by this time, however, was too crystallized by the traditions of thousands of years, too enthralled by its nobles, military leaders, and particularly by the powerful priesthood of Amon, to accept an idea so contrary to tradition. Ikhnaton, by nature not a practical man of affairs, became absorbed entirely in the religion of Aton; with the result that, through upheavals at home and invasions from without, the empire dwindled and Ikhnaton fell, the first monotheist, an idealist far ahead of his times. The power at Thebes was restored and the empire partly reorganized by Seti I (1313–1292 B.C.) and Ramses II, the Great (1292–1225 B.C.), but never firmly reëstablished. Egyptian history continues long after this time, but in art, after the time of Ramses the Great, there is little that we have not already seen in the periods we have studied.

Life in "Hundred-gated Thebes" and at Amarna, too, was luxurious and magnificent. The enormous wealth of the pharaoh enabled him to erect a palace with decorations that reproduced for him the outdoor world in which he delighted. On the floors and walls, which were painted or decorated in glazed tiles, were represented ducks swimming in the water (PL. 15 c), and the animal life of the marshes (PL. 14 B); across the deep blue background of the ceiling flew flocks of birds, and butterflies. The furniture was superbly designed, and skillfully constructed (PL. 18). Magnificent gold and silver vessels, blue faïence lotus cups, glass vases of various colors, rich jewelry (PLs. 16 and 17) — all these tell of a magnificence quite in contrast to the sterner dignity of the pyramid age.

ARCHITECTURE

As the Old Kingdom was preëminently the period of the pyramid builder, so the Middle Kingdom and Empire were that of the

---

[2] Breasted, *History of Egypt*, pp. 371 ff., where a complete translation is given, in a parallel arrangement with one of the Hebrew Psalms, which it approximates to an amazing degree.

temple builder. This was not because burial no longer demanded the elaborate care shown earlier. An even more scrupulous attention was given to the protection of the body, but in a different way. Robberies and neglect had shown the futility of the pyramid for perfect preservation; and while pyramids continued to be built by the earlier pharaohs of the period, they were small, made of brick, and today are little more than mounds, though their substructures have yielded rich finds of jewelry and other mortuary equipment.

The nobles no longer sought a locality for burial near that of

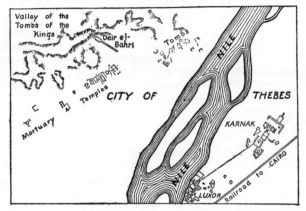

Fig. 27. Map of Thebes, showing the most important temples and tombs. The dwellings have disappeared.

the king, but hollowed out their tombs and chapels in the cliffs bordering the Nile. The pharaohs themselves, perhaps following the example of their retainers, chose for their burial site a wild, desolate valley west of the cliffs at Thebes now known as the Valley of the Tombs of the Kings (FIG. 27), where deep in the rocky hills they carved burial chambers which were reached by long corridors sometimes extending five hundred feet into the hillside (FIG. 28).[3] The entrances were carefully concealed; and because of the impracticability of making offerings at the actual tombs, the mortuary temples, which correspond to the chapel abutting the east side of the pyramid, were separated from the tombs and built on the eastern side of the cliffs along the bank of the river; but in each case the temple was on the axis of the tomb

[3] The *Tomb of Tutenkhamon*, discovered in the valley in 1922, is a rock-cut tomb of this type.

and hence in the same relative position as the pyramid chapel. Furthermore, these temples were dedicated to the gods, and each provided the king who built it with a place for worshiping his patron god during his lifetime, and then served as his mortuary chapel after his death. Hence they became elaborate and sumptuous, befitting both the kings and the gods of a mighty empire.

The noblest of these royal mortuary temples, though unique in many ways, is *Deir el-Bahri*,[4] the temple of Queen Hatshepsut (PL. 9). The site that the queen selected for her temple was a sloping bay in the western cliffs (FIG. 27), above which towered the rocks weathered into columnar shapes, the vertical lines of

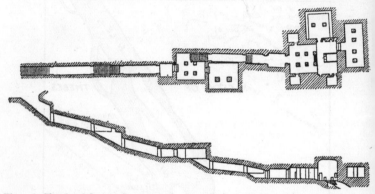

Fig. 28. Tomb of Seti I. Section and plan. Thebes, Valley of the Tombs of the Kings. XIX Dynasty (1350–1205 B.C.). (Benoit)

which contrast happily with the long horizontals of the plateau edge, while the rough surfaces afford deep shadows and a more broken mass of light and shade than is usual in Egypt. Mindful of these conditions, Hatshepsut and her architect built the temple on a triple terrace, each level consisting of an open colonnaded court with an inclined passage leading to the court above. The upper terrace abutted the cliff in which were cut the sanctuary and the shrines of the gods. Notice in the distant view how effectively the long horizontals of the lintels and the verticals of the shafts with their rhythm and light and shade repeat the horizontal and vertical lines of the great cliffs above — an example of marvelous adaptation of architectural design to the environment in which it is placed.

---

[4] *Deir el-Bahri*, meaning "the north monastery," is the modern Arab name of the locality from a monastery, now destroyed, that was built on the site.

In reconstructing in our minds this temple as it was in Hatshep-
ut's day, we must not think of these open courts as the barren
laces that they now are, but as luxuriant gardens, filled with
rankincense trees (PL. 9 c), and strange, rare plants brought
ere from the far-away land of Punt. The queen tells us in the
nscriptions and reliefs on the walls of the temple how she sent

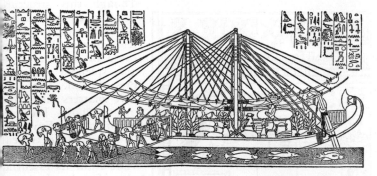

Fig. 29. Deir el-Bahri. Relief showing the loading of the ships in Punt. An
nscription reads: "The loading of the ships very heavily with marvels of the
ountry of Punt; all goodly fragrant woods of God's-Land, heaps of myrrh-resin,
vith fresh myrrh trees, with ebony and pure ivory, with green gold of Emu, with
Cinnamon wood, khesyt wood, with ihmut-incense, sonter-incense, eye-cosmetic,
vith apes, monkeys, dogs, and with skins of the southern panther, with natives
nd their children. Never was brought the like of this for any king who has been
ince the beginning." Breasted, *Ancient Records of Egypt*, II, 265. (Egypt Explora-
ion Society)

n expedition of ships to this country (FIG. 29) at the command
f Amon-Re, to obtain the plants:

I will cause you to know that which is commanded to me, I have hearkened
o my father . . . commanding me to establish for him a Punt in his house,
o plant the trees of God's-Land beside his temple, in his garden, according as he
ommanded. It was done . . . I have made for him a Punt in his garden, just as
e commanded me, for Thebes. It is large for him, he walks about in it.[5]

Not only is the general design of this temple reserved and noble,
ut the details consistently harmonize. It was this taste that
rompted the builder to use in his colonnades pillars either sim-
ly rectangular or chamfered off into sixteen sides, rather than
he more elaborate lotus or papyrus form so popular in most of
he temples of the period. The unfinished northern colonnade
f the middle terrace (PL. 9 B) is finely spaced and proportioned,

[5] Breasted, *Ancient Records*, II, 295.

reminding one of Greek work in its simplicity and quiet harmony. So too the painted reliefs reveal a high standard of decorative design (PL. 9 c and FIG. 30).

While *Deir el-Bahri* is the noblest temple in Egypt, it differs radically from the more usual pylon type, which we shall study as we find it in the *Temple of Horus* at Edfu (PL. 10 A and B).

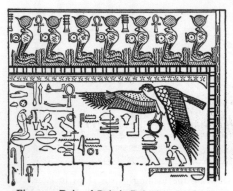

Fig. 30. Deir el-Bahri. Polychrome decoration showing the hawk of lower Egypt that hovers protectingly about the pharaoh. The motif of the border is the *uræus* combined with the sun-disc. The figures are painted in bright colors, chiefly red and blue, with a little green and yellow. (Naville)

Though this structure is of much later date, yet it affords an excellent basis for study because of its clear plan and splendid state of preservation. The date here matters little for our purpose because, when once the Egyptian had evolved his typical structure, he did not deviate from its essential plan for hundreds of years, remaining inflexible even after the Greeks and Romans became influential in the Nile valley.

As we approach the temple, the dominating feature is the great façade or pylon, simple, massive, with walls sloping inward as they rise, giving it the shape of a truncated pyramid reminiscent of the mastaba, and with no marked break in its lines except for the space left above the door. The broad surface is unbroken, except for the doorway with its overshadowing cornice, the four grooves to hold the great flagstaffs, and the low reliefs. A round molding finishes both the top and the sides. Passing through the doorway we enter a court open to the sunshine and surrounded on three sides by a colonnade. To this the crowds had access. Beyond rises a roofed hall, the hypostyle hall, for the priests and devotees, where the cool dimness contrasting with the bright sunshine of the open court, together with the rhythm of the massive shafts, inspires a feeling of solemnity. Still farther beyond lies the sanctuary, low, dark, mysterious, and secluded; for here only the priest and the pharaoh could enter. A girdle wall, beginning at the pylon, urrounds the structure. This temple at Edfu shows us then the eneral arrangement of a typical pylon temple (FIG. 31), which lways includes a pylon, an open colonnaded court, a hypostyle all, a sanctuary, sometimes surrounded by smaller chambers for he storage of the temple treasures nd for the use of the priests, and a irdle wall.

It is not surprising to find that the Egyptian temple, like the pyramid, is imple and massive, when we recall gain the geographic conditions of he country — that narrow strip of uxuriant river valley, bordered on oth sides by vast sterile deserts; a andscape of predominantly horizontal ines; and over all a continuously lear sky and overwhelming sunshine. Protection from the heat demanded hick walls with few apertures, and overed colonnades. So the temple n its outline presents a sternly simple nass of horizontal and vertical lines [6] with great unbroken surfaces of wall pace. But as we walk around the building and see its ornamentation nd reconstruct in our own minds hose parts of its decoration that are now lost, we realize that in addition o the simple mass and unbroken line here is a wealth of decorative detail which not only affords a contrast but also enhances through its rich-ness. The great reaches of wall sur-ace both inside and outside are overed with low reliefs originally painted in bright colors that were

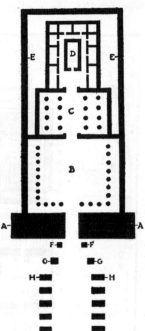

Fig. 31. Plan of a Typical Pylon Temple. *A*, pylon; *B*, court; *C*, hypostyle hall; *D*, sanctuary; *E*, girdle wall; *F*, colossal statues of the pharaoh; *G*, obelisks; *H*, avenue of recumbent animals.

oftened by the brilliant light. As the color has almost disap-peared, as many of these embellishments are lost, and as the tructures themselves are in a more or less ruined condition, let us reconstruct one of the great temples as it stood in the day of Ramses the Great. Approaching, we walk for some distance

[6] The Egyptian understood the arch (p. 56, note) and used it frequently in substructures and idden parts of the building; hence his preference for the lintel system seems to be based upon his nstinct for fitting design.

down the broad avenue bordered on both sides by statues o
recumbent rams (PL. 10 C) with metal discs between their horn:
Before us rises the massive pylon, in front of which stand the tw
obelisks (PL. 12 B) nearly a hundred feet high, covered wit
hieroglyphs, their glittering metal tips catching and reflectin

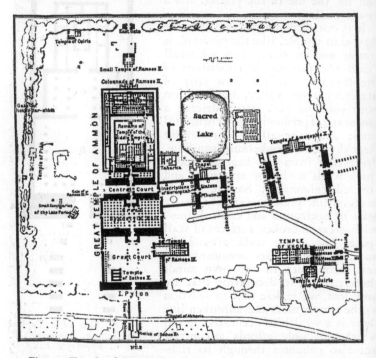

Fig. 32. Temple of Amon. Karnak. C. 2000 years in building, from the
time of the Middle Kingdom until that of the Ptolemies, I cent. B.C. Ramses I,
Seti I, and Ramses II, all of the XIX Dynasty (1350–1205 B.C.), built the great
hypostyle hall. (Baedeker)

the sunshine as they rise far above the top of the pylon. O
each side of the doorway stands a colossal statue of the pharaoh
in the grooves rest the huge wooden staffs that carry the flag:
floating above the cornice. The wall space is covered with low
reliefs brilliantly painted; the great door of cedar of Lebanon is
decorated with shining metal, while surrounding and framing
the whole structure are the rich green masses of palms and

PLATE 9

) Temple of Queen
tshepsut. Deir el-
hri. XVIII Dy-
sty (1580–1350 B.C.)

) Deir el-Bahri.
orthern colonnade.
Haskell Oriental
useum)

C) Deir el-Bahri.
rankincense trees.
Naville)

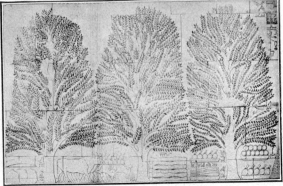

PLATE 10

(A) Temple [of] Horus. Edfu. V[iew] from the side, sh[ow]ing the pylon [and] open court. (Gad[dis] and Seif)

(B) Temple [of] Horus. Edfu. Vi[ew] from the top of t[he] pylon, showing pa[rt] of the open cou[rt,] the hypostyle ha[ll,] sanctuary, a[nd] girdle wall. (Gad[dis] and Seif)

(C) Temple [of] Amon. Karna[k.] Avenue of ram[s] leading to the pylo[n.] (Gaddis and Seif)

ropical plants. It must have been a magnificent sight, as well as ne inspiring feelings of mystery and awe.

The two most famous temples of the Empire are *Luxor* and *Karnak* (FIG. 32). If we look at these closely, we shall see that hey are merely complex arrangements of the simple plan of *Edfu;* or it became the custom for each succeeding pharaoh to add to is glory by building an additional hypostyle hall or pylon to vhat was already a complete temple. One fact only needs to be nentioned that *Edfu* does not illustrate. In the great hypostyle all of *Karnak* (PL. 11 A), the two central rows of columns are igher than the side rows, which means that the roof over the enter is higher than that on the sides. The wall space connecting these two levels is filled with perforated stone windows

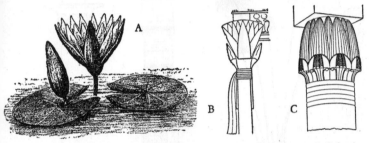

Fig. 33. *A*, Blue Lotus. *B*, Lotus Flower Column, *C*, Lotus Bud Column.
(Borchardt)

for the admission of light. Here is a fully developed clerestory, the beginnings of which we saw in the valley-temple of the *Pyramid of Khafre* (PL. 3 B and FIG. 25).

The decorative motifs that the Egyptian used in the embellishment of his temples were taken chiefly from the lotus, the papyrus, and the palm. The palm we saw used in the colonnade of the *Pyramid of Sahure* (PL. 4 A). The lotus was very popular with the Egyptian. We see children gathering it in the streams while the elders enjoy the perfume, weave it into garlands, or mass bunches of it over the water jars, to keep the water fresh. Two varieties chiefly were used as decorative motifs, the blue and the white. The craftsmen used its form to shape their cups and to fashion their cosmetic boxes; they carved it from ivory, wove it into their textiles, and molded it for glazed wall tiles. So, too, the builders employed it to decorate their columns (FIG. 33) — not with the highest success, however, as is shown especially in the lotus flower capital, where the spreading petal militate against the feeling of solidity and stability that shoul characterize a member whose function is to support. More suc cessful is the cluster of buds.

The papyrus plant (FIG. 34), now extinct in Egypt but in earl days plentiful, produced a flower whose feathery petals forme a bell-shaped mass. The columns forming the central row o the hypostyle hall of *Luxor* (PL. 12 A) have capitals the form of which has been suggested by the papyrus flower, whil the columns of the colonnade in the background are based or a cluster of papyrus buds. The stems of this cluster are tie

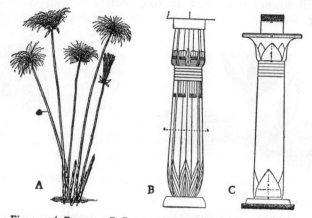

Fig. 34. *A*, Papyrus. *B*, Papyrus Cluster Bud Column. *C*, Papyrus Flower Column. (Borchardt)

tightly below the buds, whose swelling contours form the capital. Were it not for this broad band to hold the stems firmly together, the shaft would give one a feeling of insecurity by seeming incapable of performing its function of support. The shafts of both the flower and the bud type contract at the base, as does the stem of the plant; for the Egyptian, when conventionalizing his plant forms, closely observed nature. In design, proportions, and workmanship, these colonnades at *Luxor* are the noblest to be found in the pylon temples.

The more apparent does this become when we turn to the hypostyle hall of *Karnak* (PL. 11). Here, according to the usual convention, the columns of the central aisle are of the papyrus flower type; those of the side aisles, of the papyrus bud. But compare the latter with the bud type at *Luxor*. At *Karnak*, only the general contour of the cluster has been retained, producing a heavy, ungainly shaft. It is as if the architects, in haste to complete this mighty hall, were depending upon bulk and barbaric splendor to create an effect. And they were partly successful in their attempt, for notwithstanding the shabby workmanship a certain overwhelming impressiveness results from the mere number and size of these mighty shafts. Yet this impressiveness is not the same satisfying kind which we feel in the noble colonnades of *Deir el-Bahri* (PL. 9 B), in the powerful simplicity of Khafre's valley-temple (PL. 3 B), or in the subtle proportions of the *Pyramid of Khufu* (PL. 2 C).

SCULPTURE

In studying the sculpture of the Middle Kingdom and the Empire, we shall look at three portraits. In *Amenemhet III*[7] (PL. 12 C) we see a powerful characterization. Here is not only the warrior and the ruler, but the individual man who lived and thought intensely. The generalized modeling of the Old Kingdom portraits, such as that of *Khafre*, has given way to the expression of individual characteristics. In the strong mouth, the drooping lines about the nose and eyes, and the shadowing brows, we discern a man, who, though still powerful, has lost faith. "In all his energetic effigies is cast a shadow as of one who had lived to see the extinction of some great hope, or the dawn of some great threat."

In the head of *Ikhnaton* (PL. 13 B), we do not feel primarily the ruler or even the official class to which this man belongs. What is significant is the thoroughly human characterization of that remarkable young king; emphasizing, in the pose of the head, the long neck, the drooping mouth and lids, and the almost effeminate delicacy, the essential elements of his character, which was first of all that of the dreamer and idealist.

For the expression of individual charm, the head of *Nofretete* (COLOR PL. I), wife of Ikhnaton, stands preëminent. In the long slender neck, the sensitive mouth, the delicate modeling, and the charming color, one feels an aristocratic, queenly bearing combined with a simple, unaffected grace.

When we compare these three heads with those of *Khafre*, *Ranofer*, and the *Princess*, we observe a striking difference. We

---

[7] The broken ornament on the headdress just above the forehead is the *uraeus*, or serpent, the symbol of royalty in Egypt.

miss the vivacity, the alertness, and the serene grandeur of the earlier work, in which individuality, though present, is subordinated to the abstract idea of sovereignty or nobility. In its place we find that the chief aim of the artist has been to express the significant characteristics of the individual, his emotions and his inner life.

The reliefs of the period show the same tendencies. In the *Funeral Procession* (PL. 13 c), the figures are arranged as usual in zones. But the grouping is becoming a little more complex, with more overlapping of the figures. In the lower zone at the right are the two sons of the deceased, following the bier. Their figures are superb expressions of abandonment to grief, in marked contrast to the elegant formality of the nobles behind them. Such an expression of emotion in itself shows a great change in Egyptian art; furthermore, the freedom with which the body is made to express the emotion, and the surprisingly good drawing here seen, the greater ease and facility of line, in contrast to the angularity of the Old Kingdom reliefs, are indications that the sculptors were turning to nature rather than following implicitly the traditional methods of representation. The same phenomena are discernible in the figures of the servants in the upper zone.

The man of whose work we have here a mere fragment was a master of ripe and mature culture, an observer of life, whose work exhibits alike the pathos and the wistful questioning of human sorrow, recognizing both the necessity and the cruel indifference of official conventionality, and seeing, amid all, the play of the vain and ostentatious fashions of the hour. Here across thirty-five centuries there speaks to us a maturity in the contemplation of life which finds a sympathetic response in every cultivated observer.[8]

This note of freedom received powerful impetus from Ikhnaton's revolution. The new faith with its conception of a sole creator of all life turned men's attention to nature and lifted art expression out from mere traditional convention. But reaction in art as well as in religion set in after the failure of the revolution. The priests of Amon had triumphed. Not only did they attempt to eradicate the heresy by destroying the works of art created by the Amarna artists, and by removing from them all references to the hated Aton, but they enshackled the artists with their dogmatic conceptions even more securely than before. For it was the priests who controlled both the subject and the method of representation. Still, even with these restrictions, a brief period of high attainment was reached by the Egyptians

[8] Breasted, *History of Egypt*, p. 347.

PLATE II

A) Temple of
Amon. Karnak.
Hypostyle hall, central part. From a
model in Metropolitan Museum of Art.
(Metropolitan Museum)

B) Temple of
Amon. Karnak.
Hypostyle hall, central aisle. The columns are 66 ft. high,
and the capitals 22
ft. wide at the top.
XIX Dynasty
(1350–1205 B.C.).
(Gaddis and Seif)

PLATE 12

(*A*) Temple of Amon. Luxor. Right: central colonnade of an unfinished hypostyle hall; center and left: double colonnaded court. XVIII Dynasty (1580–1350 B.C.). (Gaddis and Seif)

(*B*) Temple of Amon. Luxor. Pylon, with statues of the pharaoh, and one obelisk; the companion obelisk now stands in Paris. XIX Dynasty (1350–1205 B.C.). (Gaddis and Seif)

(*C*) Amenemhet III. Obsidian. H. c. 5 in. XII Dynasty (2000–1788 B.C.). MacGregor coll., Tamworth. (*Journal Egyptian Archæology*)

PLATE 13

(*A*) Ibis on Papyrus. From a tomb at Beni Hasan. c. 2000 B.C. Detail of Fig 35. (Newberry)

(*B*) Ikhnaton. Painted sandstone. H. c. 8 in. 1375–1358 B.C. Staatliche Museum, Berlin. (Grantz)

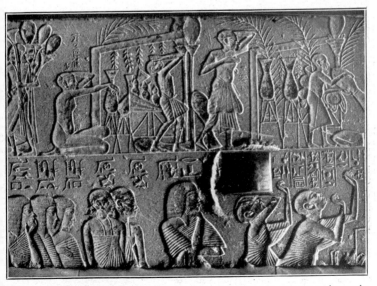

(*C*) Funeral Procession of a High Priest. Upper zone: garden scene, servants setting up the funeral booth; lower zone: funeral procession. XVIII Dynasty (1580–1350 B.C.). Staatliche Museum, Berlin. (Staatliche Museum)

PLATE 14

(*A*) Osiris and Goddesses. XIX Dynasty (1350–1205 B.C.). Temple of Seti, Abydos. (Kodak)

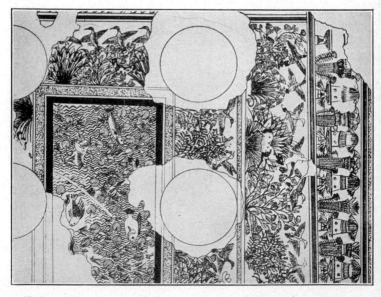

(*B*) Painted Floor Decoration. Detail. From the palace of Ikhnaton, Amarna. (Petrie)

before their art was strangled by the triumph of their crystallizing conventions.[9]

A wall decoration in the *Temple of Seti I* at Abydos (PL. 14 A) will illustrate this return to convention. The figures are painted in bright colors laid on flat; and the first impression is one of beautiful decoration. We have noted the Egyptian's skill in composition from earliest times. That it was thoughtfully planned, we know from many unfinished works where guide lines are still left upon the wall. The large central panel was spaced with due regard to the wall area and surrounded by borders that in turn were carefully paneled and decorated with figures and inscriptions. Within the central space are four standing figures and one seated. Looking at the standing figures, we see that they are highly conventional, carved with a firm, clear-cut contour line that is at the same time sure and flexible; and relief is softly rounded, giving a suggestion of shadow. Within the contour line there is very little modeling. The knowledge and expression of anatomy that we saw in the panel of *Hesire* (PL. 7 A) is no longer discernible. Instead, we have a symbol that suggests rather than represents the figure. But the beautiful cameo-like quality of the work, acquired only through a long-lived tradition, the graceful sweep of contour, the delicacy of texture, indicated by most sensitive line, the harmonious color, and the orderly composition — all these give the relief a superbly decorative quality.

Temple decoration was a primary purpose of much of the sculpture produced in this period. The pharaohs of the Empire covered their temple walls on the inside with representations of a religious nature, such as the king making offerings to the god; on the outside, with records of their wars and their hunts. Besides immortalizing their deeds in the reliefs, they placed at the entrance of the temple colossal statues of themselves (PL. 12 B) to correspond with the gigantic size of the building.[10] This architectural sculpture was carved in a very summary way. Yet it fits so admirably the decorative purpose for which it was made that it is astonishingly impressive. Animals too played their part in the architectural sculpture (PL. 10 c). In all the figures there is the dignity, repose, and enduring quality that characterize Egyptian art.

[9] The *Tomb of Tutenkhamon* is adding greatly to our knowledge of this period, for many of the works of art found there appear to have been made under the direct influence of the Amarna school.

[10] Perhaps the best known examples are the so-called *Colossi of Memnon*, nearly seventy feet high, which are portrait statues of the pharaoh Amenhotep III, and which stood with two great obelisks at the entrance of the pylon of his mortuary temple on the western bank of the Nile at Thebes.

PAINTING

Painting had been practiced in Egypt since prehistoric times, though more as an accessory of sculpture than as an independent art. The *Geese of Meidum* (PL. 6 A) was one of the exceptions, but even there, one feels the chisel in the precision of the outline. The tomb painters of the Middle Kingdom and Empire, however, came to a realization of the value of painting for itself. Hence they began to eliminate the relief and paint directly upon the tomb wall. This was due partly to the fact that the stone from which many of the tombs were excavated was coarse and rough, and unsuitable for carving. Hence they covered it with plaster and stucco to form a smooth surface, upon which they painted directly. As the brush is more facile than the chisel, permitting greater ease and freedom both of line and of color, we soon begin to see evidences of the change.

Fig. 35. Wall Decoration of a Tomb. Beni Hasan. Detail of right side showing the noble harpooning fish. (Egypt Exploration Society)

Let us look at the decoration of one of these tombs. Certain conditions were imposed upon the decorator, namely, a space with a clearly felt triple division, cut in the center by a door. But one is immediately impressed with the success of the design. Having enclosed the inscriptions in a wide border that forms a dado and frames the door, with two seated figures to give an accent at that point, the painter placed on the side panels in balanced position two similar hunting scenes, with the large figure of the noble as the center of interest. He is out in the papyrus marsh in his reed boat accompanied by his family, fowling; on the right he is harpooning fish (FIG. 35). In the narrow border below the noble' boat is a second river scene, in which there is great freedom of action. The figures are wonderfully expressive of natural movement and show a consistent profile in the drawing. This is true also of the figures of the wrestlers (FIG. 36), which reveal the greatest variety of movement and a careful observation and recording of momentary action.

The expression of bird and animal life in these Beni Hasan tombs[11] is astonishing in its observation of nature and also in its ability to represent, often by the most economical drawing, an instantaneous moment. Of many examples representing bird life, both in flight and at rest, the *Ibis on Papyrus* is typical (Pl. 13 a). The bird has alighted upon three papyrus blooms, the central one lower and nearer the left so that the bird rests easily and the grouping is compact. The drawing even in its great economy adequately expresses the bird form; and the firm, unfaltering line is beautiful in itself.

Another example of a closely naturalistic expression is found in the *Ducks Swimming* among the lotus plants (Pl. 15 c). A comparison with the *Geese of Meidum* (Pl. 6 a) brings one to a realiza-

Fig. 36. Wrestlers. Beni Hasan. (Egypt Exploration Society)

tion of the tendency of this later period. Both paintings were architectural decorations: one on a tomb wall, the other on a palace floor. Both represent fine observation of the bird form especially in movement, but the emphasis has shifted from the purely decorative quality to the naturalistic.

Of many wall paintings of Theban tombs, we shall look at two. The first represents part of a *Banquet Scene* (Pl. 15 a) where six guests are seated upon mats near a blind musician who is playing his harp. The guests wear long, thin garments, wigs held by a fillet, and on the crown of the head a conical object to contain perfumed unguent; they have wreathed lotus flowers about their heads or hold them in their hands; they all wear elaborate collar necklaces and large disc earrings, one of which a little waiting-maid is adjusting. The grouping is more sophisticated than in the Old Kingdom painting; the figures overlap; everywhere is greater freedom of pose and movement. The bright

[11] For color reproductions of these paintings, see Newberry, *Beni Hasan*. Archæological Survey of Egypt, London, 1893–1900.

color adds vivacity to the scene and also enhances the decorative quality of the wall surface.[12]

Another painting from a Theban tomb represents a fragment from a *Fowling Scene* (PL. 15 B). The noble is standing in his boat and with his boomerang is driving the birds from the papyrus swamp. In his right hand he holds three birds that he has caught, while his hunting cat, on a papyrus stem just in front of him, has caught two more in her claws and is holding the wings of a third with her teeth. His two companions, perhaps his wife and little daughter, are enjoying the lotus that they have gathered. The water is indicated by the usual wave line. The cat, the fish, and the birds are painted with the same charming naturalism as the *Ducks Swimming*. While the conventional representation of the figure, on the whole, still remains, the quality of line in these Theban paintings is superb. The painter has drawn the figure with long firm strokes that never fumble or hesitate; and more than once he has broken from tradition and has drawn a profile correctly.[13]

This tendency to naturalism received great impetus, as did sculpture, from Ikhnaton. In his own palace at Amarna, for example, the floor decoration of one room represented a pool of water surrounded by the appropriate zones of life and vegetation (PL. 14 B). In the center is the pool, with birds, fish, and aquatic plants; bordering this is the marshland with birds flying about; beyond, the meadow land with tall grasses through which calves are running. All the forms, both plant and animal, are painted with a new freedom. An illusion of nature, however, does not dominate; for the Egyptian's never failing sense of design has grouped the scenes into an orderly arrangement by inclosing them with firm lines and a conventional outer border, so that representation and decoration are happily blended. Even in the more formal ceiling decorations (FIG. 37) interesting adaptations of lotus and papyrus are interwoven with spirals and other geometric forms.

In painting, as in sculpture, emancipation from traditional convention was not very long-lived. The reaction from the worship of Aton, so fanatical that it destroyed not only the works of art but the intellectual freedom that created them, brought the painters back to the crystallizing domination of the priesthood.

---

[12] For fine color reproductions of this tomb, see Davies, *Tomb of Nakht at Thebes.* N.Y., Metropolitan Museum, 1917.

[13] In the Theban paintings of the Empire there appears to be a slight use of light and shade to express the roundness of the figure. Discoloration and chemical changes in the pigments make a final statement on this question difficult.

PLATE 15

A) Banquet Scene. From the tomb of Nakht, Thebes. XVIII Dynasty (1580–1350 B.C.)

B) Fowling Scene. From a Theban tomb. XVIII Dynasty (1580–1350 B.C.). British Museum, London. (British Museum)

C) Ducks Swimming. Fragment from a painted floor decoration of a Theban palace. XVIII Dynasty (1580–1350 B.C.). (Tytus)

PLATE 16

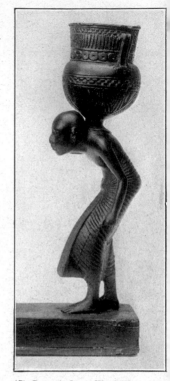

(*A*) Necklace with Pectoral of Senusert II. Metropolitan Museum, New York. (Metropolitan Museum)

(*B*) Cosmetic Jar. Wood, 8¾ in. high. XVIII Dynasty (1580–1350 B.C.). Liverpool Museum. (Liverpool Museum)

(*C*) Pectoral of Senusert II (detail of *A*). Gold, inlaid and engraved. W. 3¼ in. at the base. 1849–1801 B.C. Metropolitan Museum, New York. (Metropolitan Museum)

Like the reliefs of Seti at Abydos, moreover, later drawings reveal a superb craftsmanship that enabled the artist to draw the contour of the figure from the top of the head to the foot with one stroke of his brush and with a line that for economy and power can scarcely be equaled.

MINOR ARTS

When we think of the wealth of the Middle Kingdom and Empire and see the magnificence and luxuriousness of the palaces and temples, it is natural to expect corresponding characteristics in the articles of personal adornment and household furnishings.

Fig. 37. Painted Decoration of a Tomb Ceiling.

This is what we find in all the craft-work of the period. Jewelry played an important part in the personal adornment of the Egyptian, as we see in the sculpture and painting of all periods. The diadem of a princess (PL. 18 A) is made of gold threads, fine enough to lose themselves in the strands of the hair, along which are scattered tiny florets with blue petals and red centers. This delicate circlet is caught at intervals by crosses of blue with red centers. This cross, now known as the Maltese, is formed of four bell-shaped papyrus flowers, the sturdy contours and formality of which strengthen by contrast the delicate naturalism of the florets. Not only is the design noteworthy for its grace and daintiness, but the cutting and setting of the stones reveal great technical skill on the part of the craftsman.

The pectoral, which was a breast ornament suspended by a necklace, was a popular form of jewelry. The pectoral of Senusert II (Pl. 16 a and c) is made of an open-work gold plate engraved on the underside and inlaid with turquoise, lapis lazuli, and carnelian on the upper. In the center of the design a kneeling figure of a man is holding palm branches on which rests the royal cartouche, that is, the name of the king, flanked on each side by a royal falcon, while the intermediate space is filled with the *uræus* and sun disc, from which is suspended the sign of life. It is a design of clarity, dignity, and delicacy; in fact the central part of the design would be fragile were it not strengthened by the sturdy backs of the falcons and the firm line of the base that frames it. The birds are united very skillfully to the central design by the disc of the *uræus* above and by the claws braced so firmly against the palm branches below. The blue of the lapis lazuli and that of the turquoise are well balanced and the whole design unified by the careful distribution of the red carnelian. On the back of the pectoral the plumage and other details are finely engraved in the gold. The necklace consists of drop beads arranged in pairs in a fourfold unit of blue-green feldspar, lapis lazuli, carnelian, and gold; the gold clasp is ingeniously designed with a dovetail groove and a tongue.

Further evidence of the products of the metal worker we see in a silver wine jug (Pl. 17 b) in which the Egyptian craftsman, with his characteristic love of the out-of-doors, has revealed his imaginative power in forming the handle in the shape of a gazelle which, with hind legs resting upon the body of the jug and forelegs pressed against the neck, is eagerly stretching up to sniff the wine.

In much of the handicraft of the period is seen this happy adaptation of the forms of nature — human, plant, and animal — to decorative design. In the field of woodcarving, the cosmetic receptacles well illustrate this tendency. As the Egyptians made free use of cosmetics, we find many varieties of receptacles for this purpose. A so-called "perfume spoon" (Pl. 17 a) is shaped to represent a girl swimming and pushing along a duck whose body forms the cosmetic box, with the opening between the slightly parted wings — the whole conception a charming adaptation of the human and bird form to a utilitarian purpose. Again, the jar in Pl. 16 b furnishes another illustration of the same principle, the slave bending beneath the weight of his burden. Natural representation is there, but skillfully adapted.

The cabinetmaker was another craftsman who attained great

astery not only in the utility but in the design and the workmanship of his furniture and household utensils, combining in
is products the craft of the goldsmith, the ivory-carver, and the
lapidary. This is seen in a jewel-casket (PL. 17 D) of great beauty
nd refined taste that was found in the same pyramid as the
ectoral of Senusert II. The beauty lies partly in the color harmony — ebony, ivory, gold, blue faïence, and carnelian — but
largely in the quiet richness that results from the design, which is
ased upon carefully proportioned panels that follow the struc-
ural lines of the casket. The narrow panels are decorated alter-
ately with gold ornaments and strips of blue faïence crowned
with a square of red carnelian. Their decorative effect is height-
ned by the quiet, unadorned ivory rectangle above. The
urve of the base harmonizes with the hollow cornice and the
urved lid, in which are inlaid Hathor heads of gold, blue faïence,
nd carnelian.

Magnificent furniture has come from the tombs, some of which
pparently had been used by the deceased in his palace before it
erved him in his tomb. Typical in construction is the armchair
n PL. 18 B and C, with its feline-shaped legs, curving arms, and
loping back with an upright brace to hold it firmly. It is made
f redwood with decorations of gold leaf on plaster and with a
eat of plaited string. Similar in design, though more slender in
proportions, is the chair recently found in the *Tomb of Tutenkhamon*.[14] The wooden frame is covered with gold; the span
etween the brace for the legs and the seat originally contained,
n open-work gold, the intertwined lotus and papyrus that
ymbolized the union of Upper and Lower Egypt, as is repre-
ented in the chair in the panel. The front legs terminate in
olden lion heads broadly modeled and not only decorative but
ymbolic of the power of the king. The arms are designed of
erpents which wear the double crown of Upper and Lower
Egypt and whose partly outspread wings form the body of the
rm and appear to enfold the royal cartouche that fills the curve
t the front. The back panel not only gives us a charming scene
ut forms a pattern of brilliant color harmony. We see the king
utenkhamon and his girlish queen in a room of the palace. He
s seated easily in his cushioned chair and she bends forward
with great tenderness to anoint him with perfume from the
ittle jar that she carries in her left hand. Both are elaborately
dressed and the room in which they are is adorned with columns

[14] Reproduced in Carter and Mace, *The Tomb of Tut-ankh-Amen*, Pls. II and LXII; and in
urrent History, June, 1924. It is regretted that further reproduction of objects from this tomb
s not permitted.

decorated with lotus and papyrus flowers and a deep border through which the sun is shining, its rays terminating in hands that symbolize the god Aton; for the young wife here represented was the daughter of Ikhnaton. Early in their reign this king and queen appear to have remained loyal to Aton;[15] but they were soon brought back to the traditional worship of Amon by the power of the priesthood. The sheen of the gold and silver and the color harmony of the various insets make the panel a brilliant piece of decoration.

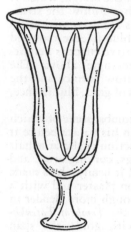

Glazing had been known by the Egyptian from prehistoric times and early had been used to cover tiles for wall decoration. It had then been applied to various objects but in the Empire it reached a climax in technical development and also in the variety of its uses — beads, pendants, scarabs, amulets, vases, figurines, and architectural decorations. The blue color, particularly deep and pure in tone, the craftsman obtained from copper by a long process that required great skill in the preparation of the material and patience in tending the furnaces during the long, even roasting, for no mechanical devices were known to regulate the heat. A typical household utensil of this glazed ware is a lotus cup (FIG. 38) of particularly elegant shape that is derived from the half-open flower.

Fig. 38. Lotus Cup. Of blue faïence.

Glass was not the common, inexpensive medium among the Egyptians that it is at present, for the blowpipe was not invented until about the first century B.C. Therefore, it was necessary to mold the hot glass over a copper and paste core that could later be removed — a slow, laborious process. Such a vase as that illustrated in PL. 17 c was made in this way. It is deep blue in color. For decoration, threads of light blue, yellow, and white glass were wound about the neck and body while it was still hot and dragged back and forth by a hooked instrument, forming the zigzag that is known as the "dragged pattern." Besides dark and light blue, a considerable number of other colors are found — violet, green, yellow, orange, red, white, and black.

[15] Evidence of this is seen in the early form of the king's name — Tutenkhaton.

PLATE 17

(A) "Perfume Spoon." Wood. Louvre, Paris. (Giraudon)

(B) Wine Jug. Of silver with engraving; handle and rim of gold. H. 7 in. XIX Dynasty (1350–1205 B.C.). Cairo Museum. (Metropolitan Museum)

(C) Glass Vase. Dark blue, with dragged pattern in light blue, yellow, and white. H. 3¼ in. Metropolitan Museum, New York. (Metropolitan Museum)

(D) Jewel Casket, Reconstructed. Ebony, inlaid with ivory, gold, blue glaze, and carnelian. L. 17½ in. XII Dynasty (2000–1788 B.C.). Metropolitan Museum, New York. (Metropolitan Museum)

PLATE 18

(*A*) Diadem of a Princess from a Roy
Tomb. XII Dynasty (2000–1788 B.C
Cairo Museum. (Metropolitan Museur

(*B*) Chair from the Tomb of a Nobl
Of redwood with decorations of gold le
on plaster. The seat is of plaited strin
XVIII Dynasty (1580–1350 B.C.). Cai
Museum.

(*C*) Chair from the Tomb of a Nobl
(back view of *B*).

SUMMARY

The Middle Kingdom and Empire were an age of great production in all the arts. Wealth and power fostered magnificence, as
the temples indicate, some of which, such as *Deir el-Bahri* and
parts of *Luxor*, are splendid examples of orderly planning with
careful regard to natural environment; are characterized by refined decoration; and are impressive manifestations of the awe
and mystery of religious belief. Others, such as *Karnak*, reveal
the tendency in the days of Ramses II to colossal size and overelegance without refinement.

The sculptors and painters had inherited the traditional conventions that had been established in the formative period and
had reached a climax in the Old Kingdom. But we miss the
vivacity, the freshness, and the sincerity that come from the
struggle through which any people passes in an archaic age when
ideas and conventions are forming. The wider outlook upon life
that characterized the period, and particularly the influence of
Ikhnaton's religious revolution, led the artists along a path that
they had already begun to discover for themselves — the path
of nature. For a brief time freedom and ease and the beauty of
the freely curving line supplanted angularity and stiffness, and
inspired the artists with new creative power. But the Egyptians
were not yet ready for so radical a change. By nature conservative, they soon fell back into the conventions that crystallized
their art. But, though they could never break from their shackles,
they always remained superbly skillful in line, whether of the
brush or of the chisel, and always superbly decorative.

In the minor arts "use and beauty are still undivided; all that
men's hands are set to make has still a fascination alike for
workmen and spectators."[16] Everywhere one discerns astounding
technical skill and fertility of imagination, combined with the
innate sense of design that admirably adapted the forms of nature
to decorative purposes.

BIBLIOGRAPHY (See Chapter II)

[16] Pater, *Greek Studies* (Macmillan, 1914), p. 197.

CHAPTER IV
BABYLONIAN, ASSYRIAN, CHALDEAN
AND PERSIAN PERIODS

c. 3100–331 B.C.

A. EARLY BABYLONIAN
c. 3100–1925 B.C.

HISTORICAL BACKGROUND

As we leave the Nile Valley, with a vivid impression of th
world's earliest civilization because of the wonderful state of
preservation of the monuments, and travel eastward to Asi
to the Valley of the Two Rivers in which arose the second grea
state, we look in vain for temples and tombs. In fact, in th
whole length of the valley we can see but one fairly well pre
served structure that today rises more than one story above th
ground — the *Ishtar Gate* at Babylon (FIG. 42). Only plain
through whose rich fields the rivers wind, and here and there
shapeless mound. Why this condition of complete ruin?

Of the two rivers that form this valley, the western, th
Euphrates, is quiet and majestic, with few tributaries, and
almost unnavigable because of the cataracts in the north and th
sand bars in the south; the eastern, the Tigris, rising in the moun
tains to the north and east, augmented by large tributaries fron
the same source, is more rapid, and forms the highway of com
merce for the valley. Today we see the modern Mesopotamia
transporting his cargo on the river in the same kind of roun
tub-shaped boat that his predecessors used thousands of year
ago. Both rivers, flooded during the season of heavy rain
bring down vast quantities of rich alluvium, as does the Nile i
Egypt, forming an amazingly productive soil. Unlike Egyp
however, this valley affords very little building stone; none i
the south, and scanty quarries of limestone and alabaster in th
north. Wood must be obtained from far-away Lebanon. S
clay bricks, either sun-dried or baked, became practically the so
building material.

While the rain and the rivers were the constructive element of the valley in that they furnished the rich soil, at the same time they proved equally destructive. For as the buildings were made of such perishable material, when they were subjected to rains and annual floods they soon fell into ruins, were buried by the sand blowing in from the desert, and today are nothing but mounds. A few of these mounds have been excavated and have yielded the evidence that pictures for us the civilization of this valley. But this picture is far from being the intimate one of everyday life in all its aspects that we saw in Egypt, not only because the remains that have been recovered up to this time are scanty, but also because, in contrast to the Egyptian, the beliefs of these people in reference to the future life were so gloomy and vague that very little attention was paid to burial equipment. As it was a civilization centered on the present life, interest lay in the palace, a more or less temporary structure built for this life, rather than in a tomb the chief purpose of which was endurance. In fact the remains of Babylonia-Assyria visualize for us the city of the living; those of Egypt, the city of the dead.

To the north and east of the valley lie mountainous plateaus where lived, as far back as we can go, a mountaineer people called the Sumerians, clean-shaven men, carrying the shield. To the west and south stretch the great reaches of the Arabian desert with its nomad shepherds, the Semites, bearded, and equipped with the bow and arrow. Both wear heavy woolen garments usually covering the whole body. The history of the valley is the story of the struggle between the mountaineers of the north and the nomads of the south for the possession of the fertile portions of the land.

Long before 3000 B.C. the Sumerian mountaineers had established walled towns in the lower half of the valley — a region that eventually came to be known as Babylonia.[1] They possessed domesticated animals and grain, metal, a system of writing, of measuring time, and of weights and measures. Gradually there drifted in from the desert small groups of Semites, who mingled freely with the Sumerians and took over their writing, government, and art. As their numbers increased, there began the struggle to determine which should be the dominating power; and from one to the other it alternated. Out of this struggle arose two mighty kings, both Semites — Sargon (active 2750 B.C.)

[1] For convenience, the name "Babylonian" is used for this early period, though strictly speaking it is not applicable until Babylon became the dominating city, under Hammurapi, about 2100 B.C.

and Hammurapi (2123–2081 B.C.), both of whose reigns indicat
a climax in the civilization of the valley.

Agriculture was the chief economic basis of the state, an
commerce was the main concern of the community. Not only wa
business controlled by the state, with the king at the head, bu
even the priesthood became an important factor in the busines
life of the country, renting out land, bartering and exchangin
the wool, cattle, birds, fruits, grain, oil, and perfumes. Religio
itself was concerned chiefly with material prosperity.

After the climax reached under Hammurapi, when Babylo
for the first time became the leading city, a thousand years c
decline set in, when the state was harassed by the Kassites,
pre-Indo-European people who came from the grasslands of th
north, bringing with them the horse. In the meantime th
struggling settlement of Assur in the northern part of the valle
was steadily gaining in strength, and ready to assume the leadei
ship upon the decline of the Babylonian power.

ARCHITECTURE

The remains are so scanty that, to study the architecture c
early Babylonia, we go to a temple some distance up the river a
Assur (FIG. 39), which, though really Assyrian, is of the sam
general type as the Babylonian. It is a massive structure, wit
thick, heavy turreted walls, built about an open court. Th
entrances are constructed of square towers with arched openings
contrasting in this respect with the work of the Egyptian, whc
with his plentiful stone, could roof over his buildings with lin
tels; while the Babylonian, with no material large enough t
span the distance between the piers, used bricks made roughl
wedge-shaped so that they formed an arch.[2] Thus of necessity th
arch, rather than the lintel, became the basic structural elemen
of his buildings. But the dominating feature of the temple i
the *ziggurat*, or tower of four stages, each smaller than the on
below and ascended by a ramp. The purpose of the *ziggurat* wa
to provide an artificial hill for the shrine of the god which ha
been built on the mountain top before the Sumerians left thei
original home. While the shrine is on the top of the tower, th
temple is on the plain. The stages of a *ziggurat* recently discovere
at Ur were covered with glazed tiles, light blue for the shrine

[2] A true arch consists of wedge-shaped blocks, usually of brick or stone, called *voussoirs*, fitte
together in order to roof over the space between two supports. The central *voussoir*, at the crow
of the arch, is called the keystone because when this block is put into place, usually last, th
arch is firmly set.

ed for the next stage, then black, and whitewash for the court.
These colors were apparently used symbolically. The absence of
columns or colonnades is to be noted.[3]

SCULPTURE

An example of the sculpture of early Babylonia is the relief of
rnina (PL. 19 c). We see the king on the left, of larger stature
than the other figures, to indicate the dignity of his position. He

Fig. 39. Temple at Assur, Restored. 1125–1100 B.C. (Andrae)

s dressed in the usual heavy flounced skirt, and carries on his
ead a workman's basket, while the members of his family stand
efore him in the conventional pose of devotion. The scene rep-
esents some ceremony in connection with the building of a
emple, corresponding, perhaps, in our day, to the breaking of
he ground or the laying of the corner stone. Below, the king is
eated, holding audience. The figures are short and stocky, with
prominent peaked nose and wide-opened eye, and are practically
like. The cuneiform signs, which tell us who is represented,

[3] The absence of the column and colonnade in Babylonia-Assyria has been noted by the best
authorities, and no evidence has hitherto been found for its use in either the ruins or the documents. The recent excavations at Kish and Ur, however, have unearthed conclusive evidence of
he colonnade in buildings dated conservatively between 2500 and 3500 B.C. These excavations
re also pushing the dates of the early Babylonian period considerably back, at least to 3500 B.C.

are carved wherever there is space, with no feeling for order
arrangement such as we found in early Egyptian work. In fa
the whole relief, though it tells its story, is very crude.

In the relief of *Naram-Sin* (PL. 19 B) the king, at the head
his army, is fighting in a mountainous country. Woods a
suggested by one tree. The army is marching up to the pla
where the king stands with one foot on two of the foe; befo
him are two others, one of whom is falling pierced by his spea
while the second stands imploring mercy. Naram-Sin is repr
sented just at the moment of lowering his spear, which indicat
that he grants the plea. The king, large of stature, as is custo
mary, stands out as a noble figure in splendid isolation, formir
a center of interest toward which the lines of the spears and th
soldiers lead. The figure is battered, especially the head, y
we can see that it is finely modeled and full of vitality, in marke
contrast to the squat proportions, conventionality, and ove
crowding of the relief of *Urnina*. The sculptor has selected
single dramatic moment, clarified and unified his compositio
and created a monument that is distinctly noble.

Sculpture in the round is best represented by a statue of *Gud*
(PL. 19 A). It is carved from hard diorite, obtained from a lor
distance. The prince is seated, clothed in the characterist
heavy skirt, here covered with inscriptions, while his mantl
falls from the left shoulder, leaving the right shoulder and ar
exposed. The hands are tightly clasped in the traditional att
tude of devotion. The figure is heavy and squat, but in the ex
posed parts of the body, particularly in the shoulder and arn
we can discern the strong modeling of the muscles and the nervou
tension in the clasped hands. The heavy feeling of the body
evident in the head too, accentuated by the woolen cap, sho
neck, and the blank expression. However, the modeling abou
the mouth, the cheeks, and the inner corner of the eye is carefu
The eyebrows, conventionally indicated by a fishbone patter
meet in a point between the eyes. In spite of poor proportion
and heaviness there is a brusque strength and dignity abou
this figure.

But when we look at these reliefs and statues, and remembe
that, at the same time that the Babylonian was making them, th
Egyptian was carving the statue of *Khafre* and the panel
Hesire, we doubt the ability of the men of the Tigris and Eu
phrates valley in sculpture, and their feeling for design.

MINOR ARTS

Turning to the minor arts, we find a somewhat different situation. There is a simple, sturdy vigor about the silver vase supported by four lions' feet (FIG. 40). Two engraved bands encircle it. On the broader one, in the center, is represented a lion-headed eagle with outstretched wings, conventionally drawn, clutching the backs of two lions symmetrically placed and walking in opposite directions. This device, which we find in sculpture as well, we know is the heraldic design of the Sumerian city of Lagash. The motif is repeated four times but varied by substituting an ibex for the lion. Each lion is biting the mouth of the animal of the next group, thus uniting the four main elements of the design. Although the result of the artist's attempt to draw the lion's face front view is grotesque, yet his drawing of the bodies and of the ibexes' heads is vigorous and sure-handed, and the essentials of the form accurately expressed. A narrow fish-bone border finishes this band. The narrower border, about the shoulder of the vase, consists of a row of half-crouching heifers all facing in one direction. Here the drawing is more naturalistic than in the heraldic design and the lines are engraved with the utmost firmness, and show no fumbling. It is the

Fig. 40. Vase from Lagash. Silver with bronze base. H. c. 14 in. C. 2850 B.C. An inscription around the neck records the name of the king who placed this vase in the temple as a votive offering. Louvre, Paris.

technical excellence in so difficult a medium as engraving on metal, together with the fine sense of balanced design and the decorative fitness of the motifs, that brings the work of the metal craftsman to so high a plane.

The firmness and delicacy of line seen in this work of the engraver reveals itself also in the products of the lapidary as we see it in the cylinder seals that formed a necessary part of the

daily equipment of the Babylonian, from the king to the com
moner. According to Herodotus, "Every one carries a seal an
a walking stick." The seal consisted of a cylindrical piece o
stone usually about an inch and a half high, pierced so that
wire could be inserted, clamped at one end and looped at th
other for the attachment of a cord. Seals were made of variou
colored stones, both hard and soft, such as hematite, black
obsidian, varicolored agate, red carnelian and jasper, blu
lapis lazuli, and creamy white alabaster; and were decorated
with a design in intaglio, so that when the seal was rolled ove
the soft clay a raised impression was made, just as in the use o
sealing wax today. With this impression the Babylonian sealed
signed, and identified his letters and documents, which were writ
ten on clay tablets. PL. 20 B shows an impression made from one
of them. At the right is represented the moon-god, Sin, indicated
by the crescent moon near by, to whom a goddess is leading a
king, followed by another goddess with uplifted hands. The god
is a dignified, bearded figure, clothed in the usual long fringed
robe hanging from the left shoulder, and wears a turban like that
of *Gudea* (PL. 19 A). The chair in which he sits is quite elaborate
the back leg being carefully carved to represent an ox's leg. The
goddesses are elaborately dressed, each wearing a pointed cap
though the gowns differ, that of the foremost being made of a
series of flounces, while that of the one at the left hangs in long
folds from the shoulders. The moon-god raises his right hand
toward the three as if in a gesture of welcome. We notice here
how well the figures are spaced and with what firmness th
engraver has cut his lines, as in the drapery particularly of th
figure at the left, and also with what delicacy he has indicated
the details such as the ox-leg, the hands, and the fringe.

In a seal of Sargon (PL. 20 C) at each end is a mythologica
figure, perhaps Gilgamesh, a demigod like the Greek Heracles
one knee bent upon the ground, holding a vase from which issu
two streams of water; in the center, back to back, are two bull
that lift up their heads to drink; immediately above the bulls i
the center is the inscription containing the name of Sargon; belov
is the conventional wavelike representation of a stream with it
banks. The scene refers to water as the gift of the gods to ma
and to beast. We perceive here, first, how the engraver worked
out the problem of unifying the necessary elements of his design
which are the god, the animal, and the inscription. The god
kneels and holds the vase in such a way that the stream o
water touches the upturned mouth of the animal, thus naturall

PLATE 19

(A) Gudea. Diorite. H. 3½ ft. c. 2450 B.C. Louvre, Paris.

(B) Stele of Naram-Sin. c. 2550 B.C. Louvre, Paris. (Mansell)

(C) King Urnina, his Family and Courtiers. H. 16 in. c. 3000 B.C. Louvre, Paris. (Stoedtner)

PLATE 20

(A) King Assurbanipal and His Queen. 668–626 B.C. British Museum, London. (Mansell)

(B) Seal of a King of Ur. c. 2400 B.C. British Museum, London. (Mansell)

(C) Seal of King Sargon I. 2750 B.C. Red jasper. H. 1½ in. Coll. de Clercq, Paris.

PLATE 21

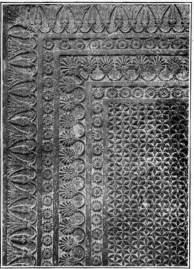

(*A*) Winged Being with a Horned Animal and Ear of Wheat for Sacrifice. 885–860 B.C. British Museum, London. (Mansell)

(*B*) Paving Slab from the Palace at Nineveh. Alabaster. C. 700 B.C. British Museum, London. (Mansell)

(*C*) Palace of Sargon II, Restored. Dur-Sharrukin (Khorsabad). 722–705 B.C. (Place)

PLATE 22

(A) Palace of Sargon. Façade (detail of PL. 21C). (Place)

(B) Dying Lioness. From palace at Nineveh. 668-626 B.C. British Museum, London. (Mansell)

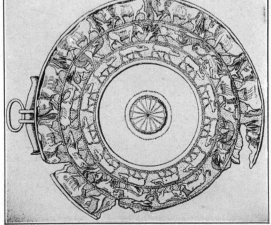

(C) Bronze Bowl. VIII cent. B.C. British Museum, London.

uniting the two figures; the curve of the head and breast of the bull is repeated in the horns, which are conventionally treated so that their tips ingeniously hold the tablet containing the inscription. The design is exactly repeated, forming a perfect bilateral balance. In the second place, the execution is most skillful, especially when we remember the tiny size of the cylinder. The modeling of the god's body with its exaggeration of muscles is very much like that in the statue of *Gudea*. In the bulls, the knowledge and expression of the animal form is superb; the bony structure, the heavy hide, and the details of the hoofs are admirably indicated. Every line, from the broad curve of the horns to the delicate lines of the hair, is carved with a fine, firm stroke.

These seals represent the highest attainment in early Babylonian art. It is an interesting observation that, when the introduction of the drill from Egypt brought the end of hand carving, the work deteriorated. Seals continued to be made through Persian times, but never do they attain the fine quality of those made by hand in the days of Sargon.

B. ASSYRIAN

c. 3000–606 B.C.

HISTORICAL BACKGROUND

While the Sumerians and the Semites were struggling over the leadership in the lower part of the valley, farther north at Assur a little settlement had been in existence as early as about 3000; but it had been too weak to make headway against its great rivals until the eighth century, when under a line of strong kings led by Sargon II it pushed outward and established the Assyrian empire over western Asia, Babylonia, and even Egypt, for a short time. Under Sennacherib, Nineveh became a great metropolis. The state was essentially military, very fierce and very cruel, probably well deserving its reputation of being the scourge of the East. Only about a century and a half did the Empire maintain its supremacy. The Chaldeans, a Semitic tribe who had slowly drifted into Babylonia and had captured Babylon, combining with the Medes and Persians who had gradually been building up a strong Empire on the plateaus to the north and east, in 606 captured Nineveh and utterly destroyed it. Then there arose through western Asia the exultant cry of Nahum (3:18–19):

Thy shepherds slumber, O king of Assyria; thy nobles are at rest; thy people are scattered upon the mountains, and there is none to gather them. There is no assuaging of thy hurt; all that hear the report of thee clap their hands over thee; for upon whom hath not thy wickedness passed continually?

Occasionally we catch glimpses of private life in Assyria. PL. 20 A shows us King Assurbanipal and his queen. The king reclines easily on a carved couch, sipping wine from a cup. He wears an elaborate robe, headband, and bracelets, and his long hair and beard are carefully curled. The queen sits stiffly in her richly carved chair, with a footstool. She too is clothed and adorned with elegant fringed, embroidered clothing. Servants stand behind them with fly-flappers. Others bring loaded trays or furnish music on the harp. They are in a garden with palm and pine trees and heavily loaded vines. Everything suggests oriental splendor and luxuriousness. But the glance of Assurbanipal is directed beyond the queen to the second tree to the left, where hangs the head of his last vanquished enemy, above which hover vultures. In Assyria even pleasure was grim. Hunting the lion or the wild horse served as the chief pastime of the king, whether in his chariot, on horseback, or with hunting dogs; and he pursued the game with the same fierceness as he did his foes in battle.

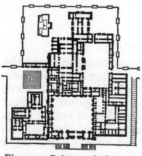

Fig. 41. Palace of Sargon. Khorsabad. (Place)

ARCHITECTURE

When Sargon II came to the throne, he selected a new site for the capital at Dur-Sharrukin, meaning "City of Sargon" or "Sargonburg," and there built his palace (PL. 21 C and FIG. 41) now usually called the *Palace at Khorsabad* from the name of the modern village near by. It is a vast rambling structure covering about twenty-five acres of ground, palace and temple combined. It rests upon a great platform which was a necessary protection against the floods. Stone, which is more accessible here than in Babylonia, for Assyria lies nearer the mountains, is used in the substructure, brick in the upper parts. There are two entrances to the platform, one by a ramp for vehicles, the other by a monumental double stairway leading directly to the main entrance. The plan shows a great many small rooms grouped about two open courts: one, reached by the main entrance, a center for the affairs of state and the royal living quarters; the other, toward the rear, serving for everything pertaining to the service of the whole establishment. At the left is the temple, at the back of which rises the usual ramp tower.

Looking at the façade more in detail (PL. 22 A), we see a massive wall space with a crenellated top broken by huge square towers between which are arched openings, a large one in the center, two smaller ones on the sides. Here we see that the structural system is that of arch rather than lintel. At the base and on each side of the main arch, like guardian sentinels, are colossal winged bulls with human heads. Around the arches and on the towers are friezes of glazed tile of brilliant coloring. The effect is one of sumptuousness and grandeur. The massiveness, the brilliance of the tiles glistening in the sun, and the impressiveness of the colossal figures all reflect the fierce might of the king, quite in contrast to the softer tones of less glaring color and the grave monumentality of the stone structures of Egypt. Dazzling brilliance seems to have been the aim of the builders, if we can judge from an inscription in which an Assyrian king says:

The splendid temple, a brilliant and magnificent dwelling, . . . I made its interior brilliant like the dome of the heavens; decorated its walls, like the splendour of the rising stars, and made it grand with resplendent brilliancy.[4]

The decorative motifs that the Assyrians used in the embellishment of their palaces were largely borrowed from Egypt, especially the lotus. Very effectively designed is a paving slab (PL. 21 B) with happily varied borders of lotus, rosette, and palmette.

SCULPTURE

The interiors of these Assyrian palaces were decorated with limestone or alabaster reliefs, arranged in zones; miles, literally, of ceremonial, military, and hunting scenes. In PL. 21 A we see a winged being who accompanies King Assurnasirpal as he performs religious rites before the tree of life. The figures, heavily clothed with fringed, embroidered robes and adorned with bracelets and necklaces, are monotonously similar, while the heads, with their conventionally curled hair, are identical. Where the modeling shows in the exposed limbs there is a great exaggeration of muscular forms which have become a conven-

---

[4] Inscription of Tiglath-Pileser I (1100 B.C.) quoted in Handcock, *Mesopotamian Archæology*, p. 142.

tional pattern. The cuneiform inscription is carved across the panel with no regard for the figure or the design. The majority of these reliefs that picture hunting, military, and traveling scenes, like the garden scene of Assurbanipal (PL. 20 A), are primarily narrative. To picture his exploits in war and in the chase seemed to be the aim of the Assyrian; and, as he was not endowed with the unfailing sense of design that was the gift of the Egyptian, his walls are covered with episodes rather than with decorations.

Among these scenes, however, are some superb representations of animal life. As we have said, hunting was one of the chief pleasures of the Assyrian, and all aspects of this sport King Assurbanipal carved on the walls of his palace. PL. 23 A shows preparations. Some of the attendants are carrying nets to hold the game, others are holding in leash the muscular hunting dogs that are struggling to free themselves for the dash. So eager are the animals that we ourselves enter into the spirit of the chase, and realize that the wild asses on the plateau must flee swiftly if they are to escape these bloodthirsty dogs. But the Assyrian's greatest sport was the lion hunt. Sometimes we see the king mounted, spearing one lion, while another, wounded, fiercely attacks a fleeing riderless horse. The vigorous movement, the excitement of the moment, the rage of the beasts — to show this was the sculptor's purpose, in which he was supremely successful.

In PL. 22 B we see a *Dying Lioness*, pierced with arrows that have paralyzed her hind legs. Her face shows pain and terror. She is fighting her last fight, dragging herself along the ground, refusing to submit. The agony and pathos are so real that we are involuntarily drawn into sympathy. The fierceness and grimness of these hunts was something in which the Assyrian reveled, and it guided the artist's hand as he chiseled the scenes.

Sculpture in the round does not appear to have been as popular as relief work. One reason for this was the difficulty of obtaining suitable stone. The most characteristic examples are the colossal human-headed bulls or lions that flanked the doorways of the palaces (PLS. 22 A and 23 B), though, strictly speaking, these figures combine the features of high relief and sculpture in the round, as they are attached to the background. All the details, such as the muscles, hair, and wings, are conventionally treated. An interesting feature here, that must relate itself to the Assyrian instinct for realism, is the presence of five legs. This does not mean that the animal had five legs, but that the sculptor wished to represent him standing from the front view, showing two legs, but moving from the side view, showing four legs; and because the representation of these two poses was impossible in one figure, he naïvely attempted to reconcile them by the addition of the fifth leg to complete the side view. While these figures are conventional and dry, yet, in their original position on either side of the doorway, they are decorative and impressive.

MINOR ARTS

As we turn to the minor arts of the Assyrians we see that the metal worker, as in Babylonia, was a skilled craftsman. A bronze bowl from one of the great palaces illustrates his work (PL. 22 c). In the center is a rosette, that ever present ornament in Assyrian art, about which move concentric rows of animals in borders that have a pleasing gradation in width. In the inner bands are gazelles, with heads bent as if to graze; in the middle band are various animals, some peaceful, some attacking, but the action is subordinate to the general trend of the procession. The outer band is decorated with bulls, all alike, as are the animals of the inner band, but they are moving in an opposite direction from those in the other two rows, thus giving a balance to the direction of movement. We notice how naturalistically the animals are represented, yet how decorative they are. This is characteristically Assyrian, combining the natural tendency for realism with the same feeling for design that we found the early Babylonian engraver using on his silver vase (FIG. 40). Concentric bands of animals as a decorative motif passed from the Assyrians to the Greeks, who used it on their early vases (FIG. 62). The technical process by which this vase was made is known as *repoussé*, which means that the design was hammered up into relief, showing concave on the reverse side. Details were added by engraving.

C. CHALDEAN OR SECOND BABYLONIAN
606–539 B.C.

HISTORICAL BACKGROUND AND ARCHITECTURE

At the fall of Nineveh, two kingdoms were established, the Chaldean in the south, the Medo-Persian in the north. Nebuchadnezzar the Chaldean built Babylon anew so that it surpassed Nineveh in the splendor of its palaces, temples, and hanging gardens. This is the Babylon of which the Greek traveler Herodotus wrote, and the city of the Hebrew captivity, for it was

Nebuchadnezzar who punished rebellious Judah with exile. Commerce and business flourished. The science of astronomy made advances. The Chaldeans divided the circle into 360 degrees, laid out the signs of the zodiac, and knew at least five planets. But the power and magnificence of Chaldean Babylon was short-lived, for in 539 she opened her gates to Cyrus the Persian.

Today very little remains of Babylon. Until recently nothing but a mound marked the traditional site of the city. Since then excavators have unearthed the *Ishtar Gate* (FIG. 42), which gives us a suggestion of the splendor of Chaldean days. It was a double

Fig. 42. Ishtar Gate, Restored. Babylon. 606–539 B.C. (Koldewey)

gate with six great towers and decorated with glazed tile. The Chaldeans, without a supply of stone, could not adopt the Assyrian scheme of decorating with stone reliefs, but utilized the available clay, molding it into low reliefs and glazing it brilliantly. So on this gate rose tier after tier of animals, forty feet into the air. The approach to the gateway was by Procession Street, along which parades passed on festive occasions, carrying the images of the gods and goddesses. The walls lining each side of the street were also decorated with glazed tile, on which were represented processions of lions (PL. 23 c), some white with yellow manes and tails, others yellow with red manes. It is the same ferocious lion we met in Assyria, but conventionalized enough to be purely decorative rather than realistic. Behind the

Ishtar Gate rose the palace of Nebuchadnezzar with its terraced garden filled with tropical plants — the famous hanging gardens of Babylon. As we walk up Procession Street past the brilliant roaring lions and approach the gate, its tiled surface flashing in the sunshine against the rich green of the gardens above and beyond, we cannot but marvel at the rich effect gained by the Babylonian in his use of glazed tile.

SUMMARY

In the architecture of the Babylonian-Assyrian period we have seen massive rambling structures built chiefly of brick on the arch system of construction. Broad platforms with monumental stairways, entrances flanked with colossal bulls and glittering with brilliantly colored tile decorations, interiors adorned with long rows of reliefs, with scenes full of life and vigor — all these created a rich and sumptuous appearance; but it was the effect of temporary barbaric splendor, rather than monumental endurance. In sculpture, while the human figure was poorly executed, the representation of animal life was superb in its realism, full of life and movement, always forceful, always impressive. The handicrafts reached their climax in the work of the engraver, the lapidary, and the bronze worker, whose sense of decoration and technical skill are seen in the silver vessels, the early Babylonian seals, and the Assyrian bronzes.

D. PERSIAN

539–331 B.C.

HISTORICAL BACKGROUND

The end of the Assyrian power and the establishment of the Chaldean had been brought about by the combined efforts of the Semitic Chaldeans and the Medo-Persians. The latter were an Aryan people who had moved southward from the grasslands of central Asia, and had gradually built up an empire on the mountainous plateaus east of the Valley of the Two Rivers. They had brought with them from their original home a beautiful conception of religion, recognizing the struggle of good and evil and the ethical value of right conduct as seen in the writings of their great prophet, Zoroaster. About 550 B.C., Cyrus, a Persian vassal of this Median Empire, threw off the yoke and with his powerful archers and daring horsemen swept over western Asia, swiftly conquering from the Persian Gulf to the

Mediterranean Sea. Before his armies Babylon fell in 539 B.C. Still further conquest added Egypt to the empire, which was thoroughly organized and enjoyed a remarkable period of prosperity under Darius. It was a humane, intelligent rule, though no rights of citizenship were extended to the people. The king's word was the one law. While these earlier emperors were rulers with a conscience and a feeling of responsibility for their rule, their followers became luxurious oriental despots. Decline set in and the decadent state fell before the armies of Alexander the Great in 331 B.C.

ARCHITECTURE AND THE MINOR ARTS

The Persians, before 550 B.C., had been a simple shepherd people, with no cities and none of the cultural traditions of city life. Babylon and Thebes must have impressed these mountaineers greatly; and when they found themselves suddenly masters of a great empire they too wished to build cities and palaces. But they had no art traditions of their own; and what they did under these circumstances, we see in the group of palaces and halls at *Persepolis*. Fragmentary as are these remains, we see at once both a difference and a similarity to what we have noticed in Babylonia-Assyria. The buildings rest upon a raised platform approached by a double monumental stairway; at the entrance stand colossal winged bulls. These features are obviously derived from Assyria. But the columns are a feature that we have not met in the Valley of the Two Rivers. Stone was accessible in this mountainous country; so the Persians, probably with the great colonnaded hypostyle halls of Egypt in mind, adopted the lintel type of architecture for their colonnaded audience halls (PL. 24 A). The elaborate columns that support the roof, while they have some features suggestive of an Egyptian influence, carry capitals which are quite original. They are made by placing back to back the forepart of the bodies of two bulls, which rest on scrolls placed vertically — a strangely incoherent and loaded design, which appears to be striving for elegance without taste. The Persians, like the Babylonians, employed glazed tile friezes to decorate their halls. In a fragment from the *Palace of Darius* at Susa (PL. 24 B), we see represented in rhythmic order the famous Persian archers. They are dressed in elaborately embroidered robes, and are armed with spears, bows, and large quivers. The bricks are glazed with brilliant harmonious colors so that the decorative effect must have been impressive.

PLATE 23

(*A*) Attendants and Hunting Dogs. From palace at Nineveh. 668–626 B.C. British Museum, London. (Mansell)

(*B*) Human-headed Bull. From palace at Nineveh. 885–860 B.C. British Museum, London.

(*C*) Lion of Procession Street, Restored. Babylon. Glazed tile. L. 7 ft. 606–539 B.C. (Stoedtner)

PLATE 24

(*A*) Audience Hall of Xerxes, Restored. Persepolis. 485–c. 465 B.C. (Perrot and Chipiez)

(*B*) Frieze of Archers. Glazed tile. From the palace of Darius at Susa. H. c. 5 ft. Louvre, Paris. (Alinari)

(*C*) Tomb of Cyrus. Pasargadae. c. 528 B.C. (Sarre)

(*D*) Armlet. Gold. H. 5 in. c. 400 B.C. British Museum, London. (Dalton)

As we turn to the *Tomb of Cyrus* (PL. 24 C) we experience immediately a feeling totally different from that produced by the buildings at *Persepolis*. Here is a very simple rectangular structure, with a gabled roof, resting on a base of six courses. Originally it was surrounded by a colonnade, scanty remains of which can be seen. The simplicity and dignity of this tomb contrast strongly with the rather garish elegance of *Persepolis*. How does this happen? Here is undoubtedly an influence from Greece, which in the meantime was rapidly developing a style of architecture, the chief characteristics of which were simplicity, dignity, and subtle proportions. Cyrus in pushing his boundaries to Asia Minor has seen tombs of this character, or possibly has brought to Persepolis some Greek architect to superintend the work.

The Persians, like the other members of the group of civilizations that rose in this valley and the near-by plateaus, were skillful craftsmen, especially in the use of metal, as a gold armlet shows (PL. 24 D). The decoration consists of two winged monsters, the bodies and hind legs of which are indicated in relief while the wings, breasts, and necks are covered with cloisons (p. 164) once filled with colored stones cut to fit the depressions — an early and interesting use of the cloison that played so important a part in Byzantine decoration (PL. 63 C and D). The animal forms are highly conventionalized, so that their simplified outline forms a bold, vigorous design peculiarly fitted to the medium. It was not the purpose of the artist here to use the charmingly naturalistic expression of the animal form that we found on the Egyptian jug (PL. 17 B), but by a severe simplification to utilize the decorative pattern that the form suggested. It is this attitude toward form as a decorative motif that we shall find in India (PL. 165 A), and not unnaturally, for the Indians were racially of the same origin as the Persians.[5]

SUMMARY

On the whole, the art of the Persians was an eclectic product. They took ideas from the different countries that they conquered, now using them literally in their original spirit, as we have just seen in the *Tomb of Cyrus;* now combining and modifying them so that the sobriety of Egypt plays its part at *Persepolis* side by side with the fierceness and brilliance of Babylonia and Assyria. But never wanting in Persian art is the feeling of luxuriance and the

[5] See p. 405, note 2.

love of brilliant harmonious color that later is to reveal itself in Persian rugs, pottery, and miniatures.

BIBLIOGRAPHY

BAIKIE, JAMES, Life of the Ancient East. N.Y., Macmillan, 1923.

BREASTED, J. H., Ancient Times. Boston, Ginn, 1916.

BRITISH MUSEUM, Pictorial postcards. Set XXXVII: Assyrian Sculptures.

BUDGE, E. A. W., Assyrian Sculpture in the British Museum. London, 1914.

CHASE, G. H., AND POST, C. R., History of Sculpture. N.Y., Harper, 1924.

FAURE, ELIE, History of Art, v. I., Ancient Art (tr. Pach). N.Y., Harper, 1921.

FLETCHER, SIR BANISTER, History of Architecture on the Comparative Method. N.Y., Scribner, 1924.

GLAZIER, RICHARD, Manual of Historic Ornament. London, Batsford, 1914.

HALL, H. R. H., Ancient History of the Near East. London, Methuen, 1920.

HAMLIN, A. D. F., History of Ornament, Ancient and Medieval. N.Y., Century, 1923.

HANDCOCK, P. S. P., Mesopotamian Archæology. N.Y., Putnam, 1912.

JASTROW, MORRIS, Civilization of Babylonia and Assyria. Philadelphia, Lippincott, 1915.

KIMBALL, FISKE, AND EDGELL, G. H., History of Architecture. N.Y., Harper, 1918.

KOLDEWEY, ROBERT, Excavations at Babylon. N.Y., Macmillan, 1914.

CHAPTER V

MINOAN OR AEGEAN PERIOD

c. 3000–1100 B.C.

HISTORICAL BACKGROUND

When Ægeus was king of Athens, Minos the great sea king of Crete, having conquered the Athenians in a war to avenge the treacherous murder of his son, levied upon her a tribute of seven youths and seven maidens to be sent every nine years to feed the great Minotaur that he kept in a vast, intricate building known as the Labyrinth. Two of these human levies had already been paid and the time was approaching for sending a third, when Ægeus' son Theseus asked to be chosen as one of the seven in the hope that he might kill the monster and so free his country from this horrible tribute. The sail of the tribute ship was black in recognition of her gruesome mission. As Theseus lifted anchor, he agreed with his father that if his attempt was successful he would carry a white sail on the return trip. When he arrived in Crete and appeared before the king, his beauty and the fate awaiting him so aroused the fair-haired Ariadne, daughter of Minos, that she assisted Theseus to enter the Labyrinth with a word by which he killed the monster; he then retraced his steps by means of a thread that she had given him. With Ariadne and his companions he fled from the island. But, in the joy of his return, he forgot to hoist the white sail; and old King Ægeus, standing on the cliffs and peering out over the sea to catch the first glimpse of the returning boat, seeing the black sail, cast himself into the sea, which, after him, was called the Ægean. And Theseus became king of Athens.

So reads the old Greek legend. Up to the year 1900, however, no remains had been found to substantiate the story. Already Heinrich Schliemann had proved that the Homeric tales of Troy were based on historic fact. Schliemann, as a child, had been told the story of the Trojan War and of the great walls that protected the ancient city; and in spite of opposition he strongly maintained his belief that those walls must still be standing. He

had acquired a small amount of education, but in the little gro-
cery-store in which he sold herring and butter, sugar and candle,
from five in the morning until eleven at night, he had not a
moment for study. However, he kept warm in his heart the love
of learning, and his dream of one day finding the walls of Troy.
One evening there entered the little shop a man who, dissatisfied
with his lot, had given himself up to drink, "— which, however,
had not made him forget his Homer; for on the evening that he
entered the shop he recited to us about a hundred lines of the
poet, observing the rhythmic cadence of the verses. Although
I did not understand a syllable, the melodious sound of the words
made a deep impression upon me, and I wept bitter tears over my
unhappy fate. Three times over did I get him to repeat to me
those divine verses, rewarding his trouble with three glasses of
whiskey, which I bought with the few pence that made up my
whole fortune. From that moment I never ceased to pray God
that by His grace I might yet have the happiness of learning
Greek."[1] Now the desire burned more fiercely than ever; but not
until middle life, when he finally amassed a fortune, was he free
to follow his dream. He then went to the locality which his
knowledge of the Iliad led him to believe was the site of Troy,
and there found nine cities built one on the remains of another.
There were ancient walls and signs of a great conflagration, and
Schliemann proclaimed that he had found the actual city. Subsequent excavations proved that the site was correct, but he
had erred in deciding that the second instead of the sixth was
Homer's Troy. Then he continued his excavating at Mycenæ,
whence sailed the proud chieftains to avenge the capture of
Helen, and his success was even more startling. Massive fortress-
palaces, elaborate tombs, great quantities of gold jewelry and
ornaments, cups and inlaid weapons — all revealed a pre-Hellenic
civilization of high culture and wide extent that has been called
Mycenæan.

But Mycenæ, after all, did not seem to be its center. Sir
Arthur Evans had long considered Crete as a fertile field for
investigation. Under Turkish rule, excavation was impossible;
but when in 1898 Crete was free from the Turkish régime, the
opportunity came, and about 1900 work began. In a short time,
Evans's faith was rewarded far beyond his expectations. His
spade did not dig very deep before it had uncovered the palaces
of these old kings. Sea kings they were. No fortified walls protected their palaces, for broad reaches of water formed their

[1] Schliemann, *Ilios, the City and Country of the Trojans*, p. 7.

PLATE 25

(*A*) Palace of Minos. Knossos. Colonnaded hall, restored. c. 1500 B.C. (Evans)

(*B*) Lion Gate. Mycenæ. Probably late Minoan.

(*C*) "Treasury of Atreus." Entrance, restored by Spiers. Mycenæ. (Anderson and Spiers)

PLATE 26

(*A*) Head of a Young Girl. Fresco from Knossos. H. c. 9 in. c. 1500 B.C. Candia Museum. (Metropolitan Museum)

(*B*) Snake-Goddess. Gold and ivory. H. 6½ in c. 1500 B.C. Boston Museum. (Bosto Museum)

(*C*) Harvester Vase. Black steatite. H. c. 4 in. The lower part of the vase is lost. c. 1500 B.C. Candia Museum. (Monumenti Antichi)

walls. Their ships plied to the three continents to which their island was a gateway. But the sea was an enemy as well; and when their craft were wrecked by the northern gales, they pictured the tragedy as a great monster swallowing the boat (Fig. 43). Of these sea kings, whose power extended over the islands of the Ægean and even the mainland, the greatest was Minos. His *Palace at Knossos* (Pl. 25 A and Fig. 45) was a large, rambling structure, in parts several stories high, built about open courts, with broad stairways, colonnaded halls, bathrooms, a drainage system, finely paved floors, oil-tinted parchment windows, and gayly decorated walls. Perhaps the very

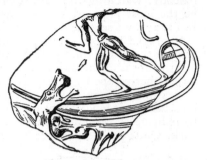

Fig. 43. Seal Representing a Sea-Monster. (*British School Annual*)

throne upon which the king sat we see in the so-called throne room of which Sir Arthur Evans writes:

Already, a few inches below the surface, freshly preserved fresco began to appear. Walls were shortly uncovered, decorated with flowering plants and running water, while on each side of the doorway of a small inner room, stood guardian griffins with peacock's plumes in the same flowery landscape. Round the walls ran low stone benches, and between these, on the north side, separated by a small interval, and raised on a stone base, rose a gypsum throne with a high back, and originally covered with decorative designs. Its lower part was adorned with a curiously carved arch with crocketed mouldings, showing an extraordinary anticipation of some most characteristic features of Gothic architecture. Opposite the throne was a finely wrought tank of gypsum slabs — a feature borrowed perhaps from an Egyptian palace — approached by a descending flight of steps, and originally surmounted by cypress-wood columns, supporting a kind of impluvium. Here truly was the council chamber of a Mycenaean King or Sovereign Lady.

Long corridors led to magazines in which huge jars stored the wine, oil, grain, and honey. Everything spoke of comfort and luxury. Pottery cups of eggshell thinness decorated both in naturalistic and in conventional designs, producing a rich harmonious effect; gold cups with reliefs of animal life (Pl. 29 A and B); finely designed gold ornaments, decorated with relief and engraving (Fig. 53); a gaming board glittering with gold and silver, ivory, and blue enamel — all these tell of wealth and splendor.

It was a proud people who ruled the sea from these luxuriou[s]
palaces. The Cretan ladies, with their flounced aproned skirt[s]
and laced bodices, flying locks, and jaunty caps, are strikingl[y]
modern in appearance. A group of these people we see on [a]
balcony, watching the games, of which bull-fighting seems t[o]
be the most popular, so frequent are the representations of it
In PL. 27 A we see one of these fights going on. Over the back o[f]
the enraged bull, a youth is vaulting toward the outstretche[d]
arms of the girl at the right. Meanwhile another girl, at the left
has the horns of the bull under her arms and in the next momen[t]
will either escape by a leap as did her companion, or be gore[d]
to death. We know which of these figures are girls and whic[h]
boys because it is a convention in Cretan painting, as in Egyptia[n]
to indicate the female flesh by a light tone and the male by [a]
dark. Quite probably we see here some of the captive youths sen[t]
by Athens forced int[o]
the bull ring to pleas[e]
the Cretan lords, a[s]
captives were used late[r]
in the gladiatoria[l]
fights at Rome.

So this picture o[f]
Cretan life substantiate[s]
the old Greek legend
The intricate maze o[f]
rooms in the palace and
the frequent vivid pic[-]
tures of bull rings i[n]
which captive youth[s]
and maidens wer[e]
literally destroyed fur[-]
nish a background fo[r]
the Theseus legend
Furthermore, the broa[d]
paved courts well may
be "the dancing-groun[d]

Fig. 44. Fragment of a Seal Showing the Transportation of a Horse (with the design completed
by dotted lines). The large size of the horse,
which is drawn over the ship rather than in it
may indicate the importance of the event. For
probably it represents the importation of the
thoroughbred horse from the Near East to Crete.
(*British School Annual*)

at Knossos for fair-haired Ariadne," while the gold cups an[d]
inlaid swords bear witness to "every form of lovely craftsman[-]
ship, resting on all things, as he (Homer) says, like the shinin[g]
of the sun."[2]

Who were the people who developed this civilization, the firs[t]

[2] Pater, *Greek Studies*, "The Heroic Age of Greek Art."

on the northern side of the Mediterranean Sea? We do not know. We may call them Ægeans. At the dawn of civilization (c. 3000 B.C.) they were there, the predecessors of the Greeks, but having no connection with them. The climate of Crete is mild and sunny, and the winter rains make production easy. Its location in the Mediterranean gives easy access both to Egypt and to western Asia, so that the Cretans became a seafaring people, controlling the commerce of the Ægean (FIG. 44). Early they had metal. Their system of writing has not yet been deciphered; when that is accomplished, we shall learn more of their origin and customs. With King Minos (c. 1500 B.C.), as we have said, the civilization reached its climax. With Egypt Crete held close, friendly connections both politically and commercially. Its culture spread to the mainland of Greece and Asia Minor, where there grew up such centers as Mycenæ, Tiryns, and Troy, where, however, conditions were somewhat different from those on the island. The warlike Greek nomads were beginning to filter in, which necessitated fortifications. As they became more numerous and more powerful, there was a restless shifting about, with frequent conflicts between the barbarian invaders and the inhabitants. Such a conflict we see in the Homeric tale of the siege of Troy. Finally, the last great wave of Greek invaders, known as the Doric invasion, swept across to Crete, burned the *Palace at Knossos*, and by 1100 B.C. conquered the Ægean world and brought to an end the Cretan civilization, which had lasted for about two thousand years.[3]

ARCHITECTURE

The architecture of the Minoans is known chiefly through their palaces. Looking at the ground plan of the *Palace at Knossos* (FIG. 45), we see that it consists of a large number of rooms grouped about a central court but with no apparent system of arrangement, and in this respect is much more akin to Sargon's *Palace at Khorsabad* than to the Egyptian structures with their ordered unity. There are living-rooms of all kinds, including bathrooms, audience halls, chapels, workshops, and huge magazines. In several places, fine broad stairways lead to upper stories; for the palace was built on a hillside and in some places was

[3] The history of Crete falls into three divisions: Early Minoan (from before 2800 to 2200 B.C.), Middle Minoan (2200–1600 B.C.), and Late Minoan (1600–1100 B.C.). In the early part of the Late Minoan occurred the reign of King Minos (c. 1500), after whom the whole civilization is named, though this term is not, strictly speaking, applicable to the periods that precede his reign. The Homeric age, so called because it is described in the Homeric poems, which were written much later, includes the period of the great migrations and conflicts from about 1350 to 1100 B.C.

several stories high. In the colonnaded hall (PL. 25 A) we see one of these stairways. The foundation and the lower parts of the building were built of huge, finely cut blocks of stone, but the columns were of wood. Each column has a small circular base and carries a cushionlike capital on which rests a square block to

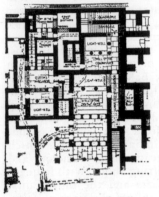

support the lintel. It tapers toward the bottom, a fact that weakens its effectiveness as a supporting member. Both the columns and walls were painted in gay colors.

Passing over to the mainland, we see that the *Palace at Tiryns* (FIG. 46), while resembling *Knossos*, differs from it in being built on a high rocky hill and strongly fortified by massive walls from twenty to thirty feet thick, built of unhewn or roughly dressed stones. So huge are these stones that later Greek legend called them the work of the Cyclopes, mythical giants. Through these walls, in some places, run galleries (FIG. 47) made of great stones in horizontal layers, roofed over by making each course project over the

Fig. 45. Palace of Minos. Knossos. Plan of the domestic quarter, with dotted lines to indicate the drainage system. (*British School Annual*)

one below until the opening is closed, the blocks roughly beveled to form what is known as a corbeled arch. This needs to be distinguished carefully from the true arch, made of wedge-shaped blocks, which we found was understood though little used in Egypt, and in Babylonia-Assyria was widely employed. At the citadel of Mycenæ, which is similar to that of Tiryns, is a remarkably well preserved entrance known as the *Lion Gate* (PL. 25 B). Here the blocks in the courses of the flanking walls are more finely cut. The door itself is formed of two great pillars capped with a huge lintel, above which the layers of stone are not solid, but by forming a corbeled arch leave a triangular opening to relieve the weight on the lintel. This space is filled with a slab on which are carved in high relief the two lions from which the gate is named.

Corbeled arch construction was used also in the so-called beehive-tombs at Mycenæ. When first discovered, it was thought these structures were storehouses for treasure; hence the most important is known as the "*Treasury of Atreus*" (FIG. 48).

Probably for the sake of protection, it was built into the hill and approached by a long passage cut through the side. Its

beehive shape is formed by corbeling courses of stone laid on a circular base. The small rectangular chamber at the side is hewn from the rock. Frequent holes in the interior seem to indicate that decorations, such as bronze rosettes, were affixed. In the monumental entrance (PL. 25 c) we find the same combination of lintel and corbeled arch construction as in the *Lion Gate*. Among the motifs of decoration, we see on the column

Fig. 46. Citadel at Tiryns, Restored. (Luckenbach)

the chevron; on the bands above, the spiral, rosette, and palmette. The columns here, as at *Knossos*, taper toward the base.

Fig. 47. Citadel at Tiryns. Corbeled gallery. (Perrot and Chipiez)

The palmette pattern we again find carved on an alabaster frieze (FIG. 49) from a vestibule at *Tiryns*. The half palmettes, surrounded by a spiral, are separated by a rectangular space ornamented with rosettes; the middle of the rosettes, the spirals, and the dentil-like pattern bordering both are inlaid with blue glass. Such a combination of blue with the creamy alabaster must have made a most effective decoration. Again these motifs appear on

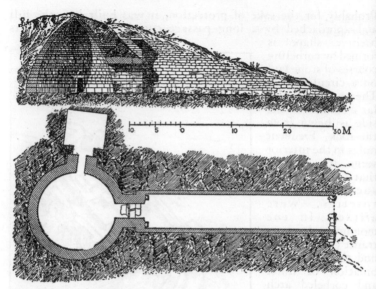

Fig. 48. Tomb Called the "Treasury of Atreus." Mycenæ. (Perrot and Chipiez)

Fig. 49. Frieze. Of alabaster with blue glass inlay. Tiryns.

the finely carved ceiling of a tomb at Orchomenos (FIG. 50), very much like that found on the ceiling of an Egyptian tomb (FIG. 37). The all-over pattern is formed of interlacing spirals and a motif derived from a combination of the lotus and palmette;[4] the ground is effectively broken by a band of double rosettes and finished by a border of single rosettes.

PAINTING

The frescoes with which the walls of these palaces were decorated furnish the chief source of our knowledge of Minoan painting. The young girl in PL. 26 A has dark curly hair loosely arranged, one lock falling over the forehead; bright red lips and a large eye, incorrectly drawn front view; and a dress looped up in the back with a bunch of bright ribbons. The execution is hasty; yet in spite of this the head and face are full of animation and have a piquancy which has earned for her the title of "*La Parisienne.*"

In the *Cupbearer* (PL. 27 B) we see a Cretan youth holding a gold-mounted silver vase. This fresco was the first picture of a Cretan man to be discovered, and the event caused much excitement, as Sir Arthur Evans tells us:

There was something very impressive in this vision of brilliant youth and of male beauty, recalled after so long an interval to our upper air from what had been till yesterday a forgotten world. Even our untutored Cretan workmen felt the spell and fascination. They, indeed, regarded the discovery of such a painting in the bosom of the earth as nothing less than miraculous, and said, "Is it the icon of a Saint!" The removal of the fresco required a delicate and laborious process of underplastering, which necessitated it being watched at night, and old Manolis, one of the most trustworthy of our gang, was told off for the purpose. Somehow or other he fell asleep, but the wrathful Saint appeared to him in a dream. Waking with a start, he was conscious of a mysterious presence; the animals round began to low and neigh, and "there were visions about"; "the whole place spooks," he said, in summing up his experiences next morning.

The youth has long hair, wears an elaborately embroidered loin cloth with a silver-mounted girdle about the waist, silver ornaments on his arms and neck, and on his wrist an agate signet with which to seal his letters. The limbs are well modeled; his pinched waist is characteristic of both the men and women of Crete. The reason for this we do not know. It is evidently a convention in the representation of Cretan people, for a painting in an Egyptian tomb at Thebes so pictures them. It may have originated in the attempt to express a lithe, athletic figure. This youth was one of a procession of cupbearers, the effect of which must have been highly decorative, as their figures moved rhythmically along against the flat, brightly colored ground in which a vivid, clear blue predominated. Although, as in Egyptian

[4] For the entire ceiling see Tarbell, *History of Greek Art*, FIG. 28.

painting, the flat tones serve the purpose of decoration, still the youth standing so erect, with shoulders thrown far back, is not cold, formal, and conventional, like the Egyptian, but full of life and keenly conscious of the pride of his race and the nobility of the ceremony that he is performing.

The *Bull-fighting Scene* (PL. 27 A) already described shows how well these painters could represent a dramatic moment, for the spirit of the incident is shown with remarkable vivacity. This quality we observe in scenes from nature which also served as subjects for wall decoration. The *Flying Fish Fresco* (PL. 27 C), in which winged fish with rhythmic movement are darting through the water among the rocks and sea plants, is full of naturalness and spontaneity. It appears to be hastily sketched, the rapid strokes showing a restlessness as if the artist was eager to finish his work and turn to something new; still that very quality gives the painting a feeling of freshness and vitality.

Fig. 50. Fragment of a Tomb Ceiling. Carved green schist. Orchomenos. (*Journal Hellenic Studies*)

SCULPTURE

Of sculpture on a large scale, very little has survived, the notable exception being the *Lion Gate* at Mycenæ (PL. 25 B). The triangular space left by the corbeled arch over the great lintel is filled with a slab on which are carved, in high relief, two lions, standing in a balanced position on either side of a shaft, on the base of which they rest their forepaws. Holes near the top indi-

PLATE 27

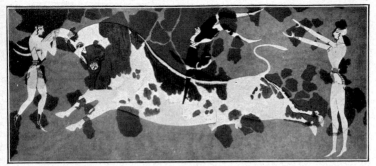

(*A*) Bull-fighting Scene. Fresco. c. 1500 B.C. Candia Museum. (Metropolitan Museum)

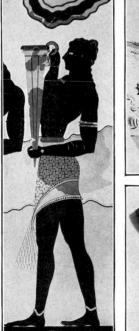

(*B*) Cupbearer. Fresco from Knossos. H. c. 5 ft. c. 1500 B.C. Candia Museum. (Metropolitan Museum)

(*C*) Flying Fish Fresco. Candia Museum. (Metropolitan Museum)

(*D*) Head of a Bull. Painted plaster relief. L. 26 in. Candia Museum. (Metropolitan Museum)

PLATE 28

(A) Palace Style Vase. H. c. 30 in. 1500–1350 B.C.
National Museum, Athens. (Metropolitan Museum)

(B) Palace Style Vase. 1600–1500 B.C.
(Seager)

(C) Octopus Vase. H. c. 8 in. 1600–1500 B.C
Candia Museum. (Metropolitan Museum)

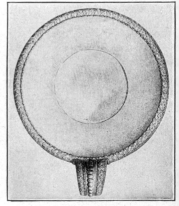

(D) Basin. Bronze. D. 12¾ in.
(Stoedtner)

cate that the heads, now lost, were made of separate pieces of stone or metal. Groups similar to this are seen on Cretan gems and probably constitute a heraldic device. The lions are well modeled and the whole design admirably fills the triangular space in which it is placed, harmonizing in dignity and strength with the massive stones that form the walls and the gate. It was indeed a fitting entrance for Agamemnon and Menelaus.

Vivacious movement characterizes much of the Minoan sculpture, as we see in the *Head of a Bull* (PL. 27 D), a fragment, probably, from a bull-fighting scene. The bulging eye and angry mouth powerfully and truthfully represent an enraged animal. Another example is the *Harvester Vase* (PL. 26 C), which is decorated with a procession of figures carved in low relief; the group is led by an old man with long hair, clad in a curious garment; near the center of the procession is an Egyptian priest with shaven head, carrying an Egyptian rattle called the sistrum. It is noticeable that he does not have the narrow waist line. He and the group behind him with open mouths are lustily singing. Almost all carry pitchforks, and three have winnowing sieves called fans. Here we have the representation of a harvest song. The swing of forward movement in the group and the exuberant joy of their song are represented in a masterly way.

A gold and ivory statuette (PL. 26 B) probably represents a Cretan *Snake-goddess*. On her head is an elaborate coronet, the holes in which indicate gold attachments, probably ornaments and the usual curls. The flounces of her skirt are banded with gold and her outstretched hands hold two gold snakes that coil about her arms. Like the *Cupbearer*, she stands proudly erect, with shoulders thrown back, firmly grasping the snakes. To the delicacy of the head is added this rugged strength of figure, which gives the goddess a forceful charm rarely equaled.

MINOR ARTS

Among the craftmen of Crete the potter was of great importance. So desirable were his vases that even the Egyptian lords procured them to place in their tombs. Of the many kinds, perhaps most noteworthy is the *Kamares Ware*, so called from the cave on Mount Ida where a large number of examples have been found. The two-handled vase seen in FIG. 51 has a lustrous black background on which is a quasi-geometric pattern of creamy white interspersed with yellow and red, forming a brilliant and harmonious piece of decoration. The tendency of the potters, as time went on, was away from geometric design toward natural-istic, as seen in a cup which is as thin as delicate china, and seems to be resting in an open water lily, the outspread creamy petals of which are outlined in red on a lustrous black ground, while above the petals runs a band of geometric design in low relief.

Sea life also furnished the potter with motifs for decoration. In the body of a "filler"[5] (Fig. 52) are rep-resented dolphins, with the intermediate space filled with the meshes of a fish net; naturalistic sprays of seaweed decorate the shoulder, neck, and inner rim of the vase. On another vase (Pl. 28 c) we have a free naturalistic piece of decoration, the main

Fig. 51. Kamares Vase. From Knossos. H. c. 9 in. 2000–1800 B.C. Candia Museum.

Fig. 52. Dolphin Filler. 1600–1500 B.C. (Seager)

feature of which is the octopus, whose body and arms, though naturalistic, are arranged with regard to the general shape of the vase, the neck, and the handles. The space is filled with marine life forming a carpetlike pattern.

Among the large jars and vases usually called *Palace Style* because many have been found at Knossos and appear to belong to the period of most splendid development, that represented in Pl. 28 a has an interesting design of skillfully interlaced birds combined with concentric circles and spirals. The bold, sweeping

5 So named because, as it is pierced at the bottom, its purpose was probably that of filling one vessel from another, like a modern funnel.

curves, though not precise, are particularly vigorous, and are highly decorative. The method of decoration is dark on a light ground, the opposite of that of the *Kamares Ware*. In stately vase (PL. 28 B) the lower part is ornamented with spiral bands; the upper part has four handles between which are conventionalized ox-heads. The double-ax motive plays through the whole design — in the shape of the handles, in the space between the handles, and between the horns of the ox, on the rim, and on the foot. It probably has some religious significance, and the vase may have been used for ceremonial purposes. Notice also the sprays of olive, an indication of the tendency of the potters toward naturalistic decorations. This relieves the formality of the design.

Another craftsman of great importance was the metal worker, as we see in a bronze basin (PL. 28 D), the rim of which is hammered out into a pattern of conventionalized lilies that spring diagonally from a beading and terminate in flamelike waving lines, the exuberance of which contrasts delightfully with the formal conventional treatment of the lilies. The same pattern decorates the finely tapering handle, to which a feeling of strength is added by the large raised beads in the center. The technical skill shown in the making of this border is superb.

Fig. 53. Gold Discs from Mycenæ. Purpose unknown. D. $2\frac{1}{2}$ in. 1600–1500 B.C.

In the work of the goldsmith some of the jewelry of gold leaf exhibits the charming naturalism so characteristic of Minoan work. In other examples, in those from Mycenæ in particular, geometric design is predominant, especially the spiral, which is used with great variety and forcefulness of line; and also such conventionalized forms as the butterfly (FIG. 53). The climax of the work of the goldsmith is found in the *Vaphio Cups* [6] (PL. 29 A and B), which are of a teacup shape like some of the *Kamares*

6 So called because they were found in a grave near Vaphio, in southern Greece.

Ware. Each is made of two plates of gold, on one of which was worked in *repoussé* the design that decorates the outside, while the other was left plain to make a smooth finish on the inside they were then fastened together and the handles riveted on some of the details were engraved. On one cup, which has a plain border at the rim and base as a finish, is represented a bull-hunting scene. In the center a bull is caught in the meshes of a net the one at the left is furiously charging a man with his horns while another man at his side is falling to the ground, probably from the back of the bull; at the right a third bull is dashing madly away from the scene. A tree beneath the handle frames the design while other trees and suggestions of landscape fill the intermediate spaces. The chief characteristic of the design is the energetic movement, carried to a point of exaggeration in the impossible position of the central bull and the stretch of the hind legs of the animal at the right. Distance is indicated by placing one object above another, as in the two trees to which the net is tied.

The second cup, which has no finishing border, is unlike its companion in that it pictures a quiet scene in which hunting takes place by means of a decoy cow. At the right a peaceful bull has been attracted and moves toward the center, where he is represented in friendly colloquy with the cow. At the left the same bull, captured and hobbled by the trapper, is bellowing in anger. There are fewer landscape details here than in the first cup, but the three scenes are well united by the trees and the trapper, and the whole design admirably composed to fit the space. It is remarkable how carefully and yet naturalistically the head of the captured bull fits into the space between the two places where the handle is riveted. Observation of nature and its truthful representation even in details are carefully shown here. The relief is just high enough to give a rich play of light and shade, to which the sheen of the gold brings additional splendor; and the design is so well adapted to the space that the ultimate effect is primarily decorative. Furthermore, the technical skill of the goldsmith who executed these cups is equaled by few craftsmen.

Another type of metal work is seen in a dagger-blade (Fig. 54) The figures are inlaid on a bronze base, with different kinds and colors of metal such as gold, silver, and some black material On one side is a lion hunt. Five men with spears, shields, and arrows are attacking the lions, two of whom are fleeing, while a third wounded, turns to attack; the foremost man has already fallen; the others advance to meet the infuriated beast. The bodies of the fleeing animals, elongated as if to accentuate their rapid movement, fit marvelously into the tapering shape. The men have the typical narrow waist line. Both men and animals are expressed with the greatest vigor. The process by which this was done, known as damascening,[7] is as follows: On the metal base, usually bronze, the design is outlined with a sharp instrument and the parts to be inlaid are cut out, leaving a depression with a slight undercutting on the edges. Into this depression pieces of different colored metal, cut to fit, are sunk and pressed firmly into the undercut edges. The surface is then smoothed and polished. Details are sometimes engraved.

Fig. 54. Dagger Blade. Bronze, inlaid with gold, electrum, and some black substance. 1600–1500 B.C. National Museum, Athens.

SUMMARY

These gifted Cretans, proud, aristocratic, pleasure-loving, and of agile mind, in the two-thousand-year span of their existence produced an art that reveals their exuberance of body and spirit. The splendor of their palaces, their furnishings and decorations, the vigorous movement in the bull-fighting and hunting scenes, the charming naturalism of their pottery and jewelry, and the magnificence of their metal work are witnesses that the descriptions in Homer of the shield of Achilles and the house of Alcinoüs were based, not on the poet's imagination, but on the actual appearance of the civilization by which he was surrounded.

BIBLIOGRAPHY

BAIKIE, JAMES, Sea Kings of Crete. London, Black, 1920.
BOSSERT, H. T., Alt Kreta. Berlin, Wasmuth, 1921.
BREASTED, J. H., Ancient Times. Boston, Ginn, 1916.

[7] From Damascus, not because the craft originated in that city but because the metal workers living there became famous for their product.

Burrows, R. M., Discoveries in Crete. London, Murray, 1908.

Evans, Sir Arthur, The Palace of Minos (Vol. I). N.Y., Macmillan, 1921.

Fowler, H. N., and Wheeler, J. R., Handbook of Greek Archaeology. N.Y. Amer. Book Co., 1909.

Hall, H. R., Ægean Archæology. London, Warner, 1915.

Hawes, C. H. and H. B., Crete, the Forerunner of Greece. N.Y., Harper, 1909.

Kimball, Fiske, and Edgell, G. H., History of Architecture. N.Y., Harper, 1918

Mosso, Angelo, Palaces of Crete and Their Builders. London, Unwin, 1907.

Pater, W. H., Greek Studies. N.Y., Macmillan, 1920.

Reinach, Salomon, Apollo (tr. Simmons). N.Y., Scribner, 1924.

Schuchhardt, Carl, Schliemann's Excavations (tr. Sellers). N.Y., Macmillan, 1891.

Tsountas, Chrestos, and Manatt, J. I., Mycenæan Age. Boston, Houghton, 1916.

Winter, Franz, ed., Kunstgeschichte in Bildern. Vol. I, Das Altertum. Leipzig, Seemann, 1912.

CHAPTER VI
GREEK PERIOD (1)
Early Greek and Archaic Period, c. 2000–480 B.C.

HISTORICAL BACKGROUND

In marked contrast to Egypt, a land monotonous with the long horizontals of alluvial plain between desert plateaus and under invariable sunshine, Greece[1] is a country of diversified geography and climate (PL. 35 A). The deeply indented bays of her rugged coast line make the country half land and half sea; mountain ridges divide it into many small units. The semitropical climate, with its varying conditions of rain and sunshine, is free from the extremes of heat and cold that drain the strength of man and stunt his intellectual growth. The atmosphere has an unusually crystalline quality, with clear distances softened by haze, and with rich colors in sky and sea. Little wonder is it that the Greeks, who were by nature sensitive to beauty and gifted with imagination, in their childlike joy in nature should people the mountains, woods, streams, the sky, and the sea with divinities, sometimes human, sometimes fantastic; that they should picture Zeus, the king of this realm of gods, as reigning from their loftiest peak Olympus; the Muses, as dwelling in the deep, cool groves on the long slopes of Parnassus and Cithæron; and Apollo, the god of wisdom, as speaking from the awe-inspiring clefts of Delphi.

These geographic and climatic conditions probably had much to do with the eager individualistic strain that was characteristic of the race. The mountains and islands, rich in marble quarries, such as Pentelicus just north of Athens and Paros hard by in the Ægean Sea, furnished a material particularly adaptable in its texture and hardness both for building and for carving.

Who were these Greeks, whom we mentioned as the destroyers of the Minoan civilization? They appear to have been Indo-European nomads, who, wandering slowly from their original home in central Asia, entered the Greek peninsula about 2000 B.C.,

---

[1] In using the word "Greek," one needs to remember that the Greeks called themselves "Hellenes" and their country "Hellas."

and mingled with the people living there. About 1500 another wave, known as the Dorian migration, more military than the first, swept into the country, conquering the earlier peoples and even passing over to Crete, where, about 1400, they burned the *Palace at Knossos*. From 1300 to 1100 these Dorian tribes gradually took possession of the lands about the Ægean Sea. To this period belong such tales as the siege of Troy, which is typical of the numerous conflicts between the Cretan strongholds like Troy or Mycenæ and the invaders. Those of the conquered peoples who had the means fled; the remainder mingled with the conquerors. Slowly they amalgamated, the barbarous Greeks, with no system of writing, taking over certain elements of the gifted Cretan civilization. It was the Greek, however, whose religion, language, and fresh energizing power triumphed. Gradually the tribal organizations developed into city states ruled over first by kings and then by nobles. From the Phoenicians, who held a monopoly of Mediterranean trade at this time, they took an alphabet; and the old Homeric legends which reflected the heroic days of their race, and which had been handed down by word of mouth through traveling bards, were finally committed to writing.

Their boldness took them out upon the sea. While establishing colonies and developing trade, from the Black Sea in the east as far as southern France and Spain in the west, they came in contact with the older cultures that were still dominant in the Near East — Egypt and Babylonia-Assyria — from which they acquired certain ideas, motifs, and conventions, as we shall see. As they were a trading people, we are not surprised to find among them the invention of coinage. In their religion, which had originally been a worship of the spirits of nature, the gods assumed a human form, with a grandeur and nobility not entirely free from human frailty. In honor of Zeus all the Greeks united every four years for athletic contests, in which the victor was crowned with a simple laurel wreath, the highest honor in the land. To him a statue was erected and odes sung. Tyrants, in the sense of benevolent despots, such as Pisistratus, succeeded the nobles in the sixth century and as great patrons aided the impulse toward creative thought, in science, art, and religion that was all ready to flower.

DRAWING AND PAINTING

In the early part of this period, when the Greek civilization was shaping itself, the people produced no monumental architecture or sculpture, but revealed their genius in their handicrafts, especially pottery. A two-handled cup (FIG. 55) is typical of the kind of pottery that the Greek was creating side by side with the Mycenæan, who was still fashioning his stately *Palace Style* vases (PL. 28 A and B) with their easy grace. The shape has a simple ruggedness and a carefully thought out scheme of decoration. The motifs, which are geometric, with the exception of the birds, are arranged in horizontal bands about the cup, the

Fig. 55. Geometric Vase. H. 4 in. Between 900 and 660 B.C. Ashmolean Museum, Oxford.

broadest one, where the handles are attached, being broken into rectangular spaces. The birds are purely conventional and used

Fig. 56. *A.* The *Amphora* (meaning to carry on both sides, referring to the two handles) was a vessel for storing provisions — wine, corn, oil, honey. It had an opening large enough to admit a ladle, and usually a cover to protect the contents. *B.* Vase painting showing two men with amphoræ, probably filled with wine for the large bowl between them.

decoratively. This ware is called *Geometric* and was made by the Greeks from about 1100 to 800 B.C., culminating in the type known as the *Dipylon.*[2] PL. 29 C shows a large amphora (FIG. 56)

---

[2] So called because these vases have been found in great numbers in the cemetery near the Dipylon gate of Athens.

with wide mouth, small handles, and slender stem. It has a vigorous shape though not the fine proportions later acquired. The
carefully planned design still contains many geometric motifs,
the meander, zigzag, concentric circles, and swastika; yet the
predominant motif is the human and animal figure. The subject
is a funeral procession. On a bier drawn by a two-horse chariot
lies the body, with rows of mourners in front and behind; below,
separated by a zigzag border, is a row of two-horse chariots. One
of the most interesting things about the vase is the introduction
of the human figure, something rarely found in the work of the
Minoan artist. To be sure the drawing is most crude, like that

Fig. 57. *A*. The *Hydria* (from the Greek word for "water") was the water jar,
used chiefly to bring water from the spring. It has three handles, two for lifting
and one for carrying. *B*. Vase painting showing two youths filling their hydriæ
at a fountain.

of a child, and is little more than a geometric pattern. The chariots the artist draws in profile, yet he shows both wheels and all
the legs of the horses.[3] Nor does he seem distressed over the fact
that the body of the chariot does not touch the wheels, nor the
wheels the ground. The rows of mourners are arranged in zones
one above the other as we saw in Egypt; for this was the artist's
means of expressing depth. In spite of these shortcomings, however, the effect is highly decorative; and that was the main concern of the painter. Its interest for us lies in the fact that out of
this crude beginning, after a long period of growth, arose a
marvelous art expression. Let us observe its growth.

Before proceeding further with the evolution of Greek drawing
as we see it on the vases, it would be well to note the six vase
shapes most frequently found, and their uses: the *amphora*, the

[3] For an explanation of this inconsistency, on psychological grounds, see Loewy, *The Rendering of Nature in Early Greek Art*.

general storage jar (FIG. 56); the *hydria*, the water jar (FIG. 57); the *crater*, the mixing bowl (FIG. 58); the *cylix*, the drinking cup (FIG. 59); the *oinochoë*, the wine pitcher (FIG. 60); and the *lecythos*, the oil flask (FIG. 61). In determining the uses of these vases, we are guided by the paintings on the vases themselves; for in these paintings the Greeks have given us an amazing revelation of their everyday life. The shapes vary in different periods and locations. Those given in FIGS. 56–61 are taken from the best period, chiefly the fifth century.

To continue our study of drawing, let us look at an oinochoë (FIG. 62). It is a well proportioned vase of firm outline, decorated with rows of animals in profile. The artist painted the silhouette

Fig. 58. *A.* The *Crater* (from the Greek verb "to mix") was the bowl for mixing the wine and water, the usual beverage of the Greek; hence it had a wide mouth. *B.* Vase painting showing the youths filling their cylixes from a crater.

of the animal in dark colors on the lighter background and then, after firing, scratched in the details with a sharp instrument, exposing the light color below. This process is called incising. But not content with his processions of animals for a decorative scheme, he filled in the background with rosettes and other geometric figures, so that the effect is of an all-over pattern, quite different from that of the austere *Dipylon* ware. The type of animals as well as their arrangement in rows is distinctly reminiscent of the Near East (PL. 22 c). So too are the rosettes. This influence is due to the fact that Greece, now in her colonizing period, was meeting these older civilizations and borrowing from them.

The same desire for completely filling the space, and this time in connection with the use of the human figure, we find in the

Euphorbus Plate (FIG. 63). The painter has cut off a segment of the space by a horizontal band decorated with the guilloche, and has filled in the segment with the tongue pattern arranged fanshape. In the remaining space he has painted a scene from the Iliad, as we know from the names painted near the figures. This plate is interesting because of the introduction into art of a mythological subject, and also because it shows what great progress the Greek had made in his ability to draw the human figure, since he painted the *Dipylon* vase at least one hundred years earlier. Yet the figure is still far from correct, for the torso is drawn front view, as is also the eye, while the remainder of the body is in

Fig. 59. *A.* The *Cylix* (from the Greek root "to roll," referring to the vases being turned on the wheel) was the chief form of the drinking cup. *B.* Vase painting showing a banquet scene; the man at the right is drinking from a cylix; the one on the left is holding his out to be filled; cylixes and oinochoæ hang on the wall.

profile. Part of the figure is done in outline and part in a solid flat tone, with no indication of folds in the dress. We notice the careful adaptation of the figures to the space. The stop-gaps which fill the background, such as the spiral, palmette, rosette, checker, and swastika, we have met in Egypt and Babylonia-Assyria.

Let us come down at least another half-century, into the sixth, when the Athenian potteries, by the quality of their fabric, so surpassed those of other cities, that from this time on until the manufacture ceased about the fourth century, Athens was the great center of production, sending her wares even to south Russia, Thebes, and Italy. The *François Vase*[4] (PL. 30 A) is a crater with volute handles, of extraordinary vigor both in its shape and in its proportion, and decorated with concentric bands

[4] Named after the man who found it in a grave in Italy.

PLATE 29

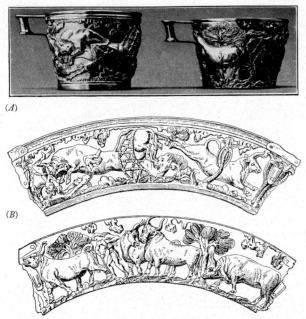

(A)

(B)

(A and B) Vaphio Cups. Gold. H. 3½ in. 1600–1500 B.C.
National Museum, Athens.

(C) Dipylon Vase, with a Representation of a Funeral Procession. H. 4 ft.
VIII cent. B.C. National Museum, Athens.

PLATE 30

(*B*) Cylix, Painted by Exekias: Dionysus Sailing over the Sea. Black-figured. D. 14½ in. 550–525 B.C. Munich. (Furtwängler-Reichhold)

(*A*) François Vase. H. c. 2 ft. First half VI cent. B.C. Archæological Museum, Florence. (Furtwängler-Reichhold)

(*C*) Amphora, Painted by Exekias: Ajax and Achilles Playing Draughts. Black-figured. 550–525 B.C. Vatican, Rome. (Furtwängler-Reichhold)

(*D*) François Vase. Detail of foot. (Furtwängler-Reichhold)

PLATE 31

(*A*) Cylix, Painted by Euphronios: Cattle of Geryon. Red-figured. D. 17 in.
c. 500 B.C. Munich. (Furtwängler-Reichhold)

(*B*) Cylix, Painted by Duris: Voting of the Greek Chiefs. Red-figured.
D. 15½ in. c. 460 B.C. Vienna. (Furtwängler-Reichhold)

PLATE 32

(*A*) Statue of a Woman. Marble. H. 6 ft. VII cent. B.C. Athens.

(*B*) Hera of Samos. Marble. H. 6 ft. C. 550 B.C. Louvre, Paris. (Giraudon)

(*C*) "Apollo" of Tenea. Marble. H. 5 ft. 8 in. Late VI cent. B.C. Munich.

(*D*) Archer. From the Temple at Ægina (PL. 33A). (Clarence Kennedy)

filled chiefly with human and animal figures. These are painted in black-figured technique, that is, in a black glaze on the natural reddish clay, which is left as a background. The vase is fired and then the details are incised with a sharp instrument, as in the oinochoë (FIG. 62); sometimes white or purple is added for detail. On the foot (PL. 30 D), between two rows of carefully executed tongue pattern is represented a battle between pygmies and cranes. Some of the pygmies are mounted on goats, others fight on foot. Animated movement and fierce conflict dominate; yet all the figures are drawn so as to fill the space in a highly decorative way. Notice the almost even line made at the top of the band by the heads and wings, and the almost equal spotting

Fig. 60. *A.* The *Oinochoë* (from the Greek verb "to pour out wine") was the wine jug. The lip is pinched into a trefoil shape, which facilitates pouring. *B.* Vase painting showing a youth pouring wine from a slender, high-handled oinochoë into a cylix.

of the lights and darks, the curves and rhythms of which contrast so happily with the regularity of the geometrical borders. On the broad band about the shoulder of the vase to which the handles are affixed is represented the procession of gods and goddesses, dressed in elaborate costumes, on their way to the wedding of Peleus and Thetis. At the extreme right stands the bridegroom receiving the guests in front of the house in which the bride is seated (not visible in this view); he is shaking hands with the centaur Chiron, who carries over his shoulder a branch from which hang three hares; then follow the other divinities, each named by an inscription near the figure. The drawing, though still crude, is spirited; and the incising is executed with delicacy and firmness. The figures and drapery are painted in flat silhouette, though in the mantles there is occasionally seen an indication of the folds of the drapery. The heads of nearly all the figures, whether riding or standing, and even the roof of the

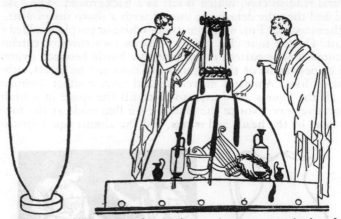

Fig. 61. . *A* The *Lecythos* (oil flask) has a long narrow neck adapted to pouring the oil slowly. It was used chiefly in funeral rites. *B* Vase painting showing two men at a tomb; on the plinth are lecythi, oinochoæ, a crater, a lyre, and a wreath.

house are on an approximately level line. The necessary distortion of natural proportion to accomplish this is known as *isocephaly*, meaning heads on a level, and was used by the Greeks

Fig. 62. Rhodian Oinochoë. (Morin-Jean)

because it produced a more decorative effect than the zigzag line that results from observing correct proportion. The use of this principle and the omission of the stop-gaps seen in the *Euphorbus Plate* have much to do with the fineness and restraint of this scheme of decoration, the predominant note of which is the human figure, to which the geometric and animal motifs have become subordinate.

An amphora painted by Exekias (PL. 30 c) shows a different scheme of decoration. Its shape, with large mouth and broad foot, is strong rather than graceful. The handles not only harmonize with the curve as an integral part of the design, but are attached in such a way that they appear to fulfill their function of supporting the weight of the vase. The surface is painted solid black, except for the band with rays just above the base, the decorated panel on the body, and the handles. In the large panel we see Ajax and Achilles seated on stools, bending intently over their game of draughts. Ajax, on the right, as the inscription tells us, calls out "Three"; Achilles, on the left, "Four." It is a close game. All the elements make for a design that is balanced, yet subtly varied; one hero is helmeted, the other not; slight differences occur in the position of the limbs and spears and the decoration of the shields. There

Fig. 63. Plate. Combat of Menelaus and Hector over Euphorbus. Black on a cream ground, with purplish color in the parts indicated by the checked lines. Late VII cent. B.C. British Museum, London.

is much greater naturalism in the pose of the figures than anything we have seen before, a better understanding of proportions and anatomy, and greater freedom in drawing. The skill and sure-handedness seen in the profusion and delicacy of the incised lines of the hair, and in the very elaborate cloaks, are a delight in themselves.

A cylix of Exekias (PL. 30 B) represents, on the inside, Dionysus sailing over the sea carrying his gifts to mankind. In the center is the dolphin-shaped boat in which the god sits leisurely and controls the bellying sail which is attached to a mast entwined with grapevines heavily loaded with fruit. Round about are dolphins, symbolizing the sea. Here the exquisite adaptation of the figures to the circular space as well as the imaginative and poetic quality make this vase one of the rare examples of the black-figured work.

As we turn to the next cylix (PL. 31 A) we notice that we are looking at a vase of different technique, for here the figures and decorative patterns are the reddish color of the clay; the details and background, black. This is known as the red-figured ware, which was decorated in the following manner: After the vase was shaped the painter with a blunt tool incised his design in the clay; he then painted a broad band around the outside of the outline thus marked off, and frequently a thin raised black line, then painted in the details, and finally filled in the background with black glaze. The advantage of this style over the black-figured ware was that the line made by a brush or a pen allowed much more freedom in drawing than that incised. The change from black to red-figured vases did not come about suddenly but by slow development. In fact some vases show a panel decorated in black on one side and in red on the other.

The cylix was a popular shape with the red-figured painters, who decorated the broad convex surface of the outside and the circular space that formed the center of the inside, as seen in PL. 31 A. On this vase the painter Euphronius represented two scenes from one of the labors of Heracles, the Cattle of Geryon. On one side we see Heracles, wearing the lion-skin and armed with his great club and bow and arrow, vigorously attacking the three-headed Geryon, who guarded the cattle with the help of the two-headed dog who has already been killed by an arrow; one of Geryon's heads has been pierced in the eye and is falling backward; behind Heracles is Athena, his friend Iolaus, and the wounded herdsman Eurytion. The figure on the right may represent some nymph of the locality. On the other side of this vase we see the cattle driven off by four armed youths. In the circular disc is represented a mounted horseman. Though the narrative element is lively, still the decorative effect is what impresses most. That was the primary purpose of the painter; and he did not allow irrelevant details to swerve him from that purpose. Particularly is this true in the herd of cattle, the flat silhouettes of whose bodies are shaped to the space as if they inevitably belonged there; and also in the central disc, where the figures of the youth and the horse form a compact pattern that seems to partake of the rotary motion inherent in the circle and at the same time to restrain that movement by the severely angular lines of the cloak. The drapery is no longer blocked out in silhouette, as in the earlier vases. The elaborate folds of the garments are arranged in a stiff conventional fashion, yet are drawn with fine firm lines that indicate a technical ability of first rank. As if the garments were transparent, the lines of the figure appear through them. The understanding of the human figure is much better and the drawing of it freer. There is no light and shade but line only is used for modeling. The drawing is not always correct; the eye, for example, is still shown front-view. The beautiful border of alternating palmettes is to be noted.

A cylix decorated by another painter, Duris, represents an incident in the Homeric story of the strife between Ajax and Odysseus over the armor of Achilles (PL. 31 B). The Greek chiefs, under the supervision of Athena, are casting their votes on the question of the disposal of the armor; the little pebbles with which they vote are piling up on the side of Odysseus, who stands on the right with hands uplifted in delight at his victory, while Ajax on the left turns aside sorrowfully in defeat. Although the incident is dramatic, it is pictured with restraint and simple directness; for example, the movement of Athena to the right makes the pile of pebbles stand out with exceptional clarity. Here, as in the work of Euphronius, we note the supremely decorative effect of the human figures, balanced on either side of Athena, yet subtly varied; for the chief on the right is turned three-quarters toward us, the one on the left, three-quarters back. The stiff folds of the drapery are now loosening up and falling more naturally, yet they are drawn with sure-handed strokes which of themselves are an element of decoration. In drawing Duris shows considerable advance. In the eye, he has pushed the pupil in toward the nose and opened up the inner contours of the lids. Furthermore, he has attempted foreshortening, as in the front view of the feet in the two end figures.

Rapidly now the Greek is becoming victor in his long struggle with his problem of how to draw the human figure correctly. We have followed him through a period of nearly four hundred years during which he has been concentrating upon this problem. By 480 B.C. he had almost learned, for the first time in the history of man, how to draw a human figure correctly from different points of view. To summarize this let us take one detail, the eye, and watch its evolution (FIG. 64). It is not easy for us living in the twentieth century to realize how many thousand years of man's existence on earth elapsed before he could do what today seems so obvious, namely, make a correct drawing of the human figure; and he learned to do it only after several hundred years of patient concentration upon the problem of foreshortening. Here are the beginnings of the traditions that form such an intimate part of our heritage that we could not escape them if we would. We can draw today because the Greek first taught us how. At no time, however, did the vase-maker forget the unity of his design as a whole, the shape of the vase he was perfecting; he gave closest attention to proportion, subtlety of curve, and method of shaping and affixing the handles, so ordering the decoration that it was a unit with the structural lines.

The Greeks, however, did not look upon these vase-makers as

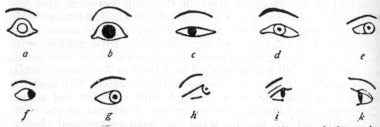

Fig. 64. Evolution of the Drawing of the Eye. In the earliest work the eye is represented front view, almost circular in form and the pupil as a circle or disc (*a* and *b*); the outline next becomes elliptical (*c* and *d*); then the lids begin to separate at the inner corner and the pupil to be pushed inward, though still circular (*e*, *f*, and *g*); finally the lids open up, the pupil becomes elliptical, the upper lid is properly shaped and the correct profile is attained (*i* and *k*). (British Museum)

great artists. Exekias, Euphronius, and Duris are never mentioned by Greek writers. They were mere craftsmen — a fact that indicates the high level of accomplishment and of taste exercised by the masses of Greek citizens. There appears to be no doubt, however, that these craftsmen were reflecting a great school of painters, all of whose works have been lost, and probably some of the designs on the vases are more or less faithful copies of these works. Apart from their own intrinsic value, then, the vases are valuable in helping us to catch a glimpse of what painting must have been in that period.

SCULPTURE

In turning to sculpture, we observe the same fascinating cycle of development. As in the vases, the problem is the representation of the human figure. A *Statue of a Woman* (PL. 32 A) represents the earliest gropings, typifying for the plastic arts what the figures on the *Dipylon* vases do for the graphic. We do not know the subject; it is a clothed female figure, whose body is rectangular like a block of marble with the edges slightly rounded off. Advance is evident in the *Hera of Samos* (PL. 32 B), made perhaps one hundred years later. The figure is rigid; the lower part seems encased in a cylindrical sheath and the toes are affixed to the line of the garment, not forming a part of real feet belonging to a structure beneath. Yet in the upper part there is life, for some form is felt beneath the drapery, and while the right arm holds rigidly to the side, the left is bent, probably holding something to the breast. With painstaking care the sculptor has indicated the drapery, the broader folds of the outer woolen mantle and the narrower ones of the thin linen undergarment. There is sincerity of purpose throughout; and the long lines, some of which are chiseled with a vigorous grace, give the figure a quiet, gracious majesty.

Early in Greek sculpture appear nude male figures; for the Greeks were an athletic people, both practicing and observing gymnastic games daily, and perpetuating this important element of their civilization in statues of the victors. Hence, the so-called *Apollo of Tenea* (PL. 32 C) may well represent some victorious youth at the games. The figure is standing in a rigid frontal position, both arms close to the side, and the left foot advanced — a pose strongly reminiscent of such Egyptian statues as *Ranofer* (PL. 3 C). The proportions are slim, yet the statue shows a careful study of the human form, for the modeling throughout, and about the knees in particular, is careful and studied. The head is quite characteristic of early archaic work, with its conventional treatment of the hair, bulging eyeballs, high cheek bones, high position of the ears, and the formation of the mouth, the upturned corners of which have that grimace known as "the archaic smile," which probably comes about from the vain attempts of early sculptors to model the difficult transition from the mouth to the cheeks.

We have now come from the seventh century to the latter part of the sixth, the age of the tyrants, a period, as we have said, particularly favorable to the arts, which, after their long period of growth, were just beginning to develop with great rapidity. This we see in the group of figures that decorate the pediment or gable of a temple at *Ægina* (PL. 33 A). The scene probably represents some episode from the Trojan war. Athena, with aegis and spear, stands in the center, yet has no immediate

connection with the fighting groups, which are arranged in
a balanced position on either side. In each group a warrior
with helmet, shield, and drawn sword attacks his falling op-
ponent, to whose help a friend rushes with outstretched arms
Behind him an archer, with bent knee, takes aim at the warrior,
while a fallen wounded soldier occupies the corner. The most
noticeable thing in the group is the freedom of movement and
variety of pose. The figures are modeled with a vigor and with an
understanding of the human physique that reflect a careful observation of nature. The *Archer* (PL. 32 D), for example, is complicated in pose, in comparison with the statues that we have
studied; but the form is so compact and so simple in outline as
to be almost geometrical. It is the contrasting direction of line
seen in the vertical of the back, the horizontal of the arm, and
the diagonal of the firmly braced leg that gives one so strong an
impression of the powerful draw upon the bow and, at the same
time, a feeling of the perfect equilibrium of the whole figure
In the fallen warrior who is endeavoring to lift himself on his
arm, the artist has attempted a difficult twisted position of the
torso, and not satisfactorily, for the line of the breast and abdo-
men is not continuous — a deficiency that is hidden by the arm
— a small detail which is most significant, for it shows how
keenly the artist realized his failure. The stiffness in most of the
figures shows that the artist has not yet been able to emancipate
himself from the domination of the stone. His supreme struggle
for freedom, however, is what makes these groups of the highest
interest.

The Greek is here attempting not only the representation of
single figures, but the grouping of them together to fill a space
the limitations of which are severe; for a pediment, besides being
long and unequally narrow, has a decided central axis from the
base to the apex of the triangle, which must be observed with
balance not too monotonous; furthermore, the narrowing angle
of each side demand low figures. At *Ægina*, the sculptor has
been just fairly successful with his problem. He is not yet facile
enough to cover the technique of his design; for we are far too
conscious of the fact that the kneeling and reclining figures are
posed as they are because of necessity.

Traces of paint on these pedimental groups remind us that the
Greek, like the Egyptian, painted his statues and reliefs. This
application of color to stone may have derived from the desire
of the artist to conceal the texture of the wood or coarse stone
from which the early statues were carved. But the fact that the

PLATE 33

(*A*) Temple at Ægina, East Pediment. Incident from the Trojan War. Conjectural restoration by Furtwängler. c. 500 B.C. Glyptothek, Munich.

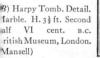

(*B*) Harpy Tomb. Detail. Marble. H. 3½ ft. Second half VI cent. B.C. British Museum, London. (Mansell)

(*C*) Figure found on the Acropolis. Marble, painted. H. c. 4 ft. Early V cent. B.C. Acropolis Museum, Athens. (Alinari)

(*D*) Figure Found on the Acropolis. Inscribed Euthydicus. Marble, painted. c. 480 B.C. Acropolis Museum, Athens.

PLATE 34

(*A*) Shallow Bowl. Bronze. L. 17½ in. with the handle. (*B*) Detail of handle. Metropolitan Museum, New York. (Metropolitan Museum)

(*C*) Jug. Bronze. H. 12 in. Metropolitan Museum, New York. (Metropolitan Museum)

(*D*) Lip of Bronze Jug (detail of *C*). (Metropolitan Museum)

(*E*) Gem: Achilles Sinking Backwards. L. ¾ in. Early V cent. British Museum, London.

(*F*) Gem: Eros Carrying a Struggling Girl. Carnelian. L. ¾ in. Early V cent. Metropolitan Museum, New York. (Metropolitan Museum)

practice continued after the introduction of fine marble is evidence of the Greek's preference for painted sculpture rather than the plain white. Though at times naturalistic, yet the fundamental purpose was decorative design; and if blue was needed at that point in the design where a man's head happened to be, the artist did not hesitate to paint the hair and beard blue.

The sculpture that we have been studying so far was produced chiefly on the Greek mainland. Let us turn aside for a moment and see what the Greeks of the east — on the islands of the Ægean and in Ionia — were producing. The *Harpy Tomb*[5] (PL. 33 B), which stood originally in Asia Minor, is a four-sided pier with reliefs at the top where the stone is hollowed out for the burial chamber. On the side where the door cuts through is a seated figure with a pomegranate in one hand and a flower in the other; three figures are approaching, carrying fruit and flowers, and holding up their chitons. They are dressed in long garments that cling tightly in the back, revealing the outline of the figure, and the long hair is elaborately arranged. They hold their fruit and flowers with great daintiness. But their soft, rounded forms are not modeled; the outline only seems to matter. A certain suavity and elegance has been the aim of the artist rather than an understanding of the form and consequent vigor of modeling. This is due to the fact that these cities of Asia Minor, partly through temperament and partly through a long-continued contact with the luxurious East, lack the force and intellectual caliber of continental Greece. The tender, gracious aspect of things appealed to their sensibilities and revealed itself in their art. We may observe here the decorative effect of the principle of *isocephaly* already noted in the vases.

This interest in the more gracious aspect of life came to Athens and appeared in a group of statues known as the "*Acropolis Ladies*" (PL. 33 C). We do not know whom they represent or what their purpose was. They all stand in the same frontal position, left foot advanced, right hand holding up the mantle, the left bent at the elbow and extended as if holding something. The lady here represented wears a linen chiton indicated by ripple marks and a woolen mantle that falls in broad conventional folds from the right shoulder. The marble is undercut along the edge of the folds, giving a feeling of depth, and is painted to represent the decorative border and the all-over pattern of the goods. The elaborately dressed hair falls down behind in con-

---

[5] On one side of the tomb are represented Harpies flying downward with figures in their arms; hence the name.

ventional waves, and a few locks, separating, fall over the breast. The long narrow face bears traces of the archaism that is rapidly disappearing. These gentle aristocrats, alluring in their charm and quaint with their elaborate coiffures and luxurious dress, have just a tinge of the austerity of Athens, where they seem as yet strangers. But they are destined to come under her sway.

This union of the gracious Ionian and the austere continental or Dorian elements we see taking place in the *Euthydicus* (PL. 33 D). Charm is still here but it has given way to a serene simplicity that is almost severe, seen in such details as the hair and the dress. The full face is beautifully modeled; the hair is undercut above the cheeks and below the ears, giving a feeling for the plasticity of the mass; the mouth, whose corners droop slightly, has an expression that is perhaps too pensive.

Thus in sculpture as in painting we have the unique spectacle of a people who, not at all daunted by the centuries which are involved in the process, concentrate upon a problem with calmness and intellectual keenness until they bring it to a marvelous perfection. This perfection we shall reach in the second half of the fifth century.

MINOR ARTS

The underlying principles and also the evolution seen in the major arts of early Greece, we find reflected in the minor, though the latter, because of their size only, cannot express the same spiritual grandeur as the former. The pottery we have already discussed, with its bearing on the development of drawing and painting.

Bronze was always a favorite medium with the Greeks, who used it widely, not only for sculpture but also for various kinds of utensils — pots and pans, dishes for the table, sacrificial vessels, tools, and weapons. An example is a shallow bowl (PL. 34 A and B) with flaring rim quite devoid of ornamentation except for the handle, which is elaborately decorated on both sides and soldered to the bottom of the bowl. At the point of attachment we see an animated boxing scene, the lithe bodies of the athletes so grouped that while they vigorously pursue their sport, yet as a group they do not interfere with the decorative purpose. Below this section is a smooth place left for the thumb when holding the handle — an indication of the fundamental feeling for utility; this is finished by a palmette which with its projecting lines terminates in a giant, whose snaky legs intertwine to form an open ring for hanging up the dish. Another bronze utensil is a jug of strongly proportioned, elegant shape, decorated on the handle and the trefoil lip only (PL. 34 c and D). The handle is attached to the body of the vase by a floral ornament, is fluted and decorated along the edges with a beading, and terminates in two couchant lions where it is riveted to the rim. The trefoil lip is edged with a tongue pattern and two rows of beading; and the inward curves are deep and rectangular, so as to make pouring easier, and are decorated with rampant lions in low relief. Both the bowl and the jug illustrate the fact that the Greek did not lavishly distribute his decoration, but concentrated it upon certain parts; first, because he was not afraid of plain, unadorned surfaces; and second, because his feeling for moderation led him toward harmony through the stern subordination of details.

Another craft of importance was that of the engraver as we find it illustrated in the coins and gems. Strange though it may seem, the finest Greek coins were struck, not at Athens nor even in continental Greece, but in Magna Græcia, particularly at Syracuse in Sicily. In the *Demarateion* [6] (PL. 35 c), on the obverse is a four-horse chariot, with a victory flying above; in the segment below, a running lion, and, about the edge, a row of dots; on the reverse a profile head, perhaps the nymph Arethusa, in a faint circle, is surrounded by four dolphins with a Greek inscription which reads in translation, "of the Syracusans." It will be noticed that the coin is thicker and less even in shape than modern coins, and that the metal runs up around the edge on one side of the reverse. This is because Greek coins were struck by hand on an anvil that held the die, without a circular frame to keep the metal from running over the edge. The relief, too, is higher; for the Greek was not hampered by the modern necessity of "stacking." What we observe first, as in the vases, is the feeling for the adaptation of the figures to the space. Though the object is small, there is a quiet orderliness and a feeling of amplitude. The circle of the disc is repeated by the dolphins and inner ring until the eye inevitably reaches the head in the center. There is clearness in the design and also austere simplicity, particularly when it is compared with the later coins decorated with the same type (PL. 44 F). Of course the skill of the engraver lay in the cutting of the die in intaglio, of which the finished coin is an impression.

---

[6] These coins are named after Demarate, wife of the tyrant Gelon. According to one story, the Carthaginians obtained very favorable terms from Gelon, after their defeat at Himera, through the influence of Demarate, to whom they gave a large amount of silver from which these coins were struck.

The same process was involved in carving the gems which were mounted in rings and used as seals. PL. 34 E shows Achilles sinking backward, wounded, his right arm still in the strap of his shield, his left pulling the spear from his heel, his one vulnerable spot; about the edge runs a cable border. In PL. 34 F we see Eros carrying off a struggling girl. In these gems there is the fine sense of design that we now see is so characteristic of all Greek work, a sensitiveness for decorating a space. The circular movement in the crouching figure of Achilles, accentuated by the repeating line of the shield, fits exquisitely the elliptical shape of the gem. In the Eros example, two figures are skillfully grouped and move rapidly to the right; yet the backward glance of Eros and the deep sweeping lines of the wings which seem to frame the figures balance the design and hold it easily in the space, although rapid movement is suggested. The modeling is exquisitely done with detail that is almost incredible, when we remember the small size of the gem. Like the coins, the gems are sculpture in miniature and exhibit, on the one hand, stiffness and inaccuracy of drawing, on the other, a freshness of observation and an eagerness for accomplishing a greater perfection.

SUMMARY

Thus it is not in the attainment of their ideal that the charm of the artists in the early and archaic period lies — for their knowledge of anatomy is deficient, and they lack the technical ability to carve or draw correctly — but in their eager striving, their earnestness, their simple directness, and vitality. These are qualities that command a greater interest, if not a greater admiration, than the supreme knowledge, the flawless technical skill, and the decorative elegance of the over-ripe periods when the artist had attained, and had begun to carry on the tradition without the spirit.

BIBLIOGRAPHY

ABRAHAMS, E. B., Greek Dress. London, Murray, 1908.
ANDERSON, W. J., AND SPIERS, R. P., Architecture of Greece and Rome. N.Y., Scribner, 1907.
BELL, EDWARD, Hellenic Architecture. London, Bell, 1920.
BRITISH MUSEUM, Guide to the Principal Gold and Silver Coins of the Ancients, by B. V. Head. London, 1895.
—— ——, Pictorial postcards. Set XXIV: Coins of Syracuse; XXVII: Types of Greek Vases; XXX: Frieze of the Parthenon; XLVI: Greek Terra-cottas; XLVII: Greek and Roman Reliefs; XLVIII: Types of Greek and Roman Statues.
BUSCHOR, ERNST, Greek Vase Painting (tr. Richards). London, Chatto, 1921.

CHASE, G. H., Greek and Roman Sculpture in American Collections. Cambridge, Harvard University Press, 1924.
—— ——, and Post, C. R., History of Sculpture. N.Y., Harper, 1924.
COLLIGNON, MAXIME, Le Parthénon. Paris, Hachette, 1914.
FAURE, ELIE, History of Art: v. I, Ancient Art (tr. Pach). N.Y., Harper, 1921.
FLETCHER, SIR BANISTER, History of Architecture on the Comparative Method. N.Y., Scribner, 1924.
FOWLER, H.N., AND WHEELER, J. R., Handbook of Greek Archaeology. N.Y., Amer. Book Co., 1909.
GARDNER, E. A., Ancient Athens. N.Y., Macmillan, 1907.
—— ——, Handbook of Greek Sculpture. N.Y., Macmillan, 1915.
—— ——, Six Greek Sculptors. N.Y., Scribner, 1910.
GARDNER, PERCY, The Principles of Greek Art. N.Y., Macmillan, 1914.
—— ——, AND BLOMFIELD, REGINALD, Greek Art and Architecture. London, Oxford University Press, 1922.
GULICK, C. B., Life of the Ancient Greeks. N.Y., Appleton, 1902.
HAMLIN, A. D. F., History of Ornament, Ancient and Medieval. N.Y., Century, 1921.
HAMLIN, T. F., Enjoyment of Architecture. N.Y., Scribner, 1921.
KIMBALL, FISKE, AND EDGELL, G. H., History of Architecture. N.Y., Harper, 1918.
LAURIE, A. P., Greek and Roman Methods of Painting. Cambridge, University, Press, 1910.
LIVINGSTONE, R. W., Greek Genius and Its Meaning to Us. Oxford, Clarendon Press, 1915.
LOEWY, EMANUEL, Rendering of Nature in Early Greek Art (tr. Fothergill). London, 1907.
LUCKENBACH, H., Kunst und Geschichte: v. I, Das Altertum. Berlin, Oldenbourg, 1913.
MARQUAND, ALLAN, Greek Architecture. N.Y., Macmillan, 1909.
METROPOLITAN MUSEUM OF ART, Handbook of the Classical Collection, by G. M. A. Richter. N.Y., 1917.
—— ——, Shapes of Greek Vases. N.Y., 1922.
NEUHAUS, EUGEN, The Appreciation of Art. Boston, Ginn, 1924.
PATER, W. H., Greek Studies. N.Y., Macmillan, 1920.
POTTIER, EDMOND, Douris and the Painters of Greek Vases (tr. Kahnweiler). N.Y., Dutton, 1916.
POWERS, H. H., Message of Greek Art. Chautauqua, Chautauqua Press, 1913.
RICHTER, G. M. A., The Craft of Athenian Pottery. New Haven, Yale University Press, 1923.
ROBINSON, J. H., The Mind in the Making. N.Y., Harper, 1921.
STATHAM, H. H., Short Critical History of Architecture. N.Y., Scribner, 1912.
TARBELL, F. B., History of Greek Art. N.Y., Macmillan, 1923.
TUCKER, T. G., Life in Ancient Athens. N.Y., Macmillan, 1906.
WALSTON, SIR CHARLES, Essays on the Art of Pheidias. Cambridge, University Press, 1885.
—— ——, Greek Sculpture and Modern Art. Cambridge, University Press, 1914.
WALTERS, H. B., Art of the Greeks. N.Y., Macmillan, 1922.
—— ——, History of Ancient Pottery, Greek, Roman, and Etruscan. 2 v. N.Y., Scribner, 1905.
WARREN, H. L., Foundations of Classic Architecture. N.Y., Macmillan, 1919.
WINTER, FRANZ, ED., Kunstgeschichte in Bildern: v. I, Das Altertum. Leipzig, Seemann, 1912.

CHAPTER VII

GREEK PERIOD (2)

The Fifth Century. 480–400 B.C.

HISTORICAL BACKGROUND

The victory won in the Persian wars, with which the archaic period closed, inspired the Athenians with an enthusiasm and idealism that found expression, under the leadership of Pericles, in the creation of great works of art. Let us try to get a picture of Athens at this time.

Like many another Greek city, Athens was situated four or five miles inland, and lay clustered about a steep rocky hill known as the Acropolis, or higher city (PL. 35 A). This hill commands a wonderful view in all directions and is easily seen from the sea, so that the gleaming tip of the spear of the bronze statue of Athena standing on its summit was the first thing seen by the sailor after he turned the cape far down the bay on his homeward voyage. In the background rise the long slopes of Hymettus, famous for its honey; farther north Pentelicus, with its great marble quarries that furnished a particularly fine material both for building and for carving. The Acropolis served as the citadel and also as the religious center of the city. It was steep and inaccessible except on the western side, where the road led up to a monumental gateway; the rather flat summit was crowned with temples, fine marble structures with painted decorations, and statues of bronze and marble, all of which gave an impression of quiet splendor. On the slope at the southern base was the open-air theater of Dionysus.

Spreading from this central point, chiefly to the north and west, lay the city within its encircling walls, from which an extension reached out on the south to the Piræus, the harbor, five miles distant. It was rather mean in appearance. The houses were unpretentious, of sun-dried brick, flat-roofed, and usually but one story high. In and out among them wound the narrow, lanelike streets, with no sidewalks and no system of sewerage or flushing. Here and there a temple loomed up, a statue, or a monument, with occasionally a garden to break the monotony. The chief open place was the agora, or market place, with its plane trees for shade, surrounded by public offices and covered colonnades called stoas. Though the market always served its primary purpose as a central place for the sale of vegetables, cheese, honey, and flowers, its actual use was much wider; for here the citizens congregated to lounge in the cool of the stoa, to discuss the latest political development, or a new philosophic idea. Outside the walls were olive groves, and the gymnasiums where the men went daily, primarily for the bodily exercise that played so large a part in the education and daily life of the Athenian. But, like the stoa, the gymnasium with its surrounding colonnades performed the function of the modern club.

Fig. 65. Scene in a School. From a cylix painted by Duris. On the left the Athenian boy is taking a lesson on the lyre; in the center he is reciting before a master who is following with his scroll; at the right sits the boy's slave, who accompanies him to school; on the wall hang cylixes and lyres. (*Archäologische Zeitung*)

Athens was a small community, of about a hundred thousand people. Commerce was the economic basis of the state, for through her colonizing in the preceding centuries Athens had established strong trade relations with the Black Sea and Egypt, Italy, and the far western Mediterranean. Still the state was by no means wealthy. An important part of the conduct of business, at times the entire responsibility, was carried on by slaves who were kindly treated and in many cases included as members of the household. This situation gave the Athenian a great deal of leisure and enabled him to spend his time in the open and to devote it largely to the commonwealth. Here in Athens, for the first time in the history of man, we see a state the management of which was in the hands of the citizens and in which the vote of the humblest craftsman was equal to that of Pheidias. This democracy revealed itself in the great religious festivals like the Panathenaic procession, in which all the citizens, men and women, old and young, were represented; or at the dramatic performances of Æschylus and Sophocles in honor of Dionysus, where the audience of citizens approved with silence or applause, or condemned with a shower of figs and olives. The comedies of Aristophanes were enjoyed to the utmost when they satirized the great of the day with a daring that would be tolerated in no city not truly democratic.

To prepare a man for citizenship in such a community was the aim of education. Writing, reading, the elements of mathematics, and a knowledge of letters, were fundamental. Music and athletics played an important part and were closely related, for dancing, wrestling, boxing, swimming, and running were frequently performed to the accompaniment of music, as we see in the vase paintings. FIG. 65 reproduces a school scene painted on a vase.

Here the boy, accompanied by his slave, is taking a music lesson and reciting

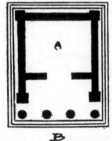

A   **B**

Fig. 66. Plans of Greek Temples. *A.* Temple *in antis*, so called because the portico is formed by the projecting side walls, *antæ*, and two columns set between them. An example is the *Treasury of the Athenians* at Delphi. *B. Prostyle* temple, so called because the columns stand out in front of the cella and extend the width of it. Sometimes an additional colonnade is placed at the back of the temple and it is then called *amphiprostyle.* An example is the *Temple of Nike Apteros* on the Acropolis at Athens.

ARCHITECTURE

Considering the fact that life was democratic and public in Athens, and that religious observances formed an integral part of it, it is natural that the Hellenic genius should find expression in civic rather than domestic building, and especially in temples. Although the temple always remained very simple, still an important evolution was going on in matters of proportion, decoration, and refinements from earliest times, many steps of which are now lost, until a climax was reached in the structures built on the Acropolis in the days of Pericles to replace those burned by the Persians when they sacked Athens in 480 B.C.

PLATE 35

(*A*) Acropolis. Athens.

(*B*) Parthenon. Athens. 447–432 B.C. Of Pentelic marble. L. 228 ft. (Alinari)

(*C*) Silver Coin of Syracuse, called the *Demarateion*. c. 479 B.C. British Museum, London.

PLATE 36

(A) Parthenon. Detail of corner.

(B) Erechtheum. North porch. c. 420–409 B.C.

(C) Parthenon, Entablature Restored.
(Fenger)

(D) Erechtheum. Entablature.

PLATE 37

(*A*) Fragment of a Cornice from the Siphnian Treasury. Delphi.
Delphi Museum. (Clarence Kennedy)

(*B*) Carving from the Erechtheum, with Honeysuckle, Bead and Reel, Egg and
Dart, and Leaf and Dart Motifs. Acropolis Museum, Athens. (Alinari)

(*C*) Temple of Zeus. Olympia. West Pediment, Battle of Centaurs and
Lapiths, Restored by Treu. c. 460 B.C.

PLATE 38

(*A*) Three-Sided Relief. Sometimes called "Ludovisi Throne." Subject unknown. Parian Marble. H. 40 in. c. 480 B.C. Terme Museum, Rome. (Alinari)

(*B*) Apollo. Olympia, West Pediment. (Kunsthist. Seminar, Marburg)

(*C*) Myron. Discobolus. Reconstructed copy of the bronze original. Terme Museum, Rome.

The Greek temple, as we have said, was simple. The essential feature was the cella (FIG. 66), the chamber for the cult statue, with an additional room, in the more elaborate temples such as the *Parthenon* (FIG. 67), for the treasure. Though the people were free to enter, the temple was not intended for congregational worship, for the sacrifices were performed at an altar outside.

According to plan, these temples fall into three classes. In the first (FIG. 66 A), the projecting walls of the cella with two columns between form a portico. Sometimes an additional portico is found at the back. In the second class (FIG. 66 B) the portico is formed by a colonnade that extends the entire width of the cella and is frequently repeated at the back; the cella walls may or may not project. In the third class, the most elaborate, the cella with its porticoes based upon either of the preceding classes, is entirely surrounded by a colonnade (FIG. 67) and hence is called peripteral. But even in this class the plan remains comparatively simple. All temples were columnar, built on the lintel system, and had sloping roofs to shed the rain. The arch, though known, was not used.[1]

According to elevation also, these temples fall into three groups known as orders: the Doric, the Ionic, and the Corinthian.[2]

The finest example of the Doric order is the *Parthenon*[3] (PL. 35 B). It stands on the crest of the Acropolis, simple and

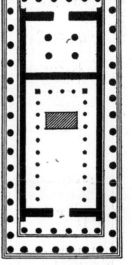

Fig. 67. Parthenon Plan. Athens. A peripteral temple based upon the plan of Fig. 66 B, but with an additional room for the treasure.

strong, its rectangular shape harmonizing perfectly with the contours of the hill, and its broken light and shade playing into the varying tones of the mountain landscape (PL. 35A). Its interior is

[1] The arched structures seen along the base of the Acropolis are of Roman date.
[2] The elements that constitute an order are the base, the column, and the entablature; the proportions, and the decoration.
[3] The *Parthenon* was the temple of Athena Parthenos, meaning Athena the maiden, who was the patron goddess of Athens. Its ruined condition is due to the fact that, at the time of the war between the Turks and the Venetians in 1687, the building was used as a powder magazine and exploded when hit by a well aimed shot. A large part of the remaining sculpture was obtained by Lord Elgin with the permission of the Turkish government, in 1801–1803, and became the property of the British Museum in 1816.

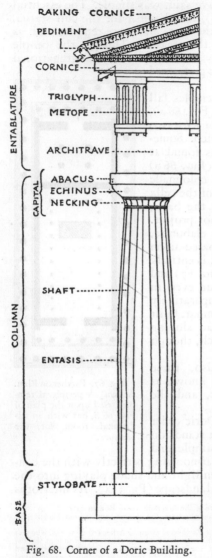

Fig. 68. Corner of a Doric Building.

comparatively limited, as were the interiors of all Greek temples, for they were not planned to accommodate the worshipers, but mainly for the cult statue, the treasure, and the priests with their attendants. The ground plan of the *Parthenon* (FIG. 67) shows the division of the cella into two parts, the larger for the sanctuary, the smaller for the treasury. Like all Greek temples, it faced the east.

Looking at the *Parthenon* from a nearer position, we note that it is sturdy, and at the same time quiet and reposeful. The subtle balance maintained between the vertical and horizontal lines has much to do with the feeling of calm it inspires. If we compare for a moment the restless lines of a Gothic cathedral (PL. 84), the difference is immediately evident.

Let us study in detail one corner of the temple (PL. 36 A and FIG. 68). The structure rests on a triple base the upper step of which is known as the stylobate. From this the columns rise directly without individual bases like trees from the ground. The omission of these bases strengthens the unity between the stylobate and the columns. The shaft diminishes in diameter as it rises and displays a very slight swelling, known as the entasis, so that the vertical edge is not a straight line but a subtle curve that prevents the feeling of rigidity suggested by a long straight line. The shafts are channeled into grooves called flutings, usually twenty, which with their soft shadows and repeated vertical lines both strengthen the rhythm and emphasize the feeling of support in the shaft, and finally individualize the columns by contrasting them with the plain wall of the cella against which they are seen. The shafts are not monoliths but consist of separate drums bonded together by dowels of wood and metal (FIG. 69) with such nicety that the joinings were scarcely visible.[4]

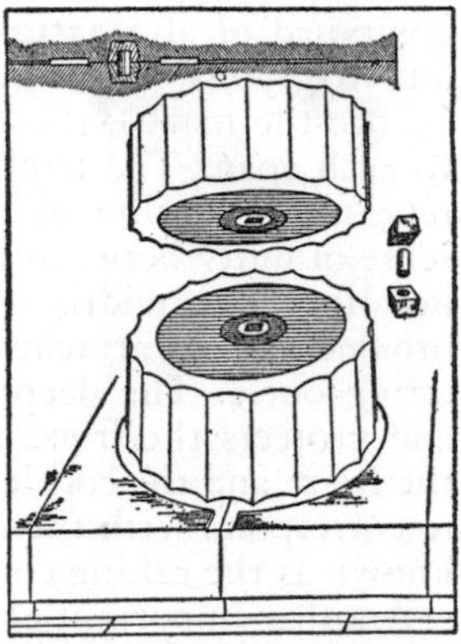

The capital consists of three parts — the necking, the echinus, and the abacus. The purpose of a capital is to form the transition between the shaft and the lintel; that is, from the vertical supporting member to the horizontal entablature. A successful capital will not make this transition too abruptly. How successful is the Doric capital? Let us see. We get our first suggestion of the horizontal in the necking; yet the vertical flutings, instead of ending at this point, play up into the capital to the point at

Fig. 69. Two drums, showing the cuttings left in the center for the bronze or wooden pivot which held the stones in place, correctly centered, and about which they were ground to secure a perfect joining. (Penrose)

which we feel more insistently the horizontal, that is, at the row of concentric ridges that separate the necking and the echinus; the simple vigorous curve of the echinus then carries the line up to the square abacus; not directly, however, for it turns inward as it meets the block, thus avoiding abruptness. The beautiful strength of this curve, rising so vigorously and then turning inward so gracefully, was not worked out by the Greek in a short time but after a long series of experiments dealing with the angle and the proportions. In the rectangular abacus we are carried easily into the architrave, the line of which is distinctly horizontal. Thus by a carefully thought out design based upon skillful interplay of direction, we pass gradually

---

[4] The clamp and dowel system of joining the blocks and of holding them firmly in place was employed throughout the building. Mortar was not used.

from the rapidly rising vertical shaft to the horizontal entablature.

In the entablature (PL. 36c), the part of the building between the columns and the roof, we find again a division into three parts — the architrave, the frieze, and the cornice. Above rises the pediment or gable. The architrave is severely plain and is separated from the frieze by a simple stringcourse. The frieze is composed of alternating metopes, squares filled with sculpture, and triglyphs, rectangular areas channeled into three grooves (hence the name); there are two whole and two half groovings to each span. The triglyphs again take up the vertical line and repeat the rhythm of the columns. In order to give a greater sense of unity between the frieze and the architrave, rectangular moldings the width of the triglyph terminating in beadlike ornaments are attached below each triglyph underneath the stringcourse. The deeply projecting cornice finishes the design and protects the frieze from the rain. Unity of design between the frieze and the cornice is obtained by undercutting the cornice to correspond with the triglyphs and metopes. A second cornice, known as the raking cornice, finishes the pediment.

Another important element of unity in the design is the color. To paint marble buildings was the usual practice of the Greeks. PL. 36c, with its varying tones, gives some hint of the effect. The color was not applied uniformly to the whole building but was concentrated upon the upper part. Red and blue predominated, with touches of green, yellow, black, and gilding. The triglyphs with the decoration both above and below were blue; the stringcourses and metopes, and the undercuttings of the cornice, red. Almost no traces of color remain on the *Parthenon* today; but the correctness of the restoration is proved on the analogy of other Greek temples, parts of which have long been buried in the soil and in this way have retained their color.

We have spoken of the curve or entasis found in the column. This variation from the straight line is characteristic of all parts of the building. The stylobate has a slight upward curve (a rise of 3⅝ inches for a length of 228 feet); the columns incline inward, and are placed, not at equal intervals, but closer together toward the corners, lending a feeling of stability at those points. In fact there is not a straight line in the building. The purpose of the Greek in avoiding straight lines was perhaps to correct certain optical illusions. For example, a long straight line appears to sag, an illusion that the slight rise in the stylobate obviates. But in addition to this, the Greek realized that the curved line was beautiful in itself and, if skillfully used, could give a building the vital quality that cannot result from mathematically straight lines.

The ornamentation of the *Parthenon*, though rich, is subordinated to the main design. Sculpture was used in the metopes and the pediments, and on a continuous frieze along the top of the cella wall (PLS. 40–42). Carved or painted moldings, especially the hawk's-beak (FIG. 70), were sparingly used, chiefly about the cornices. Thus the elements that contribute to make the *Parthenon* preëminent among buildings are the simple harmonious design based upon skillful proportion of all parts and the functional value of each detail; the rich but subordinate ornamentation of sculpture and color; the subtle variations from regularity; and the exquisite technical finish.

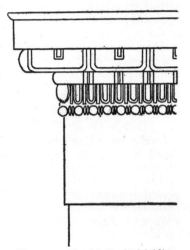

Fig. 70. Hawk's-Beak Molding from the Parthenon. Painted in red, blue, and gold. (After Penrose)

In the *Erechtheum*[5] (PL. 36 B), which stands near the *Parthenon* on the Acropolis, we find the best example of the Ionic order. Looking at the corner, we note several divergences from the Doric. In the first place, the general proportions are more slender; there is greater elegance and grace, and richer ornamentation. In detail, the columns have individual bases, one member of which is delicately carved; on the necking is an exquisite honeysuckle band; the echinus is decorated with bead and reel, egg and dart, and the double guilloche (PL. 36 D). Perhaps the most conspicuous part of the Ionic capital is the double scroll or volute inserted between the narrow echinus and the abacus. The architrave is divided into three horizontal faces and the frieze was originally covered by a continuous band of low relief, in place of the Doric triglyphs and metopes. The stringcourses and cor-

[5] The Erechtheum, so named after Erechtheus, to whom it was dedicated in part, is irregular in plan, thus differing from the usual Greek type. This may have been due partly to the irregular character of the ground on which the temple stands and also to the number of shrines that it contained. For it was said to mark the site of the contest between Poseidon and Athena for possession of Athens, and to shelter within its area the mark made by the trident and the salt spring of the former and the olive tree of the latter, as well as other sacred relics.

nices, doorway, and wall bands are delicately carved with dentils, egg and dart, bead and reel, honeysuckle, and braid patterns (PL. 37 B). This ornament, though rich, is confined to certain places and is strictly subordinated to the design of the whole. The Greek marble was particularly adaptable to the carving of moldings (PL. 37 A), which show a tempered richness and refinement. Their value, to the Greek mind, is interesting to note. Inscriptions relating to the building of the *Erechtheum* tell us that the same price was paid for carving a foot of egg and dart molding as for one human figure.

The Corinthian order, which is hardly a separate order but a development of the Ionic, was known in the fifth century but belongs primarily to a later period and will be spoken of in the following chapter (PL. 45 B).

SCULPTURE

In the preceding chapter, we followed the evolution of the Greek sculptor from his earliest efforts for a period of about two centuries to the year 480 B.C., when he was just becoming master of his material. His final struggle we can discern in the brief period between 480 and 450, known as the transitional age.

In Greek sculpture there are three important pedimental groups — *Ægina*, *Olympia*, and the *Parthenon*. We have already spoken of the pedimental design at *Ægina* (PL. 33 A). Now let us see its development in the transitional age at *Olympia*. The remains of this temple, like those of *Ægina*, are so fragmentary that restoration is hazardous. On the western pediment (PL. 37 C) is represented the battle between the Centaurs and Lapiths, where the drunken Centaurs are attempting to carry off the Lapith women. In the center stands Apollo, calmly majestic as if witnessing the scene but not of it; on each side are the combatants, in balanced groupings of twos and threes with reclining figures in the corners. Each group is a unit, so skillfully connected with the next that a movement seems to rise and flow rhythmically from the corners to Apollo in the center. In comparison with the pediment of *Ægina* the design is more complicated, and the unity among the figures and also their relation to the space are more subtle. We are still conscious, however, of the diagonal line of the roof, which seems to press down the figures toward the corners.

Let us look at the figure of *Apollo* (PL. 38 B). He stands austerely erect, the outstretched arm and turn of the head balancing the vertical of the body. The effect is monumental, almost architectural, in its severity. There is simple modeling without detail in both the figure and the drapery, which is arranged in broad folds that enhance the majestic effect. The conception is noble, and free from hampering individual traits. The figure has great vitality and at the same time poise and restraint. Both the conception and the expression harmonize in their forceful directness and sincerity. That some archaic conventions, as in the hair, still linger, matters but little in the ultimate significance of the figure. In contrast with the quiet majesty of *Apollo* is the realistic struggle of the Centaurs who fight grimly with the Lapiths, their shaggy, wrinkled, beastlike faces contrasting with the quiet beauty of the Lapith people, who maintain serenity even in the midst of the tumult.

A single statue that is typical of the transitional age is the bronze[6] *Charioteer of Delphi* (PL. 39 A). It belonged originally to a group consisting of the chariot with horses, the charioteer, and a Nike very much like that on the Syracusan coins (PL. 35 C), and was probably erected to commemorate a victory at the races. It represents a youthful aristocrat, serious but alert. He stands firmly on both feet, holding the reins in his outstretched hand. For he himself, apparently, has driven his own chariot in the races — not an ignoble thing for any aristocrat. He is dressed in the customary garment of a driver, which is girdled high and held in at the shoulders and back to keep it from flapping. The hair is confined by a band tied behind. The eyes, which are made of glass paste and shaded by lashes of hairlike strips of bronze, and the slightly parted lips, add vivacity to the face. We feel the severity of archaic work in the figure, especially in the lower part, where the folds of the dress have almost the architectural quality of a fluted column; in the sharp lines of the brow, and in the conventional way in which the hair is worked above the band. But we notice also the naturalistic curls below the band, the masterly modeling in the hand and in the feet, the toes of which are clutching the ground, the slight twist of the torso

---

[6] Bronze as well as marble and other stones was extensively used by the Greek sculptors. While small pieces were cast solid, for the larger ones the *cire perdue*, or wax process, was used. A core of clay or some crude material was shaped roughly into the form of the finished work. Over this a coating of wax was laid in which the sculptor did his finished modeling. The wax was then covered by a coat of fine pipe clay, the consistency of cream, laid on with a brush very carefully so as to reproduce, when hard, every minute detail of the wax. Successive coats were added and then layers of coarser material until a thick, firm shell was formed. Vent holes were made and the whole mass heated so that the wax was melted and drawn away, leaving in its place a thin space between the core and the pipe-clay mold. Into this the molten bronze was poured. When the metal had hardened, the shell was broken away, the core dug out, and the surface polished and sometimes details added by chasing. See Benvenuto Cellini's dramatic description of this process, p. 287 note 2.

that gives one the feeling of an organic structure beneath the dress. While the statue was set up as a portrait, yet there are but few individualistic traits about it. Broad generalization characterizes it as far as representation is concerned. But more important than the representative element is the quality that makes it a great work of art — simple dignity and reserve. The whole figure expresses the quiet control that is so characteristic of Greek art and the Greek theory of life.

These qualities of restraint and serenity are well illustrated by the so-called *Ludovisi Throne* (PL. 38 A). Neither the purpose nor the subject of this relief is understood. It may represent the birth of Aphrodite. Two women in balanced position are stooping to lift a third, apparently from the water. There are gropings and inaccuracies in the expression of the figure. But one is not deterred by these from the enjoyment of the exquisite design, balanced yet subtly varied by the difference in texture of the garments, and the position of the head of the central figure. The design is based upon the rhythmic harmony of the curves that surround the central figure and lead to it. Every part of the work is filled with eagerness to express the feeling of harmony and poise.

All the examples of sculpture that we have studied so far have been original works of art. But we have now come to the point where it is necessary to deal with copies. For the Romans, recognizing the superiority of Greek work, brought to Rome great quantities of the best sculpture to adorn their palaces and, when the supply was not great enough for the demand, copied them more or less faithfully. Because of the chaotic conditions in Italy after the downfall of the Roman Empire, much of the classical sculpture, both originals and copies, was scattered, lost, or destroyed. Out of the remnant scholars have reconstructed the story of Greek art in the great periods, with originals where possible and copies when necessary. The Greeks themselves have left us in their writings a good deal of information about their art, and on the basis of their descriptions famous statues have been identified.

Let us return to the transitional period, when for the first time we meet a well known sculptor, Myron. This artist, the Greek writers tell us, was famous for his statues of athletes. No original work of his has come down to us, but only copies. Chief of these is the *Discobolus* (PL. 38 C). The figure is complicated in pose for this period and at first sight appears to be in violent movement, but is actually represented at that instant of rest which comes

PLATE 39

(A) Charioteer of Delphi. Bronze. H. 6 ft.
Part of a chariot group. Delphi Museum.

(B) Pheidias (?). Athena
Lemnia. (See C).

(B) and (C) Pheidias (?).
Athena Lemnia. Probably a
copy of the bronze original.
Marble, over life-size. c.
450 B.C. B shows the body,
in Dresden, provided with a
cast of the head in Bologna.
(Furtwängler) (C) Head in
Bologna, which apparently
belongs to the body in
Dresden. Greek statues
were often made of more than
one piece of marble, the head
frequently of a finer quality
of stone than the draped
parts. (Clarence Kennedy)

PLATE 40

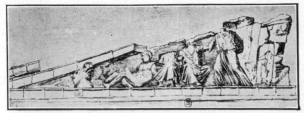

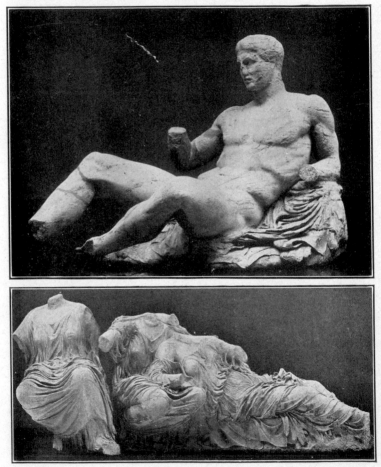

(*B*) Parthenon, East Pediment: Mt. Olympus, also called "Theseus."
British Museum, London. (Mansell)
(*C*) Parthenon, East Pediment: Three Female Figures, called the "Three Fates."
British Museum, London. (British Museum)

between the backward and forward thrust of the arm in hurling the quoit. The interesting thing about the statue is the feeling that it exhibits of tremendous energy, which is concentrated entirely within the figure — a force that moves about the periphery; for a great sweep of line begins with the quoit, moves along the right arm, the curve of the shoulders, down the left arm, is taken up in the right leg and so strongly felt that its very momentum easily carries the eye over the space back to the quoit; entirely within this great curve is concentrated a force stored up for the moment, awaiting the next movement of the throw; but of this or of any movement from without there is no suggestion. The face, contrary to what we should expect for such an intense moment, is perfectly passive and broadly generalized. It is the body in its entirety that expresses the action. The complicated pose brings into play all the muscles, which are broadly modeled with understanding and technical mastery.

A statue that brings us to the end of the transitional period is the *Athena Lemnia* made by Pheidias, of which only a copy has come down to us (PL. 39 B and c). It stood on the Acropolis at the left side of the road that leads from the great gateway to the *Parthenon*, so that her kindly glance would follow those going out or welcome those coming in. She stands erect, with the right knee bent and right foot to one side. This pose produces a little more freedom in the figure than we found in the perfectly erect *Charioteer*. She wears the woolen Doric chiton which falls in rich folds, somewhat severe, and over this the ægis. The head is turned to the right and slightly lowered. Contrary to the usual representations, she does not wear her helmet, but carries it in her hand. Thus Pheidias has emphasized her more gracious aspect — "the thoughtful Athena with the delicate cheeks," according to a Latin writer who saw the original. She impresses us with her godlike majesty; yet she looks down at us with a glance that is reassuring and kindly. The face is severely beautiful, with an exquisite curve of the cheeks and chin, delicately modeled forehead, mouth, and nostrils. The hair is held by a band that firmly confines the strands yet leaves the abundant mass free enough to frame and soften the face. The Greek ideal of divinity was man, not entirely free from human frailty, but lifted to a plane of higher majesty and power. So in the *Lemnia* we see the ideal maiden of pure, refined beauty, noble and serene.

Of Pheidias, reputed by the Greeks themselves and by many others since, to be the greatest of sculptors, we actually know but little. No work has survived that is surely of his hand. His greatest statues, the *Athena* of the *Parthenon* and the *Zeus* of the temple at *Olympia*, were made of gold and ivory, and hence have long since disappeared. The *Lemnia* probably is a fairly close copy of one of his early statues. But our knowledge of the art that Pheidias created in his prime can best be gained through the sculptural decorations of the *Parthenon*, which we know were made under his supervision, and which may be, in parts, actually by his hand.

The subject of the eastern pediment (PLS. 40 A and 41 A), the ancient writers tell us, was the birth of Athena, who sprang full-armed from the head of Zeus. War, carelessness, and wanton mutilation have destroyed most of the work; but from a drawing made by a Frenchman traveling in Athens in 1674 we can get a glimpse of part of the composition. In the left corner, the sun-god Helios in his chariot is rising out of the sea. Only the head, shoulders, and arms of Helios and the heads of the horses are shown. Yet the imagination easily supplies the rest of the group. The fiery horses, fresh with the air of early morning, approach a seated male figure turned toward them, who may personify Mount Olympus, touched by the first rays of the sun; closely connected are two seated figures whose identity we do not know, approached by a figure moving rapidly, as if conveying to them the wonderful news. The center is entirely gone. On the right are three seated female figures closely grouped, one turned toward the center. In the corner projecting over the cornice is seen the head of one of the horses of Selene, the moon-goddess, who is sinking into the west as Helios rises in the east. Even in these fragments we feel the power of the design. No longer does the cornice appear to press the figures down, as at *Ægina* and *Olympia*. Each seems to fit inevitably into its place; and each helps to form the great waves of rhythmic movement that rise majestically toward the center of interest. This is clear in the figure of *Mount Olympus* (PL. 40 B). He is reclining easily upon a rock over which his mantle and an animal skin are thrown; the thrust-back left arm and uplifted shoulder give vitality to the body and a note of virility to the easy curves of the design. Our general impression is of a youth of majestic bearing, a heroic type in perfect repose yet permeated with latent power; though in form like a man, yet both in bodily and intellectual power a god. In detail we see that the modeling is superb; the bony structure, flesh, muscles, skin — all are perfectly understood and expressed with absolute truth, but in their essential aspects only; the broad planes flow one into another not so much with delicacy, such as we shall see later in the *Hermes of Praxiteles* (PL. 45 c), as with power. The effect of the thrust-back arm upon the muscles of the back is perfectly expressed, and yet this back, placed in a gable high above the ground, was not intended to be seen. The crumpled drapery by contrast emphasizes these broad planes. The face, though battered, is as serene as the body; for the Greek expressed his thought not in the face, which plays but a small part in the art of the best period, but in the body as a whole. Neither are there indications of individuality. This is not a specific man but man in his most monumental aspect, a generalized type, expressed with moderation and serenity. Nowhere is there an unnecessary line, and nowhere exaggeration. In design the figure is compact, whether we look at the back or at the front, and is built on long curves from the top of the head to the bent knee, with subordinate harmonious curves in the arms and lower part of the legs.[7]

In this figure the sculptor has attained the ideal toward which the Greek artists had been struggling for more than two hundred years. In the *Statue of a Woman* (PL. 32 A) we felt predominantly the block of stone from which the sculptor, by gradual stages, had been freeing himself, until in the *Parthenon* figures he became complete master. This victory means, not so much that he forced the stone to do his will as that he harmonized his conception with his material, which is a fundamental principle of all the greatest art. For stone, because it is a hard, durable material, does not lend itself like pigment or clay to fleeting impressions or trivial subjects or to a perfect illusion of an object, but to those permanent monumental aspects of life that are essential and universal.

Let us see if the principles just stated apply to the *Three Female Figures* on the right of the pediment (PL. 40 c). There is the same quiet majesty; the same superb form expressed in essentials only, concealed and yet revealed by the draperies; the same ease of pose. The fact that the heads are missing is of less consequence than one would at first imagine, because here, as in the *Mount Olympus*, it is the whole body as a unit that expresses the artist's idea. This is illustrated in the drapery. The soft linen chiton clings to the figure in a multiplicity of naturalistic folds that are not distracting, because they are subordinated to the few essential lines; the heavier woolen himation is brought across the knees in broader, bolder folds, wonderfully differentiated in texture

[7] To see this design more clearly, lay a piece of thin paper over a reproduction and trace its main lines.

from the linen that appears again below; and lastly the still heavier stuff of the rug that covers the rocks has a different type of fold characteristic of very heavy material. Everywhere there is truth to nature and the technical ability to express it; but everywhere the essential aspects of form and of spirit expressed with restraint. The reclining figure is the acme of ease and relaxation, as far as stone is able to render it. Although our reasoning tells us that she is reclining so as to fit into the low space, yet so inevitable is the grouping that we are not conscious of the gable, a proof of the supreme mastery of the artist over his problem.

These same principles can be discerned in animal life (PL. 41 B). Though the *Horse of Selene* has been traveling all night, there is still fire in the dilated eye, quivering nostril, and open mouth. Everywhere apparent is a thorough knowledge of the form — the bony structure, the muscles, and the texture of the skin about the mouth and nostrils. So well does the head epitomize the essential spirit of the whole figure that the imagination easily reconstructs the body of the horse, as the Greek intended that it should.

The metopes are decorated with figures of struggling Centaurs and Lapiths, two figures in each metope (PL. 41 C). Here the Lapith is sinking to the ground, his arm still in the straps of his shield, while the victorious Centaur is about to crash down upon him the jar that he holds behind his head. The two figures are ingeniously interlocked into a compact mass not only by the pose of the figures, the arrangement of the limbs, but also by the skillful placing of the discs of the shield and jar; so that the group, although it represents a struggle, is contained within a very simple outline that traces on the flat background a pattern[8] adapted with great mastery to the square shape of the metope.

The frieze, which runs around the top of the cella wall and is not to be confused with the regular frieze of the Doric order on the outside of the colonnade, is a continuous band of low relief representing the Panathenaic procession that took place every four years when the citizens of Athens gathered in the market place and carried to the *Parthenon* the peplos or robe for the statue of Athena. On the western side of the building the procession is forming — youths are lacing their sandals, holding their horses or mounting, guided by marshals who stand at intervals and particularly at the corners to slow down the movement and guide the horsemen at the turn. On the two long sides the procession moves in parallel lines, the cavalcade of spirited

---

[8] To see this clearly, trace the main outlines of the groups and fill in the backgrounds with a dark tone.

youths, the chariots, elders, jar-carriers, and the animals for sacrifice with the attendants. The movement becomes slower and more solemn as it nears the eastern side, when, after turning the corner it approaches the seated divinities, who appear to be guests of Athena at this her great festival.[9] Let us look in detail at a few of the slabs. The cavalcade of mounted youths (PL. 42 A) is filled with rhythmic movement and spirited action. The backward glance of some of the youths gives a balance to the general forward movement of the procession; and the infinite variety in the poses of the youths and the horses free it from any feeling of monotony. There is a flat background with no distance and no unnecessary details. We have, in fact, all the essential elements of a procession of spirited youths and nothing more. Elimination of irrelevant detail is one reason why it is so satisfactory a representation. Another reason is its decorative fitness. From the point of view of design the frieze is marvelously successful. The figures both of the men and of the horses fill the space with an approximately even upper line because the sculptor has observed the principle of *isocephaly* and not natural proportion. They move against the background without crowding, and with an animated rhythm happily varied. In the slab representing the jar-carriers (PL. 42 B), for example, the insistent motif of a youth carrying a jar upon his right shoulder is repeated, making a design of decorative quality, ease, and grace of rhythm that is readily felt but only understood when one observes the subtle variations that occur in the pose of the head, the arms, the hands, and in the arrangement of the drapery.[10]

The third great sculptor of the fifth century was Polyclitus, none of whose work is extant except in copies. Greek writers tell us that he made statues of athletes, chiefly in bronze, and, unlike Myron, usually at rest; that he was particularly interested in the proportions of the human figure and made an ideal statue to illustrate the canon that he worked out. Something of the general character of his work we see in the bronze statuette of a maiden with a turbanlike headdress (PL. 42 D). The weight rests on the right foot; the left is slightly raised so that the figure is thrown into an easy pose with a charming sweep of line; the modeling is beautifully restrained and the surface finish of the bronze is exquisite.

[9] A convenient and inexpensive reproduction of the entire frieze, which is necessary for a realization of the unity of composition and the rhythmic flow of line, is published by the University Prints, Newton, Mass.

[10] Read Ruskin's appreciation of a chariot-group from the south side of the Parthenon in *Aratra Pentelici;* quoted in Gardner's *Ancient Athens,* p. 339.

It is now quite evident that the spirit of Greek sculpture of the fifth century was one of moderation and calm restraint, whatever the subject matter might be. Let us see one more evidence of it on a different type of monument, the *Grave-Relief of Hegeso* (PL. 42 c). On it is represented a woman seated, holding up a trinket that she has taken from the jewel box which her maid is handing her. Here is the same serenity that we saw in the *Parthenon*. There is no reference, even indirectly, to death. Instead, the deceased is pictured as engaged in some incident of life. The figures are carefully balanced and exquisitely adapted to the architectural background into which they fit. But the ultimate quality is the quiet restraint, which is far more profound than the melodramatic contortions that characterize many later representations of a like subject.[11]

PAINTING

In our study of Greek vases, we saw how the Greek painter from a very crude beginning slowly evolved until by 480 B.C. he could draw with fair correctness. The further great advance that we see taking place in the transitional age is largely due to the most important of the Greek painters of the time, Polygnotus, a contemporary of Pheidias, who was a painter, tradition tells us, as well as a sculptor. Unfortunately no example of the work of Polygnotus or his contemporaries is extant. So again we must rely on the vases as our criterion. A reflection of some of his innovations we can discern in such a vase as the amphora with the painting of Pelops and Hippodameia (PL. 43 B). Feeling for decoration is still there but it is not so finely and insistently realized as in the work of Euphronius and Duris. The chariot is dashing along by the sea or river, through a wooded, mountainous country. The wind is blowing back the hair and the garments. It is remarkable how much landscape detail there is here, not realistically indicated so that the figures fit into it but merely suggested by a very few lines or symbols. There is ease and freedom in the drawing and correct foreshortening in the three-quarters view of the chariot and figures; yet all is flat without light and shade. The drapery is restless. We miss the fine long lines of the earlier severe red-figured work.

Again in the crater with a representation of sunrise (PL. 43 A),

[11] An interesting comparison to illustrate this point is found in the Greek relief representing the parting of *Orpheus and Eurydice* in the Naples Museum, and the painting of the same subject by Sir Frederick Leighton; or the *Rape of the Daughters of Leucippus* by a Greek painter (PL. 49 C), and by Rubens (PL. 131 B).

the four-horse chariot decorates superbly the space between the handles. Here the sun-god Helios is rising out of the sea, as we saw him on the pediment of the *Parthenon*. As he begins his course across the sky the stars, personified as youths, dip into the sea, and the moon-goddess Selene and the hunter Cephalus disappear before Eos, goddess of the dawn. The whole representation is an excellent example of the imaginative way in which the Greek pictured the forces of nature.

MINOR ARTS

As we said in the preceding chapter, the same fundamental principles manifest themselves in the minor arts as in the major. Metal was always popular with the Greek. A mirror case is typical of his craftsmanship. The mirror itself was a disc of highly polished bronze, for reflecting-glass as we now use it was unknown to him; and it frequently had a protecting cover on which the decoration was concentrated. In Pl. 44 A we see a cover ornamented with a head in three-quarters view molded by *repoussé* work into such high relief that the metal is very thin. Some details, such as the brows, lashes, and fine hairs are delicately incised, as are the simple concentric circles forming a finishing border. Like the *Lemnia*, the face has a serene generalized type of beauty, somewhat softened by the naturalistic and highly decorative hair, which with its undulating broken mass affords a happy contrast to the smoother surface of the face and background. In spite of the feeling of a little obtrusiveness in the introduction of the hand holding a lock of hair, it balances well the abundant locks of the right side.

Another metal in which the craftsman expressed himself was gold. In speaking of Greek jewelry, we need to remember that precious stones were not in general use until the Hellenistic age, and that gold was used in the fifth and fourth centuries chiefly for its own sake. An earring (Pl. 44 B) shows what the goldsmith could do in modeling the gold. From a palmette, probably originally containing enamel, is suspended a winged Victory driving a two-horse chariot.[12] The figures are molded hollow, in order to keep the weight as light as possible. The grouping is compact; the forward movement of the Nike and the backward curve of the prancing horses bring the two as closely

---

[12] The suitability of using a chariot as a design for an earring has been questioned. This criticism has much in its favor. However, if, as has been suggested, the earring was designed for a colossal, possibly a gold and ivory, statue of a goddess, both the size and the symbolism may somewhat mitigate the charge of poor taste.

together as possible while the feet of the horses and the wings of the Nike balance the group and add lightness and delicacy to the composition. Close examination reveals careful, accurate modeling, and painstaking detail. While the goldsmith was faithful, as was the sculptor, to a generalized aspect of nature, he thought it fitting to add extremely delicate detail which never obtruded itself, but added a sensitive refinement to the whole effect. Here, for example, the Nike wears earrings and bracelets; the plumage of her wings and the horses' manes and tails are indicated with an almost microscopic finesse.

It is an evidence of supreme craftsmanship for a small work of art to retain its high qualities of design and workmanship under the magnifying lens. Ability to stand the test is characteristic of many of the works of the Greek craftsman. A notable example is found in the gems of Dexamenos. In the flying heron (PL. 44 c) we see, first, a sympathetic observation of nature, as in the erect head, the legs thrust back, and the position of the wings, so that we get a superb rendering of a bird in flight. There is firmness in the sweeping curves of the wings and a marvelous delicacy in the lines indicating the soft plumage. A simple line near the edge frames the design. As a study of bird life, as an example of a masterful technical ability, and as an exquisite design, this gem stands unrivaled. The figure completely fills the space, yet there is no feeling of its being crowded. In carving gems, the craftsman probably used a metal drill with powdered emery and oil; so that the process required not only keen eyesight, but a very sensitively trained touch, and a patience that considered neither time nor money.

Closely allied with the gems are the coins. The fifth-century coins of Magna Graecia are among the most beautiful ever struck. The Syracusan "medallion" (PL. 44 F) is obviously a development of the *Demareteion* (PL. 35 c). The head on the obverse is that of Persephone. Her hair is arranged naturalistically, with ringlets escaping here and there as if to soften the contours, and is confined by a wreath of corn leaves; the dolphins still surround it but are more subordinate because of the larger size of the head; a circle of dots encloses the design. On the reverse is the victorious four-horse chariot, seen three-quarters view, dashing forward under the lash of the driver toward whom a Victory is flying with the crown; in the segment below is a suit of armor, the prize of the race. The fact that the victorious chariot is constantly used as a type on Syracusan coins is an indication of the popularity of chariot-racing in Syracuse. The ideal beauty,

PLATE 41

(*A*) Parthenon, Eastern Pediment, Right Side. Drawing by Jacques Carrey. Bibliothèque National, Paris.

(*B*) Parthenon, Eastern Pediment: Head of the Horse of Selene. British Museum, London. (Mansell)

(*C*) Parthenon, Metope: Centaur and Lapith. British Museum, London. (Mansell)

PLATE 42

(*A*) Parthenon Frieze, North Side: metal and affixed by rivets, the holes

(*B*) Parthenon Frieze, North Side: Jar Carriers. Acropolis Museum, Athens. (Mansell)

(*C*) Grave-Relief of Hegeso. Marble, H. 6½ ft. c. 400 B.C. Ceramicus, Athens.

(*D*) School of Polyclitus. Maiden. Bronze. H. 10 in. Late V cent. B.C. Antiquarium, Munich. (Clarence Kennedy)

PLATE 43

Cavalcade of Youths. Accessories, such as the bridles and reins, were painted on or made of
for which are seen in the horses' heads. Marble. H. 40 in. British Museum, London. (Mansell)

(A) Crater: Sunrise
Scene. Red-figured.
H. 12⅜ in. c. 400 B.C.
British Museum, London.

(B) Amphora: Pelops
and Hippodameia. Red-
figured. H. 21 in. c. 420
B.C. Arezzo. (Furtwäng-
ler-Reichhold)

PLATE 44

(*A*) Bronze Mirror Cover. D. 7⅞ in. Late V cent. Metropolitan Museum, New York. (Metropolitan Museum)

(*B*) Earring. Nike driving a chariot. Gold. Nike 1 in. high. Boston Museum. (Boston Museum)

(*C*) Gem. Engraved by Dexamenos with a flying heron. Bluish Chalcedony. L. 2 in. 450–440 B.C Hermitage, Leningrad.

(*D*) Silver Coin of Syracuse. Signed by Cimon. c. 400 B.C. British Museum, London.

(*E*) Coin of Agrigentum. V cent. B.C. Munich.

(*F*) Syracusan "Medallion." Signed by Euaenetus. Late V cent. B.C. British Museum, London.

PLATE 45

(*A*) Choragic Monument of Lysicrates. Athens. 335 B.C.

(*C*) Praxiteles. Hermes with the Infant Dionysus. Marble. H. 7 ft. c. 350 B.C. Olympia. (Clarence Kennedy)

(*B*) Corinthian Capital from Epidaurus.

(*D*) Praxiteles. Hermes (detail of *C*).

PLATE 46

(*B*) Scopas. Head from the Temple at Tegea. c. 350 B.C. National Museum, Athens. (Clarence Kennedy)

(*A*) Demeter. From the temple of Demeter at Knidos. Marble. c. 350 B.C. British Museum, London. (Clarence Kennedy)

(*C*) Frieze of the Mausoleum of Halicarnassus. c. 350 B.C. British Museum, London. (Mansell)

PLATE 47

(*A*) Lysippus (?). Copy of the Apoxyomenos.
Marble. Late IV cent. B.C. Vatican, Rome.

(*B*) Nike of Samothrace.
c. 300 B.C. Louvre, Paris.

(*C*) Frieze from the Altar of Zeus at Pergamon. c. 175 B.C.
Pergamon Museum, Berlin.

PLATE 48

(A) Aphrodite of Melos. Marble. II cent.
B.C. Louvre, Paris. (Alinari)

(B) Old Market Woman. Marble. II cent.
B.C. Metropolitan Museum, New York.
(Metropolitan Museum)

(C) Eros. Bronze. H. c. 2 ft.
Morgan Library, New York. (Burlington Fine Arts Club)

(D) Tanagra Figurine. Terra cotta,
painted. H. 8 in. Boston Museum.
(Boston Museum)

the exquisite, simplified modeling and engraving, and the combination of richness and good taste make this coin one of the most notable ever struck.

A smaller Syracusan coin, but also a masterpiece, bears as the coin-type the head of Arethusa, front view and slightly turned to one side (PL. 44 D). The setting of a face in front view on a coin is a daring thing for an artist to do, as usage soon flattens the features, producing an ugly or even ludicrous effect. Hence it has not often been attempted. But the Greek die-maker is one of the exceptions. The waving locks of hair, in and out of which dolphins dart, frame the face, filling the space to the enclosing ring of dots; the finer hairs are engraved as if with a diamond point. In a coin from Agrigentum (PL. 44 E) the grouping of two eagles with contrasting movement and the adaptation of the group to the space can scarcely be equaled by any of the numerous coins of the countries that have used the eagle as a coin-type.

SUMMARY

In surveying Greek art of the fifth century, one is impressed by its simplicity. The temples are not colossal, like those of Egypt, and are of the most elementary system of construction. Sculpture and painting are narrowly restricted in subject matter, for the human figure is their chief and almost only concern. Everywhere is reserve and dignity, control of material, whether stone or metal, together with a recognition of its possibilities and limitations, and a pervading serenity and quiet joy. But careful analysis of this simplicity reveals the fact that it is based, not upon a failure to understand form with all its details, but upon that profound and comprehensive knowledge, acquired through centuries of endeavor, which could select what was essential and permanent and omit the irrelevant. Such selective power, which reveals an innate sense of balance and proportion, enabled the architect, for example, to restrain his ornament, realizing that the unity and harmony of the whole design was his primary purpose and that details of sculpture, carvings, or color must be made to serve and enhance that harmony, and not to intrude, as if ornament were an end in itself. In carving or drawing the human figure, the same qualities enabled the artist to represent a broad, generalized aspect of man. His religious beliefs, which pictured the gods as exalted human beings, shaped his conception of ideal man so that it became a figure of noble aspect in which body and spirit formed so harmonious a unit that the entire form breathed the spirit. "Give me beauty in the inward soul," prayed Socrates that summer afternoon, as he and his friend strolled along the river Ilissus, "and may the outward and inward man be at one. May I reckon the wise to be the wealthy, and may I have such a quantity of gold as a temperate man and he only can bear and carry. — Anything more? This prayer, I think, is enough for me."

The Greek's superb sense of design reveals itself not only in his monumental works, but in the everyday things of life — his household utensils, jewelry, and coins. The quality of craftsmanship as well as of design seen in these minor arts is indicative of the high standard of taste among the Greek people as a whole. With them art was as much a part of life as religion, commerce, or politics. "For we are lovers of the beautiful," said Pericles, "yet simple in our tastes; and we cultivate the mind without loss of manliness."

BIBLIOGRAPHY (See Chapter VI)

CHAPTER VIII
GREEK PERIOD (3)
The Fourth Century and Hellenistic Age. 400 to First Century B.C.

HISTORICAL BACKGROUND

The disastrous Peloponnesian War that left Greece drained of her strength brought Athens politically to a secondary place. Sparta and then Thebes took the leadership, both unsuccessfully, until Philip of Macedon, shrewdly playing upon mutual jealousies, brought the country to subjection and a semblance of unity. The work of his son Alexander was to spread Hellenic culture, by his conquests, over large areas of the East. Athens was no longer the center of this civilization, nor even continental Greece; but the great cities of Asia Minor and Egypt — Ephesus, Rhodes, Pergamon, and Alexandria.

Another result of the Peloponnesian War was to turn the Greek from his ideal of the state to that of the individual. "Know thyself," Socrates had taught as he went about daily among the people in the streets, the agora, and the gymnasium and by questioning endeavored to help them gain "wisdom," that is, to distinguish between right and wrong conduct in their own lives. Philosophers like Plato and Aristotle, following the lead of Socrates, began talking and writing skeptically of the old religious faith, and intellectual freedom began. Scientists began to pry critically into the nature of things, measuring with fair accuracy the circumference and diameter of the earth, long since known to be spherical, and discovering many facts about geometry, the natural sciences, and medicine.

While Greece had been growing, flowering, and decaying, Rome, in the Italian peninsula, had been slowly developing. Gradually she had conquered Italy, Sicily, and Carthage, and then, partly through circumstance and partly through desire for expansion, she came eastward, defeated the Macedonian power, and made Greece a Roman province. While this was a political victory, it was not a cultural one. Hellenic ideas continued to dominate both in the East and also in the West, though deeply modified by the taste of the victors; and even under new conditions furnished many of the fundamentals of medieval culture.

ARCHITECTURE

The Corinthian order of architecture, mentioned in the preceding chapter, reveals itself in the choragic *Monument of Lysicrates* (PL. 45 A). Were it not for the capitals, one would easily class this as Ionic; for the slender columns with their individual bases, the triple architrave, continuous frieze, and carved moldings are all Ionic features. The typical Corinthian capital (PL. 45 B) has a bell-shaped core decorated with two rows of conventionalized acanthus leaves from which rise volutes, the longer ones reaching out to support the corners of the abacus, the shorter uniting with a floral ornament to decorate the core. As this capital is more luxuriantly ornamental than the Doric and the Ionic, it was used sparingly by the Greeks but became the favorite of the Romans (PL. 50 B).

SCULPTURE

Greek sculpture in the fifth century had expressed a noble conception of mankind, filled with dignity and serenity, and devoid of individual characteristics. When we turn to the work of Praxiteles, we realize that we have met a new ideal. In the *Hermes* [1] (PL. 45 C) the god is represented standing, resting his weight on the left arm, a pose that gives an easy curve to the body. On this arm he holds the infant Dionysus, who reaches for the bunch of grapes that the god probably was holding in his right hand. There is a languid ease and grace throughout the figure. Hermes is looking, not at the child, but off into space, with a dreamy expression in his eyes and a half-smile playing about his mouth; the whole figure, particularly the head (PL. 45 D), is deep in the mood of reverie. Sentiment has crept into Greek art, and human charm has replaced the lofty Pheidian idealism. The modeling is exquisite. Soft shadows follow the planes as they flow imperceptibly one into another. With the utmost delicacy the marble is finished, so that over the features a fleeting expression seems to be gliding, and the delicacy is enhanced by the contrastingly rough way in which the hair is indicated. While ease and charm are predominant, intellectual and physical vigor are not lacking. The overhanging brow indicates mental power, and the broad chest and powerful muscles, bodily vigor. The infant, on the other hand, is but poorly done. The Greek does not yet un-

---

[1] This is a most important statue, for it is the only Greek statue extant that is without doubt assignable to one of the great Greek sculptors.

derstand the child, and pictures him as a diminutive man. The mantle hanging over the pedestal on which Hermes is leaning falls in deep rich folds, adding a note of elegance.

This tendency toward delicacy of finish reaches a climax in works in which brilliant technical execution almost seems to have forced the marble into expressing that which lies beyond its capacity. The surface and texture of the soft flesh are marvelously rendered. The structural form is thoroughly understood and adequately expressed; but it appears veiled, with such exquisite delicacy are the planes modeled.[2]

A head from Tegea (PL. 46 B), battered though it is, tells us of another element that entered Greek art in the fourth century. Here the upturned face, the deep-set eyes shadowed by the heavy brows, and the intense expression reveal the essence of human tragedy. The sculptor who carved this head was Scopas. Praxiteles expressed the dreaming happy moods of life; Scopas, the passionate and tragic. These fourth-century sculptors, however, did not entirely abandon the traditions of the fifth century, as we see in the *Demeter of Knidos* (PL. 46 A), in which the quiet majesty of Pheidias combines with the humanity of Scopas and Praxiteles. The goddess is heavily draped in her cloak, one corner of which is drawn up over the back of the head, throwing into relief the quietly beautiful face. But in the eyes, deep-set and shadowed, is an intent gaze filled with a human sorrow that has become calm.

In one of the friezes of the *Mausoleum of Halicarnassus*, on which we know Scopas worked, we see a battle scene (PL. 46 C) in which an impetuous Amazon at the right rushes on a Greek who recoils from her fury. The figures are thin and lithe, somewhat strained in pose, and their faces have the same expression of human passion as their bodies. The restless drapery intensifies the impetuosity that sweeps through the group. Though the figures are not crowded, they are closely related by emotion so that the unity is not so much one of composition as of feeling.

An important sculptor belonging to the generation following Praxiteles and Scopas was Lysippus, the court sculptor of Alexander the Great. No original work of his has come down to us, and even the so-called copy of the *Apoxyomenos*[3] (PL. 47 A) has been questioned. Nevertheless, it will serve to illustrate several important innovations of the time. A comparison of this figure with any of the fifth century will reveal the more slender

[2] Excellent illustrations of this surface treatment are the *Head from Chios* (Boston Museum), and the *Aphrodite* (Syracuse Museum).

[3] An athlete scraping the oil and dirt from his body after exercising. The original was bronze.

proportions and small head; the suppleness of the figure, as if of an organism that could move naturally and easily; the position of the arms extended freely from the body without fear; and particularly the fact that, seen from any point of view, the planes appear to flow into each other, giving the truly three-dimensional feeling. Greek sculptors up to this time had not succeeded in realizing that quality. The earliest sculpture was distinctly a block of stone with four faces; the *Discobolus* of Myron is felt in one plane, as a side view of the statue easily shows; even the *Hermes* of Praxiteles is best seen from one position — otherwise there are awkward passages. About 300 B.C. the scientific study of the human body through dissection began at Alexandria in the study of medicine, and the result of such work was destined to react upon the sculptors, making their modeling more scientifically accurate and bringing them more and more to a unified aspect of the figure in space.

The tendency toward an expression of restless emotion is well seen in the *Nike of Samothrace*[4] (PL. 47 B). The figure is electric with the thrill that comes from rapid, buoyant movement. The twist in the torso produces great vitality, felt through the clinging, wind-swept drapery, the restless curves and the minute folds of which are so complicated that they almost become a *tour de force*. As it is, the sculptor just saved himself by bringing the main lines into harmony with the lines of the figure in a manner that deepens the feeling of elation and the joy of swift movement. Here, as in the best Greek sculpture, the whole figure expresses the conception of the artist, which is not only the personified Nike, but an abstract expression of the very essence of victory. Because of this essential unity of feeling in all parts of the figure, the loss of the head and arms is not so disconcerting as in the case of a statue where the sculptor has concentrated upon a certain part, such as the face, to express his thought.

The tendency toward restlessness and the expression of intense feeling reached a climax in the *Altar at Pergamon*, on the frieze of which is represented the battle between the gods and the giants (PL. 47 C). Athena, moving rapidly toward the right, clutches one of the winged giants by the hair, forcing him to the ground; on the right Earth, mother of the giants, a half-length figure, looks appealingly to Athena; above her, Victory approaches to crown the goddess. It is hardly less than wild disorder that fills the group. Force is there, powerfully displayed. The artist

[4] Erected to commemorate the naval victory of Demetrius Poliorcetes over Ptolemy in 306 B.C. The pedestal has the shape of a prow. The goddess held a trumpet to her lips as we know from a coin on which this statue was used as the coin-type.

obtained it by using violent contrasts, as in the lines of direction in the bodies of Athena and the giant; by extravagant modeling; and by the agonized expression of the faces. He has filled his space, even introducing half-length figures to do so, but has not ordered them according to reason with a center of interest. Greek art has sunk to the level where disorder, extravagance, and lack of taste have taken the place of reason and monumental serenity.

The same low level of artistic conception is found in the *Laocoön* (PL. 49 A).[5] The very choice of subject shows a low ebb of taste when a sculptor wishes to perpetuate, as sculpture must do, an agonizing death struggle. To be sure the grouping is wonderfully compact, with an intense feeling for the writhing movement of the intertwining bodies and serpents; the modeling, though exaggerated, is technically excellent, showing the firm, well-knit adult figure in contrast with the soft, pliant bodies of the youths. But the ignoble conception, the exaggeration, and the striving for effect could never create a great work of art.

In the midst of this orgy, we are not surprised to find revolt on the part of those who really comprehended the noblest traditions of their race. At first thought, it seems incredible that the *Aphrodite of Melos* (PL. 48 A) could have been produced in the same age as the *Laocoön*. There is a simple dignity and calm in the erect head; the modeling is firm with no exaggeration. There is an attempt to arrange the drapery in large, quiet masses. It is a little difficult to explain the pose. The right hand probably held the drapery; and the left foot was raised and the knee bent, possibly, to serve as the rest for a shield in which the goddess is looking at herself. Though this statue has a certain noble beauty, it is not so vital and significant a manifestation of the best Greek genius as the *Parthenon* marbles or the *Olympia* pediments.

In subject matter, the work of this period is quite varied. It is not alone the gods, the heroes of the race, and athletic figures that are represented. Genre enters, now trivial or frivolous, now charming; sometimes repulsive, frequently highly realistic. In the *Old Market Woman* (PL. 48 B), for example, there is nothing idealistic or monumental about the bent, haggard old woman who is peddling her chickens and fruit or vegetables. The child, however, now comes into its own, and for the first time is rendered with a truly childlike form, as in the *Eros* (PL. 48 c) who

[5] Some of the restorations of this group are incorrect. The right arm of Laocoön should be bent back of the head; the arm of the youth at the left should curve inward limply toward Laocoön; the hand of the youth on the right should not be so prominent. These changes would make the group more compact.

moves lightly with his torch, perhaps running a torch-race. His body, perfectly and rhythmically poised, and his smiling face, filled with joy, express childhood as naturally and spontaneously as one could wish.

The *Tanagra Figurines* are the most charming examples of Greek genre. Thousands have been found, chiefly in graves, and their purpose is unknown. They represent all kinds of everyday scenes, trivial in subject but dainty in execution and bright in color. The robes are usually rose or blue, the hair a reddish brown, the shoes red, and the fans or other accessories have touches of gilding. These figurines were made in molds, several being used for one figure, so that by changing the head or the arms a considerable amount of variety could be obtained. In all of them there is a natural grace and charm; and the little lady in PL. 48 D wrapped in her cloak, with her jaunty hat and fan, is even coquettish.

PAINTING

It is difficult to get a picture of Greek painting after the fifth century. Even within the latter part of that century, the pottery industry on the continent declined, for some reason not clear. The shapes are slender and the decorations have an air of elegance; in the drawing there is great facility and freedom, but it is often superficial and hasty. Yet we know from literature that just the opposite tendency was taking place among the painters, the chief of whom was Apelles, court painter of Alexander the Great. These artists were making great strides in such fundamentals as perspective, light and shade, and color.

Let us look at a few examples which will reveal something, at least, of this great school. On an ivory panel (PL. 49 C) is pictured the *Rape of the Daughters of Leucippus*. The artist who made this drawing was a master of line. With apparent ease and yet accuracy of expression, he has indicated the essentials of the form of both horses and driver and withal has added a grace of line that has a beauty of its own. Such a figure as that of the running or the crouching woman, in the vase painting in PL. 49 B, reveals the skill of the Greek draughtsman in the expression of what is significant and essential with a minimum of means.

To study a Greek composition on a large scale, we may take the *Alexander Mosaic* (PL. 49 D), making allowance for the fact that this is probably the copy of a painting worked out in mosaic technique (p. 160). The scene represents some battle, usually thought to be that of the Issus. The center of interest is the horseman in the foreground who has been pierced by the spear of Alexander and is falling from his wounded steed. Darius is fleeing in his chariot, but he looks back at the wounded man with anguish in his face and arm outstretched as if in helpless appeal. Another horseman in the foreground has dismounted, and while attempting to hold his horse looks toward his wounded companion as if to offer his mount. Here, then, is a well defined center of interest toward which all the main lines of the composition lead. The vigor in the charge of the Greeks, the consternation of the routed Persians, the real anguish in the face of Darius, are expressed with directness. There is bold and fairly correct foreshortening, notably in the horses in the foreground. The background is flat, with no indication of landscape except a gnarled tree sketchily indicated; the upper third of the panel, perfectly flat and unadorned except for the highly decorative tree and the spears, offers an interesting contrast to the vigor and movement of the lower part.

Painting in Greece must have been, in its highest manifestation, supremely noble and monumental. It had little kinship with the realistic work of either the Renaissance or modern times; for, while the painters studied nature, their purpose was not to create an illusion of natural appearance, but to express highly generalized and significant aspects of form only; to indicate, with the highest intellectual clarity, the essentials of natural appearance and to express through them a meaning as spiritual as did the sculptor of the *Parthenon* marbles. In this respect they are one in purpose with the painters of the *Ajanta Frescoes* of India (Pl. 163 b and c) or with the Chinese (Pls. 168–9). This result they attained primarily by the use of line, making a restrained use of color, perspective, and light and shade.

MINOR ARTS

The worker in metals — bronze, gold, silver — maintained in this period the same high level of craftsmanship that he reached in the fifth century. Gold was a medium in which he delighted to work for its own sake, because, as several processes could be employed in its use — *repoussé*, modeling, filigree, plaiting — he could create a varied design. In a necklace (Pl. 50 a), for example, he has plaited five strands for the band from which hang small pendants attached by tiny starlike florets, that probably once were filled with enamel. Each petal of these florets is edged with a hairlike wire soldered to its edge; the plaited band terminates in palmette ornaments daintily executed in filigree work, to which are affixed the filigree rosettes that form the clasp; the bird suspended from a disc in the center and the pendants are modeled in the gold. Like the earring (PL. 44 B) the main design is kept simple and dignified; but subordinate to this and enhancing it, is a wealth of exquisitely wrought detail that adds a note of delicacy and refinement. With the introduction of precious stones, through the conquests of Alexander the Great in the East, the gold was no longer worked for itself, but attention was concentrated upon the use of gems, and the fine technique declined.

SUMMARY

In the fourth century we see Pheidian austerity giving way to ease and grace, and divine majesty and serenity to human sentiment. Both these tendencies developed, in the Hellenistic age, into exaggerations and found expression in a varied subject matter, often trivial. The artists were inclined to focus upon technique that often produced superb results, but at the sacrifice of that equilibrium between subject and material that had made the fifth-century works so supremely noble.

Hellenic culture was not lost by the Roman conquest. It was the main stream of subsequent European art. Sometimes the stream runs low, as in the Middle Ages, only again to rush on with tremendous power, as in the Renaissance.

When we ask what is the debt of modern art to Greek art, there is no reply. We cannot point to this idea or that, and say this is Hellenic and that is non-Hellenic. We can say this is Pheidian, that Scopaic, or this is Pergamene and that Rhodian, but to say art is Greek is simply to say it is good. For Greek art comprises every genuine effort of the artist; every statue, however cunning and ingenious, which is merely frivolous or hypocritical or untrue, is a crime against Hellenism and a sin against the light. The Greek bequest to later artists is nothing tangible; it is the soul and spirit of the artist. True art cannot be attained by rule; it demands a condition of receptivity of inspiration, in other words, of faith, in the artist; only thus can the elements of technique be so combined as to make something far greater than their mere sum total.[6]

[6] Guy Dickins, *Hellenistic Sculpture*, p. 87.

BIBLIOGRAPHY (See Chapter VI)

CHAPTER IX
ROMAN PERIOD
c. 2000 B.C. — *c.* 500 A.D.

HISTORICAL BACKGROUND

A glance at the chart (FIG. 132) reveals the fact that although the early histories of Greece and Rome run nearly parallel, chronologically, the former reached a climax in the fifth and fourth centuries B.C., while the latter was still slowly developing. The story of early Rome is a story of struggle for existence, particularly against the Etruscans, who probably came to Italy from the east and were closely allied culturally to the Greeks. Her conquest of Etruria was followed by the subjugation of the entire peninsula. When once Rome had started on her imperial policy, circumstances forced her to continue, and gradually she enlarged her boundaries until they included the entire Mediterranean basin and all western Europe. These conquests opened the way for the spread of her civilization. Roman cities sprang up especially in what is now Spain, France, and England, each a center for the propagation of Roman government, language, and customs, and closely connected with Rome by magnificently built roads.

In the main, the energy of Rome was utilized in conquest and administration, the gradual development of which culminated in the code of Justinian (527-565 A.D.), which forms the basis of modern law. Both by force of circumstance and by temperament, the Roman was warlike, practical, fond of pleasure. His life, in comparison with the simplicity of the Greek, was complex, for the demands of life were much greater.

The golden age of Rome in art and literature, though not in extent or administration, was reached under Augustus (31 B.C. - 14 A.D.). Rome was not the artistic nation that Greece was, and to her credit she conceded her indebtedness. "Conquered Greece led the conqueror captive," said Horace, a poet of the Augustan age. Shiploads of Greek marbles and bronzes were brought to Rome by generals and provincial governors to adorn their palaces, and when the supply was exhausted, copies were made or Greek artists were employed to create new ones. Thus Roman art is a continuation of the Hellenic tradition working according to Roman tastes and ideals. Yet Rome added certain things specifically her own. The practical demands arising from the administering of a great empire, such as the need of roads and bridges, as well as the erection of public buildings that would adequately express the dignity and might of their state, made the Romans great both as engineers and as builders.

With the wealth that came with conquest, there crept in pleasure-loving ideals, luxuriousness, and decay. The frontiers gave way on all sides and by 500 A.D. Rome herself had fallen before the northern tribes that had been harassing her boundaries ever since Julius Caesar had driven them back in the first century B.C.

ARCHITECTURE

In Greek architecture we discerned a concentration upon the temple; in Rome, on the contrary, as the capital of a complex world-empire, practical as well as aesthetic needs led to the erection of many kinds of buildings, secular as well as religious. The *Maison Carrée* (PL. 50 B) illustrates one type of temple derived obviously from the Greek peripteral style, but differing in the high base upon which it rests, finished with projecting moldings, and approached by a flight of steps extending across the front. Its cella is larger than the Greek, meeting the columns part way along the sides and across the back. A column thus incorporated with a wall is known as an engaged column and is found very frequently in Roman work. Another difference is the more abundant use of ornament, which produces a feeling of elegance. Still, the temple with its fine proportions, and effective irregularities, closely related to those of the *Parthenon*, bears plainly the mark of Hellenic feeling.

Another kind of temple popular among the Romans was that built on a circular plan, of which the *Pantheon* (PL. 50 c) is the most imposing example. The building is constructed of a drum without openings on which rests a dome, low and rather inconspicuous; on the front is a colonnaded portico of Greek design. As one enters the building (PL. 51 A), he is surprised at the impressiveness and the feeling of spaciousness, which are due to a very simple design carried out on a large scale — a single dome set on a circular drum, and lighted by an aperture in the crown. It was evidently the purpose of the designer to make his dome impressive from the interior, and in this he was marvelously

PLATE 49

(A) Laocoön. Marble, over life-size. II cent. B.C. Vatican, Rome.

(B) Vase Painting: Seizure of Thetis. British Museum, London. (Gardner, *The Principles of Greek Art.* © The Macmillan Company)

(C) Painting on Ivory: Rape of the Daughters of Leucippus. Hermitage, Leningrad. (Minns)

(D) Mosaic: Battle Scene Between Alexander and Darius. From the floor of the House of the Faun, Pompeii. L. 17 ft. c. 100 B.C. Naples Museum.

PLATE 50

(A) Necklace. Gold. IV cent. B.C. Metropolitan Museum, New York. (Metropolitan Museum)

(B) Maison Carrée, Nimes, I or II cent. A.D.

(C) Pantheon. Rome. Originally the walls were faced with marble and stucco and the dome covered with bronze plates. 120–24 A.D.

successful. The wall space is covered with rich marble facing; the dome is deeply coffered, and was originally decorated with bronze rosettes. Domes had been constructed before this, but never on such a scale. The Roman's conception of largeness made him daring. At the same time his practical nature made him think out his engineering problems carefully. The walls, twenty feet thick, are made of brick and concrete and are solid except for the alternating round and trapezoidal niches about which, in the masonry, are imbedded great relieving arches of brick that extend the entire thickness of the wall and carry the thrust of the dome away from the niches. The dome is constructed of

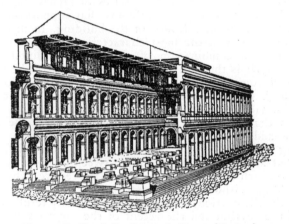

Fig. 71. Basilica Julia, Restored. Rome. (Huelsen)

horizontal layers of brick laid in thick cement and of a series of arches that converge near the crown and assist, as do those in the drum, in distributing the weight. The deep coffers not only ornament the dome but also diminish its weight.

The *Roman Forum*, about which were grouped many of the temples and civic buildings, was originally the market place where the peasants brought their fruit, vegetables, poultry, and fish for sale; booths and shops ran along the sides. But early, religious and civic activities began to encroach; the shops were crowded out to the side streets and the *Forum* became primarily the center of the city's civic life. In the open space were commemorative statues of emperors and generals, and the great platform from which public speeches were made; entirely surrounding it were imposing buildings. It was a magnificent spectacle.

Among the buildings on the south side of the *Forum* was the *Basilica Julia* (FIG. 71). The basilica was an important civic building with the Romans, ordinarily used as a law court. It was an oblong structure with a semicircular tribunal, or apse, at one end, where the judge sat, and was divided by a row of columns or piers into a central and side aisles; the roof of the central aisle was higher than that of the side aisles, thus forming a clerestory (FIG. 74). Looking at the exterior, we notice that the structural principle is not the lintel system of the *Maison Carrée* but the arcade, that is, a series of arches. Between the arches, however, are engaged columns that support an entablature running the entire length of the building. In this arrangement we find one of the most characteristic features of Roman architecture, a combination of the arch and lintel systems. Structurally it is the arch that is the vital part of the construction; the column and entablature serve only as decoration.

The highest manifestation of this system we find in the *Colosseum* (PL. 51 B). Between the arches of each story are engaged columns that support a continuous entablature, the engaged columns adding to the rhythm, and the entablature not only unifying the arched openings and binding them into a firmly felt unity but also forming a fine single sweep of curve which, repeated on each story, is dignified and impressive. The effect of the building without this decoration can be seen on the right side of the illustration, where a bare monotony results from the loss of the rhythm and the accent of the vigorous curves. The combination of structural solidity and effective decoration has created a building imposing in dignity and magnificence. On the ground story the columns are of the Doric order, on the second of the Ionic, and on the third of the Corinthian, an arrangement known as superposed orders. The fourth story is ornamented by flat Corinthian pilasters. The exterior and main corridors of the *Colosseum* are built of stone set with no mortar but clamped by iron dowels; the inner walls are of softer stone and concrete with brick facing; the stairways and substructure for seats are of concrete.

The materials used in the *Colosseum* are those found chiefly in Roman buildings. The vast size of many of their structures forbade extensive use of stone masonry. A substitute the Roman found in brick and concrete, which is a mixture of small loose material and a cement that hardens into a solid mass. The process was the same as that used today. A temporary wooden framework was built up, into which the concrete was poured. It was usually faced with brick or covered with a veneer of stucco or marble.

The impression of material power that is felt in all Roman architecture is specifically expressed in the triumphal arches and columns erected to commemorate great victories or other events. Like the *Colosseum*, the arches combined the arch and lintel system. While many have the triple opening, as the *Arch of Constantine*, for nobility of design and proportion the *Arch of Titus* (PL. 52 A)[1] is perhaps the finest. The great central opening is flanked by solid masses of masonry with engaged columns that rise from a plain base to support the entablature, which has a

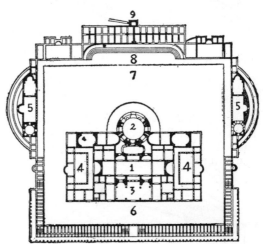

Fig. 72. Baths of Caracalla. Rome. 211–217 A.D. The central building is 750 x 380 ft. (1) *tepidarium*, or warm lounge; (2) *calidarium*, or hot room; (3) *frigidarium*, or cooling room with a swimming pool open to the air; (4) open peristyles; (5) lecture rooms and libraries; (6) promenade; (7) garden; (8) stadium; (9) aqueduct and reservoirs.

sculptured frieze uniting the three parts, though breaking to project above the columns; this forms a base for the great superstructure that contains the inscription. The decoration is restrained, and confined chiefly to the arch.

A sense of magnificence, resulting partly from size, and also an impression of engineering ability is the effect of the great *thermae*, or baths, that provided the Roman not only with his daily baths, hot, warm, or cold, but with his library and lounging place, for the numerous recreation rooms served the same function as the modern athletic club. A ground plan (FIG. 72)

[1] Erected to commemorate the conquest of Jerusalem by Titus. A bronze four-horse chariot surmounted the arch, as was customary on triumphal arches. The four bronze horses now above the entrance of *Saint Mark's* in Venice probably served such a purpose originally.

gives us some conception of the great extent of these baths and also of the orderly planning that characterizes the organization of the parts.[2] PL. 52 B reconstructs one hall of the *Baths of Caracalla*. The impression is of vast spaciousness and, in the rich

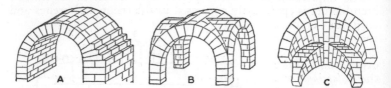

Fig. 73. *A*. Barrel vault. *B*. Groin vault seen from above. *C*. Groin vault seen from below.

marble facings, carvings, and coffered ceilings, of magnificence and splendor. The technical problem here involved was how to enclose and roof over a vast space, to give it proper illumination and still to keep the space open and free of the columns that would

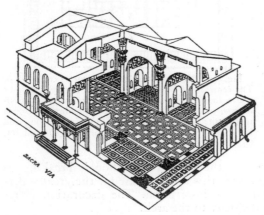

Fig. 74. *A*. Basilica of Maxentius or Constantine. Rome. 306–312 A.D. Section of a reconstruction.

be necessary were a flat roof used, as in the hypostyle halls of Egypt (PL. 11). We have seen the predilection of the Roman for the arch. Given the problem of roofing over a rectangular room by the simplest arch system, the result will be a barrel vault (FIG. 73 A) which is, in essence, a succession of arches joined together, resting directly upon the side walls, which must be thick enough to support the weight. This can be made of stone or brick masonry, or of concrete by building up a temporary wooden framework known as

[2] For the influence of the Roman baths, in plan, upon the Bank of England, see Bailey, *Legacy of Rome*, p. 405. The Pennsylvania Station in New York shows their influence in general design and spaciousness, though not in structural principle.

PLATE 51

(*A*) Pantheon. From an engraving by Piranesi. D. and H. 142 ft.

(*B*) Colosseum, or Flavian Amphitheater. Rome. 70–82 A.D. (Alinari)

(*C*) House of the Vettii. Pompeii. Peristyle, restored. I cent. A.D.

PLATE 52

(*A*) Arch of Titus, Restored on the Sides. A bronze four-horse chariot surmounted the arch. Rome. 81 A.D. (Alinari)

(*B*) Baths of Caracalla. Central Hall, Restored by Spiers. 211–17 A.D. Rome. (Anderson and Spiers)

(*C*) Temple of Castor and Pollux. Capital and entablature. Roman Forum. 117–38 A.D. From a cast in the Metropolitan Museum, New York. (Metropolitan Museum)

(*D*) Pilaster. Marble. I–II cent. A.D. Metropolitan Museum, New York. (Metropolitan Museum)

PLATE 53

(*A*) Stucco Decoration. Tomb of the Valerii, Via Latina, Rome. I cent. A.D. (Alinari)

(*B*) Ara Pacis, Altar of Peace. Erected in 13 A.D. to commemorate the victories of Augustus in Spain and Gaul. Detail of procession. Uffizi, Florence.

(*C*) Ara Pacis. Detail of decoration. Terme Museum, Rome.

PLATE 54

(*A*) Unknown Roman. Terra cotta, with traces of color. I cent. B.C. Boston Museum. (Boston Museum)

(*B*) Portrait of a Child. Marble. I cent. A.D. Boston Museum. (Boston Museum)

(*C*) Augustus. Marble, from the Villa of Livia, wife of Augustus, at Prima Porta. Vatican, Rome.

(*D*) Roman Boy. Probably a Julian Prince. Bronze. I cent. A.D. Metropolitan Museum, New York. (Metropolitan Museum)

centering, the exact size and shape of the finished vault, to hold the mass until it is set. The vaulting that we see in PL. 52 B and FIG. 74 has been made by cutting the barrel vault at right angles at regular intervals by other barrel vaults, securing what is known as the cross or groin vault, because the line of intersection is called the groin (FIG. 73 B). A barrel vault over so large an area not only would have been heavy in appearance but would have allowed no space for windows. Hence the advantage of the groin vault is not only that it is lighter in appearance because of its broken surface but that it admits of clerestory windows. Another advantage is secured by the use of the groin

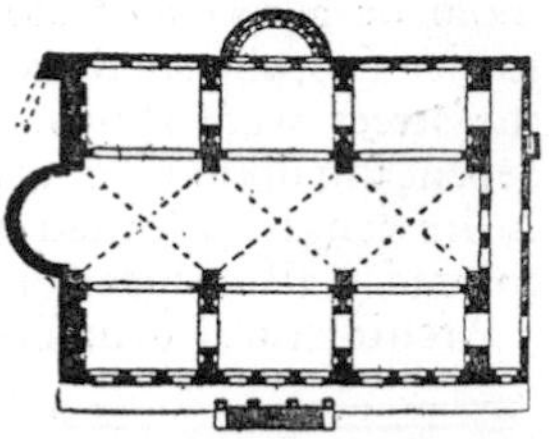

Fig. 74 B. Plan. (Luckenbach)

vault. In the barrel vault the thrust, that is, the outward force exerted by the vault, is felt along the entire wall space; in the groin, only at the points at which the groins converge. Hence it is at these points only that heavy buttressing is needed, allowing the space between to be arched over. Proper support is secured by heavy walls built at right angles, which are pierced by arches and thus form side aisles to the main hall (FIG. 74).

Domestic architecture played an important part in the lives of the pleasure-loving Romans. The typical modest Roman house we can best study at Pompeii, where many have been excavated in a fair condition, with their mural decorations still preserved and sometimes with their equipment and household utensils undisturbed. The house stood flush with the sidewalk and presented a plain, uninteresting exterior.

Fig. 75. House of Pansa. Pompeii. (1) atrium; (2) alæ; (3) tablinum; (4) peristyle; (5) garden; S, shops.

Through a narrow entrance, one entered a vestibule (FIG. 75) that led to a court known as the atrium (1), roofed over along the four sides so as to leave an opening in the center, with a corresponding sunken place in the floor to collect the rain water; along the sides were small rooms except at the end where the atrium extended the full width of the building, forming two wings, *alae* (2). Behind the atrium was the *tablinum* (3), in which the family archives and statues were kept, and which could be shut off or could afford a passage to the peristyle (4 and Pl. 51 c), a large colonnaded court with fountains and garden, about which were grouped the private apartments of the family, the atrium serving more as a reception room or a room of state. At the back there was sometimes a garden (5); the small rooms along the outer sides (s) opening on the street were shops. It is clear that the house faced inward, depending upon its courts for light and air; and, when opened, its entire length afforded a charming perspective. Of its brightly colored wall decoration we shall speak under Painting.[3]

Architectural ornament the Roman used lavishly (Pl. 52 c);

Fig. 76. Roman Rinceau.

frequently, in the attempt to obtain magnificence, overloading his buildings and concealing the structure. The restraint of the Greek in his use of moldings and decoration was too severe to suit the Roman taste, which loved display, and preferred the Corinthian capital to the more austere Doric and Ionic. In his best work, however, the Roman proved himself a master in a certain kind of decoration. This we can see best in the *Ara Pacis* (Pl. 53 c). From a central group of acanthus rises a vertical foliate form; and also curving stems that branch off so as to cover the surface with spiral forms that terminate now in a leaf, now in a flower or rosette; about the main stems entwine delicate tendrils; near the top a swan with outspread wings has alighted. A detailed study of the carving reveals a most careful observation of nature and a truthful representation of the plant both in form and in texture. Naturalistic representation has formed the basis

[3] Recent studies of the houses at Ostia make it certain that the majority of dwellings in the city of ancient Rome resembled much more closely the houses of modern Rome than the Pompeian type, which is to be regarded as Greek and south Italian rather than Roman.

of the decoration; the ultimate effect is dependent partly upon the delicacy and precision of the carving and partly upon the carver's restraint in keeping his design a clear decorative pattern. The motif of the foliate spiral rising from a bed of acanthus, known as the *rinceau* (FIG. 76), became one of the most popular in Roman decorative art, especially as applied to pilasters and borders, and later formed the basis of much of the Renaissance ornament.

Further development of naturalistic ornament is illustrated in PL. 52 D. From a vase rises a vigorous stem, the small fruit-laden branches of which cover the surface of the marble; a snake is coiling about the main stem and out on a branch toward the nest where the frightened parent birds with open mouths are crying their distress. Again the plant forms show a close observation of nature; for example, the way in which the stems issue from the main branch, the modeling of the leaf, and the bird forms. Yet this naturalism has been so tempered that the different motifs entirely cover the space with very little overlapping; and as the undercutting is but slight, a delicate light and shade plays over the surface, giving an impression not only of the charm of nature but also of decorative fitness.

Another kind of ornament used most effectively by the Romans was stucco (PL. 53 A) applied as a finish to the rough concrete barrel vaults and walls. The ceiling surface was divided by moldings into geometric patterns that frequently enclosed figures; again naturalistic spirals or other ornaments and dainty figures fill the spaces. The addition of marble dust made the stucco both durable and fine in texture. The moldings and the figures were worked in the wet stucco partly by stamps, noticeably in the moldings, and partly freehand. As in the fresco technique, the rapidity with which plaster dries requires rapid workmanship; and the figures depend for their effect, not so much upon careful modeling, as upon spontaneity, ease of workmanship, and freely flowing line.

SCULPTURE

The statement that "conquered Greece led her conqueror captive" is particularly true of sculpture. As we have said, Greek statues early were brought to Rome and the habit of making copies became common. Sometimes the copies were very faithful, but often they were adapted to suit Roman taste. The Roman was different from the Greek in temperament. He was a practical man of affairs to whom facts, the detailed record of appearance, appealed rather than generalizations and abstractions. In the sculptured reliefs of the *Ara Pacis*, for example (PL. 53 B), we see a procession of men, women, and children. In subject matter, this is close to the *Parthenon Frieze* (PL. 42), but a great difference is felt at once. Here the relief is higher in the foreground figures and lower in the background, giving one quite distinctly a feeling of depth and atmosphere; details are worked out to a greater extent and there is a considerable amount of portraiture in the faces; in fact we feel the individual figures here quite forcibly. The purpose has been to give a more realistic picture of the procession, rather than a simplified abstract one that places strong emphasis on the design, as in the *Parthenon Frieze*. Many of the Roman reliefs contain details of architecture and landscape for the purpose of lively narration and with little regard for purely decorative design.

In another field of sculpture this desire for realism is strongly apparent, that is, in portraiture. In the late Greek period, the generalization that distinguished the earlier portraits had given way to some surprisingly individualistic work. The Roman desire for literal facts together with his custom of keeping in his house, always before his eye, the *imagines*, or wax masks, of his ancestors, influenced the sculptor still further to accentuate this individuality. In the head of an *Unknown Roman* (PL. 54 A), for example, one is struck by the intensely alive quality. The bony structure of the head, the keen eye, sparse hair, the sagging skin beneath the chin, all the lines and wrinkles that designate the peculiar characteristics of an individual — all these qualities combine to give us a powerful portrait of one of those rugged men of dominant will, in the days of the Republic, who helped lay the foundations of Rome's greatness.

But when we turn to the statue of *Augustus* (PL. 54 C), the feeling is different. The emperor stands easily, with all the bearing of a leader, proud of his race. He wears an elaborately decorated metal cuirass with leather fringe over his linen tunic and carries his military cloak thrown easily over his left arm. In every part of the costume is seen wonderful skill in the rendering of texture, the soft and heavy quality of the cloths, the rigidity of the metal, and the tough nature of the leather. In his left hand he holds the scepter; his right is lifted in the direction of his glance as if he might be addressing his troops; for Augustus himself had led the army on his conquests. But the face does not characterize Augustus in detail as does the head of the *Unknown Roman*. There are no individual lines to indicate personal idiosyncrasies.

PLATE 55

(A) Vespasian. Marble. 69–79 A.D.
Terme Museum, Rome.

(B) Caracalla. Marble. 211–17 A.D. Berlin.
(Berlin Museum)

(C) Wall Decoration of a Pompeian House.
(Anderson)

(D) Cupid Riding a Crab. Fresco from the
House of the Vettii, Pompeii. (Anderson)

PLATE 56

(*A*) Cupids as Goldsmiths. Fresco from the House of the Vettii, Pompeii. (Anderson)

(*B*) Frescoes from the Villa of Livia. Prima Porta. (Stoedtner)

(*C*) Silver Cup from Boscoreale. Louvre, Paris. (Alinari)

It is rather a generalized type distinctly reminiscent of Greek work. If we recall the fact that the Augustan age was a period when the acquisition of Greek statues and the influence of Greek art was at its height, we can easily see why Roman realism had given way. The same general characteristics are found in the bronze statue of a *Roman Boy* (PL. 54 D). The youth stands with the easy grace of a Greek statue. In fact he wears the Greek cloak rather than the Roman toga; and while there is sympathy for the boy nature and that too in a boy of the aristocracy, the expression of it is not realistic but, as in the *Augustus*, generalized and reserved. There is great beauty of execution in the modeling of the nude parts and also in the drapery, which is arranged in broad, simple folds, near in feeling to the best Greek work.

The sympathetic understanding of youth and childhood is frequently to be seen in Roman sculpture. In the *Portrait of a Child* (PL. 54 B) the soft flesh and the rounding form of feature that distinguish the child are well indicated; but even more remarkable is the artist's ability to understand the workings of the child mind and to depict that characteristic moment of hesitation between a laugh and a cry that reveals itself so clearly in the quiver about the mouth. In these portraits of the youthful aristocrats of Rome, we discern the real feeling of the child, now bashful, now eager and alert.

The generalizing tendency of the Augustan age could not maintain itself long against the Roman love for literal fact. Thus the portrait of *Vespasian* (PL. 55 A) shows a return to individualistic expression. The rugged soldier whom we know Vespasian to have been is expressed with great truthfulness but with not so much of exactitude as is found in the portraits of the Republican period. There is fine feeling here for the structure of the head, and for the flesh and skin; but with a softening and blending of the features that combines Roman realism with Greek generalization.

When we come to such a portrait as that of *Caracalla* (PL. 55B), certain elements have been added to achieve greater illusion of life — the large bust that includes shoulders and arms, the turn in the head that heightens greatly the vivacity, the rough mass of hair that contrasts with the smoothly finished face. These elements, together with the expression of the face as seen in the overshadowing brow, deep-set, suspicious eyes, cynical, brutal mouth, give us a representation of life and of character that is both startling and convincing.

PAINTING

A considerable number of paintings of the Roman period has survived, chiefly the mural decorations in the palaces and villas in and about Rome, and particularly at Pompeii, where the volcanic ash has preserved their texture and color to a remarkable degree. It is in these wall decorations that we catch a reflection of the lost Greek painting, for some like the *Alexander Mosaic* (PL. 49 D) were probably copies of famous Greek works. Even when not copying, the painters, many of whom were Greeks, were working in the Hellenic tradition. In the best of these we see, beside the largeness of design and a certain measured reposefulness, a knowledge of perspective, a consistent use of light and shade and of the cast shadow, and a unity of the figure with the landscape or architecture — all fundamental principles that had been worked out by the Greek.

The Roman house, with its small number of doors and windows, offered considerable stretches of wall space for decoration; with the result that a plain, almost cell-like room not only became gayly brilliant in color, but appeared to open up vistas of garden or landscape. As we see in PL. 55 c, the wall space has assumed an architectural effect. Columns and windows have been painted on the surface in perspective, to give them an appearance of relief; in the center, this framework encloses a large painting; on the sides, architectural openings lead the eye to the charming landscape in the distance, which gives an air of spaciousness to the room.

These paintings are executed in fresco. The plaster at Pompeii was laid very thick, and by keeping moist for a considerable length of time enabled the painter to work with greater leisure than in the Renaissance, when the thin coating necessitated rapid work. The colors were brilliant and daring — red or black to throw the panels or figures into relief, with rich creamy white in the borders. A certain brilliance of surface that enlivened the effect, the Roman obtained by a careful preparation of the wall surface; for the plaster, which was specially compounded with a mixture of marble dust and laid on layer after layer, was beaten with a smooth trowel until it became very dense, and then was polished until it assumed an almost marblelike finish. The ultimate effect of the Pompeian house, with its deep vista, its open court with fountains, marble, and greenery, and the bright wall decorations seen in a subdued light, was one of gayety and richness. A panel that shows freshness and spontaneity is the black frieze above the dado of a room opening on the peristyle of the *House of the Vettii* (PL. 51 C). On this are seen groups of Cupids and Psyches engaged in various pursuits such as that of the oil merchant, the fuller, and the goldsmith (PL. 56 A), where, at the right, one Cupid is engraving a large vessel; another is at work with pincers, and another at the anvil. In the center stand the scales and trays to display the wares; beyond, a Cupid is weighing some article that the seated Psyche, a customer, has selected. The work is sketchy, but it has a spontaneity and freedom that is often lost in the ostentation that so frequently marks Roman work. In the *Cupid Riding a Crab* (PL. 55 D) there is a truly childlike dash and abandonment of everything to the intense joy of a thrilling moment.

Another kind of wall decoration we see in the frescoes of the *Villa of Livia* (PL. 56 B), where the entire wall space has been painted so as to create the illusion of a garden, as if the side of the room opened out upon the garden represented. A low fence separates the spectator from the scene and also gives solidity and unity to the composition, where trees, plants, and vines in cool green-grays stand out against a blue sky with bits of bright color in the flowers, fruits, and brightly plumaged birds flying about or enjoying the fresh water of the fountains. It is a charming bit of nature brought in from the out-of-doors to delight the life lived inside; in spirit it is closely akin to the naturalistic carvings of which the Roman was so fond.

MINOR ARTS

The skill of the Romans in the use of metal we see not only in the casting of large sculpture but also in the small bronzes such as the candelabra stands, furniture supports, and a great variety of household utensils that have been found at Pompeii. But the wealth and splendor of life made demands upon the gold and silversmith as well to furnish fine plate for luxurious tables. Much of this, of course, was looted by thieves at the time of the catastrophe or by the barbarians in later ages, but a few finds of such treasure,[4] hidden away, have come to light to give us a glimpse of the lavishness displayed at the famous Roman feasts. The silver crater from Hildesheim (PL. 57 A) for mixing the wine is finely shaped, with handles so adjusted that one feels their unity with the structural lines of the vase. Low reliefs, done in

[4] One of the rich finds of silverware was at Hildesheim, Germany; this is now in the Berlin Museum and is known as the *Hildesheim Treasure*. Another, the *Boscoreale Treasure*, most of which is in the Louvre, was discovered at Boscoreale near Pompeii.

repoussé, give a play of delicate light and shade over the surface, adding richness without overloading; at the base the relief is higher, more elaborate and compact, thus strengthening the support. The design here consists of two griffin back to back in balanced position, from which rises a conventional plant form; from this and from the sweeping wings of the griffin delicate spirals rise and spread over the surface, terminating in naturalistic forms; clinging to the stems and tendrils are tiny children attacking, with tridents, the sea animals that intertwine among the spirals. In a two-handled silver cup from Boscoreale (PL. 56 c), we see the Roman love of purely naturalistic form; for here sprays of fruiting olive have been wreathed about the cup, a charming idea giving one quite the illusion of natural appearance, as the fruit is molded in the round. The ornamentation, however, not only obscures the structural lines of the cup but by attracting interest to itself destroys the harmony that results when decoration enhances by subordination.

In Roman pottery, the most conspicuous accomplishment was the *Arretine* bowl, made of a fine reddish clay, with the decoration stamped in relief on the outside by means of molds in which the design was cut in intaglio; finally a reddish glaze was added. A sacrificial scene is represented in PL. 57 c, in which winged figures are decorating an altar to which women, clad in diaphanous drapery, are bringing offerings. These figures remind one of the stucco reliefs in their dainty charm; the relation of the figures to the space and the border designs that finish the top and bottom are close in their feeling of restrained ornamentation to the painted Greek vases.

The Roman lapidaries of the Augustan age were skilled technicians, particularly in cameo cutting, which consists of carving a design in relief from a striated stone, such as sardonyx, in such a way that each layer — and the layers usually are alternately light and dark, numbering from two to nine — shall be utilized in working out the design.

The cameo technique was carried by the Roman into the craft of the glassworker, as we see in the *Portland Vase* (PL. 57 B). Up to the second or first century B.C., glass had been molded (PL. 17 c), a laborious process. About that time the blowpipe was invented, causing a rapid growth of the glass industry; thus glass supplanted, to a large extent, the more usual pottery for everyday use. In making such a vase as the *Portland*, the glassworker shaped the deep blue vase with his blowpipe and then dipped it into opaque white liquid glass; the handles were molded

PLATE 57

(A) Silver Crater from Hildesheim. Berlin. (Giraudon)

(B) Portland Vase. H. c. 10 in. I cent. A.D. British Museum, London. (Mansell)

(C) Arretine Bowl. 40 B.C.–60 A.D. Metropolitan Museum, New York.

(D) Millefiori Bowl. Metropolitan Museum, New York. (Metropolitan Museum)

(E) Sant' Apollinare Nuovo. Ravenna. C. 500 A.D. (Alinari)

(F) Sant' Apollinare Nuovo. Nave seen from the aisle. (Alinari)

PLATE 58

(*A*) Mausoleum of Galla Placidia. Ravenna. c. 450 A.D. (Alinari)

(*B*) Mausoleum of Galla Placidia. (Alinari)

(*C*) Santa Sophia or Hagia Sophia, Church of the Holy Wisdom. Constantinople. Built by Justinian, 532–37 A.D., and dedicated on Christmas morning, 537 A.D. The minarets were added by the Mohammedans when they conquered Constantinople in 1453 A.D. and converted the church into a mosque. (Drawing by J. B. Fulton in the *Architectural Review*)

separately and added; when thoroughly hard, the white layer was cut away, leaving the raised white figures in relief against the deep blue ground. The subject is not understood. At the left a young woman is reclining on some rocks beneath a fig tree, in the usual attitude of sleep; at the right another young woman is seated on a pile of rocks holding a scepter. The figures are carved with ease and grace, making an interesting pattern against the background. The mask beneath the handle is very decorative.

Another very effective use of glass we find in the *Millefiori* or "thousand-flower" bowls (PL. 57 D), which, when held up to the light, give an impression of rich mosaic and hence are sometimes called mosaic glass. The process was as follows: Threads of different-colored glass were fused together into a larger thread, drawn out and then cut into small pieces that were fitted into a mold and fused into a solid mass. By carefully regulating his color and pattern, the glassworker could create a color harmony of surpassing richness.

SUMMARY

In Roman art we see Greek tradition evolving, under new conditions and with new demands upon it, into something radically different both in form and in spirit from the art of Athens. The serenity, moderation, and sense of perfect equilibrium and quiet joy of the Greek, gave place to large conceptions, magnificence and outward display, and massive, enduring construction. The practical Roman with his gift for organization and law produced daring, competent engineers who, with a predilection for the arch system, solved problems of enclosing and roofing great spaces with stone and concrete which they decorated sumptuously to harmonize with the luxurious life of the imperial city. These buildings — baths, basilicas, arches, theaters, temples — notwithstanding their application of structural elements to decorative purposes, as is seen in the use of the column and entablature, and their frequently lavish ornamentation, are highly expressive of the domination and the material magnificence of Rome, and were an important contribution to the art of the Middle Ages and the Renaissance. Another contribution was the naturalistic decorative motifs, particularly the *rinceau* that the Roman in his more sober moments, when he felt the restraining hand of Greece as in the Augustan age, developed most effectively and passed on to the later ages to become a fundamental motif in ornament. Finally the passion of the Roman for fact rather than ideals and abstractions led to a portraiture of astonishingly life-like character.

BIBLIOGRAPHY

AMELUNG, WALTER, AND HOTZINGER, HEINRICH, Museums and Ruins of Rome (tr. Strong). London, Duckworth, 1906.

ANDERSON, W. J., AND SPIERS, R. P., Architecture of Greece and Rome. N.Y., Scribner, 1907.

BAILEY, CYRIL, ED., Legacy of Rome. Oxford, Clarendon Press, 1923.

BREASTED, J. H., Ancient Times. Boston, Ginn, 1916.

BRITISH MUSEUM, Pictorial postcards. Set XXVIII: Select Antique Bronzes; XXIX: Room of Greek and Roman Life; XLVII: Greek and Roman Reliefs; XLVIII: Types of Greek and Roman Statues; XLIX: Portraits of Roman Emperors.

CHASE, G. H., Greek and Roman Sculpture in American Collections. Cambridge, Harvard University Press, 1924.

FAURE, ELIE, History of Art: v. I, Ancient Art (tr. Pach). N.Y., Harper, 1921.

FLETCHER, SIR BANISTER, History of Architecture on the Comparative Method. N.Y., Scribner, 1924.

HAMLIN, A. D. F., History of Ornament, Ancient and Medieval. N.Y., Century, 1921.

HUELSEN, CHRISTIAN, Roman Forum (tr. Carter). N.Y., Stechert, 1909.

JONES, H.S., Companion to Roman History. Oxford, University Press, 1912.

KIMBALL, FISKE, AND EDGELL, G. H., History of Architecture. N.Y., Harper, 1918.

LANCIANI, RODOLFO, Ancient Rome in the Light of Recent Excavations. Boston, Houghton, 1900.

LAURIE, A. P., Greek and Roman Methods of Painting. Cambridge, University Press, 1910.

—— ——, Materials of the Painter's Craft. Philadelphia, Lippincott, 1911.

MAU, AUGUST, Pompeii: Its Life and Art (tr. Kelsey). N.Y., Macmillan, 1902.

METROPOLITAN MUSEUM OF ART, Handbook of the Classical Collection, by G. M. A. Richter. N.Y., 1917.

PLATNER, S. B., Topography and Monuments. Boston, Allyn & Bacon, 1911.

SHOWERMAN, GRANT, Eternal Rome. New Haven, Yale University Press, 1924.

STATHAM, H. H., Short Critical History of Architecture. N.Y., Scribner, 1912.

STRONG, MRS. E. S., Roman Sculpture. N.Y., Scribner, 1907.

WALTERS, H. B., Art of the Romans. N.Y., Macmillan, 1911.

WICKHOFF, FRANZ, Roman Art (tr. Strong). N.Y., Macmillan, 1900.

WILLIAMS, MRS. C. L. (RANSOM), Studies in Ancient Furniture. Chicago, University of Chicago Press, 1905.

WILSON, L. M., Roman Toga. Baltimore, Johns Hopkins Press, 1924.

WINTER, FRANZ, ED., Kunstgeschichte in Bildern: v. I, Das Altertum. Fünftes/ Sechstes Heft. Griechische und Römische Baukunst. Leipzig, Seemann, 1912.

CHAPTER X

EARLY CHRISTIAN
AND BYZANTINE PERIOD

First Five Centuries A.D. *in the West*; 330–1453 A.D. *in the East*

HISTORICAL BACKGROUND

About the year 300 A.D., we see Rome still splendid outwardly — a highly organized despotism, internally weak from decay and externally hard pressed on the frontiers by barbarians or by cultivated indigenous peoples rising for self-expression. Meanwhile the Christian Church, growing at first in secret, and strengthened by persecution, emerged victorious as the real successor of Rome. Constantine, by changing the capital in 330 A.D. to Byzantium, which he renamed Constantinople, cut the empire into two rather sharply divided parts, the east and the west. Let us note a few of the important movements in each.

The lands about the eastern Mediterranean had always been Hellenic rather than Roman at heart. In many places the traditions of the old civilizations, as of Egypt and of Babylonia-Assyria, were still dominant. Long before Christianity became officially the state religion, vigorous Christian communities began to flourish in Persia, Egypt, Asia Minor, and Syria, that great highway of war, commerce, and ideas. Under the stimulus of the new faith, brilliant creative work began in church-building, unhampered by the weakening of Roman power; but Constantinople, because of her wealth and prestige, became the point at which the various eastern influences coalesced with the Hellenic and Roman to form what is known as Byzantine art, or, as it has well been called, the Christian art of the East. In the reign of Justinian (527–565 A.D.) this art reached a climax, for Justinian, beside collecting and codifying Roman law, was a great builder and a patron of all the arts. His sumptuous court and magnificent churches are an epitome of the artistic endeavors and achievements of all these eastern peoples.

Not long after the reign of Justinian the rising power of Islam began sweeping eastward, carrying with it the decree forbidding the representation of the human or animal figure. The influence of this new power, together with the aversion of the early Christian to the representation of sacred subjects as being idolatrous, culminated in the iconoclastic controversy and gave great impetus to the use of naturalistic and geometric ornament.

In the western half of the empire there was a different picture. For centuries the barbarians had been threatening the Rhine and Danube frontiers and the decaying government could no longer hold out against the strong vitality of the north. On all sides the uncouth barbarians poured in, finally reaching Rome; and though they may have had some reverence for the magnificence they saw, with no capacity for appreciation they cared little for its maintenance. The *Colosseum* was merely a mine from the stones of which could be drilled out the iron clamp to tip the spear of a Goth. Both stimulus and ability for building or creating any kind of art ceased. The one power to hold firm was the Church, the earnestness and zeal of whose leaders laid the foundations for its supremacy in the Middle Ages.

Although the history of the two halves of the empire ran so differently, yet there were close relations between them. The establishment of the exarchate at Ravenna brought a flow of Byzantine work westward. Byzantine architects came to Italy at the summons of patrons whose land was no longer producing trained artists. The iconoclastic outbreak drove artists to Italy to seek employment; while pilgrims and traders brought with them such portable objects as enamels, ivories, manuscripts, and textiles. The virility of the creative work in the East, uninterrupted by such an upheaval as was experienced in the West, thus exerted a strong influence in Italy.

ARCHITECTURE

In Italy the emergence of Christianity from secrecy was an incentive to church building. Early churches divide into two classes according to structure — the basilica and the central type. FIG. 77 shows the plan of *Old Saint Peter's*. It is a rectangular building with an open colonnaded court in front, the atrium (E), which adjoins the covered court, or narthex (D); it has a central nave (A), a semicircular apse (C), side aisles (B), and a transverse aisle (F) inserted at right angles between the nave and the apse, projecting beyond the side walls, making the plan T-shape. The nave walls rest directly on columns (FIG. 78) and rise higher than the side walls. forming a clerestory that is pierced with windows, a method of lighting, the origin of which we saw in Egypt (PLS. 3 B and 11). A great wall space is thus left between the ground-floor colonnade and the windows. Both the nave and the aisles of such a basilica carried wooden roofs, but the apse was usually made of brick or stone.

The origin of the basilica is difficult to determine. In many respects it is close to the classical basilica, the name of which it carries; yet certain elements, such as the atrium and transverse aisle, seem to be derived from the Roman private house (FIG. 75) where the early congregations met in secret and the whole arrangement of which suited the liturgical needs of the service.

Sant' Apollinare Nuovo at Ravenna serves as a typical example of the basilica. Its structure is clear from the view of the exterior (PL. 57 E). The clerestory windows are now walled up, and only traces are left of the atrium. It is built coarsely of brick, has a wooden roof, for no longer were there skilled Roman builders to erect a vault, and except for the arcadings of the side walls, presents a barnlike, unadorned exterior. This very barrenness, however, is impressive, breathing a spirit of rugged frankness. The more so does this become by contrast, as we enter the building (PL. 57 F). The light was originally more subdued than it is now, softened as it filtered through the perforated marble screens that probably filled the win-

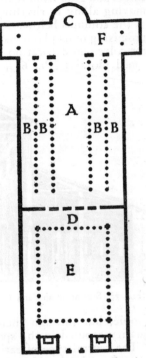

Fig. 77. Old Saint Peter's. Rome. 326 A.D. Destroyed to make way for the present cathedral. *A*, nave; *B*, aisles; *C*, apse; *D*, narthex; *E*, atrium; *F*, transverse aisle.

dows. The floor is paved with marble flags and along the nave runs a colonnade of marble columns with rudely cut acanthus capitals from which spring the arches that carry the nave walls. The old Roman buildings furnished columns for many an early Christian basilica when but few craftsmen were to be found who could use the chisel; and should one classical structure be unable to supply enough columns for a long basilica, a second would be stripped of its material with apparently little concern as to whether the capitals matched or not. The wall space above the columns and between the clerestory windows glows with rich colors and gold from which emerge figures — stately and hieratic, moving along in rhythmic order almost as purely architectural as the columns below. So while the builder left the exterior unpromising in its plainness, upon the interior he satisfied his taste for color and decoration by covering the walls with these rich-toned mosaics (PL. 61), which not only served to teach the

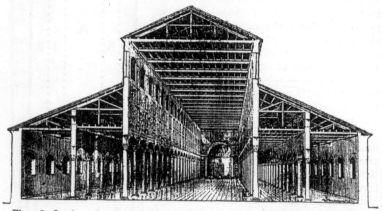

Fig. 78. Section of an Early Christian Basilica, Restored. (Dehio and Bezold)

people, but through their rich color and supremely decorative quality aroused in the spectator an emotion of deep solemnity.

The central type of early Christian church we find in its simplest form in the *Mausoleum of Galla Placidia* (PL. 58 A and B), which is built in the form of a Latin cross with a dome over the intersection of the two arms, concealed from the exterior view by a low rectangular tower. The exterior is barren, like *Sant' Apollinare Nuovo*, and unadorned except for the blind arcades and the dentils along the cornices, but the interior is entirely covered with rich mosaics except the lower part, which is faced with marble.

In the East, as we have said, the brilliant achievements of artists in various localities find a culminating expression in Constantinople and specifically in the church of *Santa Sophia* (PL. 58 C). A study of the ground plan (FIG. 79) reveals the fact that the building combines the feature of the domed central type with those of the basilica. The plan is rectangular, with side aisles separated from the nave by columns; there is an apse, a narthex (double here), and an atrium (now destroyed). The length of the nave necessitated the addition of half-domes to supplement the great central dome. The exterior is plain, the main feature being the great, low, lead-covered dome with its encircling windows, the half-domes, and the massive walls. Externally, except for the dome, the building is not interesting either for beauty of design, for technical finish, or decoration.

But as one enters (PL. 59A), he stands amazed at the wonderful spaciousness, noble and serene, and at the sumptuous decorations with their glowing color. The impression of spaciousness is obtained through the simple but daring design of the building, which consists of a harmonious arrangement of curved lines that sweep upward from the arcades of the ground story in ever increasing rhythmic curves until they meet in the great dome with its encircling windows, which seems to rest easily and lightly over the great nave. As for the decorations, let us listen to Procopius, a writer of the period, who says in describing the church, "The entire ceiling is covered with gold; but its beauty is even surpassed by the marbles which reflect back its splendor. One might think one had come to a meadow of flowers." And the poem of Paulus Silentiarius, court poet of Justinian, written to commemorate the dedication of the church, thus describes it:

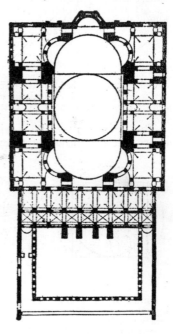

Fig. 79. Santa Sophia. Constantinople.

. . . About the center of the church, by the eastern and western half-circles, stand four mighty piers of stone, and from them spring great arches like the bow of Iris, four in all; and, as they rise slowly in the air, each separates from the other to which it was at first joined, and the spaces between them are filled with wondrous skill, for curved walls touch the arches on either side and spread over until they all unite above them. . . . The base of the dome is strongly fixed upon the great arches; . . . while above, the dome covers the church like the radiant heavens. . . .

Who shall describe the fields of marble gathered on the pavement and lofty walls of the church? Fresh green from Carystus, and many-colored Phrygian stone of rose and white, or deep red and silver; porphyry powdered with bright spots; emerald-green from Sparta, and Iassian marble with waving veins of blood-red and white; streaked red stone from Lydia, and crocus-colored marble from the hills of the Moors, and Celtic stone, like milk poured out on glittering black; the precious onyx like as if gold were shining through it, and the fresh green from the land of Atrax, in mingled contrast of shining surfaces.

The mason also has fitted together thin pieces of marble figuring intertwining tendrils bearing fruit and flowers, with here and there a bird sitting on the twigs. Such ornament as this surrounds the church above the columns. The capitals are carved with the barbed points of graceful acanthus all gilt; but the vaulting is covered over with many a little square of gold, from which the rays stream down and strike the eyes so that men can scarcely bear to look.[1]

The dome, as we have said, appears to rest lightly without effort, yet we know that it exerts a tremendous weight which is

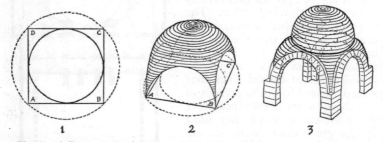

Fig. 80. A Dome on Pendentives. *ABCD* is the square area over which a dome is to be erected. If the diameter of the dome is equal to one side of the square, the area will not be covered; if it is equal to the diagonal of the square, the dome will project beyond the sides (1). The latter diameter was sometimes used and the sides of the dome cut off vertically so that the square was exactly covered; but the result was an imperfect dome (2). To secure a perfect dome the Byzantine builders conceived the idea of slicing this imperfect dome off horizontally just above the arches made by the vertical cutting, thus securing a circular base upon which to erect a true dome (3). The triangular segments of the original dome are the pendentives.

met by the massive piers that we noticed on the exterior. A dome so constructed (Fig. 80) is called a dome on pendentives, an appropriate name, for it appears to "hang" or "be suspended" in the air, as the root of the word denotes. Structurally it is very different from that of the *Pantheon* in Rome (Pl. 50c) which

[1] Lethaby, "Sancta Sophia, Constantinople," in the *Architectural Review*, XVII (1905), p. 122.

PLATE 59

(*A*) Santa Sophia. A contemporary poem, written to commemorate the rededication of the church on Christmas morning, 563 A.D., reads: "At last the holy morn had come and the great door ... ground on its opening hinges; and when the first beam of rosy-armed light, driving away the shadows, leaped from arch to arch, all the princes and people hymned their songs of praise and prayer, and it seemed as if the mighty arches were set in Heaven." (Drawing by J. B. Fulton in the *Architectural Review*)

(*B*) Santa Sophia. Carvings of capitals and spandrels Marble.

PLATE 60

(*A*) Frieze from Mschatta, a Palace in the Syrian Desert. H. 15 ft. IV–VI cent. A.D. Berlin (Berlin Museum)

(*B*) Joshua Before the Walls of Jericho. Detail from the Joshua Roll. V–VI cent. A.D. Vatican, Rome. (Muñoz)

PLATE 61

(A) Good Shepherd Mosaic. Mausoleum of Galla Placidia. C. 450 A.D. Ravenna. (Alinari)

(B) Apse of Sant' Apollinare in Classe. Mosaic. 534–38 A.D. Ravenna. (Alinari)

(C) Theodora and Her Attendants. Mosaic. Early VI cent. A.D. San Vitale, Ravenna. (Alinari)

PLATE 62

(A) Sarcophagus of Theodore. VII cent. A.D. Sant' Apollinare in Classe, Ravenna. (Alinari)

(B) Christ and Apostles. Fragment of a sarcophagus.
IV–V cent. A.D. Berlin. (Berlin Museum)

(C) Partly Ruined Enamel, Showing Depression and Frayed Cloisons. H. 4½ in. Metropolitan Museum, New York. (Metropolitan Museum)

rises directly from a circular drum. The problem of raising a dome over a square area by means of pendentives was solved brilliantly by the architects of the East and passed on by them to the West, where we meet it in *Saint Mark's* at Venice, the Romanesque churches of southern France, the great domed churches of the Renaissance such as *Saint Peter's*, and the domed buildings of modern times that have been patterned after this Roman cathedral.

Of the carvings that cover much of the stone work in *Santa Sophia*, the chief characteristic is the lacelike pattern, based chiefly on the acanthus leaf combined with other familiar classical motifs (PL. 59 B). It differs widely from the classical, however, in that it is surface carving only, almost in one plane; the under-cutting does not serve to model and give deep relief, but to provide a dark background against which the delicate pattern stands out.

This all-over carving appears to be eastern in origin. Evidence of this is apparent in the *Mschatta Frieze* (PL. 60 A). Richly carved moldings finish the edges of a long border that is decorated with a zigzag and rosettes, which, together with the entire background, are also luxuriantly carved with acanthus and vine scrolls in which are interwoven vases, animals, centaurs, and other fantastic beings. The centers of the rosettes have interesting adaptations of lotus, the pine cone, rosettes, and palmette motifs, so recurrent through the Valley of the Two Rivers. Here, as in *Santa Sophia*, the carving is done by means of drilling into the background and leaving the original flat surface cut into a pattern, rather than by undercutting and modeling with the chisel, leaving an uneven relief surface, as did the Greeks and Romans. The zigzag and rosettes give vitality and rhythm to the exquisitely delicate and fanciful all-over

Fig. 81. Byzantine Capital. Basket type.

pattern. It is like rich lace executed in stone, the decorative effect of which is superb.

Stone carving played a large part in early Christian and Byzantine ornament and was applied to capitals, screens, railings, and pulpits. Byzantine capitals (FIG. 81) appear to be derived from the classical Corinthian type, though they afford a great variety of detail. From the square abacus, the carver gradually merged his stone into the circular shape of the column and covered the surface with carvings — the basket type, because of its basket-like interlacings; the melon type in which the stone is cut in ridges like those of a melon; the wind-blown acanthus style, with its classical acanthus realistically swaying; or that with the interlaced circle motif which is so frequently found in medieval ornament (PL. 79 B). An entirely new feature, however, is the impost block, of much the same shape as the capital itself, inserted between the abacus and the springing of the arch. The purpose of this is not quite clear. It may have been to obtain greater height or to bring the weight of the arches directly upon the shaft, rather than on the outer edge of the abacus. Sometimes the impost block was richly carved; sometimes it bore simply a monogram (FIG. 81); and sometimes it was omitted, as in *Santa Sophia* (PL. 59 B). The stone railings afforded a large area for decoration. They were carved with patterns very much like those on the capitals; or with animals and birds in a balanced bilateral arrangement, a scheme of decoration that probably originated in the Near East (PL. 20 C and FIG. 40) and found great favor in all the arts (PLS. 62 A, 64 B and C, 68 A, 71 A).

PAINTING

The early Christian, before the emergence of the church from secrecy, decorated the walls of the catacombs with frescoes such as the decorative vine, which is an echo of the carved floral pattern so common in Roman ornamentation and was a favorite theme because of the frequent symbolic use of the vine in the New Testament; and also with figures, such as those representing brotherly love that are very close to the Pompeian frescoes of Cupids and Psyches in the *House of the Vettii*. In these frescoes we discern three important facts. First, there was no break in the classical tradition on the part of those who forsook the pagan faith; the early Christian painter took over what he found at hand and what had been a part of his environment. Second, he infused into it a new meaning, largely symbolical. And third, there began a rapid degeneration in the ability to represent form. The drawing is far below the Roman level; for, with mind intent upon teaching the Bible story, and with an antipathy to picturing the human figure, the artist disregarded entirely the aspect of man that had been the main concern of the Greeks and the

Romans — namely, human form. His drawing became, more and more, a symbol of the person rather than a naturalistic rendering of it.

In the miniatures of the illuminated manuscripts[2] we can best discern the characteristics and evolution of early Christian painting. An outline drawing from the *Joshua Roll*[3] shows something of the origin. Pl. 60 B reproduces a detail in which Joshua, near the walls of Jericho, is prostrating himself before the angel, in obedience to his command; in the lower right-hand corner is a female figure crowned with a tower, the personification of the city. The narrative element is lively, yet it is expressed with the same restraint that we see in the ivory angel (Pl. 63 A). Though the subject is Christian, the method of expression is Hellenic — the personification of the city, the naturalism of the figures, the way in which they fit into the landscape, and the fairly correct perspective in the architecture.

But soon the figures become flat and stiff; the landscape disappears or is highly schematic; and the background is filled with gold so that the whole picture forms a decoration that is richly ornamental. Under the influence of the Church and the monastery, which controlled much of the work, painting became conventional and stereotyped, for the artist was not left free to choose either his subject or his method of treatment. Both were prescribed in detail by the church in manuals[4] specifying which subjects should be represented in the different parts of the church; how the figures should be placed in relation to each other; the types to use for Christ or for the Virgin, with the form of face, hair, costume, and pose. Hence the similarity of type and composition quickly seen in all Byzantine painting. Such a procedure precluded any study of nature and insisted upon continual copying and recopying until the figures were so fixed in the mind that they could easily be reproduced from memory, with a consequent loss of imagination and spontaneity. The artist no longer saw with his eye but with his mind, which, bound by

[2] A miniature is a small picture that illustrates a manuscript, and is derived from the Latin verb *miniare*, to decorate with vermilion, for that was the color most popular with the painters; as the pictures were always small, the meaning has been extended to apply to anything small. To illuminate means to decorate with gold, silver, and bright color, especially the initial letters. An illuminated manuscript may or may not contain miniatures.

[3] This manuscript was originally a continuous roll thirty-two feet long and one foot wide, with pen-and-ink and color illustrations from the life of Joshua, which occupy most of the space, interspersed with the text in Greek. It has now been cut into sections and mounted for preservation. The manuscript belongs to the period when the long roll used by the Egyptians, Greeks, and Romans was being superceded by the codex, that is, a book made of separate pages bound together, the usual modern method. The change was probably due to practical considerations, for passages can be found much more readily in this form.

[4] For an interesting account of even a modern use of these manuals, see Crowninshield, *Mural Painting* (Boston, 1887), pp. 63 ff.

conventions, visualized abstractly. Though so narrowly restricted, the best artists nevertheless developed a wonderful technique and decorative quality, and imbued their patternlike figures with a mystical hieratic feeling. For when forms are but vaguely suggested by line without detail and without modeling, they become almost immaterial; and especially when the element of rich color and gold is added, they have a peculiar power of suggestion that is highly stimulating to religious emotion.

In the attainment of these two qualities — decoration and emotional feeling — the Byzantine mosaic workers were particularly successful.

The mosaics, after all, were nothing more than enlarged miniatures, executed in a different medium. By mosaic is meant a design worked out by means of small squares of colored glass or stone called tesserae, set in cement on a firm foundation. It is clear that, to carry out a design in this medium, the artist must make the drawing so simple that the form becomes almost a flat pattern, with sharp contours and little light and shade. It affords ample opportunity, however, for broad massing of color and for deep glowing tones, especially when gold is used liberally either on the surface or as a backing for the tesserae. With mosaic the early Christians decorated the great stretches of wall space in their churches. The *Good Shepherd* (PL. 61 A) was a favorite subject, for its symbolism was easily understood by the people. In the center the youthful Christ, in type like a classic Apollo and clad in royal purple, is seated on a hillside with rich vegetation; about his head is a large gold nimbus and in his left hand a golden cross. Scattered about, all looking toward him, are the sheep, one of which he lovingly caresses. The mosaic tells its story in an alluring way — in the kingdom of the *Good Shepherd* there is grace, abundance, and loving kindness. But from the point of view of decoration it is equally successful. The Good Shepherd holds the center of interest, toward which the lines of the landscape and the heads of the sheep lead. The landscape has been flattened out into practically one plane and tends to become schematic. This very flatness, the balanced though slightly varied design made by the sheep, the effective patterning of light and dark, and the deep rich color all contribute to make the lunette highly decorative.

The apse of *Sant' Apollinare in Classe* at Ravenna (PL. 61 B), like the *Good Shepherd* lunette, does not pretend to picture on the walls an illusion of nature, but to decorate the surface and at the same time to carry a message symbolically. Against the gold background is a great blue medallion, studded with gold stars and bearing a jeweled cross with a bust of Christ at the crossing of the arms; just above, the hand of God is seen issuing from the clouds, in which Moses and Elias are floating; below are three sheep looking upward. The scene symbolizes the transfiguration, the three sheep representing the three disciples who accompanied Christ to the foot of the mountain. Below, in the midst of green fields with trees, flowers, and birds, stands Sant' Apollinare with uplifted arms, accompanied by twelve sheep, forming, as they march in regular file across the apse, a wonderfully decorative base. The mysticism and grandeur of the conception, the austerity of the figures, and the splendor of deep color produce an emotion akin to that evoked by music.

Not only religious but historical subjects as well were pictured upon the walls in mosaic. In Pl. 61 c we see *Theodora*, the wife of Justinian, with her attendants, carrying a gold chalice for the performance of some ceremony, possibly in connection with the dedication of the church. She stands in front of a shell-niche with a nimbus about her head, is dressed in royal purple, richly embroidered, and wears a jeweled crown. The head has some of the individual characteristics of a portrait, with its slender neck, long nose, and thin lips. Her attendants also wear gorgeous robes and jewels. But under the straight folds there are no real bodies. As a matter of fact, the artist does not pretend to represent nature. The long stiff row is made up of gorgeous symbols of bodies highly decorative because of their very flatness, and because of the shimmer, throughout the design, of the rich colors of the embroideries and jewels.

SCULPTURE

Monumental sculpture was produced only to a very limited extent, because the statue in the round was even more closely akin to the graven images of the pagan than painting. In a rare example, the *Good Shepherd* of the Lateran Museum, we recognize an archaic Greek motif, imbued with a new significance. This again is a striking example of the continuity of the old tradition.

One of the chief expressions of sculpture we find in the sarcophagi. In some the surface is entirely covered with reliefs representing scenes from the Old and New Testaments, crowded together, one upon another, for the purpose of narration, with little regard for design or literary unity. Such a work is very close to the decadent sculpture that was being produced in the late

Roman empire. A different kind of sarcophagus is illustrated by the fragment seen in PL. 62 B. In an elaborate niche with spirally fluted columns stands the figure of Christ, as we know by the nimbus with the cross, always a symbol of divinity; on each side of the niche stands an apostle. The serenity and tranquil beauty of the figures, and the way in which the drapery falls in long sweeping folds, are very close to fourth-century Greek sculpture. The niche, however, with its elaborate decoration, drilled in flat relief, is eastern.

A third kind is represented by the *Sarcophagus of Theodore* (PL. 62 A). Here there is no crowded relief, in fact no figures, but frankly a piece of beautiful symmetrical decoration. In the center of the side is the sacred monogram[5] in a circle, facing which are two peacocks, symbols of eternity, and behind them scrolls of fruiting vines at which birds are pecking; on the lid are three wreaths enclosing sacred monograms and the inscription; rather plain moldings finish the edges.

MINOR ARTS

Great demands were made upon the craftsmen in this period both by the luxurious courts of the East and by the Church. Both needed fine silks for costumes and for hangings; jeweled ornaments; books, which, to suit current tastes, must be written in gold letters upon purple-tinted vellum or decorated with bright miniatures on gold grounds, and bound in gold, ivory, enamel, and jewels; vessels for the service, which must be of the finest material and workmanship to be worthy of the Church. Under such a patronage the minor arts flourished.

One of the most important was that of the ivory carver. For, as we have explained, sculpture as a major art practically did not exist. It was in this minor art that its tradition was carried on for a period of about eight hundred years until it again emerged to decorate the portals of the Christian churches. PL. 63 A reproduces one leaf of a consular diptych,[6] on which we see an angel standing in a niche at the top of a flight of steps, holding in his right hand an orb surmounted by a jeweled cross; in the left, a staff with a ball at each end. The arch, which is supported by fluted Corinthian columns, is carved with acanthus leaves

[5] This monogram consists of the first two letters in the Greek name of Christ, chi and rho; between the arms of the chi are the Greek letters alpha and omega, frequently used to symbolize the divinity of Christ. See PL. 78 A.

[6] A two-leaved book of ivory, carved on the outside and provided with wax for writing on the inside, like the classical writing tablets found in Pompeii. They were ordered by the consuls upon election, as gifts for friends and important officials — hence the name.

and encloses a shell on which rests a wreath tied with ribbon; in the center is a cross above an orb; the spandrels are decorated with acanthus leaves and rosettes; above is an inscription in Greek which reads in translation, "Receive this gift, and having learned the cause . . ."; the sentence probably was completed on the other leaf, which is lost. There is serenity and nobility in the figure, ease and grace in the drapery, and tranquil beauty in the face with its large eyes. The feet, to be sure, for some reason not clearly understood, awkwardly cover three steps. The craftmanship is superb. One notes the sure-handed carving, in this difficult medium, of the wings, the flutings, and other architectural details. In this ivory we see the serenity of Hellenic art linked with the rich ornamentation of the East.

A more pronounced influence of the East one observes in a bishop's chair called the *Throne of Maximian* (PL. 64 c), which is decorated on the front with five niches containing figures of Saint John the Baptist and four apostles, framed by richly carved borders. The niches are decorated with the shell pattern and spirally fluted columns very much like those on the sarcophagus in Berlin (PL. 62 B). The figures have markedly individual characteristics, varying in pose and drapery, and appear to have been studied from nature; and though they lack the serene beauty and refinement of the angel on the ivory leaf and the figure of Christ on the sarcophagus, they are akin to both. In the center of the border above the niches is a monogram, on each side of which are curving vines, intertwining peacocks, animals, and birds; in the lower border rampant lions flank a vase from which issue vines interspersed with figures; the side borders have a like motif. Both the motifs and the lacelike quality of the design, standing out flat against a dark background, are reminiscent of the *Mschatta Frieze* (PL. 60 A). Here again is the Hellenic figure work, augmented by the fantasy and rich decorative design of the East.

Although the effect of iconoclasm upon the ivory carvers was much the same as upon other branches of art, namely, to bring about a preference for secular subjects and naturalistic motifs of design, still sacred themes continued to furnish subject matter, as we see in the panel that represents *Christ Crowning Romanus and Eudocia* (PL. 63 B). In the center stands Christ upon a dome-shaped pedestal the base of which, like the dome of *Santa Sophia*, is pierced with windows. Christ is now a bearded man, not the Apollo-like youth of the *Good Shepherd* mosaic (PL. 61 A). With great benignity he places the crowns upon the heads of the emperor and empress, who stretch out their hands as if in acknowledgment of his sovereignty. The royal pair are dressed in rich ceremonial costumes that hang stiffly, quite different from the simple classical robe of Christ. To be sure, the perspective is not correct; the rich robes do not appear to cover real bodies. But this the carver was not pretending to accomplish. His aim was to express a thought symbolically; namely, that Christ consented to the rule of these two on earth while they acknowledged their allegiance to Him, the King of kings. The two represent the gorgeousness of the imperial court; He, the dignity and graciousness of the court of heaven. The design plays a large part in the expression of this feeling. The figure of Christ, forming the central axis, is placed higher than the other two, which stand in a perfect balancing on each side. As a group, they fit wonderfully into the shape of the panel with its curving top. The inscriptions fill the remaining space, for the Byzantine had a horror of vacancy. If this ivory were enlarged into a mosaic and enriched with color, it could hardly be surpassed for quiet impressiveness, both emotional and decorative. Color, however, it probably did have. Ivories were painted and gilded; for Byzantine art in all media, owing to strong influences from the Near East and to inherited traditions of polychromy, was an art of color.

Another craft, which through its technique is in harmony with the conventions of the period, is that of the enameler. Most of the Byzantine enamels are of the cloisonné type. The process of making these is as follows: First the design is outlined by soldering strips of paper-thin gold about a thirtieth of an inch wide, called cloisons, to a metal base usually gold. The cells formed by the cloisons (PL. 24 D) are then filled with enamel, that is, powdered glass of different colors, some luminous and some opaque. Then the whole plate is subjected to sufficient heat to fuse the glass on the metal. A second coat of enamel is sometimes added to fill any concavities, frequently covering the cloisons. This must be ground away until the surface becomes perfectly smooth, showing all the cloisons. If only part of the base is to be enameled, the design is depressed about a thirtieth of an inch by beating the gold into a mold in which the design has been cut in intaglio (PL. 62 c). This depression is filled up to the original surface by the cloisons and the enamel. The surface is not only smoothed off, but ground and polished to a glasslike finish, a very laborious process but one upon which depends much of the rich effect.

Because of the precious material used and the difficulty of the long, tedious process, the enamels were small and were used

PLATE 63

(*A*) Ivory Leaf of a Diptych. H. 16 in. IV cent. A.D. British Museum, London. (British Museum)

(*B*) Christ Crowning Romanus and Eudocia, Rulers at Constantinople. 1068–71 A.D. Ivory. Bibliothèque National, Paris. (Giraudon)

(*C*) Saint Peter. Enamel and gold plaque. D. 4 in. X cent. A.D. Metropolitan Museum, New York. (Metropolitan Museum)

(*D*) Halo of a Virgin. Enamel and gold. D. 4 in. X–XIII cent. A.D. Metropolitan Museum, New York. (Metropolitan Museum)

PLATE 64

(A) Chalice. XI cent. A.D. Treasury of San Marco, Venice. (Alinari)

(B) Silk Textile. VI–VII cent. A.D. Kunstgewerbe Museum, Berlin. (Lessing)

(C) Bishop's Chair Called the "Throne of Maximian." Wood, inlaid with ivory panels and borders. VI cent. A.D. Archiepiscopal Palace, Ravenna.

chiefly to adorn larger objects. To an even greater extent than with the mosaic worker, the enameler must reduce his design to its simplest terms, for the beauty of the finished product is dependent upon its line, pattern, and color. To attempt to represent the human figure in so difficult a medium is daring; for the technique requires not only utmost economy of line but, even within that, the greatest precision in placing the cloisons — a slight deviation, in the face for example, would bring about a ludicrous expression. Yet the Byzantine craftsman did not hesitate, as is seen in the plaque representing Saint Peter (PL. 63 c). With all its conventionality, a surprising amount of character has been expressed in the face framed by the white hair and beard.

Geometric design, however, is more suitable to this medium than the human figure, as we see in a halo (PL. 63 D) that probably encircled some virgin's head. Entwining bands of blue with white dots surround alternating patterns of a cross in a circle and a palmette design. The delicate colors playing through the gold are so massed that the result is an exquisite piece of harmonious color decoration. These enamels are so satisfactory because the Byzantine craftsman never overstepped the severe laws that govern the technique.

The application of enamel plaques to larger objects is illustrated by a chalice (PL. 64 A) made of sardonyx, mounted in silver and decorated with enamels, gilt, and pearls. It is finely shaped and reflects in its rich decorations the sumptuousness of the age.

Together with the ivories and enamels, textiles formed an important branch of the minor arts and proved very influential in the art of western Europe. In the early centuries of the Christian era, the Coptic textiles of Egypt show patterns in wool upon linen, sometimes woven directly in the garment or hanging, and sometimes on borders or medallions to be appliquéed, as in PL. 65 B, where the design is made up of a vine scroll, with leaves and fruit, at which birds are pecking, on a black ground. In both the plant and the bird form there is a fine underlying observation of nature; yet all the forms have been subordinated to the decorative scheme, so that the birds, the leaves, and the grapes have been flattened out, simplified, and so massed that they are splendidly adapted without crowding to fill the spaces made by the wave line of the stem. This same fundamental principle one observes in a hunter medallion (PL. 65 A), probably a Persian motif. In the center is a mounted horseman with a running hound, with no accessories of detail or landscape; in the corners of the square, in which this circle is inscribed, are knot patterns; the enclosing border is made of interlacing bands which form circles filled with lions, plants, and baskets of flowers. The forms at times are crude but expressed with great vigor, and with a lively sense of the decorative quality.

Silk fabrics, however, were the most important textile product of the East and were used for garments, hangings, vestments and furnishings, wrappings for the dead, and for the bones and other relics of numerous saints which must be shrouded in the finest material procurable. For several centuries before the time of Justinian, Persia had held a monopoly on the silk industry; she controlled not only the manufacture of these fabrics but the sale as well. Because of this oppression in the trade of an article much desired by the wealthy Byzantines, Justinian introduced the industry into the empire with the help of two monks, so the story goes, who smuggled the eggs of the silkworm out of China in hollow staves. PL. 64 B reproduces a silk textile of a repeated pattern formed of medallions with figure designs and flower-decorated borders; small circles containing a conventionalized floral design connect the medallions. The hunting scene of the medallions is frequently found on these stuffs and is evidently of Persian origin. Here a lion hunt is represented; the mounted horsemen with fluttering scarfs, armed with bows and arrows, are so arranged in the circle as to form a symmetrical balance; the lion and the horseman in each half are compactly grouped; so that while there is spirited action characteristic of the chase, the decorative design, as seen both in interesting pattern and in harmonious color, has been paramount in the mind of the weaver.

SUMMARY

To understand and appreciate early Christian and Byzantine art, we must first free our minds of the prejudice that a work of art must realistically give an illusion of nature; and, second, we must open-mindedly attempt to understand it in the light of the conditions that it reflects, and the purposes and limitations of the age. It is a complex art, a fusion of Greek, Roman, and Near Eastern elements that took on new aspects under a new environment. For example, the naturalism of Greek art in which it started became austere and schematic. Nature was lost sight of; imagination and spontaneity were smothered by conventions which became traditional. On the other hand it was always high-minded and noble. Its very austerity brought about a tranquil, somber mood. With its stately figures, its infinite depths of rich color, its sumptuousness, suggestive of the gold, jewels, and rich stuffs of the East, its keen sense of decoration — rarely has an art been so evocative of mystic and religious emotion.

BIBLIOGRAPHY

BREASTED, J. H., Oriental Forerunners of Byzantine Painting. Chicago, University of Chicago Press, 1924.

BRITISH MUSEUM, Ivory Carvings of the Christian Era, by O. M. Dalton. London, 1909.

—— ——, Pictorial postcards. Set XX: Ivories; XLI: Months' Occupations, from an English Calendar of 11th Century; XLII: Alphabet of Ornamental Initials, 12th Century Manuscripts; LVIII: Mediaeval Sports and Pastimes; LIX: Early Christian and Byzantine Antiquities.

—— ——, Reproductions from Illuminated Manuscripts. Series I–III. London, 1910.

CUNYNGHAME, H. H., European Enamels. N.Y., Putnam, 1906.

DALTON, O. M., Byzantine Art and Archaeology. Oxford, Clarendon Press, 1911.

HAMLIN, A. D. F., History of Ornament, Ancient and Medieval. N.Y., Century, 1921.

HARVARD UNIVERSITY, WILLIAM HAYES FOGG ART MUSEUM. Collection of Medieval and Renaissance Paintings. Cambridge, Harvard University Press, 1919.

JACKSON, T. G., Byzantine and Romanesque Architecture. Cambridge, University Press, 1913.

LETHABY, W. R., Mediaeval Art. N.Y., Scribner, 1904.

—— ——, AND SWAINSON, HAROLD, Church of Sancta Sophia, Constantinople. N.Y., Macmillan, 1894.

LOWRIE, WALTER, Monuments of the Early Church. N.Y., Macmillan, 1923.

MASKELL, ALFRED, Ivories. London, Methuen, 1905.

PORTER, A. K., Medieval Architecture. 2 v. New Haven, Yale University Press, 1912.

RICCI, CORRADO, Ravenna (tr. from the Italian). Bergamo, Istituto italiano d'arti grafiche, 1913.

SHOWERMAN, GRANT, Eternal Rome. New Haven, Yale University Press, 1924.

STRZYGOWSKI, JOSEF, Origin of Christian Church Art (tr. Dalton and Braunholtz). Oxford, Clarendon Press, 1923.

VICTORIA AND ALBERT MUSEUM, SOUTH KENSINGTON. Catalogue of Textiles from Burying-Grounds of Egypt: v. I, Graeco-Roman Period. London, 1920–22.

WARNER, G. F., Illuminated Manuscripts in The British Museum. London, 1899–1901.

CHAPTER XI

MOHAMMEDAN PERIOD

622 A.D. *to Date*

HISTORICAL BACKGROUND

When we think of the Mohammedans, we think not of a nation in the modern sense of the word, with sharply defined geographical boundaries, but of groups of people of varying traditions and culture, widespread geographically, but bound together by a burning and at times fanatical religious faith. The Mohammedans call this faith Islam, which means obedience to the will of Allah (God); and their creed is embodied in the prayer chanted by the muezzin from the minaret as he calls the faithful to worship: "God is great, God is great, God is great. I bear witness that there is no god but God. I bear witness that there is no god but God. I bear witness that Mohammed is the Apostle of God. I bear witness that Mohammed is the Apostle of God. Come to prayer. Come to prayer. Come to security. Come to security. God is great. God is great. There is no god but God." This religion, originating in Arabia, spread both east and west with amazing rapidity, chiefly by means of the sword; for the Mohammedan became an invincible soldier because of his fatalistic belief in the will of Allah, and because he was lured by the promise of immediate entrance into Paradise if he died upon the field of battle fighting for the Faith.

Because of geographic extent and lack of traditional unity, Mohammedan art has manifested itself in diverse ways, strongly affected by local traditions, sometimes merely grafting upon the native art a few of its requirements. At first the Mohammedan conquerors, having no arts of their own, did just what the Persians under Cyrus did when they conquered the older civilizations — adapted or borrowed what they found at hand. For example, when they conquered Constantinople, they converted the church of *Santa Sophia* into a mosque by merely inserting a niche, whitewashing the mosaics containing figure work, and erecting the minarets. Soon, however, they so transformed these

PLATE 65

(*A*) Coptic Textile. Tapestry woven in wools, chiefly purple. H. 12½ in. IV–V cent. A.D. Victoria and Albert Museum, London. (Victoria and Albert Museum)

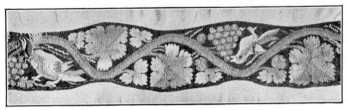

(*B*) Coptic Textile. Linen, with tapestry weaving in colored wools on black. W. 3¾ in. IV or V cent. A.D. Victoria and Albert Museum, London. (Victoria and Albert Museum)

(*C*) Mosque of Ibn Tulun. Court. Cairo. 876–78 A.D. The domed fountain is later. (Lekegian)

PLATE 66

(*A*) Mosque of Ibn Tulun. Arcades of the eastern end, with stucco borders. (Lekegian)

(*B*) Mosque of Sultan Hassan. Cairo. Court, looking toward the sanctuary. 1356–59 A.D.

(*C*) Tomb-Mosque of Sultan Kait Bey. Near Cairo. 1472–76 A.D.

(*D*) Alhambra. Hall of the Two Sisters, detail. Begun 1248 A.D. Granada.

adaptations with their own means of expression that Mohammedan art became a strikingly individual thing. Probably it is at
Cairo that this art reveals itself in its most refined and purest
form. Hence in this chapter we shall study chiefly the monuments
of that city.[1]

Egypt was a province of the Byzantine Empire at the time of
its conquest by the Mohammedans in 638 A.D., and was ruled by
governors appointed by the great Caliphates of Damascus or
Bagdad until a line of rulers threw off the domination of the
Caliph, and reached a golden age under the Mamelukes (1250–
1516 A.D.). These rulers were originally Tartar slaves in the employ
of the Caliphs and rose from servitude to become for nearly three
hundred years independent Moslem sovereigns of Egypt. Politically it was an age of intrigue and murder. The Mamelukes were
still barbarians and merciless cutthroats; rarely did a Mameluke
reign more than a few years, and very few died a natural death.
Yet the arts flourished with an amazing vigor and displayed a
rare and refined taste — one of the startling contrasts of history,
as Mr. Lane-Poole suggests.

Some of the outstanding characteristics of Moslem art were
due to the strict injunctions of the Koran, the bible of the Mohammedan, especially that which forbade any representation
of the human or other animate figure and thus turned the attention of the artists to the world of floral and geometric forms for
their motifs in decoration.

Against sumptuousness and license of all kinds the Koran
decreed puritanically. Yet these Mohammedans, particularly the
Mamelukes, with their oriental love of color, of fine silks,
jewels, and richly inlaid vessels, managed in various ways to
circumvent these decrees, so that their everyday life was that
fairy land of splendor of which we read in the Thousand and One
Nights. With great wealth at their command they adorned their
homes, and even their traveling tents of gold-shot silk, with
rich hangings, fine rugs, and at least a few exquisite utensils; and
clothed themselves in the most splendid apparel. In spite of
many fastings, prayers, and pilgrimages demanded by the Koran,
life was gay with festivals, feasts, and sports.[2]

ARCHITECTURE

Since the Mohammedan was fanatical in religious belief and
at the same time keenly zealous in the pursuit of pleasure, it is

[1] For other manifestations see the chapters on Persia and India.
[2] For a picture of Mohammedan life, see Lane-Poole, *Art of the Saracens in Egypt*, ch. 1.

natural to find his architecture devoted chiefly to the mosque and the palace. As far as worship was concerned, his needs were simple: a secluded place, away from the noise of the streets, where a fountain provided water for ablution, for he must bathe before going to worship, and a place protected from the hot sun, where, with face turned toward Mecca, he could pray. This direction was indicated to him by a niche in the wall of the mosque, beside which was a pulpit from which the Friday (the Mohammedan Sunday) sermon was preached; a little in front of these stood the raised platform from which the Koran was recited and prayers chanted. These constitute the sanctuary of a mosque (PL. 67 A).

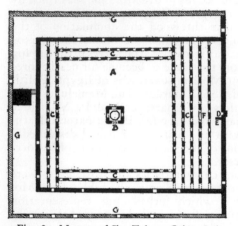

Fig. 82. Mosque of Ibn Tulun. Cairo. 876–878 A.D. *A*, court; *B*, fountain; *C*, covered arcades; *D*, niche (*mihrab*) indicating the direction of Mecca; *E*, pulpit (*mimbar*); *F*, tribune (*dikkeh*); *G*, girdle wall. The court is 300 ft. square.

The early cloistered mosque of *Ibn Tulun* (PL. 65 C and FIG. 82) adequately supplies these needs. It consists of a great open court with a fountain in the center, surrounded by covered arcades two deep on three sides but five deep on the sanctuary side, the special place of prayer, that is, the end facing toward Mecca; and a girdle wall, standing fifty feet outside the mosque walls on three sides, which gives the building added seclusion. The exterior presents a plain, massive wall with a row of small windows and simple unadorned doorways, the only decoration being a crenellated parapet. At one side rises the minaret, the tower from which the muezzin calls to prayer; it is rectangular, partaking of the same simple boldness and massiveness as the rest of the mosque. An external ramp provides a means of ascent, which carries the mind back to the ramp towers of old Babylonia (FIG. 39).[3] Entering the arcades (PL. 66 A) we see that the pointed arches supporting the flat roof rise from brick

[3] For the development of the ramp tower into the modern church steeple, see Breasted, *Ancient Times*, FIG. 272.

piers with engaged columns at the corners, covered with stucco, and decorated with floral borders worked by hand in the plaster when it was soft.

The mosque of *Sultan Hassan* is more complex in plan (FIG. 83). In the view of the court (PL. 66 B), the great sweep of the pointed arches by which the recesses open on the court is particularly noble and impos-ing. Because of the large amount of wall space, there is but little decoration. This is concentrated about the eastern recess, the sanctu-ary, and consists of inlays of colored marble and carv-ings about the niche and the pulpit, and a carved border with an inscription (PL. 69 A) at the spring-ing of the vault.

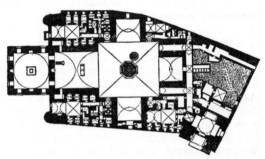

Fig. 83. Mosque of Sultan Hassan. Cairo. 1356–59 A.D. The angles formed by the recesses of the court are filled with rooms for schools, offices, and apartments for the attendants. The exterior of this mosque is built of stone from the Pyramids of Gizeh; the interior, except the great arches, of brick stuccoed. (Franz Pasha)

Smaller mosques enabled the builders to decorate more lavishly. This we see in the tomb-mosque of *Kait Bey* (PL. 66 C). That this is a tomb as well as a mosque we know from the presence of the dome that was used only to roof a mausoleum. Here the una-dorned simplicity and massiveness of *Ibn Tulun* and *Sultan Hassan* have given way to an effect of lightness and charm, with the em-phasis upon decoration. The tall arched portal is elaborately ornamented with carvings and stalactites; shallow recesses enclosing the windows break up the wall surface; the slender, graceful minaret, with projecting galleries from which stalac-tites depend, is ornamented with niches and carvings; the con-trasting dome with its virile sweep of line and its suggestion of simple mass is covered with arabesque carvings; the usual crenel-lation finishes the walls, for the overshadowing cornice rarely finds a place in Mohammedan architecture. These elements, however, do not combine to form so clear and harmonious a de-sign as we find in the Greek temple or in the Gothic cathedral.

The eastern arm or sanctuary of the mosque (PL. 67 A) opens

on the court with a pointed arch of alternating light and dark stone. The lines of the arch bend inward at its spring, making it horseshoe in form. The floor is paved with marble slabs, and the lower part of the walls is faced with variously colored marbles through which gleams mother-of-pearl; the niche is ornamented sumptuously with marble and mosaic and the pulpit with carvings; above, the wall is pierced with small windows of brilliantly colored glass; from the ceiling are suspended chains that originally held inlaid metal or enameled glass lamps. The impression of such a sanctuary with its subdued light is one of great richness of material and splendor of color.

Any study of Mohammedan mosques reveals the fact that the Moslem was not interested primarily in problems of structure. As far as climate was concerned, he needed protection from the sun; but the absence of rain and the marvelously preservative atmosphere enabled him to build rather shabbily as far as material and structure were concerned. Wood and plaster served him well. What interested him most was decoration; and this he concentrated at certain points, chiefly about the sanctuary and the portal, leaving the rest of the space, except in the smaller mosques, quite bare.

For this decoration he used chiefly plaster, stone, wood, ivory, marble inlay, and colored glass.

Plaster, used wet, was a particularly adaptable medium for the freely flowing line that distinguishes Mohammedan ornament; for here the hand could move more easily and more spontaneously than in carving in stone or wood. It appears in the earlier buildings, as we saw in the borders about the arches of the mosque of *Ibn Tulun* (PL. 66 A); but was replaced by stone or marble about the fourteenth century. The Kufic frieze[4] (PL. 69 A) that decorates the sanctuary of the mosque of *Sultan Hassan* well illustrates stone carving. The bold, angular character of the letters is particularly monumental and contrasts effectively with the delicate floral arabesques from which it emerges.

Though plaster and stone were used largely in architectural ornament and even occasionally for a pulpit, wood was the material most favored for decorating the furnishings of both mosques and palaces. It was not only carved but frequently inlaid with ivory and ebony. This is well illustrated by the mosque pulpit, which stands at the right of the niche, as one faces the sanctuary (PL. 67 A). It consists of a stairway, approached by a

[4] Kufic is the older form of Arabic writing, so called from the city of Kufa, where the best copyists lived, an early seat of the caliphate before the building of Bagdad; it is angular in form and thus differentiated from the cursive, flowing Neshky which supplanted it (PLS. 68 c and 69 A).

high door that leads to a small covered platform surmounted by a cupola. Elaborate decoration, geometric, floral, and stalactite, covers the surface. An obvious characteristic of the ornamentation is that it consists largely of small panels ingeniously fitted together. This was due, not to the impossibility of obtaining large pieces of wood or to any artistic criterion, but to climatic conditions; for, while the weather of Egypt has remarkable preservative qualities, yet the heat causes wood to shrink and warp; so that if the door or side of the pulpit is to hold together without cracking or loosening, allowance must be made for the contraction and expansion of the wood. This the craftsman learned to do by making his panel out of a large number of small pieces, lightly enough joined to allow for this change in size. The door of a pulpit (PL. 68 B) illustrates his method. Practically the entire surface is carved in low flat relief — floral arabesques with panels inserted for the inscriptions forming the border, and geometric arabesques in the doors, where the incisive angularity affords a happy contrast to the smoothly flowing line of the rest of the carving. This geometric pattern is made up of many small polygons, each carved in a floral design, and finished with a beading. Here we see ingenious and painstaking skill, together with fertility of invention in the infinitely varied way in which a few motifs are used.

A particularly rich and beautiful example of floral arabesque with inscriptions is the panel from a sheik's tomb (PL. 67 B), in which the carving is varied in motif and height of relief, and emphasized by the contrastingly unadorned moldings.

While the decree forbidding the use of human or animal figures was usually respected in Cairo, occasional exceptions occur, as in the panel from the *Hospital of Kalaun* (FIG. 84), where broadly sweeping lines intertwine and knot, now terminating in floral forms that fill the ground and now forming geometric areas that contain human, bird, animal, and griffin forms, all suggestive of the textiles of the Near East (PL. 68 A). In the large central medallion is a kneeling man carrying a slain deer on his shoulders; above him are two eagles in balanced position, and at the sides two cockatoos whose long sweeping tails harmonize with the curves of the scrolls; the four circular medallions are filled with griffin or deer on whose backs are eagles with outspread wings. Details are omitted and the forms flattened out, simplified, and pleasingly adapted to the curving lines of the geometric areas. Sure-handed technique in the carving and also appropriateness of design to the medium are evident. The all-over pattern that fills the panel is satisfying because the large units of design are clearly defined and the subordinate ones fill the ground adequately without overcrowding.

Fig. 84. Wood Panel. From the mosque-hospital of Sultan Kalaun, Cairo. 1284 A.D. (After Prisse d'Avennes)

Color and gilding played an important part in the ornament of the Mohammedan. Both stucco and wood carvings were vividly painted. Another method of obtaining color was by marble inlay and stained glass. Panels of variously colored marbles — red, yellow, black, green — perhaps combined with blue tile, or bordered with a geometric pattern of colored glass and mother-of-pearl, faced the sanctuary of the mosque or formed a dado around the palace room. A most brilliant effect of color came from the windows, which were made by filling a wooden frame with plaster about an inch thick, scooping out a pattern in the plaster while it was still soft and then filling in the perforations with bits of colored glass. In PL. 69 B the design consists of a palm tree with spreading branches that curve to fit into the arch in which it stands; below are plane trees and flowers. The process is very simple and crude in comparison with the leaded windows of the Gothic period (FIG. 96); but the harmonious masses of color when penetrated by the Egyptian sunshine are rich and jewel-like in their effect.

The Mohammedan palace reached its culmination in Spain in the *Alhambra*, which, like the typical Moslem house, was built about open courts. Here the emphasis is overwhelmingly upon decoration. The *Hall of the Two Sisters* (PL. 66 D) consists of a lofty apartment with a stalactite ceiling like a great honeycomb, surrounded by smaller rooms and balconies that overlook the courts and gardens. It was probably one of the private apartments of the Moorish kings. Around the base of the room runs a dado of glazed tile with geometric arabesques forming a deep-toned base above which rise bewildering, fairylike walls and ceilings. The entire surface is covered with arabesques and stalactites brightly colored, originally, in blue, red, yellow, and gold. Through the arabesques run inscriptions, an important motif of decoration. A typical one reads:

"How many delightful prospects I enfold! Prospects, in the contemplation of which a mind enlightened finds the gratification of its desire.
"Look upon this wonderful cupola, at sight of whose perfection all other domes must pale and disappear:
"To which the Constellation of the Twins extends the hand of salutation; and, for communion, the Full Moon deserts her station in the heavens.[5]

This stucco decoration is wrought by means of molds; hence it lacks the easy grace of the hand-wrought ornament found at Cairo. If profuse ornament that calls attention to itself is justifiable, the *Alhambra* is a remarkable revelation of that principle. The decoration is not merely haphazard; for it reveals a careful balance of line — horizontal, vertical, and curved — an effective interweaving of inscriptions, and an ingeniously varied use of geometric and floral motifs.

MINOR ARTS

In contrast with western practice, the Mohammedan needs but a few pieces of furniture for his house and but a few vessels for the embellishment of his mosque; but that little reveals both his love for the rich and sumptuous, and also his refined taste. Beautiful in itself and closely allied to the architectural carvings is the metal work of which a damascened bowl is typical (FIG. 85). Here as in the carvings and other crafts effective use is made of the Arabic calligraphy; for the chief band of decoration consists of an inscription in large letters, broken by rosettes which are made of a central whorl surrounded by a ring of flying ducks, a frequent motif in the metal work; a narrower band of scroll pattern, broken at intervals by whorls, separates the broad band from the diaper pattern with flowers and birds, on the bottom. Fre-

[5] Calvert, *Alhambra*, p. 70, where others also are quoted.

quently, in the vessels, the part of the copper or brass base not inlaid was covered with a black substance for a sharper contrast with the silver.

A craft practiced by the Mohammedans with effect was that of enameling glass. This is best seen in a mosque lamp (PL. 68 c). The glass of these lamps is blown, with many bubbles and streakings; the shape not as refined or subtle as that found in the glass and pottery of Greece, Italy, and China. The broad, tall neck tapers toward the rather squat body, which carries six loops or handles for the silver chains by which it was suspended to the beam or ceiling of the mosque. It is decorated with con-

Fig. 85. Brass Bowl. Inlaid with silver. The inscription reads: "His Excellency, generous, exalted, lordly, great Amir, wise, ruler, leonine, fighter for the Faith, warden of Islam (liegeman) of El-Melih En-Nasir" (a Mameluke ruler of the 14th century). British Museum, London.

centric bands of ornament, the two broad ones, like those on the metal bowl, containing inscriptions. That on the neck, from the Koran, is worked in blue enamel and broken by three medallions on a white ground; the one on the body of the lamp is also in blue with red edges on a gilt ground; the narrow bands contain arabesques and sexfoil medallions in blue, white, yellow, green, red, and gilt. Inside the lamp a small glass vessel, with the oil and wick, is hooked to the rim so that the light brings out the decorations with a rich soft glow. The effect of a considerable number of these lamps in such a sanctuary as that of *Kait Bey* must have been magnificent.

Another craft most successfully pursued was the writing and illuminating of manuscripts. We have spoken frequently of the

PLATE 67

(*A*) Tomb-Mosque of Kait Bey. Sanctuary, showing the pulpit (*mimbar*) and the niche (*mihrab*).

(*B*) Carved Wood Panel from the Tomb of a Sheikh.   Detail.   On the upper border and about the panels are inscriptions from the Koran and benedictions for the dead.   1216 A.D.   Victoria and Albert Museum, London.   (Victoria and Albert Museum)

PLATE 68

(*A*) Syrian (?) Silk Damask. Brocaded, partly with silver. XIII cent. A.D. Metropolitan Museum, New York. (Metropolitan Museum)

(*B*) Pulpit of Kait Bey. Door. Wood and ivory. H. 24 ft. Late XV cent. A.D. Victoria and Albert Museum, London. (Victoria and Albert Museum)

(*C*) Mosque Lamp. Enameled glass. H. 13 in. The inscription on the neck from the Koran reads, "In the house that God hath permitted to be raised for His name to be commemorated therein, men celebrate his praises morning (and evening)." XIV cent. A.D. Victoria and Albert Museum, London. (Victoria and Albert Museum)

Mohammedan's appreciation of the decorative effect of his calligraphy as shown by his constant use of it in all media. As with the Chinese, writing was a fine art. But illumination was reserved by the orthodox Moslem to adorn one book only, the *Koran* (PL. 69 c). The first and last two or three pages generally contain a richly decorated panel with the usual inscription, "Let none touch it save the purified," in Kufic letters, and a margined medallion. Frequently the text is written in gold letters. Vivid blue predominates with a little red and white, black or green to hold it, with a great deal of gold all through the design, "like sunshine on rippling seas." The splendor of the effect is perhaps equaled by the delicacy of the infinite detail, as intricate, though not as varied, as that found in the Celtic manuscripts (PL. 78 A).

We have spoken of the love of the Moslem princes for fine stuffs both for hangings and for apparel — damask, satin, silk, and the finest white cottons. Many cities in the Near East were famous for making these, such as Damascus, Bagdad, Rum in Anatolia, and Cairo. A fragment of silk, probably from Syria (PL. 68 A), is typical. Rows of eagles and gazelles are arranged in balanced position about a heart-shaped medallion, and all the intermediate space filled with floral ornament. The origin of the design, like the wood carving (FIG. 84), appears to be Sassanian. The effectiveness is due to the broad massing in the flat animal forms — what detail there is, is highly conventionalized — repeated in rhythmic order, contrasting with the more delicately designed ground that is reminiscent of the arabesques of the wood and stone carvers.

SUMMARY

Among the Mohammedans we find an art with unusually narrow restrictions. In their buildings, structural problems interested them but little, for they adapted what they found already worked out. Yet their mosques and palaces form a class peculiarly their own, suitable for a semi-tropical climate and distinctly rich in their color and decoration. There is a conspicuous absence of pictures and sculpture, and practically no figure or animal representation. In place of these are delicate carvings of stone, stucco, wood, and ivory or marble inlay, rich stuffs, fine rugs, brilliantly colored glass, and shining silver. Everywhere is line, pattern, and color. The minor arts are inextricably interwoven with the major not only in creating the ensemble but in the interchange of ideas and motifs; for the geometric inlay on the helmet finds its way to the carvings of the dome; the stone or stucco carved band on the mosque, to the pages of a Koran; and the textile design, to the silver inlay of a bowl The very restrictions of this art, however, seem to be responsible for its particular bent. For with concentration upon decoration, which appeared to be his chief interest, and that, too, dependent upon a few fundamental geometric and floral motifs, the Moslem created an endless variety of carvings, now the angular geometric pattern, now the smoothly flowing, intricate arabesque. But, in the best period, each work, no matter what the medium, is apparently a fresh and vital creation, displaying, in spite of narrow bounds, great inventiveness and amazing exuberance.

BIBLIOGRAPHY

BRIGGS, M. S., Mohammedan Architecture. Oxford, Clarendon Press, 1924.
BRITISH MUSEUM, Pictorial postcards. Set XVIII: Saracenic Metal-Work.
CALVERT, A. F., Alhambra. N.Y., Lane, 1907.
—— ——, Moorish Remains in Spain. N.Y., Lane, 1906.
FAURE, ELIE, History of Art: v. II, Mediaeval Art (tr. Pach). N.Y., Harper, 1922.
FLETCHER, SIR BANISTER, History of Architecture on the Comparative Method. N.Y., Scribner, 1924.
GLAZIER, RICHARD, Manual of Historic Ornament. London, Batsford, 1914.
KIMBALL, FISKE, AND EDGELL, G. H., History of Architecture. N.Y., Harper, 1918.
LANE, E. W., Account of the Manners and Customs of the Modern Egyptians. N.Y., Ward, 1890.
LANE-POOLE, STANLEY, Art of the Saracens in Egypt. London, Chapman, 1886.
MIGEON, GASTON, L'Orient musulman, 2 v. Musée du Louvre, Paris, Morancé, 1922.
PASHA, FRANZ, "Buildings of the Mohammedans." Baedeker's Egypt, Chap. IX. N.Y., Scribner, 1908.
RIVOIRA, G. T., Moslem Architecture (tr. Rushforth). London, Oxford University Press, 1918.
STATHAM, H. H., A Short Critical History of Architecture. N.Y., Scribner, 1912.

CHAPTER XII
PERSIAN PERIOD
226–1736 A.D.

A. SASSANIAN–PERSIAN
226–641 A.D.

HISTORICAL BACKGROUND

In the third century A.D. a new power had arisen in Persia, the Sassanian, so called from the chieftain Sassan, one of a line of Persian princes who had lived in a more secluded part of the southern Iranian plateaus and had maintained the old traditions of the race. Just as Cyrus the Great in the early days of Persia had overthrown the Median power, so Sassan vanquished the Parthian kings, secured control of all Persia, and brought about a revival of Iranian culture, especially the ancestral faith of Zoroaster. Of this line of kings the greatest was Chosroes I (531–579 A.D.), who established his capital at Ctesiphon, and was building his palace there at about the same time that Justinian was building *Santa Sophia* at Constantinople. Chosroes was a great patron of the arts and encouraged all workers in the crafts, particularly the weavers of fine silk textiles which were in demand by the luxurious Byzantine court and, through their introduction into the West, became a strong influence in the evolution of European ornament. When Justinian, in his zeal to propagate the Christian faith, closed the pagan schools of Athens, the artists and scholars fled to the court of Chosroes, carrying with them the classical traditions and learning so that the Sassanian court was one of the broadest and most enlightened of the Near East. But, notwithstanding its power and vigor, this empire was short-lived, for it was one of the first to fall before the Moslem invaders (641 A.D.).

ARCHITECTURE AND SCULPTURE

In architecture, the Sassanian looked to the older civilizations of the Valley of the Two Rivers rather than to the columnar Greek style that had entered this part of the East through the conquests of Alexander the Great and had survived under the rule of the Romans and Parthians. Hence in Chosroes' *Palace at Ctesiphon* (PL. 70 A), we see the arched buildings of Babylonia and Assyria. Most impressive, and highly suggestive of the vitality and power of the Sassanian, are the great dominating arch and elliptical barrel vault of brick. The façade is decorated with engaged columns and blind arcadings, which do not follow the superposed arrangement of the Roman style, but show a striking irregularity in the stories that reveals an unhampered versatility.

The same monumental vigor and largeness of design distinguish the best Sassanian sculpture that has survived, as illustrated by the rock-cut equestrian statue of *Chosroes II* (590–628 A.D.) at Tak-i Bostan, a villa near the modern Kermanshah that was a famous park in Sassanian times. Here, in an arched recess cut in a rock at the base of a cliff which borders a small lake, is the statue of Chosroes. His charger Shabdiz (a name meaning "black as night") is heavily caparisoned, and the rider clothed in armor. Though the statue has been badly mutilated by the Moslems, it still is monumental in spirit. A detail from this statue (PL. 70 B) illustrates both the virility of Sassanian design and also a popular decorative motif, the winged griffin enclosed in a circle. The power of the drawing and the adaptation of the figure to the space are characteristic. The truthfulness of this representation in stone of a textile design is proved by the existence of silk fabrics identical in pattern.

MINOR ARTS

Weaving, we have said, reached a high stage of accomplishment. The silk-weaving craft had made its way westward from China and became a flourishing industry in Persia, where the craftsmen wove fabrics not only for home use but for Europe as well; and so popular were these designs that they were imitated in the West throughout the Middle Ages. An all-over pattern based upon large medallions connected by small ones is a distinctive feature of these stuffs. In PL. 71 A the hunter motif appears. Two kings on winged horses, arranged with perfect bilateral balancing, are holding aloft the cubs of the lioness that they have been hunting. The forms of all the figures are so highly generalized that they have become decorative patterns splendidly adapted to the circular space. The astounding amount of vigor in the forms and the highly simplified drawing necessary for a successful textile pattern are harmonized with extraordinary skill in the Sassanian fabrics.

PLATE 69

(A) Stone Carving. Arabesque with Kufic inscription. Sanctuary of the Mosque of Sultan Hassan.

(B) Window. Stucco and glass. H. 30 in. Victoria and Albert Museum, London. (Victoria and Albert Museum)

(C) Illuminated Page from a Koran. 1368–88 A.D. Khedivial Library, Cairo. (Moritz)

PLATE 70

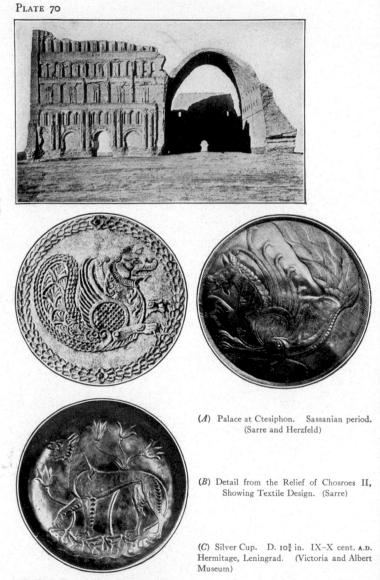

(*A*) Palace at Ctesiphon. Sassanian period. (Sarre and Herzfeld)

(*B*) Detail from the Relief of Chosroes II, Showing Textile Design. (Sarre)

(*C*) Silver Cup. D. 10¾ in. IX–X cent. A.D. Hermitage, Leningrad. (Victoria and Albert Museum)

(*D*) Silver Cup. D. 10 in. IX–X cent. A.D. Bibliothèque National, Paris. (Giraudon)

Another flourishing craft was that of the silversmith. Probably the traditions of the metal worker had never been lost in this land from earliest times when the craftsmen attained such skill as we saw in the silver vase of Babylonia (FIG. 40), and the armlet of ancient Persia (PL. 24 D). In the winged griffin, usually in a circle, one quickly discerns a similarity of motif in both the textiles and metal. In the early work it is simple and particularly vigorous; as time passes, it acquires more elaboration, elegance, and ease of line, as in the shallow cup with a plumed griffin (PL. 70 C). Grace and facility of line are seen also in another silver cup (PL. 70 D), which is decorated with a lithe animal walking along the banks of a river, indicated by swirling lines, from which rise lotus flowers to fill the vacant spaces. Here is the fierce Assyrian animal, with sharp claws and snarling face. There is not only a feeling for the animal form, but a sure-handedness in the lines that indicates a skill born of long training. The characteristic Sassanian vigor is still felt here; but added to it is a certain elegance, and an ease and suavity of curve in both the animal and the floral forms that place these cups late in the Sassanian period, if not somewhat after it. The design of both cups, regarded as adaptation of figures to a circular space, is admirably composed; it is free from a feeling of overcrowding, and the sweep of line flows into the curve of the construction line of the cup.

SUMMARY

There is little extant material by which to judge Sassanian work; but in what there is we perceive a vitality and exuberance that manifest themselves in the grandeur and monumentality of the *Palace at Ctesiphon*, and in a delight in the animal form, which is probably a heritage from ancient times, though its expression is more imaginative and fantastic, and which is used decoratively with a sound sense of design. Although the political life of Sassanian Persia was short, the influence of its art was far-reaching; for we find it as far east as India and China, and as far west as Italy, France, and Spain, where it not only dominated textile designs, but found its way to the carvings that decorated the cathedrals.

B. MOHAMMEDAN–PERSIAN

641–1736 A.D.

HISTORICAL BACKGROUND

The kingdom of the Sassanids was short-lived because of the invincible fighting power of the Moslems, who swept eastward in their conquests in the seventh century, and in 762 A.D. established Bagdad as the seat of the Caliphate. For a time the Moslem rulers remained orthodox and were strong enough to enforce the Mohammedan restriction regarding the representation of human and animal figures; but soon they became lax, for the Caliphs often were mere puppets in the hands of native rulers and so came under the sway of local associations and traditions. Bagdad became the seat of a gorgeous and pleasure-loving court, the famed city of the Thousand and One Nights. This was the age of Firdousi (940–1020 A.D.) the great epic poet who gathered together the heroic legends of the Iranian people into the *Shahnama* or Book of Kings, the greatest hero of which is Rustam; of Nizami (1141–1203 A.D.), the famous romantic poet of Persia (PL. 71 c); and of Omar Khayyam (d. 1123 A.D.), who took, for the setting of his themes, the luxurious, pleasure-seeking aspect of life.

Meantime the Mongols, or Tartars, who had been moving westward under Jenghiz Khan (1162–1227 A.D.), captured Bagdad in 1258 A.D., and came to the throne bringing with them the traditions of China. Thus Persia has been the melting-pot of many influences which have centered there in the wake of conquering armies. First were the old Babylonian-Assyrian and Persian cultures with a strong admixture of Egyptian; to this was added, through the conquests of Alexander and the Parthian empire, the classical and its descendant the Byzantine; the Sassanians revived the old Iranian traditions, to which the Moslem brought the Mohammedan element, and the Mongol, the Chinese. The Mongol rulers of the late thirteenth and early fourteenth centuries became converted to Islam and definitely established the faith. The dominating personality of the late fourteenth centuries was Timur (Tamerlane) who founded the dynasty of the Timurids (1395–1499 A.D.). This was a period of prosperity and wealth. The Timurids were great art lovers and under their patronage were produced the finest books, carpets, and armor. After an upheaval the Safawid dynasty came to the throne (1499–1736 A.D.) reaching its climax in the rule of the

Shah Abbas, another great art patron. But already there had crept in the overelegance and easy grace that marked the coming of the decline.

ARCHITECTURE

To the west [of Persia], in the upper regions which border the central desert, high above the dust, three thousand meters above sea level, and thus so much nearer the stars, the air has the transparence, the limpidity of glass. In the breath of the wind the white meadows and the pink meadows there are mottled like watered silk, and from spring to autumn the broad strips of poppies and the fields of grain run the gamut of all the uncertain color tones, from tender green to golden yellow. The skies, where the pigeons fly, and the clouds have those delicate tints that one can observe in the earliest blossoming of trees. The cities are deluged with roses.

When one approaches them their assemblies of domes, ovoid, swelling, or twisted, and their long, straight minarets that emerge from the groves of cypresses and plane trees, seem like memories already blurred by uncertainty. In turquoise blues, burnt-out pinks, pale greens, and dulled yellows the mirage has taken on the appearance of an aërial water color painted with vapor on the fleeing horizon that is known to artists who have followed the path of the caravans from oasis to oasis. . . . The enamel that clothes them, the old Chaldean enamel that ancient Persia had made known to China and that China brought back to Iran by Tartar hordes — the enamel has kept its glossy brilliancy under the coating of silicate that covers the brick. Violets, blues, and browns, ivory whites, lilacs, yellows, and greens, shine in these enamels, pure or in combinations that make rose bushes and anemone or iris flowers over white inscriptions and arabesques of gold.[1]

The imperial *Mosque of Ispahan* (PL. 71 B) illustrates this description. From a group of subsidiary cloisterlike buildings and courtyards with gardens and fountains, rises the mosque, the dominating feature. In its façade one sees the vigorous bold design of *Ctesiphon* made more slender and graceful. Arch, dome, and minaret are effectively combined to produce a design of simple directness and balance. The lofty recessed arch nearly fills the enclosing rectangle and carries the eye to the dome with the help of the minarets that also add lightness and balance to the design. Except for the arch, the façade is unbroken by cornice or molding; colored glazed tiles cover the entire surface and produce the same brilliant color harmony as did the *Palace at Khorsabad* (PL. 22 A) and the *Ishtar Gate* (FIG. 42) of which the *Mosque of Ispahan* is a descendant.

PAINTING

The best Persian painting consists of miniatures. The Persian rulers were great lovers of fine books and spared neither time nor money to obtain a copy of Firdousi's *Shahnama*, for example, penned by an accomplished calligrapher and illustrated by such

[1] Elie Faure, *History of Art:* v. 2, "Mediaeval Art," p. 248.

a painter as Bihzad (fl. c. 1500 A.D.) or Agha Mirak (fl. first half XVI cent. A.D.). In the early days of the caliphate, before Bagdad was founded, splendid copies of the *Koran* were written in the monumental Kufic calligraphy by the famous copyists of Kufa. But the popular books of the Timurids and Safawids, the truly Persian books, were secular, such as the poems of Firdousi and Nizami. Although these rulers were Moslems, their lax orthodoxy, together with influences from China, brought about a revival of figure art, so that the gay scenes of their life of pleasure — the hunt, the battle, the feast, flowers, music, and romance — fill the pages of their books. As one looks at them, he feels the joy, the luxury, the splendor, and the fleeting happiness of Omar. The cool gardens with fruit trees always blossoming and tall slender palm trees waving gently against the blue sky; the palace or mosque that gleams with enamel-like walls of lustrous faïence; or the rocky hillsides where the hunters or warriors dash by on slender horses — these form the setting for these tales.

From one of Nizami's romantic poems is the *Laila and Majnun* (PL. 71 c). The scene represents a school, which is apparently in a mosque. Seated on a rug is the turbaned priest, the teacher, lash in hand, listening to a youth reading; round him are other youths studying, all seated on their knees and heels or with one knee raised, the customary sitting posture in the East; here and there are the cross-legged book rests; in the foreground one boy is pulling his companion's ear, and at the left, near the large water jar, two are playing ball. In the middle distance are the lovers Laila and Majnun, each so obviously aware of the other's presence that the lessons are entirely forgotten and their heads droop piteously. There is a good deal of vivacity in the narrative element. The figures are drawn expressively with delicate, flowing lines; but they are flat, with no chiaroscuro, and with but a hint of perspective; the tiles in the court and the rugs on the floor appear to be hanging vertically. The painting is conceived from the point of view not of natural appearance but of decoration and color harmony. To this end the tones are kept bright and clear. The decorative quality of the miniature is emphasized by the broad margins of the page, which is tinted pale blue and flecked all over with gold. The opposite page of the book is designed to harmonize with the illustrated page, for the area containing the writing is equal to that of the miniature and the margins are of the same gold-flecked pale blue. The writing, a beautiful example of the Arabic script, is the work of a famous

PLATE 71

(*A*) Silk Textile. c. 600 A.D. Kunstge
werbe Museum, Berlin. (Lessing)

(*B*) Imperial Mosque. Ispahan.
1612–28 A.D. (Coste)

(*D*) Ewer. Brass inlaid with silver.
H. 11 in. 1232 A.D. British Museum,
London. (British Museum)

(*C*) Agha Mirak. Laila and Majnun. XVI cent.
A.D. Metropolitan Museum, New York. (Metropolitan Museum)

PLATE 72

(*A*) Carpet Loom from Persia. H. 5 ft.
Victoria and Albert Museum, London.
(Victoria and Albert Museum)

(*B*) Rhages Bowl. XIII cent. A.D.
Metropolitan Museum, New York.
(Metropolitan Museum)

(*C*) Wool Animal Rug. Detail. c. 1520–30 A.D. Metropolitan Museum,
New York. (Metropolitan Museum)

calligrapher who says in the colophon that the book was "finished with God's help by the hand of the poor and obscure Sultan Muhammed Nur."

MINOR ARTS

As we have said, the tradition of the metal worker is very old in the Valley of the Two Rivers and appears never to have ceased in spite of the rise and fall of dynasties and the changing ideas that influenced all aspects of life. In the twelfth and thirteenth centuries, after a period of suppression at the hands of orthodox Moslems, there appears to have been a revival of this work, probably due to the coming of the Tartars, who, though converted to Islam, still held but slight regard for its decrees. The center of the craft was at Mosul, from which it spread to other localities, appearing in Egypt in such a work as the brass bowl (Fig. 85), in which inscriptions and arabesques furnished the motifs of decoration. In the Mosul products, however, figure work is an important element, as we see in a ewer (Pl. 71 d). Here the figures, representing hunting and feasting scenes, are of silver and are enclosed in medallions on the neck and on the body of the vessel, while in the narrower band contending groups of men, animals, and birds are broken by octagons filled with the key pattern, which also forms the background of the medallions. This figure work gave an opportunity for fine chasing; for after the silver plate forming the silhouette of the figure had been inlaid, details such as the features, the lines of the drapery, the plumage of the birds, and the manes of the horses were indicated by the delicate strokes of the engraving tool. The effect of the contrasting metals and the delicacy of the chasing is one of rich splendor.

The potter was not so restricted as the metal worker or weaver by the technical processes of his craft. Hence in his jars and bowls we find a freer and perhaps the most characteristic expression of the freshness and exuberance of Persian art. The frequently coarse or ill prepared base, the hasty, sketchy drawing with ragged contours, the bold shapes that lack the subtlety of Greek or Chinese proportion — these very characteristics show that the craftsman was working toward one end and nothing else mattered; and that end was to create a certain effect from the imaginative and decorative quality of his motifs and from the brilliance of his color harmonies. *Rhages* pottery[2] probably best illustrates

[2] So called from the city of Rhages, near Teheran, a great center of pottery-making, and one of the most splendid cities of Persia before its destruction by Jenghis Khan early in the thirteenth century.

these qualities. The bowl reproduced in PL. 72 B has a turquoise ground upon which the figures are painted with apparent haste and indifference in dull blue and red, and touched here and there with gold; about the rim is a Kufic inscription. For the potter realized as well as the metal worker the decorative possibilities of this calligraphy. On the outside of the bowl in a cursive hand runs the inscription: "Glory, triumph, power and happiness, generosity and safety to the owner." Many of the jars and plates have a creamy glaze with decorations in a soft brown that has a peculiarly fleeting charm when covered with a transparent luster.[3] For when viewed at a certain angle there appears an iridescence of violet, dull gold, and copper. Move slightly and the sparkling color disappears. Thus it produces a subtle, evanescent form of decoration that is highly suggestive of the joy of the passing hour. Always in these vases there is decorative fitness in motif and spacing, always brilliancy and purity of color — turquoise, lapis lazuli and creamy white, sometimes combined with black or heightened by a touch of gold; or pale brown that is particularly alluring when enhanced by occasional flashes of metallic luster. There is none of the sobriety of Egypt or China, or of the intellectuality of Greece, but rather the restless joy of Minoan art. With this spirit the rapid and sketchy effect is much more in harmony than would be careful, precise drawing and technique. Delight in the happiness of the present hour that is so characteristic of Persian life well expresses itself in the sparkling, fleeting, and evanescent beauty of the luster vases.

Richness of effect through masterly design and a superb sense of color harmony are found in the Persian carpets, of which the *Ardebil Rug* (PL. 73 A) is typical. In this carpet the effective massing of large elements of design is enhanced by a wealth of detail that is kept subordinate. These main elements are the single unifying tone of the field, the central and corner medallions, and the finishing borders. The field is a rich blue and is covered with large and small flowers and leaves attached to a framework of delicate stems which weave a spiral design over all the field; the central medallion is of yellow, surrounded by small oval-shaped panels of yellow, red, and green, from one of which is suspended a mosque lamp; quarter-sections of this medallion group fill the corners; the broad border has alternating oblong and eight-foil medallions of red and yellow on a deep purple ground; the narrow borders make a happy transition from field to border.

---

[3] Luster is a very thin, transparent, metallic film added after the vessel has been glazed and decorated; it is then fired again at a low temperature.

Freedom from mechanical hardness of pattern, which characterizes modern machine-made carpets, and the rich, soft colors
were secured through the careful, painstaking process by which
these rugs were made. Rug-weaving was an inherited craft
among the Persian peasants, attained through generations of
effort. Many a pattern, or perhaps the secret of making a particularly fine dye, was handed down from father to son. The wool
was obtained from the sheep which grazed on the mountain sides
of this rugged country; and the dyes, few in number, from plant
life. The loom was primitive (PL. 72 A). When the warp had
been strung — and this required great skill, for just enough slack
must be allowed for what the weaving would take up — the
weaver would sit down on the ground with his work and begin

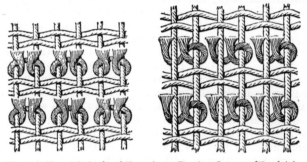

Fig. 86. Two Methods of Knotting a Persian Carpet. (Kendrick
and Tattersall)

putting in a horizontal row of knots (FIG. 86); then one or two
lines of weft, pressing it down firmly with a comblike implement
when he had woven several rows. Thus he continued putting in
rows of knots and weft, varying his color according to his pattern.
As the knots were of uneven length, the surface was cut, leaving
an even pile that concealed both the warp and the weft. Some
of the finest rugs have more than three hundred knots to the
square inch. The process was very slow. It has been estimated
that it would take a skilled worker about twenty-four years to
make the *Ardebil Rug*. In this kind of weaving irregularities and
blurred outlines are inevitable. But these are an inherent element
of charm.

In the *Ardebil Rug* there are no human or animal figures; but
another rug (PL. 72 c) from the same place illustrates how these
weavers used the animal form. Lions and other animals are

attacking spotted gazelles, while boars are running rapidly away; other animals, peonies, and various flowers fill the field. All these forms, whether flora or fauna, are simplified and flattened out, as it were. As we saw in the pottery, the designer has selected and used form in its decorative aspect only, adapting and massing his shapes and colors so as to secure interesting pattern and color harmony. For this reason the Persian rugs are primarily decorative and ornament the floor or wall as much as the finest Gothic tapestries and windows, for both are made on the same basic principles.

SUMMARY

Persian art in all its manifestations — the mosque, the rug, the illuminated page, the *Rhages* bowl, the inlaid metal — reveals its delight in the massing of color to obtain brilliant harmonious effects. It is not interested in producing an illusion of nature, or in the significance of form as the expression of physical or spiritual values; but it delights in the flat pattern suggested by the human, animal, or plant form and seen as an element of decorative power. We feel this in the hastily sketched figures on the pottery, in the silhouettes of the slender-legged horses that dash across the page of the manuscript, in the flat swaying palm trees, in the infinitely varied flowers of the rugs, and in the inscriptions of silver that shine forth from the dark metal ground. Nor are there, in this art, profound abstract expressions. It is rather a frank reflection of a life of luxury, splendor, and romance, delighting in the pleasures of the present, lively, joyous, worldly, and transitory. It is the spirit of Omar Khayyam expressed by the potter, the painter, and the metal worker. From China, from Byzantine lands, and from Moslem Egypt had come ideas that mingled with the Iranian traditions; and out of the fusion arose this art, as dazzling and as rich in color harmony as the barbaric splendor of Bagdad itself.

BIBLIOGRAPHY

BODE, WILHELM, AND KUEHNEL, ERNST, Antique Rugs from the Near East (tr. Riefstahl). N.Y., Weyhe, 1922.
BRITISH MUSEUM, Pictorial postcards. Set XVIII: Saracenic Metal Work; C7: Persian Paintings; C9: Persian and Indian Paintings.
—— ——, Encyclopædia Britannica (11th ed.), Ceramics.
FAURE, ELIE, History of Art. v. II. Mediæval Art (tr. Pach). N.Y., Harper, 1922.
FLETCHER, SIR BANISTER, History of Architecture on the Comparative Method. N.Y., Scribner, 1924.
GLAZIER, RICHARD, Manual of Historic Ornament. London, Batsford, 1914.

HANNOVER, EMIL, Pottery and Porcelain. 3 v. London, Benn, 1925.

JACKSON, A. V. W., Persia, Past and Present. N.Y., Macmillan, 1909.

KENDRICK, A. F., AND TATTERSALL, C. E. C., Handwoven Carpets, Oriental and European. London, Benn, 1922.

KIMBALL, FISKE, AND EDGELL, G. H., History of Architecture. N.Y., Harper, 1918.

MARTIN, F. R., Miniature Painting and Painters of Persia, India and Turkey. London, Quaritch, 1912.

MEYER, EDUARD, Persia. N.Y., Encyclopædia Britannica Co., 1911.

PIER, G. C., Pottery of the Near East. N.Y., Putnam, 1909.

SARRE, F. P. C., Kunst der alten Persien. Berlin, Cassirer, 1922.

VICTORIA AND ALBERT MUSEUM, South Kensington, Guide to the Collection of Carpets. London, 1915.

WALLIS, HENRY, Persian Ceramic Art in the Godman Collection. 2 v. London, Taylor, 1891.

—— ——, Persian Lustre Vases. London, Taylor, 1899.

CHAPTER XIII

ROMANESQUE PERIOD
c. 500–1150 A.D.

HISTORICAL BACKGROUND

While the long continued Byzantine tradition was following a more or less unbroken course in the East, chaos ruled in the West from about the year 500 to 1000 A.D. Through a close relation with Constantinople on the part of certain Italian cities, such as Venice and Ravenna, and through trade and pilgrimages, especially the Crusades, interchange was constantly bringing Byzantine ideas westward. During this period of chaos the elements that were to form the foundation of western Europe were meeting and mingling — Roman, Byzantine, barbarian, and Christian. Rome, through her provincial system, had built cities over a large part of western Europe, connected them by magnificent roads, and there had established her customs and culture. In swept the barbarians, illiterate but of the fresh, vigorous blood of the North. In their new environment they continued to govern by tribal methods instead of accepting Roman law; and when this law ceased, and with it order, for the kings were usually powerless, a natural outcome was feudalism; for people of necessity bound themselves to any one who could provide some measure of safety from the dangers and outrages of the times.

The one power to remain strong was the Christian Church. Steadily it was perfecting its organization and increasing both in spiritual and in temporal power. At the head of each unit of its organization stood the bishop, who lived in the largest city of his diocese. In the church of this city was the bishop's chair, called the "cathedra." Hence his church was known as the cathedral. As feudalism was the ruling power, the bishop became practically a feudal baron. With her power and wealth, the church was weakened by elements of decay, and in protest at her degradation arose the monastery. This institution with its triple vow of poverty, chastity, and obedience had originated in the East and was introduced into Italy by Saint Benedict in 526 A.D., whence it rapidly spread over western Europe. At the head stood the abbot, and his church was known as the abbey church. In FIG. 87 we see the plan of a typical monastery of the period. In the center, dominating the group, is the abbey church, of basilican type with an apse at either end and a cloister at the side. About it are grouped the living quarters, bakehouse, storerooms, shops for the goldsmith, the blacksmith, the fuller, and other craftsmen, gardens and cattle yards, hospitals and schools — a complete community in itself where daily needs were supplied

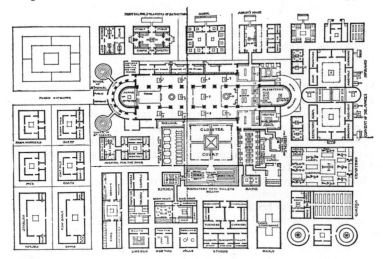

Fig. 87. Monastery of Saint Gall. Switzerland. Plan, drawn from a manuscript.
(Porter, *Medieval Architecture*, Yale University Press)

without communication with the outside world. As a protection against robbers and feudal barons, some monasteries were surrounded by a fortified wall. Thus the monastery was much more than a church. In it centered all the learning of these centuries, for it was the industrious monks who kept alive whatever ancient culture had survived. It was, in fact, the church, the school, the library, and the hospital all in one; and, furthermore, it was the steadying hand throughout the period.

With the exception of the large cities, which could withstand the attacks of the barbarians, there were few towns up to about the year 1000 A.D. The people lived in rural communities, attached, practically as serfs, to the estate of some feudal lord, abbot, or bishop; and because of the dangers of travel there was little intercommunication or commerce.

But the members of medieval society above mentioned — the feudal lord, the bishop, and the abbot — were not stable. There was constant warfare. The strife between the bishops and the abbots, who were mutually jealous of each other's power, added to the turmoil. The one brilliant spot was the reign of Charlemagne, when for a short time order was restored, education and learning revived, and the arts stimulated. But after his death Europe descended to its lowest level, and even the Church sank to deepest degradation, from which it was ultimately rescued through the influence of such monasteries as that of Cluny, which was established in 909 A.D. and for two hundred years served as the spiritual guide of Europe.

About the year 1000 A.D. a new spirit began to infuse Europe. We hear of uprisings against the feudal barons, the establishment of towns, the opening up of communication, the organization of trade guilds, and the growth of commerce. Religious faith developed into religious enthusiasm of great vitality and culminated in the First Crusade, which, though participated in by many for the sake of adventure, nevertheless was an indication of the religious faith of the age.

Intellectually, we see the beginning of the languages. Schools of learning were founded. The troubadours were singing their songs at the gay feudal courts of southern France, while the Song of Roland and the Legends of the Grail were stirring men with the ideal of chivalry.

Thus, while the first five centuries of the period were years of chaos, during which the different basic elements were fusing, the eleventh and twelfth centuries were a time when the people were able to build the foundations politically, religiously, intellectually, and artistically of a civilization which was to reach its full bloom in the thirteenth century — the Gothic age.

ARCHITECTURE AND SCULPTURE

As the monastery was the predominating power during the Romanesque period, it is chiefly the abbey churches that we shall study as examples of architecture; and we shall include sculpture under this heading, as the important sculpture of the period is that which decorates the church. Before the year 1000 A.D. there was little building, as the barbarians were incapable, and the Latins inactive because of the disorder. But

PLATE 73

(*A*) Ardebil Rug. Detail. Wool. 34½ × 17½ ft. Made by Shah Tahmasp for the tomb-mosque of his family at Ardebil. Victoria and Albert Museum, London. The inscription at the bottom of the field reads:

"I have no refuge in the world other than thy threshold,

There is no place of protection for my head other than this door.

The work of the slave of the threshold, Maqsud of Kashan, in the year 926 [1540 A.D.].".

(Victoria and Albert Museum)

(*B*) Sant' Ambrogio. Milan. Early XII cent. A.D. (Alinari)

PLATE 74

(*A*) Sant' Ambrogio. Nave. (Alinari)

(*B*) Cathedral Pisa. XI cent. A.D.

(*C*) San Miniato. Florence.
Begun 1013 A.D. (Alinari)

the new spirit discernible about that year was an incentive to church building.

In studying the architecture of the Romanesque period, one important fact must always be kept in mind — very little remains in its original condition; there are few structures with no additions or restorations of a later period. Another important fact is that the architecture is not homogeneous, but manifests itself differently in different parts of Europe. Hence we shall look at a few examples of each country, beginning with Italy.

In the sixth century the Po valley had been occupied by the

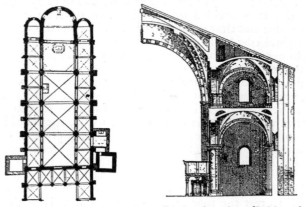

Fig. 88. Sant' Ambrogio. Milan. Plan and section. (Dehio and Bezold)

Lombards, whose name to this day designates this part of Italy. Of the buildings that they erected in the eleventh century, the most important is *Sant' Ambrogio* (PL. 73 B). It is a plain building, with an unbroken sloping roof which shows that there is no clerestory. The façade, which is approached through an atrium, consists of a two-storied arcade, flanked on either side by a sturdy square tower. The decoration consists of a corbel table along the cornices and on the tower. The whole design is one of dignity, with no suggestion of elaboration, and is saved from heaviness by its reserved decoration.

As we look at the ground plan (FIG. 88), we see a Christian basilica without a transverse aisle. Now the early Christian basilica had a wooden roof which, the builders realized, was neither permanent nor fireproof. Hence the central problem of the Middle Ages was to roof over the basilica with a vault.

This means two things — to construct the vault and to support it adequately. In studying Roman architecture, we found that the Romans constructed great barrel and groin vaults (Figs. 73 and 74) that were supported on massive walls, heavy enough to withstand the thrust of the vault. The Byzantine builders had a preference for the domical vault resting on pendentives (Fig. 80 and Pl. 59 a). This type, however, though found in western Europe,[1] did not appeal to the medieval builders so much as did the basilica.

Let us see how this problem is met in *Sant' Ambrogio*. As we look at the nave (Pl. 74 a) we see that instead of carrying a long barrel vault it is divided into sections, or bays, by transverse arches or ribs; and that each bay is covered by a groin vault with four diagonal ribs built along the lines of the groins. Why are these ribs here, and of what value are they in the construction of the building?

In building a barrel or groin vault, a large amount of centering, that is, wooden scaffolding to hold the vault during its erection, is necessary. Soon the builders discovered that by separating the long barrel vault into bays by transverse arches, they could vault one section at a time, thus economizing on the centering. Next they noticed that these arches offered a convenient ledge on which to rest the vaulting; and then it occurred to them that it would be equally convenient to build ribs diagonally across each bay, following the lines of the groins and intersecting at the crown, on which to rest the four sections of the vault. Thus they discovered that they could erect a skeleton of ribs to support the vaulting, which could be made of much lighter material than that used in a barrel or groin vault without ribs, and hence afford much greater freedom in construction. In fact, the application of the rib vault to the roofing of a basilica was the greatest discovery of the Middle Ages. The builders now had the means of lightening and raising the skeleton framework, until, two hundred years later, it reached the majestic height of the nave of the Gothic cathedral (Pl. 80 c). But they were not guided by the structural problem alone. With a sensitiveness to design, they appreciated the rhythm and decorative effect of the ribs. Compare, for example, the heaviness and barrenness of the barrel vault with the lightness, rhythm, and emotional uplift of the Gothic nave.

We have now studied the principles on which the vault in *Sant' Ambrogio* was constructed. Let us see how it is supported.

---

[1] *Saint Mark's*, Venice; *Angoulême* and *Périgueux*, France.

In PL. 74 A it will be noticed that the transverse arch springs from a pilaster rising from the floor; the diagonal rib, from an engaged column also rising from the floor; the longitudinal rib that encloses the double arcade separating the nave and aisle, from a thin pilaster; and the smaller arches of the arcade from pilasters or engaged columns. That is, each rib of the skeleton frame of the vault is supported by a member rising either from the floor or from the second story, all of which unite in forming a compound or clustered pier.

These supports, however, are not adequate of themselves to withstand the weight of the roof. Cross walls are built over the transverse arches of the aisles at right angles to the clustered pier, where the thrust of the vault is concentrated (FIG. 88). These, together with the vaulted aisles, carry the thrust to the outer thick walls, which in turn are reinforced by pier buttresses at the points where the cross walls meet them. Thus while we have in *Sant' Ambrogio* a structural principle worked out for constructing the vaults, we still have the heavy walls for buttressing them. How this problem was met, we shall see later in France (FIGS. 91, 95, and 97).

Sant' Ambrogio is important, therefore, because it is an early example of rib vaulting and clustered pier. These innovations, however, did not appear at once. The rib was known to the Roman and possibly its use was a rediscovery rather than a discovery. First these principles were tried out timidly in the aisles, then finally some courageous builder ventured to apply them in the nave. Even here at *Sant' Ambrogio* the timidity is seen in the fact that there is no clerestory, as if the builder did not dare raise the ribs high enough to allow for that. Hence the interior is low and dark.

These important structural innovations, however, did not develop further in Italy. The Lombards themselves seemed too much embroiled in political strife to continue a development so splendidly begun, while the rest of Italy appeared to be more interested in decoration. An example of this is the *Cathedral of Pisa* (PL. 74 B), a basilica with vaulting over the aisles but a wooden roof over the nave. Here one feels that interest has centered not upon structural principles so much as upon the composition of the façade and the decoration. The ground story is filled with a blind arcade decorated with marble inlays. Above this rise four arcaded galleries which present subtle irregularities in the number and spacing of the columns and in the height of the stories, which, together with the play of light and shade in the galleries, make a lively and interesting design which Ruskin uses as an example of "living architecture."[2] It is not surprising to find arcading on many of the Italian churches, for this was one of the most characteristic elements of Roman architecture and the numerous examples of it in Italy could hardly fail to impress the northerners and to suggest its use as a means of impressive decoration.

Marble inlay is characteristic of much of this central Italian work. At *San Miniato* in Florence (PL. 74 c) both the exterior

Fig. 89. Marble Inlay on the Façade of San Michele. Lucca.

and the interior are decorated in geometric designs worked out in dark marble on white. In the arcades of the cathedral of *San Michele* at Lucca (FIG. 89) some of the columns are carved, and others are covered with various designs in marble inlay — spirals, zigzags, checker — while the spandrels are somewhat heterogeneously filled with geometric, and also grotesque, animal figures in white marble on a dark ground. The interesting play of light and shade in the galleries, combined with this free and vigorous type of decoration, produces a rich, almost fantastic effect, peculiarly characteristic of the imaginative but crude vigor of the northerners.

Marble inlay as a floor decoration (PL. 75 A) shows a great variety of patterns, including animal as well as geometric forms, some of which, especially the bird or animal figures enclosed in circles, closely resemble the textiles of the Near East (PL. 68 A). A somewhat more elaborated form of inlay is found in the *Cosmati* work[3] (PL. 75 B), which consists of surrounding colored marble slabs with borders, frequently interlacing, made up of small pieces of marble and glass cut into various shapes among

[2] See Ruskin's detailed analysis in his *Seven Lamps of Architecture*.
[3] So called from the Cosmati family in Rome who were particularly skillful in this technique.

PLATE 75

(*A*) Marble Pavement. Baptistery,
Florence. (Alinari)

(*B*) Pulpit Decorated in Cosmati Work. Ravello.
XIII cent. A.D. (Alinari)

(*C*) Saint Trophime. Portal. Arles. XII cent. A.D.

PLATE 76

(A) Saint Pierre. Moissac. Tympanum. 1100–08 A.D. (Giraudon)

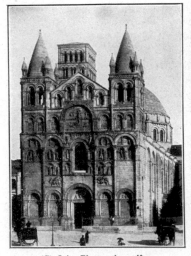

(B) Saint Pierre. Angoulême.
1105–28 A D

(C) Church at Saintes. Detail of the
doorway. XII cent. A.D (Baudot)

which the square and star are common. Even the spiral flutings of columns are so decorated. The vigor of the curving borders, the exquisite detail of the inlays, and the rich colors brought out by the light marble into which they are set produce an ornamentation both rich and highly effective.

Turning to France, here again we find widespread and diverse building in the Romanesque period, a few typical examples of which we shall study. The southern part of France had been thoroughly Latinized by the Romans. Flourishing cities existed at Nîmes, Arles, and Orange, whose theaters, arches, temples, and baths could not but influence the medieval builders. This we see in the church of *Saint Trophime* (PL. 75 c). The façade reveals a basilica type with nave, clerestory, and lower side aisles; and is quite barren except for the portal. The lower part of the portal consists of an unadorned base, above which runs a broad band of decoration, in which are statues of saints separated by columns or pilasters, resting upon bases of lions or grotesques; this band is broken by the doorway, and is surmounted by a frieze which is continuous across the portal; in the upper part a series of concentric arches, slightly pointed, enclose the sculptured tympanum over the door; otherwise the upper part, like the lower, is plain; a bracketed cornice running parallel with the roof finishes the design. We notice how effectively the builder of this portal divided his space, concentrating all his decoration on the central band like an embroidered border on a plain garment emphasized by the contrasting plain surfaces above and below, and by the strong, almost undecorated curves over the door. Looking at the portal more in detail, we see that the brackets which hold the cornice, the columns with Corinthian capitals, the fluted pilasters, the moldings decorated with acanthus leaves, and the Greek fret are strongly classical; while the saints in the niches with their stiff poses and conventional drapery are closely akin to the Byzantine ivories.

In the tympanum is the figure of Christ, seated, surrounded by an elliptical line called the aureole, one hand holding a book, the other raised in blessing. About him are grouped the four beasts of the Apocalypse, which symbolize the four evangelists — the man for Saint Matthew, the winged lion for Saint Mark, the winged ox for Saint Luke, and the eagle for Saint John. On the lintel below are the twelve apostles, seated; to the left are the blessed going to heaven; to the right the damned, chained together and being led to hell. The representation of Christ surrounded by the symbolic beasts had already become a conventional representation in Christian art and is found very frequently, not only over the doorways of the churches but in the illuminated manuscripts, the ivories, and the enamels (PL. 89 B). In fact we must remember that art in the Middle Ages was canonized, as it were, by the Church. As we shall see later, in studying the Gothic cathedral, certain subjects must be represented in a certain way and placed in a certain position on the building, while the use of symbols and attributes must be strictly adhered to. So the medieval sculptor or painter was held fast by convention and could use his individual imagination only to a limited extent.

To illustrate this let us look at the portal at *Moissac* (PL. 76 A), which consists of a vestibule, covered by a barrel vault, with both doorway and sides richly carved. In the tympanum we find the same subject and the same general arrangement as at *Saint Trophime*, except for the addition of the two angels and seated elders on either side of the central group. But at *Moissac* they are filled with life and movement; they are even twisting and writhing; the draperies are fluttering, and the elders are straining their necks toward the figure of Christ; emotion sweeps through the group, in great contrast to the restraint of the apostles and the saints at *Saint Trophime*. Thus, while the subject matter, the arrangement of the figures, and such details as attributes are the same in both, yet the feeling is very different — *Saint Trophime* is quiet, restrained, and hieratic; *Moissac*, lively, and full of emotion. In looking at these portals, one needs to recall that there had been practically no monumental sculpture produced since about 500 A.D. The continuity of the classic tradition on the one hand, and the development of Christian convention and symbolism, on the other, had been in the hands of the ivory carvers, and the illuminators of the manuscripts. But now when, about the year 1100 A.D., monumental sculpture revives, we find some of it clinging to the older traditions as handed down by the Byzantine craftsmen, and some revealing a new life of great vitality and emotion.

In comparison with *Saint Trophime*, the façade of *Angoulême* is much more ornate. This church is typical of the highest attainments of the Romanesque builders. It has a sober strength and, although the conical terminals of the towers suggest height, yet it keeps rather close to the ground, as if it lacked the assurance that would enable it to rise higher. The simple massiveness is due to solid walls having few apertures. The decorations, carved delicately in the rather soft native limestone that lends itself admirably to this purpose, are spirited and highly decorative in themselves; and, though subordinate to the design as a whole, they soften the austerity of the façade by their richness.

Romanesque ornament is always spirited and varied, often fantastic (FIG. 90), and of a decorative nature. On the lintel of the doorway of *Moissac* (PL. 76 A) we see several of these qualities. At each end of the lintel is a chimera-like creature, reminiscent of Persia and India, from whose mouth issue cords that enclose finely carved rosettes, all slightly different, unequally spaced, and with the ground carved with various motifs. Fantasy manifests itself particularly

Fig. 90. Romanesque Ornament.

in the "storied capitals," where the creatures of the imagination and characters from the Bible, centaurs, and hunters find a place, often intertwined with scrolls and foliage. Strikingly effective are many of the Romanesque recessed portals about which was concentrated much of the decorative carving (PL. 76 C).

Turning to northern France, we recall that this part of the country had been occupied by the Normans, who, like the other barbarians, had no arts of their own. Furthermore, northern France, unlike the southern part of the country, had no large Roman cities to teach them. Their own accomplishment, in which they were probably aided by builders from Lombardy who settled there, is illustrated by the *Abbaye-aux-Hommes* (PL. 77 A).[4] The first impression of the church, as we think of *Saint Trophime* and *Angoulême*, is its plainness and its rugged vigor. We notice that the façade with its two flanking square towers is divided into three vertical sections separated by pilaster buttresses and emphasized by a triple doorway, indicating a triple division on the interior, namely, a nave and two side aisles, while the doorways and two rows of windows indicate that the structure is three stories high. Notice also the almost entire lack of decoration, except the arcading in the upper stories of the towers. There is no monumental portal, no figure sculpture.

4 The spires are a later addition. The original towers rose but three stories above the roof.

As we look at the interior (PL. 77 B) we realize that here is
something that we have not seen since we left *Sant' Ambrogio*
in Milan (PL. 74 A). There is a similarity in the principles of
structure, such as the ribbed vaulting, the division of the nave
into bays, and the clustered pier. But the most distinctive difference lies in the height of the vaults. At *Sant' Ambrogio* the
builder, in his timidity, omitted the clerestory; in the *Abbaye-
aux-Hommes* the Norman with the daring blood of the old Vikings
in his veins had the courage to add it and thus to obtain both
height and light.[5]

Let us see how the Norman buttressed his vaults. A cross
section of this abbey (FIG. 91) shows us that the principle adopted

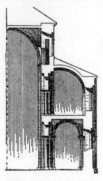

Fig. 91. Saint
Etienne, or the Ab-
baye-aux-Hommes.
Caen. (Dehio and
Bezold)

was similar to that of *Sant' Ambrogio* (FIG. 88),
that is, the heavy vaults and cross walls of the
aisles are strong enough to hold the nave
vaulting. But in the *Abbaye-aux-Hommes*, instead of a complete barrel vault over the aisle,
a half-barrel vault springs from the outer wall
to abut on the nave wall. Then the builders
realized that the thrust from the nave vaults
was not equally distributed along the entire
length of the nave wall, but concentrated at
the points where the ribs converged, that is,
at the clustered pier. Hence they realized that
much of the half-barrel buttressing vault was
unnecessary; so when they built a neighboring
church, the *Abbaye-aux-Dames*, they cut away,
as it were, the unnecessary parts, leaving those
sections only that abutted on the nave wall
where the piers stood, and thus created a rudi-

mentary flying buttress. But it was still concealed under the
sloping roof of the aisle.

Thus in Normandy we find further development of the principles established at *Sant' Ambrogio*. The nave vaults have been
lifted higher, admitting the clerestory as a means of lighting; the
principle of the flying buttress has been applied, making the
whole structure much lighter; the triple façade, with its two
flanking towers and triple portal, has become an acknowledgment of the internal structure. These principles, we shall see,
reach their culmination in the Gothic cathedral.

The Norman builders carried with them to England the

---

[5] The vaults that we now see in the *Abbaye-aux-Hommes* are later than the original roof,
but the arrangement of the piers indicates that the original plan must have been on the Lombard
principle.

principles evolved in northern France and there built such
massive, sturdy structures as *Durham Cathedral*, usually in a
picturesque setting and characterized by a massive rectangular
tower over the crossing. Norman ornament, developing apart
from the highways of trade, which, as we have said, are always
highways of ideas, was used at first very sparingly and consisted
of conventional motifs of which the zigzag, with variants, was
the most important. In England, the Norman builders produced
some very delightful doorways, such as those at *Iffley* and *Kil-
peck*. The thick Norman wall permitted a deeply recessed doorway, with a series of decorated shafts in the jambs and several
orders of decorated arches surrounding the semicircular tympanum.[6]

In Germany, the Rhine Valley became a very active center of
building as well as of other arts, for the German has always been
preëminent as a thorough craftsman. An abundance of excellent
building stone led him early toward vaulted structures, although
the great forests of Germany tempted him to wooden roofs. The
cities of the valley were strongly organized politically, economically, and religiously. The locality had rapidly become a firm
stronghold of Christianity and contained many monasteries,
abbey churches, such as the *Church of the Holy Apostles* at Cologne
(XI–XIII centuries), and cathedrals, such as *Speyer* (XI–XII
centuries) and *Mainz* (chiefly XIII century). The Rhine valley
was one of the great trade routes between northern and southern
Europe. Close relationships with Italy, especially Lombardy,
are reflected in the fine vaultings based upon the principles that
we saw worked out at *Sant' Ambrogio* and the *Abbaye-aux-Hommes;* and also in the exterior arcadings reminiscent of *Pisa*. These
cathedrals show not only structural excellence but a massive,
picturesque appearance that results from the multiplicity of
structural elements boldly and interestingly grouped. For the
apse and towers are frequently repeated at the west end of the
building;[7] a polygonal tower rises over the crossing and also at
the end. This complex arrangement gives a varied outline that
is well adapted to the varied climatic conditions. But when the
apse is repeated at the western end, as at *Mainz*, it deprives the
building of the spacious portals that so distinguish the façade
designs of the French churches.

[6] In this connection see also the carved wooden doorways of the Scandinavian churches,
reminiscent, in their intricacy, of the Celtic illuminated manuscripts.
[7] The reason for the double apsidal plan of the German Romanesque churches has not been
satisfactorily explained.

PAINTING

While great series of frescoes decorated the stretches of wall space in the Romanesque churches, these have so far disappeared that very little can be judged of them, except that they show the same type of work that we see in the illuminated manuscripts of the period, which serve as the best criterion of Romanesque painting.

MINOR ARTS

As we looked at the ground plan of the monastery of *Saint Gall* (FIG. 87), we noticed that rooms or separate buildings were provided for the various craftsmen, so that, while some of the workers were clearing the land, planting the gardens, and tending the cattle, others were carving the ivory crosiers, shaping gold chalices and reliquaries, and decorating them with jewels and enamels; others were copying and illuminating manuscripts, painting miniatures to illustrate the text, and fashioning splendid covers for them of gold and silver, ivory, jewels, and enamel. The point of view of these monks, and the relation of their art to their religion is seen in a treatise on painting, enameling, metalworking, and other crafts written by a monk called Theophilus in the eleventh or twelfth century. The prologue of the third book reads:

David, that most excellent of prophets, . . . collecting himself with all the attention of his mind to the love of his Creator, uttered this saying among others: "Lord I have loved the beauty of Thine house." And — albeit a man of so great authority and of so deep an understanding called this house the habitation of the court of heaven, wherein God presideth over the hymning choirs of angels in glory that cannot be told, . . . yet it is certain that he desired the adornment of the material house of God, which is the house of prayer. . . . Wherefore, most beloved son, make thou no long delay, but believe in full faith that the Spirit of God hath filled thine heart when thou hast adorned His house with so great beauty and such manifold comeliness; . . . Work therefore now, good man, happy in this life before God's face and man's, and happier still in the life to come, by whose labour and zeal so many burnt-offerings are devoted to God! Kindle thyself to a still ampler art, and set thyself with all the might of thy soul to complete that which is yet lacking in the gear of the Lord's house, without which the divine mysteries and the ministries of God's service may not stand; such as chalices, candelabra, thuribles, chrism-vases, crewets, shrines for holy relics, crosses, missals and such like, which the necessary use of the ecclesiastical order requireth. Which if thou wouldst fashion, begin after the manner thus following.[8]

The spirit of devotion and reverence that characterizes this prologue of Theophilus permeated not only the monastery but the community as a whole.

[8] Coulton, *Medieval Garner*, p. 166; see also Laurie, *Materials of the Painter's Craft*, p. 152.

The manuscripts were largely religious in subject — copies of the Bible, in whole or in part, prayer and liturgical books — and were written in Latin. In the early part of the period we find the illuminations and miniatures very close to the Byzantine work. In fact the tympanum at *Saint Trophime* seems to be an enlargement of a miniature carved in stone. And then we see the same development as in sculpture, as a new life begins to rise. In the *Liber Vitae*,[9] for example (PL. 77 c), the figure of Saint Peter in the lower row, like the man symbolizing Matthew in the *Moissac* tympanum (PL. 76 A), has the same twisting of the body, movement of drapery, and the same lively emotional quality; the lines cut by the chisel have the same firmness as those done in the manuscripts by the pen.

Particularly successful in another kind of illumination were the Celtic monks of Ireland and north England, who had a preference for the highly intricate initial letters that sometimes cover an entire page as we see in the *Quoniam* page of the *Book of Lindisfarne*[10] (PL. 77 D). The circular part of the Q is decorated with particularly fine spirals, while the motif of the all-over pattern filling the irregular space below is made by interlacing four birds. The upright stem of the I is divided into compartments filled with spirals, and interlacing birds. Into the two arms of the letter U, two elongated dogs are fitted. At the left of the last line of lettering the head and forepaw of a dog form a terminal for the side border filled with interlaced birds. If we follow this border to its upper end over the U, there appears the other half of the dog, his two hind legs and tail twisted into a forceful spiral. There is fine effect in the dotting as a background for the letters.

In the monogram page of the *Book of Kells*[11] (PL. 78 A), the background and also the panels within the letters are filled with various forms of decoration, some geometric, such as the interlaced bands and knots, spiral and quatrefoil; others naturalistic, as foliage, birds, reptiles, grotesques, and occasionally a human form; and all interwoven with a facility, intricacy, and a fine sweep of line that leave one astounded at the possibility of such execution. These Celtic manuscripts reveal not only a fine

[9] Literally the Book of Life, a book showing the rewards of good and evil, here seen in the action of Saint Peter, who, in the upper row, welcomes the blessed at the gate of heaven; in the middle row, he rescues a soul from the clutches of a devil whom he assails with his great key; below, he securely locks in hell the devils and the damned.

[10] This page contains the Latin word *Quoniam*, with which the Gospel of Saint Luke begins. The *Book of Lindisfarne* is also known as *Saint Cuthbert's Gospels* because it was written in honor of Saint Cuthbert, Bishop of Lindisfarne.

[11] The *Book of Kells* is a book of Gospels and miscellaneous matter that came from the monastery of Kells in Ireland. Records tell of a gold cover now lost. The monogram page contains the first three letters of the Greek word for Christ, chi, rho and iota (see p. 162, note 5). The chi occupies most of the space; the rho and iota, much smaller, are found in the lower part.

feeling for design in the spacing, lettering, and illuminating of the page, but also rich detail filled with vigor, fancy, and an infinite variety that repays long study of even one initial.

The same type of ornament we easily recognize in the Celtic metal work, though here the motifs are not so intricate as one would naturally expect in this medium. The *Ardagh Chalice* (PL. 78 B) has a round bowl shape with two handles, a short stem and broad base, a design of strength rather than of elegance. The rich ornamentation neither overloads nor interferes with the structural lines, being concentrated about the handles, on the two discs on the body of the chalice, and in the borders that decorate the top and the foot. In examining the details we discern the spirals, and the interlaced animal forms of the *Book of Kells* executed in gold and silver, worked both in *repoussé* and also in filigree of almost incredible finesse.

The marvelous minutiae that characterize Celtic work must have been attained through incredible patience and utter disregard of time. The spirit that infuses it is as far from commercialism as the mind can imagine; it is epitomized in the colophon of the *Book of Lindisfarne*, "For the love of God and Saint Cuthbert."

Boldness rather than intricacy appears in the gold chalice and plate in the cathedral of Nancy (PL. 79 A). The center of the plate is decorated with a five-lobed pattern and jewels; the border is made up of alternating enamel plaques, of both geometric and animal figures, and stones set in filigree work, and is finished on the inside with a tiny beading and on the outer edge with a braid pattern. The same general scheme of border decoration is carried out on the chalice, which is the two-handled type, but more slender in its proportions than the *Ardagh Chalice*, with a more narrow foot, and more elaborately shaped handles. The stones are unevenly matched in shape and color, and, together with the deep, luminous enamels, form a scheme of decorative quality that expresses as clearly as the church at *Angoulême* the sturdy, untrained vigor of Romanesque times.

The rich effect that can be obtained through the combination of gold, precious stones, and enamels is well illustrated by a book cover (PL. 79 C). In the center panel is the figure of Christ, done in gold *repoussé*, clearly Byzantine work, surrounded by a narrow border containing an inscription in cloisonné enamel in opaque white on a luminous blue ground; at the corners are red carbuncles. A slightly wider border is decorated with a conventionalized floral pattern set with stones irregular in size,

PLATE 77

(A) Saint Etienne, or, Abbaye-aux-Hommes. Caen. 1064–77 A.D.

(B) Saint Etienne. Nave. Vaulting reconstructed c. 1135 A.D.

(C) Page from the Liber Vitae. H. c. 10 in. XI cent. A.D. British Museum, London. (Herbert)

(D) Quoniam Page from the Book of Lindisfarne. H. 13½ in. c. 700 A.D. British Museum, London. (British Museum)

PLATE 78

(*A*) Monogram Page from the Book of Kells. H. c. 13 in. c. 700 A.D. Trinity College, Dublin.

(*B*) Ardagh Chalice. Of silver, brass, and gilt bronze, with decoration in gold and silver filigree with enamels, blue glass, and amber. D. 9½ in. c. 700 A.D. Royal Irish Academy, Dublin. (Royal Irish Academy)

PLATE 79

(*A*) Chalice and Plate. Gold, with stones, enamels, and filigree. X cent. A.D. Nancy Cathedral. (Neurdein)

(*B*) Cover of the Psalter of Melisenda. Ivory, set with turquoise and rubies. H. 9 in. 1131–34 A.D. British Museum, London. (British Museum)

(*C*) Gospel Cover. Of oak covered with plates of gold set with enamels and stones. H. 10 in. XII cent. A.D. Victoria and Albert Museum, London. (Victoria and Albert Museum)

PLATE 80

(*A*) Chartres, the Town and the Cathedral. (N. D. Photo)

(*B*) Cathedral of Notre Dame. Chartres.
Chiefly XII–XIII cent. (N. D. Photo)

(*C*) Chartres. Nave, looking east. L. 418 ft.; w.
110 ft.; h. 118 ft.

shape, and color — rock crystal, sapphire, and others. The broad outer border is made up of alternating plaques of jewel-set gold, and enamel containing conventionalized designs in opaque white on a luminous blue ground, thus harmonizing with the narrow inner enamel border. The jewels — crystal, sapphire, emerald, turquoise, and others — mostly uncut and of varying size and shape, are set in conventionalized designs of raised gold and filigree work, with pearls and tiny rubies. The shimmering gold with its raised decoration, enhanced by the massing of color, the luminous blue of the enamel, all the deeper because of the opaque pearly white and the rich color of the other stones, produces a piece of rich decoration.

Another book cover, that of the *Psalter of Melisenda* (PL. 79 B) is made chiefly of ivory. It is decorated with a design made up of six interlaced circles surrounded by a border, and set with turquoise and rubies so that the effect is one of great richness. The circles contain scenes from the life of David; the intervening spaces are filled with contesting figures which represent the Vices and Virtues; and the border is composed of vine scrolls issuing from vases, interspersed with dolphins, birds, and interlacings, arranged with a great deal of variety in details which contributes vitality to the design. For example, notice how the interlacings are not placed in the same relative position on the two long sides, but are varied on the right so as to accommodate the clasps; and while there is a foliate motif in each corner, there is considerable difference in details. The little figures both in the circles and in the intermediate spaces are depicted with dramatic power, quite characteristic of this age of the Crusades. Life is creeping into the stiff conventions of the Byzantine carvers, just as we have seen it infusing the work of the stone carvers and the miniaturists.

SUMMARY

In every aspect of the Romanesque period, we have observed vigor and versatility. Out of the chaos that marked the early part of the period, order was emerging, largely through the steadying hand of the monastery. The barbarians, Christianized, were going to school to the old traditions of the Mediterranean civilization, but were transforming them with the fresh vitality of the North. As Ralph Adams Cram says, "The awe of the dark forests and fierce seas was still on them, and strange apocryphal beasts, fantastic herbage, impossible flowers, all knotted and convoluted in runic designs, became the substance of their decorative sculpture. There is something of terror and much of grotesque in their work, but above all a brilliant decorative sense and a quality of wild freedom that, curbed at last by sound law, became the noble liberty of Gothic art."

In a certain sense, Romanesque is a preparation for Gothic. Yet of itself it is an art that displays great vitality and ingenuous power. Too robust and too serious to be overelaborate, it reveals a steady, quiet force that is not only working out problems for the future, but in its own present is accomplishing works of art which are peculiarly expressive of its simple, devout life.

BIBLIOGRAPHY

ADAMS, HENRY, Mont-Saint-Michel and Chartres. Boston, Houghton, 1913.

ALLEN, J. R., Celtic Art in Pagan and Christian Times. London, Methuen, 1912.

AMERICAN INSTITUTE OF ARCHITECTS, Significance of the Fine Arts. Boston, Jones, 1923.

BAUM, JULIUS, Romanesque Architecture in France. London, Heinemann, 1912.

BELLOC, HILAIRE, Book of the Bayeux Tapestry. N.Y., Putnam, 1914.

BRITISH MUSEUM, Illuminated Manuscripts in the British Museum, text by G. F. Warner. London, 1899–1901.

—— ——, Lindisfarne Gospels. London, 1923.

—— ——, Pictorial postcards: Set XIX: Early Enamels; XX: Ivories; XLI: Months' Occupations, from an English Calendar of 11th Century; XLII: Alphabet of Ornamental Initials, 12th Century Manuscripts; LVIII: Mediaeval Sports and Pastimes; LIX: Early Christian and Byzantine Antiquities.

COFFEY, GEORGE, Guide to Celtic Antiquities of the Christian Period in the National Museum, Dublin. London, Williams, 1910.

COULTON, G. G., Mediaeval Garner. London, Constable, 1910.

CUNYNGHAME, H. H., European Enamels. N.Y., Putnam, 1906.

DAWSON, MRS. NELSON, Enamels. London, Methuen, 1906.

FLETCHER, SIR BANISTER, History of Architecture on the Comparative Method. N.Y., Scribner, 1924.

HAMLIN, A. D. F., History of Ornament, Ancient and Medieval. N.Y., Century, 1921.

HAMLIN, T. F., Enjoyment of Architecture. N.Y., Scribner, 1921.

JACKSON, T. G., Byzantine and Romanesque Architecture. Cambridge, University Press, 1913.

KIMBALL, FISKE, AND EDGELL, G. H., History of Architecture. N.Y., Harper, 1918.

LETHABY, W. R., Mediaeval Art. N.Y., Scribner, 1904.

MASKELL, ALFRED, Ivories. London, Methuen, 1905.

PORTER, A. K., Medieval Architecture. 2 v. New Haven, Yale University Press, 1912.

POST, C. R., History of European and American Sculpture. 2 v. Cambridge, Harvard University Press, 1921.

ROBINSON, S. F. H., Celtic Illuminative Art. Dublin, Hodges, 1908.

STATHAM, H. H., Short Critical History of Architecture. N.Y., Scribner, 1912.

SULLIVAN, SIR EDWARD, Book of Kells. London, The Studio, 1914.

CHAPTER XIV
GOTHIC PERIOD
c. 1150–1550 A.D.

HISTORICAL BACKGROUND

The word "Gothic," in the meaning of "barbarian," was a term of reproach applied to medieval buildings by the architects of the Renaissance who found their only ideal in the architecture of Greece and Rome. The Gothic cathedral, however, is the highest expression of an age that was vigorous in its civic life, intensely religious, and profoundly intellectual. Rising in the midst of the houses that huddled closely about it (PL. 80 A), not only did it dominate the town, but it stood as a center for the activities of the people, all of whom it was large enough to hold when the whole town gathered for the Christmas or Easter celebration, or to see a mystery play. The market place, the shop, and the home were situated literally in the shadow of the great church; and so interwoven were religious and secular activities in the Middle Ages that life presented a unified whole rather than the segregations of modern times. Let us look at some of the factors in the civilization which thus manifested itself.

Fig. 92. Château of Coucy, Restored. (Viollet-le-Duc)

Politically stronger kings, such as Philip Augustus (1180–1223 A.D.) and Louis IX, or Saint Louis (1226–70 A.D.), were holding in check the feudal lords, though here and there such a baron as the Sieur de Coucy, protected by moat, thick walls, and a great donjon (FIG. 92), could support his boast, "I am not king, nor prince, nor duke, nor even count; I am the lord of Coucy." In distinction from the Romanesque period when life was chiefly rural and monastic, the Gothic age was one of towns with their merchant guilds, growing in number and power. Revolting from the feudal domination of the baron or the bishop, one by one they became independent communes robust and vigorous with a growing sense of freedom and expansion, resulting from the opening up of intercourse with neighboring countries and the Near East through the Crusades. Economically, this intercourse stimulated commercial activity and brought wealth.

Religiously, the thirteenth century saw the culmination of enthusiasm that had been developing since the year 1000 A.D. Under a strong line of popes, such as Innocent III, the church reached the pinnacle of temporal as well as of spiritual power. The monastery, having fulfilled its purpose of reforming the church from within, declined in power, while attention was focused upon the churches of the towns where the bishop lived. Hence we see the rise of the great cathedrals. The higher clergy had developed the creed and ritual until it had become subtle and complex, far above the comprehension of the mass of the people, whose religion nevertheless was intense, manifesting itself in the mystery and miracle plays, and in the worship of relics, many of which were believed to be miracle-working, and which, carefully protected in reliquaries (PL. 89 B) of gold and silver, inlaid with precious stones and enamels, were carried through the land, curing the sick and obtaining large sums of money for the erection of the church to house the relic. So intense was the enthusiasm that at Chartres, for example, all the people, old and young, prince and peasant, hitched themselves to carts and dragged great loads of stone to build the cathedral.[1]

But a new far-reaching element was altering religious ideas — the Franciscan movement. In 1210 A.D. Saint Francis of Assisi, in protest against the growing internal degradation of the church, clad in a rough peasant's cloak, barefoot, with no money, with his small band of followers, began traveling about, preaching the creed of poverty, chastity, and obedience, and inspiring the people with his own gentleness and radiant love for all life. The birds, the animals, the crickets, the trees, and the sun — everything in nature was a part of God's great universe, a brother, to be loved and respected. Gradually there came about a change in point of view — a change from the medieval ideal of focusing upon the life to come for which this life was but a preparation,

[1] For a full account, see the letter of Haymo, an eyewitness, as translated in Porter, *Medieval Architecture*, II, pp. 151 ff.

to a realization of the value of this life for itself, for the beauty to be seen all about and for a legitimate joy in nature. Such a realization turned men's eyes toward an observation of nature that revealed itself early in the Gothic age, and found its culmination in the Renaissance.

Another aspect of medieval life reveals itself in the cathedral — the intellectual. It was a period of great learning. Universities were springing up, and the passion of the age for encyclopedic knowledge we observe in the work of Vincent of Beauvais, who attempted to classify all knowledge under four headings, which he called "The Four Mirrors"; first, the mirror of nature, which included scenes of creation, vegetable and animal ornament, monsters and grotesques; second, the mirror of science or instruction, which included human labor, the handicrafts, and the seven arts; third, the mirror of morals, which revealed the vices and virtues; and, fourth, the mirror of history, which related the stories of the Old and New Testaments, the tales of the apocryphal books, and the lives of the saints. And the age, not content with gathering this knowledge into a book, carved it all in stone on the portals of the cathedral, on the capitals, and high up on the buttresses and towers.[2]

Everyday life in the towns was vigorous and democratic, each one contributing to the life of the community. To be sure, the streets were narrow and dark with little sanitation, so that plagues, once started, easily wiped out great masses of mankind. At the feudal courts life was festive and gay, and from hall to hall the troubadours traveled, singing their songs of love and adventure.[3]

ARCHITECTURE

As we have said, the highest achievement of the age was the cathedral, which is an epitome in stone of medieval life. Unlike Romanesque architecture, which was diverse and widely scattered, Gothic is distinctly French and in its purest form narrowly restricted to the Ile de France, though it manifested itself in varying forms in other localities.

To understand the cathedral, let us travel about fifty-five miles southwest of Paris to Chartres and there study in detail, as a

[2] For a fuller description and symbolic meaning, see Mâle, *Religious Art in France, XIII Century*.

[3] Vivid pictures of life in this period are found in the manuscripts, especially the calendars, in which the activity typical of the month is illustrated — the feast and the hawking party, sowing and reaping, and hunting the wild boar for the Christmas feast. The finest example, probably, is the *Très Riches Heures* of the Duc de Berri (PL. 87 B). Adams, *Mont-Saint-Michel and Chartres* is especially recommended for its sympathetic insight into the spirit of the age.

typical example, the cathedral of *Notre Dame de Chartres*.[4] As we approach (PL. 80 A), we notice how it looms above the compact town, a bulky mass culminating in two spires. A nearer view (PL. 80 B) reveals the façade, with a dominant note of quiet strength and majesty, for it is simple and sincere, and, with the exception of the northern tower, sober in decoration. The façade is divided vertically into three parts — a central division marked by the portal, three lancet windows, a rose and an arcade; and two flanking towers that reach up into tall spires. The design, however, is not symmetrical; the most striking irregularity being in the towers, one of which is sturdy and plain, the other higher, more slender, and ornate; and the division into stories is not uniform. These irregularities, however, which are due to different periods of building, do not disturb the balance of the composition.

Of the towers, the south, or *Old Tower*, is much the simpler and sturdier of the two, harmonizing with the general composition much more than does the more delicate and more ornate north one, which was built three hundred years afterward in the style of the later period. The effect of the *Old Tower* is marred by the arcading and rose, which bring the central part of the façade higher than was originally planned; for the tower was intended to rise freely from the third story and hence is "hunched up by half a rose and a row of kings."[5]

But we instinctively feel its sober strength, quiet harmony, and reposeful lines and proportions. It rises from a firm, square base and is decorated with blind arcades, splayed windows, and pilaster-buttresses. At the point of transition from the square tower to the octagonal spire — and this is the most difficult problem of the builder — the work becomes lighter with more frequent openings and small pinnacles that lead directly to the towering spire; but so skillfully is this transition made that one is quite unaware how gradually and subtly it took place; with the result that we have a design in this tower which for ease and unity of composition and purity of style can scarcely be equaled.

Before studying the decoration of the façade, let us look at the structural principles that produced such a cathedral. The ground plan (FIG. 93) is that of an elaborated early Christian basilica.

[4] The present cathedral dates from the fire of 1134, which destroyed the old basilica on the site. The west façade was built by 1150. To gain space in the nave (see FIG. 93), this façade, which had been built behind the towers, was moved forward until flush with the west end of the towers, its present position. The south tower was completed between 1180 and 1194, when a great fire destroyed all the church except parts of the western end. Rebuilding proceeded rapidly and the new cathedral, the present one, was dedicated in 1260. The northern and southern portals were added during the thirteenth century, and the northern spire between 1506 and 1512.

[5] Adams, *Mont-Saint-Michel and Chartres.*

By bringing the transept near the center of the nave and lengthening out the choir, the T-shape plan of the early basilica (FIG. 77) has become †, that is, cross-shape. The apse has developed into a complicated form called the *chevet* [6] which includes not only the apse itself but the surrounding aisles, known as ambulatories, or apsidal aisles, and the chapels opening from them.

With this plan in mind, we enter the cathedral (PL. 80 c). In the quiet and subdued light, one is overwhelmed by a feeling of mystery and exaltation; for by swiftly rising verticals, rhythmically repeated down the deep vista of the nave, one is lifted as if in an effort to reach heights just beyond the mysterious shadows high up in the vaults; and another note of exaltation is added by the rich color of the windows, spreading its radiant luminosity over the gray of the stone. Mechanical skill alone could not have produced such a nave. Everywhere one is aware of the sincere religious conviction that inspired it.

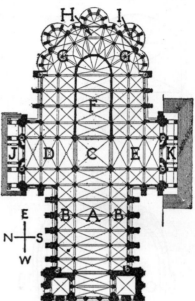

Fig. 93. Chartres. Plan. As is usual, the cathedral faces west. *A*, nave; *B*, aisles; *C*, crossing; *D*, north transept; *E*, south transept; *F*, choir; *G*, chevet; *H*, ambulatory; *I*, apsidal chapel; *J*, north porch; *K*, south porch.

As we think back to *Sant' Ambrogio* (PL. 74 A), low, dark and heavy, and even to *Saint Etienne* (PL. 77 B), where advance over *Sant' Ambrogio* came about through the daring of the Normans, we ask ourselves what enabled the Gothic builders to erect their lofty naves. It was two things primarily — the ribbed vaulting and the pointed arch — by means of which they produced a building not only uplifting and awe-inspiring in emotional appeal, but highly intellectual in organic unity.

[6] For an exterior view of a *chevet*, see PL. 83 B. Note that the apse is the full height of the nave, but the ambulatories and chapels, though vaulted, are but one story high and over them spring the flying buttresses.

Let us explain this term "organic unity" more fully. As we look again at the nave of *Chartres*, we recognize the ribbed vaulting, but we see that the arches are pointed rather than round. By studying Fig. 94 we understand why the pointed

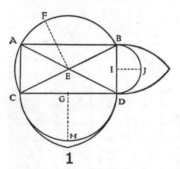

1

arch could give height and light where the round one could not; and that was what these builders were trying to secure — height for expression, and light because of the dull northern climate.

Given, then, a method of securing these two essentials, how is the vaulting stably supported in its lofty position? In Pl. 81 a we see that the great piers at the crossing are of the clustered or

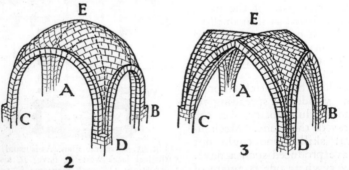

2   **3**

Fig. 94. The Value of the Pointed Arch. (1) *ABCD* is an oblong bay to be vaulted. *BC* is the diagonal rib; *DC*, the transverse; and *BD*, the longitudinal. If circular ribs are erected, their heights will be *EF*, *GH*, and *IJ*. The result will be a domical vaulting (2) irregular in shape because of the unequal height of the ribs; and with the longitudinal arch too low to admit of a clerestory. A building so vaulted is low and dark, like *Sant' Ambrogio* (Pl. 74 a). The problem, then, is to bring the crowns of all the ribs to the same height as that of the diagonal rib *E*. This can be done by pointing the lower ribs. The result is a lighter, more flexible system, affording ample space for a clerestory (3).

compound type such as we saw in *Sant' Ambrogio*, that is, each rib of the vaulting, diagonal, transverse, and longitudinal, continues upward some part of the clustered pier. The consistent application of this principle makes a massive support which is

PLATE 81

(*A*) Chartres. Crossing and nave from the transept. (Houvet)

(*B*) Chartres. Buttresses of the nave. (Houvet)

(*C*) Chartres. Western, or Royal Portal. So called because on the central tympanum is represented Christ as King of Kings. c. 1145 A.D. (Houvet)

PLATE 82

(A) Chartres. Western Portal: Kings and Queens. (Monuments Piot)

(B) Chartres. North Portal: Visitation. XIII cent. A.D. (Houvet)

(C) Chartres. Western Portal: July. (Houvet)

(D) Chartres. Western Portal: A Queen. (Houvet)

very effective at the crossing, particularly in view of the fact that the original plans called for a tower to be erected here that would need heavy supports. Had the principle been carried out the length of the nave, however, the effect would have been heavy and ungainly. Realizing this, the builders substituted on the ground floor a single shaft with four engaged columns (PL. 81 A, pier at the left), three of which rise to the capitals from which spring the arches of the ground-story arcade and the transverse arch of the aisles; the fourth, that facing the nave or transept, rises from the base to the vaulting, interrupted by stringcourses only, and at that point carries its capital, from which spring the great transverse ribs. Smaller shafts, which carry the diagonals and longitudinal ribs of the vaulting rise from the capitals of the ground-story arcade.[7]

A study of one bay in detail indicates a clearly marked division into three stories: first, the ground story, consisting of an open arch that separates the aisle from the nave; second, the triforium, a low story, separated from the first and third by stringcourses, whose wall is pierced with four arched openings separated by colonnettes;[8] third, the clerestory, which consists of tracery filled with glass, reaching to the crown of the vaulting (PL. 81 A). Notice that the ribs spring from a point about halfway up the clerestory. The most obvious characteristic of the system is the relatively small amount of wall space in comparison with the openings. The long reaches of uninterrupted surface in the basilica have given way to this light, open arrangement, with the clerestory entirely filled with apertures for the admittance of the light so much needed in the northern climate. But this suppression of wall also eliminated any space for mural decoration such as the frescoes or mosaic that so enriched the interiors of the early Christian churches. Compensation for this the Gothic builders found in stained glass, which was just reaching a climax in its development. Eagerly seizing upon its possibilities, they substituted great areas of glass for stone, producing a decoration of deep, glowing color, richer and more luminous even than the Byzantine mosaics.

We have now explained the pointed ribbed vaulting and the clustered pier from which it springs. The third vital element involved, if the vault is to stand, is efficient buttressing; other-

---

[7] A comparison of the piers of several of the great cathedrals, such as *Saint Denis*, *Senlis*, *Sens*, *Paris*, *Amiens*, and *Reims* will reveal an interesting variety of methods of treating the problem of the compound pier.

[8] As this story frequently had three openings, it became known as the triforium, meaning three-pierced; sometimes a gallery is built here over the aisles.

wise the thin walls will be pushed out by the great weight and
the whole structure collapse, like a house of cards. We have
already learned that buttressing is needed only at the points
where the thrust of the vault is concentrated. Furthermore,
experience had taught that this thrust did not concentrate at the
meeting-place of the ribs, that is, at the capital of the piers, but
manifested itself higher up, particularly at a point about a third
of the way up the curve of the rib, called the haunch.

With this in mind, let us go outside and study the buttresses
(PL. 81 B). From the ground rise massive pier buttresses, each on

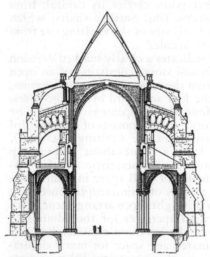

Fig. 95. Chartres. Section of the nave.

the axis of a clustered pier,
in line with the transverse
arches of both the nave and
the aisle (FIG. 93). They
diminish in thickness as
they rise, and from each
spring two half-arches, the
flying buttresses, which
abut on the nave wall, one
at and slightly above the
capital of the pier, and
the other at the crown of
the ribs. The lower arch is
double with an open arcade
between, an unusual fea-
ture. Furthermore, the nave
wall between is stiffened by
engaged columns. The but-
tresses of the *Abbaye-aux-
Hommes* (FIG. 91), hidden
beneath the roof with their

place of abutment too low, have come out into the open, frankly
revealed and efficiently constructed. Thus the thrusts of the
vaults are counterbalanced and the whole structure is stable and
sound.

An interesting feature of Gothic architecture is the marked
irregularity found in the unequal spacing of the columns, the
curves in the stringcourses, and the like. Divergence from the
vertical and horizontal line and from mathematical regularity in
spacing we have seen very subtly carried out in the *Parthenon*.
There, however, the calm, serene intelligence of the Greek carefully calculated the effect of such deviation; the Gothic builder,
on the other hand, with his emotional, impulsive nature was

probably guided more by his instinct toward a pleasing effect than by reasoning.

Structural organism alone, however, though fundamentally important, deals with but one aspect of the Gothic cathedral. Decoration plays an equally important part. Two kinds of ornament the Gothic artists used primarily — sculpture and stained glass. The purpose of the former was chiefly to enrich the portals; of the latter, to form a luminous decoration for the interior.

Turning again to the western façade of *Chartres*, we see that upon the triple portal (PL. 81 c), which occupies the central division only of the façade, are concentrated the elaborate carvings that soften the austerity of the composition, and that are themselves enhanced by the contrasting plain wall spaces.[9] The first impression is the decorative effect, like a piece of rich embroidery clear-cut in its main pattern, rich though restrained, perfectly fitted to the requirements of the whole surface. Let us examine a few details and see what means the sculptor has employed to make the portal so supremely decorative. In the central tympanum is the figure of Christ surrounded by the four beasts of the apocalypse as at *Saint Trophime* (PL. 75 c). The figure, with its stiff pose and conventional drapery, is austere; in the face there is strength and a sense of stern justice, yet a wealth of benevolence and pity for the humanity whom he is blessing. In the rows of kings and queens on either side of the doorway [10] (PL. 82 A) we discern most clearly the reason for the highly decorative effect. The elongated figures stand rigidly erect, compact, with arms close to the body, never projecting beyond the contour. The long lines of the drapery are predominantly vertical, reminiscent of flutings, so that the whole effect is that of a column. And this is what the artist was striving for — to use the human figure to adorn a column and yet not lose the feeling of the column; and in this respect he has been marvelously successful. The columnar effect is still further enhanced by the background of rich carvings on the pedestals and intermediate shafts.

But let us look at the figures as representations of kings and queens. They are richly clad in embroidered robes, befitting royalty; each carries a scepter, book, or scroll, and many wear crowns. In the heads are expressed great variety and marked individuality. One of the kings shows a "mingling of firmness, dignity, shrewdness, even a little levity and vanity in the arched brow, but also intelligence and coolness in time of peril"; while

---

[9] Compare the portals of *Notre Dame*, *Amiens*, and *Reims* in these respects (PL. 84).
[10] The unequal height of the figures is probably due to the fact that they were assembled, after the fire, from different parts of the building. The plain shafts indicate repair.

the queen (PL. 82 D) is an epitome of gracious nobility. It will readily be seen that the modeling in these figures, which are carved from building stone, has not the subtle surface modeling of the Greek; but a surprising amount of feeling has been secured by concentrating upon such a detail as the smile about the mouth or the expression of the eyes. This again is in marked contrast to the Greek, who disregarded physiognomy, making his figures in their entirety expressive of his thought.

Throughout the portal there is first, then, the feeling for decoration as seen in the restraint and conventionalization of the figure so as to adapt it to the place that it was to occupy; second, there runs through the figures a living quality of marked individuality, with a serene emotionalism born of sincere religious conviction.

Two details of the left and right doorways we must notice. Upon the orders of the arches about the left tympanum is carved a calendar. Why should such a subject be represented upon a cathedral? Recalling the "Four Mirrors" of Vincent of Beauvais, in the mirror of instruction we read that while man can be saved only through a redeemer, still he can prepare himself for redemption by labor and knowledge. Hence the sculptor pictures man's typical occupation for each month together with the appropriate sign of the zodiac. *July*, for example (PL. 82 C), is represented by a man cutting corn. In type he probably represents the peasant whom the carver saw every day in the fields; he wears a tightly fitting round cap with a plaited border; standing knee-deep in the stubble, he is cutting the grain with his sickle, a handful at a time; behind him are two trees of a conventional type but very decorative, admirably filling the space. In the niche at the right stands *April*, wreathed with flowers. In all these little pictures there is a mingling of the fanciful with the simple homely scenes of everyday life, very spontaneous, and very close to the heart of the people.

Another glance at the ground plan of *Chartres* (FIG. 93) shows that the transepts terminate in deep porches approached by a broad flight of steps. In PL. 83 A we see the north porch, a large open portico, each of its triple divisions vaulted over and capped with a pediment. As on the western portal, rows of figures flank the doorways; the tympana are filled with sculptured reliefs; all the orders of the arches are carved with figures and the intervening spaces decorated with trefoil ornament. The south porch is similar in general design. Both form effective entrances, rich in detail and harmonious in design with the whole façade.

The subject matter of the sculpture of the north porch is taken from the Old Testament and the life of the Virgin, fitting subjects for that portal which looks to the cold and dark of the north, forming a prelude to the life of Christ that finds its place on that portal which faces the warmth and sunshine of the south. On both porches are found representations of scenes from the creation, the Vices and Virtues, and the lives of saints and martyrs, thus continuing the illustrations from the Four Mirrors.

As we look at some of the figures from these north and south portals (Pl. 82 b), we realize that this is quite a different art from that of the western portal. The figures are well proportioned; they appear to stand upon their feet and turn their bodies and heads so that we feel that a bodily structure exists beneath the drapery, which falls in naturalistic folds. So, too, the carvings on the capitals and bases reveal a tendency from the conventional to the naturalistic. During the hundred years, more or less, that intervened in the construction between the western and the side portals, the Gothic sculptor had been turning to nature, and in his eagerness to imitate her had sacrificed that complete subordination to architectural needs that characterized the western portal. He has not lost his sense of design, however. The beautiful long sweeping lines of the drapery give the figures something of the architectural feeling; but they are not so impressive or so essentially a part of the building as are the kings and queens at the western doorway. In the *Visitation* particularly do we notice the sweep of line in the delicate, almost clinging drapery. In all these figures is a wonderful serenity. Each, though carved simply from building stone, is a particularly refined type of being expressive of a lofty idealism. Beneath each statue or underneath the bracket upon which it stands are small figures which not only are decorative but bear some symbolical or historical relation to the statue above. Beneath the feet of *Christ*, for example, are the lion and the dragon; for in Psalm 91: 13 we read, "The young lion and the serpent shalt thou trample under foot." These little figures are added to symbolize Christ's conquest over evil. Thus we see on these portals not only the stories from the Bible and the legends, and the illustrations from the Four Mirrors, but interwoven with them all a whole world of figures and attributes which are symbolic.[11]

Sculpture, we have seen, was used chiefly on the exterior, to adorn the portals. The second factor in decoration, the stained

[11] For the symbolic interpretation of Gothic sculpture, see Mâle, *Religious Art in France, XIII Century.*

glass, ornamented the interior. As we stand in the nave of
Chartres and look up at the three lancets and rose of the western
façade, we are aware of a mass of the richest color imaginable,
glowing like a cluster of brilliant gems, chiefly deep reds and blues
like rubies and sapphires, relieved by a little white or lighter
hue. Upon closer inspection, however, we find that these windows are carefully worked out pictures full of meaning and

Fig. 96. Window of Saint
Anne and Saint Joachim.
Le Mans. (Hucher)

symbolism (Fig. 96). To illustrate
this we shall study the *Tree of Jesse*
window.[12] In the lowest panel Jesse
is lying upon a couch; from his loins
rises the stem of a tree that branches
out into somewhat conventional
scrolls enclosing seated figures of the
sons of Jesse, the ancestors of Christ,
holding the branches; the next to the
upper panel contains the Virgin, and
the upper, the figure of Christ, much
larger, with the dove descending from
above; on either side of the panels in
semicircular spaces are prophets who
foretell the coming of Christ; a border
of interlacing lines and conventionalized flowers resembling those in the
central panel completes the design.
The first and greatest impression that
this window makes is one of radiant,
harmonious decoration. Its chief
characteristics are the lack of background, of landscape, or any feeling
for distance; all is linear in one plane,
with a considerable amount of simplification and conventional representation, both in the human figures and in
the forms of nature. The purpose of the glassmaker was not to
give a naturalistic representation with background and distance,
but to keep his design flat with all details subordinated to design
and color harmony.

Let us follow a glassworker as he makes such a window. With
the dimensions of the window in hand, he draws his design in full
size upon the whitened boards that form the bench upon which he

[12] For a reproduction of this window in color, see Adams. *Mont-Saint-Michel and Chartres,*
frontispiece.

is building up his window, indicating with heavy black lines the iron bars that are necessary to hold the window firmly; for a large sheet of glass and lead is too pliable to withstand the force of the wind and weather. These bars must play into the design and not obstruct it; hence by cutting the space into small areas they determine the main lines of the composition. Having drawn in the figures to fill these areas, he begins putting in the glass. At hand he has sheets of glass which has been colored, not by being painted, but by having coloring matter, chiefly metal, added while the glass was in a molten state. From these sheets, with his hot iron or diamond point, he cuts tiny pieces, usually not more than an inch long, to fit his designs, a separate piece for each color or shade of color, piecing them together with strips of lead, because this metal is soft and pliable; soldering the strips where they join. Thus he builds up his design, piece by piece, always mindful first, as he works in his reds and blues with whites, yellows, and greens, of the harmony that will result when the light penetrates the window and blends the tiny pieces into a unified whole. Hence he does not hesitate, when his design calls for an illustration of the Prodigal Son feeding the swine, to make one pig green, two blue, and one red because it is more important for the final effect to have those colors at certain spots than to follow the color of nature. And again, with the final effect in mind, when he wants a rich purple he does not always make purple glass, but places side by side small bits of red and blue, allowing the eye to mix them at a distance, and so obtaining a much richer hue than by coloring the glass purple. Thus the twelfth-century glassmakers used the same principle as the French Impressionists of the nineteenth century who juxtaposed their red and blue pigment on the canvas for the eye to mingle into purple from afar. Here and there in the designs he needs somewhat larger pieces of glass on which must be painted a face, a hand or a bit of drapery. With a brownish enamel, in fine, firm strokes, he draws these details and then fires the pieces, thus fusing the enamel with the glass, and then leads them into the design. Thus the glassworker was guided by the same principle as the sculptor, namely, decorative value determined by architectural needs.

While sculpture and stained glass formed the chief decorative elements of the cathedral, polychromy and certain accessories also played an important part. Color and gilding were applied, apparently, to any available wall space, to capitals, ornamental details, and statues. Of this, because of time and the destructive

northern climate, nothing but faint traces now remains. Furthermore, accessories of the service — the rich robes of the clergy,
the gold and silver jeweled crosses, reliquaries, and chalices, the
carved ivory crosiers, and the great tapestries — testify to the
love of color and contribute to the magnificence expressive of
the religious exaltation of the times.

Many other great Gothic cathedrals were built, particularly
in the thirteenth century in France, the most noteworthy of

Fig. 97. Reims. Buttress of
the chevet, spanning a double
aisle.

which were *Notre Dame* in Paris,
Amiens, and *Reims*[13] (PL. 84). Each
was constructed on the same basic
principles as *Chartres*. Only in detail
and ornamentation do they differ.
All are incomplete and the impression
of squatness produced in some ob-
servers would have been eliminated
had the towers been carried up by
spires to the intended height. In
façade composition, the tendency is
toward elaboration. *Notre Dame* has
sobriety and repose due to the almost
classic balance of line and the quiet
unadorned spaces of wall and buttress; at *Amiens*, there is richness of
detail, effective interplay of line, and
richness of light and shade; at *Reims*,
decoration has become excessive and
the vertical line predominant; at
Rouen, ornamentation is supreme.
We notice in all of these façades the
decorative beauty and the suggestion
of welcome in the deeply recessed
portals that extend the width of the porch. The flying buttress
also developed from the simple, robust type of *Chartres* into the
lighter and more elaborate type of *Reims* which, with its niches,
pinnacles, crockets, and finials (FIG. 97 and PL. 83 B), contributes
to the soaring quality of the cathedral.

The sculpture of these great thirteenth-century cathedrals,
while akin to that of the north and south portals of *Chartres*,
still shows marked differences. The *Vierge Dorée* (PL. 85 A), a
gracious virgin, stands holding the child and playfully smiling;

[13] As each of these cathedrals bears the name *Notre Dame*, it has become the habit to designate
them by the towns in which they are located, with the exception of the Paris example, which has
persisted to a greater degree than the others in retaining its original name.

PLATE 83

(*A*) Chartres. North Porch. The Gift of Philip Augustus, Blanche of Castile, and Saint Louis. c. 1205–70 A.D.

(*B*) Reims. North Side. Reims, as planned, would have carried seven spires, two at each of the portals and one over the crossing. (N. D. Photo)

(*C*) Capital of a Clustered Pier. Reims. (Giraudon)

PLATE 84

(*A*) Notre Dame. Paris. 1163–1235 A.D.

(*B*) Amiens. 1220–88 A.D.

(*C*) Reims. 1211–90 A.D.

(*D*) Rouen. 1200–1507 A.D.

PLATE 85

(*A*) Vierge Dorée, the Gilded Virgin. So called because the statue was originally covered with gilt. XIII cent. A.D. Amiens, South Portal.

(*B*) Smiling Angel. XIII cent. A.D. Reims, Western Portal. Practically destroyed during the War.

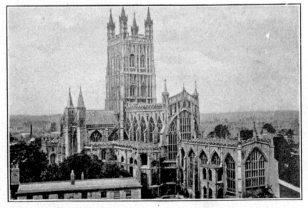

(*C*) Gloucester Cathedral. Transept and choir, 1331–37 A.D.

PLATE 86

(A) Church of Notre Dame. Louviers. South porch.

(B) Gloucester Cathedral. Choir. Rebuilt, 1331–37 A.D., on the lines of the older Norman cathedral with thick walls.

(C) Charles V. Stone, formerly painted. XIV cent. A.D. Louvre, Paris. (Giraudon)

(D) Claus Sluter. Moses, from the Well of the Prophets. Between 1389 and 1439 A.D. Monastery of Champol, near Dijon.

three angels, two in rapid movement, hold the shell-adorned nimbus. She stands so that the figure is built on a great sweeping curve; the drapery, girded high, falls in broad folds. The delicate naturalistic carvings and the fluttering angels enhance the graciousness of this gentle, smiling queen. In his tendency toward naturalism, the sculptor has altered his type, and for the austerity and dignity symbolic of the queen of heaven of the eleventh and twelfth centuries has substituted elegance and the serene joy of the more human type of mother and child. Possibly the most characteristic figure to illustrate the temperament of these sculptors is the *Smiling Angel* of *Reims* (PL. 85 B). The tall, slender figure stands in an attitude of ease and grace; the swing of the body is accentuated by the long sweeping curves of the drapery. The tilt of the head, the movement of the uplifted hand, the sweep of the wings that frame the head — all these give a charm to this angel who is so tender and so joyful. While the statue is not so impressively architectural as the kings and queens of the western portal of Chartres, it still retains with its naturalism a sense of decorative fitness; with the exception of the wings, it stands within the space bounded by the two engaged columns, the vertical of which is repeated in the long straight fold of the cloak.

Although the subject matter, general treatment, and location of the major sculpture of the cathedrals were dictated by the church,[14] the imagination of the carvers found free play in the naturalistic carvings which are inconspicuously tucked away on the capitals, pedestals, up on the towers — in all the nooks and corners. This decorative carving, as well as the statues of the portals, reveals a return to nature. The capitals of the clustered piers of *Reims* (PL. 83 C) are covered with foliage in which animals and fantastic figures are intertwined; the leaves, deeply undercut or standing out in the round, appear to have been just fastened up on the stone and to be still quivering with life. The grotesques (FIG. 98) that live high up on the balustrades of the towers peering out over the city — half man, half beast, crow, elephant, the three-headed Cerberus — were born probably of pure fancy, and show that the fantastic and chimerical forms of the world of imagination also belonged to the mirror of nature, and for this reason are found tucked away in the corners all over the cathedral.

The Gothic cathedral reached its highest culmination in the thirteenth century, continuing in the fourteenth without great changes. The fifteenth-century cathedrals, however, such as

[14] See Mâle, for a full exposition of this.

Rouen (PL. 84 D), reveal quite a different aspect. The feeling of structural significance and the intellectual sanity of the thirteenth century have given way to lightness and elegance and an over emphasis upon decoration for its own sake. *Notre Dame* in Paris has the profound calm of a great epic; *Rouen* and *Louviers* (PL.

Fig. 98. Grotesques. Notre Dame, Paris.

86 A) display all the fancy and delicacy of a lyric. The emphasis upon decoration is well illustrated by the latter with its exquisite carving, lacelike in delicacy. The restless line finds recurrent expression in the ogee arch, which is not structurally an arch but is formed by two moldings with reversed curves that unite and terminate in a finial. So too the foliage, departing from the pure naturalism of *Reims*, now twists and turns in wavy, flamelike lines, so that the work of the late Gothic period became known as the flamelike or Flamboyant age.

Although Gothic architecture was primarily French, its influence spread to England, the Low Countries, Germany, Spain, and to some extent was felt in Italy. These manifestations varied with local conditions and traditions. In England the most characteristic was the perpendicular style, well illustrated by *Gloucester Cathedral* (PL. 85 C). In many ways the English cathedral differs from the French. As in the Romanesque *Durham* it generally has a more open, picturesque setting; it is more sturdy because of its thick Norman walls, which, with the help of pier buttresses or low flying buttresses, frequently hidden, could carry the thrust of the vault; and also because of the rectangular tower over the crossing. The restless searching spiritual quality of the French was replaced by something more earthly and more complacent. The choir (PL. 86 B) shows the fine designing ability of the English builders. The composition is based upon the vertical line; the piers rise without interruption even on stringcourses from floor to rib; the stone paneling harmonizes as does the stone tracery of the eastern end that holds the great area of glass. In the vaulting the ribs spread out in great sweeping lines from the capital, and with the help of intermediate ribs weave an elaborate design on the ceiling — a system known as lierne vaulting. A few of these ribs are structural, but most of them are decorative.

In the Low Countries, particularly Flanders, although typical Gothic churches were built, the most individual expression was the secular building, especially the Town Hall and the Cloth Hall.[15]

In Germany, Gothic building was generally imitative of the French. In the Romanesque period, the builders in the Rhenish cities had developed a particularly virile, original style of church architecture. The Gothic was arbitrarily accepted rather than naturally evolved. So, *Cologne Cathedral* (1248–1880 A.D.), although it imitates *Amiens* quite consistently, lacks the imagination and spontaneity of the indigenous French cathedrals. As in most German work, its craftsmanship is highly skillful. The most original accomplishment of Gothic Germany was the *Hallenkirchen* or Hall churches, in which the vaults of the aisles equaled in height those of the nave, giving the building a simple outline and mass. Decoration in German Gothic in its zeal for naturalism lost the finely decorative quality that always distinguishes the French and English carving.

In Spain, the Gothic style — *Burgos* (founded 1226 A.D., spires begun 1442) and *Seville* (begun 1401 A.D.) may be taken as typical — shows distinct contrasts with the French, due partly to different climatic conditions. The hot, dry climate did not require the steeply pitched, protecting roofs of the northern cathedrals. Hence the vaults were either left exposed or covered with tiles, giving a flat or low-sloping shape to the roof. Because of the hot, brilliant sunshine, the large number of openings needed in the north was diminished, thus increasing the plain wall space. Frequently the clerestory was omitted or the windows blinded, so that the interiors are gloomy. Decoration, especially in the late period, shows characteristic Spanish exuberance and love of overloading, especially about the choir and altar (PL. 127 c and d). An elaborate polygonal lantern often rose over the crossing. Spanish decoration frequently combined Moorish and Christian motifs; and though spirited, lacks the restraint and refinement of the French.

SCULPTURE

The greatest sculpture of the Gothic age, as we have already seen, is that used to embellish the cathedral, and so intimate a

[15] See Chap. XX, and PLS. 128 c and 129 A.

part of the structure was it that it cannot be isolated. Hence we have studied it in conjunction with architecture. There did exist, however, a certain amount of independent sculpture. The tendency to realism noted in the thirteenth century found expression in a demand for portraiture, as seen in *Charles V* (PL. 86 c), where the sculptor has given expression to the benevolence and humility of the king by the stooping shoulders, the slight droop of the head, and the kindly smile. In his study of nature, he has observed and expressed only the broad, significant aspects of the figure; the modeling is simple, yet the bodily structure is adequately expressed. It is this large, quiet simplicity, untrammeled by insignificant detail, that makes the portrait so effective.

This becomes more apparent if we turn to the figure of *Moses* (PL. 86 D) on the *Well of the Prophets*, by Claus Sluter (died c.1406 A.D.). It is a majestic figure, full of powerful energy; the large head with its heavy beard is set upon a short squat body so swathed with massive drapery that the anatomy is not felt beneath. There is a restless vigor in those folds, and an exaggerated realism in the expression of the face with its deep wrinkles. This bold realism, untempered by the idealism and suavity of line that make for the grace found in such statues as *Charles V*, is due to the influence of the Flemish working at the court of Burgundy, who aimed at realism at the expense of other qualities. However, in the expression of tremendous individuality and passionate energy, Claus Sluter was successful.

PAINTING

Because of the suppression of the wall space and the lavish use of stained-glass windows, the Gothic cathedral offered but little opportunity for the exercise of mural painting. Hence we must depend upon the miniatures as the chief criterion of painting. The craft of bookmaking no longer centered in the monastery. A flourishing school in the thirteenth century had developed in Paris, where the university was attracting men of learning. Although secular books, such as treatises on medicine, romances, and histories, were appearing, liturgical and theological material was still by far the most usual, such as the psalter, a collection of the psalms usually accompanied by a calendar, the litany, and prayers, and the book of hours, a varied collection of calendar, lessons, prayers, and psalms for private devotional use.

A culmination of bookmaking was reached in France in the fourteenth and fifteenth centuries. In looking at the manuscripts

II. PAGE FROM A BOOK OF HOURS

With a Miniature of Saint Eutropius. French, First Half of the Fifteenth Century.
Collection of C. L. Ricketts, Chicago.

of the time (Color Pl. II), one is impressed with the glowing color, probably influenced by the stained-glass workers, the shimmer of gold over the page, the fine spacing, and the exquisite delicacy and refinement of every part. The ivy was a popular form of border decoration. Its foliated sprays were semi-naturalistic, spreading out in delicate curves to form a flat pattern. Occasionally a single leaf was covered with gold slightly raised, giving a delicate richness to the page. In among the sprays one frequently finds tiny figures of animals, birds, and grotesques that are another evidence of the fancy of the medieval artist that revealed itself in the cathedral grotesque.

The tendency toward naturalism that we saw in sculpture played its part in painting also. The miniature representing December from the *Très Riches Heures* (Pl. 87 b) gives us a naturalistic and intimate picture of the boar hunt in preparation for the Christmas feast. In the foreground the hunters in gay costumes with their dogs are closing in upon the boar; behind them is a dense forest with leaves in their autumn color of golden bronze, above which rise, in the distance, the towers of one of the Duke's châteaux, over against a deep blue sky; above the miniature, in a semicircle, is the chariot of the sun with winged steeds, surrounded by the sign of the zodiac for the month. Besides the incomparably delicate, brilliant coloring there is a freshness and spontaneity of vision in the little scene which is as sympathetic an expression of life as the calendar of *Chartres* (Pl. 82 c). The gold background of the illuminations of earlier centuries has given way to landscape. Realism is there, but only in so far as it is consonant with the feeling of decoration, with which it so superbly harmonizes. French miniatures reach their culmination in this work; for soon the coming of the printing-press supplanted the craft, one of the most vigorous and beautiful of the Middle Ages.

Painting proper was closely allied to the miniatures. In fact we know that some of the great painters, such as Fouquet, practiced both. The products of the formative years of painting in western Europe have been lost; but the results of those efforts we see in the fifteenth century when France, although torn by the Hundred Years' War, still maintained centers of patronage for painters in unconquered localities, as in Burgundy, Touraine, and southern France. We must remember that in western Europe at this time national lines were forming, and distinct schools were beginning to be established. Of the Flemish, we shall speak in the chapter on Flanders; of the French we shall look at one example, a *Pietà* (PL. 87 A). Above a low-lying landscape, with the towers of Jerusalem at the left, three figures rise against a gold background — the Virgin in the center with Mary Magdalene and John on either side bending toward the dead body of the Christ, which, gaunt and angular, lies across the lap and outspread mantle of the Virgin. In the left-hand corner is the kneeling figure of the donor; the halos and upper half of the panel are finished with decorative borders. The picture is filled with a feeling of deep pathos at the realization of the tragedy. The successful expression of this feeling is accomplished, not by a highly realistic expression of agonized grief in the position of the figures and in the expression of the faces, but by the powerful arrangement of the lines and masses that make the composition. The low horizon line gives a feeling of spaciousness for the figures, producing a sense of the universal that the flat gold background deepens by preventing the wandering of the eye to details of landscape. Thus the mind must focus upon the group in the foreground where the dead body with its bony structure and gaunt angularity, and its diagonal lines cutting sharply across the panel, contrast with the rounding, simplified masses of the living and intensify the poignancy of the scene. The figure of the donor balances the figure of Christ and also elongates the design, which evokes a more profound emotion because of the quietness of the predominantly horizontal lines. This vital, accomplished French painting, with its feeling for structure, its tempered naturalism, and its sense of design, was soon to be overwhelmed by the coming of the influence of the Italian schools.

MINOR ARTS

It is not surprising, when we recall the intensely vigorous life of the Gothic period, to find the craftsmen in metal, enamel, textiles, wood, and ivory flourishing, especially as the products of their hands were in demand to embellish the cathedral and to enrich its ceremonies. One of the most productive we have already mentioned in our study of painting — that of the illuminator. Close to the sculptors were the ivory carvers — that craft which had maintained the old traditions through the long centuries when sculpture, as a major art, had not been practiced, and now with the revival of the latter was becoming secondary in importance. The *Virgin* was a popular subject. In PL. 87 c we see her seated, with her right arm holding the child, who is standing on her lap, one hand playing with the cord on her mantle, and on whom she looks with a playful smile — a charming group of a happy mother and child. The figure, though seated, has the long swinging line noticed in the *Vierge Dorée* and the *Smiling Angel of Reims*, and this curve balances the figure of the child. Furthermore, this ivory is important in that it still retains a great deal of the original color that was applied to the surface — blue, red, and gilding; for it was the usual practice to conceal the texture of the ivory in this way. In fact, the mellow tone of old ivory, so popular with us, is due to time and continued handling. Secular subjects as well occupied these carvers. Ivory covers for the little mirrors that the ladies carried attached to their girdles by gold or silver chains were decorated with love scenes, very popular among which was the storming of the castle of love. These little pictures were carved with all the freshness and spontaneity of the love songs of the troubadours.

The work of the wood carvers we see in the furniture, both secular and ecclesiastical. Gothic furniture impresses one with its sturdy simplicity and strength. Great oak forests furnished an abundance of timber of superior quality and massiveness; one feels to what an extent this medium has determined the general character of the product. There were not many kinds of furniture made. The rooms were rather bare, one piece — a great oak chest, for example — serving not only as a receptacle but also as a seat and bed. The chair in PL. 88 B combines the function of chair and chest, though it is not more massive, because of this double function, than many a Gothic chair. Its simple outline appears to be determined by great oaken beams which also give it mass and solidity. The decoration consists of carved panels on the back and base, whose motifs are clearly derived from late Gothic architecture — the tall slender lancet window and the ogee arch.

In ecclesiastical furniture, the choir stalls (PL. 88 A) gave the wood carver ample opportunity to exercise his craft. The carving of the canopy and the background is derived from flamboyant stone carvings, with the ogee arch predominating. In the misericords and the arm rests particularly, the carver gave free rein to his fancy and fashioned the knoblike rests to represent the washerwoman, the baker, and Reynard the Fox.

The ceremonial vessels needed for the church rites demanded especially the skill of the metal worker. Chalices we have noted in each period since the founding of the Christian Church (PLS. 64 A, 78 B, and 79 A). The *Chalice of Saint Remi* (PL. 88 C) in comparison with these reveals a departure from the ruggedness of the

earliest examples toward a greater elegance in shape and proportion. This elegance, together with a certain regularity and precision about the details, indicates that the rude vigor of the
northerners had been disciplined by the intellectual quality of
the southern civilizations with which it had come in contact. In
this chalice a larger amount of the surface is decorated than in the
earlier ones, for the filigree, stones, and cloisonné enamels cover
a considerable amount of the broad base, stem, and cup. The
shimmer of the gold, the light and shade in the filigree bands,
deepened by the rich color of the stones and the deep luminous
tones of the enamels, make this chalice a superb example of the
skill of these goldsmiths.

Cloisonné enameling was still used, but another, the champlevé, was practiced very successfully. The process was as follows:
on a metal plate the design was drawn in a fine line and then the
metal cut away to a depth of from a sixteenth to a thirty-second
of an inch, leaving a narrow raised metal ridge to indicate the
outline of the design. The depressions were usually roughened so
as to hold the enamel more securely, and then filled with the
enamel, usually opaque, which was fused and polished as in the
cloisonné method.[16] The reliquary seen in PL. 89 B is made according to this process. It is architectural in form, suggesting
the steep roofs of this northern country. In the long panel is the
figure of Christ in an aureole surrounded by the four symbolic
beasts; in niches on both sides are saints; above are angels on
either side of a circle containing a lamb and the cross. The chief
colors of the enamel are dark blue, light blue, and green, with
a few touches of red. The metal base is delicately chased with a
foliate motif, enriching the background of the figures. In general
there is more boldness and vigor in the champlevé method, more
delicacy and elegance in the cloisonné, a difference naturally
resulting from the difference in the early stages of the process,
for greater facility is possible with cloisons than with the more
rigid lines left by cutting away the metal field.

Another metal used with highly artistic results was iron,
which when hammered partakes of the pliability of softer metals
and is free from the feeling of rigidity which is sure to result
when the metal is cast in a mold. One of the finest examples is
the iron hinges of two of the doors in the western portal of
Notre Dame (PL. 89 A). Here the elaborate, elegant design, like
the Chalice of Saint Remi (PL. 88 C), has retained just enough

---

[16] The name champlevé means raising up the field, which had been cut away, to the original
level.

PLATE 87

(*A*) Pietà. Middle of XV cent. Louvre, Paris. (Giraudon)

(*C*) Ivory Statuette of the Virgin and Child. Painted. XIII cent. A.D. Villeneuve-les-Avignon.

(*B*) Pol de Limbourg and His Brothers. December, from the *Très Riches Heures* (the *Very Rich Book of Hours*) made for the Duc de Berri, c. 1416 A.D. Musée Condé, Chantilly. (Giraudon)

PLATE 88

(*A*) Choir Stalls. Amiens. 1508–19 A.D.

(*B*) Gothic Chair. Metropolitan Museum, New York. (Metropolitan Museum)

(*C*) Chalice of Saint Remi. Gold, with cloisonné enamels, gems and filigree. H. 7 in. Late XII cent. A.D. Reims. (N. D. Photo.)

reserve to save it from the weakness of overdecoration. The fine, strong scrolls, uniting firmly with the main stem, suggest the strength that should characterize a hinge. Function and design here are admirably harmonized. Within and about these scrolls, but subordinate to them, are minor details of naturalistic decoration, such as birds and serpents, which reveal again the fantasy of their designers.

Of supreme importance in the Middle Ages were the great tapestries, the purpose of which was to decorate the walls. Tapestry weaving is a very old craft. In ordinary weaving the weft runs continuously across the warp from side to side and the result is a fabric showing both the vertical and the horizontal threads, that is, the warp and the weft. In tapestry, the weft is pushed down very tight so that the warp is entirely covered, with only a ridge left to indicate its presence. Furthermore, each weft string does not pass entirely across the loom from side to side but only so far as the color requires (FIG. 118). Each color of the weft has its own shuttle, which is left hanging loose until its color is needed again. The openings left between the patches of color are sewed together. In PL. 89 c we see one of a series of six that have to do with the *Lady and the Unicorn*. In the center, in front of a low rose-covered fence, stands the lady, tall and slender, gowned in very rich stuff and bedecked with necklace and chain; on her train sits her pet dog; on her left hand rests a falcon; her right she dips into the cup which her attendant, also richly gowned, holds out to her. On one side is a lion and on the other a unicorn, each holding a standard bearing the heraldic device of a certain French family. These animals with their standards and the trees frame the central group, while a great curve unites them as if enclosing some enchanted garden spot. Not only the enclosed span but all the background is filled with plants and flowers, among which one sees rabbits, birds, a fox, a dog, a monkey, and other animals — all expressed with the greatest freedom and naturalism. How alertly the rabbits are listening! Yet all the figures of this background are flat outline drawings with no distance or perspective expressed; even the figures of the ladies and large animals are kept flat, so that the whole surface is frankly ornamental. Thus the tapestries, like the windows, with their charming color harmonies and freshness of conception, and with their designs based upon a sound feeling for decorative fitness, reveal to us the high standard of wall decoration to be found in the Middle Ages.

SUMMARY

A summary of the Gothic age is the Gothic Cathedral, which is, first, an organic structure, revealing itself frankly and to a remarkable degree. Its chief structural features are the basilica plan, ribbed vaulting with pointed arches, clustered pier, flying buttresses, triple façade, and a consistent effort to suppress wall space and to obtain height. Second, its chief decorative features are its sculpture and stained glass, both of which are based not upon naturalistic representation but upon architectural needs, so that each statue and each window fulfills its primary purpose of decorating the place for which it is made — each, in addition, being charged with meaning, symbolic or other. Third, the cathedral in its feeling is highly expressive of the Middle Ages. This feeling reveals itself in the predominantly vertical lines, restless and upreaching; in the ever increasing height of the nave, with its feeling of mystery, of awe, and of inspiration; in the deep, rich, radiant beauty of the glass, which adds to the effect of exaltation; in the sculpture, intellectually and emotionally profound; and in all the multitude of accessories, "the adornment of the material house of God," as the monk Theophilus called them. It is a truism that the cathedral is medieval thought and inspiration in stone. It was probably this that led the Abbé Suger to say as he entered *Saint Denis*, his own cathedral, upon whose structure and decoration he had labored earnestly: "When the house of God, many-colored as the radiance of precious stones, called me from the cares of the world, . . . I seemed to find myself, as it were, in some strange part of the universe, which was neither wholly of the baseness of the earth, nor wholly of the serenity of heaven; but by the grace of God, I seem lifted in a mystic manner from this lower, toward that upper sphere. . . ."

BIBLIOGRAPHY

Adams, Henry, Mont-Saint-Michel and Chartres. Boston, Houghton, 1913.

American Institute of Architects, Significance of the Fine Arts. Boston, Jones, 1923.

Armstrong, Sir Walter, Art in Great Britain and Ireland. N.Y., Scribner, 1909.

Arnold, Hugh, Stained Glass of the Middle Ages in England and France. London, Black, 1914.

Bond, Francis, Introduction to English Church Architecture. London, Milford, 1913.

British Museum, Pictorial postcards: Set XIX: Early Enamels; XX: Ivories; XLII: Alphabet of Ornamental Initials; XLIII: Miniatures from the Psalter of King Henry VI; LI: Months' Occupations, from Queen Mary's Psalter; LVIII: Mediaeval Sports and Pastimes; C10: Christmas.

BROOKS, A. M., Architecture and the Allied Arts. Indianapolis, Bobbs-Merrill, 1914.

BUSHNELL, A. J., Storied Windows. N.Y., Macmillan, 1914.

CRAM, R. A., Substance of Gothic. Boston, Jones, 1917.

CUNYNGHAME, H. H., European Enamels. N.Y., Putnam, 1906.

FAURE, ELIE, History of Art: v. II, Mediaeval Art (tr. Pach). N.Y., Harper, 1922.

FFOULKES, CHARLES, Decorative Ironwork. London, Methuen, 1913.

FLETCHER, SIR BANISTER, History of Architecture on the Comparative Method. N.Y., Scribner, 1924.

FRANCIS OF ASSISI, SAINT, Little Flowers of St. Francis. (Everyman's Library.) N.Y., Dutton, 1917.

GARDNER, ARTHUR, French Sculpture of the XIII Century. London, Warner, 1915.

HAMLIN, A. D. F., History of Ornament: Renaissance and Modern. N.Y., Century, 1923.

HERBERT, J. A., Illuminated Manuscripts. N.Y., Putnam, 1911.

HOURTICQ, LOUIS, Art in France. N.Y., Scribner, 1911.

HOUVET, ETIENNE, Monographie de la Cathédrale de Chartres. Chelles, Faucheux, n. d.

JACKSON, T. G., Gothic Architecture in France, England and Italy. Cambridge, University Press, 1915.

KIMBALL, FISKE, AND EDGELL, G. H., History of Architecture. N.Y., Harper, 1918.

LETHABY, W. R., Mediaeval Art. N.Y., Scribner, 1904.

MACQUOID, PERCY, History of English Furniture. 4 v. N.Y., Putnam, 1904–08.

MÂLE, EMILE, Religious Art in France, XIII Century. N.Y., Dutton, 1913.

MARRIAGE, MARGARET AND ERNEST, Sculpture of Chartres Cathedral. Cambridge, University Press, 1909.

MASKELL, ALFRED, Ivories. London, Methuen, 1905.

—— ——, Wood Sculpture. London, Methuen, 1916.

MOORE, C. H., Development and Character of Gothic Architecture. N.Y., Macmillan, 1906.

POLLEN, J. H., Ancient and Modern Furniture and Woodwork. London, Wyman, 1908.

PORTER, A. K., Beyond Architecture. Boston, Jones, 1918.

—— ——, Medieval Architecture. 2 v. New Haven, Yale University Press, 1912.

POST, C. R., History of European and American Sculpture. 2 v. Cambridge, Harvard University Press, 1921.

STREET, G. E., Gothic Architecture in Spain. 2 v. N.Y., Dutton, 1914.

TAYLOR, H. O., Mediaeval Mind. N.Y., Macmillan, 1911.

THOMSON, W. G., History of Tapestry. N.Y., Putnam, 1906.

VICTORIA AND ALBERT MUSEUM, South Kensington. Smith, H. C., Catalogue of English Furniture and Woodwork: Pt. I, Gothic and Early Tudor. London, 1923.

WEST, G. H., Gothic Architecture in England and France. London, Bell, 1911.

WETHERED, NEWTON, Mediaeval Craftsmanship and the Modern Amateur. London, Longmans, 1923.

CHAPTER XV

THE RENAISSANCE IN ITALY
c. 1300–1600 A.D.

HISTORICAL BACKGROUND

Renaissance, meaning rebirth, is the name applied to the movement that began stirring Italy in the thirteenth and fourteenth centuries, reached its climax in the fifteenth and sixteenth, and then spread with different manifestations over western Europe, continuing into the nineteenth century, and even today exercising a strong influence in our life. Two aspects of this movement stand out preëminently — the delight in life and the enthusiasm for classical antiquities. The former received great impetus from Saint Francis with his exuberant love and enjoyment of nature; the latter gradually increased as the Italians opened their eyes to a great civilization that lay all about them. In the early Renaissance the church, working largely through the two great monastic orders, the Franciscan and Dominican, was the dominating power, and religious matters were inextricably interwoven with the other everyday affairs of life.

Under these new influences, we see a gradual turn in the tide of thought from the medieval point of view that looked toward the future life, to a realization of the value of the present for itself, and to a vision of the joy and the beauty of this life. The Renaissance, then, meant essentially a new attitude toward life and, because of the recognition of the value of this life, led to a development of the individual and a greater freedom of thought, a natural consequence of which was the attitude of curiosity toward nature. Hence we find ourselves in an age of scientific research and invention. The introduction of gunpowder, probably early in the fourteenth century, changed methods of warfare; the invention of the printing-press, about the middle of the fifteenth century, meant the gradual substitution of printed books for manuscripts. Interest in man's surroundings naturally led to voyages of travel and discovery like those of Columbus (1492–1504 A.D.), which had been prompted by the earlier journeys of Marco Polo in China (1260–1295 A.D.) and by the tales

PLATE 89

(*A*) Iron Hinge. XIII cent.
Notre Dame, Paris.

(*B*) Reliquary. Limoges champlevé
enamel on copper. XIII cent. A.D.
Metropolitan Museum, New York.
(Metropolitan Museum)

(*C*) Tapestry. The Lady and the
Unicorn. Early XVI cent. A.D.
Cluny Museum, Paris. (Les
Archives photographiques d'art et
d'histoire)

PLATE 90

(*A*) Cathedral of Florence, or Santa Maria del Fiore (Saint Mary of the Flower).
So called because of the lily in the coat-of-arms of the city.   1296–1462 A.D.

(*B*) Sant' Andrea.   Mantua.   Alberti,
architect.   1472 A.D.

(*C*) Medici-Riccardi Palace.   Florence.   Built
for the Medici, 1444 A.D., and later taken over
by the Riccardi family.

that he brought back of the fabulous riches of the East. The result of such voyages was a wider knowledge of geography, colonization, development of commerce, with the wealth that followed. Leonardo da Vinci (1452–1519 A.D.) with insatiable curiosity about man, animals, plants, and mechanical devices as well, attacked great engineering problems, even discovering some of the principles of flying machines and submarines. Copernicus, the Polish astronomer (1473–1543 A.D.), discovered the revolution of the earth and the planets about the sun; and Galileo (1564–1642 A.D.), watching a swaying lamp in the cathedral of Pisa, deduced from its movement the law of the pendulum.

This freedom of thought was not accepted by the Church, which saw in it the undermining of its authority. But this very freedom, attacking the profligacy of the Church, brought about a certain amount of reform within, and also the revolt from its authority known as the Reformation, which swept northern Europe but made little headway in Italy.

Politically, it was a period of upheaval and turmoil, for the republics of Italy found it necessary to ally themselves with one or the other ruling power of Europe, that is, with the Papacy or the Empire.

The heart of the Italian Renaissance was the city of Florence, which today, except for the loss of its walls, presents much the same appearance as it did in the fifteenth century. It was a city of about one hundred thousand people, compact, with narrow streets. In picturing it to ourselves and feeling our way into the point of view of the fifteenth century Florentine — which we must do if we are to appreciate rightly his art — we must always remember to eliminate the majority of things that today we take for granted as necessary to our welfare. These are based chiefly upon the application of steam, gasoline, and electricity to machinery. In the great days of Florence not a mile of railroad traversed Europe, not a telegraph wire; there was no telephone, no electric or gas lamp; no steam-driven loom, no large-scale farm implement, no newspaper. Letters and merchandise were carried by courier, ship, or caravan; clothing and furniture were hand-made and hand-decorated; books were written and illustrated by hand until the coming of the printing-press.

Economically, Florence was a great commercial and industrial center, in fact the commercial center of western Europe, with her agents in all European countries as well as the Near East. All her various activities were conducted by thoroughly organized guilds, such as the woolen manufacturers, the merchants of foreign stuffs, the bankers, the judges and notaries, and the doctors and apothecaries.[1]

Politically, Florence was an independent commune, or republic; but there was almost constant warfare, not only with neighboring communities like Pisa and Siena but also at home, for the noble families, each keen for the power, kept the city in a turmoil with their feuds, not at all deterred by the sight of the bodies of the vanquished hanging in the public square, or, hardly less gruesome, painted on the walls of the palace of the chief magistrate as became the custom, so that one artist commissioned to paint these effigies after one of the periodic uprisings, won for himself the name "Andrea of the Hanged."

In spite of these frequent political upheavals, the various activities of life continued uninterrupted and with amazing vitality. Education was not confined to the nobles alone, but was universal (FIG. 99); intellects were keen and quick; the people were industrious and ambitious; the mediocre would not satisfy.[2] Thus the great sculptor, Donatello, refused to remain in Padua after he had completed his commissions there with marvelous success, because, as he said, he was too much praised by Paduans, and felt the need of the continual censure of the Florentines as an incentive to greater glory.

Fig. 99. A Florentine Lecturer and His Pupils. A woodcut from a book printed at Florence c. 1500 A.D. British Museum, London.

Outwardly, life was festive.[3] The great palaces of the nobles (PL. 90 c), though massive and fortresslike for defense, contained

---

[1] See Staley, *Guilds of Florence*, for a full description of the guilds as well as interesting illustrations.

[2] Read the introductory paragraphs to Vasari's *Life of Perugino*.

[3] George Eliot's *Romola* furnishes a fairly accurate picture of Florentine life in the fifteenth century. For contemporary illustrations of everyday life, see Kristeller, *Florentine Woodcuts;* or court life, Castiglione, *Courtier;* Cartwright, *Isabella d'Este;* and Ross, *Florentine Palaces.*

comforts and elegances (PL. 92 A). Festivals and pageants of various kinds were frequent.[4] Now we hear of an *Adoration of the Magi* or an *Annunciation;* now of an *Age of Gold* or the *Car of Death.* Jousts and weddings not only furnished entertainment for the people, but together with the pageants kept the artists busy decorating banners, fashioning jewelry, painting the marriage chests, designing the scenery, costumes, and cars for the festivals — all of which in turn quickened the fancy.

Among the artists of the great days of the Renaissance in Florence life and training too were quite different from what we find them today. One striking characteristic is their versatility. An artist was seldom only a painter, or sculptor, or goldsmith, or architect, but usually combined two or more of these crafts in his profession. Specialization was the exception, not the rule. Art meant not simply to erect a building or to carve a statue or to paint an altarpiece or to decorate the walls of a chapel, but also to set a jewel, to carve and paint a chest, to decorate a banner with the heraldic device of a noble family or brotherhood, to fashion costumes and properties for a pageant or church festival, to make designs for embroideries and tapestries, or to illumine a book.

Their training, these artists had acquired through the apprentice system.[5] Each well known artist had a shop, a *bottega*, as it was called — there may have been from twenty to thirty in Florence in the fifteenth century — and to the artist a boy was apprenticed when he was ten or twelve years of age. He spent his time grinding the colors, preparing the gold, transferring the cartoons, the master's preliminary drawings, to the panel or wall; preparing the panel of seasoned wood for a painting. Thus years were spent in laying a solid foundation of craftsmanship. As the apprentice became proficient in the fundamentals of these crafts, he was permitted to work somewhat more independently and even trusted to paint minor parts of a great altarpiece or to make the jewel-set brooch, according to his master's design; and finally, after many years of such training he might leave his master's shop to set up one of his own.

In those days, art was very much more a matter of public and official concern and enthusiasm than today. The archives of fifteenth century Florence reveal to us what a great amount of time the council spent upon art projects, such as the competition for the dome to be erected on the *Cathedral*, or the bronze doors for the *Baptistery*, or the location of Michelangelo's statue of

---

[4] See Baldwin Brown, *Fine Arts*, Pt. I, Ch. III, for a description.
[5] See Cennino Cennini, *Book of the Art of Cennino Cennini;* Brown, *Fine Arts*, sections on a Florentine workshop, Pt. I, Ch. III; and Blashfield, *Italian Cities:* "The Florentine Artist."

David. And the people as a whole felt and appreciated art as a vital part of life, so that much of the art criticism came from the masses. When Ghiberti was making his plaque in the competition for the doors of the *Baptistery*, he invited people to come to his shop and criticize his work as it progressed; when Duccio's *Majestà* (PL. 104 A) was completed there was a holiday in Siena, and a great procession of priests and citizens in holiday dress, with candles, and with the sound of bells and musical instruments, carried the altarpiece to its place in the cathedral; and when Leonardo had made his cartoon of the *Madonna with Saint Anne*, "the chamber wherein it stood was crowded for two days by men and women, old and young; a concourse, in short, such as one sees flocking to the most solemn festivals, all hastening to behold the wonders produced by Leonardo and which awakened amazement in the whole people."

The general appearance of the city had a stimulating effect upon both the people and the artists. In their love for it and in their pride, the Florentines adorned their city with works by the greatest artists, many of which were placed in view of the public along the thoroughfares and in the open squares. Here, at the entrance of the municipal palace facing the piazza, stood Michelangelo's *David;* niches in *Giotto's Tower* and *Or San Michele* held statues made by Donatello, Ghiberti, and Verrocchio; Ghiberti's *Gates of Paradise* faced the piazza, in front of the cathedral, in the heart of the city; along a narrow street was a lunette filled with a Luca della Robbia *Madonna and Child* in rich blue-and-white glazed terra cotta, or a painted terra cotta *Nativity* by Donatello; just inside the churches and the monasteries were great cycles of mural paintings; while above all soared the powerful lines of Brunelleschi's dome. With mind and eye trained by daily acquaintance with all these, it is little wonder that the average Florentine was a keen art critic.

ARCHITECTURE

In architecture particularly we can see how the classical tradition, dormant for eight or nine hundred years, revived and then became the dominant influence. The revival, however, was not sudden. The virile medieval tradition of building continued well into the fifteenth century in spite of the emergence of the classical culture. Then the architects, whose eyes had been opened to the ancient civilization, the material remains of which lay everywhere about them, began looking at the ancient monu-

PLATE 91

(*A*) Cancelleria, or Palace of the Chancellor. Rome. Attributed to Bramante. 1495 A.D.

(*B*) Farnese Palace. Rome. Architects, Antonio da San Gallo, 1530–34 A.D.; Michelangelo, 1546 A.D., who designed the cornice; and Giacomo della Porta, who completed the palace c. 1580 A.D.

(*C*) Farnese Palace. Court.

PLATE 92

(*A*) Davanzati Palace, Restored. The Great Hall. XIV–XV cent. A.D. Florence. (Alinari)

(*B*) Vendramini Palace, Venice. Pietro Lombardo, architect, 1481 A.D.

(*C*) Garden of the Villa Lancellotti. Frascati. The garden terminates in a semicircular "water-theater" with high stone walls, fountains, and cascades, just out of view in the foreground.

PLATE 93

(*A*) Carving from the Ducal Palace, Urbino. 1468–82 A.D. (Alinari)

(*B*) Carved Pilaster from Santa
Maria dei Miracoli, Venice. By
Pietro Lombardo. 1481–87
A.D. (Alinari)

(*C*) Doorway from the Ducal Palace, Urbino.
Showing door of inlaid wood. 1468–82 A.D.
(Alinari)

PLATE 94

(*A*) Saint Peter's Cathedral. Rome. View from the west. 1506–1626 A.D.

(*B*) Saint Peter's Cathedral. Rome. Nave.

(*C*) Basilica. Vicenza. Andrea Palladio, architect. 1549 A.D.

ments to which they had been oblivious before; as the young Brunelleschi, who went to Rome with his friend Donatello,[6] and in amazement at what he saw there eagerly spent day and night among the ruins, drawing ground plans, vaults, cornices, and moldings. As a result, the architects began to introduce into their building the classical decorative motifs, so that the two traditions for some time went hand in hand, the older clinging with tenacity, the younger, though quiet at first, gradually gaining strength. The early Florentine architects, who were the leaders in the new movement, freely intermingled the old and the new with a freshness and at times a daring that are indicative of the freer attitude toward life that characterized the early Renaissance.

This daring is characteristic of the genius of the young Brunelleschi (1379–1446 A.D.) in his design for the dome of the *Cathedral*[7] (PL. 90 A), which is perhaps the first distinctive note of the new order; for this great dome spans both the nave and aisles and was erected without centering. There is little wonder that the council of Florence shook their heads over the seemingly impossible proposal of this youth.[8] To roof over a structure with a dome had been accomplished successfully many times before, notably in the *Pantheon* (PL. 50 c) and *Santa Sophia* (PL. 58 c); but a comparison of these two domes with that at Florence reveals at once a sharp difference, namely, that the former are partly concealed from the exterior view and aim at interior effect chiefly; the latter purposely emphasizes the exterior, to dominate not only the cathedral but the city. This dome is octagonal in shape. From a rather fussy base, the small half-domes of the apses lead the eye directly to the drum, pierced by circular openings for light, which supports the dome itself, the great stone ribs of which rise with a curve of great beauty and strength to converge on the circular apex holding the lantern. Partly because of its size and partly because of its simple design, the dome dominates with its serene grandeur; not with the mystic, aspiring quality of the Gothic cathedral, nor yet with the perfect equilibrium of the Greek temple, but with a frankly pagan note of the mastery of power. Thus the daring ingenuity of Brunelleschi, victorious after a long struggle, made possible many beautiful later domes of which the one at Florence was the prototype.[9]

[6] Read the account of this in Vasari's *Lives of Brunelleschi and Donato* (Donatello).
[7] The Cathedral of Florence is Gothic, begun in 1296. Giotto, appointed architect in 1334, designed and began the Campanile, which was continued by Andrea Pisano and others. The dome was erected by Brunelleschi, 1420–34; the lantern added in 1462; the present "unforgivable" façade, in 1875–78.
[8] Read the account in Vasari's *Life of Brunelleschi.*
[9] Notably those of *Saint Peter's* in Rome, *Saint Paul's* in London, the *Panthéon* in Paris, and the *United States Capitol* in Washington.

A more direct inspiration from the antique reveals itself in the façade of the church of *Sant' Andrea* in Mantua (PL. 90 B) built by Alberti (1404–1472 A.D.), who was not only an architect but a writer and classical scholar as well. The design is taken from the Roman triumphal arch with its triple division, having a large central opening and two smaller side ones, and finished by a purely classical entablature and pediment — the old Roman idea of the combination of the arch and lintel systems. Fluted Corinthian pilasters at the entrance, rising directly from the floor, support an entablature from which springs the central arch. On either side, two gigantic pilasters rise from individual bases to the crowning entablature that unifies the triple division below. There is a largeness and a quiet nobility in this façade due chiefly to the balance of the long horizontal and vertical lines and to the clarity and unity of the design. Here one feels that the artist was not dominated by religious emotion, as was the builder of the Gothic cathedral, but by a desire for quiet, harmonious design based upon orderliness and proportion. Details are used sparingly, show a fine reserved taste, and are entirely subordinate to the design.

Another departure from medieval tradition was the greater attention given to secular architecture, for, with the point of view shifted from medieval aspiration for the future life to the consideration by the individual of the present life, the palace and civic building claimed equal attention with the religious. The Florentine palaces best illustrate the early period: the *Medici-Riccardi* (PL. 90 C), for example, built for Cosimo de' Medici by Michelozzo (1396–1472 A.D.) who was a successful sculptor as well as architect, collaborating with Donatello in important commissions. The building impresses first by its simple dignity, massiveness, and strength; for, while feuds still menaced, a palace must serve as a fortress as well as a habitation. Hence it faced not toward the outside through its heavy walls, but to the great inner court open to the light and air. Situated in the heart of the city, it stands flush with the street and presents an austere front divided into three stories, decreasing in height with a pleasing gradation, and crowned by a great cornice. The blocks of stone are uneven both in length and in height; and on the lower story are rusticated, that is, left unfinished in the rough, producing a shimmer of light and shade over the surface and adding to the feeling of rugged strength. The arched windows, separated into two divisions by a mullion, contrast happily with the single large arch of the ground floor. The fact that the window is divided by a mullion, and that it does not project beyond the wall but is flush with it, is characteristic of medieval architecture. But the strongly marked horizontal divisions and particularly the great overshadowing cornice with its decoration of dentils, egg and dart, and acanthus, are strongly classical. Thus in secular architecture, as well as in religious, we see the medieval tradition continuing while the classical is fusing with it.

This tendency we see developed in the *Cancelleria* (PL. 91 A), which, if not built by Bramante himself (1444–1514 A.D.), is very close in spirit to his work. The stones are evenly cut and laid; pilasters have been introduced in the two upper stories grouped by twos with unequal spacing and supporting an entablature; the larger intervals between the pilasters are occupied by the windows, which are no longer subdivided as in the *Medici-Riccardi Palace;* the single opening is flanked by pilasters supporting an arch which with its spandrils is crowned by a cornice surmounted by a decorated disc, all projecting beyond the surface of the wall. Both the windows and the separating pilasters rise from a rather high base running the length of the façade above the cornice of the story below. The original door, its cornice resting on carved brackets recalling the north door of the *Erechtheum* (PL. 36 B), is distinguished by great simplicity of design. The composition of the façade, with its long, quiet lines, the careful proportioning of its parts, and the interesting rhythm due to the unequal spacing of the pilasters, aims at an effect of quiet reserve and dignity. Ornamentation, which is used very sparingly, is strictly classical.

The *Farnese Palace* (PL. 91 B) is highly typical of Renaissance design. Here the pilasters have been omitted and the great smooth wall space left unbroken except for the windows, framed by projecting niches, the doorway, and the stringcourses. This sheer vertical façade is strongly enclosed by the rusticated quoins, as the angle blocks on the ends are called, and the deep rich cornice above; within this frame the long lines of windows, marching across it in even ranks, are differentiated vertically by the varying design on each story, while those on the main floor afford a broken rhythm by their alternately round and triangular pediments. The central point of the design is the massive doorway of rusticated blocks, surmounted by a balcony and the Farnese coat of arms. The ornamental details, such as the cornice, stringcourses, carved brackets supporting the colonettes, and the window decorations, are rich but refined; and though kept in subordination, emphasize the design and play their part in producing a façade of regal dignity.

All these palaces are built about an open court (FIG. 100) which was as semi-public as is the modern yard or grounds. As the modern house faces outward toward these grounds, so the Renaissance palace faced inward toward the court. In the *Farnese Palace* (PL. 91 c) the court has an open arcade on the ground story only. The design of the court façade is strongly classical in design, combining, like the *Colosseum*, the arch and lintel systems, and using superposed orders, Doric engaged columns on the ground floor, Ionic on the second and Corinthian pilasters on the third, each order being finished with a complete decorated entablature. But the windows with their pedimented niches are peculiarly Renaissance.

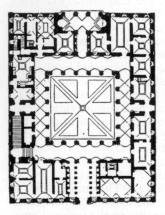

Fig. 100. Farnese Palace. A covered arcade surrounds the court. The ground floor of the Renaissance palace was generally used for storage and business; the second and third stories, for living-rooms that opened off the court. (Anderson)

The interior of these palaces harmonizes with the exterior. A typical fifteenth century Florentine room is the great hall of the *Davanzati Palace* (PL. 92 A). It has a spaciousness and simple dignity; is restful and at the same time warm and gay with color. The beamed ceiling is a revelation of the actual wooden structure. The plastered walls, having simple openings without trim for the doors and windows, furnish an unobtrusive background for painted decorations or especially the tapestries that formed so effective an ornamentation. An important part was the fireplace, a great open hearth crowned by a high hood that sloped toward the chimney. The furniture, like the room itself, is simple and massive, a few pieces supplying adequately all needs. In the late Renaissance the tendency was toward more elaborate decoration.[10] The ceilings began to hide the construction and became rich with cofferings, panels which sometimes enclosed figure painting, and stucco, and the walls were beautified with mural paintings. Doorways were decorated with carved pilasters and cornices (PL. 93 c), and the doors made of inlaid wood. A love of ornament characterized Renaissance work. The motifs were

[10] Typical examples are the *Piccolomini Library*, Siena; the *Borgia Apartments* of the Vatican Rome; the *Villa Madama*, Rome.

PLATE 95

(*A*) Santa Maria della Salute. Venice.
1631–82 A.D.

(*B*) Arena Chapel. Padua. (Alinari)

(*C*) Giotto. Joachim Returning to His Sheepfold. Fresco. 1305 A.D.
Arena Chapel, Padua. (Alinari)

PLATE 96

(*A*) Giotto. Pietà. Fresco. 1305 A.D. Arena Chapel Padua. (Alinari)

(*B*) Giotto. Obsequies of Saint Francis. Fresco. c 1320 A.D. Santa Croce. Florence. (Alinari)

(*C*) Masaccio. Tribute Money. Fresco. c. 1425–28 A.D. Brancacci Chapel of Santa Maria della Carmine, Florence. (Alinari)

chiefly classical — the acanthus, the *rinceau* (PL. 93 A), the candelabrum (PL. 93 B), garlands, and Greek moldings, all carved with the greatest naturalism and spontaneity and combined with the utmost freedom (PL. 118 c).

The Venetian palace forms a class by itself. Venice, in her isolation, was slow to accept the influence of the Renaissance; and, being free from internal feuds because of her remarkably stable government and also from external foes because of her geographic location, she did not need to make her palaces fortress-like as did the Florentines. Hence in a typical example, the *Vendramini Palace* (PL. 92 B), we are struck with the lightness and openness of the building. It stands on the Grand Canal, its ground story being almost at the water level to afford a convenient landing both for people and for merchandise. The façade is three stories high. The ground story, with the door in the center, is somewhat massive and serves as a base for the lighter construction of the main and upper stories, which consist to a large extent of two-light rounding windows with mullions and circular tracery. The main story has a balcony and each story carries its own cornice, the upper cornice more widely projecting, serving to finish and unify the entire design. Horizontally, the double shafts of the superposed orders divide the façade into three parts, the central division containing three groups of windows separated by single columns, balanced on either side by a single group with double columns at the ends. Through the symmetry, proportion, and rhythm of these parts, the façade presents an effective design. The windows with their mullions and tracery are Gothic; while the superposed orders, cornices, and decorative detail are classic.

One more element of Italian domestic architecture is noteworthy — the garden. Its development was due to the fact that comparatively peaceful times were making unnecessary the compact, strongly fortified palaces in the cities and were making life in the country possible. The Italian garden was formal, consisting of beds of flowers laid out geometrically, often with fountains, and usually, for the enjoyment of the color, situated near the house; beyond these, regular compartments, chiefly of greenery with closely clipped hedges of box; and, as a finish, masses of trees, ilex or pines, or a stretch of wooded land in its natural state that served as a background for the formal parts and also afforded the desired shade. Frequently statues and stone benches found a place in these gardens. But there is always present a sense of design in the arrangement of the parts, in the massing of the bright color of the flowers, the green of the foliage, and the clear-cut paths; and always a feeling of restfulness (PL. 92 c).

The Renaissance palaces and villas with their gardens reveal the splendid designing ability of the Renaissance architects. They fused the old and the new with the greatest freedom and in a spirit that reveals their eagerness and their delight in this new expression of life. But in the fifteenth century was discovered a treatise on architecture by the Roman Vitruvius, who fixed very definitely what he considered the principles and proportions that governed classical architecture. Believing that this was an infallible guide for erecting a perfect building, many of the architects adhered literally to its canons. Another group opposed such a restrictive tendency, desiring individual freedom though still adhering to classical design.

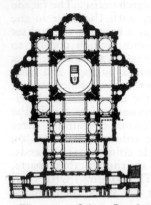

Fig. 101. Saint Peter's Cathedral. Rome. The dotted line shows approximately the front line of the building according to the plans of Bramante and Michelangelo.

One of the most influential of the opposing group was Michelangelo (1475–1564 A.D.), whose work on *Saint Peter's Cathedral* is the climax of Renaissance church building.

This new church of Saint Peter, built on the site of the old basilica, was originally designed by Bramante on the plan of a Greek cross with four apses and a great dome on pendentives over the crossing.[11] This plan was the one essentially carried out by Michelangelo, with the exception of the dome, which is his own design, and the eastern arm of the cross which was afterward lengthened out so as to make the ground plan as it now stands a Latin cross (FIG. 101). The inharmonious façade, a later addition, is somewhat mitigated by the noble piazza, which, with its curving double colonnades, forms an impressive approach. The view that offers the clearest idea of the original plan and the best view of the dome is the western, the back of the church (PL. 94 A). The three arms of the cross with their apses are clearly discernible. Huge Corinthian

[11] Ten architects worked upon this cathedral, chief of whom were Bramante and Michelangelo. The plan is essentially that of Bramante. The dome was designed by Michelangelo and completed from his drawings after his death. The great court with double colonnades was added by Bernini, 1655–67.

pilasters carry the plain entablature that finishes the ground story, above which rises the story of the vaultings with unadorned pilasters. This simple design, with its rather insistent horizontal afforded by the shadowing cornice, forms a massive dignified base for the dome, the culminating point of the composition, which gathers the lines together and rises like a majestic symbol of universal authority. The high drum carries at intervals double colonnettes like buttresses, from which the ribs spring, firmly bound together by the frieze above. These with their rhythm and unity have much to do with the impression of strength; while the external ribs, placed at frequent intervals, and steeply pitched, contribute to the soaring quality.[12]

The interior view (PL. 94 B) shows that a barrel vault, divided into bays, roofs the nave as it does the other three arms of the cross. Gigantic fluted Corinthian pilasters support an entablature with a cornice, corresponding to the exterior design, from which springs the vaulting. Colored marbles and stucco reliefs richly adorn all the available space. If one can forget the too elaborate decoration, colossal and bizarre in effect, he realizes that Bramante's conception, if carried out, would have produced a marvelous structure of noble, harmonious design, fully expressive of the dignity and power of the world-church; for " in a fine domed church you can no more help turning your eye to the dome than you can help marching to music." The minor elements of the design, such as the curves of the ground-story arcades and the lines of the vaults, would thus have led up rhythmically to be united in the spaciousness of the great dome, and the result would have been an overwhelming impression of majesty. This we found accomplished in *Santa Sophia*. But the length of the nave both in the *Cathedral of Florence* and in *Saint Peter's* does not enable one to see the dome from the entrance, and this militates against the effect at which the architects were aiming; for it was probably the desire to express by a spacious dome the power and majesty of the Church that led them to adopt the central type of edifice rather than the basilica.

This striving for effect became the aim of many of the seventeenth century architects, and in their lands was known as the baroque.[13] This century, we must remember, was the time when the Church, by means of the Counter Reformation, had again

[12] Compare this dome with that of the *Pantheon* (PL. 50C), which is a few feet greater in diameter, and with that of the *Cathedral of Florence* (PL. 90 A).

[13] Meaning irregular or fantastic. The style was predominant in Italy from about 1580 to 1730 A.D., and as it characterized the churches built by the newly founded order of the Jesuits it is sometimes called the Jesuit style.

been successful in redeeming itself, in southern Europe if not in northern. To hold and to strengthen this victory it dazzled the eyes of its adherents with outward splendor. In both ecclesiastical and secular life it was an age of pomp and ceremony. The expression of such an age could not be classically simple and quiet, as was the early Renaissance. A typical church is *Santa Maria della Salute* (PL. 95 A), which is picturesque partly because of its splendid location on the Grand Canal and partly because of the sumptuous effect of its design and ornamentation. It is octagonal, with a great central dome and a smaller one over the chancel. The dome is the unifying element, and the climax of the design; but apart from that, the eye wanders restlessly about, attracted by the complicated patterns, the irregular rhythm, the broken light and shade, the fantastic scrolls, the free-standing figures, and other ornamentation. The decoration does not form a part of a unified design, but appears rather like an excrescence the purpose of which is in itself. The baroque, then, is a consistent expression of the age that produced it. Imaginative, surprising, and gay, richly decorated with colored marbles, carvings, paintings, and gilding, it sought to attract attention by a striking and picturesque appearance. And in that it was successful.

Thus there were established in late Renaissance architecture two tendencies, one holding fast, even rigidly, to the canons of Roman laws of architecture; the other free, knowing no restraint, striving for complexity and effect. Chief of those who clung consistently to the purely classical tradition was Palladio of Vicenza (1518–80 A.D.). The Gothic town hall that he remodeled on the lines of a Roman basilica, hence called the *Basilica* (PL. 94 C), shows clearly this origin. Like its prototype, the building has a two-storied open arcade with superposed orders, thus combining in the Roman fashion the arch and lintel system. The intercolumniations, however, are not spanned by the arch alone, but contain smaller columns set two deep from which the arch springs, the space between them and the great shafts being spanned by a lintel while the spandrels above are pierced with circular openings. The bays, whose width was determined by the old building, are unusually wide for their height, but in reducing the width to be arched by the insertion of the smaller columns, Palladio not only attained superb proportions for his arches but brought about a rich play of light and shade where the smaller columns group around the larger pier. The order of the ground story is Doric with a frieze of alternating triglyphs and metopes; that of the second, Ionic with the characteristic en-

PLATE 97

(A) Paolo Uccello. Battle Piece. c. 1456 A.D. National Gallery, London.

(B) Fra Angelico. Coronation of the Virgin.
c. 1430 A.D. San Marco, Florence.

PLATE 98

(A) Baldovinetti. Madonna. c. 1460 A.D. Louvre, Paris. (X Photo.)

(B) Antonio Pollaiuolo. Heracles Slaying the Hydra. 1460 A.D. Uffizi, Florence.

(C) Unknown artist. Portrait of a Lady. c. 1460 A.D. Poldi Pezzoli, Milan. (Anderson)

(D) Fra Filippo Lippi. Madonna. c. 1457 A.D. Uffizi, Florence.

tablature. In both stories the entablature is not continuously horizontal but projects at each column, thus making more insistent the vertical lines which form the main accents of the horizontal rhythm and also carry the eye upward to the statues adorning the balustrade. At the corner, Palladio narrowed the intercolumniation, but not the arch, by placing the smaller shafts near the large, and doubled the columns at the corners, thus giving a feeling of strength and solidity at this point.

SUMMARY

Renaissance architecture was a return to the classical. Yet, notwithstanding the fact that Bramante and other architects asserted their independence of the "barbarous" medieval styles, their product was a fusion of the two. As their knowledge of the classic was neither profound nor broad, they did not so much slavishly copy as take ideas — a decorative detail, a vaulting, a ground plan, or a profile — and transform them by their own genius while carrying on the old tradition. Thus, although the medieval and particularly the classic elements were basic, yet the final synthesis was something new. Emphasis was placed not so much upon structural principles as upon design and ornamentation, which at first were held in restraint, but later became ends in themselves and degenerated into the baroque. The influence of Renaissance architecture has been very great all through northern Europe and America (PLS. 137 A, 138 B, 139 B, 140 A and B, 143, 151 B, 152), and one needs but to look to see evidences of it on every hand.

BIBLIOGRAPHY

General

ADY, JULIA (CARTWRIGHT), Beatrice d'Este. N.Y., Dutton, 1903.
—— ——, Isabella d'Este. London, Murray, 1903.
BIAGI, GUIDO, Men and Manners of Old Florence. London, Unwin, 1909.
BLASHFIELD, E. H. AND E. W., Italian Cities. N.Y., Scribner, 1912.
BROWN, G. B., Fine Arts. London, Murray, 1920.
BURCKHARDT, J. C., Civilization of the Renaissance in Italy. N.Y., Macmillan, 1909.
CASTIGLIONE, BALDASSARE, Book of the Courtier (tr. Opdycke). N.Y., Scribner, 1903.
CELLINI, BENVENUTO, Memoirs of Benvenuto Cellini (tr. Symonds). N.Y., Appleton, 1899.
—— ——, Same (tr. Macdonell; Everyman's Library). N.Y., Dutton, 1919.
CENNINI, CENNINO, Book of the Art of Cennino Cennini (tr. Herringham). London, Allen, 1899.

FAURE, GABRIEL, Wanderings in Italy. Boston, Houghton, 1919.

FRANCIS OF ASSISI, SAINT, "The Little Flowers" and the Life of Saint Francis (Everyman's Library). N.Y., Dutton, 1917.

JAMESON, MRS. A. B., Sacred and Legendary Art. 2 v. Boston, Houghton, 1889.

ROSS, JANET, Florentine Palaces and Their Stories. London, Dent, 1905.

STALEY, J. E., Guilds of Florence. London, Methuen, 1906.

SYMONDS, J. A., Short History of the Renaissance in Italy. N.Y., Holt, 1894.

—— ——, Renaissance in Italy: the Fine Arts. N.Y., Holt, 1882.

TAYLOR, H. O., Thought and Expression in the Sixteenth Century. 2 v. N.Y., Macmillan, 1920.

VASARI, GIORGIO, Lives of Seventy of the Most Eminent Painters, Sculptors and Architects (tr. Blashfield and Hopkins). 4 v. N.Y., Scribner, 1909.

—— ——, Lives of the Most Eminent Painters, Sculptors and Architects (tr. de Vere). 10 v. London, Warner, 1912–15.

Architecture

AMERICAN INSTITUTE OF ARCHITECTS, Significance of the Fine Arts. Boston, Jones, 1923.

ANDERSON, W. J., Architecture of the Renaissance in Italy. London, Batsford, 1909.

BELCHER, JOHN, Essentials in Architecture. N.Y., Scribner, 1907.

BERENSON, BERNHARD, Study and Criticism of Italian Art. London, Bell, 1902.

BLASHFIELD, E. H. AND E. W., Italian Cities. N.Y., Scribner, 1912.

FLETCHER, SIR BANISTER, History of Architecture on the Comparative Method. N.Y., Scribner, 1924.

GILMAN, ROGER, Great Styles of Interior Architecture. N.Y., Harper, 1924.

GROMORT, GEORGES, Italian Renaissance Architecture (tr. Waters). Paris, Vincent, 1922.

HAMLIN, A. D. F., History of Ornament, Renaissance and Modern. N.Y., Century, 1923.

HAMLIN, T. F., Enjoyment of Architecture. N.Y., Scribner, 1921.

JACKSON, T. G., Renaissance of Roman Architecture: v. I, Italy. Chicago, University of Chicago Press, 1922.

KIMBALL, FISKE, AND EDGELL, G. H., History of Architecture. N.Y., Harper, 1918.

MOORE, C. H., Character of Renaissance Architecture, N.Y., Macmillan, 1905.

SCOTT, GEOFFREY, Architecture of Humanism. N.Y., Scribner, 1924.

STATHAM, H. H., Short Critical History of Architecture. N.Y., Scribner, 1912.

TRIGGS, H. I., Art of Garden Design in Italy. London, Longmans, 1906.

VAN PELT, J. V., Esssentials of Composition as Applied to Art. N.Y., Macmillan, 1913.

CHAPTER XVI
THE RENAISSANCE IN ITALY
c. 1300–1600 A.D.

PAINTING IN FLORENCE

The history of Italian painting centers about three cities — Florence, Siena, and Venice; and the kind of work produced in each differs widely according to native temperament and varying conditions of life.

In the early Christian and Byzantine period, when last we spoke of painting in Italy, we saw that there were two traditions current. First was a decadent type of the Roman in which the human form, which had been so significant in classical times, lost all but the shadow of its significance and was used symbolically. The other tradition was the Byzantine, hieratic and conventional, gorgeous in color, and majestic in effect (PL. 61), well suited to express the dogma of the medieval church. These two art traditions form the basis upon which the new spirit worked to produce the painting of the Renaissance.

The first great Florentine painter was Giotto (1276–1336 A.D.). The Florence into which he was born was the medieval Florence in which already were felt the beginnings of the new era. His heritage was the Byzantine and decadent Roman traditions of which we have already spoken; the fresco technique; and the practice of covering the interior walls of the churches with long series of frescoes for a didactic as well as a decorative purpose. His work we can best study by going to the city of Padua, whither Giotto was called to decorate the *Arena Chapel*.[1] The building is a plain structure; and as one enters he is surprised to find himself in a barrel-vaulted room (PL. 95 B), the entire wall space of which is brilliantly decorated. The blue ceiling is ornamented with golden stars and medallions; the walls are covered with frescoes which, with their broad, rhythmic masses, flat tones, and uniform deep blue background, produce a quiet har-

---

[1] So named because it stands on the site of an ancient Roman arena or amphitheater. It is also called the *Scrovegni Chapel* because Enrico Scrovegni, the son of a wealthy Paduan who was so avaricious that Dante placed him in the seventh circle of hell among the usurers, had built the chapel as if to atone for the reputation of the family.

monious effect. These frescoes are arranged in a triple line about the room and represent scenes in the lives of the Virgin and Christ. We shall look at a few typical examples.

In PL. 95 c we see the aged shepherd Joachim returning sadly to the sheepfold after the offering of a lamb which he had brought to the temple had been refused by the priests because he and his wife Anna were childless. So absorbed in grief is the old man that he does not respond even to his dog, who runs out to greet him; while the shepherd lads look inquiringly at each other, wondering at the depression of their master. The rocky landscape with its trees and sheepfold are merely suggested, and are not meant to give a naturalistic setting for the figures, while the flat deep blue background cuts off any feeling of distance. Let us look more closely at the figure of Joachim. His sadness is expressed not so much in the face as in the bent shoulders and the drooping head; in fact, it permeates the whole figure. Giotto has here taken a dramatic event and expressed it with a lucidity that leaves no doubt in our minds as to the meaning; and he has done this by eliminating every detail which does not relate to the central idea, so that we feel the significance of the incident in an unforgettable way. Again, the figures of the three men are to be noticed. They do not form merely a flat pattern, as did the figures of the Byzantine painters, but make us realize that beneath the broad sweeping lines of the drapery there is a body. We feel the three-dimensional mass as a reality.

In another fresco, the *Pietà* (PL. 96 A), we see the dead body of Christ held and surrounded by mourning women and men. There is the mere suggestion of a barren landscape — a rocky hillside and a dead tree — while the sky is filled with angels who are giving themselves up to unrestrained grief. The feeling that impresses us as we look at the picture is one of intense grief over some tragedy; not superficial nor melodramatic, but deep, profound, and universal. How is it that Giotto brings about this feeling so directly and so clearly? The center of interest is the head of Christ, toward which all the lines lead the eye inevitably — the curves of the bending figures, the line of the hillside, which is broken by one of the figures and hence not too obvious, the vertical folds of the drapery just above the Virgin, and even the glance of the two upright figures on the right. The function of these figures is to balance the group on the left and to form, in an almost architectural way, a framework for the central group. Hence every figure in the panel plays its part as if it were an architectural member. Each is bounded by great sweeping lines. Not a single gesture or detail is irrelevant to the central idea. Looking at the individual figures, we see how few lines are used to express the figure and yet how convincingly the body is felt beneath the mantle and how adequately its volume is realized. Let us compare, by way of contrast, the flatness of the figures in the work of Duccio and Simone Martini (Pls. 104, 105), and notice what slight use Giotto makes of light and shade. It is his masterful line, that is, the line that indicates the structure in its essential aspects boldly and without fumbling, that serves his purpose.[2] Very little attention is paid to individualized facial expression or to the hands and feet. They are very much alike in all the figures. This is because Giotto, seeing the figure or the incident in its large aspects, generalized both his types and his action. Hence the spiritual significance expressed so directly and so convincingly in this *Pietà* is universal in its appeal.

Let us take one more illustration of Giotto's work (Pl. 96 b), the *Obsequies of Saint Francis*, which is perhaps an epitome of his style. One needs to study the picture but a short time before he realizes the simple directness and profound calm of the representation. In this fresco Giotto built up his composition with astonishing skill. In the center upon a bier lies the body of the dead saint, over which his followers are bending in adoration and grief. At each end of the bier stands a group of monks, in front of a building, forming a framework for the central group. Behind these figures stretches a paneled wall, the long horizontals of which, repeated in the line of the bier, are balanced by the vertical panels. The diagonal line of the banner, cutting across the horizontal line and thus somewhat relieving it, leads the eye to the small figure of the saint above carried heavenward by angels. The upward glance of the monk at the left is sufficient to connect that side of the picture with the group above, for so strong an accent as the banner at this point would have detracted from the center of interest, the head of the saint, which is significantly isolated by the falling line of the figures and the unrelieved quiet space above. If one analyzes this picture thoroughly, he will find that there is not one line, one figure, or one gesture wrongly placed or irrelevant to the central action. Everything takes its place inevitably. The idea which Giotto aims to convey and the means which he takes to convey it are in perfect harmony.

So in Giotto we find a man who saw things clearly in their

[2] Mr. Roger Fry calls attention to the fact that when we realize the great significance of Giotto's line, the famous story of Giotto's O seems credible. For this story see Vasari's *Life of Giotto*.

large essentials. Going directly to the heart of an incident, he composed the elements of which it was made up with such insight and such economy, with such careful emphasis upon the center of interest through the elimination of all inessential detail, that there is no misunderstanding either as to the action or as to its spiritual significance. In his individual figures Giotto was a revolutionist in that he started the movement toward natural appearance which was to dominate the Florentine school. Instead of being flat patterns symbolic of men and women, they give one a sense of real mass existing in space.

Giotto's influence had been tremendous, not only in Tuscany but in all parts of Italy. Followers arose who imitated him but who were not great enough to comprehend his principles. Hence the movement which he initiated found no great further expression for nearly a hundred years, until the time of Masaccio (1401–1428 A.D.).[3]

In his *Tribute Money* (PL. 96 c) the disciples are grouped about Christ, who is directing Peter to go and cast his line, saying that in the mouth of the first fish he will find a coin with which he is to pay the tax. In the foreground, back to the spectator, stands the publican. The two concluding incidents are also shown in the panel, for at the left Peter is seen dragging the fish from the water, while at the right he is giving the publican the coin. The group stands in a landscape which is rugged and barren except for a few trees, but has great depth and spaciousness. It is not abbreviated or symbolic as in Giotto but bears a real relationship to the figures which fit into it. This is what Vasari felt when he said that Masaccio was the first artist to attain to the imitation of things as they are. But the scene is not merely an imitation of nature; it is an exceedingly dignified and monumental conception. The figure of Christ is the center of interest toward which the lines lead — the disciples look toward him, the lines of the hills, the trees, and the architecture converge there. Not only is the group convincing because of its monumental dignity, its relation to the landscape, and its largeness of design, but the individual figures give one a sense of massiveness and of existence in space, as did Giotto's, and also a sense of bodily structure. In this respect Masaccio advances beyond Giotto. This may be

[3] Masaccio's real name was Tomaso; but because of his careless disregard for his personal affairs, his forgetfulness of his debtors and equally of his creditors, he won the nickname Masaccio, a shortened form of Tomasaccio, meaning "clumsy Tom." The Florentines frequently gave expression to their fun-loving disposition by applying appropriate nicknames to their citizens, which became so current that they have taken precedence over the real name. Thus in the case of Donatello, this sculptor's name was Donato, to which the suffix -*ello*, denoting endearment, was added, signifying the loving esteem felt by the Florentines for him. For the life of Masaccio, see Vasari.

noted particularly in the figure of the publican, in which there is real expression of a structural organism. The weight of the body is resting on the left leg with the right foot raised. One feels that there is a bony framework, muscles, joints, and articulations which enable this organism to support itself and move. As Vasari said, "Masaccio made his figures stand upon their feet." We notice also Masaccio's use of the cast shadow, and of perspective in the architecture and the foreshortened arm of the publican. To us these innovations may not seem unusual. But upon the Florentines who had been used to the flat, unreal painting of the preceding centuries, they made so tremendous an impression that the *Brancacci Chapel*, where Masaccio painted this fresco, became the school of the Florentines.

While Masaccio was painting these epoch-making frescoes, another Florentine artist was producing an entirely different kind of picture — Fra Angelico (1387–1455 A.D.). As his name implies, he was a Frate, a monk, brought up in the tradition of the Middle Ages that was fostered in the monasteries. In his *Coronation of the Virgin* (PL. 97 B), Christ and the Virgin are represented seated upon a throne of clouds from which radiate golden rays. This central group is surrounded by circling angels with censers and musical instruments, and an outer circle of angels and saints. The panel is aglow with gold, radiant, harmonious color, and beautiful sweeping lines, and expresses just what Fra Angelico wished to express — a resplendent, celestial scene.[4] To be sure there was nothing profound or monumental in his work, for Fra Angelico appeared to see but one aspect of life — the happy, the serene, the heavenly. His success is due largely to his feeling for fine design. We mark how effectively the drapery of the angels nearest the central group encircles it; how the rhythm is repeated in the outer circle of angels and saints, and relieved by the kneeling saint in the left foreground and the angel with the harp on the right; and how the long trumpets very effectively fill the space above. Line, pattern, and color are predominant; with the Gothic emphasis on line for its own sake rather than for its capacity to model form. Yet Fra Angelico was not entirely apart from his contemporaries who were striving for realism; for in some of the figures in the foreground especially,

---

[4] It was because of these simple radiant visions that this painter, whose name was Fra Giovanni da Fiesole, received the name Angelico, meaning angelic or beatific. An interesting document tells us that when the guild of the linen weavers commissioned Fra Angelico to paint a Madonna, they stipulated that the tabernacle and shrine were "to be painted inside and outside with colors, with gold and silver, the best that could be found — and for all his trouble and work of hand, he was to receive 180 florins of gold or less, according to his conscience." (Douglas, *Fra Angelico*, p. 37). For other contracts, see Mather, *History of Italian Painting*, pp. 56 and 106.

there is a naturalistic rendering of drapery beneath which a figure is felt, while individual character is indicated in many of the faces.

Thus we see established in Florence, early in the fifteenth century, two tendencies which, though not the only ones, dominated the work of the century. One was that established by Masaccio, which was of overwhelming influence in such fundamental principles as the proportion of the human figure, anatomy, perspective, light and shade, and the expression of individual character. The other, exemplified by Fra Angelico, is the continuation of the medieval tradition which emphasizes rhythmic line, pattern, and color. Very few artists belong exclusively to either group, though in many one tendency strongly predominates.

First let us study a few of the painters who were particularly interested in the first tendency — Paolo Uccello, Antonio Pollaiuolo, and Baldovinetti. In a *Battle Piece* (PL. 97 A) of Paolo Uccello (1397–1475 A.D.) we are impressed first with the decorative quality of the panel. The simplified and sharply defined outlines of the horses, the interesting spotting of the surface with lights and darks, the juxtaposition of sharply contrasting masses, the effective diagonals of the spears and banners — all these contribute toward this end. But if we look more closely at the details, there is forced upon us the thing in which Paolo Uccello was most deeply interested — perspective. It is not only the skillfully foreshortened dark horse and rider at the right of the center and the receding lines and figures in the background, but more obviously the prostrate body at the left, and the spears and armor lying about on the ground, that tell the story.[5]

The sharp outlines to which we have referred are due partly to Paolo Uccello's interest in pattern and partly to the technical method used most frequently by the early Florentines, namely tempera. The foundation of a tempera painting was a panel of carefully selected wood, often covered with linen, on which was laid a thin coat or several coats of gesso, that is, fine plaster of Paris mixed with glue. This was rubbed down until the surface was marblelike. A detailed preliminary drawing, called the cartoon, was made to size and transferred to the panel. The pigments, in dry powder form, were mixed with egg and slightly thinned. First a coat of underpainting in green or brown was

---

[5] Vasari, in his *Life of Paolo Uccello*, tells us how this painter used to sit up all night drawing plans and elevations of buildings, and figures receding according to scientific principles. Whether true or not, the tale indicates the eagerness and enthusiasm of these early Florentines. Here also we read of Paolo Uccello's great love for animals and especially for birds; hence his name, which means "Paul of the Birds."

put in with shading to model the form. Over this were added the colors applied in small strokes and with painstaking care, for the pigment dried quickly to a hard surface finish and gave no opportunity for making changes such as are possible when oil is used. The result of this method was definite outlines, slight shading, a hard enamel-like surface, and a generally decorative effect.[6]

About the middle of the century a very important workshop was that of Baldovinetti (1425–1499 A.D.); for not only was he the teacher of some of the greatest artists of the second half of the century, but he carried on valuable experiments in color and media, especially oil. In fact, some of his work is more scientific than artistic. This is not true, however, of a *Madonna* in the Louvre. In this painting (PL. 98 A) we see the Virgin seated just behind a parapet and looking down in adoration at the Child, who is resting partly on her lap and partly on the parapet. To be sure, the Child is not particularly attractive and is proportionately too small. But there is a winsome charm in the Madonna. Behind her is a low-lying, spacious landscape, which, with its winding streams, woods, and hills, recedes into a blue misty distance. The tiny cloudlets emphasize the spaciousness and suggest a mood of exaltation. If we look at the picture carefully we can find many faults — the proportions of both figures are awkward, there is almost no modeling. The effect is due rather to the artist's sensitive feeling for design, through which he was enabled to express a charming sentiment. The two figures form a compact triangle with a strongly marked vertical axis, and an emphasis on the vertical line reminiscent of the predominant line of the Gothic cathedral, so suggestive of emotional uplift. The eye is carried toward the apex of the triangle by the elongated proportions of the figure, by the uplifted hands, and by the lines of the veil; and then is turned back by the line of the halo, the downcast eyes, and the beautiful curve of the face repeated in the neck of the dress. The type of the Madonna is particularly winsome, and her charm is enhanced by the exquisitely delicate veil that softly frames the face. The landscape shows what advance the Florentines were making in this subject. It does not serve, however, as a setting into which the figures fit naturalistically, but rather as a tapestry background against which they are silhouetted. The colors, especially the reds and

---

[6] The unpleasantly greenish tone of many Italian paintings is due to the wearing away of the surface pigments, leaving the underpainting exposed. Also the brownish tone found in so many paintings even down to the present is due to the fact that the brown underpainting controls and unifies the hues applied over it.

blues of the Madonna's robes,[7] are clear and bright and add greatly to the decorative effect of the panel.

Another artist who was interested in the absorbing problems of the day was Antonio Pollaiuolo (1429–1498 A.D.). Trained as a goldsmith, he became equally successful as a sculptor, particularly in bronze, as a painter, as an engraver, and as a designer of tapestries. A small panel represents *Heracles Slaying the Hydra* (PL. 98 B). Heracles is rushing upon the monster, is grasping one of the heads in the left hand, and is about to bring down his club with the right. The two figures nearly fill the panel and stand out against a low-lying landscape with winding rivers in much the same way as in Baldovinetti's *Madonna*. Heracles' face is tense and unpleasant, and so is the body with its exaggerated muscles. Yet where can one find such an expression of fierce energy? One leg is bent to a right angle and firmly placed, with toes clutching the ground, to carry the weight of the body and also to withstand the encircling tails of the monster; the other is stretched to its utmost as he concentrates his energy upon the attack. We feel the tenseness of the muscles and the articulation of the joints as every part of the anatomy responds to the demand of the moment. Even the lion's skin sweeps backward to suggest the fierceness of the onslaught. As Berenson says, Antonio Pollaiuolo was "one of the greatest masters of movement that there ever has been and one of the ablest interpreters of the human body as a vehicle of life-communicating energy and exulting power." We know that he made searching studies in perspective and in anatomy, especially through dissection. What interested him particularly was how the human figure would act in violent movement. For this reason he usually selected subjects that gave an opportunity for action. And so directly do his figures express an intense energy that as we look at them we feel in our own bodies like sensations of strain and force.[8]

One of the most charming paintings of the early Renaissance, which seems to have been painted by one of the group we are studying is the *Portrait of a Lady* (PL. 98 c).[9] The idea of portraiture is here clearly combined with that of design, if not dominated by it. This is due partly to the tempera technique, of which the panel is an excellent example. The face and neck are

---

[7] Convention and symbolism play a large part in the color of Italian painting. For example, the Madonna's dress is usually red and her mantle blue: red, the color of the ruby, symbolizing divine love; blue, the color of the sapphire and emblem of the heavens, symbolizing heavenly love, truth, and fidelity.

[8] For an exposition of Florentine painting as an expression of this tactile quality, see Berenson, *Florentine Painters of the Renaissance*.

[9] This portrait has been variously attributed by different authorities: to Antonio Pollaiuolo, to Verrocchio, to Piero della Francesca, and to Domenico Veneziano.

exquisitely modeled with minute strokes in delicate flesh tones, which indicate the essentials of the structure but no superfluous details. The ornaments and the pattern of the sleeve have been painted with painstaking but not niggling care. The flat blue ground is relieved by a few cloudlets. Against this ground the profile is placed in such a way that the whole forms an almost flat and very decorative pattern.

Thus the so-called realists of the fifteenth century — Masaccio, Paolo Uccello, Antonio Pollaiuolo — deliberately put themselves to the task of working out the fundamental principles of their craft, and made possible the later accomplishments of Leonardo, Raphael, and Michelangelo.

As we turn from this virile work to that of Fra Filippo Lippi (1406–1469 A.D.), we relax into the easy enjoyment of a charmingly gracious aspect of life (PL. 98 D). The Madonna is seated on an elaborate chair with a cushion, in an attitude of adoration of the Child, whom two roguish angels are holding up to her; through the open window appears a landscape with a river, winding roads, rocks, and distant towers. It is an intimate, happy group of mother and children, quite devoid of religious feeling, but winsome and appealing. This charming aspect of life was the main interest of Fra Filippo; and we feel it in the type of Madonna and in the exquisite delicacy with which he has painted the elaborate headdress, of the softest blue.

Emphasis upon line and the use of line as a medium of expression reaches its climax in Fra Filippo's pupil, Botticelli (1444–1510 A.D). The *Birth of Venus* (PL. 99 A) challenges attention because of its subject matter. Pagan themes were now claiming the attention of the painters, for religious fervor was waning and was being supplanted by interest in classical literature and art, particularly at the court of the Medici. A tradition tells us that Botticelli used an antique statue in the Medici garden as a model for the figure of Venus. Be that true or not, the pose is nearly that of the classical Venus. In the center of the picture the goddess stands lightly and with the utmost ease on a shell which is being blown to the shore amid a shower of roses by two vigorous zephyrs; at the right a nymph is hurrying with a mantle to meet her. The composition is built on a great semicircle that rises along the figures of the winds, reaches its crown in the head of Venus, follows the fluttering hair, and is carried down by the arm of the nymph and the line of the mantle — a semicircle that is repeated in the upper curve of the shell. In the interlocked winds there is great movement in the quick rhythmic curves of the limbs, the fluttering drapery, the great sweep of the wings, and the quick conventional lines of wavelets. This slows down in the tall, slender figure of Venus with its long quiet lines, standing somewhat isolated against a low horizon. The figure is rather flat, and the contour lines, while they model the form, still with their long graceful curves have a beauty of their own, and are emphasized by the movement in the great mass of hair twisting and fluttering, and framing the drooping head, whose expression of wistful melancholy is so characteristic of Botticelli. As the flying locks carry the eye to the nymph, the movement again rises in the impatient, whimsical curves of the drapery, which are all the more restless in contrast with the straight, conventional lines of the tree trunks, the little promontories, and the horizon. After all, the significance lies in line and pattern. While the lines model, in so far as they express the essentials of form, still they have a quality of their own. Now they are long and quiet, now short and capricious, now whimsical, and always rhythmic.

Probably the works of Botticelli in which we can see the this use of line in its purest form are the drawings for the *Divine Comedy*. In the drawing that illustrates Canto I of Il Paradiso (PL. 99 B), "the daintiest trees ever drawn wave softly over a smooth meadow"; through the circle that they form Dante and Beatrice rise toward heaven, their upturned faces filled with ecstasy. The trees and figures are drawn with a few exquisitely delicate lines. What modeling there is, is done by the contour line only. The drawing does not give us a reproduction, an illusion of nature, nor a conventionalization of natural form; nor is it a sympathetic illustration of the *Divine Comedy*, for the temperament of Botticelli was altogether different from Dante's, which was profound, majestic, and dramatic. These drawings are made of the same "stuff" as music. That is, they evoke the same exquisite emotion as a delicate melody does when drawn by a master from a rare violin. In spirit Botticelli approaches the Chinese, especially in their landscapes; for they sought, not to reproduce nature realistically, but by use of the simplest essential elements only to express an interpretation or a mood of nature (PL. 168 A).

The two tendencies that we have seen developing in Florence unite definitely in the two great culminating Florentine geniuses, Leonardo da Vinci (1452–1519 A.D.) and Michelangelo Buonarroti (1475–1564 A.D.). This we can see taking place in the workshop of Andrea Verrocchio (1435–1488 A.D.), the most important *bottega* in Florence in the third quarter of the fifteenth century.

The drawing of the head of a woman (PL. 100 A) shows us something of Verrocchio as a draughtsman. There is feeling for structure and for the softness of the flesh; the hair is drawn with both sureness and delicacy. The firmly plaited coils accentuate the free loose ringlets which have such living quality, and frame the face into a highly decorative way. It is easy to recognize here the master into whose shop came the boy Leonardo da Vinci.

In a rapid pen-and-ink sketch of a *Madonna and Child* (PL. 100 B) we find some of the characteristics of Leonardo. The Virgin is seated holding the Child, who is putting his left hand into a dish which she holds, and with his right is caressing her cheek. Leonardo has caught a single passing moment of delightful intimacy between these two — a very human mother and child — and with great rapidity and freedom has transferred his vision to the paper with entire spontaneity and apparently the slightest effort. With extraordinary delicacy and with an amazingly small number of lines, except for the fumbling in the legs, he has modeled the baby form with its folds of soft flesh, its infantile face, head, and lock of curly hair. The same kind of fleeting vision he has expressed in the head of an angel (PL. 100 C), though here with greater finish. Here is the same winsome beauty, the same penetrating vision and facile technical ability as in the preceding drawing. With perfect ease he has indicated the structure of the head, both in the modeling and in the contour line, which itself models so adequately. These drawings of Leonardo are valuable, as are all drawings of great masters, in that they reveal a closer, more spontaneous expression of the artist's mind and hand than do the finished works.

But let us study two finished paintings of Leonardo — though they are really unfinished, for Leonardo never completed anything — and in these try to discern the elements of his genius. First, the *Last Supper* (PL. 101 A). In a simple, spacious room, at a long table, Christ and the twelve disciples are seated. Christ, in the center, with outstretched hands, has just said, "One of you will betray me." At this statement a wave of intense excitement passes through the group as each asks, "Is it I?" The force and the lucidity with which this dramatic moment is expressed are due to the masterly composition. In the center is the figure of Christ, in perfect repose, isolated from the disciples because it is framed by the central window at the back and emphasized by the curved line over the opening — the only curved line in the whole architectural framework. The lines of the walls, which are relieved by vertical panelings, and the beams of the ceiling converge upon the head of Christ, while the long horizontal of the table adds to the quiet tone of the architectural setting. Into this reposeful framework is fitted the group of agitated disciples. The twelve are separated into four smaller groups, each occupying one-fifth of the length of the space, the same as that occupied by Christ alone, and united within themselves and also to each other by a movement of the hand, a gesture of the arm, or a turn of the head. The two figures at the ends are more quiet, as if to frame in the movement and hold it imprisoned. The excitement grows more intense as it approaches the figure of Christ, whose quietude at the same time halts and intensifies it. Thus we see that it is the carefully thought out composition even more than the skillful execution that gives this picture its great power. We know that Leonardo had been working on the subject for years, for a number of preliminary drawings are extant which help us follow the workings of his mind not only in the general arrangement but also in his studies for the individual heads.

The second work of Leonardo that we shall study is the *Mona Lisa* (PL. 100 D). Mona Lisa is seated in an armchair on a loggia in front of a stone parapet from which rise two columns, forming a framework for the picture. In the background is a misty, fantastic landscape. The composition is the same as in Baldovinetti's *Madonna* (PL. 98 A) — a pyramidal mass, with a strongly defined central axis, occupying most of the canvas and set over against a distant landscape. This mass is so sensitively placed in reference to the frame that, change the distance ever so little between the top of the head and the upper line of the frame, and the effect is not the same. The definitely felt axis falls from the forehead along the nose to the point where the hand crosses the arm, connecting the two masses of interest, the face and the hands. The outline of the figure is of almost geometrical simplicity, the curve of the head forming a sharply defined semicircle. Mona Lisa is very simply dressed. Her hair falls in loose ringlets and is covered by a thin veil. She wears no ornaments and her dress has but a simple border about the neck. She is seated with the utmost ease; yet the erectness of the figure and the slight turn in the body contribute to the effect. The whole figure is realized as an organic structure, existing in space. The face is modeled with the utmost subtlety, but not realistically, with the emphasis of definite traits of character. Over the delicate surface, especially about the mouth and eyes, ripples almost imperceptibly an elusive expression, perhaps a smile, which makes this face an enigma.[10] Just as exquisitely modeled and just as important in the picture are the hands — delicate, aristocratic hands suggesting a life of luxury and ease; and their soft roundness is all the more emphasized by the crumpled satin sleeves. From the figure the eye wanders off into the landscape, reaching far into the distance, fantastic, mysterious, misty, and dreamlike. The vague outlines of the rocks and waters contrast with the strongly expressed head, but at the same time are in harmony with the enigmatical, fleeting expression of the face.

A noticeable difference between the *Mona Lisa* and most of the paintings that we have studied up to this time is to be seen in the depth of the shadows, the greater softness of outline, and the more gradual transitions from light to shade. This is due to the oil technique. The Florentines had been experimenting with the mixing of pigment with oil since the middle of the fifteenth century, if not earlier, and had found that with it they could obtain not only richer color but bolder brushwork and deeper shadows. So, by the time of Leonardo, we begin to see the incisive outlines that distinguish the tempera technique become blurred and indefinite and the figure appear to reproduce more faithfully the enveloping light and air; and a shifting of the emphasis upon visual appearance rather than upon decoration. This very indefiniteness harmonized with Leonardo's desire to express fleeting, momentary feelings, and the mysteries into which his curiosity led him to delve.[11]

Before studying Michelangelo, let us turn aside a moment and look at a painting by Andrea del Sarto (1486–1531 A.D.) which is typical of the tendencies which were making themselves evident early in the sixteenth century. In the *Madonna of the Harpies* (PL. 101 B) the stately figures almost fill the canvas, yet there is a feeling of spaciousness and reposeful grandeur. The Madonna stands upon a high pedestal, assisted by two winged *putti*. With her right arm she supports the Child; with her left hand she holds a book close against her bent leg. One does not feel sincere religious conviction here, nor the tenderness of the human mother and child, but stateliness and queenly greatness. The Madonna is accompanied by two saints so placed that the three figures form a pyramidal group rich and complex in color, line,

---

[10] Read Walter Pater's famous passage in his essay on Leonardo in *The Renaissance*.

[11] No study of Leonardo is adequate without a realization of his universal type of genius. He was not exclusively or even primarily a painter, being also a sculptor, architect, engineer (particularly military), mathematician, a student of all forms of mechanical and physical science and of anatomy, a writer, and a musician. See his notebooks with drawings that form a visual commentary to the text. See also the letter which he wrote to the Duke of Milan commending himself as worthy to receive the commission for an equestrian statue that the Duke was planning to erect — in Richter, *Literary Works of Leonardo*, III, p. 395.

and strongly contrasting masses of light and shade. Certain parts are highly illuminated and others cast into deep shadows in which the contours are lost. The richness of the group is emphasized by the quiet, unadorned background, the spaciousness of which is amplified by the fact that the niche and pilasters, cut off by the frame, suggest extension beyond it. Each figure is sculpturesque and full of varied movements of head, arm, torso, or uplifted foot, thus powerfully suggesting the organic structure, and increasing the effect of regal power. The broad, sweeping folds of drapery add to this effect. This is a Madonna of great splendor, but after all grandiose rather than grand. We miss the sincerity and spontaneity of the fifteenth century which has been supplanted by a striving for effect.[12]

In Michelangelo we find the culmination of the fifteenth century as well as the tendencies of the sixteenth century, and the beginnings of the baroque. This we have already seen in his architecture. Michelangelo considered himself a sculptor; and when Pope Julius II ordered him to decorate the ceiling of the Sistine chapel[13] (PL. 101 c), he rebelled. But the Pope was insistent. The result looks as if Michelangelo were getting even, as if he had said, "Well, if the pope will have his ceiling, let him have it; but," as Woelfflin suggests, "he will have to stretch his neck to see it." As a scheme of decoration, this ceiling is an absurdity, a penance alike to the artist while he painted it, and to the spectator who wishes to look at it. A vast complex of humanity thunders down upon him, drowning out everything else, and the frescoes on the walls pale before it. On the other hand it is a marvelous composition scarcely to be equaled (PL. 102 c). Though the first impression is bewildering, a brief study easily resolves the mass into a great pattern, the motifs of which are rhythmically repeated and inextricably coördinated. The eye is carried from human figure to human figure; prophets and sibyls sit in niches flanked by pilasters on which are *putti* who serve, Caryatid-like, to hold up the projecting cornice which runs the length of the vault and forms a framework for the central panels and a connecting link between the prophets and the panels; for on this cornice rest the blocks on which the nudes are seated, a pair at each corner of the smaller panels, holding between them, by means of bands, round me-

---

PLATE 99

(*A*) Botticelli. Birth of Venus. c. 1485 A.D. Uffizi, Florence. (Alinari)

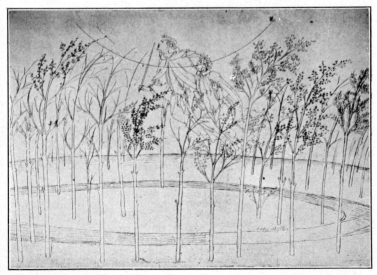

(*B*) Botticelli. Drawing to Illustrate Dante's Divine Comedy, Paradiso I. 1492–97 A.D. (Lippmann)

PLATE 100

(*A*) Verrocchio. Drawing of the Head of a Woman. Black chalk. Life-size. British Museum, London.

(*B*) Leonardo. Drawing of Madonna and Child. Pen and ink. Louvre, Paris. (Giraudon)

(*C*) Leonardo. Drawing of the Head of an Angel. Silver-point. C. 1483 A.D. Turin. (Anderson)

(*D*) Leonardo. Mona Lisa. 1503–06 A.D. Louvre, Paris. (Alinari)

PLATE 101

(*A*) Leonardo. Last Supper. c. 1495–98 A.D. Refectory of Santa Maria delle Grazie, Milan. (Alinari) The doorway in the foreground was cut through later. The ruined condition of the Last Supper is due partly to careless restoration and vandalism and partly to the fact that in this painting Leonardo appeared to be experimenting, as was his habit, in media, and painted in oil upon a surface wrongly prepared for it. So that even early in the sixteenth century it had begun to flake and show signs of ruin. Recently expert specialists have scientifically removed the dirt and restorations, regulated the humidity, and very delicately but firmly bound to the wall what remains of Leonardo's work.

(*B*) Andrea del Sarto. Madonna of the Harpies. 1517 A.D. Uffizi, Florence. (Alinari)

(*C*) Sistine Chapel. Vatican, Rome. (Anderson)

PLATE 102

(A) Michelangelo. Jeremiah.
Sistine Ceiling.

(B) Michelangelo. Drawing. Study for a Resurrection. British Museum, London. (Berenson)

(C) Michelangelo. Sistine Ceiling, Detail. 1508–12 A.D.

dallions. These figures serve a decorative and unifying purpose, each pair with the help of the medallions carrying the eye, by their repeated rhythmic pattern, from the larger to the smaller panels all the length of the ceiling.

The marvel of gathering so many figures into a harmonious unit would have been impossible except for the extremely simple, though strongly marked, architectural framework, all in mono-chrome, which holds the mass together, so that the eye can wander about among the figures and yet feel the unity of the whole. It is always the human figure, sharply outlined against the neutral tone of this architectural setting, or the plain back-ground of the panels. Why did Michelangelo decorate the ceil-ing in this way? It was because to him the most beautiful, the most expressive thing in the whole world was the human figure. It was beautiful not only because of its form but because of the spiritual and ethical significance that its form could so success-fully express. The fifteenth century painters as well as the sculptors had been striving to render it in all its tectonic life, both at rest and in movement. Now Michelangelo, with his wonderful knowledge of anatomy, acquired by his studies in dissection, found it perfectly facile in his hands, so that he took another step and used it not simply for itself, but to ex-press a state of mind or soul. In doing this, he represented it in its most simple, elemental aspect, that is, the nude or simply draped, with no background, no ornamental embellishment, and an idealized physiognomy. "Simple people," he called the prophets. Let us look at one of them, *Jeremiah* (PL. 102 A). The prophet is seated in a niche, his head bowed upon his uplifted right hand, sunk in deep thought. The line of the shoulders is repeated in the drapery across the lap. This broad sweep of line, producing a massive, monumental effect, is strongly rem-iniscent of Giotto (PL. 96 A). In fact, Michelangelo, in many respects, is Giotto plus the scientific knowledge which the Florentines had gained in the two hundred years intervening. The vertical line of the beard, emphasizing the central axis of the figure and giving it a sense of equilibrium, the droop of the right shoulder, the weight of the bowed head on the right hand, and the marvelous left hand resting so limply on the lap, a limpness that emphasizes by contrast the intensity of con-centration of mind — all these contribute to an impression of deep thought. Nor are there any details to individualize this prophet; everything is so generalized that we feel that this is not only Jeremiah brooding over Israel, is not only Michelangelo himself, pondering in isolation and melancholy, but is every human being, who, probing with his own soul beneath the surface of things, ponders over the problems and mysteries of life. Thus the figure, in its last analysis, is a universal expression of the serious man's thoughtfulness before the unfathomed ways of God.

It was probably in the twenty *Nudes* that Michelangelo was happiest, for here he had the opportunity of reveling in his ideal — the human nude. Although they perform the same decorative purpose, still they are very different. PL. 103 B shows one in which the outstanding impression is that of strain and stress. The mighty back, the thrust-out right arm and shoulder, the bent left leg by which the figure is supporting itself, the tousled hair, the sharply defined profile with the open mouth — all these combine to create a single, unified impression of struggle. The figure in PL. 103 A, on the other hand, though very complex, is all idle ease and complacency. The complex pose calls for bold foreshortening that reveals Michelangelo's superb ability as a draughtsman.

So far we have studied single figures only. Now let us take one of the panels as an example of Michelangelo's power of composition. In the *Creation of Adam* (PL. 103 C) we find the space divided into two masses, which stand out clearly against the perfectly flat background. Adam, on a hillside — the hill is merely suggested, again a Giottesque quality — is just awakening, still dreamy, but his physical perfection is impregnated with latent physical power. The right shoulder thrust back, the turn of the head, the twist in the torso, and the bent leg indicate capacity for powerful movement. The comparative serenity and quiet flow and rhythm of line in this figure are reminiscent of the Parthenon marbles, the *Mount Olympus*, for example (PL. 40 B). Michelangelo probably never knew anything about the Parthenon marbles. But while, as a youth, he lived at the palace of Lorenzo de' Medici, he studied the classic gems and statues which Lorenzo had gathered into his garden and imbibed something of their fundamental spirit. His own restless, bitter spirit, however, forbade his ever attaining the complete serenity and moderation of the Greek. The second group, that of God with his attendant spirits, is full of vigor and movement. These two contrasting masses, one filled with quiet calm and the other with powerful movement, are unified by the wonderful connecting link of the two hands, each marvelously expressive of the mood of its possessor — Adam's limp and lifeless, God's tense with active power. This touch of finger to finger is the act of creation.

In Michelangelo's painting we find the same essential qualities as in his sculpture. In fact, one feels that these mighty figures on the ceiling are highly plastic and sculptural. He himself says in a letter written while he was discouraged and depressed about the ceiling: "This is not my profession. I waste time without any results. God help me." In all his work one looks in vain for quietude, and everywhere is made to feel restlessness or violence — something of the bitterness and conflict which distracted this artist's soul.

In one of his late drawings, a study for a *Resurrection* (PL. 102 B), we see less of the struggle. It is more a manifestation, perhaps, of his sublime religious faith. From the open tomb the soldiers start back in amazement and awe as the majestic figure of Christ floats upward into space, with a deep calm all the more powerful because of the contrasting agitation of the soldiers. The figure of Christ is studied with the greatest care and its plastic quality emphasized by the floating drapery behind it, not finished as the figure is, but suggested only. So, too, the head and hands are merely indicated. This lack of finish, however, stimulates the imagination, thus enhancing rather than detracting from the poetry and the majesty of the conception. The drawing, as it is, is a complete expression of what Michelangelo wished to say. Why, then, add finished details?

In Michelangelo we reach the climax of Florentine painting. He had gathered up all that the fifteenth century had learned and then by his own sheer genius lifted it to so lofty a plane that it overwhelmed all the artists of the time, who were so impressed by this new revelation that they forsook their own paths to follow in his; with the result that we have empty copying of his forms entirely lacking in the creative spirit. Hence came the decadence which followed his death.

SUMMARY

Florentine painting is highly typical of the Renaissance in its loftiest attainment. The painters were craftsmen who could work equally well in various media. Beginning with the Byzantine and ancient Roman traditions, under the guidance of classical art, and influenced by the new attitude toward life, with its widening interests, they discovered, or rediscovered, the fundamental principles that govern the representation of the figure. Their art was primarily a figure art. The subject matter was religious, for religious subjects were commissioned by the church, the nobles, and the guilds, all of them the great art-patrons of the time. In the fourteenth and early fifteenth centuries the medieval tradition was still strong and religious faith still fervid. At times, in the eager searching of the age, the scientific interest almost smothered the artistic. Yet the majority of the artists were great enough to maintain their sense of monumentality, spiritual significance, and design. The sincerity, joy, and ethical value that result from striving toward an ideal make early Florentine art analogous to early Greek art. Both were more vital and more significant than the later more accomplished creations which were an outgrowth of their endeavors. Although not unmindful of color, still the Florentines were primarily draughtsmen, for their ultimate purpose was incisive drawing which recorded the essential, monumental aspects of form and of the outward manifestation, through form, of the inner life. By the late fifteenth century, the problems had been solved and the passion of endeavor cooled, for accomplishment was easier. The oil technique was making possible greater richness in every way. The medieval faith was weakening, and the classical subjects both in spirit and in subject were engrossing the attention of all. Under these conditions highly accomplished works were executed; but too often a superficiality, a striving for effect, or an emphasis upon technical accomplishment alone, marks the decadence.

BIBLIOGRAPHY

In addition to the general books listed in Chapter XV:

BERENSON, BERNHARD, Florentine Painters of the Renaissance. N.Y., Putnam, 1909.
BROWN, A. V. V., AND RANKIN, WILLIAM, A Short History of Italian Painting. N.Y., Dutton, 1914.
COX, KENYON, Classic Point of View. N.Y., Scribner, 1911.
CROWE, J. A., AND CAVALCASELLE, G. B., New History of Painting in Italy. 3 v. N.Y., Dutton, 1908–09.
CRUTTWELL, MAUD, Antonio Pollaiuolo. N.Y., Scribner, 1907.
—— ——, Verrocchio. N.Y., Scribner, 1904.
DOUGLAS, LANGTON, Fra Angelico. London, Bell, 1902.
FRY, ROGER, Vision and Design. London, Chatto, 1920.
GRONAU, GEORG, Leonardo da Vinci. N.Y., Dutton, 1902.
HOLROYD, CHARLES, Life of Michael Angelo Buonarroti. London, Duckworth, 1903.
HORNE, H. P., Alessandro Filipepi, Commonly Called Sandro Botticelli. London, Bell, 1908.
LAURIE, A. P., Materials of the Painter's Craft. Philadelphia, Lippincott, 1911.
MATHER, F. J., JR., Estimates in Art. N.Y., Scribner, 1916.
—— ——, History of Italian Painting. N.Y., Holt, 1923.

PATER, W. H., The Renaissance: Studies in Art and Poetry. London, Macmillan, 1910.

ROLLAND, ROMAIN, Michelangelo (tr. Street). N.Y., Duffield, 1912.

—— ——, Life of Michelangelo (tr. Lees). N.Y., Dutton, 1912.

RUSKIN, JOHN, Mornings in Florence. Boston, Caldwell, 1912.

SIRÉN, OSVALD, Giotto and Some of His Followers. Cambridge, Harvard University Press, 1917.

—— ——, Leonardo da Vinci. New Haven, Yale University Press, 1916.

STRUTT, E. C., Fra Filippo Lippi. London, Bell, 1906.

THIIS, J. P., Leonardo da Vinci. London, Jenkins, 1913.

WOELFFLIN, HEINRICH, The Art of the Italian Renaissance. N.Y., Putnam, 1913.

CHAPTER XVII
THE RENAISSANCE IN ITALY
c. 1300–1600 A.D.

PAINTING IN CENTRAL AND NORTHERN ITALY

Siena, though situated in central Italy only about thirty miles from Florence, always remained medieval at heart. Her attitude toward pagan thought and influence is illustrated by the story of the statue of Aphrodite that had been found buried near the city and set up to decorate the public fountain. A long series of disasters subsequent to the coming of Aphrodite was laid to her malevolent presence. Hence the council decreed her removal; and not only to free themselves from further disaster but also to bring ill fate upon their enemy Florence, they saw to it that the statue was taken far enough away from the city to be buried in Florentine ground. Siena's history is one of struggle not only with Florence but over internal feuds, so that a note of grimness is detected in the pleasure-loving life of her people, who were at the same time intensely religious. They adored Saint Catherine, who lived among them; and they laid aside their frivolity and gayety under the homely, vigorous eloquence of San Bernardino. As a commercial center in the twelfth and thirteenth centuries, Siena came into contact both directly and indirectly with Byzantine art and there found a type of expression peculiarly fitted to her emotional, mystical temperament.

A typical manifestation of the Sienese school at its climax is found in Duccio di Buoninsegna (1255–1319 A.D.). His altarpiece for the Siena cathedral, the *Majestà*, was double, so placed that the front (PL. 104 A) faced the nave, and the back, with its small pictures (PL. 104 B), the choir.[1] Let us look at the front. In the center, the Madonna and Child are seated on an elaborate throne decorated with *Cosmati* work; standing or kneeling in rows that seem unending are angels and saints, all turned toward the central group; over the back of the throne four angels are bending graciously. The Madonna's robe is a deep, rich blue contrasting with

[1] For an account of the festive occasion when this altarpiece was carried from the shop to the cathedral, see Douglas, *History of Siena*, p. 336.

the softer tones of the throne; the background and halos are gold. The flowing line, the gold and jewel-like color, the splendid isolation of the central figure standing out large and patternlike against the background, the successful appeal to the worshiper's adoration — all contribute to produce a sumptuous piece of decoration and a deep expression of religious emotion. This is largely Byzantine, yet if we examine the drapery of the Madonna's robe, we see that the stiff folds are gone and the cloth hangs naturally. There is a certain amount of modeling, too, in the figure, and a feeling for life in the body. In the droop of the heads and in the easy sweep of line there is a stately grace. Thus, while the picture carries the old Byzantine form, it reveals also a new feeling for naturalism. It was in the thirteenth century that the conventional, hieratic kings and queens of the western portal of *Chartres* were giving way to the naturalistic figures of the northern and southern portals (PL. 82 A and B). The observation of nature to which Europe was turning afresh was manifesting itself in Siena as well as in France and in Florence. It is to be noticed in Duccio, however, that while this naturalism softens the hieratic quality, it does not change the essentially Byzantine character of the work.

The narrative and decorative quality of Duccio's work is seen in the *Three Marys at the Tomb* (PL. 104 B). The angel is sitting on the open tomb, his figure framed by the rugged barren hill behind; on the left stand the three Marys who have come with their jars of ointment and who shrink back, startled at the sight of the angel and the empty tomb. There are no details here to detract from the simplicity and the dramatic power with which the incident is told. The figures, while they show some feeling for form and naturalistic rendering of drapery, still are quite flat, the angel being very close to the *Good Shepherd* mosaic (PL. 61 A); the hills of the background are conventional, with no depth, symbols, as it were, of landscape; the flat background is gold. Here rhythmic line, pattern, and bright color with a liberal use of gold have combined to make the panel essentially decorative.

An important follower of Duccio was Simone Martini (c. 1285–1344 A.D.). In his *Annunciation* (PL. 105 A), at the left, is the angel Gabriel kneeling. He has just alighted and is eagerly pressing forward with the branch of olive to deliver his message to the Virgin. She sits on an inlaid throne, her finger marking the place in the book where she was reading when interrupted by the angel, and she shrinks at his message. Between the two stands a vase of flowers; above in the central arch is a circle of cherubim surrounding the dove. The flat gold background, without a suggestion of landscape, keeps the interest centered upon the two figures. Looking at these more closely, we see how flat they are; the Virgin's robe does not seem to cover a real figure, but forms a dark pattern made up of harmonious curves rhythmically repeated. In the face, too, there is almost no modeling, and the beautiful line that marks its contour, as well as the curves of the drapery, is used primarily for its own sake. There is more restlessness in Gabriel, expressed in the pattern of the rich brocade of his robe, in the quick rhythmic curves of fluttering drapery, and in the broad sweeping lines of the wings; and he offers an effective contrast to the quiet, dark silhouette of the Virgin. We notice how skillfully the vase of flowers joins the figures; eliminate it, and the unity is disturbed at once. The relation of figure to space, particularly to the triple arch of the frame, is carefully thought out. What Simone Martini is attempting in this picture is not to give a realistic reconstruction or an illusion of the incident of the annunciation, but to make a beautiful piece of decoration by means of flowing line, pattern, and color, and by this means to create an atmosphere of religious emotion, abstractly, in a manner closely akin to the Chinese. Compare this *Annunciation* with the *Pietà* that we studied in the Gothic period (PL. 87 A). Although the French picture contains more realism, yet the tragic pathos surging through it is obtained by the same means that Simone used.

To appreciate the painting of Siena, we must approach it as we do Byzantine mosaics, with a mind freed from the common prejudice that a picture to be successful must give us an actual reproduction or illusion of nature. The Sienese took the conventions of the Byzantine mosaic and miniature painters and, playing upon them, produced an art now hieratic, as in Duccio, now exquisite, as in Simone Martini; but always noble, and always decorative. This they accomplished by the use of pure line, flat tones, beautiful dark silhouettes rising with rhythmic curves against a gold background, and exquisite jewel-like color. By these means they also attained to an emotional, mystic quality that the beholder is free to feel because the attention is not focused upon the recognition of naturalistic detail. As the Sienese came under the influence of the Florentines and attempted to graft upon their own art the Florentine naturalism, they brought upon it a blight, for theirs was the culmination and the end of a great tradition, while the Florentine was the beginning of a new, founded on entirely different principles. Duccio had been great

PLATE 103

(*A and B*) Michelangelo. Decorative Nudes. Sistine Ceiling.

(*C*) Michelangelo. Creation of Adam. Sistine Ceiling.

PLATE 104

(*A*) Duccio. Majestà. Detail of the center. Originally it had an elaborate Gothic frame.
1308–11 A.D. Siena Cathedral. (Alinari)

(*B*) Duccio. Three Marys at the Tomb. A panel from the back of
the Majestà. Siena Cathedral. (Alinari)

PLATE 105

(*A*) Simone Martini (assisted by Lippo Memmi). Annunciation.
1333 A.D. Uffizi, Florence. (Alinari)

(*B*) Perugino. Crucifixion. 1493–96 A.D. Santa Maria Maddalena
dei Pazzi, Florence. (Anderson)

PLATE 106

(*A*) Piero della Francesca. Federigo da Montefeltro, Duke of Urbino. 1465 A.D. Uffizi, Florence. (Alinari)

(*B*) Raphael. La Belle Jardinière. 1507–08 A.D. Louvre, Paris.

(*C*) Piero della Francesca. Visit of the Queen of Sheba to King Solomon. Fresco. 1452–66 A.D. San Francesco, Arezzo. (Alinari)

enough to accept naturalism only in so far as it did not interfere with the tradition upon which his art was based. But when his lesser followers attempted to make it their sole purpose, their art sank into decadence.

Besides Siena, the cities of Umbria and the Marches — Perugia, Assisi, and Urbino — were important art centers in central Italy. These provinces are mountainous, and their hilltop towns have wide views over hills and river valleys with olive groves and gardens. "It seems as if life must be easy here, and the horizon itself, bounded on every side by a line of harmonious hills, attunes the soul to peace. A light breeze is blowing and its murmur is soft as that of the wind among the reeds of Thrasymene. . . . 'Gentle Umbria' is really no mere conventional phrase, especially if we take the word in its widest and strongest sense. Umbria is 'gentle' because it is peaceful, because its rhythms are quiet and equable, because the admiration it inspires is without terror, because it is truly human. I understand why the joy of life held a larger place in the religion of S. Francis than the fear of death."[2]

Local schools had sprung up here and there, strongly Byzantine in general character; but their currents were destined to mingle with those of the great centers of Florence, Siena, and Venice. In the northern part of Umbria, which lies close to Florence, there was a group of painters who came directly under the influence of that city. Chief of these was Piero della Francesca (1416–1492 A.D.). To study Piero, let us go to the town of Arezzo, and look at the fresco that represents the *Visit of the Queen of Sheba to Solomon* (PL. 106 c). At the right the queen, surrounded by her attendants, is kneeling before a bridge,[3] the whole group being accentuated by the tree behind them. The kneeling queen is emphasized by the contrasting tall, erect figures of the attendants. From the one to the other the eye is carried by the alternating light and dark masses, and by the long sweeping lines of the drapery to the group on the left, that of the grooms and horses also accentuated by a tree. Here the white horse turns the eye inward, where it is caught by the light hat, the black horse, and by the small figure of a serving boy until it again reaches the first group. Every figure seems to fit inevitably into the place where it stands. There is ample space in the landscape although it does not have the illimitable quality of Leonardo, but is somewhat sharply cut off in the middle distance, keeping the whole

---

[2] Gabriel Faure, *Wanderings in Italy*, Part III, p. 141.
[3] This fresco is a detail from a series that illustrates the story of the cross on which Christ was crucified. In this scene the bridge before which the Queen is kneeling was made from the tree that was destined to furnish the wood for the cross.

wall space flat. There is a certain profound repose in the scene. The figures are austere and quite devoid of emotion. The drawing and modeling are reduced to the simplest terms possible; all details not vitally necessary to the design are eliminated; the hands, feet, and faces are almost conventionally treated and vary but little. Piero shows here a lofty disregard of natural appearance, yet he communicates a deeply convincing feeling of reality. This is because as a student of mathematics and perspective he builds up his design by means of the application of severe scientific laws; for every figure and every object is placed with mathematical precision as regards both linear and aerial perspective; the lights and darks are massed with careful regard for design and for the easy guidance of the eye from figure to figure; elimination of detail and simplification of form have been carried as far as possible without losing literary content. The result is a fine piece of decoration in which calm, austere figures stand up in an intensely real space. This space, however, is not deep enough to produce the illusion of piercing the wall, but is kept flat so that, with the interplay of the sharply contrasting light and dark masses and the exquisite adjustment of every part of the composition to the whole, it produces an effect of monumental grandeur and establishes an unequaled ideal of mural decoration.

A painter of Piero's temperament is not likely to be successful as a portrait painter, for severe simplification eliminates those very details that differentiate the individual from his fellows and express his character. Hence a portrait painted by this type of artist is particularly interesting, and we find in the *Duke of Urbino* (PL. 106 A) what we would expect — primarily design. The figure with its bright red cap and robe occupies most of the panel, rising with rugged strength and princely dignity against a low-lying landscape and great expanse of sky. But subtly interplaying with this feeling for design is a certain amount of character expression. There is strength, firmness, and benevolence in the face with its great nose, thin lips, firm mouth, and prominent chin. The precise drawing and modeling of a few essentials have brought out the expression, while the rest is suggested in a large and simple way. It is an austere but compelling portrait because of its remarkable balance between design and subject matter. Piero may well be called Florentine-Umbrian. His art was coldly intellectual, lofty, and more austere even than that of the naturalistic group of Florentines which included Paolo Uccello, and Antonio Pollaiuolo, with whom he belongs artistically.

More typically Umbrian was Pietro Perugino, the Perugian

(1446–1524 A.D.). The peace and harmony of so winning a manifestation of nature as Umbria affords seem to have penetrated his very fiber, and were never lost even when he came to Florence and was strongly influenced by a far more intellectual kind of art. In his *Crucifixion* (PL. 105 B), although the subject is dramatic and tragic, the dominant note is one of quiet repose. The painter has divided the wall to be decorated by covering it with three sweeping arches, a use of the space which is in itself a quiet rhythm. The center one is filled with the cross bearing the figure of Christ, which stands out against the clear sky above a low horizon; in the side arches are figures of the Virgin, John, and saints, so placed that with the figure of Christ in the center they form a triangle of long base and long, reposeful sides; the kneeling figure of the Magdalen not only emphasizes the height of the cross but also breaks what would otherwise be a too monotonous balance of figures. Behind them, unifying the whole composition, stretches a landscape of hills and valleys and rivers and trees, above which are reaches of sky, whose spaciousness is suggested by the tall slender trees at the left. The lines of this landscape are far-extending and quiet, and the distance is immersed in a bluish haze. Everything is very much simplified. Were all the little irregularities and details that actually exist in nature indicated here as the camera would indicate them, the result would not be one of tranquil repose such as Perugino here communicates. This applies to the figures as well. They are not significant structurally; but they fit into the landscape almost architecturally, like a column or a pediment into the design of a building, and the whole composition becomes a unified poetical expression of a quiet mood of nature.

To Perugia and into the shop of Perugino came the young Raphael Sanzio (1483–1520 A.D.) from his home in Urbino. A little later he made his way to Florence, and for a few years, as his drawings show, was a very diligent student not only of Leonardo and Michelangelo but of the earlier Florentines also — Masaccio, Donatello, and Pollaiuolo — all of whom were tremendous revelations to him.

The whole series of Raphael's Madonnas, from the *Granduca* to the *Sistine* is indicative of the way in which the Florentine masters were shaping this docile, charming Umbrian talent. In *La Belle Jardinière* (PL. 106 B), for example, the influence of Leonardo appears in the compact pyramidal grouping of the figures;[4] that of Michelangelo, in the restless twisting pose of the Christ

[1] See Leonardo's *Madonna of the Rocks* (Louvre), and the *Madonna with Saint Anne* (Louvre).

Child.[5] The group is set in a charming landscape with the Umbrian feeling for tranquillity and spaciousness. In fact there is a compelling realization of this spaciousness and of the possibility of walking out into the landscape and of breathing deeply there. Yet the Madonna dominates the picture. Notice how suggestive of the dome of the sky is the curve of the frame, and with what a masterly feeling for design the pattern of the group fits the space. The *Sistine Madonna*[6] derives its effect from the carefully studied composition with its effective use of contrasts. The traditional pyramidal arrangement is there; the Madonna and Child, masterfully grouped and balanced, are all the more majestic because the saints on either side are kneeling; the figure of one is turned inward, the other, by his gesture, outward; one looks down, the other up. The sincerity of religious conviction found in the early Renaissance has disappeared. Although the painters still produced pictures with religious subjects because the church commissioned them to do so, their interest was frankly human and largely pagan. Conscious skill had taken the place of sincerity of faith and of struggle.

Raphael's sensitiveness to design reveals itself best in his *Vatican Frescoes*, of which the *Disputà* is typical (PL. 107 c). The great lunette occupies the entire side of the room. Wherever the eye rests upon the wall, it is caught by a sweeping curve, and is carried by the receding steps, or by the vertical line of the axis inevitably to the altar on which stands the monstrance over against a brilliantly illuminated sky. Above the arc of clouds is represented the heavenly scene. In the center Christ sits enthroned between the Virgin and Saint John, God the father above, and the dove below; seated on each side in a semicircle are saints; above, a second parallel arc is suggested in the flying angels and clouds filled with cherubim. There is a calmness and serene majesty in the heavenly group, contrasting with the variety and movement in the lower. This also is built along an arc that approaches but does not meet the upper. About the altar are the four fathers of the church, Jerome, Gregory, Ambrose, and Augustine, and ranged on each side are dignitaries, old men and young, reading or exhorting, meditating or writing, some in stately repose, others in vigorous movement. Each figure, though interesting in itself, is significant chiefly for the part it plays in the whole group; for every pose, every gesture of all this multitude is carefully thought out with regard to the whole.

[5] See Michelangelo's *Madonna and Child* (Bruges).
[6] Painted for the monks of Piacenza and called *Sistine* because of the prominent figure of Pope Sixtus.

For example, at the extreme left two figures are leaning on a railing absorbed in a book, except that the elder is turning toward the youth who looks back and at the same time is moving and pointing toward the altar; the connection between the two being also helped by the gesture of the man standing just behind them. Were it not for this the figures at the left would appear to have no place in the group. By such means Raphael has tied his figures together and at the same time kept the movement working toward the center of interest, the altar. Here a climax is reached; the quiet dignity of the fathers is enhanced by the impetuous zeal of the youths just behind them, who point so eagerly to the host, the gesture of the one on the right serving as an important connecting link between the upper and lower parts of the composition, though the chief unifying element of the two great arcs is the serene landscape with its great open reaches of sky. Even in a monumental mural decoration such as this, Raphael has not lost his Umbrian feeling of spaciousness.

Thus we have seen Raphael as an accomplished designer of great wall decorations. In another field also he was a master — in that of portraiture. In the *Castiglione* (PL. 107 A) we feel a quiet elegance. The subdued harmony of the grays and blacks, the rich costume relieved by the soft white shirt-front, the placidly folded hands, the steadfast but quiet gaze — all contribute to a truthful impression of this calm, modest humanist, a perfect embodiment of what Castiglione himself describes as the perfect courtier.[7]

Northern Italy includes the centers of the Po valley — Milan, Verona, Mantua, Ferrara, Bologna, Padua, and, chief of all, Venice.

Venice was more isolated than any other Italian city. The islands on which it was built in the midst of salt marshes near the head of the Adriatic Sea offered a refuge for the peoples of north Italy from the barbarian invaders of the fifth century. Segregated from the rest of Italy, it developed quite independently. The Venetians early became a seafaring people, establishing close relations with the East and sending their artists to execute commissions at the court of Constantinople. Venetian markets were full of the rich brocades, silks, jewels, metal goods, and slaves of the Near East. Politically, Venice was sound; and, though autocratic, was peaceful and free from the periodic feuds that were constantly rending other Italian cities. Religiously,

---

[7] In *The Courtier*, in which the reader is introduced intimately to the life of the court of Urbino, one of the most enlightened and refined of the Renaissance.

too, Venice was more independent. Safely remote from the papal power at Rome, she centered her religious life about the worship of her patron, Saint Mark, quite independent of papal bulls.

Venetian life was the antithesis of Florentine, for it was dominantly gay and luxurious. A fervid patriotism made strong demands upon its citizens for the glorification of the state. There were gorgeous pageants and ceremonies both religious and civil, besides private banquets and pompous balls,[8] the richest costumes of stiff brocades, gold embroidery, and lavish lace and jewels. This extravagance and love of display was not conducive to intellectual pursuits. A humanist was shabbily treated and even starved in Venice, and a profoundly religious man found no sympathy there.

Gay and isolated as she was, however, her art did not remain uninfluenced by the great stirrings that were revolutionizing Italian art. Up to the fifteenth century Venetian painting was strongly Byzantine with the love of color a predominant quality, as one might expect in a city so closely connected with the East. Nevertheless, it received strong enough impulses from outside forces, particularly Florentine, to steer its course into other channels. This influence we see first early in the fifteenth century, when Venice through the conquest of Padua began to establish closer relations with the rest of Italy. Now Padua, an old Roman colony, had always had a strong intellectual and religious strain in her culture; her pride in being the birthplace of the great Roman historian Livy led her naturally toward an enthusiasm for things classical; at the same time her religious fervor led her to respond as easily as the Sienese to San Bernardino. Furthermore, Padua had been close to Florence artistically, for Giotto was painting in the *Arena Chapel* about 1305; in the first half of the fifteenth century Paolo Uccello was working in this general locality; and in 1443 Donatello came to decorate an altar and to make the equestrian statue of *Gattamelata*.

All this we see reflected in the drawings of the so-called "father of Venetian painting," Jacopo Bellini (died 1470 A.D.). In his notebooks of drawings[9] we are struck by his fancy, and by his lively joy in nature — trees, hills, flowers, particularly animals, both real and fantastic. Jacopo had been touched by the naturalistic movement, and also by the growing passion for classical subjects, for sheet after sheet in these notebooks shows

---

[8] See the paintings of Gentile Bellini, Tintoretto, and Veronese.
[9] See Ricci, *Jacopo Bellini e i suoi Libri di Disegni*, Florence, Alinari, 1908.

III. GIORGIONE

Madonna with Saint Francis and Saint George.
1504 A.D. Castelfranco.

drawings of architectural details, antique statues, centaurs, and satyrs.

The greatest successor of Jacopo Bellini at Venice was his son, Giovanni Bellini (1430–1516 A.D.). In an early *Madonna* (PL. 107 B) the Virgin, filled with human tenderness, is adoring the Child who lies on a parapet asleep. Behind her is a low-lying landscape, above which she rises with serene grandeur, almost filling the curved panel. The slight turn of her body from the frontal position and the inclination of the head give one a sense of the structure of the form; yet that is not the quality in the picture that impresses us most. Nor is it the wonderful blue of the robe, nor the quiet landscape and pearly sky of the background. The quality that makes this Madonna so impressive is the expression of a mood of profound serenity. Line, pattern, and color are all ordered toward this end — the sleeping child, the low horizon, the balanced vertical and horizontal lines, the rather arbitrary verticals in the drapery that frame the hands almost architecturally. It is as if everything were hushed, and one could hear the deep tones of a great hymn.

Emotion of a different kind, but just as sincerely felt, Giovanni expressed in a *Pietà* (PL. 108 A). A low-lying landscape with no great depth and an expanse of sky marked by horizontal cloudlets form a quiet background for concentration upon the tragic grief expressed by the three figures represented half-length in the foreground just behind a parapet. The Virgin and Saint John are supporting the body of the dead Christ, whose head is turned toward the Virgin's. Both figures are brought together into such a compact physical unity that one feels intensely the tender, intimate, personal relationship existing between them. This is emphasized by the fact that Saint John is turning away, unable to share this intimacy but deeply aware of the pathos of the tragedy. To be sure, there is a disquieting angularity and hardness about the contours and the drapery. This shows that Giovanni, while in Padua, had caught both the emotional fervor that pervaded this city and also the intellectual intensity which, among the artists, found expression in an intensive study of form. Their figures appear hammered-out and schematic, with hard lines and a tendency to formal design. In the *Pietà*, however, Giovanni has shown himself enough of an artist to simplify his forms and mass his lights and darks broadly. Thus his design contributes much to the profound feeling which is the most significant thing about the picture — the superb expression of "the tenderness and intimacy of grief."

In the *Frari Madonna* (PL. 108 B), Giovanni is more truly Venetian. The composition suggests a scene in a church. In the center is the apse, decorated in gold brocade, where the Madonna sits on a lofty throne. On each side four saints turning toward her are standing in the aisles that surround the apse, separated from it by columns. Thus the architectural unity suggested by the church building, and the psychological unity of the two groups of saints with the Madonna, bring about a singleness of effect. The elaborate frame covered with typically Renaissance carvings, the rich chiaroscuro, the sumptuous stuffs, and mellow, harmonious color produce a picture of truly Venetian splendor. But there is no profound emotional quality, no religious feeling. The Madonna is very stately and very human. The heavy silk of her robe falls in rich, heavy, somewhat angular folds, suggestive of the texture of elegant stuff. It is an impression of happiness, wealth, and worldliness.

An important tendency not only in Giovanni but in the Venetian school as a whole is seen in a small *Allegory* (PL. 109 A). Here, in the foreground, is a paved enclosure in the center of which are children playing around a tree; men and women stand about apparently without unity of action. The rest of the panel is filled with a landscape in which is a mountain lake surrounded by rocky hills. It is evening; only the rocks catch the light, and the lower hills are in the shadow. There is a feeling for atmosphere in the softened contours. What the scene represents is quite unimportant. The significant thing is that here we have a charming landscape that is an expression of joy in one of the moods of nature. This impression is heightened by the jewel-like color. The tendency illustrated here is the increasing importance of landscape. For it is now being valued more and more for itself, with the figure subordinate to it, and is being less used as a tapestry-like background against which the figure is silhouetted (PLS. 98 and 100 D).

Into the shop of the aged Giovanni came the two youths who were to add new elements to Venetian painting and to bring it to its culmination — Giorgione and Titian. Giorgione (1478–1510 A.D.) left but few paintings, for he died young. His *Castelfranco Madonna* (COLOR PL. III) is detached and serene in feeling. In the center is a lofty throne on which the Madonna is seated, holding the Child; on each side in front of an enclosing wall stand two saints, Francis and George; behind the wall a landscape stretches into the distance, over which is the glow of early-morning light. The figures are absorbed, each in himself, and,

PLATE 107

(*A*) Raphael. Baldassare Castiglione.
1515 A.D. Louvre, Paris.

(*B*) Giovanni Bellini. Madonna. 1450–
60 A.D. Estate of Theodore Davis,
Metropolitan Museum, New York.

(*C*) Raphael. Disputà. 1509–11 A.D. Vatican, Rome. (Alinari)

PLATE 108

(*A*) Giovanni Bellini. Pietà. c. 1460 A.D. Brera Milan. (Alinari)

(*B*) Giovanni Bellini. Madonna. 1488 A.D. Church of the Frari, Venice. (Alinari)

PLATE 109

(*A*) Giovanni Bellini. Allegory, possibly from a medieval poem, the Pilgrimage of the Soul, and representing in the foreground the earthly paradise. c. 1490 A.D. Uffizi, Florence. (Alinari)

(*B*) Titian; attributed also to Giorgione. Concert. Pitti, Florence. (Alinari)

PLATE 110

(*A*) Titian. Bacchus and Ariadne. 1523 A.D. National Gallery, London.

(*B*) Titian. Portrait of an Unknown Man ("Young Englishman," or "Duke of Norfolk") c. 1540–45 A.D. Pitti, Florence. (Alinari)

(*C*) Titian. Pope Paul III and His Grandsons. c. 1545 A.D. Naples. (Alinari)

although knit together into a pyramidal grouping, still they have no psychological connection. There is nothing to disturb the dreamy mood. How did Giorgione accomplish this? In the first place by the large simplicity of the design, which is built up on long, restful lines — a triangle over against happily balanced verticals and horizontals; while the diagonal line of Liberale's banner, cutting sharply across one side of the triangle, gives the note of vigor and makes the transition easier from the group in the foreground to the background. The landscape gradually fades off into the distance, as quiet and as dreamy as the figures. The feeling of spaciousness is obtained through the lofty position of the Virgin set over against the landscape. Toward her the lines converge, and the floor and steps of the throne recede. The feeling of height is enhanced by the fact that the throne is cut off by the upper edge of the picture, yet the eye is held by the downward glance of both the Madonna and the Child and by the strong horizontal of the enclosing wall. The large masses of warm red are relieved by the equally cool masses of green, blue, and blue-green — a color scheme frequently found in Italian painting. There is no profound religious or intellectual quality about this Madonna; but rather the use of a religious subject for the expression of a mood, merging both figures and landscape into a harmonious expression of serenity.

This expression of mood is one of the characteristics of the Venetian school. We have seen it in Giovanni Bellini's *Allegory* (PL. 109 A). But in Giorgione it reaches an expression that is highly lyrical, approaching music in its emotional appeal.[10]

Titian (1477–1576 A.D.), as we have said, was a fellow student of Giorgione in the shop of Giovanni Bellini. The close relation existing between these two young artists is evident from an early painting of Titian, the *Concert* (PL. 109 B), in which Giorgione possibly had a share. Here are represented two monks who have been playing and are still under the spell of the music, particularly the younger one, who turns his head in response to the hand laid upon his shoulder. It is but a physical response, however, almost involuntary, for the emotions aroused by the music still completely dominate him. Here the young Titian has caught a moment of rapture as it lingers a little, with its enthralling power. The third figure is somewhat problematical. Possibly the rich costume and the disinterestedness evidenced by the glance outward emphasize by contrast the intensity of the emotion in the

---

[10] One should not fail to read "The School of Giorgione," Walter Pater's subtle analysis of Giorgione and the relation of his work to music, in *The Renaissance*.

others; while, for specifically artistic reasons, it is evident that the light masses of the plumes and linen are needed to balance the light garment of the monk with the viol.

Titian did not long continue in the spirit of Giorgione. More characteristic of his robust nature is the *Bacchus and Ariadne* (PL. 110 A). Movement dominates the panel, exuberant yet restrained by a master. It comes sweeping in at the right in a great curve as the band of revelers emerge from the woods following the car of Bacchus. This curve carries the eye, with the help of the trees, to the figure of the god silhouetted against a clear sky. The frenzied movement in every part of his body is emphasized by the rich color and crumpled folds of the drapery and the dark masses of the foliage. This right half of the picture is filled with broken masses of light and shade, while the left contains a quiet expanse of cool sky, below which is the figure of Ariadne. She turns toward Bacchus with a startled gesture, thus bringing the eye back toward the center. The exuberance of the scene is obtained through the masterly composition and the vivacious contrasts of hot and cool color.

This rich color, the deep shadows, and the soft outlines of the forms are due to the oil technique which found such favor with the Venetians. The oil technique, in comparison with the tempera, had far greater possibilities for expressing Venetian ideals of worldly splendor. By means of it, the painter could easily obtain gorgeous color, marvelous textures, subtle transitions and deep shadows, and strong contrasts. He could use a broad brushstroke, or paint directly upon the canvas with little or no preliminary drawing. Thus a typically Venetian painting throbs with the warmth of emotion and of splendor. A typically Florentine tempera painting (PLS. 97–99), on the other hand, with its softer, paler tones, its painstaking brush strokes, soft shadows, and incisive contours, reveals essentially the draughtsman and the cool, intellectual temperament with controlled emotions.

Titian's magnificent altarpieces, such as the *Assumption of the Virgin* and the *Pesaro Madonna*, are always finely designed and powerful in color, and produce an overwhelming, grandiose effect. All the pomp, splendor, and worldliness of Venice is there. Pictures of this kind had a great influence upon the painters of northern Europe, who were beginning to visit Italy and were taking back with them visions of this splendor, which in some cases did only harm to their native talents.

Long years and great vitality enabled Titian to produce a large number of masterpieces which are remarkably varied in subject matter. Holding a high place among them are his portraits. Portrait-painting results from the swift, eager life of the Renaissance that called for the expression of the individual in distinction from the medieval expression of the community as a whole. The early Florentine *Portrait of a Lady* (PL. 98 c) is generalized and decorative. But in proportion as the individual assumes more and more importance, the demand for portraits increases, and the likeness becomes more keenly realistic. In the *Young Englishman*, so called (PL. 110 B), for the identity of the subject is unknown, we see a young man represented half-length, dressed in a black costume relieved only by the heavy gold chain and delicate white ruffles at the throat and wrists. His right hand holds his gloves; his left is held somewhat restlessly on his hip. With the greatest simplicity and reserve, Titian reveals the pride and aristocracy of this young man, and his fine sensitive nature, dreamy and wistful. The half-length figure admirably fills the square frame; the eye travels back and forth with the help of the chain and the contours of the arms from the face to the hands, which are as expressive of this young man's character as the face itself.

The unfinished portrait group of *Pope Paul III and His Grandsons* (PL. 110 c) reveals another aspect of Titian's ability as a portrait-painter. In the center is the aged pope, seated, wearing his red cap and cape, and white silk, fur-lined robe; one hand rests on the table where stands an hourglass, the other nervously clutches the arm of the chair as he leans forward toward the youth who so superciliously bends toward him. Another grandson in his cardinal's robes stands at the left, his hand resting on the pope's chair, and looking out toward the spectator as if not vitally interested in the tense situation which seems to exist between the other two. The bent old man shows fire in his face and anger in his body as if he felt intrigue working against him. In the knowledge of subsequent history, which tells us that a few years later Paul III died after his family had treacherously risen against him, we can see how penetratingly Titian grasped the psychology of the situation and with what unsparing frankness he expressed it. This, it has been suggested, is the reason why the picture was never finished. Thus in Titian's portraits we always find a penetrating vision and an intellectual grasp both of individual character and of the psychology of a situation. This result is accomplished not entirely by expression of the face but also by a few characteristic details of costume, pose, or some accessory that contributes to the creation of an environment which is as expressive of the individual as is the face itself. When psychology is combined with superb technique, the result is always a portrait of great distinction.

In passing from Titian to Tintoretto, we pass to an entirely different personality, as the great canvas of the *Crucifixion* shows (PL. III A). In the center is the figure of Christ upon the cross, with the executioner's ladder still against it; huddled about the base are a group of mourning friends; on the left, the cross of one of the thieves is being raised with ropes; on the right that of the second thief still lies on the ground, receiving its victim; the sides and background are filled with crowds of people — horsemen, workmen, spectators; and behind all is a lurid sky with flashes of brilliant light. Everywhere is animation; nowhere, repose. The impression is one of tremendous movement and excitement. Instead of the organized thought and coolly calculated design of Mantegna's representation of this subject (PL. III B), we feel the impetuous haste, the tremendous energy, and the imagination of Tintoretto,[11] which bring with them a certain power of their own. The painter accomplishes this largely by his powerful chiaroscuro. The light falls brilliantly on certain spots; then all else sinks into the deep shadow which is the unifying principle.

In other centers of north Italy — Verona, Ferrara, Brescia, Milan — vigorous schools more or less closely connected with Venice were producing noteworthy artists. Of these we can speak of but two painters — Mantegna and Correggio.

Andrea Mantegna (1431–1516 A.D.), the son-in-law of Jacopo Bellini, was brought up in Padua under two influences that had much to do with his art: first, the intensive study of form, and second, the strongly classical influence which was one of the passions of Padua. In his *Crucifixion*[12] (PL. III B) we see both working. In the foreground, on a rocky hill, the place of a skull, stand three crosses. The immediate spectators are in two groups: on one side, the soldiers casting lots for the raiment, quite unaware of the significance of the occasion; on the other, the friends

[11] Tintoretto's impetuosity and his habit of working directly upon the canvas without preliminary sketches is well illustrated by Vasari's tale of the decoration of the ceiling of the Scuola di San Rocco. This confraternity had commissioned three painters, Tintoretto among them, to present competitive designs for the ceiling. When the council assembled to judge of the design and award the commission, they found that Tintoretto had painted his directly on a full-sized canvas and already had it put into place, saying that that was his way of doing it and if they did not wish to recompense him he would make them a gift of the painting.

[12] This small picture is part of the predella of Mantegna's *San Zeno Altarpiece*. The predella was the long, narrow panel that rested directly upon the altar and served as a decorative base for the altarpiece. It consisted usually of several small paintings related in subject matter to the large painting above. Many of these predellas were scattered when the altarpieces in course of time were dismembered. An example of an altarpiece that still retains its predella is the *Annunciation* of Fra Angelico at Cortona.

PLATE III

(*A*) Tintoretto. Crucifixion. 1565 A.D. Scuola, or Confraternity, of San Rocco, Venice. (Anderson)

(*B*) Mantegna. Crucifixion. 1459 A.D. Louvre, Paris. (Alinari)

PLATE 112

(*A*) Mantegna. Gonzaga Family. A tablet in the room bears the following inscription: "To the illustrious Marquis Lodovico II, most worthy prince, invincible in the faith, and to his illustrious Lady Barbara of incomparable renown; their Andreas Mantegna of Padua has completed this humble work to their honor in the year 1474." Castello, Mantua.

(*B*) Correggio. Madonna and Saint Sebastian. 1525 A.D. Dresden.

(*C*) Nicola d'Apulia. Pulpit. 1260 A.D. Baptistery, Pisa. (Alinari)

of Christ, overcome by the pathos and tragedy of the event. The two end figures, both looking inward, and the perspective view of the crosses of the thieves serve as a framework; in the middle distance people are coming and going; rocky hills form the background. In the sky, the horizontal cloudlets give a feeling of restful spaciousness. Here is a dramatic scene expressed with noble dignity, largely through the means of a carefully thought out composition built up on two diagonals intersecting at the central cross on which the figure of Christ is lifted above the landscape, which is lowered at this point, giving the cross a sense of isolation not only physical but spiritual. Further emphasis is afforded by the soldier's spear at the right, and by the fantastic vertical rock on the left. The group at the right, held together by the rocky hill of the middle distance, consists of hardy Roman soldiers, the types being taken from Roman portrait heads and clothed in Roman costumes both military and civilian. Here Mantegna had an opportunity to make use of his knowledge of Rome. So passionate was the archaeological zeal of this "old Pagan" that his highest ideal seemed to be to reconstruct classic times — Roman architecture, costume, type, and detail, even though the subject were entirely Christian. Individual figures, such as the horseman seen from behind, the soldier with the spear, or John — what incisive drawing and what a feeling for structure! In the bodies on the crosses the proportions are elongated, the torso sharply and schematically outlined.

In this austere and searching study of form, Mantegna accomplished for north Italy what Donatello and Masaccio did for Florence. Classical sculptures, examples of which he had in his own collection, served as his models, and though at times his passion for archaeology dominated his art, he nevertheless brought a tonic influence to schools whose predominant interests lay in the splendor of color, the texture of fine stuffs, the pride of their city, or the mood of the sunset hour.

This searching observation and uncompromising recording of facts is evident in his portraits. On the walls of one of the rooms in the castle at Mantua is a portrait group of the *Gonzaga Family* (PL. 112 A) who employed Mantegna for many years as court painter. At the left sits the Marquis Ludovico Gonzaga, holding in his hand a letter just brought to him by his secretary, to whom he turns as if giving some direction. At the right the Marchesa sits rather stiffly, looking toward the Marquis as if with some concern as to the contents of the letter; a little girl holds up an apple toward her, without attracting her attention; at her left is a dwarf whose task was to furnish amusement; grouped about are members of the family and court. Here is a quiet family scene, dignified and serious. The incident of the letter is a minor matter. What impresses the spectator is the exceeding reality of all these people, a reality that brings out sternly and incisively the character of each one, with no idealizing. The Marquis is a lofty-minded man, a conscientious and successful ruler; his secretary, with his squinting eyes and huge nose, a clear-headed, shrewd, and capable assistant; the stately Marchesa a thoroughgoing housewife and helpmeet. In every figure one feels Mantegna's penetrating observation and his uncompromising fearlessness in recording the facts.

The other painter of north Italy, outside Venice, of whom we shall speak is Antonio Allegri, called Correggio (1489?–1534 A.D.), the painter whose work expresses lyric joy. His frescoes in the dome of the Parma cathedral carry one up ecstatically with the same astonishing, dazzling quality that underlies baroque work. For Correggio well illustrates the Jesuitical era. His color is not warm and resplendent like the Venetian, but of a silvery tone. His drawing and composition derive from Mantegna, Raphael, and Michelangelo. In this respect he foreshadows the Eclectic school of the next century. Of his panel paintings the *Madonna and Saint Sebastian* (PL. 112 B) is typical. The Madonna is seated aloft on the clouds over against a brilliant radiance which blends into cloud forms filled with joyful angel heads; on either side are youthful angels looking down to the saints below and pointing out to them the Madonna and Child. At her feet cherubs quivering with exuberant life ride the clouds or plunge through them. There is no repose here. Each figure abandons itself to rapturous joy. Much of this feeling Correggio secured through radiant light, daring foreshortenings, and powerful chiaroscuro.

Chiaroscuro we have seen developing in Italian painting from Giotto, who, though he used the shadow for modeling, still expressed both mass and space chiefly by line. The early fifteenth century painters of Florence — Masaccio, Fra Angelico, Baldovinetti, and Pollaiuolo — used it moderately to express the structure of the figure and space, so that their work, whether in fresco or tempera, had an even tonality without strong contrasts of light and shade. This was due partly to the medium and partly to interest in the structural line, for the Florentines were principally draughtsmen. In Leonardo the use of the oil technique reveals itself in the deep shadow and soft transitions. In Venice the development was rapid. Rich chiaroscuro aided

Titian to obtain greater movement and more resplendent color harmonies. Tintoretto built up his compositions in terms, not of line, but of masses of lights and darks. Correggio carried this idea to a greater extreme, almost making it an end in itself, as in the *Holy Night*. Brilliant illumination brings out certain parts vividly and darkness envelops the rest. Surprising, dazzling, at times purely rhetorical, effects are obtained by him in this way.

The last giant of Italian painting was Tintoretto. Brief mention, however, should be made of the painters of the late sixteenth and the seventeenth centuries, though not so much for their intrinsic worth as for their historical value. Two tendencies are to be noted. First, there were the Eclectics, centered at the art school which they established at Bologna. These painters attempted to combine into a perfect art the best qualities of the great masters — the drawing of Michelangelo, the noble types and composition of Raphael, the color of Titian, and the chiaroscuro of Correggio. Such an unnatural method, which copies external appearance and fails to grasp fundamental principles, is destined to lack imaginative and ethical qualities. Thus the altarpieces of these Bolognese, chiefly the Caracci, are rhetorical and melodramatic in effect.

The other tendency was that of the realists, chief of whom was Caravaggio (1569–1609 A.D.) who, in revolt against the weakness of the followers of Raphael and Michelangelo, selected his types from the lowest classes, and painted figures and scenes with a realism that characterizes with incisiveness but is lacking in the refined and noble qualities fundamental to fine art. His chiaroscuro, suggested by Correggio, is abnormally dark and murky. The influence of Caravaggio, however, was powerful, especially at Naples, and was carried thence to Spain to become the heritage, through the refining influence of Ribera, of the Spanish master Velasquez.

SUMMARY

Painting was a peculiarly characteristic expression of the Italian people. They were an eager, vivacious people, who lived in a country rich in the colors and forms of nature. They had a particular gift for seeing and feeling. They delighted in the gay spectacles of frequent pageants and festivals and hence in the painted decorations of churches, palaces, and public buildings; and they learned their chief lessons from this same source. Of the important centers of central Italy, Siena and Umbria, Siena always remained medieval, only slightly influenced by the new movement but aroused enough by it to bring to a culmination the Byzantine tradition upon which her art was founded. Superb decoration, based upon line, pattern, and jewel-like color, interested her most, and often became an expression of intense feeling. The Umbrian painters were usually more or less under the influence of Florence, if not actually working there; but they never quite lost the sweetness and charm and the feeling for spacious landscape taught them by the quietly beautiful hills and valleys of Umbria. In northern Italy, the chief center, Venice, was less touched by the power of the Church and the Renaissance movement, and evolved more freely and naturally. Her wealth, fondness for pleasure, civic pride, and close connections with the Near East inspired an art that was ostensibly religious but actually worldly. Now it revealed the mood of an idyllic scene or the poetry of the sunset hour, now a gorgeous pageant which pictured well the magnificence of both public and private life. In this respect it was a consistent expression of the late Renaissance. The Venetian painters were not primarily draughtsmen like the Florentine, but were great craftsmen in handling the oil technique, so that by the strong massing of resplendent color and rich light and shade, they produced paintings of surpassing splendor and magnificence, which were their greatest contribution to the arts.

BIBLIOGRAPHY

In addition to the general books listed in Chapter XV:

BERENSON, BERNHARD, Central Italian Painters of the Renaissance. N.Y., Putnam, 1909.
—— ——, Essays in the Study of Sienese Painting. N.Y., Sherman, 1918.
—— ——, North Italian Painters of the Renaissance. N.Y., Putnam, 1907.
—— ——, Venetian Painters of the Renaissance. N.Y., Putnam, 1909.
—— ——, Venetian Painting in America. N.Y., Sherman, 1916.
CROWE, J. A., AND CAVALCASELLE, G. B., History of Painting in North Italy (ed. Douglas, Borenius). 6 v. London, Murray, 1914.
CRUTTWELL, MAUD, Andrea Mantegna. London, Bell, 1901.
DOUGLAS, LANGTON, History of Siena. N.Y., Dutton, 1902.
FRY, R. E., Giovanni Bellini. N.Y., Longmans, 1901.
GARDNER, E. G., Painters of the School of Ferrara. N.Y., Scribner, 1911.
GRONAU, GEORG, Titian. N.Y., Scribner, 1904.
HARVARD UNIVERSITY, WILLIAM HAYES FOGG ART MUSEUM, Collection of Mediaeval and Renaissance Paintings. Cambridge, Harvard University Press, 1919.
HEYWOOD, WILLIAM, AND OLCOTT, LUCY, Guide to Siena, History and Art. London, Unwin, 1903.
KRISTELLER, PAUL, Andrea Mantegna. London, Longmans, 1901.
MOORE, T. S., Correggio. N.Y., Scribner, 1906.

PERKINS, F. M., "Some Sienese Paintings in American Collections." *Art in America*, v. VIII (1919–20), pp. 195, 272 ff.; v. IX (1920–21), pp. 6, 45 ff.

PHILLIPS, CLAUDE, Earlier Work of Titian. N.Y., Macmillan, 1897.

PHILLIPPS, E. M., Tintoretto. London, Methuen, 1911.

RICCI, CORRADO, Art in Northern Italy. N.Y., Scribner, 1911.

—— ——, Antonio Allegri da Correggio (tr. Simmons). N.Y., Scribner, 1896.

RUSKIN, JOHN, Modern Painters. Boston, Estes, 1913.

—— ——, Stones of Venice. Boston, Estes, 1913.

SCHEVILL, FERDINAND, Siena. N.Y., Scribner, 1909.

CHAPTER XVIII
THE RENAISSANCE IN ITALY
c. 1300–1600 A.D.

SCULPTURE

We saw in the Early Christian and Byzantine period how monumental sculpture, because of religious prejudice, ceased to be produced; and how it was revived in the eleventh century, especially in France, where its purpose was to adorn the great abbeys and cathedrals, upon the portals of which the sculptors carved enlargements of the Byzantine ivories (PLS. 75 c and 76 A). Into these the Gothic artists infused new life based upon an observation of nature (PLS. 82, 85 A and B).

While the sculptors in Italy shared somewhat in this movement, the great sculpture of the Renaissance, like the architecture, had its origin and its greatest stimulation in the classical tradition. Its beginnings, however, appear nearly two hundred years earlier than in architecture, in the works of a family living and working in the city of Pisa and so known as the Pisani. Nicola (c. 1203–c. 1280 A.D.)[1] made and decorated a pulpit (PL. 112 c) for the Pisa Baptistery. It is hexagonal, resting on columns that rise alternately from the floor and from the backs of lions and support the trefoil cusped arches above which rise the sculptured panels. In design and spirit the work is Gothic. Let us study one panel, the *Nativity* (PL. 113 A). It is crowded with figures, placed one above another with no regard for perspective. Several scenes are represented: in the upper left-hand corner, the Annunciation; in the center, the Nativity with the Virgin on her couch, before whom attendants are bathing the Child; behind her, the annunciation to the shepherds, who are adoring the Child. The cold, unemotional types of the figures, the stiff angular folds of the drapery, the crowding of the space — all these show clearly the origin of Nicola's inspiration, the Roman sarcophagus.

Nicola's son, Giovanni Pisano (c. 1250–1328 A.D.), also made a pulpit, but for the church at Pistoia. It was much like Nicola's

[1] Known as Nicola d'Apulia probably because of his early residence in southern Italy.

in general design, but of more slender proportions, with pointed instead of round arches. Comparing the panel representing the *Nativity* here (PL. 113 B) with that of Nicola, we see at once a great difference in feeling. In Giovanni's the figures still crowd the space but are smaller and of slighter proportion; they stand in higher relief and seem to be twisting and bending, so that the effect is that of a spontaneous emotion running riot over the panel. In these figures we seem to feel the naturalism and swing of line as well as the emotional quality of the Gothic.

In the bronze[2] *Doors of the Baptistery* at Florence (PL. 114 B), made by Andrea Pisano (c. 1270–1348 A.D.), a Pisan who had been summoned to Florence to execute this work, the overcrowding is gone, and so is the cold calm of Nicola's Virgin and the warm emotionalism of Giovanni's. Andrea has made his doors decorative in the first place by means of a repeated geometric motif, one found in Gothic sculpture and illuminations, which forms a carpetlike pattern. Within the pattern he has placed low reliefs of simple composition, with smoothly flowing lines admirably adapted to the spaces, and in no way detracting from the main decorative pattern. One of Andrea's reliefs on the Campanile, *Weaving* (PL. 113 C), is typical of his work. At the left a woman sits at a loom weaving; at the right stands a lady holding out her hand as if seeking to purchase the stuff. A gentle charm pervades the figure, like the serenity of a Greek gravestone; so simple, direct, and quiet is it.

Before continuing in Florence, where was produced most of the greatest sculpture of the Renaissance, we need to turn aside a moment and look at the work of a somewhat isolated sculptor whose influence, however, was important — Jacopo della Quercia (1375–1438 A.D.). In his *Allegorical Figure* (PL. 113 D) we see a powerful form, strong, erect; the broad folds of the drapery, realistic and not adapted to the swing of line, accentuate the massive figure. Here is a robust vigor.

Yet to Jacopo has been attributed[3] the sarcophagus of *Ilaria del Carretto* (PL. 114 A), one of the exquisite monuments of the early Renaissance. The attribution can hardly stand, however, because the inherent feeling in this monument is so different from all Jacopo's known work. Ilaria lies easily with her head upon a double cushion and at her feet a dog, the symbol of fidelity;

---

[2] For an account of bronze-casting as practiced by the Renaissance sculptors, see Benvenuto Cellini's dramatic account of how he cast his *Perseus*, in his *Memoirs of Benvenuto Cellini*, Everyman's ed., pp. 402 ff.

[3] "Attributed to" indicates that there is doubt as to whether the artist mentioned is the correct one.

her face, with its exquisite oval framed by the turban and the high collar, is perfectly serene; the drapery is arranged in long lines whose reposefulness is enhanced by the quicker rhythm of the winged *putti* with garlands that decorate the body of the sarcophagus. These chubby little *putti*, all different, stand in naturalistic pose holding up their garlands, which are obviously too heavy, with sorrowful faces and pensive droop of the head. The predominantly horizontal lines produce a peacefulness and a stillness that evoke a profound emotion akin to that felt before French Gothic art.

We have already seen something of Florentine sculpture in the work of Andrea Pisano. Andrea, however, was essentially medieval and Gothic. The true Renaissance in Florence begins with Donatello (1386–1466 A.D.). In the *Saint George*[4] (PL. 115 A) we see a youthful knight clad in armor standing firmly on both feet, and with furrowed brow looking keenly toward the left. The carelessly tied cloak with its heavy naturalistic folds contrasts happily with the stiff armor and helps to make the outline simple, as does the shield also, which by hiding the triangular space made by the legs at the same time adds firmness to the design. The figure, though of compact silhouette, through its firm pose, slight twist in the torso, and turn of the head, communicates the impression that beneath the closely fitting armor is a living anatomy. As Vasari said, "Life seems to move within that stone." This young knight is spiritedly alive, and his Christian chivalry is expressed by his face, by his firmly planted feet, in fact by his whole body, with a directness and a restraint that are classic.

Donatello, with Brunelleschi, had steeped himself, at Rome, in a study of all the classic remains available. Of sculpture there were not as yet many examples; for a large number of those well known to us today were then still buried in the ground or covered by ruins. It was the small objects such as gems and coins that first attracted notice. In fact Donatello and Brunelleschi while digging around the ruins in Rome, according to Vasari, found an ancient vase full of coins and thereafter were known as the "treasure-seekers." Such they were, but their treasure was the ideas by which Brunelleschi was enabled to build the great dome of the Cathedral and Donatello to carve living statues. The lesson that the antique taught Donatello was to return to nature. This keen youth saw that the ancients had created their superlative

---

[4] Saint George was the patron saint of the Guild of the Armorers, who commissioned the statue for a niche on the exterior of the church of Or San Michele. The original statue has been removed to the Bargello for safe keeping, and a reproduction placed in the niche.

PLATE 113

(*A*) Nicola d'Apulia. Nativity, from Pulpit at Pisa (detail of PL. 112 C). (Alinari)

(*B*) Giovanni Pisano. Nativity, from Pulpit at Pistoia. 1298–1301 A.D.

(*C*) Andrea Pisano. Weaving, from the Campanile of the Cathedral, Florence. 1334–38 A.D.

(*D*) Jacopo della Quercia. Allegorical Figure. 1409–19 A.D. Siena Museum. (Alinari)

PLATE 114

(*A*) Unknown sculptor. Tomb of Ilaria del Carretto. 1406 A.D. Lucca Cathedral. (Alinari)

(*B*) Andrea Pisano. South Doors of the Baptistery, Florence. In the panels are scenes from the life of Saint John, and Allegorical figures. Bronze. 1330 A.D. (Alinari)

works through a careful observation of nature and if he were to produce equally fine statues he must go to the same source; and he did it with a decisiveness and in a thoroughgoing manner undreamed of by the French Gothic sculptors, who had also begun to travel the same road.

In doing this Donatello did not always, like the ancients, keep within the bonds of restraint, which his passion for realism burst. In the *Zuccone* (PL. 115 B) we see an eccentric-looking old man walking forward, ugly and sad. He wears a heavy mantle that falls from the left shoulder in massive folds of great power as well as realistic and plastic beauty. The bared right shoulder droops and the hand clutches the cloak with an almost convulsive movement of the wrist, revealing the structure in a most convincing way. In fact, the superb modeling of the throat, the bared shoulder, and the arm reveal an intimate study of the human figure as an organic structure. This, however, is not an end in itself but a means for the expression of a character highly individualized even if ugly in appearance. Thus here, the wrinkled face with its large mouth, the inclination of the head toward the uplifted right shoulder, the slouching left shoulder, and the bent wrist, the whole restless pose of the figure — all combine to express vividly the individuality of this curious old man. But with all its realism, the statue is not photographic; for Donatello well understood the value of using enough generalization to accentuate the essentials and to eliminate details. His own feeling toward this statue is evident in the phrase that he used to express strong conviction on any subject: "By the faith that I put in my Zuccone."

Another characteristic of Donatello, the expression of child life, we see in the *Cantoria* (PL. 115 C). The architectural setting is classical in its details. The continuous frieze is decorated with *putti* dancing against a gold mosaic background, and broken by double colonnettes placed above the supporting brackets that provide the needed vertical lines to balance the design. These colonnettes also are finished in gold mosaic, which is carried up into the border with the vases and down into the lower parts of the gallery, thus playing through the whole composition as a unifying factor. Against this gold background the *putti* swing across the choir, now forward, now backward, each in a different pose but each filled with vibrant life that cannot contain itself but impetuously bursts forth in an abandon of movement. To control this exuberance and emphasize its rhythm is another purpose of the colonnettes, the severity of which, by the law of contrast, also heightens the feeling of movement behind them. We saw how the Greek, in the Hellenistic age, learned to represent a truly childlike form (PL. 48 C). But to Donatello we owe the expression of the exuberant spirit that manifests itself in the spontaneous, riotous play of children.

In the equestrian portrait of *Gattamelata* (PL. 116 A) we meet one of the two great equestrian statues of the Renaissance, the other being Verrocchio's *Colleoni* (PL. 119 B). Gattamelata sits easily in the saddle, looking out as if watching his troops, unhelmeted, his uplifted right hand holding a truncheon diagonally across the horse's head. The man and the horse are a compact unit, the design being made of curved lines, the only exception to which are the spurs, the truncheon, and the sheathed sword. Not only do these curves knit the two together but they keep them firmly upon the pedestal without the unpleasant feeling, sometimes prompted by equestrian statues, that the horse is walking off. The bent back of the rider, the turn of the head, the feet firmly held in the stirrups, give a realization of the organic structure of the body beneath the armor. But more than this, the figure of the rider with its poise and relaxation is suggestive both of great physical and intellectual power. The fact that Gattamelata is bare-headed deepens this impression. We feel ourselves in the presence of a character quietly strong and masterful in every way. The face indicates this; but, what is far greater, the whole figure is a unified expression of it. Donatello succeeded in conveying this impression partly by great simplification, knowing that the statue on its high pedestal was to be seen from a distance. Detail is there: the saddle is decorated with little *putti*, and the cuirass with a magnificently worked Medusa head; but the sculptor has created a truly monumental group by emphasizing only the significant in form and character.

The revolutionary ideas of Donatello tending strongly toward realism, to which a study of the antique had led him, were of tremendous influence upon both painters and sculptors of the fifteenth century. Side by side with these, however, the medieval traditions continued to live, particularly in their greatest exponent Lorenzo Ghiberti (1378–1455 A.D.). In the second *Doors of the Baptistery*,[5] Ghiberti followed the all-over pattern of Andrea Pisano in the first doors (PL. 114 B). In the *Temptation* (PL. 116 B)

---

[5] There are three sets of bronze doors to the *Baptistery* at Florence: the first (PL. 114 B), made by Andrea Pisano for the eastern doorway, which faced the cathedral, were moved to the south door to make way for those made by Ghiberti in 1403–1424 (PL. 116 B); these in turn were moved to the north door in order that the second pair made by Ghiberti, the famous *Gates of Paradise* (PL. 116 C), might be placed in the eastern, the most important entrance.

we see that the sculptor was not interested in expressing the organic structure of the figure, nor in representing its monumental aspect; but was concerned rather with the swing of line and with the beautiful pattern that his figures could weave within the enclosed space. The broken foreground merges gradually into the flat background. Vertically the design is divided into two parts, built on arcs of circles that approach but do not meet, symbolizing both a physical and a spiritual separation between Christ and the devil, the cringing movement of the latter emphasizing the nobility of the former. We may notice the Gothic sway of line particularly in the drapery of the devil, and the exquisite manner in which his wings are adapted to fill the space and to balance the group of ministering angels. Ghiberti, through the use of line, has succeeded not only in creating a beautiful design but in exhibiting a great amount of dramatic power.

Ghiberti, however, was not entirely untouched by the naturalistic movement of the day. He was a great lover of the antique. We read in Vasari of a collection of ancient marbles, bronzes, and vases brought by him from Greece. Evidence of this appears in the *Gates of Paradise* [6] (PL. 116 c). Here he has abandoned the all-over pattern of the earlier doors and divided the space into rectangular panels set in plain frames. In the niches are evidences of his interest in the classic. The one on the right in PL. 117 A, for example, is a nude figure that appears to have been taken directly from some classical Heracles.

Let us look at the panel that illustrates two episodes from the life of Abraham (PL. 117 A). In the upper right-hand corner Abraham is about to slay Isaac on the altar, when the angel appears to stay his hand; at the foot of the hill the servants and ass are waiting for the master; on the left Abraham kneels before the three angels who appeared to him before his tent near the oaks of Mamre; in the background Sarah stands at the door of the tent. It was not unusual to combine two or more episodes into one panel. But Ghiberti has united them with astonishing ease. Emphatic lines, like those of the rocks and trees, carry the eye up to the scene of sacrifice or down to the group of angels. The planes recede, showing higher relief in the foreground with sharper transitions of light and shade, and lower relief in the group of the sacrifice, with gentler transitions, thus producing an effect of aerial perspective. The trees are conventional, their foliage in particular showing the goldsmith's technique. The

[6] So called because Michelangelo, standing before these doors, said, "They are so beautiful that they might fittingly stand at the gates of Paradise."

figures of the servants are modeled with a considerable amount of feeling for the form, and the ass is admirably foreshortened. The angels, however, with their long folds of drapery and sweeping wings carry one back to the angels of *Amiens* and *Reims*. Thus, while Ghiberti here shows a tempered naturalism, his primary purpose has been to make a design that was beautiful in line and pattern, and he was successful. The graceful curves of the figures, contrasting with the tall slender tree-trunks, and the delicate interplay of light and shade over the surface create what we might call a melody in bronze.

More akin to Ghiberti than Donatello was Luca della Robbia (1400–1482 A.D.). In his *Cantoria* the singing, dancing, and music-making boys are not placed in a continuous frieze as were Donatello's but in panels, one of which (PL. 117 B) represents seven boys singing. The two smaller ones hold the choral book while three others look over their shoulders. All are so absorbed in their chant, and are singing so earnestly that we almost catch the waves of sound. The youth at the right beats time with his hand, and the little fellow next to him, with his foot. The seven stand easily, not crowded though compactly grouped, and fill the space admirably. The flat background and the elimination of detail, the sincerity and reserve of representation, and the religious seriousness pervading it make this panel highly expressive of a beautiful rhythmic chant. The modeling of the figures, though not so incisively realistic as Donatello's, shows that Luca had profited by the lessons of the early fifteenth century; his elimination of picturesque detail, and his simpler and more direct approach to his subject, differentiate him from Ghiberti, and bring him nearer than both his great contemporaries to the true spirit of the Greek.

Luca is best known, perhaps, for his introduction, into the field of sculpture, of another technical method, that of glazed terra cotta. The process of glazing had been known since early Egyptian times, but had been used for small objects only. The chief value of its application to the major art was in its cheapness, in comparison with stone or bronze. A typical example in this medium is the *Frescobaldi Madonna*[7] (PL. 117 C). The background is a rather deep blue, and the figures creamy white, except for the natural color applied to the eyes and hair, and for the gilt borders of the robes. The modeling, which is obviously based upon a study of nature, is broadly generalized, as would be necessary for glazing. The Madonna is a simple, wholesome, girlish

[7] So called because it was formerly in the possession of the Frescobaldi family in Florence.

PLATE 115

(*A*) Donatello. Saint George. Marble. 1416 A.D.
Bargello, Florence.

(*B*) Donatello. Zuccone, meaning
"pumpkin-head." 1416-35 A.D.
Campanile, Florence. (Alinari)

(*C*) Donatello. Cantoria, or Singing Gallery. 1433 to c. 1440 A.D. Florence Cathedral.

PLATE 116

(*A*) Donatello. Erasmo da Narni, called Gattamelata, a nickname meaning "honeyed cat." Bronze. c. 1446 A.D. Padua. (Alinari)

(*B*) Ghiberti. Temptation of Christ. Panel from north doors of the Baptistery. Bronze. 1403–24 A.D. Florence. (Alinari)

(*C*) Ghiberti. "Gates of Paradise." The scenes represented are taken from the Old Testament. Bronze. 1425–52 A.D. Baptistery, Florence.

PLATE 117

(*A*) Ghiberti. Episodes from the Life of Abraham. From the "Gates of Paradise" (PL. 116 c).

(*B*) Luca della Robbia. Panel from the Cantoria. 1431–38 A.D. Cathedral Museum, Florence. (Alinari)

(*C*) Luca della Robbia. Frescobaldi Madonna. Glazed terra cotta. H. 28 in. Kaiser-Friedrich Museum, Berlin. (K.-F. Museum)

PLATE 118

(*A*) Desiderio da Settignano. Marietta Strozzi. Kaiser-Friedrich Museum, Berlin. (Kaiser-Friedrich Museum)

(*B*) Desiderio da Settignano. Laughing Boy. Benda coll. Vienna.

(*C*) Desiderio da Settignano. Tomb of Carlo Marsuppini. c. 1455 A.D. Santa Croce, Florence. (Alinari)

type, tender but neither profound nor sentimental. In the quiet figures of both the mother and the child there is a sweet serious-ness and a gentle reverence. It is this tender, serene, human qual-ity infused with a religious feeling to make it reverend, that gives the works of Luca their great appeal.

In the second half of the fifteenth century, a marked tendency seen among a considerable group of sculptors both in marble and bronze is illustrated by the work of Desiderio da Settignano (1428–1464 A.D.). The *Laughing Boy* (PL. 118 B) shows a sympa-thetic and spontaneous conception executed with the greatest deli-cacy of modeling. The laughing eyes, the soft flesh of the cheeks, the charm of the rollicking, childlike spirit — in all this we feel that the chief interest of the sculptor lay, not in the uncompro-mising realism of Donatello, but in the joyous, gracious aspects of life, exemplified particularly in the heads of the aristocratic youths of the noble families of Tuscany. Their alluring charm comes from subtle modeling and exquisite surface finish rather than from realism in anatomy or from the permanent in form or feeling. *Marietta Strozzi* (PL. 118 A), with high forehead, accord-ing to the fashion of the day, arched brows, wide-open mischie-vous eyes, is instantly recognized as a fearless, aristocratic girl. The head is particularly captivating in its momentary alertness.

Nor is this smiling charm absent in the tombs designed and carved by Desiderio. Florence honored her dead — statesmen, humanists, artists, churchmen — with burial in her churches and with monumental tombs made by the greatest artists. In the *Tomb of Carlo Marsuppini* (PL. 118 c), the sarcophagus, with an effigy of the dead reclining on a bier, stands in a niche formed by two fluted pilasters that rise from a decorated base to the entablature, whence springs a round arch surmounted by a can-delabrum, from which garlands are suspended. The back of the niche is filled with four panels of colored marble, which balance the horizontal line of the sarcophagus and base and afford with their plain surfaces a restful contrast to the rich, delicate orna-ment that covers all parts of the tomb. The decorative motifs are the familiar classical ornament and moldings. All this ornament is carved in low relief so that the light and shade flits over the surface gently with no great contrasts, and produces an effect of elegance and refinement without a feeling of overloading. Figure sculpture also plays an important part. The broad base furnishes space for the two *putti*, who hold shields decorated with the coat of arms of the deceased; in the lunette are the Madonna and Child with two adoring angels, and at the base of the arch two youths who support the garlands. In all these figures is the sweetness and charm typical of Desiderio's work.

Side by side with those sculptors who were interested in the charming aspects of life were some who carried on Donatello's searching studies of the human figure. Chief of these was Antonio Pollaiuolo (1429–1498 A.D.), in whose painting we have already seen a zeal for the expression of the human figure in movement. The bronze statuette of *Heracles and Antaeus* (PL. 119 A) shows this artist applying himself to the same problem as it regarded sculpture in the round. The group appears to have been left just as it came from the mold, without the usual detail and finish that a sculptor usually bestows upon a bronze. For this reason, perhaps, suggestion rather than finish of detail heightens the impression of the energy that surges so mightily through both combatants.

Another pupil of Donatello, whose workshop as we have seen became the center of artistic activity in Florence in the second half of the fifteenth century, was Andrea Verrocchio (1435–1488 A.D.). He is best represented by the equestrian statue of *Colleoni* (PL. 119 B), who was one of the greatest soldiers of the age and at the same time a prince of great wealth, living part of the time in the midst of camp hardships, and part of the time in the luxury of a magnificent court. We see Colleoni in full armor sitting rigidly in the saddle, from which he seems to be half rising, the feet pressing firmly upon the stirrups which bear the weight of the body, in marked contrast to Gattamelata, who relaxes into the saddle. The violent twist of the figure suggests the bodily structure and adds to the impression of impetuosity. The helmet is so adjusted that it but slightly shades the face, revealing the sharply cut features and particularly the piercing eyes. Every detail contributes to a brilliant expression of the forceful energy and power that are felt to permeate not only the figure of the man but the horse also, where they are seen in the arched neck, the angular tail, and exaggerated modeling.

By the time of Verrocchio, the fundamental principles underlying the plastic expression of the figure both at rest and in movement had been solved; and, as usually happens after such a conquest, ease, grace, and facility followed. All this accomplishment of the fifteenth century was the heritage of Michelangelo (1475–1564 A.D.), who in the first half of the sixteenth century brought Florentine sculpture to its climax. The *Moses*[8] (PL.

---

[8] The Moses was carved to decorate the tomb of Pope Julius II that was never completed as planned. The horns on the head, traditional in representations of Moses, are due to an incorrect interpretation of the passage in Exodus that describes the rays about the head of the prophet as he came down from Mount Sinai.

120 A), though an early work, illustrates his characteristics. Here we see a colossal figure, seated; the head, made all the more massive because of the shaggy hair and heavy beard, is held erect and turned toward the left; the left foot is drawn back, as if something toward which he is looking had caught his attention and he were about to rise. This in itself makes a restless figure; but that quality is further accentuated by the nervous way in which the right hand holds the beard, and by the sharply contrasting lines of the heavy drapery that falls in deep folds over the knees. The rugged form, with deep-set eyes, the great muscles of the arms, the hands finished with marvelous delicacy and with almost incredible anatomical accuracy, the mighty torso and projecting knee, emphasized rather than hidden by the clothing — all communicate a wonderful feeling for the structure of the body. Although the outline is compact, yet within it the contrasting lines and masses militate against any feeling of repose such as we find in Donatello's *Saint George* and *Gattamelata*, but infuse it with a feeling of conflict and struggle, which, aided by the colossal scale of the statue, is overpowering.

This note of restlessness we see again in the *Tomb of Giuliano de' Medici* (PL. 119 c), especially if we compare it with Desiderio's *Tomb of Carlo Marsuppini* (PL. 118 c). In the latter we noticed that the deceased was represented reclining asleep above the sarcophagus, which was placed within the niche and architecturally subordinate to it, while all the surface shimmered with the play of delicate decoration. In the Medici tomb we see three figures so placed that they form a unified triangular group standing out against an architectural background. It is a question in the spectator's mind whether the sculpture is subordinate to the architecture or the architecture to the sculpture. The rounding lid of the sarcophagus is decorated with two volutes upon which rest colossal figures of Day and Night. Back of these rise an architectural setting cut horizontally about one-third way up by a cornice, above which is the figure of Giuliano seated in a niche that is very simply finished by a horizontal cornice while the side niches have rounding pediments supported by curved brackets, and have also decorative garlands. Thus the ornamentation is kept away from the figure, about which are almost plain, unbroken surfaces. The three figures, although placed in different planes, present a unity within the bounding triangle, for the feet of Giuliano are on a level with the heads of Day and Night, which break the cornice just behind them that would otherwise entirely separate the group. Giuliano wears a suit of armor magnificently ornamented with a mask and other classical decorations and exquisitely finished in the marble; over the seat and across one knee is his military cloak. He holds a marshal's baton somewhat listlessly across his lap, and looks toward the left as if something were attracting his attention for a moment. The left shoulder droops and the left leg is thrust back as if he were about to rise — a restless, momentary pose very much like that of the *Moses* (PL. 120 A). The face is generalized, with apparently no purpose of portraiture. In fact the whole figure is more a symbol than a characterization of Giuliano.

Day is a great superhuman figure just arousing himself as if for his day's work. Above the mighty muscular shoulder the head, vertically erect, peers out with sudden alertness. Parts of the figure, such as the back and shoulder, are highly finished, revealing with scrupulous care the bony structure, the joints and muscles; other parts, such as the head and left hand, are still in the rough, giving one the feeling that this vigorous giant is trying to wrest himself from the block of stone as the chisel of the master actually had done. The figure is represented in a very complicated pose, twisting as if it were revolving about a central axis — the head toward the right, shoulder and arms toward the left, and legs toward the right. The thrust-out shoulder and the left leg, bent at almost a right angle with the main line of the body, produce an impression of tremendous vigor. The same twisting, rotary movement we feel in Night, though not quite so strikingly. Her head droops as it rests upon the bent arm, and the face is thus brought very effectively into the shadow. But her sleep is not the calm, restful one of *Ilaria* (PL. 114 A). The whole figure expresses the slumber of utter weariness, and the sleep is a troubled one, although the owl sits quietly beneath the bent knee and the foot rests upon a wreath of poppy heads, symbolic of slumber. It is the mask, whose eyes never close but follow one fascinatingly, that truly symbolizes her restlessness.

In both these figures we can observe two fundamental characteristics of Michelangelo. First was his knowledge of the human figure. Jacopo della Quercia (PL. 113 D) had given the form robust vigor and monumentality. Donatello and his school with their sincere, searching studies had added immensely to the scientific understanding of form and structure. Equipped with this knowledge, Michelangelo continued the study until he knew the form anatomically as no one before him and possibly no one after him. His statues reveal the bony structure with its joints, the muscles, and the surface texture. But to represent this alone was not the purpose of Michelangelo; it was merely a means to an end. For, second, he took the figure and so breathed meaning into it that it became symbolic, as we have said, of a state of mind or soul.

We can best illustrate this by his so-called *Bound Slave* (PL. 120 B). Here the figure is not so restless, nor the modeling so exaggerated, nor is a momentary action expressed. The lines lead the eye rhythmically to the bent arms that frame the head, which is pressed backward in a movement of despair; for despair is the significance of the figure, and the enslaving character of despair is made still more vivid by the bands tightly drawn across the breast, while hopelessness is expressed also by the ease of the pose and the limp right hand. The face is highly generalized and free from expression except for the closed eyes, which help to emphasize and concentrate within the figure its inherent quality, so that the whole statue becomes an expression of the hopelessness of struggle. In this use of generalized form to express abstract quality and feeling, Michelangelo is akin in principle to the Greeks of the fifth century. In content, he is far removed from them. With the fifth century Greek, all is quietude and serenity; with Michelangelo, all is restlessness and struggle.

SUMMARY

Thus we have seen how the Italian sculptors, guided by classical models, turned to the study of nature and infused life into their statues. Their intellectual strength, their earnest searching for fundamental principles, and their ability to recognize essentials kept them from becoming mere realists and enabled them to make their figures monumental, though some of the later sculptors came perilously near sinking to mere prettiness. Finally Michelangelo, in the sixteenth century, profiting by the knowledge of the human figure gained by the fifteenth century, went one step further and used the figure to express the spiritual. This expression was usually one of conflict, for Michelangelo's spirit was always in torment and his art a very personal manifestation of his spirit; but it was always powerful. His followers, seeking to emulate his work, failed, like the followers of Giotto, to grasp the fundamental principles of their master, and so reproduced the outward appearance without the spirit. The great age of Renaissance sculpture in Italy was over.

MINOR ARTS

We have already said that one of the most striking character-istics of the Renaissance artist was versatility. This was because every artist, through the apprentice system of education, was a craftsman trained in the fundamentals of working in several media. Another reason for this versatility was the demand of the times on the master's shop. All through the Middle Ages fine vessels and books were made of the most precious material for the church service, jeweled regalia for the clergy, and tapes-tries to decorate the cathedral. This need still continued; and to it were added the needs of wealthy nobles and merchants as secular life became more important and the mode of living more luxurious and ostentatious. Carvings, tapestries, and painted decorations were in demand for the palaces, as well as more elab-orate furniture and gold and silver plate, and fine cloths, velvets, and brocades for costumes, and jewelry and fine armor. Books in particular, with the widening of knowledge, scientific research, and passion for the literature of Greece and Rome, assume an im-portance unknown before. As most of these things came from some *bottega*, it is easily seen that the artist must be versatile; and, as public taste was of a high order, he must produce works of quality both in design and in technique.

Metal — bronze, iron, gold, silver — was an important me-dium, and skill in casting, molding, chasing, and engraving it was essential. The use of bronze we have seen in the *Doors of the Baptistery* (PLS. 114 B and 116 C) and in the equestrian statues of Donatello and Verrocchio (PLS. 116 A and 119 B). Sometimes the casting was done by the artist himself,[9] sometimes by a fellow craftsman. Among smaller works of art in bronze, the medal be-came important and reached its climax in the work of Antonio Pisano, known as Pisanello (c. 1395–1455 A.D.). The purpose of the medal was commemorative; and the fact that the medals of the Renaissance were personal, that is, that they commemorated persons rather than events, is another illustration of the individ-ualistic strain that we have already noticed manifesting itself in portrait painting.

Among the finest medals of Pisano are those of Leonello d'Este, Marquis of Ferrara, who, contemporary writers tell us, was a cultivated man and a lover and patron of the arts. On the obverse of our medal (PL. 120 C) is the portrait of the Marquis, a profile of extraordinary ugliness, with thick lips, receding forehead,

[9] P. 287, note 2.

curiously shaped cranium, and abrupt line of the hair and of the nape of the neck; and Pisano has not softened the ugliness by idealizing lines. Through the beauty and dignity of his design, however, he has lessened its unpleasant features. The size of the head is happily related to the size of the disc, and about it is relieving space that adds quietude and dignity. The finishing border contains the inscription, in letters superbly shaped and spaced, broken by sprays of fruiting olive. The smooth modeling of the face and neck and the unadorned ground counterbalance the broken masses of the hair, embroidered gown, and border, thus giving a design that is well balanced, reposeful, and rich in the play of light and shade. While the obverse of these medals is quietly, almost severely dignified, the reverse shows charming humor, as in the marriage medal made to commemorate the union of Leonello and Maria of Aragon in 1444 A.D. (PL. 120 D). As Leonello was fond of music and himself an accomplished musician, he is here represented as a lion, a pun on his name, standing complacently before a Cupid who is teaching him to sing from the scroll of music that he holds in his hands. The adapting of the complicated design to a circular disc is splendidly accomplished. The broken foreground gradually emerges into the flat background with little suggestion of distance; the emphatic vertical lines of the shaft supply the need of a strong accent, for with this exception the design is built upon curved lines that flow into the curve of the frame.

Among metal workers the goldsmith was very important. In fact it was as a goldsmith that many a painter and sculptor began his career. The processes used were substantially the same as those employed in the Middle Ages — *repoussé*, chasing, jewel-setting, and enameling; and the character of the work in the early Renaissance had the same quality of sound design construction-ally, with decoration subordinate and contributory, as in the best medieval work. But increasing luxury and desire for display in all aspects of life are reflected in the changed taste seen in the late Renaissance. Of this period, the famous bronze and gold worker, Benvenuto Cellini (1500–1571 A.D.), is typical, and the salt cellar (PL. 122 A) with figures representing the Sea and the Land that he made for Francis I well illustrates his work. The artist himself describes it in his autobiography.[10] There is no question about the superb technical skill here shown, the great ease and facility of handling the medium and of finishing it. But who would conceive of this exquisite bit of work as a container for

[10] *Memoirs of Benvenuto Cellini*, Everyman's ed., p. 340.

salt and pepper? Here is a lack of sound craftsmanship. To astonish and delight by exquisite finish or decoration and to surprise by ingenious motifs seems to be the aim. It is as baroque in design as the Jesuitical churches, and like them very characteristic of the age that produced it.

Iron was frequently used as a medium of artistic expression. The strength of the metal makes it valuable for grilles and gates where strong protection is needed, and at the same time light and air. Technically, it can be worked by several processes, for it can be hammered, molded, welded, carved, chased, and stamped. The necessary tools are few and simple — a forge and bellows, hammer and anvil, tongs and chisels. An important fact in designing in this medium is that the metal must be worked in the plastic state, that is, at red or white heat, and must be worked quickly. Hence virility and breadth must control a successful design, though the chased ornament may be added at greater leisure. This harmony of material, process, and design is well seen in the standard holders and lanterns found on many of the Florentine palaces. The lantern of the Guadagni Palace (PL. 121 c), for example, with its curving branches, is fittingly strong and architectural in feeling; and its decoration, done by fine chiseling, is entirely in keeping with the main design.

A product of the *bottega* that required a knowledge of several media, or was the work of a group of craftsmen, was the furniture. In the early Renaissance it was of simple, massive wood construction like that of the medieval period. It consisted of but a few pieces, most important of which was the great chest or *cassone* (PL. 121 A) that served as a clothes closet, a storage place for the family plate or books, a seat, a bed, a table, if high enough, and a trunk, if small enough. Its massiveness and its dignity harmonized with the room in which it stood. The early *cassoni* were very much like the Gothic chests in their almost severe rectangularity with a few carved moldings for decoration. In the example seen in Pl. 121 A this severity is modified by the bracketlike carved ornaments which are covered with gesso and gilded, by the cornice-like projection of the lid, and the brightly painted panel on the front. Rarely has an important piece of furniture attained the splendor and dignity of the Italian *cassoni*. The panel was frequently painted by one of the best artists of Florence — Paolo Uccello, Botticelli, Pier di Cosimo, or Leonardo [11] and with the tapestries provided color for an otherwise somber room.

[11] Many of these panels have been stripped from the chests and now hang as isolated pictures in galleries and museums.

PLATE 119

(*A*) Antonio Pollaiuolo. Heracles and Antaeus. Bronze. Bargello, Florence. (Clarence Kennedy)

(*B*) Verrocchio. Colleoni. Bronze. 1481–88 A.D. Venice.

(*C*) Michelangelo. Tomb of Giuliano de' Medici. 1524–33 A.D. Sacristy of San Lorenzo, Florence.

PLATE 120

(*A*) Michelangelo. Moses. c. 1505 A.D.
San Pietro in Vincoli, Rome.

(*B*) Michelangelo. Bound Slave.
c. 1513 A.D. Louvre, Paris. (Alinari)

(*C*) Pisano (Pisanello). Leonello d'Este. Bronze. 1441–50 A.D. British Museum, London. (British Museum)

(*D*) Pisano (Pisanello). Reverse of the Marriage-Medal. 1444 A.D. British Museum, London. (British Museum)

PLATE 121

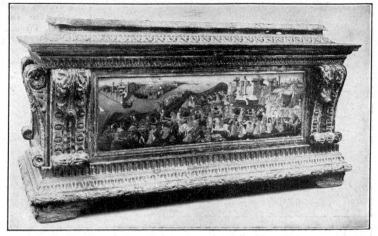

(*A*) Cassone. Florentine. c. 1475 A.D. Metropolitan Museum, New York. (Metropolitan Museum)

(*B*) Liberale da Verona. Aeolus. Historiated initial from a choir book. Piccolomini Library, Siena. (Alinari)

(*C*) Iron Lantern. Guadagni Palace, Florence. (Alinari)

PLATE 122

(*A*) Benvenuto Cellini. Salt Cellar. Of gold with chasing and enamel; the base is of black ebony with figures in gold. Vienna. (Plon)

(*C*) Orazio Fontana. Majolica Plate. XVI cent. A.D. Metropolitan Museum, New York. (Metropolitan Museum)

(*B*) Velvet. Italian, XV cent. A.D. Metropolitan Museum, New York. (Metropolitan Museum)

Another source of color in the Italian houses was the majolica,[12] which is earthenware covered with a whitish, opaque glaze on which the decoration is painted. The colors used were intense, and their effect was heightened by an additional coating of rich transparent glaze and by a luster of amazing brilliancy. Very fine majolica in the " grotesque style" was made in the sixteenth century at Urbino by the Fontana family, showing the influence of Raphael in its decoration. A plate of Orazio Fontana (PL. 122 c) contains in the center a mythological scene closely related both in design and in spirit to the paintings of Raphael. Surrounding this are two borders of grotesque forms — winged lions, birds, half-human figures — combined with garlands, medallions, and scrolls painted with a sweep of line and delicate grace that remind us very much of the stucco decorations used by the Romans (PL. 53 A) and adopted by the late Renaissance architects.

Fine fabrics played an important part in Italian life, as the paintings show.[13] Silks, velvets, brocades, and tapestries were much in demand for costumes, both for ecclesiastical and secular purposes, and for hangings. We have seen how Persia had been a center for weaving, especially of fine silks; how Justinian introduced the craft into Europe; and how the Mohammedans became expert weavers. In their conquests westward the Moslems brought the craft with them to Spain, to Sicily, and thence to Italy, where luxuriant stuffs were woven which in pattern, color, and motifs were entirely of the tradition of the Near East (PLS. 64 B, 68 A, and 71 A). In the fifteenth century, however, the Italian weavers, quite in accordance with the spirit of their times, broke with this old tradition. In their velvets and brocades, which are the culmination of this craft, they limited themselves chiefly to one pattern, but within it used a great variety of detail. This pattern consisted of the pomegranate motif enclosed in a leaf-shaped border (PL. 122 B). The boldness and vigor of these fabrics conveys a distinctive quality that is in harmony with Florentine life and art.

In the field of bookmaking, the Italians made valuable contributions. We have been following the evolution of the book from the long rolls of the Egyptians, Greeks, and Romans to the codex (p. 159, note 3), which became in the early Christian era most

[12] Probably derived from Majorca, one of the Balearic Islands, a calling-place of the ships that brought to Italy the glazed and lustered wares of Spain.
[13] See particularly the paintings of Domenico Ghirlandaio, Benozzo Gozzoli, the Bellini, Crivelli, Titian, and, in fact, most of the Venetian painters, whose works reveal so clearly the love of the Venetians for fine stuffs.

sumptuous in its writing, decoration, and binding, and formed one of the most charming and expressive products of the Middle Ages. Probably the highest expression of the Italian scribes and illuminators is seen in the great choir books that reached their culmination in the late fifteenth century. Like other liturgical books, they were decorated with gold and bright colors. The most characteristic part of this decoration is the initial letters, which sometimes are painted in bright colors with white tracery, foliate ornament, and gold; but frequently because of their large size are historiated, that is, contain a miniature within the form of the letter. Many of these were painted by well known artists, as the *Aeolus* (PL. 121 B). Within the letter and wonderfully adapted to the shape is a representation of Aeolus sweeping forward with all the energy that characterizes the north wind. The use of a classical subject is interesting here as well as the spontaneous naïve conception so characteristic of the fifteenth century attitude toward Greek and Roman subjects. The rich foliate decoration surrounding the initial is typical of Italian work, which often became too heavy and florid to have the perfectly decorative quality of the French and Flemish manuscripts.

Meanwhile, one of the most far-reaching inventions was about to bring to an end the handmade book, that is, printing. This invention was not made by one man or at one place, but was the growth of centuries. Some of the underlying ideas, such as using a stamp for initial letters, had long been known. Paper was becoming common in the fourteenth century, making inexpensive books possible, though vellum and parchment were long used for fine books. What we know is that in the decade from about 1450 to 1460 A.D. printing with movable type became established at Mainz, and by the end of the fifteenth century was being practiced in all the countries of western Europe. The earlier books, such as the *Gutenberg Bible* of c. 1456, traditionally called the earliest printed book, closely resembled the manuscripts of the period in composition, form of letters, and decoration. In fact printing was used for the small letters only; the initials and the decorations were added in color by hand after the printing was done, so that the general effect of the page was the same as that of the manuscript.

For nearly a century, the printed book very closely followed the tradition of the manuscript. It had no title page, no chapter heading, no running title, no pagination. The early printed books of Italy show clearly the Italian sensitiveness for unity of design, especially the small pamphlets issued at Florence, known as

Rappresentazioni (FIG. 102) because they reproduced the plays given on saints' days. In place of a title page, they had a woodcut with the representation of an angel as a herald to announce the play, and perhaps a characteristic scene from the life of the saint who was being celebrated. These Florentine books are among the most successfully illustrated books ever made, because the illustration illustrates and at the same time harmonizes with the letterpress. Its purpose was to elucidate the text or to emphasize some point by visualization, and not to call attention away from the text to itself as an end. The Florentine realized that to keep this unity his illustration should harmonize with the printing, and that nothing could accomplish this end as adequately as purely linear work, as light and simple as possible, with little detail.

Among early printed books, the *Hypnerotomachia Poliphili* (FIG. 103) holds an important place. The intrinsic worth of the book does not lie in the content of the text, which is dull and long drawn out, nor in

Fig. 102. Title Page of Lorenzo de' Medici's *Rappresentatione di San Giovanni e Paulo*. Woodcut. Printed at Florence.

the woodcuts themselves, for the drawing is frequently bad, but in that complete and satisfying unity of composition in which the letterpress, margins, type, and illustrations are all harmonious. This unity is as important in bookmaking as it is in picture making, unless one looks upon a book merely for its content, and not as a work of art. As in the Florentine pamphlet, so in the *Hypnerotomachia*, the simple line of the wood block adds variety to the printed page but at the same time maintains the unity of the page composition.

Another kind of illustration used by the Italians was the engraving. The process is as follows: A copper plate is beaten smooth and highly polished; on this the engraver incises his design with a sharp instrument called the burin. The plate is then inked by passing over it an inked roller that fills the incised lines of the design. Then a sheet of paper is laid on the plate and subjected to pressure that sucks the ink out of the plate, leaving the design in raised lines on the paper. The fact that many printings, or impressions, can be made from one plate made the process appeal to the Italians as a practical method of making many copies of a design to serve as models for their apprentices. The origin of engraving, as of printing, is uncertain. The Netherlands, Germany, and Italy claim priority in its use. Not many of the first-rate Italian painters made use of the medium, though two notable exceptions were Antonio Pollaiuolo and Mantegna, both of whom were interested in that intensive study of forms that finds free expression in incisive line. Perhaps the greatest Italian master of engraving was Giovanni Battista Piranesi (1720–1778 A.D.). Piranesi was strongly attracted to the monuments in Rome, in which he saw a manifestation of monumentality and splendor.

Fig. 103. Page from the *Hypnerotomachia Poliphili*, or *Strife of Love in a Dream*. Printed by Aldus at Venice, 1499 A.D.

To express this character was the purpose of many of his engravings. The large size of his plates contributes to such an expression; but even more than that, the splendid massing of the blacks and whites, and the strong, bold contrasts which he obtained by this means, contribute to the feeling of monumental and imperial dignity he endeavored to have the scene inspire (PL. 51 A).

SUMMARY

In this and the preceding chapters we have seen how the Renaissance transformed Italy, penetrating to the very roots of its social, economic, intellectual, religious, and artistic life. It was an age of great fecundity of work in every line. Its roots lay in the Middle Ages with their sobriety, their emphasis upon the community rather than upon the individual, their vitality, their religious fervor, and their imaginative power. But the new attitude, which recognized a legitimate delight in this life and the inspiration of the classical civilization, proved to be a great stimulation to the artists and spurred them on to a stern struggle for the attainment of means adequate to express their new ideals. Thus experimental struggle with the fundamental problems of expression characterized the early Renaissance. In the late fifteenth century attainment came. No longer was there the moral stimulation of great endeavor; religious fervor weakened; pagan ideas captivated men to the detriment of sterner ideals. Life became more complex, swift, and eager, and called for the expression of the individual; it delighted in the splendors of this world. Art expression like life became rhetorical. The Renaissance had always maintained a high standard of craftsmanship, but now there was a growing tendency to make technical display and ornamentation ends in themselves. Thus high attainment became the beginning of decadence.

BIBLIOGRAPHY

Sculpture

In addition to the general books listed in Chapter XV:

BODE, WILHELM, Florentine Sculpture of the Renaissance. N.Y., Scribner, 1909.

CHASE, G. H., AND POST, C. R., History of Sculpture. N.Y., Harper, 1924.

HOLROYD, CHARLES, Michael Angelo Buonarroti. London, Duckworth, 1903.

MARQUAND, ALLAN, Luca della Robbia. Princeton, Princeton University Press, 1914.

MEYER, A. G., Donatello. Leipzig, Velhagen, 1904.

POST, C. R., History of European and American Sculpture. 2 v. Cambridge, Harvard University Press, 1921.

SCHUBRING, PAUL, Donatello. Stuttgart, Deutsche Verlags-Anstalt, 1907.

—— ——, Luca della Robbia. Leipzig, Velhagen, 1905.

Minor Arts

BRITISH MUSEUM, Pictorial postcards: Sets I–III, Sforza Book of Hours; V, Early Florentine Woodcuts; XI, Florentine Picture Chronicle; XII, Florentine Engravings; XXVI, Medals by Pisanello and Pasti.

FABRICZY, CORNELIUS VON, Italian Medals (tr. Hamilton). London, Duckworth, 1904.

FFOULKES, CHARLES, Decorative Ironwork. London, Methuen, 1913.

FORTNUM, C. D. E., Majolica. London, Chapman, 1882.

HERBERT, J. A., Illuminated Manuscripts. N.Y., Putnam, 1911.

HILL, G. F., Portrait Medals of Italian Artists of the Renaissance. London, Warner, 1912.

HIND, A. M., Giovanni Battista Piranesi. London, Cotswold Gallery, 1922.

KRISTELLER, PAUL, Early Florentine Woodcuts. London, Paul, Trench, Trübner, 1897.

ODOM, W. MacD., History of Italian Furniture. 2 v. N.Y., Doubleday, 1918.

POLLARD, A. W., Early Illustrated Books. London, Paul, Trench, Trübner, 1917.

—— ——, Fine Books. London, Methuen, 1912.

POLLEN, J. H., Gold and Silversmiths' Work. London, Clay, n.d.

—— ——, Ancient and Modern Furniture and Woodwork. London, Wyman, 1908.

SOLON, L. M., History and Description of Italian Majolica. N.Y., Cassell, 1907.

CHAPTER XIX

SPAIN

From the Gothic Age to the Nineteenth Century

HISTORICAL BACKGROUND

While the Renaissance had been transforming Italy, the rest of western Europe had been living in the medieval tradition and had been naturally evolving that tradition to meet new conditions, each country in its own way. The seventeenth, eighteenth, and to a large extent the nineteenth centuries saw the impact of the Italian movement upon these traditions. Sometimes this influence was assimilated. But usually its power was entirely transforming, and frequently it was robbing the native art of its charm and individuality. Often it was imposed by arbitrary monarchs. For this was the heyday of the monarch and the aristocrat, under whose influence art became a fashion rather than a genuine expression with vital significance. But the Renaissance had a far wider influence than this. The love of independent thought that was the heart of the movement permeated religious life, bringing about a revolt from the Church and the establishment of Protestantism; it stimulated scientific activities, laying the foundation of critical thinking that has resulted in unparalleled scientific development, and also, through the industrial and economic revolution which has come from the introduction of machinery, has struck at the very roots of the creative impulse; and it entered political life, too, bringing about the overthrow of absolutism and the coming into power of the middle classes and the masses. Europe and America are still suffering from this almost complete revolution in all phases of life; for readjustment is slow.

The great complexity of such a movement as this prevents detailed study of it in the space of one volume. Hence in the succeeding chapters we shall see in only a general way how the Renaissance came to the other nations of Europe, and how in each country certain local conditions reacted upon its influences; how some artists succumbed and became empty imitators; how some accepted the new ideas but were great enough to create, with their help, not merely copy; and how some rebelled against an unnatural and unsympathetic environment.

Spain, because of her geographic position and the mountainous character of her territory, is more isolated than most of the other countries of Europe. Yet she has been particularly the prey of the foreign conqueror — Roman, Goth, and Moor — and of foreign influences, from Flanders, Italy, and France. But the Spaniard has always infused them with his own temperament, which is conservative, holding fast to traditions of long standing. The coming of the Moor and his long residence in the peninsula was a provocation to the Christians, whose long struggle against the infidels, combined with native conservatism, made them grim fighters for the faith in dealing with all forms of heresy. The Church has always been the dominating power in Spain, of a narrow conservative type and with a fanatical priesthood. Hence the Inquisition could flourish in Spain as in no other country of Europe. This constant struggle and religious fervor made the Spaniard brutal and fanatical on the one hand and emotional and mystical on the other.[1]

It was not until after the fall of Granada in 1492 A.D. that any semblance of unity in the peninsula was possible. By the sixteenth century, largely through marriage and inheritance, Spain had become a first-rate power, holding large sections of Europe in fief and acquiring great wealth through her newly discovered possessions in America. Through Seville, the trade center of southern Spain, flowed the gold and silver from the new world. Here, too, nature was less austere than in the barren, mountainous plateaus of the central part of the peninsula. The warm sunshine, fertile soil, and romantic temperament were more conducive to geniality. Southern and eastern Spain were also closer to Italy because of possessions in Naples and Sicily. But constant wars, mismanagement, and shortsighted policies controlled by a bigoted Church rapidly exhausted her wealth. Her religious fanaticism led to the expulsion, in 1609 A.D., of the Mudéjares and Moriscoes and deprived the country of its chief industrial class and its most skillful craftsmen, thus crippling the nation both economically and artistically. By the beginning of the seventeenth century, the greatest days of Spain were past.

ARCHITECTURE

Spain, like other European countries, accepted the influence of the Renaissance upon its architecture, adapting it to local conditions and bringing about a particularly ingenious fusing of it

---

[1] The picture of Spanish life given in Cervantes' *Don Quixote* is invaluable.

PLATE 123

(*A*) University of Salamanca.
Portal. c. 1530 A.D.

(*B*) El Greco (Domenico
Theotocopuli). Assumption of
the Virgin. 1577 A.D. Art Institute, Chicago. (Art Institute)

(*C* and *D*) Archiepiscopal Palace. Alcalá. Plateresque carvings
of the patio. 1534 A.D. (Moreno)

PLATE 124

(*A*) El Greco. Burial of the Count of Orgaz.
C. 1584 A.D. Santo Tomé, Toledo. (Anderson)

(*B*) El Greco. Pentecost. 1604–
14 A.D. Prado, Madrid.

(*C*) Velasquez. Surrender of Breda. 1639 or 1641 A.D. Prado, Madrid.

with the native temperament, especially in the matter of ornament. In the early Renaissance, when the continuity of the Gothic tradition in structure was still unbroken, a new spirit revealed itself in the plateresque style,[2] which is well illustrated by the entrance of the *University of Salamanca* (PL. 123 A). Plateresque ornament was often concentrated about the doors and windows and its decorative value increased by the plain surfaces that surrounded it. At the Salamanca entrance a richly decorated panel rises above the double portal. The ornament is arranged in three zones separated by double stringcourses and crowned by an elaborate cresting. Engaged clustered shafts frame the panel and furnish the needed vertical lines. The carvings increase in depth and boldness as they rise and are broken by portrait medallions, heraldic emblems, and a sculptured group. The motifs include *putti*, masks, and grotesques, and predominantly the *rinceau*, showing an influence from Italy. More typically Spanish is the ornament of the *Archiepiscopal Palace* at Alcalá. The walls of the patio, the open court, appear at first sight to be rusticated, but on close inspection are found to be carved in low relief (PL. 123 C) with animals, birds, masks, griffin, and *putti* expressed in vigorous movement that is characteristically Spanish. The balustrades and capitals (PL. 123 D) are also carved with the same delicacy and give one the impression of richness and quiet taste.

The plateresque was the most original accomplishment of the period, and its short life of only about half a century was due to external causes. It was still vigorous and spontaneous when Philip II came to the throne in 1556. But it was too imaginative, exuberant, too emphatic in its ornament to please the austere, morose monarch. So, by royal order, the cold, unadorned classic ideal was imposed upon Spain, and the warm, typical Spanish style gave way to a grim and solemn majesty exemplified by the *Escorial*, a monastery built by Philip thirty miles from Madrid. The Spanish love of luxuriant ornament, however, did not long bow to this severe ideal; and the baroque style, with its excessive decoration, which appealed both to the native temperament and also to the religious zeal of the people, succeeded the cold severity of the purely academic style, revealing itself particularly in the elaborate altarpieces, such as that in the Seville Cathedral (PL. 127 C and D).

---

[2] A name derived from *platero*, a silversmith, and applied to the style because of the delicate execution of its ornament.

PAINTING

Although the Spanish evolved so charming and individual a style in architecture as the plateresque, created polychrome wooden statues of a surprising emotional intensity, and proved themselves exceptionally skilled in the crafts, still it was in the field of painting that they reached their highest accomplishment, and that in the seventeenth century, following their political and economic climax. Foreign influence was strong; but, as we have said, this was always swung by the intense Spanish temperament into the current of its own tenacious traditions.

There were numerous local schools in the fifteenth century whose work was religious in subject, dramatic in character, and highly decorative with bright colors and a lavish use of gold and gesso relief throughout the panel.

The sixteenth century experienced a direct influence from the great masters of the Italian Renaissance, as we see in Domenico Theotocopuli (1545?–1614 A.D.), a Cretan. He was probably an apprentice of Titian, saw the works of Michelangelo, and then settled in Spain, where he was popularly known as El Greco, the Greek. His *Assumption of the Virgin* (PL. 123 B) shows the influence of Michelangelo in the sculpturesque figures, especially in the lower group. The design of the panel is obviously based upon Titian's painting of the same subject. The space is divided into two parts; below are the disciples grouped about the empty tomb, some in consternation, others with gestures of amazement at the glory of the vision above, where the Virgin standing on a crescent moon is rising upward on the clouds with angels attending her, the whole group being placed high upon the panel and splendidly filling the curving space. All the elements — rich color, careful design, and rapid movement — unite in creating an impression of ecstatic religious emotion. The figures are vigorous and restless, with a tendency to elongated proportions. There is a sharp cutting of the broad planes; abrupt transitions from light to dark; and along these lines, many of them predominantly angular, the eye is rapidly carried upward. These were the means that El Greco used to attain his purpose — the expression of a heightened emotion.

In the *Burial of the Count of Orgaz* (PL. 124 A), we find a like division of a large curved panel into two parts, the one devoted to the scene upon earth, the other to that in heaven. As the priest is reading the burial service, Saint Stephen and Saint Augustine miraculously appear to take charge of the burial. We see them, clad in the most gorgeous vestments, gently lifting the body of the Count, the three figures forming a compact circular group with which the others are united by gesture or glance. At the right a priest wearing a robe stiff with rich embroidery and holding a gold, jeweled cross, is reading the service; beside him another one of the clergy, in filmy robe, stands with outstretched hands, transfixed by the vision above. At the left in balanced position are two monks wondering at the miracle; behind is a row of mourners dressed in black robes with lacy ruffs about the neck and wrists. Some look up, others at the central group; each is a superb character expression; nowhere among them is there a display of overwhelming grief but a self-contained restraint. The whole lower part forms a compact horizontal mass filled with calmness and restraint, in strong contrast to the upper half of the panel, where swift lines leap up to the crown of the arch, creating an impression of tremendous movement and intense emotion. Here is the scene of the reception of the soul of the Count into heaven. Everywhere is restless movement, expressed by the same means as we saw in the *Assumption* — sharp cutting of planes, and high lights sharply picked out against the dark background with the unexpected startling effect of lightning.

El Greco's religious intensity more and more dominated him, finding expression in an arrangement of lines, planes, and color masses, tending strongly toward abstract design. *Pentecost* (PL. 124 B) illustrates this. The panel is high and narrow, curved at the top. At the head of a stairway is the Virgin seated, and grouped about her are the disciples and the two other Marys, upon whom the spirit, symbolized by the dove, is descending in tongues of fire. The spectator is carried at once into that realm of fiery emotion which the group as a whole is experiencing. The group is almost rigidly rectangular, enclosing a triangle made of the two foreground figures and the Virgin. The upper horizontal line of the rectangle is broken by the uplifted arm, which also connects the group with the effective space above that emphasizes the descent of the spirit and is singularly suggestive of the meeting-place of the uplifted spirit of man with the descending spirit of the divine. The lights and darks are strongly contrasted, the one changing very abruptly into the other; the proportions of the figures are elongated, especially in the foreground; for, as we have already seen, El Greco used his lines, planes, colors, and chiaroscuro to express emotion rather than significant form and structure. Hence the latter is sacrificed to obtain the former. His fundamental principle of expression is that of the Byzantine painters whose tradition was his native inheritance. The result, though not always pleasing and at times rhetorical, is powerful.

In El Greco we have seen a super-religious Spanish temperament expressing its emotion, not by means of a literal rendering of nature, but rather by means of the elements of pure design. In Velasquez (1599–1660 A.D.), on the other hand, while we find a superb balance between design and content, we perceive a cool, objective, impersonal attitude toward a more realistic representation of nature. In his *Surrender of Breda*[3] (PL. 124 C), Justin of Nassau, the Flemish governor, is handing to Spinola the keys of the town. Spinola places his hand on Justin's shoulder as he graciously praises him for his gallantry. Each commander is accompanied by his retinue. In the middle distance are seen the Flemish troops marching out from Breda; in the background are the long reaches of the lowland country with winding rivers and occasional glimpses of bulwarks and conflagrations, all finally lost in a misty horizon and low-lying clouds. Spinola has just dismounted. He is dressed elaborately. There is a feeling of elegance in the rich silken sash, gloved hands, plumed hat, and tightly fitting riding-boots. Justin also is dressed as befits the occasion, with the typically northern broad lace collar and cuffs, and the heavy, clumsy boots. The two figures are brought into bold relief by the high light on the marching troops against which they are silhouetted. The figure of Justin is built on a strong diagonal line that is again suggested in the flag, which neutralizes the balanced massing with predominant verticals and horizontals. One feels that great crowds accompany the commanders, though few figures are actually seen. This is suggested among the Spanish troops by the lances, which would also be to a Spaniard a symbol of victory. The compactness of the Spanish group contributes to the feeling of victory in distinction to the uncertain, loosely knit group of the Flemish. All appear to be looking toward the center, or, with turned head, intently listening to the words exchanged. But not only has Velasquez told his story simply and clearly; he has also made his canvas a highly decorative work of art. Against the cool misty blues and greens of the background he has placed the warm tones of the groups, keeping the composition rather flat with large masses of lights and darks, so that the final effect is that of a tapestry of large,

---

[3] During the struggle between Spain and Netherlands in the seventeenth century, the town of Breda, a key to Flanders, was still in possession of the Flemish. To the Marquis of Spinola the Spanish king Philip II had said: "Spinola, you must take Breda!" After a siege that was brilliant alike for defense and offense, the town surrendered.

PLATE 125

(*A*) Velasquez. Don Balthasar Carlos on Horseback. 1635 A.D. Prado, Madrid.

(*B*) Velasquez. Maids of Honor. 1656–57 A.D. Prado, Madrid. (Anderson)

PLATE 126

(*A*) Goya. Family of Charles IV. 1800 A.D. Prado, Madrid.

(*B*) Goya. Portrait of His Wife. 1811–14
A.D. Prado, Madrid. (Anderson)

(*C*) Goya. Caprice: "Why Hide Them?"
(Calvert)

warm masses on a cool ground. The lances, playing up into this background, not only connect the figures with the sky but contribute to the decorative quality of the picture.

As court painter to Philip IV, Velasquez was engaged largely with the portraits of the royal family. In PL. 125 A we see the six-year-old *Don Balthasar Carlos* cantering over the hilly country of the royal hunting grounds, with the snow-capped mountains in the distance. He sits proudly in the saddle, foot firmly set in the stirrup, and right hand holding a baton with infantile seriousness that is almost comic. He wears a rich green coat embroidered in gold and silver, with a delicate pink sash, and a black hat set jauntily on his head; the saddle bow is blue. The bright color, flowing mane, and floating drapery give a feeling of youthful vivacity, which is increased by the blue-green tones of the landscape lightly sketched in broad, generalized masses with diffused light, and by a strong note here and there, as in the snow-capped peaks and white cloudlets. To be sure, the pony might be criticized for its rotundity, which is too devoid of modeling. In spite of this, however, we realize that the painter has expressed very sympathetically a truly elegant, self-confident young king. But it is not character expression alone that is significant in the picture. Velasquez's sense of design has admirably fitted the figures into an almost square frame and so united it with the landscape that the feeling of unity is unusually satisfying.

Let us look at a group of this family, the *Maids of Honor* (PL. 125 B). We are in a room in Philip's palace looking at a group, the center of which is the little Infanta Margarita, accompanied by two maids of honor, young girls from the noblest Castilian families. One is kneeling, and with charming grace is offering the princess a cup of water on a golden salver; the other is courtesying. At the right are two dwarfs, popular playthings of the Spanish court, one of whom, rotund and misshapen, accentuates by contrast the dainty aristocracy of the little princess; the other is kicking a very sleepy mastiff who even with this provocation refuses to forgo his comfortable doze. Behind this group stand two attendants. At the right of the picture we see the edge of a great canvas before which stands Velasquez himself with his palette and brushes. In the background at an open door the grand marshal of the palace looks towards the group as he pushes back a curtain. Two more people, however, are present, though but indirectly represented; for the king and queen stand in the same position as we, the spectators, their likenesses reflected in the mirror hanging beside the door in the background.

Probably Velasquez was working upon a portrait of the king and queen, who, wearied with sitting, asked to have the little Margarita brought in as a diversion. Towards them the princess is looking and to them the maid of honor is courtesying. As we look at the picture we feel that this is not an artificially posed group but that by some good chance we have been permitted a glimpse into an intimate scene, a bit of everyday life snatched from reality and placed on the canvas. Certain conventionalities, to be sure, are there; but these are due to the fact that the scene is taken not from the life of the average home, but from that of a royal court whose most intimate actions were controlled by rigid rules. The little princess forms the center of interest; the light from the open window at the extreme right falls directly upon her; the other figures stand in the more or less softened light of the shadowy room. About them the light and air play freely, filling the space above and softening the outlines of the figures. One feels that there is ample space to walk about. Wherever the eye rests, it is carried back by figure, object, or receding line to the open door at the back, where a flood of brilliant outdoor light by contrast reveals the softened quality of the inside light.

In this picture it is the exceeding reality of the illusion that captivates. By what means was Velasquez able to create such an illusion? Close inspection shows that the coarse canvas is but thinly covered with broad, apparently hasty painting. But the secret lies in the fact that Velasquez, with an eye rarely equaled for its accurate observation of nature, had trained his hand to follow the eye and to tone each object exactly according to the amount of light that it received. For every object receives a different amount of light in proportion to its distance from the source of light. If a painter is to succeed in creating a feeling of distance, he must be careful that the far-away objects are not so strong in tone and that the contours are not so sharply defined as those near by. These differing tones due to the difference of amount of light received are known as values. Velasquez was the first great master to give accurate values to his paintings. Even the great space that occupies about half the canvas and at first glance seems to be of no use, apart from offering a quiet contrast to the liveliness of the lower half of the panel, is so subtly toned that it plays its part just as vitally as the figures in drawing the eye back into space. Try eliminating even part of this vacant half, and its vital importance will become apparent. Such an illusion does not mean a literal transcription of nature.

Together with keen powers of observation, Velasquez, like all great masters, possessed the power of selection that enabled him to simplify by disregarding most of the detail and emphasizing a few essentials, frequently accomplished by a stroke or two of heavy pigment.

In his late work, Velasquez's palette became more and more restricted so that some of his canvases are subtle harmonies of neutral grays and rich blacks. But every part of these pictures is permeated with atmosphere, showing, as did the *Maids of Honor*, that Velasquez was a master in the expression of the figure existing in space and enveloped by atmosphere. There is always superb modeling accomplished with a minimum of means, that is, with a few brush strokes apparently hasty but really of consummate skill, by means of which the painter expressed all the essentials of form and character, and that too with a poise and restraint that are masterly.

After the seventeenth century there is very little that is noteworthy in Spanish painting until it flames up once more in Goya (1746–1828 A.D.), who for a considerable part of his life was the favorite painter of the Spanish court. In the *Family of Charles IV* (PL. 126 A) we see that Goya was as faithful to truth as was Velasquez; but in contrast to Velasquez's impersonal poise, Goya paints into these portraits his high scorn of this sham court degenerate both in body and mind. Prominent in the foreground is Charles, much bedecked with regalia, "the pompous futility of a king," and his queen Maria Luisa, masterful and dominating, surrounded by the other members of the royal family, whose elegance of costume only heightens their weakness. At the left in the background stands the painter at his canvas. How an artist who was so fearless of truth and so bold in his expression of it could be tolerated at such a court is a puzzle. Either Charles was too stupid to understand or he was too lazy to resent. Besides the characterization here, we discern Goya's power to paint exquisitely the silks, jewels, velvets, and lace, each with its own texture and all together producing a delicate color harmony.

A contrasting characterization as warm in its sympathy as the family portrait was bitter in its satire, we find in the *Portrait of His Wife* (PL. 126 B). She is sitting stiffly with conventional propriety, her gloved hands folded over her lap. The frank eyes and erect head give strength to the sweetness and charm of the face. The soft hair playing so naturally about the face, and the exquisite lace shawl, save it from austerity. It is a convincingly truthful expression. Not only this, but Goya carefully planned the placing upon the canvas. The figure forms a rather sharp triangle occupying most of the space with a strongly felt vertical axis. The base of the triangle is strengthened by the curving back of the chair, which balances the hands.

But nowhere else do we appreciate Goya's insight into the life about him and his fearlessness in expressing it so clearly as in the *Caprices*. In this series he pictures with stinging satire the weakness of the State, the greed and corruption of the Church, the hypocrisies of the people, and the social rottenness. In the foreground of *Why Hide Them?* (PL. 126 c) a miser with snarling face tightly clutches his money bags, bending over them as if to protect them from the four men who stand laughing at him. He is probably one of the clergy; for the great wealth and greed of the Church at that time were commonly known.   Goya's draughtsmanship is as incisive as his satire is biting. With a few strokes he has suggested in a most convincing way the volume of the figure and its cramped position, as well as an ample spaciousness for the other figures. Besides using line most economically he has massed the lights, darks, and half-tones in such a way that the essential fact stands out with amazing lucidity and at the same time the composition becomes an interesting pattern of tones.

SCULPTURE

In sculpture as in painting we see a reflection of the emotional Spanish temperament, the strong religious bias, and the working of foreign influences. Although stone and particularly bronze were used by the sculptors, wood was always a popular material and was ordinarily painted in natural colors and gilded. The painting of the statue was considered to be of equal importance with the carving, if we may judge from the fact that well known painters were employed for this part of the work. The contracts made by one sculptor stipulated that he himself was to select the painter to color his statues.

Alonso Berruguete (c. 1486–1561 A.D.) well illustrates the fusion of the Spanish temperament and foreign influence. Although he studied in Rome not only sculpture but architecture and painting, and was a pupil of Michelangelo, he returned to the native polychrome wood sculpture when he came back to Spain. In his figures Spanish fervor is expressed in terms of Michelangelo; that is, to Michelangelo's superb realization of form, vigor, and restlessness is added an ecstatic emotion typically Spanish. Somewhat less emotional than some is the *Saint Peter*

(PL. 127 A), though even in this figure there is a tenseness in the lean, almost skeleton-like hands and feet and the expressive face. The drapery sweeps about the figure in massive folds, their broad simplicity accentuating the emaciation of the body.

Another sculptor in wood whose work is particularly compelling is Pedro de Mena (1628–1688 A.D.). In his *Saint Francis* (PL. 127 B) he has expressed fervid piety with sincerity and conviction and without being overemotional. The long monk's robe and hood completely clothe the quiet figure and frame a face which in its expression of asceticism is typically Spanish. This interpretation of the Italian Saint Francis, who made all creatures his "little brothers," is peculiarly Spanish. Granted the interpretation, the simple directness of expression harmonizes well with the conception.

MINOR ARTS

In Spain as in Italy, the minor arts were closely interwoven with the major; in fact, the distinction here implied did not exist, for all artists were craftsmen. As among other peoples, the trade guilds were of paramount influence. "The formula of admission to a Spanish brotherhood was very quaint in its punctilious and precise severity. . . . It was required that the candidate for admission should be a silversmith, married in conformity with the canons of the church, a man well spoken of among his neighbors, and not a recent convert to the Christian faith. The day prescribed for choosing or rejecting him was that which was consecrated to Saint John the Baptist, coinciding with the festival of Saint Eligius or San Loy, 'the patron and representative' of silversmiths, who in life had been a silversmith himself."[4] We hear of Berruguete assisting in the decoration of the palace at Alcalá, carving wooden panels for the choir stalls at Toledo, as well as making marble tombs for counts and cardinals, and statues for altarpieces. Juan de Arfe is equally famous for the delicate workmanship of his silver *custodias* and for his bronze sepulchral statue of *Don Cristobal*. The famous iron-grille makers were sculptors and architects as well.

In discussing sculpture we spoke of the popularity of wood as a medium. It was plentiful and cheap. Besides carving statues from it, the Spaniard used it for the choir stalls and the great retables that are so unique a feature of the Spanish cathedrals. The origin of the retable is the simple altarpiece. With the help

---

[4] Williams, *Arts and Crafts of Older Spain*, III, p. 222. Then follows a description of the method of voting by beans or almonds.

of the Spanish love of splendor and decoration, it expanded until it spanned the bay or nave and lifted its top well toward the vaulting. Not only did it become large but it furnished, as a background for the altar, a surface of the richest ornament, covered with carvings which were painted and gilded. In the retable of Seville (PL. 127 c and D) vertical shafts and horizontal bands divide the space into panels which have richly carved niches and figure sculpture. Every inch of the surface is decorated. The motifs are chiefly Gothic, but mingled with them are Moorish domes and arabesques. The impression is of overloading; there is no reposeful plain surface, and the elaboration would be intolerable but for its position in a spacious cathedral where the unadorned surfaces of pier and vaulting and the dim light afford compensating relief.

For metal work Spain had numerous mines of gold, silver, iron, and jewels that supplied her with material even before the vast resources of America were opened up. The silversmith, the *platero*, labored with greatest care and utmost skill upon the *custodia*, the large templelike receptacle that contained the monstrance and was carried in processions. The *custodias* made before the Renaissance influence became dominant well illustrate the Spanish love of ornament (PL. 128 A). From a polygonal base, this gold and silver structure — for the design is primarily architectural — rises lightly and delicately, gradually diminishing in circumference. It is all decoration — reliefs with representations of both sacred and secular subjects, figure work, and Gothic ornament, all executed with great technical skill. Whether or not overloading with ornament is ever justifiable, it is done here with a fairylike grace that almost disarms criticism.

Although the silversmiths attained great skill, yet it was the iron worker who in the making of the *rejas*, or grilles, brought his craft to an unrivaled perfection, almost exceeding the possibility of the material, so light and delicate are his crestings. The purpose of the *reja* was to enclose a chapel or altar in such a way that it could protect the treasures within and still leave them visible. To make such a grille it was necessary for the craftsman not only to work his material dexterously but to have a sense of architectural fitness in his design. The *reja* of the *Capilla Mayor* (PL. 128 B) of the Seville Cathedral, reaching from pier to pier, encloses the altar with the great retable (PL. 127 c and D), and appears " glittering in the dim light like vast bits of gold lace heavy enough to stand of themselves on edge." Together with the retable, which is itself wondrously rich in delicate carvings, color, and gilding, it helps to make the ensemble of the whole bay one of indescribable splendor. The design is arranged in two stages with decorative borders and a cresting. Vertically the *reja* is separated into five panels, the central one wider than the others. The vertical shafts on the lower stage are colonnettes covered with delicate reliefs reminiscent of silver work, and carrying capitals; in the second tier they are carved balusters, and in the cresting, candelabra. In the decorative borders the chief motif is the scroll containing figures, while the intervening space is filled with the typically Renaissance *rinceau;* similar motifs appear in the cresting with flying angels and cherub heads. The artistry of such a *reja* consists of the happy balance of vertical and horizontal lines, the great richness of detail held in strict subordination to the main lines of the design, the architectural fitness of the design, and the facility and easy grace of the detail accomplished by the patient use of the hammer and chisel.

Another craft that added to the sumptuousness of Spanish houses and churches was that of the leather workers, particularly those of Cordova. Their painted and gilded leathers were used for hangings, cushions, furniture, and coverings for chests. The leather was moistened and the designs were worked up in relief like *repoussé* by means of molds, the details added by engraving, and color applied — red, green, blue, black, and white. If silver or gold was used, the sheet metal was applied with oil sizing to the leather before the relief was stamped so that the silver or gold relief stood out against the natural color of the leather or the brighter pigments.

SUMMARY

In Spanish art the emotional character of the people is clearly seen. It is an expression that comes from the heart of a race both mystic and gay, and strongly biased and narrow in religion. Exuberant love of ornament is one manifestation of this temperament. In the plateresque decoration, a certain restraint through concentration at doors and windows makes the rich detail all the more charming; but in the great altars, choir stalls, *custodias,* and vestments, ornament frequently so overloads that it becomes an end in itself. The Spanish were recklessly lavish in both time and material to express this feeling for exuberance. Love of color and of gold and a strong love of reality characterize both sculpture and painting. In painting, strong color, a liberal use of gold, and an extravagant chiaroscuro derived from the late Italians, formed the foundation from which rose the great masters. Because of their strong feeling for reality they enveloped their figures in light and air, observed the accurate values of each object, and depicted individual character with great penetration. At the same time they wove exquisite color harmonies, often those subtle harmonies of grays, blacks, and silver that have had so strong an influence on painting ever since.

BIBLIOGRAPHY

BERUETE Y MORET, A. DE, Goya as Portrait Painter (tr. Brinton). London, Constable, 1922.
—— ——, School of Madrid (tr. Erskine). N.Y., Scribner, 1909.
—— ——, Spanish Painting (tr. Spence). London, The Studio, 1921.
—— ——, Velasquez. London, Methuen, 1906.
BYNE, ARTHUR, AND STAPLEY, MILDRED, Spanish Architecture of the Sixteenth Century. N.Y., Putnam, 1917.
—— ——, Spanish Ironwork. N.Y., Hispanic Society of America, 1915.
CAFFIN, C. H., Story of Spanish Painting, N.Y., Century, 1917.
CALVERT, A. F., Goya. London, Lane, 1908.
—— ——, Sculpture in Spain. N.Y., Lane, 1912.
—— —— AND HARTLEY, C. G., El Greco. N.Y., Lane, 1909.
COSSIO, M. B., El Greco. Barcelona, Thomas, n.d.
DIEULAFOY, M. A., Art in Spain and Portugal. N.Y., Scribner, 1913.
FLETCHER, SIR BANISTER, History of Architecture on the Comparative Method. N.Y., Scribner, 1924.
HARVARD UNIVERSITY, WILLIAM HAYES FOGG ART MUSEUM, Collection of Mediæval and Renaissance Paintings, Cambridge, Harvard University Press, 1919.
HARTLEY, C. G., Record of Spanish Painting. London, Scott, 1904.
HIND, C. L., Days with Velasquez. London, Black, 1906.
JUSTI, CARL, Diego Velasquez and His Times (tr. Keane). Philadelphia, Lippincott, 1889.
KIMBALL, FISKE, AND EDGELL, G. H., History of Architecture. N.Y., Harper, 1918.
MATHER, F. J., JR., Estimates in Art. N.Y., Scribner, 1916.
POST, C. R., History of European and American Sculpture. 2 v. Cambridge, Harvard University Press, 1921.
RIAÑO, J. F., Industrial Arts of Spain. London, Chapman, 1890.
RICKETTS, C. S., Art of the Prado. Boston, Page, 1907.
ROTHENSTEIN, WILLIAM, Goya. N.Y., Longmans, 1901.
STEVENSON, R. A. M., Velasquez. London, Bell, 1912.
STOKES, HUGH, Francisco Goya. N.Y., Putnam, 1914.
WILLIAMS, LEONARD, Arts and Crafts of Older Spain. London, Foulis, 1907.

PLATE 127

(*A*) Berruguete. Saint Peter. 1543
A.D. From the choir stalls of Toledo
Cathedral.

(*B*) Pedro de Mena. Saint
Francis. Wood. Toledo
Cathedral.

(*C*) Retable. Detail. 1482–1564 A.D.
Of wood with polychromy and gilding.
Seville Cathedral.

(*D*) Retable. Upper part, showing the crest of the
reja (PL. 128 B) in the foreground. Seville
Cathedral.

PLATE 128

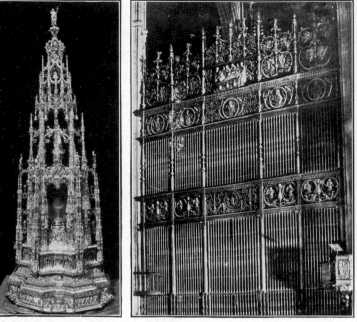

(A) Custodia, Restored. Gold and
silver. 1513 A.D. Cordova.

(B) Reja. Of hammered iron, gilded. H. 21 ft.
1518–33 A.D. Seville Cathedral.

(C) Cloth Hall. Ypres. XIII cent. A.D. Destroyed, 1914 A.D., in the Great War.

CHAPTER XX
FLANDERS
From the Gothic Age to the Seventeenth Century

The lowlands facing the North Sea near the mouth of the Rhine were the home of hardy, industrious people, hardy because of their continual struggle with nature for self-preservation. Their knowledge of the sea and their courage in braving it early made them traders and hence manufacturers. Their ships not only brought the raw wool but carried away the fine woolen cloth famous throughout Europe. Of the several provinces included in the term Lowlands or Netherlands, Flanders up to the seventeenth century was the most important, with many great manufacturing centers such as Ghent, Louvain, and Ypres, and with Bruges not only as the chief market of the lowlands but one of the great trade centers of Europe. Some of the trade went overland by the Rhine and Brenner Pass to Venice and other Italian cities; some by sea around western Europe by Gibraltar. An arm of the North Sea, now silted up, reached inland to Bruges as late as the fifteenth century.

Bruges (meaning the city of bridges) was the typical Flemish city of medieval times, large, industrious, and wealthy. "In the fifteenth century buyers and sellers from every land resorted to Bruges for their trade. The merchant of Venice and the Jew of Lombard Street encountered one another on her quays and in her exchanges. Sailors and traders from all parts of the world made her streets lively with the varied colouring of their bright costumes. They came and went, and each left something behind him. The wealth of England met the wealth of the East in the market-halls of Bruges. The representatives of twenty foreign princes dwelt within the walls of this capital of the Dukes of Burgundy, at the crossroads of the highways of the North. 'In those days,' says Mr. Weale, 'the squares [of Bruges] were adorned with fountains; its bridges with statues of bronze; the public buildings and many of the private houses with statuary and carved work, the beauty of which was heightened and brought out by gilding and polychrome; the windows were rich with stained glass, and the walls of the interiors adorned with paintings in distemper or hung with gorgeous tapestry.'"[1]

Though technically Flanders was a fief now of a duke and now of a king, these great Flemish industrial cities were only loosely united, for each was a strong civic unit, thoroughly organized through its merchant guilds, which were not only industrial but social, religious, and political as well. The cult of the individual, so prominent in Italy in the fifteenth century, had not yet reached Flanders. To pursue a craft, a man must belong to the guild controlling that craft. For example, to be a painter, he must be a member of the guild of Saint Luke — each guild had a patron saint — which included the painters, saddlers, and glass and mirror workers. To secure membership in such an organization, the education of a boy was directed. Early he was apprenticed to a master, with whom he lived as a son, and who taught him the fundamentals of his craft — how to make implements, how to prepare the panels with gesso, and how to mix colors, oils, and varnishes. When the youth had mastered these problems — for there was no supply house where a painter could purchase ready-made pigments and implements — and had learned to work in the traditional manner of his master, he usually spent several years as a journeyman, traveling about from city to city, observing and gaining ideas from other masters. He was then eligible to become a master of his craft and was admitted to the guild. Through the guild he obtained commissions; the guild inspected his painting for honest, craftsmanlike materials and workmanship; and the guild secured him adequate payment.[2] The result of such a system was the sound, sober craftsmanship that characterizes the best work of Flanders.

By the end of the fifteenth century, Bruges was losing her prestige because of the silting up of her harbors and because of political disturbances. Antwerp now became her successor as a center of the political, industrial, and artistic life of Flanders. Antwerp was more cosmopolitan than Bruges, and more eager to receive the stimulation to trade that was being felt because of the discoveries in the new world. Life became more exuberant, and more sympathetic toward the new ideas which were penetrating northern Europe from Italy. Just at this time, however, Flanders, as a fief of the Spanish crown, was drawn into the religious wars. The Renaissance in northern Europe had emphasized the right of the individual in religious matters as opposed to the authority

[1] Conway, *The Van Eycks and Their Followers*, p. 85; for an excellent picture of Flemish life in the Middle Ages see Chs. VII and VIII.
[2] For the guild system see Conway, *The Van Eycks and Their Followers*.

of the church. Many of the provinces of the lowlands had turned Protestant. Spain, however, was strongly Catholic and Jesuitical. Hence she directed against these heretics the Spanish Inquisition. Antwerp was the center of the struggle, and much of the wealth and vigor of Flanders was spent in these wars. In the seventeenth century, however, after the Peace of Westphalia, a renewed vitality produced the last great school of Flemish art.

ARCHITECTURE

In studying Gothic architecture, we mentioned the town halls of Flanders as one of the most important manifestations of secular Gothic. Although the Flemish built fine cathedrals such as that of Antwerp, still the most characteristic buildings of these wealthy industrial cities were the town and cloth halls. The simple vigor and dignity of the *Ypres Cloth Hall* (PL. 128 c) is characteristic of the sturdy traders who built it. It is a large rectangular building with a steeply pitched roof; four small turrets with spires rise at the corners, and a massive square tower with turrets crowns the building. The small amount of decoration is inconspicuous. The impressiveness of the hall is due to the quiet balance of line and the harmonious massing of the parts. We feel the unity of the tower and the body of the structure, and the importance of the four turrets, which repeat the motif of the tower and also finish or frame the design as a whole. The relatively large number of apertures contrasts happily with the plain expanse of the great roof. The windows and the roof remind us to what an extent climate may condition architecture. To shed the rain and snow and to admit all possible light are needs of buildings in northern countries; while the flat roof and thick wall with few openings to keep out the sun and heat characterize the buildings of the warm southern countries where there is little rain.

The *Ypres Cloth Hall* with its restraint and quiet nobility has become more slender, more elegant, and more ornate in the *Brussels Town Hall* (PL. 129 A). Here again is illustrated the development that we noticed in studying the Gothic cathedral, a tendency toward lightness, elegance, and decoration. We see this in the tower and turrets, in the roof broken by frequent dormers, and in the light and shade of the façade made rich by the carvings and niches the original statues of which were painted and gilded. This decoration, however, is not carried to the point of overloading. There is enough restraint to keep a clear impression of the unity of design.

PAINTING

The *Ghent Altarpiece*[3] (PL. 130 A), painted by the Van Eyck brothers, Hubert (c. 1370–1426 A.D.) and Jan (c. 1385–1440 A.D.), is the culmination of a series of efforts on the part of a school which had grown out of medieval miniature painting, long practiced by the Flemish with great success. In fact, when the Van Eyck brothers were painting this altarpiece, Flemish miniature painters at the court of the Duke of Burgundy were producing such books as the *Très Riches Heures* (PL. 87 B). Let us look at the large lower panel. In the center, in a meadow gay with violets, lilies, daisies, and cowslips, stands the altar with the Lamb, from whose heart flows a stream of blood into a chalice; around are kneeling angels. In front is the fountain of life with the apostles grouped about it, kneeling. Toward the center from the four corners great throngs of people approach, clad in rich robes, through a country where rosebushes and vines are laden with flowers; in the background stretches a varied landscape with richly wooded hills, rivers, and towns, and above this an early-morning sky. Over the altar appears a dove from which rays descend to all the groups below. Here we have a powerful, poetical expression of the medieval idea of the redemption of man, as sincere and majestic as the account in the book of Revelation. The deep, glowing colors in the trees and flowers, meadow, and landscape, in the robes with rich embroideries, and in gold miters set with jewels, deepen the emotional effect.

The same feeling is inspired by the figure of the Virgin in the upper panel on the left. It is a majestic representation of the queen of heaven, calm and tranquil. She is thoughtfully reading a book; her hair falls loose over her shoulders; the elaborate crown is jeweled with rubies, topaz, and pearls and decorated with roses, lilies, and harebells, symbolic of her virtues; seven shining stars scattered over the inscriptions of the arch form a super-crown; her robe of richest blue is trimmed with an elaborately jeweled border, each jewel painted with minute delicacy; behind her is a panel of gold and black brocade. The soft texture of the hair, the luster of the pearls, the gleam of the other jewels, in fact all the details, are indicated with such finesse that one is almost led away by them from the larger conception.

Taking the altarpiece as a whole, however, one is impressed most by the grandeur and poetry of the conception, which are enhanced by the exquisite harmony of the rich jewel-like color. This

[3] This altarpiece was commissioned of Hubert in 1415, left unfinished at his death in 1426, and completed by Jan in 1432. It seems impossible to disentangle the work of the two brothers.

PLATE 129

(*A*) Town Hall. Brussels. 1401–55 A.D.

(*B*) Jan van Eyck. Esquire of the Order of Saint Anthony, also called Man with a Pink.   c.   1436   A.D. Kaiser-Friedrich   Museum, Berlin

(*C*) Jan van Eyck; also attributed to Hubert. Madonna of Chancellor Rolin. H. 27 in.   c. 1432 A.D.   Louvre, Paris.   (Alinari)

PLATE 130

(*A*) Hubert and Jan van Eyck. Ghent Altarpiece, or Adoration of the Lamb. Central Panel. W. 8 ft. 1415–32 A.D. Church of Saint Bavon, Ghent.

(*B*) Rogier van der Weyden. Descent from the Cross. 1435–50 A.D. Escorial, Spain.

color and the marvelous state of preservation of the panel are due to the technical methods employed by the Van Eycks. They did not invent the oil medium, for documents prove that painters had long been experimenting on the problem of mixing pigment with oils, and of using successive coats of transparent glaze. The Van Eycks continued these experiments to a point where they could produce rich, glowing surfaces of great durability.[4]

This lustrous surface is also found in the *Madonna of Chancellor Rolin* (PL. 129 c). In a loggia with tiled floor, rich carvings, and stained glass the Madonna is seated with the Child. She is of peasant type, heavily draped in a richly bordered mantle which spreads in great folds over the pavement about her; an angel is about to place upon her head a marvelous gold crown. On the left side of the loggia Chancellor Rolin, the donor of the picture, dressed in richest stuffs, kneels before a prayer desk. Through the columns one looks out on a garden with flowers and birds to a parapet where two passers-by are looking over toward the town on both sides of a winding river; the landscape fades away in the distant blue hills. The detached and imaginative quality of the *Ghent Altarpiece* is gone. The eye delights in the rich color harmony, but it wanders from detail to detail, each of which is rendered with the greatest minuteness; the texture of fabric, stone, hair, gold, and flower is marvelously expressed. As if through a telescope we can look down into the town and see the people walking about the square and passing to and fro across the bridge. The portrait of the Chancellor is incisive; sincerely and uncompromisingly Jan has painted the strong, rather grim features. All through the picture we feel that interest has centered upon the details. With the greatest patience and care the artist has endeavored to express as faithful a picture as possible of the life about him.

From a painter of this kind we might expect portraits of great realism. In the *Esquire of the Order of Saint Anthony* (PL. 129 b), who is as unprepossessing a person as one could wish, Jan has not softened the rather coarse type, the ugly mouth, puffy eyes, and huge ears. The Esquire wears a fur-trimmed coat, with a bit of brocade and fine linen showing at the throat, and a high, broad-brimmed beaver hat; about his neck is a chain with the insignia of the order of Saint Anthony; in his right hand he holds three wild pinks. Jan has observed his model most keenly and placed upon the panel a faithful picture of his subject with no hint of idealization.

[4] For the technical methods of the Van Eycks, consult Laurie.

A Fleming of the fifteenth century whose work is of a different type from that of the Van Eycks is Rogier van der Weyden (c. 1400–1464 A.D.). In his *Descent from the Cross* (PL. 130 B) the eye is not lured from detail to detail, but is focused upon the central figure of Christ, to which the rhythmic sweep of line and mass inevitably leads it by the line of the dark cross, by the light mass of the figure, and by the contrastingly dark masses surrounding it. Furthermore, a common intense emotion fuses all the figures, giving a sense of psychological unity to the group. There is no landscape background. Against a flat surface, the figures stand out with strong plastic feeling. The subordination of details and the predominant sense of design based upon sweeping line and balance of mass relate Rogier to the French. In fact his home was in the Walloon country in the southern part of Flanders, which was much more intimately connected with the French than the northern part.

A third painter of Bruges was Hans Memlinc (c. 1430–1494 A.D.), who was a different kind of personality from either the Van Eycks or Rogier van der Weyden, as we see in the *Marriage of Saint Catherine* (Pl. 131 A). In the center are the Madonna and Child enthroned, a panel of rich damask behind them and a fine oriental rug on the floor; saints and angels are grouped symmetrically on each side; at the top of the panel two small angels are floating down with a crown to place on the Virgin's head; on both sides are kneeling angels, one with a musical instrument, the other holding open a book, the leaves of which the Madonna is turning over. At the right Saint Barbara with her tower sits reading intently; at the left Saint Catherine reaches out her hand to receive the ring from the Christ Child; behind stand Saint John the Baptist with the lamb and Saint John the Evangelist with his poison cup; through the columns and piers we catch glimpses, in typical Flemish surroundings, of scenes from the lives of these saints. We feel the northern realism here, in the detailed painting of the pattern and texture of the fine rug, the rich brocade of the panel, the angel's robe and Saint Catherine's dress of black and gold brocade, the red velvet of the sleeves, and the delicate veil, so exquisite that it is scarcely discernible in a photograph. Still the total impression is not so much an insistence upon minute detail as it is the expression of a charming sentiment. Every one here is serene and happy. Saint Catherine, with her gorgeous raiment, is the daintiest of figures. There is all the poetry of the story of their mystic marriage, but it is lyrical, far removed from the austerity and lofty conception of the *Ghent Altarpiece*. There is here no profundity, not even a psychological unity among the figures; for Saint Barbara is intent upon her reading, and the Virgin turns the leaves of her book rather idly, without regard for the action of the Christ Child and Saint Catherine. Still the sweetness, grace, refinement, and harmonious color are alluring. The same characteristics are found in Memlinc's other pictures. No trouble, no future tragedy shadows his world, which is a paradise of serenity and delight.

It will be apparent, at this point in our study of Flemish painting, that there are certain well defined types that govern the appearance of the figures, except in the case of an actual portrait. The Madonnas, for example, are much alike. The face with its high forehead, long nose, and small mouth is conventional. The Child is like a diminutive man with a large head, a face as mature as the Madonna's, and a wizened body quite without structure. So an appreciation of fifteenth century Flemish painting must recognize that these expressions are largely conventional, a part of the tradition of the school. Form is something in which the early Flemings were not interested, as were the Italians.

The great century of true Flemish painting was the fifteenth, as we have seen it in the work of the Van Eyck brothers, Rogier van der Weyden, and Memlinc, centering chiefly in Bruges. During this century communication between Flanders and Italy was becoming much more frequent. Not only did these countries have a common trade interest, but the Flemish artists began to journey to Venice and to Florence, while the Italians depended on the Flemish weavers, the most expert in Europe, to translate their cartoons into the great tapestries to decorate the walls of their halls and palaces. Evidences of this contact we see creeping into Flemish art — an interest in the figure as expressed in the nude, Renaissance architecture and architectural detail, Italian landscape, a feeling of worldliness quite in contrast to the mysticism and religious sincerity of the native art. Thus the sixteenth century saw two main currents of art: first, the native tradition with its insistence upon realism which, when severed from the religious subject, became genre, sometimes charming, sometimes satirical of contemporary life, and in the hands of some painters displaying a tendency to sink into the vulgar and repulsive; second, the Italian imitation, the ideals of which did not well assimilate with northern ideals.

But this Italian influence, as in the other countries of Europe, had come to stay. The seventeenth century produced men who could learn fundamental principles from it without merely imitating. Such an attitude was the result of the sheer genius of Peter Paul Rubens (1577–1640 A.D.), who lived in Italy for eight years as the court painter of the Duke of Mantua.

The *Descent from the Cross* (PL. 132 A) indicates Rubens' characteristics. What we see first, as we stand at a little distance from this altarpiece, is a bold design in which a great diagonal massing of brilliant light stands out from the midst of darker masses, black, green-black, and red, over against a dark, unobtrusive background with a light spot at the low horizon. A closer study shows that the light mass is the body of Christ, which Joseph of Arimathea and some of the disciples, with the help of a winding-sheet, are lowering from the cross. Its limpness and lifelessness are emphasized by the vigorous action or pose of the other figures. The drooping head forms the center of interest to which all the lines lead; for these figures, so varied and individual, still are so grouped that they form a compact mass turning toward the central figure and framing it in. The transition from one to another is not abrupt, for the light penetrating the dark brings out a face here and a hand there or the sheen on a satiny texture, strengthening the unity of the group. The ease, breadth, and unity with which Rubens has composed his details is one of the important lessons which he learned in Italy. Another is the feeling for the figure. Here is a realization of form such as we have not met in the Flemish school. The figure of Christ is an accomplished study, giving one a tremendous impression of inert weight; everywhere else is the feeling of living organisms — in the figure of John as he strains backward to receive the weight of the body, his foot clutching the rung of the ladder; in the back and the arm of the disciple on the cross who has just released his hold of the body; in the head and shoulders of Peter, as he stops for a moment with his gaze fixed upon the head of Christ. The whole impression, though spectacular, is powerful.

In the *Rape of the Daughters of Leucippus* (PL. 131 B) like characteristics may be noted — the selection of a dramatic subject as the best suited to a certain exuberance of nature that must find expression; a finely composed, compact group of dark masses about a bright central mass, the complete unit admirably fitted into its square frame. A certain feeling of spaciousness, of room for this impetuosity, comes from the low horizon line, another lesson learned in Italy, we realize, when we recall the predilection of the Flemish for a horizon line placed high upon the canvas (PLS. 130 A and 131 A). The two figures of Leucippus' daughters form the center of interest and reveal Rubens' ability to paint the female form, which, in his work, has abundant flesh, soft, warm, and wonderfully luminous, though at times it is coarse. This warmth and luminosity is emphasized by the dark figures of the men and the horses with their brilliant color masses. The splendor of Rubens is characteristic of the Counter-Reformation carried on so zealously by the Jesuits, whose policy was to hold adherents to the Church through display. Flanders, we remember, remained Catholic.

It is a great contrast to pass from Rubens to Anthony van Dyck (1599–1641 A.D.), for it is to pass from dazzling joy, impetuosity, and frequent coarseness to sobriety, taste, and refinement. In any one of Van Dyck's portraits — for his portraits are his greatest work — one can discern these qualities. There is great distinction in such a picture as *Maria Louisa de Tassis* (PL. 132 B), suggestive of Van Dyck's study of Titian. There is not only elegance in the costume — the rich fabrics, fine lace, jewelry, and feathered fan — but color harmony, decorative fitness, and aristocratic bearing. In judging Van Dyck's work we must remember the character of his sitters — stately, elegant, self-centered people whose life was superficial; and must realize that these portraits were painted to decorate palaces and to harmonize with the life lived there. There is no vigor either of character or of form in his figures, but rather an aristocratic detachment and somberness, with an execution showing the painter's delight in surface and in texture, and his refined taste. This is true of the *Children of Charles I* (PL. 132 C), who are real children in a somber mood but thoroughly at ease as they stand dressed in satin and lace, the richness and shimmer of which Van Dyck so loved.

MINOR ARTS

The carefully worked out details in the painting of Flanders serve to picture the minor arts of the Flemish, whose versatility and skill made them famous and influential throughout Europe. As in painting, everything was produced under the control of the guilds, with a like result of sound craftsmanship. The crowns and miters, jewels, and ceremonial vessels reveal the same skill of the goldsmith as we saw in the Gothic period; the pages of the illuminated manuscripts, glowing with color and gold, richly decorated initial letters, and miniatures, rival the panels of the altarpieces. Their skill in the carving and paneling of wood made a wide market for their furniture and carried their workers to many parts of Europe to execute orders on the ground. But it is perhaps in the craft of tapestry weaving that the Flemings showed their greatest skill.[5] In the Gothic tapestries (PL. 89 c) we saw that the same fundamental principles controlled the weaver as the sculptor and the glassworker, namely, decorative fitness through the insistence upon line, pattern, and color. Although the tendency toward naturalism was making itself felt and a love of minute detail was inherent in the Flemish artists, still they observed these fundamental laws by disposing their figures skillfully into large units for the ultimate effect, and by keeping the detail subordinate. The tapestries became very large, and more complicated in composition. Classical, historical, and pastoral subjects entered. Dyes of intermediate tones, which were now becoming available, enabled the weavers to obtain more brilliant color and more pictorial effects. The borders become wider and more complicated and often give delightful representations of foliage, fruit, and flowers (PL. 132 D), as well as heraldic devices and inscriptions.

SUMMARY

In Flemish art we have seen two distinct phases. First, there was the native Flemish, which created splendid town and cloth halls, monuments to the vigorous industrial and civic life of the times, and produced a school of painting in the tradition of the Middle Ages. This was marked by certain conventions, by brilliant, robust color, and by an insistence upon minute detail. It was saved from mediocrity by its sincerity and sound craftsmanship; and was important historically because of its place in the perfecting of the oil medium. This same sound craftsmanship is apparent in the minor arts as well, especially in those of the illuminator, the goldsmith, and the tapestry weaver. The second phase, which we might call Italianized Flemish, at first appeared as an imitation of the Italian elements that had been grafted upon the native art; but culminated in a fusion of Italian and Flemish in the hands of Rubens and Van Dyck, with their mastery of form, composition, and color.

[5] There were two important centers for tapestry weaving: Arras and Brussels. Arras was the chief center from early in the fourteenth century until 1447, when Louis XI seized the town. The Arras hangings were famous all over Europe, and some of them were designed by the Van Eycks and Memlinc. After the fall of Arras, Brussels became the center of the craft, which there operated under royal patronage. Painters such as Rogier van der Weyden and Rubens made cartoons for the weavers. Charles V required that the tapestries be signed by the master weavers. Of these Willem de Pannemaker was the most famous, and his signature appears on the great series made for Charles, such as the *Conquest of Tunis* in the Royal Palace at Madrid.

BIBLIOGRAPHY

CONWAY, SIR W. M., The Van Eycks and Their Followers. N.Y., Dutton, 1921.

CUST, L. H., Anthony van Dyck. London, Bell, 1906.

FRIEDLAENDER, M. J., Pictures of Rogier van der Weyden in America. *Art in America*, IX (1921), pp. 62 ff.

FROMENTIN, EUGÈNE, Masters of Past Time (Les Maîtres d'autrefois).

—— ——, Old Masters of Belgium and Holland (Les Maîtres d'autrefois, tr. Robbins).

HARVARD UNIVERSITY, WILLIAM HAYES FOGG ART MUSEUM, Collection of Mediæval and Renaissance Paintings. Cambridge, Harvard University Press, 1919.

HOLME, CHARLES, ED., Sketches by Samuel Prout. London, The Studio, 1915.

HOURTICQ, LOUIS, Rubens (tr. Street). N.Y., Duffield, 1918.

HUNTER, G. L., Tapestries, Their Origin, History, and Renaissance. N.Y., Lane, 1912.

LAURIE, A. P., Materials of the Painter's Craft. Philadelphia, Lippincott, 1911.

ROOSES, MAX, Art in Flanders. London, Heinemann, 1914.

—— ——, Rubens (tr. Child). 2 v. London, Duckworth, 1904.

THOMSON, W. G., History of Tapestry. N.Y., Putnam, 1906.

VALENTINER, W. R., Art of the Low Countries. Garden City, N.Y., Doubleday, 1914.

WEALE, W. H. J., AND BROCKWELL, M. W., The Van Eycks and Their Art. N.Y., Lane, 1912.

CHAPTER XXI

HOLLAND

In the Seventeenth Century

HISTORICAL BACKGROUND

The country now called Holland constituted the northern and eastern part of the group of provinces known as the Lowlands or Netherlands, while Flanders occupied the southern and western part. There was a racial difference between the two, the Hollander being closer to the German, the Fleming to the French. Like Flanders, these northern provinces were the fief now of one lord and now of another. At the time of the religious and political struggle with Spain, however, the northern provinces, which had quite generally accepted Protestantism, revolted from the Spanish crown, forming the nucleus of modern Holland, whose independence was recognized by Spain in the Peace of Westphalia in 1648. Under the early part of the Spanish rule the Dutch, like the Flemish, had flourished. The East India Company had been formed and the discovery of the new world had opened up further opportunities to them for trade and colonization. Their great commercial cities, such as Haarlem and Amsterdam, had thus been stimulated, and were rapidly acquiring great wealth. Life was not unlike that in the neighboring Flemish cities. Civic pride was strong, and supervision by guilds and similar organizations effective.[1]

Religiously, however, there was a great difference. Protestantism gained a strong hold among the Dutch. Further, the Protestants were puritanical toward art. Religious pictures and sculpture found no place among them, nor pagan myths, nor even historical subjects. As we think back over the art of the Middle Ages in all parts of Europe and of the Renaissance in Italy, Spain, and Flanders, we realize that to eliminate the religious subject means to eliminate most of the art and one of the chief motivations of art. What then was left for these wealthy Hollanders, with their strong love of independence, national pride, and religious convictions? Fromentin has answered the question thus:

[1] See G. B. Brown, *Rembrandt*, Ch. III, for a picture of Holland in the seventeenth century.

PLATE 131

(*A*) Memlinc. Marriage of Saint Catherine. 1479 A.D. Hospital of Saint John, Bruges.

(*B*) Rubens. Rape of the Daughters of Leucippus. 1619 or 1620 A.D. Munich.

PLATE 132

(A) Rubens. Descent from the Cross.
1612-14 A.D. Antwerp Cathedral.

(B) Van Dyck. Maria Louisa de Tassis.
Liechtenstein Coll., Vienna.

(C) Van Dyck. Children of Charles I,
detail. 1635 A.D Turin. (Anderson)

(D) Flemish Tapestry. Detail of the month of
August. XVI cent. Metropolitan Museum, New
York. (Metropolitan Museum)

PLATE 133

(A) Hals. Laughing Cavalier. 1624 A.D.
Wallace Coll., London.

(B) Hals. Young Man with a Slouch Hat.
1660 A.D. Cassel.

(C) Rembrandt. Supper at Emmaus. 1648 A.D. Louvre, Paris. (Giraudon)

PLATE 134

(*A*) Rembrandt. Young Girl at an Open Half-Door. 1645 A.D. Art Institute, Chicago. (Art Institute)

(*B*) Rembrandt. Portrait of an Old Woman. Hermitage, Leningrad.

(*C*) Rembrandt. Christ Healing the Sick, called the Hundred Guilder Print. c. 1649 A.D. Metropolitan Museum, New York.

A writer of our time, very enlightened in such matters, has wittily replied that such a people had but one thing to propose — a very simple and bold thing, . . . and that was to require that they [the artists] should paint its portrait. This phrase says everything. Dutch painting, it is quickly perceived, was and could be only the portrait of Holland, its exterior image, faithful, exact, complete with no embellishment. Portraits of men and places, citizen habits, squares, streets, country-places, the sea and sky — such was to be, reduced to its primitive elements, the programme followed by the Dutch school, and such it was from its first day to the day of its decline. . . . [2]

PAINTING

Thus it comes about that the great accomplishment of the Dutch lay in the field of painting, and this, too, in a brief space of time, the seventeenth century, following hard upon the independence of Holland. Two artists stand preëminent — Frans Hals (1580–1666 A.D.) and Rembrandt van Rijn (1606–1669 A.D.).

The *Laughing Cavalier* (PL. 133 A) illustrates one of Hals's individual portraits. Is he laughing? The self-confident soldier with a suggestion of bravado looks out at us with a very direct glance, while over his face ripples a momentary expression that is difficult to analyze. The plain surface of the broad flaring hat brings out this highly expressive face and emphasizes by contrast the rich detail of the coat. The lacy quality of the fine ruff is indicated by skillful strokes, while on the cuff the pattern is painted in such careful detail that one could easily reproduce it. In the upper part of the cuff and on the sash again is the broad slashing brush work.

Momentary surface expression, caught in passing and frequently of a jovial nature, is characteristic of much of Hals's work, and his technical methods are particularly suitable to his purpose. How much he could say by means of a few of his vigorous brush strokes, the *Young Man with a Slouch Hat* illustrates (PL. 133 B). He is sitting in a chair with his arm over the back; his eyes sparkle; an infectious jollity spreads over the face, which the easy, unconventional position of the body and angle of the hat accentuates. The planes are roughly blocked out and the transitions abrupt; the high lights are daubed on, but daubed with utmost skill. Goya's artistic creed might well be applied here, "A picture is finished when its effect is true," and the effect of sparkling vivacity, the living expression of a passing moment, would not be more effective if the details of the hand, for instance, were more carefully worked out.

The other great painter of portraits is Rembrandt, who devel-

[2] Fromentin, *Masters of Past Time*, p. 130.

oped a peculiar medium of expression suited to himself alone. This is apparent in the *Supper at Emmaus* (PL. 133 c).[3] Four men are grouped about a table, Christ in the center, with clasped hands, uplifted eyes and worn face, perfectly quiet and serene. The disciple at the left sits with hands folded in adoration as he recognizes the guest; the one at the right has made a quick movement as recognition dawns, but remains transfixed as if still doubting; the stolid serving boy hesitates, puzzled at the scene. The room is dim except for the brilliant light that falls on the tablecloth and the face and hands of Christ, touches the hands of the disciple at the left, and brings out the faces and hands of the two at the right. About the head of Christ is a deep glow subtly blending into the shadows; in the background is a great unadorned arch with lateral pilasters. The light carries the eye directly and forcibly to the center of interest — the figure of Christ — and plays into the other figures, tying them into a psychological unity with the central one; the contour lines are blurred and finally fade into the shadows. This shadow is not a dead gloom, but luminous and vibrating, filled with living air, enveloping the shadowy forms so that we feel their mass and significance as forcibly as if they were sharply defined in clear light. The upper half of the panel, at first glance apparently quite empty, not only adds a note of quietude contrasting with the more lively lower half, but by its suggestion of spaciousness and elevation deepens the emotional quality and hence the spiritual significance of the incident.

It is evident here that an important characteristic is the way in which light is used. It is not a natural illumination either from the sun or from an artificial light, but is something unique born of Rembrandt's imagination. He seemed to visualize in terms of this light, a term which in fact includes the shadowy parts of the picture as well, for these darker portions glow with light which is only of a different intensity from that of the brilliantly accented parts. This was Rembrandt's peculiar means of expression, just as the human figure was Michelangelo's, and line was Botticelli's.

One may question here why, after what has been said about the aversion of the Dutch Protestants to representing sacred themes, we have as the subject an incident from the life of Christ. Rembrandt, as individual in religious thought as in artistic creed, evidently cared little for the dogma of the times and the decrees of the Church. The fierce struggle of the Jesuits and Calvinists did not trouble him. But his representation of the Bible story was

[3] See Fromentin's famous description in *Masters of Past Time*.

vastly different from anything we have met before. For he chose the types of his characters from the life about him, and usually gave them local setting and dressed them in Dutch peasant costume. Many of the paintings with religious themes during the Italian Renaissance, with their splendor and idealism, were made at the command of the Church as outward manifestations of its power. Then in the Spanish painters and Rubens the message of the Church, in its attempt to stem the tide of the Reformation, became pompous and grandiloquent. How very simple and sincere then, in contrast, is Rembrandt's everyday story told in the language of everyday man!

Let us see whether the characteristics seen in the *Supper at Emmaus* hold for Rembrandt's portraits. In PL. 134 A we see a *Young Girl* standing at a Dutch door, the upper half of which is open, her hands resting upon the lower closed part. She wears a tightly fitting bodice with linen guimpe gathered closely about the throat, and full skirt, and about her neck a double string of beads. She stands looking out toward her right with youthful awkwardness rather than grace, and with a shyness and reserve that is not unfriendly as one judges from the suggestion of a smile about the mobile mouth. Rembrandt has pictured this simple, unsophisticated girl with an appropriate simple directness. A brilliant illumination concentrates upon the side of the face, one hand, and the wall behind the figure, against which the arm is so sharply silhouetted. Thence a glowing light envelops the figure, blurring the outlines and merging the other parts in shadow, but with such subtle gradations and such true emphasis on essentials that we feel strongly both the surrounding atmosphere and the plastic quality of the figure. Thus Rembrandt both draws and models by means of light.

This ability to treat his subject with keen penetration and warm sympathy is characteristic of Rembrandt. Take, for example, the *Portrait of an Old Woman* (PL. 134 B). She is sitting wearily in her chair with folded hands and dreaming eyes which look at nothing in particular. In the bent shoulders, listless hands, and the head too weary to be held erect, are expressed utter weariness and the patience of long years. The illumination is more concentrated here than in the *Young Girl*, emphasizing the face, the kerchief, and the hands. All the rest is sunk in shadow, yet one easily realizes the whole figure, so clearly has the artist stimulated the imagination by the indication of a few essentials. Though this is probably a portrait, still Rembrandt has here become abstract enough in his expression to make it universal in its appeal. Here again we see amazing draughtsmanship and modeling, not of the kind practiced by the Florentines, but highly individualized and expressed in terms of chiaroscuro.

The use of line as a means for the expression of form was not unknown to Rembrandt, as his etchings show. The process of the etcher is this: Upon a polished copper plate is laid a thin coating of a mixture of wax, gum, and rosin called the ground, in which the etcher draws his design with a sharp needle, exposing the copper below. This plate he then immerses in an acid, known as the mordant, which bites the copper along the lines exposed. The ground is then removed and a print made as in engraving. The difference between the processes of engraving and etching is that greater ease and facility can be obtained by the needle working freely in the soft wax than by the burin cutting directly into the hard metal. These two processes are analogous to the two techniques of the black- and red-figured Greek vases, where we saw that the Greek abandoned the black for the red in order to attain greater freedom in drawing.

That this use of line appealed to Rembrandt is clear from the large number of etchings that he made. His subject matter he took from the life round about him — the landscape of Holland, the beggars of Amsterdam, peasants, and the common folk of all kinds. In the *Hundred Guilder Print*[4] (PL. 134 c) there is great facility in the expression of form and character, with the greatest economy of line. Here we have an example of Rembrandt's method of unifying several contrasting groups into a whole. The center of interest is the figure of Christ, toward which the figures on both sides inevitably lead and which is further emphasized by the brilliant illumination contrasting with the dark background. Christ is raising his hands with tenderness in welcome to the woman carrying a little child whom Peter is attempting to push aside; just behind her comes another woman with a baby, urged on by an eager child. In the crowd at the left in the open diffused light are the fat, supercilious Pharisees and the sneering crowd; one youth, however, sits on the ground with his head resting on his hand, pondering deeply. At the right are grouped the sick; apparently a crowd of them are coming through the opening in litters and wheelbarrows, or limping along with the help of friends. The pictorial effect of this side of the print is due to the same kind of illumination that we have seen in Rembrandt's paintings. The light accentuates now one

---

[4] The subject of the print is *Christ Healing the Sick. Hundred Guilder Print* is a title probably derived from the price which the print brought at an auction sale.

form and now another, contrasting them sharply with the shadow, which, though dark, is filled with atmosphere and with forms. Here again Rembrandt draws and models with chiaroscuro. On the left side of the print his method is different; with line only, now extremely delicate, now more firm, yet always unerringly precise, he expresses not only form and texture but, with a few essential strokes, as penetrating a characterization as we found in his portraits, and each one markedly individual. These two contrasting parts of the print he blends by using intermediate tones in the central group. As in the *Supper at Emmaus*, the emotional appeal is heightened by these contrasting effects of the chiaroscuro.

In another line the Dutch excelled — genre, which after all is part of the portrait of Holland. More than any other nation they have left us a picture of their homes, their courtyards and streets, and their everyday life. The *Pantry Door* by Pieter de Hooch (1629–1678? A.D.) is typical (PL. 135 A). We are in one of these Dutch homes, and see a young woman just outside the pantry handing a small jug to a little girl. There is the usual beamed ceiling and tiled floor; in the room beyond is a chair, and above it a portrait near the half-open window where the light and air pour in, flooding the room and permeating even the darker corners of the foreground. Here the title matters but little. There is nothing monumental, nothing of spiritual significance about the picture. What interests us is the masterful way in which the artist makes us feel the interior. The bright outside light coming through the half-open window and the smaller one in the pantry emphasize, by contrast, the dimmer light inside and so true are the artist's values here that we get a living impression of the air-filled space and distance. The drawing of the figures is rather feeble; but they are placed very effectively against the wall space.

A climax of Dutch genre painting, in which homely scenes are lifted to a plane of exquisite beauty and poetry, is reached in Johannes Vermeer of Delft (1632–1675 A.D.). In his *Young Woman at a Casement* (PL. 135 c), there is pictured an everyday scene of no particular moment. A young woman is standing at a partly open window by a table, one hand resting on the window, the other holding a pitcher. There is perfect poise and serenity in the picture and a feeling of great coolness and restfulness that comes partly from the quiet balance of design and partly from the subtle harmony of blue and white tones that almost fill the canvas. The dress is deep blue; the cloak thrown over the back of the chair is lighter blue; blue plays through the linen headdress and the window glass. A cool white covers the wall; while the rich red of the rug on the table furnishes a complementary note of warmth and strength. The structure of the figure is well indicated, as are the form and texture of the different kinds of cloth, the rug, the glass, and the map. The light from the window fills the room, unifying all objects. The luminosity is one of the superlative qualities of the picture. The light falls upon the wall with the subtlest gradations of tone, maintaining a balance with the other half of the picture. For ability to express with pigment exquisitely modulated values in an unbroken wall surface upon which the light falls, Vermeer stands unrivaled. Against this background is patterned the figure, revealing the artist's sense of design. So complete is the illusion of reality here, in fact so heightened and so poetical is the expression of it, that we forget that the panel is only eighteen inches high.

This sense of design is predominant in the *Head of a Young Girl* (PL. 135 B) who wears a turbaned headdress of yellow and blue, a yellow dress with a little white about the neck, and a large pearl earring. She looks over her shoulder toward the spectator with a momentary glance. The frank questioning eyes and the parted lips give to the face an expression of ingenuousness and wonder. The ability to impart this mobile expression is only part of the charm of the picture. There is a fine feeling for structure here, yet only in its essentials; the modeling is kept rather flat, and the massing of the parts carefully calculated in relation to the space. Notice the exquisite line of the face, sharply defined against the dark background; the strong vertical line of the loose end of the turban which gives virility to a design composed entirely of curves; and finally the charming, simple color harmony of blue and yellow that plays through the design. Vermeer has given us here a rare blending of content, pattern, and color harmony.

In the field of landscape, the Hollanders made a great contribution. What that was we shall find in the work of Jacob van Ruisdael (1628/9–1682 A.D.). In his *Swamp* (PL. 136 A) we are looking across a marshy place in the woods, surrounded by great gnarled trees whose trunks are reflected in the open stretch. Water plants, grasses, and lilies fringe the edge of the swamp and float on its surface; a duck flies off to the left where two others are swimming; the light illumines a great log half in the water, a slender birch sapling, and a gaunt oak; behind the trees clouds roll up into a blue sky. A great calm and stillness permeate the scene with a suggestion of melancholy. One feels that the artist has a sympathy and an intimacy with nature which have enabled him to conceive the scene not merely as a transcription but as a poetical interpretation. There is nothing gay here, nothing evanescent; but everywhere quiet strength. In order to express his concept convincingly, Ruisdael worked out the composition with great care, massing his darks strongly at the corners, allowing the light and air to penetrate freely in the center; while the high-lights strike important accents and unify the scene. There has been a careful study of the forms of nature, as we see in the structure of the trees, which are painted with a considerable amount of careful detail, and in the texture and illumination of the clouds, with their feeling for mass and movement through space. The color is somber, browns and greens predominating both in the light and in the shadow. The noteworthy fact here is that this is not an idealized scene born of the imagination but a native landscape approached with sympathy and expressed with poetry. This was the Hollanders' unique contribution to the history of landscape. To appreciate this fact we need to remember the imaginative, heroic landscapes which Ruisdael's contemporary, Claude Gellée, was painting in France (PL. 147 B).

SUMMARY

One could hardly summarize the painting of Holland better than Fromentin,[5] has done, a brief quotation from whom appeared at the beginning of this chapter. It remains only to stress the general tone of sincerity and sobriety, which is lighted up only occasionally with imagination, poetry, or idealism; and to emphasize the fact that these Dutch pictures, though usually small, for their purpose was not to decorate spacious walls but to embellish the modest home of a Dutch burgher, are examples technically of marvelously fine painting, whether they are the expression of character, the illusion of light and air-filled space, or the representation of the texture of a rug or a lace collar. In these qualities the Dutch were wonderful craftsmen.

BIBLIOGRAPHY

BODE, WILHELM, Great Masters of Dutch and Flemish Painting (tr. Clarke). N.Y., Scribner, 1909.
BROWN, G. B., Rembrandt. N.Y., Scribner, 1907.

[5] Although some of the statements and opinions expressed in the *Masters of Past Time*, written in 1875, have been superseded by later research, still Fromentin remains the most fundamental and penetrating critic of the Dutch and Flemish schools and, in fact, one of the few great art critics.

CAFFIN, C. H., Story of Dutch Painting. N.Y., Century, 1911.

DAVIES, G. S., Frans Hals. London, Bell, 1904.

FROMENTIN, EUGÈNE, Masters of Past Time (Les Maîtres d'autrefois). N.Y., Dutton, 1913.

—— ——, Old Masters of Belgium and Holland (Les Maîtres d'autrefois, tr. Robbins). Boston, Osgood, 1882.

HIND, A. M., Rembrandt's Etchings. London, Methuen, 1924.

—— ——, History of Engraving and Etching. Boston, Houghton, 1923.

HOLMES, C. J., Notes on the Art of Rembrandt. London, Chatto, 1911.

KNACKFUSS, HERMANN, Rembrandt. Leipzig, Velhagen, 1906.

LUCAS, E. V., Vermeer of Delft. London, Methuen, 1922.

MICHEL, EMILE, Rembrandt (tr. Simmons). N.Y., Scribner, 1903.

ROBINS, W. P., Etching Craft. N.Y., Dodd, 1923.

VALENTINER, W. R., Art of the Low Countries (tr. Van Rensselaer). Garden City, N.Y., Doubleday, 1914.

PLATE 135

(*A*) Pieter de Hooch. Pantry Door. H. 27 in. 1658 A.D. Rijksmuseum, Amsterdam.

(*B*) Vermeer. Portrait of a Young Girl. H. 18½ in. The Hague.

(*C*) Vermeer. Young Woman at a Casement. H. 18 in. Metropolitan Museum, New York. (Metropolitan Museum)

PLATE 136

(A) Ruisdael. Swamp. Hermitage, Petrograd.

(B) Dürer. Saint Jerome in His Study.
Engraving. 1514 A.D.

(C) Dürer. Four Preachers,
detail. 1526 A.D. Munich.

CHAPTER XXII

GERMANY

From the Gothic Age to the Nineteenth Century

HISTORICAL BACKGROUND

In the Middle Ages we noted the vigor of the Rhenish craftsmen in many of the arts. They built finely constructed and vaulted churches with bold picturesque outlines and with more decoration than many of the churches elsewhere in northern Europe. Among the crafts their textiles and metal work were equal to any produced in Europe. The impulse toward independent thought that was basic in the Renaissance movement in Germany touched chiefly religious and intellectual life, and resulted in a revolt from the authority of the Church in Rome and the establishment of the Protestant Church. The result of this Reformation was hostility to Rome and, perhaps unconsciously, to all things Italian. Probably for this reason the traditions of the Middle Ages persisted longer in Germany than in any other country of Europe.

The landscape of Germany, in comparison with Italy, is drab. The character of her people is solid, practical, and usually tends toward the unimaginative. In the race, as in many of the races of north Europe, is a deep-rooted love for fact, that is, for reality; a passion for painstaking detail which in art is likely to result in sacrifice of the essential. In their workmanship, the German craftsmen have always been patient and skillful.

The highest expression of the Renaissance in Germany is found in the first half of the sixteenth century in the paintings, engravings, and drawings of Dürer and Holbein the Younger. Almost immediately after this Germany was plunged into a series of disastrous religious wars which so drained her energy and her resources that she was unable to make any notable contribution to the arts of Europe. In the eighteenth and nineteenth centuries, however, there rose the other great expression of her people, perhaps her loftiest — music. Bach, Händel, Mozart, Beethoven, Wagner — this has been her chief glory.

341

ARCHITECTURE

German buildings always appeared to have a predilection for the picturesque — irregular outlines, abnormally high, steeply pitched roofs with dormers, and abundant decoration in the form of bright color, gilding, and carvings. When the influence of the Renaissance came, late as we have said, it came in the form of the baroque, which with its love of ornament made a strong appeal to German taste and stimulated that taste to extravagant decoration and to an emphasis upon detail rather than upon construction and design. It was in secular architecture particularly, upon the town halls and the houses of the wealthy merchants, that this influence made itself felt. The reformed church had little zeal for building. In the houses — the *Peller House* in Nuremberg (PL. 137 A) is a typical example — the high gable has retained the essentials of the old traditions but has accepted some of the outward forms of Italy. The arrangement of the doors and windows is symmetrical; the doorway is placed in the center and is emphasized by a bay above it; the stories with superposed orders to frame the openings continue up into the gable and are decorated fantastically with scrolls, pinnacles, and statues.

PAINTING AND ENGRAVING

The wealthy middle-class burghers, who erected houses of this type, were the chief art patrons — a fact that influenced the work of the painters. For a commission from this class of patrons was likely to insist upon the story and realistic details rather than upon the specifically artistic elements of line, pattern, and color. Thus much of the German painting lacks unity, because it is so cluttered with detail. More than often it focuses upon many interesting details rather than upon one centralized significant fact or feeling. Two painters, however, were great enough artists to rise above this plane, and one of these remained at the same time essentially German — Albrecht Dürer (1471–1528 A.D.).

While Dürer was still a young man, the printing-press was beginning to make books available. Paper was becoming better in quality and cheaper in price. Illustrations began to be used commonly in printed books as early as about 1475 A.D. The demand for these illustrations, especially for religious books, coincided with Dürer's ability. His conceptions, like those of Hubert van Eyck, were of the Middle Ages. The *Apocalypse* series reveals the intensity and sincerity of his convictions and his imaginative powers. The woodcuts also illustrate his highest attainment, for they are free from that excessive detail that mars the engravings. This is largely due to the necessities of the medium. The design is drawn on the block of wood in ink; then the wood is cut away, leaving the ink lines raised. Such a process demands elimination of detail on the part of the designer, and patience and skill on the part of the cutter.[1] In Dürer's woodcuts there is a robust,

brilliant, and convincing quality that is due to the bold vigor of his draughts-manship, to the vivacity of his clear crisp lines, and to the decorative effect of his massing of pure blacks and whites with no half-tones (FIG. 104). In producing this effect lies the power of the really successful wood-cut.

A different conception we meet in the *Saint Jerome in His Study* (PL. 136 B), as well as a different technique. This print is from an engraving on copper. Here is a delightful atmosphere of

Fig. 104. Dürer. Saint Christopher.
Woodcut. 1511 A.D.

peace, quiet, and orderliness — an atmosphere conducive to meditation. The sun streams warmly through the little round panes. The Saint sits at his desk absorbed in work, quiet and disregardful of the movement of the sands in the hourglass behind him. The lion and the dog are dozing in perfect repose. The books, the cushions, and even the slippers underneath the bench suggest relaxation and comfort. It is this feeling of wholesomeness and sweetness that is the outstanding impression. But the more one looks at the print the more he realizes Dürer's fidelity to minute detail — the knots in the beams of the ceiling, the scissors and writing materials on the wall behind the Saint; the fine discrimination of texture in the wood, the glass, the fur of the animals, and the different stuffs. All this detail Dürer has been able to hold somewhat in subordination by means of a cer-

---

[1] Some illustrators cut their own blocks; others do not. In Dürer's case it seems probable that this part of the work was done by a professional cutter.

tain amount of clear, unifying line — the arch of the window, the beams of the ceiling, the shadow of the table on the floor. So that the astounding thing here — the work of genius — is the fact that with all this infinite detail there is a concentrated feeling of quiet orderliness. In the hands of any other engraver this was not likely to result.

Like Leonardo, Dürer was an inquirer. In his eager curiosity about everything, he belonged to the Renaissance. He traveled in Italy, and was much impressed with the painters and with the beauty of the country. "How I shall freeze after this sun!" he wrote to his friend at Nuremberg. But Dürer's fiber was too strong for him to be lured away from native traditions, as were many northerners, to their destruction. Some influence of Italy, however, is seen in a late painting, never finished, the *Four Preachers* (PL. 136 c). The conception is as lofty, majestic, and powerful as that of his earlier works, but the treatment is simpler. The broad massive folds have an ease and freedom about them; and while there is detailed individuality in the faces, on the whole there is less of that over-insistence on detail that was Dürer's birthright.

Hans Holbein the Younger (1497–1543 A.D.) like Dürer, belonged to Renaissance Germany. But in his greatest work, his portraits, Holbein alone of his nation had the selective ability. In his *Wife and Children* (PL. 137 B), for example, one is deeply impressed with the honest, straightforward representation of living people. It is not merely the external appearance that we see but the real life of each, understood with great insight and painted without compromise. There is the serious mother, sweet and capable, her plain face softened by the delicate veil; the eager lad, and the sober baby. We feel the volume of each figure and its structure — the hard bone, firm muscle, and soft flesh, as well as the essentials of the personality. This truthfulness of appearance and character Holbein attained not with the infinite detail of Dürer, but by the selection and emphasis of essentials. What he saw and said, he saw and said precisely, but he learned that many things, after all, are irrelevant. The three figures form a compact group, the pattern of which is sensitively related to the frame. This sensitive relation of a group or a single figure to the canvas is characteristic of Holbein, and reveals his innate feeling for design. Technically, Holbein belongs to the Flemish school of the fifteenth century. His surfaces are as hard and lustrous as enamel, and before them one is thrilled with admiration for the master craftsman.

PLATE 137

(*A*) Peller House. Nuremberg.
1605 A.D.

(*B*) Holbein the Younger. Holbein's Wife and
Children. c. 1528 A.D. Basel. (Hanfstaengl)

(*C*) Holbein the Younger.   Dance of
Death: The Old Man. Woodcut. c.
1526 A.D. Metropolitan Museum, New
York. (Metropolitan Museum)

(*D*) Holbein the Younger. Drawing: Man in a
Broad-brimmed Hat. Basel.

PLATE 138

(*A*) Compton Wynyates. 1520 A.D. England.

(*B*) Longleat. 1567–80 A.D. England.

(*C*) Hampton Court. Great Hall. 1515–40 A.D. London. (Nash)

Holbein's marvelous vision and masterly draughtsmanship are clearly evident in his drawings. These are largely preliminary studies for the long series of portraits that he painted for the English court, whither he was called by Henry VIII. The line, usually red or black chalk, is drawn with the greatest delicacy and at the same time with unflinching accuracy in essentials. Thus he models the structure of the head and analyzes the character in its permanent aspects. At times he puts in a few minutely worked details of pattern or color as if they were notes for future reference. His hand worked so spontaneously and so unerringly that one feels the ultimate *rightness* of the result. In such a drawing as the *Man in a Broad-brimmed Hat* (PL. 137 D) the strong silhouette of the hat not only is interesting as pattern but serves to emphasize the sensitive face and keen eyes. Thus Holbein combines in a most surprising way frank, unequivocal honesty and pure artistry. The forty-one woodcuts known as the *Dance of Death* (PL. 137 C) not only illustrate Holbein's lucid thought and expression but disclose a remarkable dramatic power and an exuberant inventiveness. Death, in the form of a skeleton that is never anatomically accurate but marvelously imbued with natural life and alert movement, always plays his part with grim irony as he mockingly enters into the activity of each individual.

SUMMARY

The artists of Germany were craftsmen with superb technical ability, but placed emphasis upon minute and infinite detail. Their strength, honesty, and fidelity to the facts of a scene or character led them too strongly in this direction. They overloaded their buildings with ornament which made them fantastic and extravagant. Decoration runs riot over their altars, doorways, iron grilles, wood carvings, and even the pages of their early printed books. The highest manifestation of the race appears in two groups of artists: first in the two great painters and draughtsmen, Dürer and Holbein. The former was thoroughly German and medieval in conception and technique, but also Renaissance in eager curiosity and profound individual thought. Holbein combined with a real ability to select and emphasize essentials a masterly draughtsmanship. After the death of these two masters, largely on account of exhaustion from war there was very little production, until the second great manifestation of the German people came in the music of the eighteenth and nineteenth centuries.

BIBLIOGRAPHY

BRITISH MUSEUM, Pictorial postcards: Set XXXI, German Woodcuts of the Sixteenth Century; Set LXI, German Engravings of the Nativity and Epiphany.

CARRINGTON, FITZROY, ED., Prints and Their Makers. N.Y., Century, 1912.

DAVIES, G. S., Hans Holbein the Younger. London, Bell, 1903.

DICKINSON, H. A., German Masters of Art. N.Y., Stokes, 1914.

DÜRER, ALBRECHT, Records of Journeys to Venice and the Low Countries. Boston, Merrymount Press, 1913.

FAURE, ÉLIE, History of Art: v. 3, Renaissance Art. N.Y., Harper, 1923.

GANZ, PAUL, Work of Hans Holbein. N.Y., Brentano, 1921.

HARVARD UNIVERSITY, WILLIAM HAYES FOGG ART MUSEUM, Collection of Mediæval and Renaissance Paintings. Cambridge, Harvard University Press, 1919.

HIND, A. M., Albrecht Dürer, His Engravings and Woodcuts. N.Y., Stokes, 1911.

LA FARGE, JOHN, Higher Life in Art. N.Y., McClure, 1908.

POLLARD, A. W., Fine Books. London, Methuen, 1912.

SHERER, VALENTINE, Dürer. Leipzig, Deutsche Verlags-Anstalt, 1906.

TAYLOR, H. O., Thought and Expression in the Sixteenth Century. N.Y., Macmillan, 1920.

WEITENKAMPF, FRANK, How to Appreciate Prints. N.Y., Scribner, 1921.

CHAPTER XXIII

ENGLAND

From the Gothic Age to c. 1900 A.D.

HISTORICAL BACKGROUND

The accomplishment of England in the fine arts since the Gothic age has been supreme in one field — literature. Some admirable work is found in architecture, but in sculpture, painting, and the handicrafts, the attempts, on the whole, have been mediocre. Much of the vigorous art of the Middle Ages had been created under the stimulus and patronage of the Church. But when, in the sixteenth century, Protestantism secured a strong foothold and the monasteries were destroyed, this patronage ceased and England was deprived of a large class of skilled craftsmen. Protestantism in general, as we saw in Holland, was averse to religious representation. This attitude attained an extreme among the Puritans, becoming even iconoclastic when the Commonwealth succeeded in overthrowing the monarchy. The restoration of the king and nobles, however, gave added zeal to the aristocracy, who cared little for the people and for religion. Wealth increased greatly through the acquisition of large colonial possessions. These conditions proved an incentive to the building of fine mansions on great estates.

Except in building, however, there was a dearth of native talent, so that the kings and lords were obliged to call in foreign artists to paint their portraits. It was not until the eighteenth century, a hundred years after the Renaissance had begun to influence architecture, that England evolved a school of painting of her own. This, like that of the Dutch, was devoted to portraiture and landscape; but, unlike the Dutch, was strongly under the influence of Italy and existed for the aristocracy.

The eighteenth century also initiated a revolution that was far-reaching in its effects upon the arts, not only of England, but of the world — the industrial revolution. For at that time machinery, driven by steam, began to replace the handmade or really *manufactured* product. The movement spread rapidly to France, America, and other countries, and vitally affected all the arts; for it took away from the vast majority of the workers the creative faculty and the ideal of craftsmanship that was vital because it was a part of life. Art was now confined chiefly to building, to painting, and to sculpture, and was fast becoming something apart, something that was looked upon as a luxury, to be enjoyed at certain times and in certain places rather than as an integral factor of life. In the period of readjustment due to this new situation, which affected life socially and economically as well, taste declined. In 1857, when William Morris and Burne-Jones installed themselves in London as "artists" (a profession then looked upon as odd and hardly respectable) and attempted to furnish their rooms, all the furniture and hangings that could be purchased were so ugly that they were driven to make everything themselves — the designs, the dyes, the textiles, and the furniture. Thus began the Morris movement, which was essentially a revolt against the artificiality of the times and against the spiritually unhealthy conditions under which the creative impulse was feebly trying to express itself.

ARCHITECTURE

Gothic art in England was strong, versatile, and long-lived. The first suggestions of the Renaissance were seen, as in France, in decorative details, and in the greater symmetry of ground plan and of design, especially in the great houses of the Tudor age. For with the coming of Protestantism church building almost ceased. At the same time the greater security throughout the country and the increasing wealth of both nobles and merchants from the confiscated properties of the monasteries and from the colonial possessions encouraged the building of country places. The typical English manor of this period, such as *Compton Wynyates* (PL. 138 A), is set in a great park with stretches of green lawn, masses of elms and oaks, and gardens, all carefully designed with an informality that is patterned after nature. There is an air of comfort, geniality, and freedom from conventionality about both the manor and the surrounding park that is peculiarly English. The variety of materials used in the construction — brick, wood, stone, and plaster — and the irregularity of the exterior and the plan (FIG. 105) give the manor a picturesque appearance. In the early Renaissance, the Tudor age, a terrace was sometimes substituted for the outer side of the court and the rooms were grouped symmetrically on either side so that the plan assumed an H-shape.[1]

---

[1] *Montacute House* and *Hatfield House* are good examples of this plan.

The Renaissance influence reveals itself more clearly in such a house as *Longleat* (PL. 138 B). The plan shows how balance and symmetry, fundamental principles of the Renaissance, were controlling the arrangement. The exterior, with its flat roof, superposed orders, regularity, and proportions, is due to the Italian

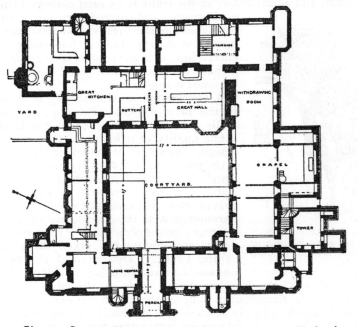

Fig. 105. Compton Wynyates. Warwickshire, c. 1520 A.D. Notice the irregularity of the plan. At the left are the rooms of service; at the right, the great hall that served as the chief living-room of the household. At one end was a raised dais where the lord and lady dined, while the servants and retainers occupied the space below; the hearth was often in the center of the room. Beyond the great hall were the private apartments of the owner, and the chapel. (Garner and Stratton)

influence; the large number of openings, the bays, and mullioned windows, to the medieval English tradition.

The interiors of these English houses indicate the wealth of the country in timber — oak and other hard woods — and also the taste and skill with which it was used. The open timber ceiling, the wainscoting, and the stairways were perhaps the three most characteristic uses. The open timber ceiling, which is the ceiling and roof combined (Fig. 106), is best seen in one of the great halls, such as that at *Hampton Court* (Pl. 138 c). The room is two stories high and of fine proportions. At the end and along the sides are large windows filled with perpendicular tracery, placed high, thus leaving space below for the tapestries that provided warmth and added color; at the right is an oriel entirely filled

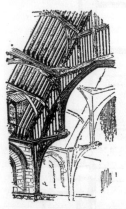

with tracery and covered with fan vaulting; above is the highly decorative hammer-beam ceiling, rich in fine sweep of curved line, in tracery, and carvings. It is a hall of conservative good taste and dignified magnificence.

A fine example of wainscoting is found in the *Bromley* room[2] (Pl. 139 a). The walls are entirely sheathed in panels of a fine quality of oak in a simple, restful design. The center of interest in the room is the great fireplace with its carved stone lintel above which rises the overmantel elaborately ornamented with the royal coat of arms. The ceiling of molded plaster harmonizes with the mantelpiece and adds

Fig. 106. Hammer-Beam Ceiling. Westminster Hall, London. (Viollet-le-Duc)

another element of richness. Although the flat plaster ceiling had taken the place of the vault, it still retained the most obvious feature of the lierne vaulting (Pl. 86 b), that is, the intricate design made by the ribs.

When the Renaissance came as an effective force, it came quickly and in a purely academic form, chiefly that of Palladio. This was due very largely to the dominating personality of Inigo Jones (1573–1652 A.D.). The new style is evident in the *Banqueting Hall of Whitehall* (Pl. 139 b). The façade is designed in two orders with columns in the center and pilasters near the ends, doubling at the corners; the entablature of both orders breaks about the supporting members and is finished with a balustrade. All these characteristics are suggestive of Palladio's *Basilica* (Pl. 94 c). The window treatment is peculiarly Renaissance, with alternating rounding and triangular pediments on the ground story and horizontal cornices supported by scroll consoles on the second. The rusticated masonry gives a feeling of strength and solidity; and the ample window openings furnish the light needed in a

---

[2] The palace is now destroyed, but this room has been re-erected in the Victoria and Albert Museum, London.

northern climate. Inigo Jones, then, availing himself of the elements and principles of the Renaissance architects, combined and adapted them to the needs of London. Like all accomplished designers of buildings, he has kept his decoration subordinate. Everywhere there is fine proportion, dignity, and restraint.

The second great architect of the English Renaissance was Sir Christopher Wren (1632–1723 A.D.). Wren, like Inigo Jones, fell under the spell of Italy, as we see in *Saint Paul's Cathedral* (PL. 140 A). Here the emphasis has been placed upon an effect of picturesqueness and majesty rather than upon a frank expression of structure. The artist realized that a church located in the heart of London with no space as a setting but viewed from the irregular streets leading to it, and in a city whose climate is uncertain, dull, and foggy, if it were to dominate, must be vigorous, bold, and even picturesque in its composition. Wren used the basilica plan with a great dome spanning both the nave and the aisles, as at *Saint Peter's* in Rome, and two towers with many columns that harmonize with the encircling colonnade of the dome and form the transition between the body of the church and the dome. A classical portico with a sculptured pediment decorates the façade. The two stories, which are carried consistently about the building, hiding the vaults, are rusticated and are decorated with coupled pilasters, and with strongly profiled and ornamented cornices to give the needed shadow. *Saint Paul's* is an interesting example of a discreet and skillful artist who could adopt and use the classical style with a frank acceptance of conditions of location and climate different from those of its original home.

Very characteristic of this period that followed the Restoration are the mansions and country houses of the aristocracy. They vary from the great palaces such as *Hampton Court* and *Blenheim* to the modest manors whose setting in a great park constitutes one of the chief causes of their charm. But now purely academic forms prevailed, particularly the Palladian design used in the *Villa Rotonda* at Vicenza, in which a great pedimental portico rising two stories in height formed the dominating feature of the design. This style of architecture was carried by the English to the American colonies, where it became popular, especially in the South (PL. 151 B).[3]

The interiors of these houses are perhaps more characteristic of the elegant formality of the times than the exteriors. The im-

[3] The period from c. 1720–1780 A.D., covering roughly the reign of the Georges, is frequently called *Georgian*.

portance of design was now emphasized. Monumental proportions were sought after and from this endeavor pomposity frequently resulted. The most refined aspect of the late Georgian age is found in the work of Robert Adam, an influential architect and designer (PL. 140 B). Adam retained the spaciousness that is characteristic of the times, but lightened the detail. Stucco ornament based upon classical motifs — garlands, scrolls, vases, candelabra — he arranged in panels frequently oval, for curved lines predominated. Even the room was sometimes made oval. The delicacy and daintiness of this ornament carries one back to the Roman stucco decoration (PL. 53 A). White was the prevailing hue, or the pale tones of green, tan, and gray. Invigorating color was supplied by the rugs, the hangings of velvet and chintz, and the mahogany of the furniture.

The furniture of the late eighteenth century, *Chippendale*, *Hepplewhite*, and *Sheraton*,[4] was made under the influence of Robert Adam, and harmonized perfectly with the architectural setting. The *Chippendale* chair (PL. 141 A) shows solid construction and, at the same time, lightness, and finely carved decoration: for Chippendale was a skillful wood carver. The legs often are straight and efficient in appearance, though sometimes the front ones are cabriole, that is, curved, much like those of the French furniture (PL. 144). The back has an open-work splat extending from the top to the seat, variously designed, sometimes after Gothic window tracery.

The *Hepplewhite* chair (PL. 141 B) is contrastingly light, delicate, and more severe in its lines. The legs taper. The heart-shape back does not meet the seat. The decoration is unobtrusive, frequently consisting of inlaid wood instead of carving. Of a more extreme delicacy and severe balance is the *Sheraton*, which has inlays of various kinds of wood and dainty paintings of floral decoration.

PAINTING

Although, as we have said, painting reached a high plane of attainment in the Middle Ages among the illuminators and miniaturists, it did not develop into a school of painting, as in France and Flanders. With the exception of the charming miniature portraits of the Oliver family in the seventeenth century, so great was the native poverty in painting that Henry VIII and Charles I were obliged to summon foreign artists — Holbein from

---

[4] Thomas Chippendale (died 1779 A.D.) and George Hepplewhite (died 1786 A.D.) were cabinetmakers with shops of their own; Thomas Sheraton (c. 1751–1806 A.D.) was primarily a designer, famous chiefly for his publications of designs for furniture.

PLATE 139

(A) State Room from Bromley-le-Bow. 1606 A.D. Victoria and Albert Museum, London. (Victoria and Albert Museum)

(B) Whitehall Palace. Banqueting Hall. Inigo Jones, architect. 1619-22 A.D. London. (Blomfield)

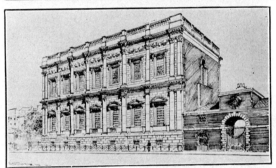

(C) Hogarth. Marriage à la Mode: The Marriage Contract. 1745 A.D. National Gallery, London.

PLATE 140

(A) Saint Paul's Cathedral. London. Sir
Christopher Wren, architect. 1668–1710 A.D.

(B) Dining-Room. Detail. London. Designed
by Robert Adam. (Swarbrick)

(C) Gainsborough. Morning Walk.
Lord Rothschild's coll., Tring Park.

(D) Chaucer. Printed by William Morris;
illustrated by Burne-Jones, 1896. Ryerson
Library, Art Institute, Chicago.

Germany and Van Dyck from Flanders; and while their work is of a very high order, it is the work of Holbein and Van Dyck, not that of the English. The development of a truly English school was largely due to the vigor and independent thought, often expressed in writing, of William Hogarth (1697–1764 A.D.). It was the age of Addison and Steele, the *Spectator*, and the early novelists. The middle classes had been growing in power at the expense of the nobility. There were the Puritans, whose life was drab and intolerant; and the Cavaliers, who were trivial, artificial, and licentious. In the life and manners of these eighteenth century people, Hogarth, like Addison, found his subject matter. Hogarth's paintings and engravings, like Goya's (PL. 126 A and C), were a satirical commentary upon the coarseness, debauchery, and frivolity of certain classes of people. The current stage productions seem to have influenced the artist, so that the dramatic as well as the psychological aspect of the situation is evident. The series called *Marriage à la Mode*, or a marriage after the fashion of the day, is typical.[5] The first of the series is the *Marriage Contract* (PL. 139 C). At the right is seated the viscount elaborately dressed, his gouty foot resting on a stool, his family tree conspicuously displayed on a scroll at his left. At the table sits the alderman, as his gold chain betokens, an awkward grasping bourgeois, scrutinizing the contract. The pile of money on the table and the papers held out by the notary are the price paid. On the left are the young couple. The heir to the title, a sleek, effeminate dandy, is unconcernedly taking a pinch of snuff as he views himself in the mirror; the prospective bride is twirling her ring on her handkerchief as she listens to an admirer. The characterization in all its details reveals with biting humor the psychology of a situation. The power of Hogarth's satire is helped partly by the delightful little details that suggest so much more than they represent, and partly by the placing of the two groups in about the same plane with little depth in the background to detract. Each group is busied with its own preoccupation, but is psychologically reacting upon the other and is artistically united to it by the surface patterning of darks and lights.

Hogarth's refreshing sincerity had a tonic influence on the English school, and prepared the way for the eighteenth century school of portraiture of which Sir Joshua Reynolds (1723–1792 A.D.) and Thomas Gainsborough (1727–1788 A.D.) are the

[5] The series consists of six paintings, later engraved, setting forth in racy fashion the story of the marriage of the daughter of a wealthy alderman to the worthless son of the titled but bankrupt Viscount Squanderfield.

chief representatives. But Reynolds was more a theorist than an artist, especially in his attempts to attain the color harmonies of the Venetians. Upon ideas gathered during his travels in Italy and his deep and appreciative studies of Italian masters, he built up a "grand style" in which he painted the portraits of the fashionable people of the day. An artificial society found in him its artificial painter; for he imitated the appearance of form instead of building up form on scientific and artistic principles.

Gainsborough, though he too painted the fashionable people of the time, gave the artificiality of life artistic expression (PL. 140 c). His canvases are composed, to be sure, usually after the Italian fashion of the day, with masses of foliage, or a column, with a glimpse of the distant landscape as a background for the figure. In spite of the artificial elegance, there is a sensitiveness and spontaneity here and an ease of line. Light and air play about the figures. The textures of the satin, lace, velvet, and plumes are wonderfully rendered, and the enchanting color, delicately and spontaneously laid all over the surface, produces a glowing iridescence. There is nothing profound or monumental in the art of Reynolds and Gainsborough, no great character study or psychology, and no study of the form. It is surface painting only, too imitative of the Italian masters, but at the same time charming in its airy grace, its atmosphere of elegance, and its color harmonies.

If the English school of portrait painting attained a superficial excellence only, the landscape painters made definite contributions and attained lofty results. Most important of them were John Constable (1776–1837 A.D.) and Joseph Mallord William Turner (1775–1851 A.D.). Constable, like Ruisdael, found delight in direct contact with his native landscape — in the light and warmth of the sunshine, the cool of the shadow, and the movement of the wind and rain. The *Hay Wain* (PL. 141 c) reveals the quiet charm of the country at noon. In the foreground a hay wagon is fording a stream near a house behind which are luxuriant trees that cast cool shadows; at the right stretch the meadows glowing in the sunshine; clouds fill the spacious sky, the darker masses at the left prophesying a storm. Something of the vibrant quality of the light, the warmth, and the air appears in this picture that was lacking in Ruisdael's. This Constable attained by his technical method, and thereby he made a great contribution to landscape painting. He abandoned the traditional method of putting on his colors smoothly and shading with gray and brown, and for it substituted heavy strokes and dots of pigment;

for by roughening the surface in this way he could obtain the vibrating quality of the light and air, and the movement of the foliage and clouds. The colors of nature he also followed more closely, especially in the shadows, which he saw were not the conventional gray or brown used by the Continental painters. He not only used the colors that his honest observation revealed to him, but gave them intensity by juxtaposing them without the subtle blending of the traditional method. In these innovations Constable was one of the forerunners of the French Impressionists of the late nineteenth century.

Turner also was interested in light and air, but in an entirely different way from Constable, as is clear from a study of the *Fighting Téméraire* (PL. 141 D). In the light of a sunset of tremendous brilliancy, with the moon just rising above the horizon, the old, worn-out battleship is being towed down the harbor by an efficient, puffing little tug to the wrecking yards to be broken up. The poetry of the subject and the poetry of the sunset hour are in harmony. It is a "song of time and eternity." The composition is free and unconventional. The forms are hardly more than suggested. That Turner understood the fundamental principles of composition and also the structure of the forms of nature is clear from his drawings. But his interest lay, not in the reproduction of nature, but in an interpretation, a poetical expression of the majesty that he felt in the sun, the sky, and the sea. In such pictures as the *Fighting Téméraire* and *Ulysses Deriding Polyphemus*, the human interest, in a highly imaginative way, associates itself with the landscape. Later, however, Turner grew away from this and made his pictures the expression of his own ecstatic visions. He felt and he painted, as few have done, the vastness, power, and grandeur of space with its light, air, and color. Technically, Turner, like Constable, contributed to the methods used in the oil medium, for he too juxtaposed rough dots of pure color upon the canvas for the eye to blend, instead of mixing them upon the palette and applying them with a smooth finish.

One more movement is important in English painting, that of the Pre-Raphaelite Brotherhood and its sympathizers. In 1848 seven young men[6] formed this brotherhood. To break away from the bad taste and empty artificiality of the times was the purpose of the movement, and to substitute real ideas, a sincere study of nature, and sound craftsmanship. The brotherhood sought to

[6] Best known of the group were Dante Gabriel Rossetti and William Holman Hunt; in close sympathy were Ford Madox Brown, Sir Edward Burne-Jones, and William Morris. A champion of the cause was John Ruskin.

regain the spirit of the ages that preceded Raphael and to bring back the old ideal of the craftsman who could make things not only useful but beautiful in shape, line, pattern, and color. This group of men worked as craftsmen along various lines, for they made stained-glass windows, textiles, dyes, and furniture, decorated walls, painted panels, designed cartoons for tapestry and wall paper, and printed and illustrated books (Pl. 140 d). The value of the movement lay chiefly in its protest against the results of the segregation of art from life, and in its efforts to make art again a vital, spontaneous expression manifesting itself in the chair and the book as well as in the building and in the statue. The chief figure in this aspect of the movement was William Morris, who in the zeal of his unstinted endeavor made an important contribution to the attempt to solve the problem that is still engaging attention — the place of art in contemporary European and American culture.

SUMMARY

In England we meet a people who had developed strong, healthy native traditions in all lines during the Middle Ages and who through their natural conservative and practical nature were not as easily influenced as the French by the splendor of Italy. Besides their literature, which is the loftiest manifestation of their genius, the architecture of their churches and especially of the great manor houses with their parks, under the leadership of real artists like Inigo Jones and Sir Christopher Wren, shows how the influence of the Renaissance fused with the tenacious native traditions both in design and in ornament and transformed the earlier style without, on the whole, too great a sacrifice of taste and design. Sculpture in England was negligible. In the field of painting, there was either great poverty or foreign domination until the eighteenth century, when portraiture developed in a strongly Italianized form with little or no imaginative power. In the early nineteenth century a strong landscape school appeared that made important contributions to technique and in Turner reached a lofty poetical expression. While in England there began the world-wide industrial revolution that together with the baneful aspects of the Renaissance has well-nigh overwhelmed true spontaneous art expression, in England also there have arisen against this unhealthy condition some of the strongest protests, which, if not always justifiable in detail, in the main have done much to turn attention toward higher standards and to stimulate the ideal of honest craftsmanship.

BIBLIOGRAPHY

ARMSTRONG, SIR WALTER, Art in Great Britain and Ireland. N.Y., Scribner, 1913.
—— ——, Gainsborough and His Place in English Art. N.Y., Scribner, 1913.
BLOMFIELD, REGINALD, History of Renaissance Architecture in England, 1500–1800. London, Bell, 1897.
BROWN, G. B., William Hogarth. N.Y., Scribner, 1905.
CESCINSKY, HERBERT, Old-world House, its Furniture and Decoration. 2v. N.Y., Macmillan, 1924.
DOBSON, AUSTIN, William Hogarth. N.Y., Dodd, 1902.
FLETCHER, SIR BANISTER, History of Architecture on the Comparative Method. N.Y., Scribner, 1924.
GILMAN, ROGER, Great Styles of Interior Architecture. N.Y., Harper, 1924.
GOTCH, J. A., Early Renaissance Architecture in England. London, Batsford, 1914.
HAMLIN, A. D. F., History of Ornament, Renaissance and Modern. N.Y., Century, 1923.
HIND, C. L., Landscape Painting from Giotto to the Present Day. 2v. London, Chapman, 1923–4.
HOLMES, C. J., Constable. N.Y., Longmans, 1901.
JACKSON, T. G., Renaissance of Roman Architecture: II, England. Cambridge, University Press, 1922.
KIMBALL, FISKE, AND EDGELL, G. H., History of Architecture. N.Y., Harper, 1918.
MACQUOID, PERCY, History of English Furniture. 4v. London, Lawrence, 1904–8.
MACARTNEY, MERVYN, English Houses and Gardens in the Seventeenth and Eighteenth Centuries. London, Batsford, 1908.
MOORE, GEORGE, Modern Painting. N.Y., Scribner, 1893.
MULLINER, H. H., Decorative Arts in England, 1660–1780. London, Batsford, 1924.
RUSKIN, JOHN, Modern Painters. 5v. (Everyman's Library.) N.Y., Dutton, 1906.
SPEED, HAROLD, Science and Practice of Oil Painting. London, Chapman, 1924.
SWARBRICK, JOHN, Robert Adam and His Brothers. N.Y., Scribner, 1915.
TRIGGS, H. I., Formal Gardens in England and Scotland. London, 1902.
VALLANCE, AYMAR, William Morris: His Art, His Writings, and His Public Life. London, Bell, 1909.
VICTORIA AND ALBERT MUSEUM, SOUTH KENSINGTON, DEPARTMENT OF WOODWORK. PANELLED ROOMS: I: Bromley Room. London, 1914; II: Clifford's Inn Room. London, 1914; V: Hatton Garden Room. London, 1920.
—— ——, Catalogue of English Furniture and Woodwork. I: Gothic and Early Tudor, by H. C. Smith. London, 1923.

CHAPTER XXIV
FRANCE
From the Gothic Age to c. 1900 A.D.

HISTORICAL BACKGROUND

We last spoke of France in the late Gothic period, when life was still a unit of community and religious elements and when virility and craftsmanship still dominated the work of the artists. But cosmopolitanism was taking the place of medieval exclusiveness. The exchange of commodities and of ideas was establishing a broader attitude toward life. Political interrelations were taking the French kings to Italy and ended in bringing Italian ideas to dominate France. There is little wonder that the warmth and splendor of Italy captivated the northerners, even those who came primarily on political missions, as Charles VIII, who, in his expedition to Italy in 1494, lived for some time in the Medici palace in Florence. Even more influential was Francis I (1515–1547 A.D.), a great patron of all the arts, who not only brought ideas from Italy but induced Italian artists like Leonardo da Vinci and Benvenuto Cellini to come to France, and there execute commissions for him.

For it was the king and not the Church that now held the balance of power in France. The religious art of the Middle Ages was being superseded in the attempt to glorify the State and to flatter the monarchs, who were now arbitrary and now whimsical, and usually under the spell of Italy. Hence upon the native artists the kings imposed a foreign art.

Politically and economically, the rapid tendency toward the final suppression of the feudal lords and toward the concentration of power in the hands of the monarch reached its climax in the famous statement of Louis XIV, "I am the State." Religious wars and persecutions, the unendurable burden of taxation, and chiefly the injustice of class privilege — these the people endured to the breaking point; finally they rose in tumultuous wrath, to overthrow the old order by means of the Revolution. This great movement is reflected in French art.

ARCHITECTURE

The tendency in France from religious to secular interests, even before the coming of a direct influence from Italy, brought about a greater demand for châteaux and civic buildings. Protection, an important function of the medieval château (FIG. 92), was no longer necessary. Yet some of its features, such as the towers and battlements, had become so traditional in the thought of the people that they still persisted. Climatic conditions also determined several characteristic features — steep roofs to shed the

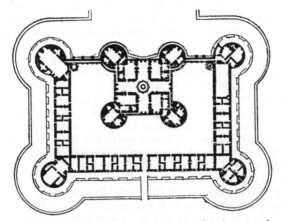

Fig. 107. Chambord. 1526–1544 A.D. In the central building were the rooms of state; in the side wings, the servants' quarters, kitchens, and pantries. There was little in the way of convenience or sanitation. The stables were near the living-rooms and the kitchens far from the dining-room. (Du Cerceau)

rain and snow; a large number of windows to provide the light needed in the north; chimneys and fireplaces to give heat.

The working of Italian influences on the native architecture we see at *Blois* (PL. 142 A), in the wing built by Francis I. The steep roof with its dormers and chimneys, the large windows with mullions, the niches containing statues, the gargoyles — these are French. The Italian reveals itself in the greater regularity of design, the greater repose that comes from the balance of vertical and horizontal lines, and the classical pilasters and carvings. Traditional love for the Gothic verticality, however, has made the builder break his entablatures with pilasters.

Perhaps most typical of the early Renaissance châteaux is *Chambord* (PL. 142 B). It stands out on the open plain, as did most of these châteaux; for they were great country places usually built near a forest so as to serve as hunting lodges. Its plan (FIG. 107) shows regularity and symmetry — a central square building with four rounded towers at the corners, set in a court, surrounded by an outer line of rooms with towers at the corners, all surrounded by a moat. The exterior design shows marked simplicity and regularity of spacing and balance in the lower stories, with a strongly felt horizontality of stringcourse and with pilasters for the only ornament. To compensate for this restraint, the roof rising from a rather elaborate cornice presents a fantastic group of steep surfaces, with dormers and chimneys, about a central lantern.

The rooms of the early Renaissance châteaux (PL. 142 c) were large; the ceilings, when not vaulted, showed the structural wooden beams, which were richly painted; the walls, whether of stone or plaster, were covered with tapestries that served two purposes — decoration and warmth. The only source of heat in this cold climate was the huge fireplace, which not only served this utilitarian purpose, but was also a center of decorative interest; for the overmantel that usually reached to the ceiling was elaborately carved, giving a strong accent to the design and a note of elegance to the entire room.

Thus the architecture of the early Renaissance, as illustrated by *Blois* and *Chambord*, is still French at heart. Afterward, in the reign of Henry II (1547–1559 A.D.), came translations of treatises by Italian architects and even architects themselves; and study and travel in Italy on the part of the French. This brought about a more thoroughgoing revolution, though it never entirely eliminated the French elements. The building that best illustrates this period is that part of the *Louvre* (PL. 143 A) which was built by the architect Pierre Lescot (1510?–1578 A.D.) and the sculptor Jean Goujon (died before 1568 A.D.). The typically French charm and grace of this façade are somewhat lost in the large court that it now faces, four times the size of the original one; for the projections, the shadows, and the detail are too delicate to carry a great distance. Each story forms a complete order, the pilasters no longer breaking through the entablature as at *Blois*. The cornices project enough to furnish the balancing horizontal line. The projecting central and corner pavilions that characterize all parts of the *Louvre* are partly a reminiscence of the traditional tower-pavilions and central gate of the early fortresslike château,

PLATE 141

(*A*) Chippendale Chair. Metropolitan Museum, New York. (Metropolitan Museum)

(*B*) Heppelwhite Chair. Metropolitan Museum, New York. (Metropolitan Museum)

(*C*) Constable. Hay Wain. 1821 A.D. National Gallery, London.

(*D*) Turner. Fighting Téméraire. 1839 A.D. National Gallery, London.

PLATE 142

(*A*) Château of Blois. Wing of Francis I. 1515–19 A.D. (N. D. Photo.)

(*B*) Château of Chambord. 1526–44 A.D. (N. D. Photo.)

(*C*) Chaumont. Dining-Room, restored. (Saint-Saveur)

especially where they terminate in high roofs, and partly a development of the projecting end bays of the Roman palace (PL. 91 A). The arcading on the ground story is the French echo of the Roman idea of combining the arch and lintel; artistically, it is recessed enough to produce more shadow than the upper stories, thus strengthening the base of the design. On the second story the pilasters rising from bases, and the alternating curved and triangular pediments supported by consoles, carry one directly to the Roman palace; but the lower height of the stories, the larger size of the windows, and the sloping roof are northern. Sculptured decoration verging on over-ornamentation plays a large part in the composition, delicately carved in low relief and distinctly architectural in its design. In this façade we have the best of French Renaissance architecture, showing masterly design both in the balance and in the proportions of the large elements, as well as delicacy, charm, and fine taste in the details and ornamentation.

A more literal dependence upon classical design is evident in the façade of the *Louvre* (PL. 143 C) built by Claude Perrault (1613–1688 A.D.). The design not only displays effective composition, but has strongly influenced columnar façade design ever since. The general impression is one of imposing nobility combined with quiet restraint. There are five divisions, bilaterally balanced — the projecting central pavilion, emphasized by a great arched doorway and crowned with a pediment; the projecting end pavilions, and the two connecting colonnades of fluted Corinthian columns, set in pairs. The unifying line is the horizontal of the cornices, relieved by the projecting pavilions and pediment. The severely plain ground story with its quiet surface not only serves as a base but emphasizes by contrast the richness of the broken light and shade of the colonnade. The varying light and shade that plays over the different parts of this façade is carefully regulated. In the colonnades it is deepest because of the open loggia behind the columns; in the center, where the columns stand close to the walls, there is more light; on the corners, where they are engaged, or supplanted by pilasters, there is little shadow, except in the central niche that takes up the tone of the colonnade, binding the two into greater unity. Thus there comes about a varying degree of light and shade like the different values in a painting that add richness and unity to the design.

In ecclesiastical architecture as well as in secular, the classical tradition finally supplanted the Gothic. In the chapel of the *Hôtel des Invalides* (PL. 143 B), which is typical of a large group of churches, we find a thoroughly Renaissance base surmounted by a dome that derives from that of Michelangelo on *Saint Peter's*.

While the exteriors of these buildings were so purely classical, the interiors were a free expression of the personal taste of the monarch. This is particularly true of the buildings erected during the reigns of Louis XIV and Louis XV. Louis XIV (1661–1715 A.D.) was a great builder who paid special attention to decoration and to furnishing so that the whole ensemble was an unusually harmonious unit. Louis was able to do this because he had entire control over the Gobelins establishment, purchased in 1662, which at that time did not limit its productions to tapestries, but made furniture, metal work, jewelry, and textiles. The Grand Monarch's ideal was somber dignity and magnificence; and as art was at the service of the State for the purpose of pleasing and glorifying the monarch, the palace at *Versailles* in all its aspects, from the architectural design of the buildings to the metal decorations of the furniture, is sober, symmetrical, and stately. The *Galerie des Glaces* or *Hall of Mirrors* (PL. 144 A) has lofty proportions and stately lines, sober color enriched by brilliantly painted ceilings, hangings of silk, velvet, and tapestry, and an abundance of ornament such as colored marbles, plaster relief painted and gilded, carvings, and metal fittings. The vast scale and the general exuberance that desired to load with ornament show the influence of the Italian baroque. It is all very magnificent. The furniture was consistently heavy and rich (PL. 144 C). Much of this furniture was of simple, massive construction but was elaborately veneered with fine woods or tortoise, sometimes inlaid with metal, and usually decorated with ornaments of various alloys much like gold in appearance, which showed highly skilled workmanship.

At the death of Louis XIV, the nobility threw off this heavy dignity, and turned to the gayety, frivolity, and sparkling light-heartedness that characterized the reign of Louis XV. One feels this in the slender proportions and in the graceful curves both of the architectural ornament and of the furniture, as if the artists were afraid of a straight line and a right angle; in the white color with much gilding, and in the mirrors that add vivacity with their reflections.[1] Dainty rooms for conversation or card-playing or boudoirs are most typical (PL. 144 B). As in the reign of Louis XIV, the furniture harmonizes in its lines and spirit. A typical console (PL. 144 D) shows a design based entirely upon

[1] From the frequent use in this reign of rock-work ornament, *rocaille*, the decoration is frequently called *rococo*.

curved lines. Its slender proportions, its dainty decorations of flowers and garlands, and its gray-white color are quite suggestive of the age.

The French gardens that formed an integral part of the plan and the life of the château were as formal as the age itself. Those laid out at *Versailles* (PL. 145 A) by André le Nôtre (1613–1700 A.D.), the landscape artist employed by Louis XIV, illustrate how magnificent the gardens had become. Water played an important part, its use demanding a knowledge of hydraulic engineering. A great basin lay near the palace to catch the reflections of the buildings. Fountains, large and small, cascades, and canals with smooth reaches all played their part. Bronze and marble statues of river gods and playing children decorated the fountains or relieved the tall clipped hedges that bordered the garden. Great ornamental vases of lead rising above the low box hedges gave an accent to the design. Broad walks and long avenues afforded fine distant views. Behind the hedges trees were massed to give a setting to the design.

SCULPTURE

In studying the sculpture of the Gothic age (PLs. 82, 85, and 86 c) we saw how grace and swing of line dominated the work, even in the case of portraiture. This native quality was combined with the Italian influence in the work of Jean Goujon (died before 1568 A.D.). On the decorative panels of the *Fountain of the Innocents* (PL. 145 B), nymphs are carved in low relief. The easy grace of the "rhythmic figures, bending here, curving there, haunting but elusive," the elongation of the proportions to obtain free sweep of line, the soft clinging drapery that suggests the flow of water, the emphasis upon the sinuous line accentuated by the rigid verticals of the fluted pilasters that frame the figures — all this reveals Jean Goujon as a master of decorative sculpture.

Of the next two centuries, the seventeenth and the eighteenth, the outstanding figure is Jean Antoine Houdon (1741–1828 A.D.), who was a somewhat independent artist with an unusual gift for expressing the essentials of character in the portraits that constitute his best work. In his seated figure of *Voltaire* (PL. 145 c), there is virility in the structural forms, nervous tension in the bony hands that clutch the arms of the chair, and poignant expression in the lean face with its gleaming eyes and scornful smile. The restless pose and the tremendous realism of face, throat, and hands are both enhanced and relieved by the broad simple fold of the mantle. In artistic principle, *Voltaire* is close to Donatello's *Zuccone* (PL. 115 B).

Much of the sculpture of the eighteenth and early nineteenth centuries is feminine both in subject matter and feeling — figures of goddesses all ease and grace and with exquisite surface finish expressive of the texture of flesh or fabric. But too often this finish is superficial, mere sentimental prettiness. This was the result of the autocracy of the French Academy, which narrowly restricted the subject matter and the technical methods of the painters and sculptors. Revolt against the artificiality and convention of the typical work of the day came in the powerful personality of Auguste Rodin (1840–1917 A.D.). His bold realism appeared all the more rugged by contrast with the popular smooth modeling of the day. In contemplating Rodin, one almost inevitably thinks of Michelangelo, for their artistic creeds had many points in common. Each was a thinker and a poet, and a rebel against the times in which he lived. Both were interested mainly in the human figure as a means of conveying spiritual or emotional significance. The *Thinker* (PL. 146 A) illustrates this. A brutelike man sits pondering with such intensity that his toes clutch the ground. The inherent significance of the statue is not the representation of primitive man, but that abstract expression of penetrating thought which Michelangelo revealed in his *Jeremiah* (PL. 102 A). In his lyrical subjects also, for which he used marble instead of bronze, because he could work the stone to a more delicate finish, it is emotional significance that the figure aims to convey. Where two figures are used, as in the *Kiss*, within a simple compact contour there is a rhythmic movement of line like the flow of music; the light and shade play in the surface with exquisite delicacy, so subtle is the modeling. Yet these delicate figures are far from the anemic nudes of the Academy, for their lyricism is as powerful as is the brutal strength of the *Thinker*. This artistic principle of contrast between a simplified contour and a rapid movement of line within it, we saw in Myron's *Discobolus* (PL. 38 C). As the concentration of physical energy was there heightened by this device, so here by the same means the concentration of emotional ecstasy is enhanced. Another element of contrast that Rodin uses frequently is the lack of finish in parts of statues. The figure appears to be emerging from a block of marble, the rough surface of which acts as a powerful foil for extreme delicacy of modeling.

PLATE 143

(*A*) Louvre. Court, showing the façade of
Lescot and Goujon. 1546–76 A.D. Paris.

(*B*) Hôtel des Invalides. Chapel.
Mansart. 1692–1704. Paris.

(*C*) Louvre. Façade of Perrault. 1665 A.D. Paris.

PLATE 144

(A) Versailles. Galerie des Glaces. Louis XIV.

(B) Hôtel Soubise. Louis XV. Paris.

(C) Table. Louis XIV. Metropolitan Museum, New York. (Metropolitan Museum)

(D) Console. Louis XV. Metropolitan Museum, New York. (Metropolitan Museum)

PLATE 145

(*A*) Gardens of Versailles. Basin of Latona from the Terrace. (Rigaud)

(*C*) Houdon. Voltaire. 1781 A.D.
Comédie-Française, Paris.

(*B*) Goujon. Panel from
the Fountain of the Inno-
cents. 1547–49 A.D. Paris.

PLATE 146

(*A*) Rodin. Thinker. 1904 A.D. Bronze replica in reduced size made by Rodin after the colossal bronze standing in front of the Panthéon, Paris. Metropolitan Museum, New York. (Metropolitan Museum)

(*B*) Brocade. XVIII cent. Metropolitan Museum, New York. (Metropolitan Museum)

(*C*) Sèvres Porcelain. Metropolitan Museum, New York. (Metropolitan Museum)

(*D*) Chardin. Saying Grace. Louvre, Paris.

PAINTING

In the sixteenth century, native French painting (PL. 87 A) experienced an overwhelming influence from Italy, the reason for which we have already explained. The Italian ideal we see dominating two painters who lived most of their lives in Italy and hence were more under the influence of that country — Nicolas Poussin (1594–1665 A.D.) and Claude Gellée (1600–1682 A.D.) also called Claude Lorrain. Poussin's *Shepherds in Arcady* shows this (PL. 147 A). In an ideal landscape are three shepherds and a woman grouped about a tomb on which the older man is tracing an inscription, "Et ego in Arcadia" (I too have been in Arcady). Imagination has carried Poussin into this realm of fancy, which he sees and paints through the medium of Raphael and the antique. The latter influence is seen in the plastic quality in the figures, suggestive of classical reliefs; the former, in the composition which has been thought out with great care for the harmonious grouping of the figures, each of which is so placed in relation to the others, to the landscape, and to the frame that it plays its part in the design in true Raphaelesque fashion; the eye is carried easily and rhythmically by the suave flow of line from figure to figure to the center of interest, the inscription. Yet, notwithstanding this conscientious, studied organization, one cannot escape the feeling of cold artificiality.

In Claude Gellée the figures give way to an absorbing interest in the landscape for its own sake. To be sure, in the *Egeria* (PL. 147 B), as in many of Claude's paintings, there are a few figures that serve as an excuse for the title. The picture is as thoughtfully and carefully built up as Ruisdael's (PL. 136 A), yet the feeling is very different. There is not as close an intimacy with nature here nor as profound a knowledge or feeling for the structure of her forms, but she is made to appear in a magnificent, imaginative aspect, great stretches filled with light and air and the freshness of early morning. At the sides Claude has massed his trees and buildings, to serve as a framework for the opening through which we are carried far into space. Light fills the picture, falling brightly on the buildings at the right, reflected by the smooth surface of the water, penetrating the deep shade of the trees where it plays about the nymphs and flickers among the branches and foliage. Against the concentrated mass of light the trees silhouette interesting patterns. It is an artificial landscape. The group of buildings at the right consists of a ruined classical structure with great Corinthian columns, a round classical temple, so usual in Claude, and in the distance on a hill a ruined castle, the dark mass of which carries the eye inevitably off into luminous space. The trees on the right perform this same function. In fact, the composition is largely the skillful, balanced arrangement of light and dark masses, which despite its formality gives an impressive sense of heroic grandeur.

While Poussin and Claude were painting their ideal landscapes in Italy, in France art was becoming more and more the monopoly of the privileged class. The establishment in 1648 of the French Academy of Sculpture and Painting gave official sanction to the dictates of the autocracy which ruled France during the seventeenth and eighteenth centuries to further its own selfish interests. The elegance and profligacy of these privileged few are reflected by the painters. In Antoine Watteau (1684–1721 A.D.) we see its highest manifestation, particularly in the period of Louis XV. Watteau's *Embarkation for Cythera* (PL. 147 c) is representative of its spirit. In the delightful cool shade of a park, couples are idly loitering; winged loves hover about, cling to a statue of Venus, and dance around a dainty, gilded ship toward which the couples are making their way to journey to the island of love far away in the golden, misty distance. All is light-heartedness and gayety, charming grace and elegance. But Watteau was too much of an artist to express merely this idea. His feeling for balance, for the interesting pattern of trees against the luminous distance, for the easy rhythm of the line that begins in the figure of Venus, follows the groups across the canvas, and then turns inward again in the rollicking cherubs in the sky at the left, and, perhaps most of all, his feeling for the harmony of exquisite color — all this is the real Watteau.

This gayety, extravagance, and frivolity of the French court continued quite disregardful of the ever increasing rumblings soon to swell into the terrific storm of the thinkers and the masses of people rising against the old, worn-out system of class privilege. A reflection of this is to be discerned in an earnestness and severity that was finding its ideal in classical subjects. Attention had already been turned in that direction by the excavations at Pompeii (1755 A.D.), by the publication of Winckelmann's "History of Art Among the Ancients," the first ever written on the subject, and by the popularity of Piranesi's engravings of Roman buildings. What the French saw in these revelations seemed to accord with the temper of the times and so became the expression of that temper. Hence it is not surprising that the pictures of the Classicists, such as the *Oath of the Horatii* by Jacques Louis David (1748–1825 A.D.), were received with great enthusiasm. In spite of the cold and rhetorical effect, people found in just such work a gratifying reaction against the "pink and blue gallantries" of the day.

Another painter, Jean Auguste Dominique Ingres (1780–1867 A.D.), was more or less closely connected with the Classicists, though it was the draughtsmanship of the Florentines that served as his inspiration. For, as we see in the *Portrait of Madame Rivière* (PL. 148 A), line and linear design became his primary means of expression. What impresses one most here is the harmonious rhythm of the sweeping lines of the shawl as it winds over the shoulders and falls across the figure with a single great curve through which minor harmonies interplay; and the admirable adaptation of the whole design to the oval frame. Ingres' famous saying laconically summarizes his artistic creed, "Drawing is everything; color is nothing."

Meanwhile the storm had broken and the people had risen to free themselves from the injustices of centuries. The result of the Revolution was to liberate powerful energy and tumultuous feelings that could not find expression in the cold severity of David's and Ingres' classical ideals. Hence rose the Romanticists in literature, music, and painting, of whom, among the painters, Eugène Delacroix (1798–1863 A.D.) is typical. The *Entrance of the Crusaders into Constantinople* (PL. 149 A) in the first place is a dramatic subject which is characteristic of the Romanticists who found their ideals in history and literature. In the foreground a group of mounted crusaders are advancing with flowing banners; on every side are scenes of killing and pillage, or pleading for mercy; low-lying in the background is the city of Constantinople, with the smoke of fires rising from the houses and the ships in the harbor; above are threatening clouds. A feeling of tumultuous movement runs through the picture. The composition is based chiefly upon the balance of lights and darks, and upon color masses. The warmth of vivid hues appealed to Delacroix, who declared that "gray is the enemy of all painting." Hence color, mass, and rich chiaroscuro rather than incisive line became his medium of expression. Something of color he had been learning from the English landscape painter Constable (PL. 141 C), and both artists were experimenting in laying on the colors in small brush strokes to be blended at a distance by the eye, thus obtaining greater intensity of hue.

While Paris was being swayed now by the Classicists and now by the Romanticists, away from the city in the forest of Fontainebleau, in the vicinity of the little village of Barbizon, a small group, the "Men of 1830," were quietly playing their part in the revolution that was going on in French painting. Most important of these were Théodore Rousseau (1812–1867 A.D.), Jean-Baptiste Camille Corot (1796–1875 A.D.), and Jean François Millet (1814–1875 A.D.). All felt a close intimacy with nature and painted directly from nature in the open, away from the studio. Because this is the method usual among painters today, it is perhaps difficult for us to realize what a revolutionary idea it was in the early nineteenth century. Rousseau was interested in the heroic aspect of nature as he saw it symbolized in the sturdy oaks, the life and vigor of which he painted with such sympathy. Corot was drawn toward the lyrical aspect, especially as he saw it in early morning and evening when the landscape is enveloped by a grayish mist from which the trees half emerge, ghostlike. Although Millet maintained the same attitude toward nature, he chose his subject matter from the French peasants, as we see in the *Sower* (PL. 148 c). A peasant, in rough clothes, with hat pulled down over his eyes, swings along over the field scattering grain from his bag. We do not know what kind of individual this man is. The highly generalized expression of the figure makes the type as well as the action universal. In this respect Millet is in the tradition of Michelangelo, Giotto, and the Greeks. What interests one primarily is the feeling for volume and for the rhythmic movement of the stalwart figure as it strides forward, the pattern that it weaves against the background with its sensitively placed diagonal horizon line, and the adaptation of the figure to the shape and size of the frame. It is partly the subject matter and partly the type, but largely the purely artistic qualities of line, balance, pattern, and color, expressed with honesty and sincerity, that make the "grave and noble poetry of Millet." This group of men at Barbizon, then, in their quiet, honest return to nature, gave great impetus to the naturalistic movement that was soon to transform French painting.

In Paris, however, orthodox academic standards still held sway in spite of the heresies of Delacroix and of such a realist as Gustave Courbet (1819–1877 A.D.), who boldly turned for his subject matter to the living world about him — which to the Academy was in itself a novel idea. The slender tradition of medieval sobriety, in secular as well as in ecclesiastical art, the ideal of art as a spontaneous expression, and the realization of

PLATE 147

(*A*) Poussin. Shepherds in Arcady. Louvre, Paris.

(*B*) Claude Gellée (Lorrain). Egeria. 1669 A.D. Naples. (Anderson)

(*C*) Watteau. Embarkation for the Island of Cythera. 1717 A.D. Berlin.

PLATE 148

(A) Ingres. Madame Rivière. 1805 A.D. Louvre, Paris. (Giraudon)

(B) Daumier. Souvenir du Cholera-morbus. An illustration for Fabre, *Némésis Médicale*. 1840 A.D. Metropolitan Museum, New York. (Metropolitan Museum)

(C) Millet. Sower. 1850 A.D. Boston Museum (Boston Museum)

(D) Puvis de Chavannes. Saint Genevieve Watching over Paris. 1874-76 A.D. Panthéon, Paris.

beauty and poetry in the everyday affairs of life, had never been entirely lost in the wave of artificial monarchical art based upon the Italian tradition. We see it in isolated painters now and again, as in Jean-Baptiste Siméon Chardin (1699–1779 A.D.), who, at the time that Watteau was giving expression to the court life of Louis XV, was quietly painting those charming scenes of French middle-class people and interiors (PL. 146 D), so serene, unassuming, and poetical, and such fine examples of the technical handling of pigment to express the subtle gradation of tone in light and in texture. In this respect Chardin approaches the seventeenth century Dutch masters of genre, by whom he appears to have been influenced.

Another revolutionary was Honoré Daumier (1808–1879 A.D.), who, like Goya, expressed himself best in his cartoons and other illustrations for periodicals. The skill with which Daumier could say much with the simplest means is well shown by his woodcut illustrations, *Souvenirs du Cholera-morbus* (PL. 148 B), for the *Némésis Médicale*. Silence and melancholy pervade every part of the scene so directly and so forcibly that they easily stimulate the imagination to realize all the terrible results of a great plague. Yet the elements of expression are simple, a splendid example of the high art of the elimination of everything except a few essentials, which are portrayed with such power that anything else would be entirely unnecessary. The feeling for form is significant as seen in the inert figure in the foreground. Sometimes this form is distorted to emphasize the central fact, as in the dog and the elongated necks of the horses. There is great skill in so arranging the blacks that the eye is inevitably carried to the distance.

Still, the majority of the French painters remained passively hedged about by strict rules. For the Academy dictated the subject matter by limiting it chiefly to religious or legendary material, especially classical; and also the method, by insisting upon a smooth handling with careful blending of light and shade. "High art," this was called. But it was very empty and very unconvincing. Such official domination and such an ideal, however, did not accord with the new spirit that was rising in France. So when Édouard Manet (1832–1883 A.D.), gifted with unusual vision and a healthy interest in the everyday life about him, began to place upon the canvas pictures taken from the real world and painted in the brilliant colors that he saw in nature, he found himself the object of ridicule and scorn on the part of the upholders of the old traditions. And he spent most of his life in a battle for the recognition of the right to paint real life as he saw it. His subject matter shocked the Academicians, for it was taken, as we have said, from the living world — a bull-fight, a girl tending the bar, a horse race, a group on a balcony, a man in a boat, everyday people in everyday clothes. Manet's method was as revolutionary as his subject matter. He used vigorous planes with sharp transitions, and bright colors with but few intermediate tones.

Manet's struggle against the traditional art of the Academy made him the leader of a group of men who shared his convictions. Most important of these were Claude Monet (1840–), Camille Pissarro (1831–1903 A.D.), Alfred Sisley (1839–1889 A.D.), and Firmin Auguste Renoir (1841–1919 A.D.). Primarily they were landscape painters, working in the open directly from nature, and particularly interested in reproducing light and color as they saw it in nature. The fundamental principles upon which all these men worked were very much the same. We may therefore take Monet as typical of them all.

Monet knew very well that light, and therefore the appearance of nature, changed every moment as the light shifted. So, in his insatiable desire to understand thoroughly the appearance of an object under varying lights and atmospheric conditions, he used to paint the same subject from the same point of view a great many times, going out at sunrise with twenty canvases so as to be able to catch quickly the elusive changes. And the results are astonishingly different. Each is a realistic rendering of a fleeting impression. Hence the term "Impressionist" [2] well suggests the character of the work of these painters.

This kind of fleeting impression is what we see in Monet's *Westminster* (PL. 149 B). On the farther side of the Thames River the buildings only half emerge from the mists. But the canvas vibrates with an effect of living light and air that envelop them and blur their outlines. We do not get a sense of structure or a feeling of design, that is, of the ordering of the elements of formal composition into a harmonious unit, so characteristic of Italian painting. There is nothing permanent, monumental, or imaginative in the picture. It is frankly a momentary impression of *Westminster* at a time when the buildings were half hidden in a mist; or, more specifically, it is a painting of vibrating light itself as it envelops the buildings.

[2] This term was not invented by the Impressionists themselves. In 1874 Monet exhibited a sunrise scene to which he gave the title, "Impression: soleil levant." As this title seemed quite expressive of the methods of the group, the term soon became current but was used at first in a sense of reproach and scorn for the painters who were the "ignorant and extravagant iconoclasts of established principles."

This living, vibrating quality of light is the significant element of Monet's paintings and was obtained by his technical methods. Approach the picture and it becomes unintelligible — a rectangle of canvas covered with streaks and dabs of thick pigment. But move across the room and the objects appear, enveloped in glowing, shimmering light. This has happened because the little dabs of pigment were placed so accurately as regards tone and value that, when the eye mixes them at the proper distance, they reproduce the shape of the objects, the texture of the water, the color in the shadows, and, because of their rough surface, the vibrating quality of the light. Furthermore, the juxtaposition of colors on the canvas for the eye to mix at a distance produces a more intense hue than the mixing of the same colors on the palette, just as we saw was true in the making of Gothic stained-glass windows.

The paintings of the Impressionists are as truly and sincerely realistic as the work of Jan Van Eyck or Dürer. The difference, apart from technique, is that the Flemish and German painters put in with the greatest minutiae all the details that their minds told them existed, and sharply defined the contours. The French recorded what the eye actually saw of things blurred by the envelope of light and air. Technically, the French method required not only keen powers of observation but also a scientific knowledge of the properties of color. The French also saw, for the first time, that shadows are full of color. Landscape painters down to Constable had used black, gray, or brown shadow. Even Ruisdael with his intimate knowledge of nature had filled his pictures with dull greens and browns. But Manet and his followers saw that the shadow beneath the tree was not gray or brown, but green, blue, violet or some other hue.

Another characteristic of these painters was their real love of nature and their joy in it. The warm, bright sunshine, the sparkling water, the cool shadow, are often found represented with an astounding reality in the paintings of Sisley, especially those of streams with willows dipping in the water; or the sweet fresh smells of spring in a landscape by Pissarro, with the pale green foliage of the blossoming trees and the soft blue of spring in the sky.

Renoir was the one member of the group possessed by an absorbing interest in the human figure, especially the nude. He took sheer delight in unaffected feminine charm and frankly expressed his joy in it. He could take a simple subject, such as the *Lady at the Piano* (PL. 150 A) and make something enchanting out of it. One almost inevitably thinks of Watteau, for it is charming grace expressed spontaneously and with marvelous workmanship — "a pool of iridescent loveliness." This lady is dressed in a fluffy gown of pale blue with a narrow border of rich black as if to give it strength. She is sitting at the piano entirely absorbed in her music. The brush strokes indicate with great accuracy the textures of the stuffs, the hair, and the sheen of the polished wood. The room is rather shadowy but there is an amazing feeling in it of depth and atmosphere. There is nothing affected, elegant, or monumental about the picture; but the great masses of rich, luminous color that seem to melt into each other, the suave line, the ease and spontaneity both of composition and of technique, make the canvas enchanting.

Another French painter of importance, who lived quiet and serene, apart from the turmoil of conflicting ideas, was Pierre Cécile Puvis de Chavannes (1824–1898 A.D.). Typical of his work are the mural decorations in the Panthéon representing the life of Saint Genevieve. These paintings almost inevitably recall those of Piero della Francesca (PL. 106 c). Like Piero, like the Gothic glassmakers and tapestry weavers, and like Giotto, Puvis de Chavannes never forgot that he was decorating a wall, not creating a pictorial illusion. For this reason he did not carry the eye far into the distance, but kept the painting flat, in a very few planes. The figures he simplified until they became almost geometrical silhouettes fitted into the landscape like architectural members of a building. Nowhere are there deep shadows or violent contrasts, but the harmonious massing of soft silvery tones — blue, rose, green, and white. Even the night scene of *Saint Genevieve Watching over the Sleeping City* (PL. 148 D) conforms to these principles, and also shows how much poetic and imaginative quality there was in the painter's conception of the scene as the aged Saint, the patron saint of Paris, stands almost ghostlike by the parapet watching with great tenderness over her loved city. Thus Puvis de Chavannes in his wall paintings with their serenity, poetic imagination, intellectual clarity, and quiet decorative beauty, has set a standard for modern mural decoration.

The Impressionists and their immediate followers, after all, were luminists and scientists. Perugino had expressed the spaciousness of nature; Giovanni Bellini and Giorgione had given it poetry and mood; Velasquez had filled it with atmosphere; Claude and Turner had painted ecstatic visions of light and air. It was the accomplishment of the French Impressionists really to

PLATE 149

(*A*) Delacroix. Entrance of the Crusaders into Constantinople.
1841 A.D. Louvre, Paris. (Giraudon)

(*B*) Monet. Westminster. 1901–04 A.D. Ryerson Loan Coll., Art Institute,
Chicago. (Martin A. Ryerson)

PLATE 150

(A) Renoir. Lady at the Piano. Coll. of Martin A. Ryerson, Chicago. (Martin A Ryerson)

(B) Cézanne. La Montagne Victoire. Private Coll.

succeed in conveying the impression of light itself. To be sure, other artists, Constable, Turner, and Delacroix in particular, had been groping toward this end. The accomplishment was possibly more scientific than artistic, based upon the principle of a rough impasto and division of color. Charming as the paintings of the Impressionists are, still they have little or no imaginative quality, design element, or spiritual significance.

It was against this phase of Impressionism that revolt came from Paul Cézanne (1839–1906 A.D.). This painter did not find in the works of the Impressionists the structure, the significance, or the profundity in nature that he so mightily felt and wanted to express. "I want to make Impressionism something solid and permanent, like the old masters." Hence alone, in southern France away from Paris, he worked out his problems. Many times he painted *La Montagne Victoire* (PL. 150 B). In looking at the painting, we realize that we do not see here a changing, momentary aspect of the scene. The suggestion of time or season has all been eliminated. Here is the permanent, unchanging mountain, solid and massive; and reduced, after all irrelevant details have been eliminated, to geometric form. This underlying geometric pattern we have found basic in the work of many of the greatest artists: in the Greek archer from Ægina, in Giotto's frescoes, in Piero della Francesca, in Michelangelo, in Vermeer, in Rodin, and in Puvis de Chavannes. Cézanne's planes cut sharply and truly, giving one a heightened sensation of volume; and the color is so true that the feeling of distance is most remarkable. In addition to the feeling of the ultimate reality of the scene, there is a conscious recognition of design in nature and a grouping of the elements of design — line, pattern, and color — into a harmonious decorative effect. Cézanne's paintings, like those of Piero della Francesca, are austere. They have power rather than charm. They brought back into painting those elements of pictorial art that the Impressionists had lost — structure and design. Thus Cézanne was the culmination of the nineteenth century in France and was also the starting-point of the various schools that have arisen in Europe since about the year 1900.

MINOR ARTS

Because of the state control instituted by the establishment of the Gobelins, there was unity and standardization in all the arts. The artists were part of a great system, under which artificiality and conventionality were inevitable. One misses the charm, spontaneity, and sincerity of the fifteenth century. An excellent result, however, was the high standard of workmanship that characterized the furniture, porcelain, silks, tapestries, and metal work.

We have already spoken of the furniture because it formed so intimate a part of architectural and decorative design. Another important factor in this architectural design was the great series of tapestries that covered the walls and contributed so much to the color. We have seen the splendid accomplishments of the Flemish as tapestry weavers. Under Louis XIV, the craft was established at Paris; and the Gobelins, since its purchase by Louis in 1662 A.D., has been the center for the finest production. The tapestries of the period were of great size. Their subjects were taken chiefly from history and mythology, and the compositions were designed by the most important artists of the day. Technically, they show the great skill of the weavers in their complicated compositions and elaborate borders. But artistically many of them fail to attain their purpose of decorating the wall, as the Gothic tapestries so successfully did, because they sought primarily not so much to produce a decorative color harmony as to create an illusion of reality after the fashion of a painting with the use of distance, perspective, light and shade, and thus transgressed their medium.

Other textiles also reveal a deviation from tradition. The all-over design consisting of large repeated pattern that originated in the Near East began to break up into a lighter framework and by the time of Louis XV had taken on the form of a delicate pattern of vines, garlands, flowers, and ribbons that well harmonized with the interior decoration and the furnishings of the period. The brocade reproduced in PL. 146 B makes an exquisite pattern of blue, light and dark rose, and green and gold on a ground of ribbed white. These brocades and silks were made largely at Lyons, which had become an important center for silk textiles; and, like the tapestries, they show the great technical skill of the weavers.

Another important product of the French craftsman was porcelain. Chinese porcelains had made their way to Europe perhaps as early as the eleventh or twelfth century; and, because of their thinness and translucency, were greatly admired. The potters did not understand the process of their manufacture until finally in the eighteenth century both the German and the French potters discovered the nature of true porcelain. Of several important factories, the royal establishment at *Sèvres* is best known. For decorating the royal palaces, it produced ornate, elegantly shaped vases. A typical example (PL. 146 c) is covered with a deep blue enamel, flawless in its finish, and is heavily ornamented in gold, with a panel reserved on which a dainty miniature is painted with picturesque effect. The vase harmonized well with the grandeur and artificial elegance of the age, and shows superb technical skill. But as a truly artistic product of the potter's craft it is not to be placed beside the genuinely spontaneous expressions of the Persian Rhages ware, the Greek red-figured vases, or the Chinese porcelains. For in these the shape of the vase, that is, the constructional element, performed the function both of use and of beauty. Where decoration appeared it recognized both the shape and the material and lent itself to that in its broad, flat massing of the figure and its economic line.

SUMMARY

The late Gothic age saw France still vigorous in all the fine arts. The heightened fervor of the Middle Ages had indeed somewhat cooled, and decoration as an end in itself was occupying a more prominent place. A vigorous school of native painting had grown out of miniature-painting and a school of independent sculpture had developed, both of which showed a tempered naturalism and a sincere feeling for fine design. Upon this native art the Renaissance was forced by arbitrary monarchs who had been captivated by everything Italian. The result was an artificial and conventional art, entirely under the control of the monarch and existing for the sake of the monarch, but, because of state supervision and requirements, maintaining a high standard of technical excellence. Styles followed each other rapidly with the change of rulers. Revolt against the frivolity and injustice of the ruling class revealed itself in the classical movement. Classicism in turn weakened, toward the end of the Revolution, before the impetus of Romanticism. The most important tendency of the second half of the nineteenth century was the revolt against the tyranny of the Academy and a return to naturalism both in subject matter and in technique. This movement found its strongest manifestation in the Impressionists among the painters and in Rodin among the sculptors. Immense advance was made technically, especially in the science of color Out of this situation have grown revolt and counter-revolt, resulting in the unexampled individualistic freedom and confusion in the life of the arts today.

BIBLIOGRAPHY

BLOMFIELD, REGINALD, Studies in Architecture. N.Y., Macmillan, 1905.

BROWNELL, W. C., French Art. N.Y., Scribner, 1905.

CAFFIN, C. H., Story of French Painting. N.Y., Century, 1915.

DILKE, LADY, French Architects and Sculptors of the XVIII Century. London, Bell, 1900.

—— ——, French Furniture and Decoration of the XVIII Century. London, Bell, 1901.

DURET, THÉODORE, Manet and the French Impressionists. Philadelphia, Lippincott, 1910.

FAURE, ELIE, History of Art: v. 4, Modern Art (tr. Pach). N.Y., Harper, 1924.

FRIEDLAENDER, WALTER, Claude Lorrain. Berlin, Cassirer, 1921.

FRY, ROGER, Vision and Design. London, Chatto, 1923.

FURST, H. E. A., Chardin. London, Methuen, 1911.

GILMAN, ROGER, Great Styles of Interior Architecture. N.Y., Harper, 1924.

HAMLIN, A. D. F., History of Ornament, Renaissance and Modern. N.Y., Century, 1923.

HAMLIN, T. F., Enjoyment of Architecture. N.Y., Scribner, 1921.

HIND, C. L., Landscape Painting from Giotto to the Present Day. 2v. London, Chapman, 1923–4.

HOURTICQ, LOUIS, Art in France. N.Y., Scribner, 1917.

JACKSON, T. G., Renaissance of Roman Architecture: III, France. Cambridge, University Press, 1923.

LISTER, REGINALD, Jean Goujon: His Life and Work. London, Duckworth, 1903.

MARRIOTT, CHARLES, Modern Movements in Painting. London, Chapman, 1920.

MAUCLAIR, CAMILLE, French Impressionists. N.Y., Dutton, 1903.

—— ——, Great French Painters (tr. Konody). N.Y., Dutton, 1903.

MICHEL, ANDRÉ, Puvis de Chavannes. Philadelphia, Lippincott, 1912.

MOORE, C. H., Character of Renaissance Architecture. N.Y., Macmillan, 1905.

PHILLIPS PUBLICATIONS, 2. Honoré Daumier. N.Y., Dutton, 1923.

POST, C. H., History of European and American Sculpture. 2v. Cambridge, Harvard University Press, 1921.

SARGENT, WALTER, Enjoyment and Use of Color. N.Y., Scribner, 1923.

SPEED, HAROLD, Science and Practice of Oil Painting. London, Chapman, 1924.

TILLEY, A. A., Dawn of the French Renaissance. Cambridge, University Press, 1918.

TRIGGS, H. I., Garden Craft in Europe. N.Y., Scribner, 1913.

VICTORIA AND ALBERT MUSEUM, SOUTH KENSINGTON, DEPARTMENT OF WOODWORK. Panelled Rooms: III, Boudoir of Mme. de Sérilly. London, 1915.

WARD, W. H., Architecture of the Renaissance in France. 2v. London, Batsford, 1911.

WRIGHT, W. H., Modern Painting: Its Tendency and Meaning. N.Y., Dodd, 1922.

CHAPTER XXV
AMERICA
The United States from Its Colonization to c. 1900 A.D.

HISTORICAL BACKGROUND

The short three hundred years since the Pilgrims landed in America have been devoted chiefly to the development of the country, at first along the seaboard under primitive conditions that left little energy for anything except necessities. But even when those necessities were provided, colonial culture, because of the iconoclastic nature of its religion, particularly in the North, was generally drab and forbade the theater and frowned upon art. When the colonies began to flourish and were aroused by the war of independence to a new feeling of nationalism, with energy and zeal they pushed west of the first barrier of mountains to explore and utilize the vast resources of the West. The growth and development of the country, even under pioneer conditions, has been an amazing accomplishment. The Civil War that threatened the unity of the nation resulted in the strengthening of it. Since then the growth of industrialism, with its consequent unprecedented wealth, has been the chief attainment.

Intellectually and artistically, the United States has kept close to European traditions and movements. This was natural. The majority of American students have gone to Europe for their training. The United States is still too young and too heterogeneous in its population to have blended and fused its varying traditions into what might be called a truly American tradition.

ARCHITECTURE

Architecture in America has been determined by European tradition modified to a considerable degree by local conditions. Its earliest manifestation is found in the charming houses that are the highest expression of the colonial period. Wood always played an important part in building construction, as the great forests surrounding the colonies provided an abundance of timber of excellent quality. At first it was used for the entire building; and even after clay pits and quarries began to supply brick and stone, wood still was used for pillars, porches, cornices, panels, and carvings both on the exterior and interior. The forms worked out in stone by the English architects were translated in the colonies into wood and hence became more slender and delicate.

The New England domestic architecture of the eighteenth century is represented by the *Peirce-Nichols House* (PL. 151 A). There is an atmosphere of dignity and well-being about the house that is reserved and even severe. The façade is designed with a feeling for regularity and balance, and is framed by great fluted pilasters that finish the corners, and by the overshadowing cornice with its balustrade. The pedimented porch holds the center of interest. The carvings of the pilasters, cornices, and portal are classical and show both skill and restraint. This detail takes us back to England, which at this time was experiencing the Adam phase of the classical revival.

On the interiors of these colonial houses (PL. 151 c) the wood-work — paneling, fireplaces, and stairways — is an important element of interior design. There was an abundance of pine especially adaptable for carving because it was rather soft and fine-grained and at the same time durable. It was painted some-times gray, but usually white. The work of Samuel McIntire, one of the best known carvers, reflects that of Robert Adam (PL. 140 B) in the delicacy of its low-relief carvings. But the ceilings are plain and the general effect is much less stately and more plainly domes-tic than the English prototype.

In the southern colonies a somewhat different type of building is found, as typified by *Woodlands* (PL. 151 B). The general im-pression is one of dignity and stateliness, like that of the *Peirce-Nichols House*, but more genial. The southern colonists were not as austere as the New Englanders. Life was more luxurious and gay. The warmth of hospitality and welcome is felt in the two-story pedimented portico with its lofty columns. The strict regularity is broken by the circular bays on the sides and by the great arched window of the ground story, Palladian in its design. Most of the houses of the period were placed with careful regard for natural surroundings. Trees, hedges, spacious lawns, and gardens contributed to the qualities of the building itself.

The national feeling that inspired the country because of the War of Independence became an incentive for breaking from England artistically as well as politically. Very influential in this movement was Thomas Jefferson, himself a designer and draughtsman of considerable ability. He turned to the classical tradition for inspiration, and gave the country such a powerful impetus in this direction that up to 1850 this style prevailed. Now it was the tradition of Rome, now of Greece, now of Palladio. The *Bank of the United States (Custom House)* at Philadelphia is modeled directly after the *Parthenon*. The *Capitol of the United States* at Washington (PL. 152 A) was designed and constructed by successive architects upon classical and Renaissance models. Through the balanced massing of the parts, the monumental stairway, and the crowning dome, the building fittingly symbolizes the power of the State just as Brunelleschi's dome in Florence and Michelangelo's in Rome symbolized the domination of the Church.

The period from about 1850 to 1900 reveals various movements, each having its origin in some European tradition. Now it was the Italian Renaissance that furnished the inspiration, now the French, now the Romanesque, again the classical, and then the Gothic. Thus, unfortunately for the American cities, along many of the main thoroughfares there is imitation after imitation of European "styles" instead of a homogeneous appearance reflecting the conditions of life out of which building should have naturally evolved. To be sure, European cities also are not free from this criticism, because exotic styles there too have been grafted upon the native growth.

While European tradition has formed the basis of American architecture, still the architects of real merit have at times infused into the older styles a distinct personality. This was perhaps inevitable in view of the fact that these older styles must be subjected to new conditions quite different from those out of which they grew. Geography and climate play an important part. The type of building that met the demands of the warm bright climate of southern Europe, in coming to our severer climate must submit to openings for light and protection from the cold. Available material is another important factor. When stone technique is translated into wood or vice versa, where machinery takes the place of hand carving, where steel and terra cotta enter into the structural elements, great changes are destined to appear. Again, the complexity of civilization in modern America has increased enormously the uses to which buildings are put. If a Greek temple is to serve as a modern bank in a great metropolis, certain changes must be made; if the Romanesque style with its thick walls and small number of windows is to serve a great business establishment, it must be so modified that large openings for light and display are possible. Another important feature in American civilization that directly affects its architecture is the concentration of the population into great cities, so that more and more thought has been concentrated upon city planning, not only for beautifying by parks, broad thoroughfares, and waterfronts, but for handling the intricate transportation problems where great masses of people are huddled together. All this has entered into the work of the American architect. And in the translation of these older styles into the American vernacular some of the architects have shown great originality.

Let us illustrate. A reflection of the Romanesque is seen in the *Marshall Field Wholesale House* (Pl. 153 A), which despite the large openings made necessary by the northern climate and the business purpose of the building, still maintains the sturdy massiveness of its prototype. The walls of finely cut stone are frankly constructional and are made interesting by the great variety shown in the disposition of openings. The *Boston Public Library* (PL. 152 B) reveals the early Italian Renaissance both in the quiet dignity of its design and in the details of its composition and decoration. *Saint Patrick's Cathedral* in the heart of New York City is a close copy of a Gothic cathedral. The *World's Columbian Exposition*, especially the *Fine Arts Building* (PL. 152 C) shows one of the latest returns to the classical ideal. In its long quiet lines, low domes, and harmonious grouping of the central part and the wings, it reveals a quiet nobility and an unusually distinctive feeling for architectural design.

Probably the most typical American buildings have been those that function directly with commerce and industry, particularly the skyscraper. Three elements have contributed toward the evolution of the skyscraper: the rapid rise in land values, which have strongly tended toward increasing the height of the building; scientific developments in elevator service, lighting, and heating, which make the occupancy of the upper stories both safe and comfortable; and the employment of steel, reinforced concrete, and fireproof brick as structural material. In such a building the walls no longer perform a structural function as they do in the *Marshall Field Wholesale House* (PL. 153 A) but form an encasing shell dependent upon the steel frame and thus make possible the large openings necessary in a northern climate and in a building devoted to business purposes. The problem of designing such a building is a difficult one. To indicate structural lines sufficiently to suggest stability and strength, to provide

PLATE 151

(*A*) Peirce-Nichols House. Salem. c. 1790 A.D. (Essex Institute)

(*B*) Woodlands. Philadelphia. Rebuilt 1788–89 A.D. (Copyright by Detroit Publishing Co.)

(*C*) Peirce-Nichols House. East Parlor (Essex Institute)

PLATE 152

(*A*) United States Capitol. Washington. 1818–65 A.D. (Copyright by Detroit Publishing Co.)

(*B*) Public Library. Boston. McKim, Mead and White, architects. 1888–95 A.D. (Copyright by Detroit Photographic Co.)

(*C*) Fine Arts Building. World's Columbian Exposition, Chicago. 1893 A.D.
C. B. Attwood, architect. (Copyright by A. G. McGregor, Chicago)

PLATE 153

(*A*) Marshall Field Wholesale House. Chicago.
H. H. Richardson, architect.

(*B*) Prudential (Guaranty) Building. Buffalo. c. 1895 A.D. Louis Sullivan, architect.
(Detroit Publishing Co.)

(*C*) Inness. After a Summer Shower. 1894 A.D. Butler Coll.,
Art Institute, Chicago. (Art Institute)

PLATE 154

(*A*) Inness. Rosy Morn. 1894 A.D. Ryerson Loan Coll.,
Art Institute, Chicago. (Martin A. Ryerson)

(*B*) Whistler. Nocturne, Southampton Water. Art Institute, Chicago. (Art Institute)

ample light, and at the same time to give the tall façade harmony, balance, and variety is no mean task. One of the first really successful solutions was that of Louis Sullivan in the *Prudential* *(Guaranty) Building* (PL. 153 B). Here one feels the framework of vertical shafts and horizontal beams revealed by the lines of the encasement and the massing of larger non-structural units to form an effective base to the design.

PAINTING

In the early colonial days, hard life under primitive conditions, together with a puritanical prejudice toward art, militated against creative work in painting, sculpture, music, and the drama.

The story of painting in America, as of architecture, has been a series of influences from Europe. It was the English portrait school, especially of Gainsborough and Reynolds, that provided models for the early portrait painters. The landscape painters found their source of inspiration in Ruisdael, Claude, and the Barbizon group. Some figure artists followed the French Academy; but many figure and landscape painters, the French Impressionists. All this has been due largely to study and travel in Europe. Some artists have continued to live there permanently, notably Whistler and Sargent, and possibly belong to Europe rather than to America. This means merely that nationalism has been superseded by cosmopolitanism.

We shall look at the works of four American painters—Inness, La Farge, Whistler, and Sargent — as typical examples of the best work that has been produced. Landscape has been a popular subject, receiving a strong impulse in the first half of the nineteenth century from the Hudson River school of painters who were filled with genuine enthusiasm over the new spirit of nationalism and, recognizing the natural beauty of the land, sincerely attempted to express their feeling for it. While their efforts seldom rose above mediocrity, they were influential by arousing interest in the subject among painters of greater powers. Among them George Inness (1825–1894 A.D.) stands preëminent. *After a Summer Shower* (PL. 153 C) shows us that his attitude toward nature was not unlike that of Corot in that he responded sympathetically to her moods. Over a rural landscape, with a broad reach of flowering meadow land, a few trees, and distant buildings, a storm is just passing; the dark clouds at the right are still heavy with rain; the rest of the sky is filled with masses of broken clouds through which a rainbow is seen. Everywhere we breathe the fresh air and smell the sweet smells that follow showers. This is the ultimate significance of the scene — an intimate expression of one of nature's moods. The successful expression of this feeling is due partly to the careful composition, especially in the balancing of the light and dark masses, and partly to the adequate expression of essential form. The structure of the gnarled tree in the center, of the masses of foliage beyond, and of the clouds and the sky is shown with great skill. Another distinctive quality is the color harmony.

In some of the morning and evening scenes of Inness, the forms melt with the softest gradation into the enveloping atmosphere, and the trees make interesting, wavering patterns against a silver or rosy sky, as in *Rosy Morn* (PL. 154 A). Here we feel the fresh morning air and the damp coolness. The rosy light is reflected on the water, the house, and the grass, and as it plays through the canvas, it unites all the forms into a color harmony. The elements of the design — the trees, river, house, and distant banks — compose into a harmonious pattern that forms an arabesque against the sky. But again, what impresses one most is the revelation of a penetrating and sympathetic insight into nature and the ability to give it poetic interpretation.

In John La Farge (1835–1910 A.D.) we have an artist whose training was broad and varied. His school was not only the ateliers and the galleries of Europe, where he steeped himself in the principles of the great masters, but also the primitive, exotic, and colorful civilization of the South Sea Islands, and the almost unknown gardens and treasure houses of Japan. Too virile to be a mere copyist, he assimilated these experiences. His work shows his genuine respect for the value of tradition — the design of the Italians, the color and movement of Delacroix, the asymmetrical balance of the Japanese. But it was light and color, viewed scientifically as well as aesthetically, that became problems of the highest importance to La Farge. Independently he was reaching conclusions in pigment very much like those of the French Impressionists. It was in glass, however, that he found his best medium of experimentation and expression. He was able to produce such a masterpiece as the *Peacock Window* [1] because, in the first place, through an intimate study of such medieval windows as those of *Chartres*, he mastered the fundamental principles that enabled the twelfth century glassworker to make the most perfect windows known; and second, because he pur-

[1] For a description, see Cortissoz, *John La Farge*, p. 200.

sued an ideal of broad, sound craftsmanship. For he realized that the finest design could be ruined by less skillful or by mechanical assistants. Hence he either carried out the design with his own hands or very carefully supervised every detail that passed through the hands of his assistants. Every piece of material that went into the window, he chose or even made with the utmost care. The success of La Farge's work was in large measure due to his recognition of these sound principles of craftsmanship.

James Abbott McNeill Whistler (1834–1903 A.D.) like La Farge, worked in several media — oil, water color, pastel, etching, lithograph — and covered a wide range of subject matter. It was in his portraits and landscapes that he attained his greatest achievement. In the portrait of *Miss Alexander* (PL. 155 A) there is characterization, to fulfill the purpose of portraiture, but one feels that after all Whistler was primarily interested in the harmonious arrangement of line, pattern, and color. Evidence of this is found in the titles that he gave many of his portraits: *Arrangement in Gray and Black*; *Symphony in Flesh-Color and Pink*. The Alexander portrait is entitled *Harmony in Gray and Green*. The young girl is represented standing in front of a paneled background of gray and black, none too happy over the long hours of posing. She wears a fluffy white dress with a green sash draped about it, and carries a hat with a green plume. A robe is thrown carelessly at the left; a few daisies break into the frame at the right; and butterflies hover above. If we try to change the proportions of any of the parts or remove any detail, even the butterfly in a circle at the left, Whistler's signature, we realize that something is wrong. Gray and green and also black and gold play through the composition, sometimes in strong masses, again subtly suggested by faint strokes, so that Whistler's own title is a fitting one.

Of the influences that have entered into the work of Whistler, two in particular are paramount — Velasquez and the Japanese. Velasquez we see in *Miss Alexander* in the full-length figure placed as it is upon the canvas, in the blacks and grays, in the outlines softened by the enveloping air, and in the values and texture of the white expressed by a few masterful strokes of the brush. Japanese art in the form of the Japanese color print was just coming to be known in Paris through the accidental discovery in 1856 of a volume of Hokusai. The unusual point of view, the asymmetrical balance, the color harmony, the tendency toward abstraction, even the subject matter, appealed strongly to Whistler. In *Miss Alexander*, for example, the spray of flowers entering the panel at the right, suggesting to the imagination the plant just out of vision, is characteristic of the art of Japan.

These qualities are particularly noticeable in Whistler's landscapes, which he preferred to call *Nocturnes*, *Harmonies*, and *Arrangements*. Here we find the highest abstraction. Whistler himself best expresses their significance in his *Ten O'Clock*:

. . . Nature indeed contains the elements in colour and form of all pictures, as the keyboard contains the notes of all music. But the artist is born to pick and choose and group with science these elements, that the result may be beautiful — as the musician gathers his notes and forms chords, until he brings forth from chaos glorious harmonies. . . .

And when the evening mist clothes the riverside with poetry, as with a veil, and the poor buildings lose themselves in the dim sky, and the tall chimneys become campanili, and the warehouses are palaces in the night and the whole city hangs in the heavens, and fairy-land is before us — then the wayfarer hastens home; the workingman and the cultured one, the wise man and the one of pleasure, cease to understand as they have ceased to see; and Nature, who for once has sung in tune, sings her exquisite song to the artist alone, her son and her master — her son in that he loves her; her master in that he knows her. To him her secrets are unfolded; to him her lessons have become gradually clear. He looks at her flower, not with the enlarging lens, that he may gather facts for the botanist, but with the light of one who sees in her choice selection of brilliant tones and delicate tints, suggestion of future harmonies. . . .

The very titles suggest that Whistler's emotional reaction to these aspects of nature and that of the spectator in looking at his interpretations are closely akin to that of music. They appeal to the imagination, suggesting the essence of the scene rather than the facts of it. In the *Nocturne, Southampton Water* (PL. 154 B) four tones are laid on flat, in very thin pigment; modeling, structure, and form are all suppressed in the pursuit of a color harmony that suggests the beauty, poetry, and mystery of a moonlight scene in Southampton harbor. Rarely have fluid technique and ephemeral representation been carried so far.

John Singer Sargent (1856–1925 A.D.), though a successful mural decorator, as his paintings in the Boston Public Library show, possibly attained his climax in his portraits. In these there is a certain feeling of distinction, a sense of orderly design, and a superb technical ability in handling pigment. His single portraits are usually more successful than his groups. The *Portrait of Mrs. Swinton* (PL. 155 B), for example, well illustrates these points. The characterization is inclined to be one of external appearance rather than a penetrating study. The feeling of quiet elegance comes partly from the dignified pose, and partly from the luxuriousness of the dress and the surroundings. Sargent was particularly successful in creating a certain atmosphere in his portraits through the texture of elegant stuffs and through a well organized design. In this portrait, the curving chair and the sweeping drapery at the right make a firm base of rhythmic curves above which the figure rises with great stateliness. Sargent was not a draughtsman as were the Florentines, as Goya, or Ingres, but an accomplished wielder of the brush modeling by planes rather than by line and cutting his planes vigorously rather than by subtle gradations, more in the gusto manner of Frans Hals. Thus his canvases have a sparkle and a dramatic quality that is captivating.

SCULPTURE

Out of unpromising conditions, the sculptors in the United States have produced some notable work, preëminently that of Augustus Saint-Gaudens (1848–1907 A.D.). Of the long series of portraits that Saint-Gaudens executed, the *Lincoln* (PL. 155 c) embodies his characteristics. The statue represents Lincoln standing before his chair about to speak. His left hand clutches his coat. The large circular architectural setting around the pedestal suggests the audience chamber. He is looking down with an expression of noble seriousness and perhaps a little sadness. The pose is easy and naturalistic. The modeling is broadly generalized, especially in the modern garments that offer but little incentive for artistic treatment. The outline is simplified and the mass compact. These characteristics show that Saint-Gaudens was loyal to the fundamental laws of great sculpture. In all his work he recognized the integrity of his material, that is, he realized that stone or bronze, by its very nature inflexible and enduring, limits the expression to one that must be enduring and monumental. Therefore it is the essential and not the ephemeral or transitory that is suitable to such a medium. Hence mass, significant structure, and essentials of character govern any sculptor working under these laws. In the *Lincoln*, there is a notable serenity and restraint, with nothing to startle or astonish. This simple monumental expression harmonizes fittingly with the profoundly monumental character of Lincoln.

These characteristics are just as applicable to the *Adams Monument* (PL. 155 D), though in this statue the subject matter takes us from portraiture to the realm of poetry and mystery. Profound poetic emotion expressed in terms of monumental sculpture has rarely been attained in America. But in this statue Saint-Gaudens has been marvelously successful. A mysterious figure almost hidden in a great mantle sits with her chin resting upon her right hand. There is monumental simplicity in the powerful folds and a brooding suggestiveness in the half-hidden face. It does not need a name. Its mystery, its stillness, and its suggestion of inevitability, its bare simplicity, its freedom from distracting representational qualities and irritating detail, arouse in the spectator a feeling that leads him toward the regions of pure thought and mysticism. If he is a poet, he will enter; if not, he will return.[2]

SUMMARY

In the three hundred years of the life of the American nation, the best art that has been produced has been chiefly in imitation of European styles, as in architecture and furniture, or work so close to that of contemporary European movements, in painting especially, that there is very little to differentiate it. This was the situation down to c. 1900. With an unprecedented development of resources and of material prosperity, why is this so? Three reasons, at least, stand out clearly. First, the unfortunate conditions, artistically, into which the nation was born; second, the youth of the nation; and third, the diversion of all energy into the development of the natural resources of the country. The American nation happened to be born into an age in which art production everywhere was at low ebb, and in which art was rapidly being segregated from the affairs of life chiefly because of the industrial revolution. England was entering upon that age of bad taste and mediocre imitation against which the Pre-Raphaelites protested. France, under the domination of the Academy, had also reached the low level of emptiness and artificiality against which the naturalists and Impressionists revolted. Lifeless imitation of Italian art everywhere stifled natural creative expression. It was inevitable that the colonists should bring with them the inherited traditions of the home country. And it was also inevitable that these traditions should develop, perhaps with provincial mediocrity, to their logical end — empty copying — unless some vitalizing force should evolve new ones. But the youth of the nation has operated against this. The heterogeneous elements found among the American people have not yet fused into a unity — political, social, religious, and intellectual — to create fundamental tradi-

[2] See Cortissoz, *Augustus Saint-Gaudens*, p. 30, for a very sympathetic analysis and appreciation of this statue.

tions, to establish capacity for appreciation on the part of the mass of the people, and thus to create a demand for the real artist. The energies of the nation have gone into the development of the country — again the inevitable condition of a colonizing people — which has led into an age of great mechanical and scientific industrialism, with a materialism frequently preponderant at the cost of the spiritual, ethical, and intellectual. The creative impulse, under these conditions, has found comparatively little encouragement.

BIBLIOGRAPHY

AMERICAN INSTITUTE OF ARCHITECTS, Significance of the Fine Arts. Boston, Jones, 1923.

CAFFIN, C. H., American Masters of Painting. N.Y., Doubleday, 1903.

—— ——, American Masters of Sculpture. N.Y., Doubleday, 1913.

—— ——, Story of American Painting. N.Y., Stokes, 1907.

CHASE, G. H., AND POST, C. R., History of Sculpture. N.Y., Harper, 1924.

CORTISSOZ, ROYAL, American Artists. N.Y., Scribner, 1923.

—— ——, John La Farge: A Memoir and a Study. Boston, Houghton, 1911.

—— ——, Augustus Saint-Gaudens. Boston, Houghton, 1907.

COUSINS, FRANK, AND RILEY, P. M., Colonial Architecture of Philadelphia. Boston, Little, 1919.

—— ——, Colonial Architecture of Salem. Boston, Little, 1920.

DURET, THÉODORE, Whistler (tr. Rutter). Philadelphia, Lippincott, 1917.

EBERLEIN, H. D., Architecture of Colonial America. Boston, Little, 1915.

HIND, C. L., Augustus Saint-Gaudens. N.Y., Lane, 1908.

INNESS, GEORGE, JR., Life, Art, and Letters of George Inness. N.Y., Century, 1917.

ISHAM, SAMUEL, History of American Painting. N.Y., Macmillan, 1910.

KIMBALL, FISKE, Domestic Architecture of the American Colonies and of the Early Republic. N.Y., Scribner, 1922.

—— ——, AND EDGELL, G. H., History of Architecture. N.Y., Harper, 1918.

LA FARGE, JOHN, Considerations on Painting. N.Y., Macmillan, 1901.

MUMFORD, LEWIS, Sticks and Stones: A Study of American Architecture and Civilization. N.Y., Boni, 1924.

PENNELL, E. R., AND J., Life of James McNeill Whistler. Philadelphia, Lippincott, 1919.

POST, C. R., History of European and American Sculpture. 2v. Cambridge, Harvard University Press, 1921.

SAINT-GAUDENS, AUGUSTUS, Reminiscences of Augustus Saint-Gaudens Edited and Amplified by Homer Saint-Gaudens. N.Y., Century, 1913.

TAFT, LORADO, History of American Sculpture. N.Y., Macmillan, 1923.

VAN DYKE, J. C., American Painting and Its Tradition. N.Y., Scribner, 1920.

WHISTLER, J. A. McN., Ten O'Clock. Boston, Houghton, 1888.

CHAPTER XXVI

ABORIGINAL AMERICAN ART

From Earliest Times to the Seventeenth Century A.D.

HISTORICAL BACKGROUND

The study of the aborigines of America is still in its infancy, and many of the important problems are unsolved. An Asiatic origin seems probable. The subsequent history was a series of migrations, frequently of nomad hunters, each tribe in turn taking and assimilating the elements of civilization found among the settled agricultural predecessors whom it conquered. Out of shadowy mists where facts and legend confusedly mingle, at least five important centers of civilization emerge — Mayan, Toltec, and Aztec of Middle America, that is, Mexico and Central America; and the pre-Inca and Inca of South America. Though literary record is wanting, the art remains of these peoples tell us much of their culture. As the relation of the South American civilization to that of Middle America is not clear, we shall study these two divisions separately.

A. MIDDLE AMERICAN

For the purpose of this study Mexico and Central America constitute a unit. Here we find a great variety of geographic and climatic conditions. The country lies in the belt of dry and rainy seasons. Great reaches of plateau land, fertile for raising maize and wheat wherever water can be secured, rise to heavily forested mountain slopes and thence, at places, to perpetual snow; or descend to the tropical, unhealthy jungles of the coastal plains. These plains are marvelously rich agriculturally if man can only clear the land and steadily pursue his battle against the rank luxuriousness of nature. The country is a volcanic region; and the volcanic rock, now coarse and now finely grained, together with plentiful limestone furnished abundant material both for building and for decorative carvings.

Of the three civilizations mentioned, the Mayan reached the highest point of development and was also the most influential.

PLATE 155

(*A*) Whistler. Portrait of Miss Alexander. 1872 A.D. W. C. Alexander Coll., London.

(*B*) Sargent. Mrs. Swinton. Art Institute, Chicago. (Art Institute)

(*C*) Saint-Gaudens. Lincoln. Bronze. 1887 A.D. Lincoln Park, Chicago.

(*D*) Saint-Gaudens. Adams Monument. Bronze and Granite. 1887 A.D. Rock Creek Cemetery, Washington.

PLATE 156

(*A*) El Castillo, Pyramid Temple of Kukulcan Chichen Itza. H. 105 ft.; the base covers one acre. XIII or XIV cent. A.D. (Carnegie Institution, Washington)

(*B*) Temple at Mitla. Detail of the façade, showing stone mosaic decoration in geometric patterns. Aztec.

(*C*) House of the Governor. Detail of the façade, showing stone mosaic decoration. Uxmal. L. 320 ft.

PLATE 157

(A) Stucco Ornament.
Palenque. (Maudslay)

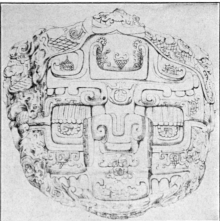

(B) Great Dragon or Turtle of Quirigua.
View of the top. W. 11½ ft. (Maudslay)

(C) Pyramid Temple at Xochicalco. Detail of the decoration of the base, from a model. H. 12 ft. Toltec period.

(D) Great Dragon of Quirigua. H. 7 ft. 3 in.

PLATE 158

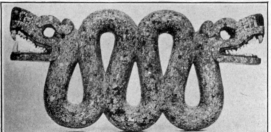

(*A*) Peruvian Pottery. American Museum of Natural History, New York. (American Museum of Natural History)

(*B*) Gold Water Jar. Inca. American Museum of Natural History, New York. (American Museum of Natural History)

(*C*) Double-Headed Serpent. Mosaic. L. 17¾ in. Probably Aztec. British Museum, London.

(*D*) Peruvian Textile. American Museum of Natural History, New York. (American Museum of Natural History)

This tribe occupied the lowlands of Central America, chiefly what is now Yucatan and Guatemala. In the early centuries of the Christian era the Maya were there, a primitive people at a stage of civilization that presupposes a development of centuries. Their first great climax came between 300 and 600 A.D. at such centers as Copan, Palenque, and Quirigua. After a period of civil war, of decadence, and shift of habitation to northern Yucatan, a second climax was reached between about 1000 and 1200 A.D., with Chichen Itza and Uxmal as influential centers. Though the Maya were an agricultural people, all the activities of life were dominated by religion. The government was in fact a theocracy and the cities were great centers where gorgeous cere-

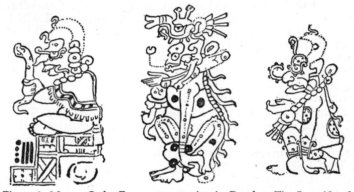

Fig. 108. Mayan Gods. From a manuscript in Dresden. The Long-Nosed God of Rain, the Death God, and the Sun God. (Spinden)

monies and the display of magic power overawed the people. The gods such as the sun god, the wind god, the maize god, and the death god (FIG. 108), personified the processes of nature. Some of these gods represented the powers of evil and some the powers of good. They were constantly at war with each other, and the power of good, at times, unless supported by other powers of good, might fall a victim to some evil power like that of death. In form these gods combined human, bird, and animal features. A very important deity, Kukulkan, for example, called Quetzalcoatl by the Aztecs, was a combination of the quetzal, a plumed bird, with the serpent, the coatl. In his bird manifestation he appeared to typify the winds and thus had to do with the sky and the four directions; while in his serpent manifestation he was connected with water and rain. Sometimes he had the teeth of the jaguar and in his mouth a man's head, all of which involves an intricate symbolism at times unintelligible and for this reason militating against an appreciation of the art in which it plays so large a part. Apparently another means of symbolic expression was color — blue for the sky god, yellow for the sun, green for the sea, and red for war.

An important factor in the Mayan culture is the system of hieroglyphs. This tribe quite early developed an intricate and amazingly accurate method of reckoning time, that is, a calendar, the purpose of which, apart from agricultural necessities, was chiefly to assist the priests in their elaborate systems of religious observances and festivals.[1] Another surprising fact is that these people at their climax and even at the time of the Spanish conquest were in a stone age. Metal tools, if known at all which is doubtful on account of the rarity of copper, were negligible.

Another center of culture was on the plateau of Mexico. Recent excavations point to an early occupation of this locality, probably thousands of years ago, by men in a primitive stage of culture. Apparently the first tribe to reach a comparatively high stage of civilization was the Toltec (c. 750–1050 A.D.), about whose power and splendor there is much legend but little known fact. Though the Toltec culture was maintained in some localities, still the power was broken by decay and civil war and the supremacy passed to the intensely warlike Aztecs, who set up their capitol at Tenochtitlan (now Mexico City), and dated their rule from their first warrior king in 1370 A.D. Like most of the Indians, the Aztecs were predominantly religious; but more than any other tribe they carried religious fanaticism to the hideous extreme of human sacrifice. After conquering the Toltecs and other tribes they settled in the region as an agricultural people, assimilating the culture they found there, and developing a state that was wealthy and peaceful, though in many respects barbarous and never reaching the level of culture attained by the Maya. More than once they have been compared to the Romans. As Spinden says:

The Aztecs, like the Romans, were a brusque and warlike people who built upon the ruins of an earlier civilization that fell before the force of their arms and who made their most notable contributions to organization and government.[2]

[1] Only a part of these hieroglyphs have been deciphered, those indicating the calendar signs, numerals, the gods, and the four directions. See Morley in the *National Geographic Magazine*, Feb., 1922.

[2] Spinden, *Ancient Civilizations of Mexico and Central America*, p. 181. See also the sections on the music and poetry of the Aztecs, in which a note of sadness and grimness prevails.

ARCHITECTURE

As the highest state of culture reached by the American tribes is found among the Maya, we shall study the buildings of this people chiefly.[3] As religion was the dominating power, it is the temple almost exclusively that we find, though there are so-called palaces, buildings composed of groups of rooms evidently used for habitation, perhaps for the priests or nobles. The homes of the people were probably thatched huts. An abundance of excellent building material favored the Maya, who, we remember, were still in the Stone Age. They had quarries of evenly grained limestone that could be cut with stone tools, and an abundance of stone already weathered by vegetation and climate into small pieces for making cement and concrete. Great forests of wood furnished ample timber and also firewood for the preparation of lime.

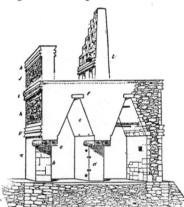

Fig. 109. Section of a Typical Mayan Building. (Holmes)

The most characteristic building was the pyramid-temple, of which *El Castillo* (PL. 156 A) is typical. The structure rests upon a high pyramidal base and is approached by a broad flight of steps on each side. The base is made of a solid mass of concrete faced with stone. The walls of the temple (FIG. 109) are very thick and, like the substructure, are made of concrete faced with stone blocks smoothed on the outer face but left roughly pointed on the inner, to hold more tenaciously in the concrete. On the interior the courses project inward, forming two corbeled arches that spring, over the doorway, from wooden lintels. Rooms so constructed could not be more than about twelve feet wide, but might be of unlimited length. Hence the temples consist of two long, narrow compartments, the inner one of which, the sanctuary, is sometimes divided into smaller units. Above the flat roof rises, in some buildings, a false front or a

[3] The rank vegetation of Yucatan has been the great enemy of these structures. Plants began to grow around and over the temples almost as soon as they were abandoned, and their roots have pried the stones apart and loosened them, so that today it has been necessary to cut away dense jungles to extricate the ruins.

pierced roof-crest for decoration. The construction of such a building — the quarrying of the stone, the transporting and lifting of it to its high position — represents a prodigious amount of labor. The stone tools were primitive, and there were no transportation facilities, not even beasts of burden.

Decoration played an important part in these temples. Stucco, stone mosaic, and carvings — naturalistic, conventional, and geometric — adorned the broad wall surfaces of both the platform and the temple, the columns, lintels, and interior walls. All these surfaces were painted brilliantly with black, blue, red, yellow, and several shades of green. The lofty position of the building as it rises above forests of the richest tropical greenery gives an impression of aloofness, of striving toward a power above. With the massive base, the gay color, the broken outlines made interesting by moldings, relief, and the crest, the effect must have been both gorgeous and impressive.

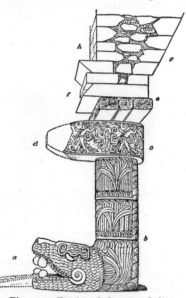

Fig. 110. Feathered Serpent Column, Restored. H. 7 ft. 9 in. Chichen Itza. (Holmes)

Let us look at a few characteristic details of ornamentation. The feathered or plumed serpent column is found frequently at the entrance (Fig. 110). The base is formed of the head, with open mouth; the tongue, made of a separate piece of stone, extends two feet forward; the eye, of polished shell with pupil painted black, adds to the ferocious appearance of the monster. The shaft, which is short and heavy, represents the body with the feathers indicated in low relief. The capital is formed by the tail, the projecting top of which, now broken off, probably showed the rattle, for the rattlesnake served as the model; on the sides of the capital are carved figures which appear to be supporting the wooden painted lintels above. Originally these columns were painted in bright colors.

The feathered serpent formed one of the most common motifs in Mayan art. Seldom is it found used naturalistically, but it is highly simplified and conventionalized until it appears almost as a geometric pattern. Its sinuous form adapted itself to a generally rectangular shape, as on the base of the temple at *Xochicalco* (PL. 157 c). This was a settlement of the Toltec whose patron god was Quetzalcoatl. The decorative band of both the pyramidal platform and the temple is based upon the sinuous folds of great plumed serpents, between the coils of which are human figures and hieroglyphs, all standing out clearly against the colored ground.

Fig. 111. Mosaic Stone Patterns. Mitla. (Holmes)

Another kind of decoration was stone mosaic. The *Governor's Palace* at Uxmal (PL. 156 c) well illustrates the general effect. This long, rectangular flat-roofed building has a façade that is boldly designed and extremely decorative. Like the typical Mayan building it is made of rough concrete and is faced with finely cut, light gray limestone. A bold triple cornice divides the façade into two bands. Below is a plain stone facing; above, an elaborate design in relief the dominant motif of which is the fret against a lattice ground with an elaborate ornament over the doorway; a simple wave-line border finishes the composition. The design is not carved from the stone but is built up of stone mosaic in relief; that is, small pieces of stone were cut and fitted, each individual piece to its own place, and set in mortar, a process involving an enormous amount of patient labor. The ornament over the doorway consists of a human figure, life-size, seated in a niche with a curving base, surmounted by an enormous plumed headdress; from this central figure extend horizontal bars enclosing hieroglyphic inscriptions and terminating in conventionalized profile serpent heads.

Another example of stone mosaic worked out in geometric

motifs but interestingly varied we find at *Mitla* (PL. 156 B and FIG. 111). The sloping base is made of blocks that are unequal in size but finely cut and joined. Here for some inexplicable reason, mythological and naturalistic subjects and sculpture were entirely eliminated, and all the decoration, both exterior and interior, is purely geometric. The tough yet easily worked stone of this vicinity lent itself well to the technique. The small pieces of stone, at most a few inches in size, were carefully cut and finished on the face, which projected only about one and one-half inches, with the back left rough and deeply triangular in form so as to adhere more firmly to the mortar bedding. The long façade above the inclining lower courses of stone is broken into panels, each filled with this mosaic, with great variety of motif.

Another kind of ornament used very skillfully by the Maya was stucco, particularly at Palenque, where the native stone was usually too hard to work with stone tools. Commonly it was employed to smooth over stone that had been roughly dressed by pecking only. But it was also used plastically for decorating the sides of pyramidal bases, piers, and crests. When the relief was high, the rough wall was covered with plaster in which small stones were set to give a framework for the figure. Holes were sometimes cut in the foundation stone to give a firm hold for this stone skeleton. On this the plaster was molded; and the final coat of fine quality was polished and painted so that the surface was brilliant and shining. Typical of this work is a monumental relief from Palenque (PL. 157 A). In the center stands a figure in marvelous ceremonial costume and enormous plumed headdress, carrying a staff surmounted by the conventionalized serpent. The two seated figures reveal the power of draughtsmanship as seen in the foreshortening. They also strengthen by their seated position the importance of the central figure. The brilliant color of the relief was probably determined by symbolical as well as artistic criteria.

SCULPTURE

Sculptural decoration was applied to the so-called stelae and altars found at many sites. These stelae are rectangular monoliths up to twenty-six feet high elaborately carved with figures and inscriptions, and are thought to have a chronological significance. The altars, such as that at Quirigua (PL. 157 D), are low, massive forms, also monoliths. The *Great Dragon*,[4] as it

---

[4] Also called the *Great Turtle* because in general shape it resembles a gigantic turtle.

is called, is entirely covered with intricate carvings in both high and low relief. The most conspicuous part of the design on the north face is the seated human figure, dressed in rich garments and wearing an enormous elaborate headdress of serpent masks, plumes, scrolls, and symbols. A perfect serenity dwells in the figure, reminiscent of the expression of inward poise that is so characteristic of the oriental Buddha. It is seated in the mouth of a great dragon; the lower jaw forms the base, with the fangs showing on either side below the hands; the upper jaw with its fangs frames the figure and is covered at the top by the headdress; near its base are the two deeply cut eyes; on its carved surfaces are inscribed hieroglyphs. The placing of a human head or figure in the jaws of a reptile is quite common in Mayan art and undoubtedly has a symbolic meaning, possibly the endowing of the serpent with human intelligence, thus combining in the god the highest type of mind with any type of material body. The top of the altar (PL. 157 B) presents a magnificent piece of decorative design based upon a highly conventionalized form of the serpent. The virile lines that indicate the features stand out from the intricate decoration about them with a dominating power. What impresses one most here is the perfect harmony between content and design, that is, between the expression of life with its symbolic meaning, and the method of representation.

Some examples have been found of sculpture in the round, one of which, a head now in the Peabody Museum of Harvard University, is impregnated with a profound quiet and a spiritual intensity that is again suggestive of the concentrated spirituality of the oriental Buddhas.

PAINTING

Mural painting was an important form of decoration with the Maya. The stone surface was covered with a whitish plaster coating and highly polished, giving a fine even ground upon which the painter drew his figure in outline and then filled in with colors — red, blue, green, yellow, white, black, and purple — applying them sometimes to the wet plaster, that is, fresco technique, and sometimes dry. At *Mitla* (FIG. 112) we see figures of the gods drawn in red on a white ground and the background filled in with dark red and finished by a simple border. The draughtsmanship of the Mayan we can judge from a painted vase (FIG. 113) on which is represented a chief receiving a visit from an inferior. The former with an elaborate headdress, very much like that seen on the stucco relief from Palenque, is seated on a dais, bending toward the visitor with outstretched hand; the latter is kneeling and offering a pouch of copal; behind him stands an attendant. The interesting and surprising thing here is not only the quality of the line, so sure-handed and firm, but

Fig. 112. Frescoes. Mitla. (American Museum of Natural History)

particularly the skill shown in foreshortening, as seen in the figures of the two chiefs. Notice how closely the drawing of the eye approximates that of the Greek painter in the late archaic period (Fig. 64). In his sculpture as well as in his drawing

Fig. 113. Drawing from a Mayan Vase. (Joyce, *Mexican Archaeology*, G. P. Putnam's Sons)

the Mayan shows many affinities with the state of culture represented by this period of the Greek.

MINOR ARTS

The people of Middle America proved themselves able craftsmen in several fields, notably those of the goldsmith, lapidary, and potter. Gold mines furnished an abundance of metal which the goldsmith fashioned by molding, hammering, wax-process casting, and engraving into pendants, necklaces, anklets, and other ornaments that were used not only for personal adornment but as amulets to charm away evil spirits, for burial with the dead, and for sacrifices to the gods. They are fashioned after various forms — the butterfly, crocodile, toad, birds, lizards, monkeys, human figures. In all these objects, the form has been highly conventionalized. In general it is the pattern suggested

Fig. 114. Painting from a Mayan Vase Showing the Quetzal and Hieroglyphs. (Spinden)

by the form that is used rather than a naturalistic representation of it (Fig. 116).

The skill of the lapidary reveals itself in the mosaic work, an example of which we find in a large breast ornament, perhaps a ceremonial ornament of a priest, representing the double-headed serpent (Pl. 158 c). Upon a wood foundation the tesserae are fixed with gum. The coils are of turquoise and other stones; about the head are massed red and white shell; the holes for the eyes were probably filled with discs of glowing stone. The ornament shows a splendid vigorous design both in line and in massing of color. When we remember that these tesserae were cut and polished probably with stone implements only, we feel that the patience required to make such an ornament must have been infinite.

The Mayan potters made vessels of various shapes — plates, bowls, and vases. The decoration consisted of human (FIG. 113) and animal figures, birds, and the serpent drawn quite naturalistically, or, especially in the case of the serpent, highly conventionalized and superbly decorative. Geometric patterns and hieroglyphs are also frequent. Such a design as that illustrated in FIG. 114 shows the bold vigor and fitting character of Mayan

Fig. 115. Pottery of Central America. Yale University. *A* and *B*. Armadillo Ware. In *A* the armadillo is used as shoulder ornaments. In *B* the neck is decorated with alternating groups of armadillo tail and eye motifs. *C*. Lost-Color Ware. The handle is broken off. (MacCurdy, *Chiriquian Antiquities*, Yale University Press)

ceramic ornament. Farther south among the Chiriqui or Talamancans, several fabrics were produced which are particularly interesting. One of these is the *Armadillo* ware (FIG. 115), of vigorous bowl shape, with handles or tripod feet, and named from the fact that the armadillo furnished the chief decorative motif. Another ware, the *Lost-Color* (FIG. 115), is finely shaped and boldly decorated, and serves as an example of an interesting technique. The vase was shaped and then covered with a cream slip upon which the design was painted in wax; the whole vase was then covered with black paint and boiled; as the wax melted it carried off with it the paint from the parts it had covered, leaving the design in the cream ground color. The vigorous spirals that dominate the decoration appear to be derived from the alligator.

SUMMARY

"If art is great, in proportion as it reveals experiences of life, then this Mayan art is great art." It is the profound expression of a people who were overpowered by religious problems and practices, by the fundamental questions of man, nature, and God, and by the manifestation of these in ritual and gorgeous ceremony. At first sight it appears fantastic and weird; for the subject matter, types, costumes, and apparent symbolism all seem so strange and unintelligible. Yet in many of the examples there is an unmistakable expression of intense spirituality. Ceremonial and religious intensity kept the expression formal. Symbolism controlled the motifs of decoration and the use of color. Primitive conditions of life also limited technical accomplishment. But even with these restrictions we find the people of Middle America not only untiring workers and patient craftsmen but bold decorators and skilled draughtsmen. The design and construction of their buildings are bold and massive; the

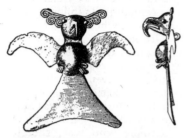

Fig. 116. Gold Ornament. Probably derived from the sacred parrot. The head is surmounted by a snake. (MacCurdy, *Chiriquian Antiquities*, Yale University Press)

carved and painted decoration, luxuriant, brilliant in color, and architecturally fitting. The minor arts too are vigorous in form and color and show the same sensitiveness to decorative design as the architecture.

B. SOUTH AMERICAN

In South America, both on the coast and on the highlands, there developed a series of cultures, the origin and the interrelation of which are not clear. South America, like Middle America, presents great contrasts of climate and geography. The narrow coastal plain is a hot desert, habitable only along the rivers that bring water from the mountains. Of the numerous settlements of this coastal strip, two stand out prominently — Nasca in the south and Chimu in the north. As air-dried brick furnished their building material, little is left of their architecture to judge. Pottery is the chief evidence of their culture. The highlands of the Andes contain two physical conditions of life —

the high, bleak regions, and the intermediate valleys where climatic conditions are less stern and more conducive to the development of a high state of culture. Both on the coast and in the highlands these cultures were developing in the early years of the Christian era. On the lofty mountains a climax was reached, from about 200 to 900 A.D., called Tiahuanacan because of the important remains at Tiahuanaco near Lake Titicaca in Bolivia. As Tiahuanaco declined, the Incas, a tribe who lived in the valley of Cuzco, gradually developed and established their culture, finally incorporating into their empire the coastal regions as well. This Inca empire was at a climax and was spreading its influence from Argentina and Chili to Colombia and Brazil, when it was conquered by the Spanish, about 1520 A.D.

Although the Inca is the best known of the South American civilizations, it probably does not illustrate the climax of culture attained. Its place is analogous to that of the Aztec; for, like the latter, it shows a warlike tribe conquering and taking over the older civilizations, but never itself attaining their artistic level. The Inca civilization was autocratic and theocratic. The sun-god was the chief divinity and was represented on earth by his son, the ruler, who was, therefore, absolute both politically and religiously.

ARCHITECTURE AND SCULPTURE

An abundance of fine hard stone is a basic fact in the architecture of the mountain peoples of South America. The simple massive gateway of Tiahuanaco is evidence of this. Its highly formal, austere decoration harmonizes with the general character of the gateway. Both suggest the bare massive mountains in which the city is located.

The best example of this kind of decorative carving is the *Greater Chavin Stone* [5] (FIG. 117). The first impression is of an elaborate conventional pattern consisting of a central vertical motif from which radiate diagonal lines terminating alternately in spirals and serpent heads, the whole forming a perfectly bilateral design. Closer study reveals the fact that at the base is a figure, in frontal view, short, and built on rectangular forms except for the arms and legs, which are slightly modeled; the features are so highly conventionalized that it is difficult to identify them; in each hand is held a bunch of staves. The panel above this figure is occupied by three grotesque, masklike faces with protruding decorated tongue and fangs. To see them it is

[5] A carved monolith found at Chavin, a town in central Peru.

necessary to reverse the illustration. The first and lasting impression of this carving is its severely formal character, its angularity, its intensely conventional and decorative quality, and its suggestion of an austere people. In this respect it contrasts sharply with the curving line and the rich luxuriousness of Mayan decorative art.

The highest attainment in building in South America — and it was a very high one — is found in the granite walls of the Inca city of Machu Picchu.[6] This city, with palaces, temples, fountains, baths, stairways, and terraces, was built upon the crest of a mountain that rose in a secluded and almost inaccessible mountain valley about sixty miles from Cuzco. The work shows not only great engineering ability but also astonishing skill in cutting the stone both for rectangular and for round buildings, and laying it without mortar in courses that gradually decrease in width as they rise, making a wall that is marvelous in its solidity, texture, and finely cut angles.

Fig. 117. Greater Chavin Stone. H. 6 ft. Museo Nacional, Lima.

MINOR ARTS

In three fields particularly, the South American people produced highly artistic work — in pottery, metal, and textiles. Geographic location appears to have had some influence upon these crafts as well as upon architectural decoration. Pure Inca art is conventional and largely geometric. Down on the coastal plains the pottery shows more freedom, naturalism, and a wealth of showy color (PL. 158 A). In the early ware made when these tribes were independent, there is a charming naturalism, especially in the drawing of the animal figures. Domination from the mountains, however, exercised a strong influence in the direction of formalism. The drawing is careless and free. The rich colors — white, yellow, black, violet, blue-gray and intermediate tones — stand out against a whitish ground, or a red, or a black. The bold decorative effect, together with the hasty but spontaneous

[6] For illustrations of Machu Picchu see Bingham, "In the Wonderland of Peru," in the *National Geographic Magazine*, April, 1913.

appearance of the painting, reminds one of the *Kamares* ware of Crete.

The finest textiles of South America show the highly formal character of the art of the mountain people in addition to the necessities imposed by the medium. Several processes were used — tapestry, pile knot like the Persian rugs, fancy weaves like those produced by a modern Jacquard loom, and embroidery. Both cotton and wool were used, the latter being obtained from the llama, alpaca, and vicuña. The tapestry weave is commonly found. Looms as well as the textiles themselves have been found in graves (Fig. 118). The colors are soft, largely red, brown, violet, blue, and green. Among the decorative motifs used are various geometric patterns and also conventionalized animals, birds, fish, and human figures (Pl. 158 d) often used symbolically. A reserved wealth of color harmony and fitting decorative motifs, combined with great technical skill, give a rare charm to these textiles.

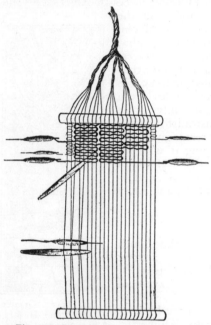

Fig. 118. Peruvian Loom. American Museum of Natural History, New York. (American Museum of Natural History)

The skill of the goldsmith is well illustrated by a gold water jar (Pl. 158 b) in which there is the same vigor and formality that we saw in the textiles. Two bands of geometric design form a most effective ornamentation. It is interesting to note how close in form this gold jar is to the pottery.

SUMMARY

The art of South America, like that of Middle America, was the expression of a theocratic people and was determined to a considerable extent by religious symbolism. The early Tiahuanacan culture of the loftiest mountain regions was especially austere in its formality and angularity, as if the very souls of the people were permeated by the rigor of the climate and the bare might of the mountains. The Incas who succeeded the Tiahuanacan, living in more tempered mountain valleys, retained something of this formality. They conventionalized into geometric patterns all the forms of nature and made use of subdued and harmonious color. Their skillful workmanship is especially evident in the superb masonry of their buildings and in their textiles. It was on the plains that naturalism and a luxuriant wealth of rich color manifested themselves, as we see in the pottery, the chief criterion of art expression, which is vivacious and startling in its decorative effect.

BIBLIOGRAPHY

BINGHAM, HIRAM, "In the Wonderland of Peru." *National Geographic Magazine*, XXIV (1913), pp. 387 ff.
—— ——, "Story of Machu Picchu." Op. Cit., XXVII (1915), pp. 172 ff.
—— ——, "Further Explorations in the Land of the Incas." Op. Cit., XXIX (1916), pp. 431 ff.
BRITISH MUSEUM, Pictorial postcards: Set LXV, Ancient Maya of Central America.
—— ——, Guide to the Maudslay Collection of Maya Sculptures. London, 1923.
HEWETT, E. L., "America's Archaeological Heritage." *Art and Archaeology*, IV (1916), pp. 257 ff.
HOLMES, W. H., Ancient Art of the Province of Chiriqui. Bureau of American Ethnology, Report VI. Washington, 1888.
—— ——, Archaeological Studies Among the Ancient Cities in Mexico. Field Columbian Museum, Anthropological Studies: I, Publications 8, 16. Chicago, 1895-97.
JOYCE, T. A., Central American and West Indian Archaeology. N.Y., Putnam, 1916.
—— ——, Mexican Archaeology. N.Y., Putnam, 1914.
—— ——, South American Archaeology. N.Y., Putnam, 1912.
LEHMANN, WALTER, Art of Old Peru. N.Y., Weyhe, 1924.
MacCURDY, G. G., Study of Chiriquian Antiquities. New Haven, Conn., Yale University Press, 1911.
MARKHAM, SIR CLEMENTS R., The Incas of Peru. N.Y., Dutton, 1910.
MEANS, P. A., Survey of Ancient Peruvian Art. New Haven, Conn., Yale University Press, 1917.
MORLEY, S. G., "Foremost Intellectual Achievement of Ancient America." *National Geographic Magazine*, Vol. XLI (1922), pp. 109 ff.
—— ——, "Chichen Itzá, an Ancient American Mecca." *National Geographic Magazine*, Vol. XLVII (1925), pp. 63 ff.
SPINDEN, H. J., Ancient Civilizations of Mexico and Central America. American Museum of Natural History, Handbook Series 3. N.Y., 1922.
—— ——, Study of Maya Art. Cambridge, Harvard University Press, 1913.

CHAPTER XXVII
INDIA

India[1] comprises a continent within itself, surrounded by water except on the northern boundaries, the only gateway for invaders until recent times. The country divides geographically into three distinct units: first, the mighty wall of the Himalayas, a barrier, and also the source of vital river systems, and the home of the gods; second, the northern river valleys, generally known as Hindustan, including the basins of the Ganges and the Indus, very fertile, densely populated, the home of the Aryan invaders and the seat of the strongest political powers; third, peninsular India, comprising the Deccan and the Tamil states in the extreme south, tropical tablelands south of the northern river basins and naturally separated from them by mountains and forests, and the home of the Dravidian races.

Among these divisions are great variety and extremes of climate, geography, and economic conditions, from tropical heat to perpetual snow and glaciers; from desert conditions to the heaviest rainfall in the world. Economically, greatest poverty stands opposed to greatest wealth — wealth still kept in the form of the family treasure, gold and jewels. The northern river basins have a wonderfully productive soil and the mountainous regions are rich in stone, woods, ivory, gold, and precious stones.

Likewise, among the people, numbering nearly three hundred million, there is great diversity of race, language, and custom. Politically India has always been divided into many minor principalities and only rarely in its long history has any considerable area been unified for more than a brief time.

Unity, however, is not lacking; that is, a deeper and more fundamental unity than that manifested in political coöperation, and in uniformity of dialect and custom. This is evident in the religious and cultural life of India — in the Brahman faith, the national sacred literature, the caste system, and the Hindu atti-

[1] This name is derived through the Greek and the Persian from the Sanskrit word *sindhu*, a river, referring preëminently to the Indus River. The name is not indigenous. The Hindus apparently have never evolved a title to include all India.

PLATE 159

(*A*) Buddhist Assembly Hall. Karle. c. I cent. B.C. (India Office)

(*B*) Temple of Vishnu. Khajuraho. L. 109 ft.; H. 116 ft. c. 1000 A.D. (India Office)

(*C*) Subrahmanya Temple. Dedicated to the Son of Shiva. Tanjore. c. 1000 A.D.

PLATE 160

(*A*) Hoysalesvara Temple. Halebid. Detail of the carving. Between 1117 and 1268 A.D. (W. E. Clark)

(*B*) Taj Mahall (Crown of Palaces). Agra. 1632-53 A.D. (W. E. Clark)

(*C*) Carved Marble Window. Ahmadabad. XV cent. A.D

PLATE 161

(*A*) Buddha. Of dolomite. Colossal size. V or VI cent. A.D. Anuradhapura, Ceylon.

(*B*) Gate at Sanchi. II cent. B.C. (India Office)

(*D*) Avalokiteshvara. Bronze. H. 3⅝ in. VII cent. A.D. Boston Museum. (Boston Museum)

(*C*) Shiva as Nataraja. Bronze. H. c. 4 ft. X–XII cent. A.D. Madras Museum. (*Ars Asiatica*)

PLATE 162

(*A*) Death of Hiranya-kasipu. c. VIII cent. A.D. Elura. (India Office)

(*B*) Buddha Expounding the Law to His Mother, Maya. Borobudur.

(*C*) Women at the Fountain. Borobudur. c. IX cent. A.D.

tude toward fundamental spiritual truths. For perhaps no people have felt so profoundly and pondered so deeply over the fundamental problems of life; and with no people have spirituality and spiritual significance taken precedence as they have in India.

About the time when the Kassites were moving from the tablelands of Asia in the vicinity of the Caspian Sea southwest into the Valley of the Two Rivers (c. 1700 B.C.), another Indo-European people, the nomad Aryans, from the same tablelands were slowly making their way southeast toward the valley of the Ganges.[2] But their coming was not uncontested; for in these lands lived the Dravidians, a dark-skinned people who appear already to have reached a highly developed state of civilization. These the Aryans drove to the highlands south of the Ganges. Then they settled down as as agricultural people. They had villages, knew the use of metal, had domesticated horses and chariots, and were organized into a tribal state with the family as the unit. They worshiped the powers of nature — the sun, the sky, and the rain — gradually personifying them as did the Greeks. This we see in their most ancient hymns, the Vedas, the title of which means knowledge, that is, sacred knowledge or lore. The ritual connected with the worship of these forces was first performed by the father as head of the family; but soon it became the prerogative of the priests called the Brahmans, who developed it into a system with elaborate rites and sacrifices, and infused into it philosophical ideas in the endeavor to explain the fundamental problems of existence. The poet-priests also gathered together the legends of their race into the great Aryan epic poems, the *Mahabharata* and the *Ramayana*, just as the Greek poets collected their national legends into the *Iliad* and the *Odyssey*. The *Ramayana* tells of the deeds of the prince Rama during his exile, brought about by court intrigue, and the recovery of his lost bride Sita.[3] The *Mahabharata*, like the *Iliad*, deals with a war between two clans, the Kurus and the Bharatas. But inserted, frequently at a later date than the first collecting of the legends, are such religious treatises as the *Bhagavad-Gita*, or the *Lord's Song*, which is probably the highest expression of the fundamental tenets of Hindu belief. The knowledge of a few of these is necessary for an understanding of Indian art. The first is that every deed in this life plays its part in determining the next life; for, second, individual souls pass at death from one body

---

[2] For these great movements and the relationships existing among them, see Breasted, *Ancient Times*, FIG. 112.
[3] For the story of the *Ramayana* and the *Mahabharata* see Macdonald, *Iliad of the East;* and Nivedita and Coomaraswamy, *Myths of the Hindus and Buddhists.*

to another (the doctrine known as the transmigration of souls). Good deeds reward the soul by reincarnating it in a higher form of life; evil deeds bring it into a lower, so that existence is one continuous succession of rebirths, the goal of which is Nirvana, that is, freedom from existence by absorption into Brahma, the ultimate, the only reality. The conception of this one universal reality the writer of the *Bhagavad-Gita* expresses when he says:

There is naught higher than I, O Wealth-Winner; all this universe is strung upon Me, as rows of gems upon a thread.

I am the taste in water, O son of Kunti; I am the light in moon and sun, the *Om* in all the Vedas, sound in the ether, manhood in men.

The pure scent in earth am I, and the light in fire; the life in all born beings am I, and the mortification of them that mortify the flesh.

Know Me to be the ancient Seed of all born beings, O son of Pritha; I am the understanding of them that understand, the splendor of the splendid.

The might of the mighty am I, void of love and passion; I am the desire in born beings which the Law bars not, O Bharata-prince.[4]

The young Prince Siddhartha (died c. 543? B.C.), brought up in this traditional Brahman faith, looking about him, became much impressed with the suffering that he saw everywhere. To attain Nirvana one must pass through an almost endless succession of reincarnations, each with its own suffering. So he put himself to the problem of seeking relief from it. Leaving his family and his luxurious surroundings, he gave himself up to the life of an ascetic and through meditation obtained the knowledge that enabled him to bring a means of salvation to his people. Hence he became a Buddha,[5] that is, an enlightened one. Gautama's solution was to recognize that the individual was an illusion only and that suffering was due to self-interest, that is to the assertion of the interests of the individual rather than to the submersion of the individual in the larger universal life that embraces all nature in its fellowship and is the only reality. The means of escape from the fetters of the individual into this supreme universal life lay, not in the elaborate sacrifices prescribed by the Brahman priests, but partly in meditation, in order to bring the soul through retirement and concentration into union with the divine; and partly through moral actions done in a spirit of complete selflessness. This is the path that leads to the conquest of self, to peace of mind, to wisdom, and to release from bondage.

---

[4] *Bhagavad-Gita* (tr. Barnett), p. 119.

[5] Gautama Buddha, the only historical one of the seven Buddhas of the Hindu faith. He is sometimes spoken of as Gautama, his family name, or as Shakyamuni, the monk of the Shakyas, the clan to which his family belonged. For an account of Buddha and Buddhism, see Coomaraswamy, *Buddha and the Gospel of Buddhism*.

Buddhism spread rapidly; and when the great Asoka (273–232 B.C.) came to the throne, he made it the state religion, organized councils to gather together the sacred literature and to decide upon points of creed, and sent out missionaries to propagate the faith. Buddhism was not the foe of Brahmanism, for it did not run counter to the tradition of the older faith, but was rather a heresy existing alongside the latter, and was finally absorbed by it, about the eighth century A.D. Through missionaries and colonists, however, it had penetrated Ceylon, Java, China, and Japan, and there became a dominant factor of civilization and a mighty stimulus to the creation of great art.

Of the large number of gods worshiped by the Brahmans in their desire to win salvation from continual rebirth, the fundamental trinity consisted of Brahma the creator, Vishnu the sustainer, and Shiva the destroyer; but it was about the worship of the last two as manifestations of the supreme God that the two great Hindu sects gathered. This religious faith, which permeated every act of life, was so vital an element in Indian culture that it is impossible to think of the Hindu apart from it. With him life was a complete synthesis of its religious, social, and economic aspects.

One element in particular in Hindu society needs mention, the caste system, which has been described as "a group of families united by peculiar rules for the observance of ceremonial purity, especially in matters of diet and marriage." Thus the Hindus are divided into more than twenty-five hundred social groups, admission to which comes by birth. Change from one to another is practically impossible, and violation of caste rules results in expulsion from the caste, which means social ruin as well as serious hardship. This system is of great antiquity, and evolved out of natural conditions. To the Hindu mind it is a part of the natural order of things; and while it militates against unity, social, political, or religious, stimulates class pride, and restricts individual liberty in many ways, still it has steadied and deepened the strong race feeling that is so characteristic of India. Under such a system, tradition and the sacrifice of the individual to the good of the larger social unit are fostered much more effectively than among the more cosmopolitan and more individualized nations of the West. Hence we may expect to find tenacity of conventions in the art of such a nation, and an expression that is racial rather than personal.

While this national evolution was taking place within the life of India, foreign influences from the West were strong enough to assert themselves; for the Greeks under Alexander had penetrated to northwest India and later the Sassanian-Persians. Evidences of these influences are somewhat apparent in Indian art; but in 320 A.D. a native dynasty was restored and this, the Gupta period, together with the reign of Harsha, forms the golden age of Hindu culture (320–647 A.D.). A Chinese pilgrim writing of his travels in India in the fifth century, describes the rich and prosperous condition of the country. He tells of charitable institutions and hospitals, institutions of learning, great monasteries, rich palaces with carved and painted ornamentation; of a mild, adequate government, and religious toleration. Fine buildings were erected, only to be destroyed later by the Mohammedans; sculpture and painting reached a climax of attainment as did music, science, and Sanskrit literature. For this was the period of the most famous poets, of whom Kalidasa was the greatest. Europe just at this time (FIG. 132) was being plunged into chaos by the fall of the Roman empire and the inroads of the barbarians; and although the Byzantine empire was flourishing under Justinian at Constantinople, still India at this time in the sum total of her broad culture was the most enlightened nation in the world.

Upon the decline of the Gupta and Harsha empires the Tartar invaders from central Asia who had penetrated to the northern plains of India succeeded to the power under the name of Rajputs, while native dynasties ruled in the south.

About the year 1000 A.D. the Mohammedans were pushing eastward into India. By 1526 they had overrun most of the country, and had established the great Mogul empire, which was the ruling power over large areas until the coming of the English and the French in the eighteenth century and the establishment of the English rule in 1818.

ARCHITECTURE

Of the early cities of India of which we read in Hindu literature, nothing is left. The earliest structure that has survived is the Buddhist *stupa*, a mound of solid brick or stone to mark some sacred place or to hold some relic. Most representative is the great *Sanchi Stupa* (FIG. 119). It is hemispherical, with a flattened top, and rests upon a high circular terrace; a massive balustrade surrounds the dome, the usual method in India of protecting a sacred place; at the four cardinal points are ornamental gateways, lavishly carved (PL. 161 B). Originally a

balustrade surrounded the terrace, which served to guide the
pilgrims in their procession, or circumambulation, about the
shrine, an early practice common in Hindu religious ceremony.
A double stairway with balustrades afforded an entrance to the
terrace. On the flattened top of the dome was another balustrade
surrounding the reliquary, which was surmounted by an umbrella, the symbol of royalty. Both the balustrades and the
gateways appear from the construction to be stone copies of
wooden rail fences and gates. They are, in fact, the work of the
carpenter executed in stone. This gives us a clue to why earlier
examples of architecture have not survived: they were of wooden

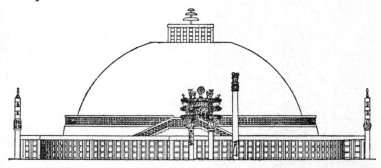

Fig. 119. Sanchi Stupa, Restored. D. 121 ft. III cent. B.C. (Archaeological Survey
of India)

construction and could not withstand the destructive climate
of India.

Another important type of Buddhist building was the assembly
hall [6] for congregational worship. Probably many of these halls
were of wooden construction; those that are now extant are
rock-cut, that is, hollowed out from the side of a cliff. Rock-cut
churches, monasteries, and temples were popular in India, as
they afforded excellent shelter both from the heavy rain and
from the glaring heat. Though chiseled from the solid rock, they
imitated the form of the wood or masonry structures. Such a
hall we find in *Karle* (PL. 159 A). The hall consists of a nave with
a semicircular end, and with aisles from which it is separated
by a row of columns; at the circular end within the nave stands
the shrine in the form of a *stupa*, which was the symbol of the
faith in the early days of Buddhism before statues of Buddha

---

[6] Sometimes called a *chaitya hall*, that is, a temple or hall containing a *chaitya*, a monument,
which in the early Buddhist churches took the form of a *stupa* (PL. 159A).

were made. The roof is in the form of a great barrel vault with ribs which reproduce the bamboo construction of its prototype. Originally there were fresco mural decorations and painted banners hung from the roof. One large leaf-shaped window was placed above the entrance in such a way that the light fell directly upon the *stupa* and brought out the rich colors of the decorations before it was lost in the dim shadows of the high vaulting.

Fig. 120. Sanchi Stupa. Pier of the east gate. (Grünwedel)

In the decoration of these early Buddhist structures we discern a native characteristic of Indian ornament — exuberance. The gates at *Sanchi* are typical (PL. 161 B). Rectangular piers covered with reliefs are surmounted by four elephants from whose backs rise the uprights that hold three slightly curving bars, graduated in length and width as they rise, and terminating in vigorous spirals that by contrast bring out the richness of the carving and also turn the eye inward. Animals, winged griffin, and human figures in the round fill the spaces between the bars, which, like the supports, are entirely covered with reliefs. On one of the piers (FIG. 120) the lotus [7] is the motif of decoration. Here the design is held effectively by the central panel of repeated discs formed from the conventionalized section of the lotus, with the space about them filled with the buds, fruit, or flowers; the outer borders contain a waving stem from which issue lotus leaves, flowers, buds, and fruit arranged naturalistically and filling the space, but with practically no overlapping. The carving is kept low and flat, and forms a rich and effective panel of decoration.

[7] The lotus was the favorite flower of India and was used symbolically. Growing up out of the mud, undefiled it blossoms in the pure light of the sun. Just so the human spirit growing out of the material conditions of life finds liberation in Nirvana. The open lotus with down-turned petals, so frequently found in domes, capitals, and the pedestals of the statues of Buddha, suggested the vault of heaven. The section of the fruit, which is the shape of a wheel, symbolized the universality of Buddha's law.

The Brahmanical temples, dedicated to the worship of Vishnu and Shiva chiefly, were not intended for congregational worship as were the Buddhist assembly halls. In India, as in Egypt and Greece, the people lived and worshiped chiefly out of doors. Only the priest entered the shrine. Hence all that was necessary was a room to hold the statue and a small portico for the guardian. For this reason also the decoration, which was didactic as well as ornamental, was placed on the exterior rather than on the interior. But the Hindu temple served a much wider purpose than that of a shrine. For here the king gave audience, the village assembly met, religious and philosophical discussions took place, as well as the recitation of the great epics, songs, and dances. Hence many temples had one or more assembly halls called *mandapams*, roofed over but open on the sides.

Fig. 121. *A*. Section of a Typical Brahmanical Temple. (Archaeological Survey of India)

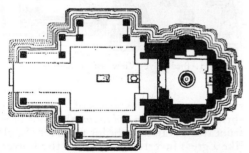

Fig. 121. *B*. Plan of a Typical Brahmanical Temple. (Archaeological Survey of India)

Of these Brahmanical temples there are three important classes: the Vaishnava temples, dedicated to Vishnu, found chiefly in the north, where this sect was strongest; the Shaiva, dedicated to Shiva, located chiefly in the south; and a group in the Deccan, sometimes called the Chalukyan,[8] that combines features of the other two, implying a use by more

---

[8] So called because they are found in the district ruled by the Chalukya dynasty; they are also called Hoysala, because some of the finest were built by the kings of the Hoysala dynasty.

than one sect. In fact, all these temples reflect religious movements and though dedicated to one god do not preclude a change
to the worship of another.

A typical Vaishnava temple (FIG. 121) shows that the essential
parts are the shrine and the assembly hall, or *mandapam*, which
takes the place of the simple portico when the temple consists
of a shrine only. The walls and roofs are thick and massive, and
sometimes contain a hollow chamber to protect from the heat;
the cornices are deep and hollow for the same reason, and awnings
frequently are added to shield from the glare and the dust. The

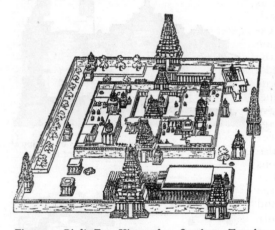

shrine is square
and is covered by
a high tower, the
shikara, with curv-
ing ribs the origin
of which is the
bamboo frame-
work of the primi-
tive shrine from
which the stone
building was de-
veloped; it is
crowned by a flat
round member,
derived in shape
from the fruit of
the blue lotus, sur-

Fig. 122. Bird's-Eye View of a Southern Temple.
(Fergusson)

mounted by a vase;
the lower courses
of the tower are

richly carved, with statues of gods and goddesses. In front of the
shrine stands the *mandapam*, the roof of which is built up into a
truncated pyramid in order to cover the elaborate ceiling, which,
like a great inverted blue lotus, the flower of Vishnu, symbolizes
the dome of the world. On the *mandapams* the Hindu builders
lavished their decorative skill. Some were made of white marble,
with every inch of the surface of the ceiling and the supporting
columns carved in all kinds of ornament — figure work as well as
floral and geometric design — so that the effect was one of lavish
richness.

An elaboration of this type of temple is found at *Khajuraho*
(PL. 159 B). Here the temple is built upon a raised platform.
The rather plain base unifies all the parts of the building; the

roofs, so rich and complex, culminate in the lofty tower over the shrine. The tower itself has become complex by the addition of smaller towerlike members which encircle the base, fill the angles, and with their varying height carry the eye upward rhythmically.

In the second class of Hindu temple, the southern, the shrine is enclosed in an immense walled quadrangle (FIG. 122) and surrounded by minor temples, bathing pools, halls, and cloisters, so that frequently the shrine itself appears small and out of proportion, especially beside the great towering gateways, called *gopurams*, by which one enters the enclosure. The shrine differs from the northern type in that its tower is built up by horizontal stories and surmounted either by a barrel roof or by a small stupalike dome, as we see in a temple at *Tanjore* (PL. 159 c) which is splendidly designed though profusely ornamented.

Elaborate decoration showing exuberance and no restraint characterizes the southern temples. On the great gateways monsters, many-armed gods, animals, floral and geometric ornament, all crowded together, overload the architecture to its very summit.

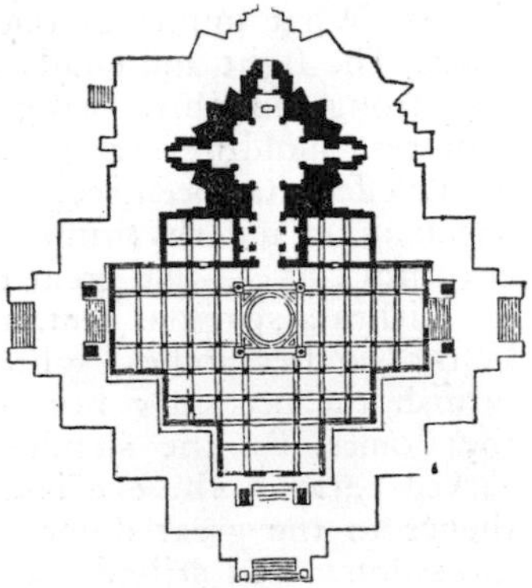

The third type of Hindu temple is like the northern in plan except that it has become star-shaped (FIG. 123), so that it pre-

Fig. 123. Plan of a Chalukyan Temple. (Fergusson)

sents a varied and picturesque outline from whatever point it is viewed. Like the southern temple, however, it is built horizontally and roofed with low towers. The decoration is very profuse, as at *Halebid* (PL. 160 A), where the horizontal zones are deeply undercut and carved with elephants, grotesques, mounted horsemen, gods, and human figures, worked in relief so high that they are almost in the round. Occasionally a band of floral or geometric ornament adds variety.

When the Mohammedans had established their empire in India, their wealthy rulers, the great Mughals, or Moguls, erected magnificent tombs and mosques, palaces and audience halls. These Moslems had brought with them certain traditions from the West, such as that of the dome over the tomb, the great pointed arch, the minaret, and other features of the typical mosque. In India as in other lands, we see the Moslem plastic, and ready to adopt whatever features he finds in his conquests. So it is the fusion of his own tradition with the native Hindu that produces the buildings of the Mughal period.

The highest embodiment of Mughal architecture is the *Taj Mahall* (PL. 160 B), the "Crown of palaces," the tomb built by Shah Jehan, one of the great Moguls, for his beautiful and gifted young wife, Mumtaz-i-Mahall, a name that means "exalted of the palace," from which the name of the building is derived. The main structure is square and is covered by one large and four smaller domes. It stands upon a platform at the corners of which rise four minarets terminating in domes similar in design to those of the main building. It is set in the midst of a rich tropical garden. What impresses one most is its exquisite delicacy and grace. The light and shade play softly about it, with contrasts just strong enough to bring out the main features of the design. Cornices, moldings, and carvings have been suppressed. The whole effect has been secured through beauty of proportion, the harmonious and rhythmic massing of parts, and the sweep of beautiful curves. The great central arch, finely proportioned and set within a spacious rectangle, is a dominating motif repeated in the smaller arches, which are arranged in two stories and furnish the necessary horizontal lines to form a firm base for the domes. By the slender minaret-like pinnacles above the carved parapet, the eye is carried to the four small domes and thence to the great dome, which unifies the design. It is the lotus dome, not stilted like the Mohammedan domes in Cairo (PL. 66 c) but contracted at the base. It springs with an exquisitely beautiful curve from a row of conventionalized lotus petals and terminates in an inverted lotus. The minarets, standing like sentinels, play so integral a part in the ensemble, in their design, proportion, height, and spacing, that without them the balance of the composition is vitally marred.

Looking at the building more closely, we see that the spandrels of the arches are inlaid with delicate floral designs worked out with precious stones — agate, bloodstone, and jasper; inlaid inscriptions border the frames of the arches; the platform and wall spaces at the back of the arches are paneled and delicately sculptured in low relief with geometric or floral motifs. All this decoration, of such exquisite taste, is kept entirely subordinate to the design of the tomb but enhances it with its inconspicuous richness.

In the interior, which is as exquisitely wrought as the exterior, a subdued light filters through delicately carved marble windows. Beneath the great dome are the cenotaphs of Mumtaz-i-Mahall and Shah Jehan, surrounded by a screen of marble which has been carved into a lacelike design and bordered with floral inlays. Fine material and expert craftsmanship are evident everywhere. While Shah Jehan and the other great Mughals were not strict Mohammedans, for they had been in India long enough to adopt much of Hindu thought and the Hindu point of view, still the aversion to representing the human figure in sculpture was deeply ingrained in their traditions. One feels that Shah Jehan, instead of representing his queen by sculpture or by painting, erected this building as a symbol of her beauty and of his passionate love.

An important element of decoration in the Mohammedan buildings was the marble screen or window, made by carving the slab of marble until it was entirely perforated by a delicate tracery, sometimes with geometric, sometimes with naturalistic motifs. Such a window from *Ahmadabad* (PL. 160 c) illustrates the patient, skillful craftsmanship of these carvers.

SCULPTURE

In the early days of Buddhism, Buddha was not represented in sculpture but was referred to by symbol, as by the *stupa*, or by stories of his former incarnations when he was a bird or an elephant,[9] as in the reliefs on the *Sanchi Gates* (PL. 161 B). It was not for several hundred years after his death that statues of Buddha began to be made.[10] He was frequently represented as the Yogi, that is, the ascetic who devoted himself to meditation. Through this practice he turned his mind and sense organs from outward things and directed them inward, thus bringing reality into closer relationship with the soul and acquiring that knowledge and enlightenment that would enable him to attain salvation. Such is the pose of the *Buddha* in PL. 161 A. He is seated with legs crossed, hands folded easily in his lap and eyes downcast. He is not asleep, for the body is too erect for that. We feel the perfect poise and self-control through the complete

---

[9] Known as the *Jataka Tales*. For these stories see Francis and Thomas, *Jataka Tales;* and Burlingame, *Buddhist Fables*.

[10] Due partly to the influence of Greece that had penetrated to northwestern India through the conquests of Alexander the Great and had strongly influenced the sculptors of Gandhara, who combined the Indian conception with the Greek method of expression. The result is interesting historically, for it penetrated to China also. But it is curiously exotic and typical neither of Greece nor of India. The attributes of Buddha, in the sculpture of India, China, and Japan, are the protuberance of wisdom on the top of the head; the split and elongated ear lobes; and the mark on the forehead, often a jewel, that symbolizes the third eye of spiritual vision.

withdrawal of the self inward. The figure is not entirely nude; a thin drapery falls from the left shoulder, indicated by the diagonal line across the breast. There are no individual lines in the face; the whole body is expressed with the highest simplification of modeling; with great sweeping lines the sculptor has indicated the easy erectness of the backbone, the articulation of the head and arms with the body, and the relaxed wrists. The Indian artists carefully studied the human figure, worked out canons of proportions for drawing and carving it, and at times modeled with precise detail. Hence such simplification, which eliminates details and suppresses any desire merely to imitate nature, is intentional, and reveals a point of view that one must comprehend if he is to understand oriental art. Here the aim has not been to tell us what the Buddha looked like physically, but to make us realize the spiritual realm to which he attained, so that the statue becomes an abstract expression of a state of perfect control and perfect quiet. "As a lamp in a windless spot flickers not, such is the likeness that is told of the strict-minded man . . . when the mind, held in check, comes to stillness . . . and when he knows the boundless happiness that lies beyond sense-instruments and is grasped by understanding, and in steadfastness swerves not from Verity, than which, once gotten, he deems no other boon better . . ."[11] This stillness is not the negation of power, but the acquisition of the greatest spiritual values.

This *Buddha*, with its lofty conception and monumental grandeur of expression, brings us as near as we can come to pure Hindu primitives. As sculpture developed toward a climax in the classic age (IV–VIII centuries A.D.), it became more dramatic, and more tender and suave, though it did not lose its power of expressing, primarily, spiritual truths. This we see in the reliefs of *Elephanta* and *Elura*. The cave-temples of India were decorated with sculptured reliefs representing the various gods and scenes from sacred lore, such as the great series mentioned. One of these (PL. 162 A) represents the moment when the god in the form of a man-lion appeared to King Hiranyakasipu, who had sneeringly denied him.[12] Here the sculptor has expressed with convincing power that dramatic moment when the king, still derisive, is recoiling before the sudden apparition. Battered though the relief is, it reveals powerfully the might of an angry god who is destined to vanquish the king. Furthermore, the largeness of design and the suppression of irrelevant matter

[11] *Bhagavad-Gita*, (tr. Barnett) p. 114.
[12] This legend forms the basis of the ballad called "Prehlad," in Toru Dutt, *Ancient Ballads and Legends of Hindustan.*

intensify the feeling. Of these reliefs which decorate the rock-cut temples it has well been said, that all these images, without hesitation, awkwardness, or any superfluous statement, perfectly express by their action the passion that animates them.

A small bronze statuette of *Avalokiteshvara* (PL. 161 D) is equally expressive. This Bodhisattva [13] is seated in an easy pose, the weight borne by the left arm, and the right hand, supported by the raised leg, held in the traditional gesture of teaching. The shoulders are broad and strong, the waist narrow, the limbs rounded and skin smooth; on the head is the protuberance of wisdom, here covered with a crown, and the ears are elongated. All these are traditional characteristics. Convention, however, has not hindered the sculptor from making his figure expressive of the serenity, the youthfulness, the physical and spiritual power that is characteristic of representations of Buddha and the Bodhisattva and particularly of the infinite compassion of this gracious god.

A statue that illustrates Brahmanical symbolism is *Shiva as Nataraja*, that is, as *Lord of the Dance* (PL. 161 C). Shiva is poised with one foot upon a dwarf. He has four arms. In one hand is a drum; in another, fire. A ring of fire (broken off in our illustration) rising from the lotus pedestal surrounds the figure, touching it at the hands with the drum and the fire. The meaning is that when Shiva dances with the drum and fire, he awakens the powers of nature to the dance, that is, to life. But in turn he destroys these powers with fire and they return to rest. The movement of the dance symbolizes the rhythmic energy of the cosmos. Its purpose is perpetual creation and then destruction, but a destruction that is change, not annihilation, and results in the release or salvation of soul.[14] In the movement of this dance, as in the *Buddha*, we see that an orderly rhythm controls every part of the body. The figure is poised upon one foot, in the ankle of which is concentrated firm strength. The other limb moves with incomparable ease and grace, and the whole body is under the control of the animating impulse.

Bronze as well as stone, we have seen, was used by the Hindu sculptors. In fact they were such expert bronze casters by the *cire-perdue* process that some of their casting cannot be equaled by the best modern methods.

[13] A Bodhisattva is a being who is destined at some time to become a Buddha; even at present he is an active force for salvation and his worship is the center of a cult. Avalokiteshvara, "the Lord who looketh down in great compassion," is one of the most important Bodhisattvas not only in India but, under a different form, in China and Japan also.

[14] For a detailed description of the statue and of its symbolism, see Coomaraswamy, *Dance of Siva*.

Let us look at two examples of Indian sculpture outside the boundary of India. We have noted that the Buddhist colonists carried their art to Java, where it manifested itself in its highest form at *Borobudur*. This shrine was an elaborated *stupa*, with five procession paths along which were sculptured in low relief the stories of the Buddhist faith for the instruction and stimulation of the pilgrims, just as the early Christian churches were decorated with carving, mosaics, and frescoes representing the life of Christ and the saints. In PL. 162 c we see a group of Javanese women coming to the fountain near the temple for water; at the left, they are moving away with filled jars; one is pulling hers up from the water covered with lotus; on the other side another group is approaching, while at the extreme right one has put her jar down and sits motionless drinking in the words of the master, who with uplifted hand is bringing her his message. The scene is appealing in its naturalism. Out of the rather coarse native stone, the sculptor has carved this everyday scene with an ease and truthfulness in the pose of the individual figures and also in the arrangement of them into groups. To be sure, the work is done in a summary fashion with but little individual expression; everything is generalized, with only slight attention to detail. There is a disregard of proportion between the women and the temple and trees that shade the fountain. That is not because the sculptor did not realize the discrepancy, but because to carve it as he did not only served his narrative purpose but also helped the decorative effect. For rich decoration as well as convincing narrative seemed to be the purpose of these carvers (PL. 162 B.)

Another great example of Indian art, both architecture and sculpture, outside India is the work of the Khmer people in Cambodia. This race, originating in Indo-China, had settled in Cambodia, whither came Hindu colonists who became the ruling class and developed a high type of civilization from the ninth to the thirteenth century, when they appear to have been annihilated by some other race. In the jungles of tropical Cambodia they built their capital city, Angkor, with marvelous temples and palaces. A fine native limestone served their purpose both for building, being cut and laid with great precision, and for carving the low reliefs that decorate the walls. In PL. 163 A we see a detail from the palace where are represented from the old Hindu legends of the *Mahabharata* the battles between the Kurus and the Bharatas. The relief is very low, in that respect unlike the work at *Borobudur*, and also more archaic in its drawing. But how one feels "the cadenced sound of marching troops," the slower movement of the great elephant, and the eagerness of the mounted riders! They are marching through the jungle, the lacelike quality of the foliage forming a delicate background that makes more vivid the movement and rhythm of the army. The whole design is kept flat and the ultimate effect is that of an exquisite decorative pattern, like a musical composition in which the cellos weave a deep-toned melody through the more delicate tones of the wind instruments.

PAINTING

Indian painting falls into three general groups — Buddhist, Rajput, and Mughal; and according to this classification we shall study it. As in many lands, so in India, painting because of its perishable nature has not preserved its beginnings. When we first meet it in the *Ajanta Frescoes* (third or second century B.C. to seventh century A.D.) the craft is already highly developed. The Ajanta caves are Buddhist cave-temples that formed a monastic retreat in a far-away lonely ravine in central India. Here the painter-priests covered the walls with stories of the Buddhist faith, just as the sculptor-priests at *Borobudur* carved the walls of their procession path with the same tales. These they pictured, as was natural, in terms of the everyday life with which they were familiar, just as the fifteenth century Florentine painters used the men and women, costumes, and setting of Florence for their Biblical stories.

Most popular among Buddhist stories are the *Jataka Tales* that we have already seen carved on the *Sanchi Gates* (PL. 161 B). PL. 163 B illustrates a scene from the tale of the *Golden Geese*.[15] The fowlers, at the order of the king, are seeking the golden geese of which the queen dreamed and are capturing the goose-king himself, who is the Buddha in a former life. After the goose-king was taken before the king and talked to him he was released to return to his mountain home, as another fresco in the same cave shows. In these frescoes the dramatic element is expressed with great spontaneity and lucidity. The love and understanding of nature are profound, based upon that intimate kinship with all animate life that is so vital a part of the Buddhist faith. In the human figures there is ease and grace at times languorous, very expressive hands with long slender fingers in which so much of the expression is concentrated. These are

[15] For this tale see Brown, *Indian Painting*, p. 67.

aristocratic beings, noble, dignified, and filled with deep emotion. As in the *Elura* sculptures (PL. 162 A) the figures express perfectly the passion that dominates them. In largeness of design, rhythmic sweep of line, and monumentality these paintings are closely akin to the *Elura* reliefs, revealing the ability of the artists to express only the significant and essential. These characteristics remind us of what the great Greek paintings, which we saw reflected in the Greek vases, must have been. The subject matter may be very different, but the means of expression and the way of looking at things are much the same in the disregard for an illusion of nature; in the large, generalized aspect of form, feeling, or situation, with the suppression of detail; in the flat silhouette use of the figure, based upon line and used with a high regard for its decorative possibilities; and also in the capacity to express in their entirety spiritual values that are universal in their appeal (compare PLs. 49 B and 163 C).

One easily discerns that this painting is based upon the use of line with a negligible use of chiaroscuro. How much the Indian painter could express by this one means alone, we can see frequently at Ajanta. The figure of a woman seated with her back to the spectator (PL. 163 C), for example, is drawn with the greatest skill. One feels convincingly the mass of the figure, the firmness of the left wrist as it supports the weight of the body, and the supple ease and exquisite grace of the right hand. The expression of so much with a minimum of means must have been the result of long generations of training, and required the skill of a very great master. These paintings, we have said, were frescoes; the technique is essentially that used in Italy, except that the surface was smoothed and polished until it acquired a marblelike finish. When we remember that the fresco technique requires rapid, accurate workmanship, we realize all the more the supreme technical skill in the use of line attained by these painters.

The *Ajanta Frescoes* are almost exclusively Buddhist and carry us to about the middle of the seventh century A.D. From then on for about a thousand years, no paintings have survived to us, though traces of the continuity of the tradition are being found in recent discoveries in Turkestan and Tibet, where the art was practiced as it spread along the great highways toward China in the early centuries of the Christian era. It is not until c. 1550 A.D. that we again find examples of Indian painting. In the meantime important events had taken place. Buddhism had been absorbed by Brahmanism and the cults of Vishnu and

PLATE 163

(*A*) Angkor-Wat. Cambodia. Detail of the carving. XII cent. A.D. (Giraudon)

(*B*) Jataka Tale: Scene from the Golden Goose. VII cent. A.D. Ajanta Caves. (India Society)

(*C*) Seated Girl. VII cent. A.D. Ajanta Caves. (India Society)

PLATE 164

(*A*) Krishna Quelling the Serpent Kaliya. Rajput. XVIII cent. A.D.
Coomaraswamy Coll., Boston. (A. K. Coomaraswamy)

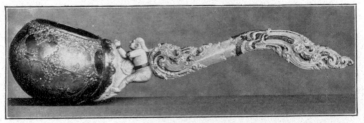

(*B*) Ceremonial Dipper. Silver and ivory. L. 18 in. Victoria and Albert
Museum, London. (Victoria and Albert Museum)

(*C*) Necklace Pendant. Coomaraswamy Coll., Boston. (A.
K. Coomaraswamy)

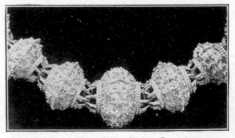

(*D*) Detail of a Silver Girdle Chain. Coomaraswamy
Coll., Boston. (A. K. Coomaraswamy)

PLATE 165

(*A*) Nut Slicer. Brass, inlaid with silver. L. 8½ in. Coomaraswamy Coll., Boston. (A. K. Coomaraswamy)

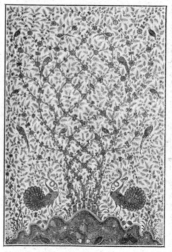

(*B*) Embroidered Muslin.

(*C*) Palampore. XVIII cent. A.D. Victoria and Albert Museum, London. (Victoria and Albert Museum)

(*D*) Cashmere Textile. Detail. Metropolitan Museum, New York. (Metropolitan Museum)

PLATE 166

(*A*) Temple of Heaven. Peking. XVIII cent. A.D.

(*B*) Maitreya. Limestone, originally painted. H. 6½ ft. Northern Wei dynasty, early V cent. A.D. Boston Museum. (Boston Museum)

(*C*) Kuan Yin. Limestone, originally painted and gilded. H. 8 ft. Late VI or early VII cent. A.D. Boston Museum. (Boston Museum)

Shiva had been developing. The Mohammedans had conquered large parts of the country and established the Mogul Empire, bringing with them strong influences of the art of the West. The paintings fall into the two classes mentioned above, Rajput and Mughal. The Rajput, so called because it was practiced chiefly in the Rajput domain, particularly in the Himalaya valleys beyond the reach of the Mohammedan power, was a purely indigenous art and appears to continue the traditions of the *Ajanta Frescoes*. In it, however, we find a wider expression of Indian life, for there we see pictures of everyday life, stories from the heroic days of the *Mahabharata* and *Ramayana*, and illustrations from the lives of the gods, particularly Vishnu. Another difference between these paintings and those at Ajanta is that they are small, though their largeness of design may well suggest lineal descent from the great Buddhist frescoes. *Krishna Quelling Kaliya*, a poisonous serpent (PL. 164 A), is a typical example. Krishna, one of the numerous incarnations of Vishnu, stands holding the body of the serpent easily, through his god-like power, pressing upon it with his foot; on each side are grouped the wives of the serpent, half human, half reptile, tenderly grieving for him and pleading with Krishna to spare him; on the bank Krishna's family and the cowherds are frantically rushing to the edge of the pool; in the background the herds are peacefully grazing. To appreciate the beauty of this painting one needs the color particularly, for the sheet presents a brilliant, glowing color harmony.[16] The massing of the parts into a rhythmic design is clear everywhere, particularly in the Krishna group. The god himself framed by the serpent forms the center of interest, with the wives arranged in balanced grouping on either side, each expressing by pose and gesture her tender love or earnest pleading. At the same time each figure, especially the long sweeping curve of the reptilian form, plays its part in the beautiful composition of rhythmic mass and line, which is enhanced by the conventionalized waves of the pool which serve as a background for the design.[17]

The third group, the Mogul or Mughal, is less Indian than the others. When the Mongols came to India, they brought with them painters who had been trained in the Persian school, and their art, combining with the native Hindu elements, formed the

[16] Reproduced in color in the *Burlington Magazine*, v. 20, p. 315. For the story, see Nivedita and Coomaraswamy, *Myths of the Hindus and Buddhists*, p. 226.

[17] A very interesting aspect of Rajput painting is its relation to music. Many examples, whatever the representation, display a deep feeling of tenderness, and are of a lyrical mood that evokes the same emotion as music. Thus they are known as *ragas*, or *raginis*, that is, a melody or a musical theme. On this see Coomaraswamy, *Rajput Painting*, or *Arts and Crafts of India and Ceylon*.

foundation of Mughal painting. But while Rajput painting was lyrical and religious, having its roots deep in the soil of native traditions, Mughal painting was secular. It was a miniature art chiefly. Its interest lay primarily in the picturesque aspect of human life, chiefly that of the palace; for it flourished under the patronage of the Mogul rulers and nobles, and aimed to give a vivid picture of court scenes and persons, hunts and night scenes, animals and flowers.

MINOR ARTS

The Hindu craftsman held an important place in Indian life. As part of the feudal system, he did not have to think of the economic aspects of life, for the system provided that. The monastery had its painters, sculptors, and metal workers to decorate its buildings, and perhaps sent them on to another monastery when its own work was done. The noble had, as part of his household, his goldsmith to make the jewelry and plate for his family. The boy inherited his father's calling and belonged to the guild which was under the protection of the king.[18]

Among the metal workers the goldsmith was of great importance. For jewelry played an important part in Indian costume, of the men as well as of the women.[19] It was used not only for personal adornment but for the trappings of state elephants and for palace hangings. Girdle chains (PL. 164 D) originated in the old Hindu custom of decking the body with garlands of flowers and seeds. In order to keep the chain light in weight the beads were made hollow and in filigree. Like the Greek, the Indian recognized the value of gold and silver as a medium for expression of itself without the addition of jewels. When he used gems, he did not facet them but only smoothed them off, thus obtaining a deep and glowing rather than a flashing effect. Another use of gems was made by inlay. Tiny pieces of ruby, sapphire, emerald, or topaz were embedded in a thin gold plate, producing the effect of enamel. In this the Indian revealed his skill in massing color harmonies, and out of almost valueless bits created an unsurpassed piece of rich decoration. The pendant to the chain in PL. 164 C is an example of this. The general shape is suggested by a bird with outspread wings. There is no thought of giving a realistic representation of the bird form, but the aim is to use the essential elements only to obtain decora-

---

[18] On this situation see Coomaraswamy, *Indian Craftsman*, and *Mediaeval Sinhalese Art*.
[19] See Coomaraswamy, *Arts and Crafts of India and Ceylon*, p. 151, for a description of the costume of the maids of honor of an Indian queen.

tive beauty. "To wear a real bird . . . would be barbarous; to imitate a real bird very closely . . . would be idle; but all that is beautiful in the general idea of a bird, colour, form, and poise, can be suggested."[20]

Another kind of metal work successfully practiced was damascening. The betel-nut slicer (PL. 165 A) shows not only great technical skill but vigorous imaginative quality in the design that adapts to everyday use this fantastic figure with the head of a lion and the body of a bird.

Further evidence of the Indian love of ornament we see in the wood and ivory carvings. The sacrificial dipper (PL. 164 B), for example, is an elaborate design of curves. One great sweeping curve forms

Fig. 124. Indian Textile Design. (After Coomaraswamy)

the structural line of the handle; but it is varied and emphasized by minor curves swirling now this way and now that, but entirely subordinated to the main line of direction. The bowl of the dipper shows the skill of the silversmith, for the rich design is superbly executed. The union of the two parts, however, is not successfully accomplished by the curious, elaborately bejeweled little figure that distracts and weakens the construction at that point.

One of the most important crafts of India has always been weaving, and the chief material, cotton. The muslins from Dacca are so sheer that they have received poetic names such as "running water" or "evening dew," the latter because the fabric is so delicate that if laid on the wet grass, it is scarcely visible. When these delicate muslins are embroidered they have the effect of exquisite lace (PL. 165 B). Cotton textiles served

[20] Coomaraswamy, *Mediaeval Sinhalese Art*, p. 211.

not only for garments and turbans but also for hangings, bed-spreads, and other furnishings. From their native names are derived many of our own words for cotton fabrics, such as chintz and bandanna. For decorating these cottons, several processes were employed, chiefly printing and painting. PL. 165 c reproduces a *Palampore*, or calico bedcover. The ground is formed of interlaced branches and foliage with peacocks and various birds arranged in a balanced position. The cotton was first sized with buffalo milk to keep the color from running. The design was drawn on paper and punched on the prepared cloth. Some of the colors were painted in by hand; others, especially the blue, were dyed so that the color would be more permanent. To do this, all the parts except those to be colored blue were covered with wax, and the entire piece put into the dye-pot. The wax was then removed with boiling water, and successive colors added with paint or dye. In case of a repeat pattern wood-block stamps were sometimes used. The colors of the old Indian cottons are very lasting, and their soft tones of rose, blue, and blue-green have been acquired through time and frequent washing.

Fig. 125. Indian Brocade.   (After Coomaraswamy)

In some of the woven fabrics (FIGS. 124 and 125) beauty of fitting design was obtained by means of the same attitude toward natural appearance that characterized the jewelry. Simplification of form was carried to the point where abstract design was paramount and the bird or animal form suggested only. One other kind of textile needs mention, the *Cashmere* (PL. 165 D). The weavers of Cashmere, in northern India, well up in the Himalayas, used the goats' wool for these shawls, weaving them on small looms in long strips, which they sewed together so skillfully that the seaming is scarcely perceptible. The characteristic motif is the pine pattern, probably originating in the cypress tree of Persian art, while the ground or border is filled with small floral designs. The beauty of color and design in these shawls is equaled by the supreme skill shown in the weaving.

SUMMARY

The greatest art of India, whether a building, a statue, a fresco, or a piece of gold work, was hieratic and strictly obedient to accepted canons of technique and representation. The artist was a "pious craftsman" who "should understand the Atharva Veda, the thirty-two Śilpa Śastras, and the Vedic mantras by which the deities are invoked. He should be one who wears a sacred thread, a necklace of holy beads, and a ring of *kuśa* grass on his finger; delighting in the worship of God, faithful to his wife, avoiding strange women, piously acquiring a knowledge of various sciences, such a one is indeed a craftsman. . . . The painter must be a good man, no sluggard, not given to anger; holy, learned, self-controlled, devout and charitable."[21] Convention was partly a natural tendency of race and partly a canonical requirement; and though it determined the outward form of expression, it really only provided the craftsman with a general mode or instrument by means of which he could suitably express his own convincing experiences.

An appreciation of Indian, in fact of all oriental art, presupposes an acceptance of the principle that great art is not necessarily an imitation or illusion of nature, but that a generalized, conventional, or symbolic representation of man and of nature can express both the form and the spiritual forces that dominate it. Western, that is, European art, on the whole has followed the canon of the representation of nature, yet has produced great art wherever the artists have been able to be selective and to reproduce nature in her universal aspects as expressive of a controlling spirit within. At times western art has approached the eastern ideal of generalization, convention, and spirituality, as in the best Byzantine mosaics, and the paintings of Simone Martini and Botticelli. In fact, the Hindu author, Dr. Coomaraswamy, quotes from the writings of Leonardo in speaking of the art of his own country: "That figure is most worthy of praise which by its action best expresses the passion that animates it." The difference between the art of East and West is not so great as it appears to be at first sight, but is rather a difference of emphasis, the West concentrating more

---

[21] From the Shilpa Shastras, or the canonical books of the artificer (Shilpan), quoted by Coomaraswamy in *The Dance of Śiva*, p. 26. Compare, in spirit and attitude toward work, the treatise of the monk Theophilus, p. 202.

upon the physical aspect, the East, with much greater simplification of form, upon the abstract expression of the inner, dominating passion.

BIBLIOGRAPHY

BARNETT, L. D., TR., Bhagavad-gita. (Temple Classics.) London, Dent, 1920.

BINYON, LAURENCE, AND ARNOLD, T. W., Court Painters of the Grand Moghuls. London, Oxford University Press, 1921.

BIRDWOOD, SIR G. C. M., Industrial Arts of India. 2 v. London, Chapman, 1884.

BOSTON. MUSEUM OF FINE ARTS, Synopsis of History. Boston, 1922.

BRITISH MUSEUM, Pictorial postcards: Set C4, Indian Paintings, Mughal School; C9, Persian and Indian Paintings.

BROWN, PERCY, Indian Painting. London, Oxford University Press, 1918.

—— ——, Indian Painting Under the Mughals. Oxford, Clarendon Press, 1924.

BURLINGAME, E. W., TR., Buddhist Parables. New Haven, Yale University Press, 1922.

COHN, WILLIAM, Indische Plastik. Berlin, Cassirer, 1923.

COOMARASWAMY, A. K., Arts and Crafts of India and Ceylon. London, Foulis, 1913.

—— ——, Buddha and the Gospel of Buddhism. N.Y., Putnam, 1916.

—— ——, Catalogue of the Indian Collections in the Museum of Fine Arts, Boston. Boston, 1924.

—— ——, Dance of Śiva. N.Y., Sunwise Turn, 1918.

—— ——, Indian Craftsman. London, Probsthain, 1909.

—— ——, Mediaeval Sinhalese Art. Broad Campden, Essex House Press, 1907–8.

—— ——, Rajput Painting. 2 v. London, Oxford University Press, 1916.

DUTT, TORU, Ancient Ballads and Legends of Hindustan. London, Trench, 1885.

FERGUSSON, JAMES, History of Indian and Eastern Architecture. 2v. London, Murray, 1910.

FLETCHER, SIR BANISTER, History of Architecture on the Comparative Method. N.Y., Scribner, 1924.

FRANCIS, H. T., AND THOMAS, E. J., Jataka Tales. Cambridge, University Press, 1916.

FRAZER, R. W., Indian Thought, Past and Present. London, 1915.

GILES, H. A., Travels of Fa-hsien (399–414 A.D.), or Record of the Buddhist Kingdoms. Cambridge, University Press, 1923.

GRUENWEDEL, ALBERT, Buddhist Art in India (tr. Gibson). London, Quaritch, 1901.

HAVELL, E. B., Ancient and Medieval Architecture of India. London, Murray, 1914.

—— ——, Handbook of Indian Art. London, Murray, 1920.

—— ——, Himalayas in Indian Art. London, Dent, 1924.

—— ——, Ideals of Indian Art. London, Murray, 1911.

—— ——, Indian Architecture: Its Psychology, Structure, and History. London, Murray, 1913.

—— ——, Indian Sculpture and Painting. London, Murray, 1908.

KALIDASA, Shakuntala and Other Works (tr. Ryder; Everyman's Library). N.Y., Dutton, 1920.

MACDONALD, FREDERIKA, Iliad of the East. N.Y., Lane, 1908.

MONIER-WILLIAMS, SIR MONIER, Indian Wisdom. London, Luzac, 1897.

NIVEDITA, SISTER, AND COOMARASWAMY, A. K., Myths and Legends: Hindus and Buddhists. N.Y., Holt, 1913.

OMAN, J. C., Great Indian Epics: the Ramayana and Mahabharata. London, Bell, 1906.

PERCIVAL, MacIVER, Chintz Book. London, Heinemann, 1923.

SMITH, V. A., History of Fine Art in India and Ceylon. Oxford, Clarendon Press, 1911.

——, Oxford History of India. Oxford, Clarendon Press, 1920.

WATT, SIR GEORGE, Indian Art at Delhi, 1903. London, Murray, 1904.

WITH, KARL, Java. The Hague, 1920.

CHAPTER XXVIII

CHINA

In studying Chinese art we are dealing with a people whose native conservatism has preserved their fundamental traditions for more than four thousand years — a unique case in the history of civilizations. To be sure, foreign influences have entered China and become powerful, but eventually they have been absorbed or assimilated by the truly Chinese thought and action.

China is vast both in population and in geographic extent, a land of probably more than four hundred million people, with an area, including Tibet, Chinese Turkestan, Mongolia, and Manchuria, of more than twice the size of the United States, though China proper includes a little less than half this area. The fertile eastern plains are traversed by two great river systems that have their rise in the mountains of the west. The Hoang-ho, or Yellow River, with swift current brings down great quantities of silt that is still building up the alluvial plains, now providing rich agricultural lands, now destroying farms and people with its floods and erratic change of course. The Yangtze-kiang, or Blue River, through its navigability serves as the great artery of commerce. As one would expect in so large a country, there is great variety of climate, vegetation, language, and custom. North China, centering about Peking, has a cool, dry climate and many stretches of plain; south China, centering at Canton, is moist and tropical, and the mountains near by afford a summer refuge from the enervating heat. To the west and north are vast areas of desert plateau. Agriculture forms the economic basis of life; even in the mountainous regions small patches of tillable land are intensively cultivated. The natural resources are enormous — mines of gold and other metal, quarries, "jade mountains," and formerly great forests, now destroyed.

The old civilization centered in the valley of the Hoang-ho in the Shensi province, and comprised perhaps one-fifth of present China. The people, when not at war, were primarily agricultural, and for this reason interested in the powers of nature — the sky, the stars, the wind, and the rain. About these powers their religion centered. The dragon, in varying forms one of the most important motifs in Chinese art, and the emblem of the emperor, possibly had its origin in the great alligators that infested the rivers and early became objects of worship, symbolizing the coming of spring and rain. So also the phoenix, because of its fabulous renewal of life from its own ashes, symbolized the sun and warmth that brings about the ever recurrent life in nature.

Added to nature worship were two fundamentals in this early civilization which have persisted as basic elements of Chinese culture. First, the social basis, the unit of which was the family and not the individual. The customs of one's ancestors constituted the established law and the perpetuation of the family was the vital necessity. To this the rights and freedom of the individual were sacrificed. He was but one link in the social chain; and the chain was the paramount thing. Such an attitude fostered the second fundamental, which was a pious reverence for the dead, a continual looking to the past rather than to the future, and an acceptance of the past as the ultimate authority. The result of such a culture was unity and harmony; and, in art, an expression that was racial rather than individual.

Early Chinese culture reached a climax in the Chou dynasty (1122–255 B.C.).[1] The social system that had been evolving for many centuries was ready to be formulated by the early fifth century, at just about the time that the Greek civilization was reaching a climax of expression in the age of Pericles (FIG. 132). This formulation was the work of Confucius (551–479 B.C.). While Confucianism is frequently classed as a religion, it is neither religious nor philosophical, but a social and ethical system that aims to secure a stable society by regulating human relationships. Its ideal is communism, as worked out among an

---

[1] Chinese civilization may be traced back to about 3000 B.C. The important periods are as follows:

Hsia dynasty	2205–1766 B.C.
Shang dynasty	1766–1122
Chou dynasty	1122–255
Ts'in dynasty	255–206
Han dynasty	206 B.C.–221 A.D.
Wei and the Six dynasties	221–618
T'ang dynasty	618–907
Sung dynasty	960–1280
Yüan or Mongol dynasty	1280–1368
Ming dynasty	1368–1644
Ts'ing or Manchu dynasty	1644–1911

The spelling and the dates used in this chapter are those of Giles. For maps illustrating the geographic extent of China in the various dynasties, and the old trade routes, see E. H. Parker, *China* (N.Y., Dutton, 1917).

agricultural people. The affairs of everyday life, that is, right conduct in human society, and even such details as "the right sort of a bonnet to wear or the most genteel way to lie in bed," are so regulated by law and custom that a harmonious and peaceful society results.

Meanwhile, in the valley of the Yangtze-kiang, the "land of thorns," lived the "jungle barbarians," of a different race and a different conception of life. Among them grew up a sect known as the Taoists, that is, followers of the Tao, the impersonal force or principle identified with nature. These dwellers of the Blue River had an intense love of nature, of the mountains, rivers, mists, and clouds that are characteristic of that part of China. They claimed as their founder Lao Tzu (570?–490 B.C.), a contemporary of Confucius but a teacher who recognized the individual to a far greater extent, for he taught that the self must be recognized in order to be brought into harmony with the great impersonal force permeating the universe which was the ultimate good.

While these two ideals were taking root among the Chinese, the Ts'in, a Tartar people who were living on the boundaries and serving the Chou as horseherders and charioteers, finally became the dominating power and the king of Ts'in became the first emperor of China (246 B.C.). The situation is analogous to that of the Tartar slaves of the Mohammedans, who eventually became the Mamluke rulers of Egypt. The Ts'in consolidated the empire, set up a strongly centralized government, built the Great Wall as a protection against the Mongolian nomads, and, in order to abolish local patriotism, burned the written books. They also gave to the country the name by which we know it — China, which is Ts'in — or Chin — land. They, in turn, were overcome by the Han, who by dividing the land set up a feudal state. The Han were the great supporters of Confucian ideals, and established Confucian writings as the exclusive classical literature of China. Under the Han, China expanded westward to protect herself against the barbarous tribes of central Asia and also to keep open the great trade routes over which her silks and other products were carried west even to the Roman empire.

These highways were most important in the history of Chinese civilization. Along them traders, pilgrims, and armies traveled between eastern and western Asia. While in China proper the native culture had been developing until it had formed established traditions, over these highways the Buddhist faith was slowly making its way as the Buddhist monks and missionaries established their monasteries farther and farther eastward, especially in eastern Turkestan, which had become a Chinese protectorate. Here in the oases that formed a chain of cities across the desert plateaus the religion of India met the culture of China, and the fusion of the two formed the basis of the great art of China.

Buddhism, during the thousand years since its founding, had developed into something much more comprehensive than the simple teaching of Shakyamuni. As a strongly missionary religion, its conception of salvation included the whole universe; and, in this aspect, perhaps even more important than the Buddha were the Bodhisattvas, particularly Avalokiteshvara, the lord of pity, who under the name Kuan Yin, became one of the most important of the Chinese and Japanese Buddhist deities. With well established traditions, China was ready for the stimulation that the emotionalism and mysticism of Buddhism could give her. The ground had been prepared by the Taoists, whose ideas were somewhat akin to those of the Buddhists. We read of pilgrims such as Fa-hsien traveling through India (399–414 A.D.) visiting sacred places, learning of the faith, and collecting literature about it. The translation of the Indian idea into Chinese mode of expression we see developing in Turkestan. But its full assimilation and ultimate expression took place in China proper in the T'ang dynasty (618–907 A.D.), a golden age in all the arts — painting, sculpture, metal work, poetry, music. Toward the end of the T'ang period, a conservative reaction set in against Buddhism and other religions that had secured a foothold, and developed into a revolution that demanded a return to the Confucian system. The success of the revolutionists (845 A.D.) brought about the destruction of temples and monasteries with their great series of frescoes, and general ruin of all works of art; and this is why so little real T'ang art has survived. Another reaction in favor of Buddhism restored many of the temples and monasteries in the tenth century, but by that time most of the paintings were irretrievably lost.

The second golden age of Chinese art, following closely upon the T'ang, was the Sung (960–1280 A.D.), a period perhaps analogous to our Renaissance, in that both ages produced great statesmen, philosophers, poets, art critics, painters. Like the Italian Renaissance, the Sung dynasty looked to the archaic periods, as we see in the deep study that the commentators made of the canons of Confucius, and the Chou motifs that we find on the slender, typically Sung-shaped bronzes. In this period, however, philosophy, poetry, and painting together produced the finest of the Chinese landscape paintings.

An important source of inspiration of this art was Zen Buddhism. Zen, derived from the Indian word meaning meditation in supreme repose, was brought to China by an Indian prince in the sixth century, and, as many of its ideas were close in spirit to those of the Taoists, took deep root especially in southern China.

Their [Zen Buddhists'] training was centered on the methods of that self-control which is the essence of true freedom. Deluded human minds groped in darkness, because they mistook the attribute for the substance. Even religious teachings were misleading, in so far as they set up semblances for realities. This thought was often illustrated by the simile of monkeys attempting to seize the reflection of the moon in water; for each effort to snatch at the silvery image could but ruffle the mirroring surface, and end in destroying not only the phantom moon but also themselves. . . . Freedom, once attained, left all men to revel and glory in the beauties of the whole universe. They were then one with nature, whose pulse they felt beating simultaneously within themselves, whose breath they felt themselves inhaling and exhaling in union with the great world-spirit.[2]

The fundamental principle of . . . Zen Buddhism may be summed up in the expression that *the universe is the scripture of Zen*. . . . Actual scripture is worthless in the letter, and only valuable for that to which it leads; and to that goal there are other guides than the written page or the spoken word. It is related, for example, of the sage Hüen Sha that he was one day prepared to deliver a sermon to an assembled congregation, and was on the point of beginning, when a bird was heard to sing very sweetly close by; Hüen Sha descended from his pulpit with the remark that the sermon had been preached. . . .

. . . It is the very heart of "culture" and religion to recognize the eternal, not as obscured but as revealed by the transient, to see infinity in the grain of sand, the same unborn in every birth, and the same undying in every death. These thoughts find constant expression in the poetry and art inspired by Zen thought. The Morning Glory, for example, fading in an hour, is a favorite theme of the Japanese poet and painter. What are we to understand by the poem of Matsunaga Teitoku?

"The morning glory blooms but for an hour, and yet it differs not at heart
  From the giant pine that lives for a thousand years."

"It is the same with the pine as with the morning glory, but as the life of the latter is shorter, it illustrates the principle in a more striking way. The giant pine does not ponder on its thousand years, nor the morning glory on its life of a single day. Each does simply what it must. Certainly the fate of the morning glory is other than that of the pine, yet their destiny is alike in this, that they fulfil the will of Providence, and are content. Matsunaga thought his heart was like their heart, and that was why he made that poem on the morning glory."[3]

The Sung were overthrown by an invasion of the Mongols, who, under Jenghis Khan and his son Kublai Khan, set up the Yüan or Mongol dynasty (1280–1368 A.D.). This was in turn supplemented by the Ming (1368–1644 A.D.), which looked to

---

[2] Okakura, *Ideals of the East*, p. 162.
[3] Coomaraswamy, *Buddha and the Gospel of Buddhism*, pp. 254 ff.

the T'ang for its inspiration and created some admirable works
in the spirit of T'ang but lacked its depth, its nobility, and its
grandeur. With the passing of the Ming, the days of the greatest
art of China were past.

ARCHITECTURE

Chinese architecture well illustrates the natural conservatism
of the race, for one type of building has served all needs, religious
and secular, public and private. It has accepted minor elements
of construction and decorative motifs from without, but it has
remained fundamentally the same in design for thousands of
years. To a considerable extent, it has retained its early building

material, wood, though it
has at times translated this
construction into stone and
tile. In this respect the
history of Chinese architecture is different from that
of painting and sculpture,
which have been profoundly
influenced by other civilizations.

Fig. 126. Sacrificial Hall of Yung Lo.
XV cent. A.D. Ming tombs, near Peking.
(Paléologue)

The most striking feature
of the design (FIG. 126) is the
roof, broadly overhanging
and steeply pitched. It is four-sided, built in two sections with
the corners curving slightly upward. The shape is due to climate,
for the steep pitch easily sheds the rain; the broad overhanging
protects from both the sun and the rain. The reason for the upturned corners is a subject of controversy. According to some it
goes back to the tents of prehistoric days, for the tent cloth,
spread over upright spears, sagged enough to form such a curve.
According to others, it is the natural outcome of the overlapping
of the horizontal layers of bamboo that was the chief building
material in early times. Whatever its origin, it has remained
constant in Chinese architecture, and has the advantage of admitting more light while at the same time offering protection.
The roof is of open timber construction, covered with S-shape
tiles laid in beds of mortar. It rests upon lintels that are supported by columns with projecting brackets which take the place
of the capital in occidental architecture. The hall is but one
story high, though the roof is at two levels and each section is

supported independently by its own set of columns, those for the upper section not visible from the exterior. This is characteristic of Chinese buildings, which do not rise above a single story. If additional space is needed, the building is enlarged horizontally, by adding wings, for example. The walls, which are of no structural value, are occupied by folding doors filled with tracery. It is a kind of architecture that impresses through its dignity and sobriety, its rhythm of line, its quiet and simple massing of parts.

To these characteristics one more must be added — splendor of decoration, particularly color. The roof tiles of royal buildings are yellow, the imperial color in China. Sometimes the tiles are blue or green; and the choice is determined by strict laws, indicative of the rank of the owner and symbolic in meaning. The ridgepoles are decorated with dragons, phoenixes and grotesques, as if to break the long lines. The beams and undersides of the projecting roofs and the interior are elaborately ornamented with gold and vermilion, carvings, lacquer, and inlay, so that the effect is one of solemn splendor.

Structurally the same as our type building is the *Temple of Heaven* (PL. 166 A), the Chinese name for which means "temple of prayer for the year"; for here each spring the Emperor went to offer sacrifices and prayer for a propitious year not only to heaven but to the imperial forefathers, to the sun, moon, and stars, and to the spirits of nature in the winds, the clouds, the rain. Here again color and form are determined by symbolism. As blue is the color of heaven, so the tiles of the temple are a deep cobalt and, during the ceremonies of the spring sacrifice, blue dominates the interior, for the ceremonial vessels are of blue porcelain, the worshipers are clad in blue; in fact a blue tone is cast over everything by Venetian blinds made of blue glass which cover all the doors and windows. So too is the unusual circular shape symbolic of the spherical appearance of the heavens. The temple is an imposing structure, its triple roof with gilded ball pointing with assurance toward the heavens. This impressiveness is increased particularly by the location of the building; for it stands upon an elevation, surrounded by encircling marble terraces and broad stairways, set at the cardinal points of the compass, with ornamented balustrades.

A characteristic feature of Chinese landscape is the pagoda, a Buddhistic structure, some of whose forms originated in the umbrella, that symbol of royalty in India which usually terminated the *stupa*, often in a multiple form (FIG. 119). These pagodas often formed a part of the temple group, but frequently served as memorials without religious significance. Some of these pagodas are of a vigorous, massive type, with as many as thirteen stories. Others are more slender (FIG. 127), with elegance of proportion, interesting variety in the shape of the three stories, and rich ornamentation. One of the famous "porcelain" pagodas is faced with glazed tiles in five colors — deep purplish blue, rich green, yellow, red, and turquoise-blue — so that the effect as it stands in the open surrounded with greenery is most charming. It is called "porcelain" incorrectly, because of the glazed tile facing, a method of ornamentation that we saw carried out so effectively in Egypt and Babylonia-Assyria, and it is quite probable that the Chinese of the Han dynasty, as they pushed their boundaries westward, learned of its use from these western peoples.

Another characteristic architectural form in China is the gateway, the *pailou*, made of wood with tile roofs, or of stone imitating the wooden structure. Like the pagodas, these appear to be derived from the gateways of the *stupas* in India, but the silhouette of the upper part has been determined by the typical curved line of Chinese roof. Unlike the Indian *stupa* gate, these arches are not necessarily entrances but

Fig. 127. Pagoda. Near Peking. (Paléologue)

may be independent structures, erected only by special permission as memorials to distinguished Chinese, both dead and living.

PAINTING

The chief forms of Chinese painting are frescoes, hanging scrolls (*kakemono*), and long scrolls (*makimono*). The frescoes, which formed great series of wall decoration, majestic and hieratic like the *Ajanta Frescoes* and the early Christian mosaics, have disappeared, as we have explained, from China proper and we can judge of them only through the wall paintings of Turkestan and Japan, which reflect something of their nature. Most of the Chinese painting that has survived belongs to the second and third classes, the panels and scrolls. The framed picture, with which we are so familiar, is practically unknown in the Orient.

Another important difference between eastern and western painting lies in the method of exhibiting it. The Chinese panel or scroll was not kept on view continuously, but formed a part of the family treasure to be exhibited for a short time in a place of honor or brought out for a brief period of enjoyment or for some connoisseur to examine and to affix his seal.[4] It was then rolled up and put away in a place of safety. Thus the place and use of paintings in China was perhaps analogous to that of rare books with us.

Of early Chinese painting, nothing remains. Something of its nature we learn from a *makimono* in the British Museum attributed to Ku K'ai-chih[5] (fourth and fifth centuries A.D.), whom the Chinese writers consider one of their great painters. The subject of the painting was taken from a Chinese writer, who explains the principles that an instructress in the royal palace would teach to the princesses under her care. This we know from the inscriptions that accompany the paintings. The detail reproduced on PL. 168 B represents the Lady Feng rescuing the emperor from a bear that had broken loose from the circus ring. At the right sits the emperor, perfectly calm, surrounded by his courtiers; at the right two men are attacking the bear, in front of which fearlessly stands Lady Feng, her lithe figure with its draperies billowing about her feet a perfect epitome of courageous self-sacrifice; for that was the lesson that this episode sought to inculcate in the minds of the princesses. The secular subject is interesting; but perhaps the most striking characteristic is the great amount of expression with a minimum of means. There is a sense of structure and movement in the figures; a great deal of expression in the hands and faces; and rhythmic sweep of sure, unfaltering line. All is expressed by line with no shading, no expression of depth, with little color, and with suppressed detail and accessories. The technique has strongly influenced the character of the work. The figures are painted on silk with a brush in Chinese ink, which is not the ink with which we are familiar, but a solid kind that the Chinese made by burning certain plants and combining the soot thus obtained with glue or oil. It was then molded into a cake and dried. If a particular kind of surface was desired, other ingredients were added — pulverized oyster shells, for example, to obtain a dead finish. The process of making the finest ink was a secret, often a care-

---

[4] See the seals of about fifty former owners or famous connoisseurs on the scroll in the British Museum attributed to Ku K'ai-chih.
[5] For interesting stories of this painter see Giles, *Introduction to Chinese Pictorial Art*, p. 18, and Waley, *Introduction to the Study of Chinese Painting*, p. 45.

PLATE 167

(*A*) Votive Tablet. Detail of the upper part. 534 A.D. Metropolitan Museum, New York. (Metropolitan Museum)

(*B*) Kuan Yin. Sung dynasty. Buckingham Coll., Art Institute, Chicago. (Art Institute)

(*C*) Buddhist Votive Stele. Erected in 554 A.D., "as a means of securing the happiness and welfare of the donors, their ancestors, their posterity, their relations, and friends, the Emperor in particular and the Chinese people in general." Boston Museum. (Boston Museum)

PLATE 168

(A) Tung Yüan. Landscape. Sung dynasty, late X cent. A.D.

(B) Ku K'ai-chih. Lády Feng and the Bear. Detail of the Admonitions of the Instructress. Probably a T'ang copy. Late IV or early V cent. A.D. British Museum, London. (British Museum)

(C) Sacrificial Jar. Bronze. H. 7½ in. Shang dynasty. Parish-Watson Coll., New York. (Parish-Watson)

PLATE 169

北苑真筆

Boston Museum. (Boston Museum)

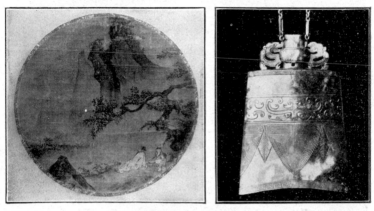

(A) Ma Yüan. Landscape. Ming dynasty. Boston Museum. (Boston Museum)

(B) Jade Bell. H. 8 in. Ch'ien-Lung period (1736–95 A.D.). Field Museum of Natural History, Chicago. (Field Museum)

(C) Sacrificial Vessel. Bronze. L. 12¾ in. Chou dynasty. Buckingham Coll., Art Institute, Chicago. (Art Institute)

PLATE 170

(*A*) Flower Vase. Jade. 1736–95 A.D. Metropolitan Museum, New York. (Metropolitan Museum)

(*B*) Porcelain Jar. Ming dynasty. Potter Palmer Loan Coll., Art Institute, Chicago. (Art Institute)

(*C*) Horiuji, a Monastery near Nara. Kondo and Pagoda. 586–607 A.D.
(*Japanese Temples and Treasures*)

fully guarded heritage. To use this ink, the painter moistened the cake on a slab, thus obtaining a semi-fluid. Great skill was needed both in rubbing the cake and in applying the ink to the brush.

This ink was used for writing as well as for painting. For writing, among the Chinese, was one of the highest arts (PL. 168 A). The characters were made with the brush, not the pen, and required a skill attained only through long years' practice. The hand did not hold the brush as we hold a pen with the thumb and two fingers to be manipulated by wrist movement, but vertically in the fist, the whole arm as well as the wrist guiding the movement from the shoulder. The writer or painter did not work at a table or easel, but sitting on his heels and knees with his work spread out on the floor before him. The ink might be used thick or thin; and the strokes were now bold and strong, now abrupt, now diminishing to a hair line, and sometimes of surpassing delicacy. The characters were originally pictographs, like the Egyptian, which in the process of a long evolution were so highly simplified that they became abstract symbols of the original form. In the mental make-up of the calligraphist, then, abstract form was an important element. Now the greatest painters were poets, philosophers, or priests, and the same type of literary training furnished the background in the education of all; so Chinese painting is akin to literature. And, as the same materials were used to write poems and to paint mountain scenery, we may expect to find in painting the same simplification and abstraction as in calligraphy. Of one famous painter a Chinese writer said, "I can taste in the poem something of the picture's flavor; and in the picture I see something of the poem." Another fact of technique that we need to consider is that the figures and landscapes were usually painted on specially prepared silk, though paper was sometimes used, and when once the stroke of the brush had touched the silk, it could not be altered. This demanded of the painter not only perfect control in handling the brush, but also a careful thinking out of his work before he applied the ink.

Looking at the painting of Ku K'ai-chih again, we understand that the restraint and the directness of statement are due to this peculiarly Chinese technique, the conditions of which are more stringent even than those of fresco.

Thus an accomplished school of painting had developed early in China of which Ku K'ai-chih is the climax. Such skill as is here seen reveals a long past during which the painters were achieving, as were the archaic Greek artists, mastery of expression. Another characteristic that reveals accomplishment and not merely endeavor is the feeling of elegance and graceful charm of figure and of gesture and the suavity of line.

While native Chinese painting was developing toward this climax, the Buddhist faith was slowly moving eastward, as we have explained, to fuse with the Chinese traditions. This we see accomplished in the paintings of *Paradise* that have come from the monastery caves of Turkestan. These paintings represent that paradise where Amida Buddha lived in gorgeous surroundings, attended by Bodhisattvas and believers.[6] For Paradise and its pleasures were conceived in terms of an earthly court of great splendor and joy. A lofty mood permeates all the figures, "the spell of a single mood of immaterial felicity and peace." In the drawing there is the same firmness and delicate grace that characterized the work of Ku K'ai-chih.[7]

These *Paradise* panels give us some hint of the lost T'ang painting, which was a fusion of the powerful native Chinese tradition and the energizing spirit of Buddhism. For Buddhism had brought to China a new conception of deity. Buddha in his contemplative aspect, with his conquest over self and also his universal love and pity for suffering mankind as expressed in the Bodhisattva Kuan Yin, was particularly appealing. What we learn from literary sources, added to examples of Japanese art which we know took T'ang art as their prototype, tells us that this was a hieratic art of "tingling austerity," concerned not with the visual facts of natural appearance but with those highly simplified, essential aspects of form that could express that inner life whose fervor was so intense that it had become calm, somber, and majestic.

Chinese writers tell us much of the numerous painters of the T'ang age, among whom the greatest was Wu Tao-tzu [8] (born c. 700 A.D.). His most important works were the series of frescoes in the Buddhist temples that were destroyed in the revolution.[9]

Another aspect of Buddhism that influenced Chinese painting

[6] Amida, or Amitabha, Buddha means the god of boundless light. This worship may have originated among the sun-worshipers of Parthia, for Buddhism, as it penetrated northwestern India, there received some Greek and Iranian influences (p. 415, note 10), which it carried along into Turkestan. There we see a mixed culture. Manichaeans, Buddhists, and Christians were living together peaceably; yet Buddhism was the dominating element.

[7] The *Horiuji Frescoes* of Japan (PL. 173 B), are very close in style to these paintings.

[8] For stories of Wu Tao-tzu, see Giles, *Introduction to Chinese Pictorial Art*, pp. 47 ff.; and Waley, *Introduction to the Study of Chinese Painting*, pp. 112 ff.

[9] Probably none of the great T'ang painting is extant. The situation is analogous to that of Greek painting, which we could study only as we found reflections of it in the vases and Roman copies at Pompeii.

profoundly was its attitude toward nature. We saw in India how Buddhism recognized all life as a unit. Some of the poets and philosophers of southern China had already realized something of this kinship with nature; and their spirit, intensely augmented by the powerful Buddhist belief in the universal brotherhood of all forms of life, laid the foundation of those schools of landscape painting culminating in the Sung period that have been one of the great accomplishments of Chinese art.

The Chinese had not only an intimate knowledge of the facts of nature but also a deep love for her. They "did not merely love nature; they were in love with her . . ." Kuo Hsi, a painter who was born c. 1020 A.D., wrote:

> Wherein lies the reason that good men so much love landscape? It is because amid orchards and hills a man has ever room to cultivate his natural bent; because streams and rocks never fail to charm the rambler who goes whistling on his way. It is because fishing and wood-gathering are the natural vocations of the hermit or recluse, hard by where the flying birds and chattering apes have made their home. Noise and dust, bridles and chains — these are what man's nature is ever weary of. Haze and mists, saints and fairies — for these man's nature pines eternally, and pines in vain." [10]

The Chinese word for landscape means "mountains and rivers." This is not surprising to any one who has looked over a considerable number of Chinese paintings, so frequently are these the subject matter. Let us take for study, as a typical example, a painting of Tung Yüan (PL. 168 A). It is one of those long scrolls, peculiar to Chinese and Japanese painting, the origin of which is uncertain, though the plausible suggestion has been made that this long roll, the original form of the book, is an imitation of geographic maps, as the same word in Chinese is used for a map and for a picture or design of any kind. The scroll is not unrolled and viewed as a unit, but is rolled up at one end while it is unrolled at the other, so that only a section of it is seen at one time. This requires that there be both unity in the parts and continuity in the whole, which demands extraordinary skill on the part of the painter. As we slowly unroll the painting, there is spread out before us a panorama of great spaciousness quite characteristic of the bold mountainous landscapes of China. In the foreground is a sparsely wooded stretch with a pavilion and at the left a river; in the background rise rugged, majestic mountains, receding into the distance, and the valleys between the crags are filled with mists. But it is very unlike a map; for it is not certain facts about this mountainous country that

---

[10] Waley, *Introduction to the Study of Chinese Painting*, p. 189.

hold us. Visual facts are there — the structure of the rocks, the mighty upward thrust of the mountains, their mass and solidity; the form of the tree trunks, and the shapes and masses of foliage that weave interesting patterns against the distance; the enveloping of all forms in atmosphere, and the precise values in the trees and mountains as they recede into the illimitable distance. But mere visual truth is subordinate to the mood, to the emotional power that fills the picture. We can easily imagine how Tung Yüan from a somewhat elevated position like that of the spectator sat meditating upon this scene, as we see a sage meditating in PL. 169 A. Days and perhaps months he spent in this way until, as the accidental and ephemeral appearance was lost sight of, he *felt* and so he saw the scene as the interpretation of a rare, noble mood of a harmonious and infinite nature. So attuned was he finally to this poetic mood, and so trained was his hand technically to follow his mind and his emotions, that he quickly, spontaneously, and unerringly transferred his feelings to the paper. And we, if we gradually and sympathetically feel ourselves into the picture, will find that it evokes in us the same noble reposeful mood as it did in Tung Yüan, a mood that is close to that of music. This idea Dr. Laufer has expressed with extraordinary insight when he says:

Such creations . . . no doubt belong to the greatest emanations of art of all times. . . . The T'ang masters were not naturalists, idealists, romanticists nor were they one-sidedly given to any of our narrow -isms exclusively. They were, in the first place, symphonists in the sense of our music. . . . There is but one giant in our art to whom Wang Wei and Li Se-sün can be adequately compared, and that is Beethoven. The same lofty thoughts and emotions expressed by Beethoven . . . find an echo in the works of those Chinese painters. The Adagio of the Fifth Symphony is the text interpreting the noble transcendental spirit pervading the painted scenery of Li Se-sün, and the Pastoral Symphony is the translation into music of the *Wang ch'uan t'u*. We shall better appreciate Chinese painting, if we try to conceive it as having no analogy with our painting, but as being akin to our music. Indeed, the psychological difference of Chinese painting from our own mainly rests on the basis that the Chinese handle painting, not as we handle painting, but as we handle music, for the purpose of lending color to and evoking the whole range of sentiments and emotions of humanity. In depth of thought and feeling, the great T'ang masters, in their symphonic compositions, vie with Beethoven, and in line and color almost reach Mozart's eternal grace and beauty. . . . Chinese pictorial art, I believe, is painted music, with all its shades . . . of expressive modulation.[11]

For the expression of the facts of nature, the Chinese had certain formulas that were taught as fundamentals of art education. For example, there were sixteen ways of drawing mountains,

[11] Berthold Laufer, "A Landscape of Wang Wei," in *Ostasiatische Zeitschrift*, v. 1 (1912), p. 54.

differing according to the geological formation, flora, and season — the sixteen "mountain wrinkles," the Chinese called them. The names of a few of them — "wrinkled like hemp fibers," "wrinkled like tangled hemp fibers," "wrinkled like a thunder head," "wrinkled like eddying water," "wrinkled like horses' teeth"— reveal a keen observation of nature and also a direct, suggestive method of expressing the idea.[12] Likewise there were laws governing the painting of water.

In regard to painting moving waters, whether deep or shallow, in rivers or brooks, bays or oceans, Chinanpin [a Chinese teacher] declared it was impossible for the eye to seize their exact forms because they are ever changing and have no fixed definite shape, therefore they can not be sketched satisfactorily; yet, as moving water must be represented in painting, it should be long and minutely contemplated by the artist, and its general character — whether leaping in the brook, flowing in the river, roaring in the cataract, surging in the ocean or lapping the shore — observed and reflected upon, and after the eye and memory are both sufficiently trained and the very soul of the artist is saturated, as it were, with this one subject and he feels his whole being calm and composed, he should retire to the privacy of his studio and with the early morning sun to gladden his spirit there attempt to reproduce the movement of the flow; not by copying what he has seen, for the effect would be stiff and wooden, but by symbolizing according to certain laws what he feels and remembers.[13]

This quotation is valuable not only because it gives one a notion of the formulas that governed the painters, but also because it explains something of the way in which the Chinese painters worked. Meditation, that is, mental preparation, combined with a highly trained memory, played an important part in the creation of a painting. The great Wu Tao-tzu, a well known story says, was ordered by the emperor to paint for him one of his favorite scenes of river and mountain landscape. Thither the painter went. When he returned and was asked for his sketches, he replied, "I have it all in my heart."

Less panoramic than the scroll and perhaps even more expressive of the quintessence of mood and inner meaning are some of the small round album leaves such as the *Mountain Scene with a Sage Meditating* (PL. 169 A). In the foreground a sage is reclining beneath the spreading branches of a gnarled tree looking toward the precipitous towering cliffs that fill the background and gradually fade into the distance. A note of quiet meditation and of noble sentiment pervades the picture. The whole scene has been painted with a few skillful strokes. The composition is broad and free. Ma Yüan has arranged the elements of composi-

[12] For drawings to illustrate the sixteen ways, see essay by Sei-Ichi Taki, in *Kokka*, Heft 196; Petrucci, *Encyclopédie de la Peinture Chinoise*, pp. 134 ff.
[13] Bowie, *On the Laws of Japanese Painting*, p. 61.

tion without crowding and has successfully balanced the mass on the right with the space on the left.

These paintings are as imaginative and evocative of mood as Chinese poems. For example:

> On Lady's Table Mountain-top spring snows melt;
> By the roadside apricot-flowers bud on tender twigs.
> My heart is ready; I long to go. Yet when shall the day be?
> Sadly I watch the homeward coach roll over the field-bridge.
> — *By Yang E-Shih (c. 800, written when detained in the city).*[14]

> From the thick bamboos the last rain-drops drip;
> On the high hill-top lingers the evening light.
> —*By Hsia-Hou Shen (8th century, 2nd half).*[14]

This purpose on the part of the Chinese painters to emphasize the inner significance of things rather than the external appearance is particularly true of the paintings of flowers and birds. Probably no people have felt so deeply and so sympathetically as the Buddhists the unity and harmony of all animate life. The Zen Buddhists in particular arrived at an expression of this significance that is amazing in its intimate knowledge of form, its simplicity and subtlety. It is interesting to note that these lovers of nature did not personify her forms. The mountain, the bird, or the flower is an entity with its own attributes as personal, as majestic, or as delicately graceful as human life, and as important a member of the universe as man. Hence it was not necessary to visualize it in terms of man. Technically, these paintings of the Zen Buddhists are astonishing. Color was usually abandoned and ink only used, applied with a few quick but amazingly accurate strokes. Rarely has the world seen such a marvelous expression, so ephemeral and at the same time so quivering with life, accomplished with such a minimum of means.

SCULPTURE

Monumental sculpture was short-lived in China in comparison with the other arts. When Buddhism began to stimulate life, sculpture became one of its greatest expressions, reaching a climax in the period extending from the Wei dynasties until late T'ang. Even then and in the Sung period some good work was produced, but it foreshadowed a decadence.

The influence exerted by Buddhism upon sculpture was a good deal the same as that upon painting — a fusing of the new ideas with the traditional native art, creating a product that was

[14] Waley, *Introduction to the Study of Chinese Painting*, pp. 193–94.

inherently Chinese. Such a process we see working in a votive stele (PL. 167 c) in which the figures of the donors in the two lower zones and on the back and sides are incised and the ground cut away to give contrast, the traditional method of tomb decoration; while the middle and upper zones of the face which contain Buddhist subjects are carved in relief and show strong Indian influence. Above the inscriptions that make a broad, firm base are four seals forming a square surmounted by a reliquary, four donors with their horses, worshipers, and lions. In the middle zone, Buddha, with uplifted hand symbolic of his teaching, is seated in a canopied niche with two disciples, Bodhisattvas, and guardians. The upper zone contains Buddhas and Bodhisattvas under a canopy and scenes connected with the life of Buddha. Just above this zone, the stele is broken. The first and the lasting impression of the monument is its superbly decorative beauty, tempered by Chinese sobriety and thus rich without the exuberance that is so characteristic of Indian ornamentation. The space is filled but not crowded, and an occasional plain background brings a note of restfulness. The drapery is conventionally arranged with a distinct feeling for a bold rhythmic sweep of line in the flat folds, a quality that finds particularly fine expression in the design of the reliquary and in the narrow border that contains the lotus canopy of the Buddha's niche. But besides decorative beauty, the scenes are filled with a feeling of sincerity that reveals as earnest a religious conviction on the part of these sculptors as did the kings and queens of the western portal of *Chartres* (PL. 82 A), with which they are comparable in many ways.

An illustration of the decorative beauty of these Wei sculptures as well as their ecstatic feeling is found in the upper part of a votive tablet that is filled with angels carrying musical instruments (PL. 167 A). The floating figures are suggested, not naturalistically rendered. The conventional drapery fades off into very low relief and sweeps around in flamelike lines into the curving edge of the tablet.

A single figure that exhibits this spiritual quality and also the early conventions of its expression is a statue of *Maitreya* (PL. 166 B), the Bodhisattva who is destined to become the next Buddha. He is seated with legs crossed and hand uplifted in the traditional Indian pose of the teacher. The statue breathes forth the sincerity of faith that dominated the sculptor. We feel convincingly the perfect calm and poise attained through the concentration that the lowered lids suggest; and the great benignity and assurance of salvation in the uplifted hand. The powerful stimulation that a burning faith arouses demands something higher than the illusion of natural appearance. To be sure, lack of mastery over his material accounts partly for the character of the expression, as seen in the extreme awkwardness in the leg and the foot. But far more overpowering than correct representation of form was the desire to express spiritual significance. This the artist has done by reducing the modeling to the point of bare essentials only; the features are conventionally treated with planes sharply cut; except for the head and hand the figure is so flat that it gives one more the impression of relief than the round. The drapery, plaited and girdled high, and the streamers of the cloak that cross in front in an almost geometrical pattern, fall over the pedestal in a conventional way with a distinct feeling for sweeping, rhythmic pattern. It is the nobility of the artist's conception and the superb balance between this conception and the mode of expression that give this statue and others of the Wei period a rare spiritual quality.

A *Kuan Yin* [15] (PL. 166 c) shows how the sculptor was gaining control over his material; for the figure, though still somewhat flat, shows a more naturalistic appearance and a more facile technique. The deity stands easily upon a lotus pedestal, guarded by four lions. The high tiara with a tiny statue of the seated Buddha in front, the lotus buds in the right hand and the bottle of ambrosia in the left, are the usual attributes of a Bodhisattva. The lofty, abstract, spiritual quality felt in the *Maitreya* has softened into a stately graciousness that is seen in the expression of the face, in the pose of the figure, and in the sweeping lines of the drapery. For now we see ease and grace rather than austerity in the pattern of the folds. Originally both the statue and the pedestal were covered with gilding and brilliant color. One pitfall the sculptor has not escaped in his desire to attain a gracious type of beauty; and that is overdecoration. The chains and ornaments are both fussy and profuse. Apart from this, the statue is a splendid expression of a noble and dignified majesty combined with serene benignity; but not so mightily felt as in the austere *Maitreya*.

Of T'ang sculpture, very little has survived because of the anti-Buddhist revolution, as we have explained. Its characteristics were a natural evolution of what we have seen in the art of the

---

[15] The Bodhisattva Avalokiteshvara, as his worship passed over into China under the name of Kuan Yin, assumed first a sexless and then gradually a feminine form.

Wei and Six dynasties, that period when certain conventions were fixed that continued as permanent traditions. Perhaps the most important of these were the highly simplified modeling and the conventional arrangement of the drapery. Completely satisfactory simplification of the figure requires a sophisticated and accurate knowledge of such fundamentals as proportions and organic structure. This the Chinese had now so mastered that his expression of it was facile. But his purpose was not to represent the figure as an end in itself, to give an illusion of its visual appearance, but to express the inner meaning or the dominating passion. If we apply this principle to the method of representing the drapery, we see that the conventional arrangement of folds, which emphasizes line, pattern, and design, enhances the abstraction of the figure by harmonious rhythm. The difference between T'ang sculpture and the *Bound Slave* of Michelangelo (PL. 120 B) is not so great after all. Except for such minor differences as racial characteristics, costume, and creed, both statues are manifestations of universal spiritual truths: the *Bodhisattva*, of beneficence, the serenity and freedom of soul; the *Bound Slave*, of despair, the tragedy of soul. The former is distinctly more impersonal and national in its expression, and tends to greater suppression of natural appearance; the latter is more personal, and emphasizes more the organic structure. It is partly a difference of how near to the visual appearance of nature the artist decided to come in expressing a spiritual truth. The Chinese chose to keep afar; the Italian to come closer. And it is partly a difference of temperament. The Chinese is calm; the Italian emotional. But in the last analysis these differences too are minor. What really matters is the concentration upon the ultimate spiritual significance; and, in subordinating everything else to this end, both were obedient to the fundamental laws of great art that are applicable alike to all people and to all times.

The tendencies already noted — the more naturalistic modeling, elaboration of detail, easy grace — become more pronounced in the Sung period. The fire of Buddhism was burning lower and the Zen aspect of the faith that so stimulated the landscape painters of the Sung age had little to offer the sculptors. Dignified and noble figures were still produced, such as the *Kuan Yin* (PL. 167 B). The statue is carved from wood, which was a more popular medium than stone at this time, covered with gesso, and painted. The pose is inherited from India (PL. 161 D). The erect posture and the right arm, which supports the weight, give strength and dignity to the figure. The drapery falls naturalistically in broadly flowing curves even entwining the arms as if to obtain additional curving lines. The pattern of the fine stuff of which the robe is made is indicated by gesso worked in relief, gilded and painted; the high tiara well suggests the skillful work of the goldsmith; the chains hang naturalistically; the fussy bow does not harmonize with the rest of the costume. These are minor details; but they are inclined to hold the attention and to interfere with that perfect harmony of content and expression which, we have said, made the earlier sculpture so supreme.

MINOR ARTS

Among the earliest and at the same time the loftiest manifestations of the Chinese race are the bronzes. From a remote antiquity the Chinese have been skillful molders and chiselers of this metal. But above the superb technical skill revealed is a noble spirit that breathes from these bronzes, apparently due to the fact that this was not an industrial art only. The vessels were sacrosanct because they were used in the ritual connected with ancestor worship. So deep-rooted was this feature of Chinese civilization that it afforded a profound stimulus for art production. It also determined the forms, designs, and symbols used in the decorations.

Something of this spirit we discern in the frequent inscriptions found on the bronzes, as on one of the bells that were used to summon the spirits of the departed, or the guests to the banquet, or to serve as one of the instruments of the orchestra:

I, Kuo-Shu Lü, say: Grandly distinguished was my illustrious father Hui Shu, with profound reverence he maintained a surpassingly bright virtue. He excelled alike in the rule of his own domain and in his liberal treatment of strangers from afar. When I, Lü, presumed to assume the leadership of the people and to take as my model the dignified demeanor of my illustrious father, a memorial of the event was presented at the Court of the Son of Heaven, and the Son of Heaven graciously honoured me with abundant gifts. I, Lü, humbly acknowledge the timely gifts of the Son of Heaven and proclaim their use in the fabrication for my illustrious father Hui Shu of this great sacrificial tuneful bell. Oh, illustrious father seated in majesty above, protect with sheltering wings us who are left here below. Peaceful and glorious, extend to me, Lü, abundant happiness! I, Lü, and my sons and grandsons for ten thousand years to come, will everlastingly prize this bell and use it in our ritual worship.[16]

The finest bronzes belong to the early periods — the Shang, the Chou, and the Han dynasties. A sacrificial jar (PL. 168 c) is typical both in shape and in decoration. Its proportions are

[16] Bushell, *Chinese Art*, I, p. 73.

vigorous; its curves suggest strength rather than grace. The
decoration in the broad central band consists of the highly conventionalized form of the eyes and nose of an animal, probably
of a mythological nature; the upper and lower borders contain
a tiger head and what seem to be conventionalized birds. The
meaning of this kind of decoration is uncertain, for much of the
mythological history of China is still unknown. The decorative
beauty of the design, however,
which quickly brings to mind
the *Dragon of Quirigua* (FIG.
157 B), like the latter is powerful.

A shape that is quite un-
usual is a double sacrificial
vessel (PL. 169 c) which is rectangular with flaring top and
bottom, both of which are the
same in size and shape, with
arched openings cut in each
side. The two parts are so
shaped that together, as in
the illustration, they form a
harmonious unit or separately
serve as two independent
vessels. The shape is rectangular and apparently derived from the basket that
held the millet for the ancestor worship. The arched

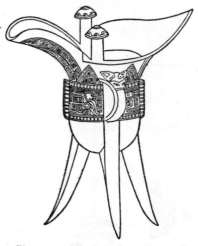

Fig. 128. Libation Cup. Shang dynasty, 1766–1122 B.C. (*Ostasiatische Zeitschrift*)

openings cut in the flaring top and bottom relieve the solidity,
and, with their strongly curved lines, act as a foil to the predominant angularity of the design. On the short ends are conventionalized animal heads that serve as handles; the two small
heads on the long sides that are attached to the upper half and
project over the lower keep the parts from slipping. The entire
body of the vessel is incised with a meander pattern that, with
its fret motif infinitely varied, gives a feeling of liveliness without obtruding or in any way interfering with the structural lines.

The meander or fret is a frequent motif of decoration in these
bronzes. The fret in early Chinese art symbolized the elements,
especially thunder and lightning. Small triangular patterns
found at the top of a vase represented mountains and, when
filled with thunder and lightning motifs, mountains surrounded

by clouds. Probably an all-over decoration based upon the fret represented a cloudy sky; the lanceolate pattern, the winds; and when eyes in the form of knobs were added, the Chinese saw the Storm God against the background of a cloudy sky.

A shape frequently found is that of the libation-cup (FIG. 128), which was used in the rites of Heaven and Earth and also in ancestor worship. Its shape not only is strong but shows fine proportions and an unusual unity between the parts and continuity of structural line as inevitably as did the Greek vases.

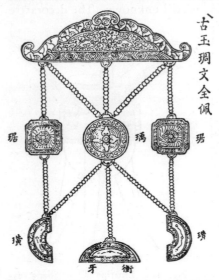

古玉琱文全佩

琚　瑀　珩

璜　璜

牙衡

Fig. 129. Drawing of a Complete Jade Girdle Pendant. (Laufer)

In all these early bronzes we feel a spirit that is too noble, too lofty and sincere for anything trivial, superficial, or pretty. There is never suavity, but always marvelous strength expressed spontaneously and directly because it was born of deep-rooted conviction. The shapes and decorative motifs early became fixed, but continued as traditions, even after the symbolism was lost, down to comparatively recent times, and were copied by the workers in jade (PL. 169 B) and ceramics. One element of charm in these bronzes is accidental, for the rarely beautiful blue, green, and iridescent color was not planned by the original artist but is due to the patina.[17]

Another medium in which the Chinese made notable achievement is jade, which they obtained from the mountains of western China and from the rivers that had their rise near these quarries and washed the jade pebbles and boulders for some distance down their courses. Particularly fine boulders were kept in the temples, in early days, as precious relics, and some of these were carved in the eighteenth century into bells, vases, and bowls. Jade was

[17] A patina is a crust that forms on a bronze during a long period of time because of the chemical action of the alloys that compose the bronze, and the atmosphere or material in which the article is buried. It may be thin or thick, rough or smooth, and of great variety of color.

used for personal ornaments, insignia, and charms, and also for vessels and utensils of various kinds.[18]

Jade carving is a very old art in China, going back to legendary times, and may possibly be traced to the work of the lapidary in early Babylonia as we saw it in the cylinder seals. The tools were few, simple, and even crude — saws for cutting and shaping the objects; iron discs and drills, worked by treadles, for carving it; and several kinds of abrasives for polishing, such as quartz, garnet, emery, and, hardest of all, ruby dust. These were applied with wood, leather, or gourd-skin, for the entire surface, even in the deepest crevices, must be free from all irregularities and from all marks of the tools.

The early jades, like the bronzes, were stimulated by religious ideas and their decorations determined by religious and emotional symbolism. This is seen in the personal ornaments, perhaps the most interesting of which are the girdle pendants (Fig. 129). Seven pieces of jade formed the pendant, which tinkled as the bearer walked. Each was a token of love and friendship, as an old song says:

> Who will give me a quince, I shall return to him a central side-ornament of fine jade for the girdle-pendant. It is not meant as an act of thanks, but I want to render our friendship everlasting. Who will give me a peach, I shall return to him the red jade *yao*. . . . (with the same refrain). Who will give me a plum, I shall return to him the black jade ornament *kiu* . . . (with the same refrain).[19]

These ornaments were sometimes buried with the dead as emblems of the parting of death and also of an eternal love. For this purpose the finest and most beautifully colored stones were used. Such a burial girdle ornament is seen in Fig. 130. On the right is a phoenix on a cloud-form, looking down toward the long slender hydra, with a

Fig. 130. Girdle Pendant. Jade. Han dynasty, 206 B.C.–221 A.D. (Drawing after Laufer)

bird's head, on the lower left side; above, along the upper edge, cloud bands carved in long firm curves. Here as in the bronzes, are simplification and conventionalization of form,

[18] Something of this variety is suggested by reading the table of contents of a Chinese book on the subject, in one hundred volumes, quoted in Bushell, *Chinese Art*, v. 1, p. 132.
[19] Laufer, *Jade*, p. 198.

virility of line, and harmony between the medium and the motif of decoration.

Something of the character of these early pieces we find in later examples such as a jade bell (PL. 169 B) that is very close, in shape, to the Chou bronze bells, and, to a less degree, in its decoration. As jade is resonant, it was used both for single bells and for chimes, and in this form was a favorite gift for congratulation of any kind. For in a Chinese pun, "to strike a musical stone" may be interpreted as "may blessings attend you." The bell was suspended by a silk cord from a wooden frame and, like the bronze bells, was struck with a hammer. This bell was carved from a single boulder of jade, and was hollowed out with a tubular drill, as the interior shows. The upper and lower edges are decorated with a fret pattern; the body contains a border with a highly conventionalized monster's head, similar to those found on the early bronzes (PL. 168 c) but based upon sweeping curves rather than rectangular mass; below this is a border of leaf-ornament, the larger motif being subdivided and filled with concentric lines; on each side of the handle are dragons. The bold simplicity of the design reflects the Shang, Chou, and Han vessels.

The eighteenth century was a renaissance period when the artists looked to these ancient dynasties for their prototypes, imitating both the shapes and motifs of the early work. The spacing of the borders, the confident firmness of line, the fine and at times even severe taste, the fitness of the design to the material — all this belongs to the long, deep-rooted tradition of the craftsmen. But as much of the symbolism and hence the dynamic power that produced the great spontaneity and sincerity of the earlier work was lost, the result, though finely decorative, is not so convincing in its spirit.

The eighteenth century jades, however, reveal a remarkable technical climax. This is apparent in a flower vase (PL. 170 A) which well illustrates the easy grace of the naturalistic design, graceful but not powerful like the earlier pieces. It also shows the soft evanescent effects that may be obtained in this medium, and the waxy luster that the Chinese call "mutton fat."

Ceramics is another field in which the Chinese have been preeminent, ranking with the few master potters of all ages. So widespread and deeply rooted is their reputation in this line that the ware of their country has become a common name in our language, applied loosely to various kinds of pottery. Ceramic products were highly prized by the Chinese, and imperial

IV. CELADON VASE

Height About Three Feet. Chinese, Sung Dynasty (960–1280 A.D.).
Buckingham Collection, Art Institute of Chicago.

patronage constituted a stimulation. Some of the kilns produced for the imperial household alone and some of the famous wares were named after the emperor whom the kilns served. Shortly before the establishment of the Sung dynasty a fabric was manufactured called Ch'ai, after the emperor who ordered it. According to Chinese writers, the emperor required that it be "as blue as the sky, as clear as a mirror, as thin as paper, and as resonant as a musical stone of jade." Judging from the extraordinary praise with which these writers describe it, this imperial order must have been well met. No example of it is extant as far as we know. It evidently served as a challenge to the Sung potters, as we discern some of these qualities in the fabrics of that period.

Sung pottery was usually porcelain,[20] which seems to have been known in China as early as the Han dynasty. Shape, color, and texture were its chief characteristics. The color was applied in the glaze and most frequently as a monochrome covering the entire surface. Where further decoration existed, it was quiet, harmonious, and unobtrusive. The objects, shapes, and color were varied. There were the imperial bulb bowls, like deep plates with a flaring rim, and the hexagonal flower pots, noted for their thick glaze of rich purples and reds. Then there were the Ting bowls and slender vases, potted so thin that they were translucent and covered with a rarely beautiful creamy white glaze, and sometimes decorated with an inconspicuous relief or incised design under the glaze. Perhaps the best known to westerners are the *Celadons*.[21] These fabrics were glazed with a soft green color that the Chinese likens to young onion sprouts. In the color, and in the smooth texture of the glaze, the celadons are not unlike jade and may have originated in an attempt to reproduce the more valuable stone in a less expensive medium. For if a person wanted to compliment a potter highly upon his vase, he would tell him that it looked like jade. In the *Celadon* reproduced in COLOR PL. IV there is quiet elegance and refined taste. It has a sturdy strength because of the careful proportioning of the parts, especially of the finely curved lip and the

[20] Porcelain is composed of three elements — kaolin, *petuntse*, and glaze. Kaolin is a fine white clay, named after the locality (Kaolin, or the High Hill) where it is found; it is infusible and forms the body of the vessel. *Petuntse*, the Chinese word for a square block of stone, is a vitreous stone that fuses at a high temperature and makes the fabric hard, translucent, impervious, and resonant. The purpose of the glaze is esthetic, not structural, to give a smooth lustrous surface and color. Thus porcelain combines the features of pottery and glass.

[21] *Celadon*, meaning sea-green, was originally the name of the shepherd in a seventeenth century French novel. In the plays of that period the shepherds usually wore sea-green costumes and the name was applied to the color and then to the Chinese ceramics of this color which were then coming to the notice of Europeans. The term is European, not Chinese.

slightly spreading base, the profile of which is reminiscent of the base of an Ionic column. From the base rise conventionalized lanceolate leaf forms, the severity of which emphasizes the easy grace of the peony scroll on the body; on the neck a tapering peony pattern meets a broad band of concentrated ridges. This decoration is all in low relief and everywhere plays into the structural lines of the vase. It is entirely covered by a soft green glaze which with its uniform tone produces a quiet, reposeful harmony.

The climax, technically, of porcelain manufacture was reached in the Ming dynasty. Great imperial kilns were established in 1369 A.D.; and each emperor in turn patronized and encouraged the output and the development of the craft. The Sung monochromes, except the white, were largely replaced by polychromes in which pictorial designs were worked out in different colored glazes and enamels. A large Ming jar (PL. 170 B) well illustrates this ware and some of the technical methods of the potters. For their problem lay largely in the question of how to keep the different-colored glazes from running together at the edges. This they accomplished partly by the cloisonné process, that is, by working out the design in raised clay threads like cloisons, leaving slightly depressed areas to hold the glaze. Another way was to incise deeply the design, forming a tiny trench to prevent the glaze from flowing beyond. The color used on the Ming jars is strong, chiefly a rich, turquoise blue, violet, and dull white, with a green glaze on the inside, producing a striking decorative quality rather than the quiet elegance of the Sung ware.

SUMMARY

In studying Chinese art we are studying the art of a sober, patient, conservative people whose law is the custom of their ancestors. Therefore art and art education looked to the past. Training consisted of copying the masters. The attitude of the Chinese on the matter of copying Dr. Laufer explains thus:

Where and what is the original, after all? Of these Chinese copies and copies of copies, the word of Holmes (*The Autocrat of the Breakfast Table*) holds good: "A thought is often original, though you have uttered it a hundred times," and Emerson's saying: "When Shakespeare is charged with debts to his authors, Landor replies, 'Yet he was more original than his originals. He breathed upon dead bodies and brought them into life.'" Thus, it is no wonder that Carl Gussow of Munich could not believe Huang Hao's Red Carp of 1811 to be a copy, though expressly stated so by the artist on the painting; the entire conception, he thought, was so free and independent that it was bound to be an original (Hirth, *Scraps from*

PLATE 171

(*A*) Howodo, or Phoenix Hall. Byodoin, near Uji. 1053 A.D.
(*Japanese Temples and Treasures*)

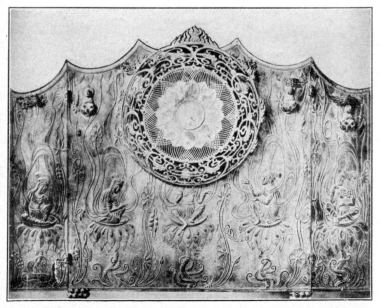

(*B*) Screen of the Trinity of Tachibana Fujin. Bronze. Early VIII cent. A.D.
Horiuji. (*Japanese Temples and Treasures*)

PLATE 172

(*A*) Yumedono Kwannon. Wood, originally covered with gold leaf. H. 7 ft. Early VII cent. A.D. Horiuji.

(*B*) Maitreya. Wood. Suiko period. Chuguji Nunnery, Nara.

(*C*) Fugen, an Attendant of a Buddha. Detail. Wood. Horiuji.

These three plates are reprinted by permission of the Cleveland Museum of Art from *Japanese Sculpture of the Suiko Period*, by Langdon Warner, published by the Yale University Press.

PLATE 173

(A) Scripture Case. Fudo as a Dragon and Two Worshipers. Lacquer. Probably Fujiwara period. Taemadera Monastery. (*Japanese Temples and Treasures*)

(B) Buddhist Frescoes. Detail. c. 712 A.D. Horiuji. (Kokka)

(C) Jocho. Amida, Central Figure of a Trinity Group. XI cent. A.D. Howodo of Byodoin. (*Japanese Temples and Treasures*)

PLATE 174

(*A*) Sesshu. Landscape Scroll. Detail. Coll. of Prince Mori, Tokio. (Taki)

(*B*) Cryptomerias and Cedars on a Snowy Hillside. XVII cent. A.D.
Freer Gallery, Washington. (Freer Gallery)

(*C*) Korin. Waves at Matsushima. Boston Museum. (Boston Museum)

a Collector's Notebook, p. 44). As everything Chinese is pervaded by an atmosphere different from our own, so also a Chinese copyist is framed of a different mould; his work is creative reinvention, not purely receptive, but partaking of the spirit permeating the soul of the master.[22]

The Chinese people had developed a native art of power and skill when Buddhism, coming from India, proved to be the great stimulating factor that brought sculpture and painting to the loftiest plane of attainment. Sculpture in the Wei period was conventional and austere but compelling in the clear flame of its spiritual significance. In the T'ang age, though it became somewhat more naturalistic, it was still formal, lofty, and noble, revealing, as did the Wei, a marvelous harmony between content and design. In the Sung age there entered a disquieting charm that allows the eye and mind to wander to the beauty of technique, of surface, and of ornament. It is charming, but not mighty. Painting, inseparable from music and poetry, under the fervor of Buddhism produced in the T'ang age paintings of Buddha and Bodhisattvas, now lost, that must have been impressive in their austerity, majesty, and fervor; and also those sympathetic and imaginative interpretations of the moods of nature that are one of the world's greatest accomplishments. Furthermore the Chinese developed a magnificent technique in painting upon silk and paper with Chinese ink; neither hesitating nor fumbling in the most difficult technical problems. The same skill is apparent in all the minor arts. But of greater importance than technical accomplishment is that unity of handiwork with deep convictions, profound thought, and lofty taste that, working together, create a great work of art.

BIBLIOGRAPHY

BINYON, LAURENCE, Flight of the Dragon. London, Murray, 1914.
—— ——, Painting in the Far East. London, Arnold, 1923.
BOSTON. MUSEUM OF FINE ARTS, Synopsis of History. Boston, 1922.
BRITISH MUSEUM, Pictorial postcards: Set VIII, Chinese Art; C8, Chinese Porcelain.
BUSHELL, S. W., Chinese Art. 2 v. London, Victoria and Albert Museum, 1921.
CRANMER-BYNG, L. A., Lute of Jade. N.Y., Dutton, 1923.
FLETCHER, SIR BANISTER, History of Architecture on the Comparative Method. N.Y., Scribner, 1924.
FRY, ROGER, AND OTHERS, Chinese Art: Painting, Ceramics, Textiles, Bronzes, Sculpture, Jade, etc. (Burlington Magazine Monograph). London, Batsford, 1925.
GILES, H. A., History of Chinese Literature. N.Y., Appleton, 1915.
—— ——, Introduction to the History of Chinese Pictorial Art. London, Quaritch, 1918.

[22] Laufer, *Jade*, p. 326.

GROSSE, ERNST, Ostasiatische Tuschmalerei. Berlin, Cassirer, 1922.

HANNOVER, EMIL, Pottery and Porcelain. 3 v. London, Benn, 1925.

HETHERINGTON, A. L., Early Ceramic Wares of China. N.Y., Scribner, 1922.

HIRTH, FRIEDRICH, Ancient History of China, N.Y., Columbia University Press, 1923.

—— ——, Scraps from a Collector's Notebook. N.Y., Stechert, 1905.

HOBSON, R. L., Art of the Chinese Potter. London, Benn, 1923.

—— ——, Chinese Pottery and Porcelain. 2 v. N.Y., Funk and Wagnalls, 1915.

KOOP, A. J., Early Chinese Bronzes. London, Benn, 1924.

KUEMMELL, OTTO, Kunst Ostasiens. Berlin, Cassirer, 1922.

LAUFER, BERTHOLD, Jade. Field Museum Publication 154, Anthropological Series v. 10. Chicago, 1912.

—— ——, "Religious and Artistic Thought in Ancient China." *Art and Archaeology*, VI (1917), pp. 295 ff.

MEYER, A. E., Chinese Painting. N.Y., Duffield, 1923.

OKAKURA-KAKUZO, Ideals of the East. London, Murray, 1920.

PETRUCCI, RAPHAEL, Chinese Painters (tr. Seaver). N.Y., Brentano, 1920.

SIRÉN, OSVALD, Chinese Sculpture. 4 v. London, Benn, 1925.

TAKI, SEI-ICHI, Three Essays on Oriental Painting. London, Quaritch, 1910.

WALEY, ARTHUR, Introduction to the Study of Chinese Painting. London, Benn, 1923.

—— ——, 170 Chinese Poems. N.Y., Knopf, 1919.

YETTS, W. P., Symbolism in Chinese Art. Leyden, Brill, 1912.

CHAPTER XXIX

JAPAN

HISTORICAL BACKGROUND

The origin of the race of Yamato (the native name of Japan) is problematical. As far back as we can trace the Japanese, they are an energetic, warlike people, yet "gentle in the arts of peace"; possessed of a primitive worship of the powers of nature, especially the sun-goddess, and of ancestors, known as Shinto. Their country is one of great natural beauty. "The waters of the waving rice-fields, the variegated contour of the archipelago, so conducive to individuality, the constant play of its soft-tinted seasons, the shimmer of its silver air, the verdure of its cascaded hills, and the voice of the ocean echoing about its pine-girt shores — of all these was born that tender simplicity, that romantic purity, which so tempers the soul of Japanese art, differentiating it at once from the leaning to monotonous breadth of the Chinese and from the tendency to overburdened richness of Indian art. That innate love of cleanness which, though sometimes detrimental to grandeur, gives its exquisite finish to our industrial and decorative art, is probably nowhere to be found in Continental work."[1]

But the chief element of inspiration in Japanese culture came from Buddhism. The impulse of Buddhism had already flooded and transformed Chinese thought, and then in the sixth century, under Chinese rather than Indian mode of expression, passed on with equal power of stimulation to Japan. With the religion came echoes of the art of India; and not only a strong influence but at first a close imitation of Chinese art by way of Korea; in fact Korean artists came to Japan to execute the work.

The story of Japanese art is a story of successive waves of influence from China, followed by periods of retirement. At no time, however, has Japan been a mere imitator. Just as China assimilated and molded to her own mode of thought and expression the ideas of India, so the native culture of Yamato,

[1] Okakura-Kakuzo, *Ideals of the East*, p. 16.

though a heavy debtor to both India and China, still is an individual racial product.

Buddhism came first in the Suiko period [2] from China of the Six dynasties, especially the Wei, and manifested itself as something spiritual and mysterious, conceived in terms of abstract form. The second wave came from T'ang China, bringing with it a spirit of grandeur and exaltation that we discern in the majestic, contemplative Buddhas and the gracious and all-merciful Bodhisattvas. The lofty idealism of this art began to give way, toward the end of the period, to a more human and a more naturalistic type. The third wave came from Sung China, in the Kamakura and Ashikaga periods, in the form of Zen Buddhism with its revolt from ritual and its emphasis upon the meditative element through which one attained insight into the ultimate spirit of the universe. This was a golden age in all the arts but especially in painting and the minor arts.

While Japanese culture was receiving and assimilating these outside influences, the barons were usurping the political power of the Mikado and setting up a military feudalism. Early in the thirteenth century they vanquished the Mongol hordes of Kublai Khan, the legend tells us, by the help of their Sun-goddess.[3] The shoguns, their commanders-in-chief, became military regents and established a complex feudal system that under the Tokugawas became a tyrannical autocracy. The astute statesman Iyeyasu, founder of the line, and his followers strengthened their own power by creating a new nobility of daimios (landed barons) and samurai (military barons), who were loyal because they were under obligation to the shogun for their existence. The Tokugawas also consolidated and increased the power of the people, and granted religious toleration. Partly through an appeal to patriotism and partly because of the Mongol and Moslem power in China, the Tokugawas cut off relationship with the continent and established that policy of isolation that continued until the downfall of the Shogunate in 1868.[4] While such a policy brought about a marvelous consolidation, its strict discipline crushed out vitality. With the rise of power among the masses, a demand came for a more democratic art. So, as the power of Buddhism waned, the native art that had always existed, though overshadowed, reasserted itself. The

[2] The chief periods of Japanese art are: Suiko, 552–645 A.D.; Hakuho, 645–709; Tempyo, 709–793; Jogan, 793–900; Fujiwara, 900–1190; Kamakura, 1190–1383; Ashikaga, 1383–1603; Tokugawa, 1603–1868.

[3] For this story see Okakura, *Ideals of the East*, p. 21.

[4] For the reasons for this event and the great change in Japan during the last half-century, from the point of view of a native, see Okakura, *The Awakening of Japan*.

lofty taste and the deep fervor of earlier days gave way to over-decoration to please the lords, and the easy charm of the wood-block print to please the people.

ARCHITECTURE

Though Shinto temples exist in Japan, the Buddhist temple and monastery stand as the highest manifestation of Japanese architecture. A typical monastery is *Horiuji* (PL. 170 c) near Nara, which was both the capital and the center of Buddhist religion and learning. At the left stands the *Kondo* or *Golden Hall* containing the principal shrine; at the right, the pagoda; in the middle distance the gateway of the surrounding wall, similar in design to the *Kondo*; outside this wall are grouped subsidiary structures such as administrative buildings, treasure houses, and cloisters, for the monastery served several purposes. Like the medieval monastery of Europe, it was a church, a charitable institution, a hospital, and a center of learning where philosophy and music were taught as well as religious subjects.

The general style is close to the Chinese (FIG. 126). There is the same massiveness, especially in the dominating roof, the same somber dignity. Yet one feels here, especially in the pagoda, a more subtle feeling for proportion and a delicacy in the sweeping curves of the eaves that suggest the Japanese element. The details and the restrained decoration are very refined, with careful spacing and proportioning of the members and an entasis in the columns. The construction is essentially of wood. Great wooden columns from two to three feet in diameter support heavy beams, the angle of joining being filled with a simple bracket. On these rests the open timber roof covered with tiles. The wall space is filled partly with plaster and partly with sliding screens. Such a structure is not only suitable to the climate of Japan but, as is revealed particularly in the pagoda, is loosely yet firmly enough constructed to withstand the frequent earthquakes to which the country is subject.

The interior of these monasteries is very splendid. On a platform is a gilded statue of the Buddha (PL. 173 c) with attendant Bodhisattvas, above whom hangs an elaborate canopy with angels carrying musical instruments; the timbers are decorated with vermilion, blue and green, and with gilding and lacquer; the walls are covered with frescoes representing the paradise of Amida Buddha. The rich color harmony adds to the mystic calm of the Buddha, so that the whole effect suggests a plastic representation of the paradise seen in the T'ang paintings.

This group at Horiuji represents the period when Japan, by assimilating Chinese influences, was developing a new national expression which we discern in the *Kondo* of the monastery of *Byodoin* at Uji (PL. 171 A), known as the *Howodo* or *Phoenix Hall*.[5] One is immediately struck by the beauty of the spot and the feeling of unity between the building and its surroundings. The heaviness and somber massiveness of the Chinese model has given way to a lightness and delicacy; the roofs have become lower and

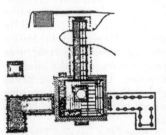

Fig. 131. Howodo of Byodoin.
(*Japanese Temples and Treasures*)

less dominating; there is a quiet grace throughout and an exquisite curve of line. The building is long and low; yet with no suggestion of monotony, for the predominant horizontal line is interestingly varied. The strong accent of the central mass is repeated in the end pavilions; and interwoven in this balance of mass is a harmonious rhythm of sweeping curves. In the matter of decoration, the exterior is very simple and restrained; but the interior, like that of *Horiuji*, is gorgeous in its splendor. Carvings and black lacquer inlaid with ivory, mother-of-pearl, and silver cover the coffered ceiling; below is rich color and gilding. In the softened light the effect is one of rich somber glow, comparable to, if not surpassing, the Byzantine mosaics.

Interiors of marvelous richness are seen in the shrines and mausoleums at Nikko, which represent the later Tokugawa period and lack the restraint and refinement of the age that produced the *Phoenix Hall*. Decoration runs riot, at times concealing the structural system, and, though powerful in effect, reveals the degeneracy in taste that characterized much of the Tokugawa work.[6]

SCULPTURE

Sculpture in Japan, like architecture and painting, had its rise in the coming of Buddhism from China in the sixth century; and its highest manifestations were created under the stimulus of the Faith. So we find much the same subject matter and the

---

[5] So called because its plan (FIG. 131) suggests a phoenix with outstretched wings, symbolic of the paradise of Amida Buddha. The *Phoenix Hall* served as the prototype of the Japanese buildings of the World's Columbian Exposition. These buildings are still one of the most attractive features of Jackson Park, Chicago.
[6] For Japanese domestic interiors, which are unique and "curiously satisfying," see Cram, *Impressions of Japanese Architecture*, Ch. VI; and Okakura, *Book of Tea*, ch. on the Tea Room.

same conventions of expression as in China, but softened by the less stolid Japanese temperament.

It was the Chinese art of the Wei and Six dynasties that came first as is evident in the *Yumedono Kwannon*,[7] (PL. 172 A). The deity stands upon an inverted lotus pedestal; on the head is a high, delicate, jeweled crown, and behind is a large lotus-leaf halo. A marvelous feeling of beneficence breathes from the whole statue.[8] The figure is thin and flat, like the *Maitreya* (PL. 166 B); the drapery is indicated by long straight conventional folds, arranged strangely like those on the archaic Greek vases and reliefs, and carried out, on the sides, into a series of sweeping curves that give a broad base to the statue to balance the massive halo. In the face the planes meet sharply, and a smile results, as in archaic Greek sculpture, because of the inability of the sculptor to model the difficult curves of the mouth and cheeks. The bronze crown, once covered with gold leaf, is perforated into a lacy pattern. Behind the statue rises the carved wood halo, the flamelike lines of which carry the eye to the apex. The rich ornamentation both relieves and enhances the severe, unadorned simplicity of the figure. The design is consummate, and the ultimate expression of beneficence is obtained chiefly through purely artistic qualities — proportion, balance, harmonious rhythm of line.

The tendency of the Japanese sculptor, as of the fifth century Greek sculptor and the Chinese Wei sculptor, was in the direction of a more naturalistic representation of the figure. A *Fugen* (PL. 172 C), an attendant, illustrates this. But one does not think of form first. Most appealing is a far-away, mysterious, ethereal quality, suggesting perfect poise and gracious beneficence. While this quality is expressed by means of the human figure, it is the quality and not the figure that speaks. The form and features have better proportions and modeling, though the highly arching brows and the hair are still conventionally treated; the folds of the garment are more deeply undercut, giving a feeling of cloth; the uplifted hand is beautifully modeled and exquisitely gracious.

Just as mysterious and abstract is a seated *Maitreya* (PL. 172 B). Here is an expression of inner peace, the consciousness of self-conquest, combined with great tenderness. The *Bodhisattva* is seated upon a high lotus pedestal; the left foot rests on a lotus,

---

[7] Kwannon is the Japanese name for Kuan Yin of China and Avalokiteshvara of India. The *Yumedono*, or *Hall of Dreams* is the sanctuary of Horiuji where Prince Shotoku, founder of the monastery, used to practise Buddhistic meditation.

[8] This statue has been held in great veneration in Japan even to the present time. Mr. Fenollosa tells the story how, when Okakura invited him to be present at the opening of the shrine where this *Kwannon* is kept, a loud clap of thunder warned the priests of the sacrilege.

the right is crossed over the knee and lightly held by the hand; the chin rests meditatively upon the uplifted right hand. The figure is finely proportioned, and modeled with great simplification of form; the drapery falls in conventional folds marvelously conceived as pure design, and carved with a sure-handedness that is without a trace of fumbling. In this statue naturalistic drapery would have been ruinous both to the significance and to the design. The deeply felt harmony of line that accords with the harmony of feeling could never have been attained by any other means than that used here. It is one of the rare illustrations of perfect harmony of content and means of expression. The additional skill in the rendering of the figure and the drapery does not force itself here to the detriment of spiritual significance any more than did the lack of skill in the *Yumedono Kwannon*. Neither matters vitally. The artist felt mightily the passion of benevolence. To express that passion was his one concern.

Japanese sculpture took the same general course of development as the Chinese. As the Wei sculpture of China was the source of inspiration for the Suiko period in Japan, so Chinese T'ang art strongly influenced the Japanese work of the Hakuho and Tempyo periods. As in China, it was a Buddhistic art. Of the various deities that found their way to Japan, Amida Buddha was the most popular. He was usually represented as seated upon the lotus in the posture of meditation or with one hand uplifted signifying his preaching, and accompanied by two or more Bodhisattvas (PL. 173 c). Behind the figures rise the elaborate lofty halos shaped like a leaf of the Bodhi tree [9] and decorated with flame-motifs and small seated Buddhas; immediately behind the seated statue is a double halo, one for the body and one for the head, decorated with a conventionalized lotus. Although this statue shows a tendency away from the austere conventions of the *Yumedono Kwannon* and the *Maitreya* toward greater naturalism, still the modeling is highly generalized and conventional, as is the drapery about the figure and the folds that hang over the pedestal. Rhythmic flow of line and pattern remained a convention for the expression of spiritual content, with only a partial acceptance of naturalistic representation.

Most of the great Trinity groups are of bronze and reveal the magnificent skill of the Japanese bronze founder. An outstanding example is the screen, containing the halo, that served as a background for the small *Tachibana Fujin Trinity* (PL. 171 B).

---

[9] The tree under which Buddha sat when he attained enlightenment; hence it was called the tree of enlightenment (Bodhi).

The base of the shrine represents, half realistically and half conventionally, the surface of a pond from which rise on curving stems three lotus flowers that serve as pedestals for the Buddha and two attendants.[10] The design of the base is carried up into the screen. For from it rise five lotus flowers on undulating stems in low relief, with delicate engraving. Each lotus, with inverted petals, supports an angel who turns toward the Buddha in adoration. The space is entirely covered but not crowded with gently flowing lines exquisitely suggestive of quietly moving water. This design is one of the most delicately sensitive ever wrought in bronze. The artist was gifted with imagination and intensely refined feeling, and he never lost sight of the medium through which he was expressing his idea. He had no desire for pictorial effect or the illusion of natural appearance. Still, by exquisite flow of line, delicate relief, and engraving he expressed all the essence of the forms. In contrast to the delicate surface of the screen is the virile pattern of the halo. In the center is the lotus, as is usual, to frame the head of the Buddha immediately in front of it. Surrounding this are perforated borders of interlaced and geometric patterns. Along the edge are flames that swirl toward the apex.

PAINTING

As in architecture, so in painting, the advent of Buddhism was the great stimulating factor. In the *Kondo of Horiuji* we find wall paintings (PL. 173 B) as typically Chinese as the building itself. The subject is one of those celestial scenes in which Amida Buddha is sitting upon a lotus, wrapped in meditation and surrounded by saints, deities, and disciples representative of the "vast community" of the Buddhist faith. One cannot but think of Ajanta, for there is the same stateliness and tenderness, the same charging of the figure with deep religious emotion. This is attained by the superlative quality of line, mass, and color.

It was the T'ang art of China that brought this impetus to Japan. As the Japanese temperament, however, is more eager and energetic than the Chinese, the austerity of T'ang was softening into something more human, more tender, and more sumptuous in color and decorative value, when another mighty wave of influence surged into Japan from Sung China in the form of Zen Buddhism. The result of this was the most exquisite and

10 The figures have been removed in PL. 171 B in order to show the design of the screen.

refined landscape, flower, and bird paintings that Japan has produced. The simplicity and directness of Zen thought led these painters to use ink rather than the sumptuous color and gilding characteristic of Yamato art. Perhaps the greatest of these painters was a Zen priest, Sesshu (c. 1420–1506 A.D.). In a detail taken from a landscape scroll (PL. 174 A), we find ourselves looking from an elevated position over a panoramic scene. At the right is a gnarled pine tree clinging to the side of a cliff and overhanging a misty valley with mountains on the farther side. Against this background the pine weaves a pattern that is lightninglike in its darting angularity. From the mists emerge other pines, climbing the steep hillside, and buildings with a pagoda, and, at the left, a rocky plateau with angular cleavage like hard basalt, crowned with tall, slender pines. One is struck at once with the crisp, powerful black stroke with which Sesshu defines his rocks and trees. Each line forces upon us a realization of the special character and inherent quality of the rock, tree, mountain, and building. Sesshu's definition of an artistic triumph illustrates precisely what this painting reveals: "It means to so represent an object or scene as to express its essential attributes with the least possible use of strokes." Subtle gradations and accurate values, as in the Tung Yüan scroll (PL. 168 A), bring a realization of infinite spaciousness. It is not as reposeful as the Chinese. The feeling of vibrant life, the eager, dashing brush strokes, the particularly decorative patterning of the trees and the massing of the darks and lights, the arresting parallelism of vertical line in the sheer cliff and the pagoda forming a center of interest — all this shows that while Sesshu had learned much from the Chinese landscape painters, he was still essentially independent.

Thus we have seen two kinds of painting produced in Japan: the majestic, hieratic Buddhist figure paintings under the influence of Chinese T'ang art, and the landscape painting, inspired by the Chinese Sung. Alongside these the native painting of Yamato continued to exist, at times quite overshadowed by Chinese influences, again strongly reasserting itself in the hands of great masters. It interested itself chiefly in court and military life, loved action and movement, delighted in rich and splendid color made all the more sumptuous by abundant use of gilding, and reveled in a keen sense of decorative values.

One very characteristic manifestation of the native art was the folding screen, which served, like the sliding screen, as a partition. Hence any ornamentation required decorative qualities.

Furthermore, the fact that it folded demanded attention to the unity of composition in each section as well as in the whole. This is successfully accomplished in a sixfold screen on which is represented a winter scene (PL. 174 B). The calm majesty of the great cryptomerias, and the lofty spirit of the entire panel as well as the decorative quality of the design, are due to the simple massing of snow, hills, tree trunks, and pines. Each section is a unit of design, yet all together compose into a pattern of great breadth and monumentality.

More daring both in imagination and in decorative quality is the work of Korin (died 1716 A.D.). Such a screen painting as his *Waves at Matsushima* (PL. 174 C) shows how far he disregarded form and at the same time revealed the essence of life. All the forms are boldly and even fantastically conventionalized. Yet the solidity of the rocks, the power of the tumultuous waves, and the quiet security of the pines on their lofty sites are surprisingly real. Korin's technique was undoubtedly influenced by his work in lacquer, in which he was an expert craftsman. One feels, however, that when he painted this screen he was following quite implicitly the teaching of the great masters on the painting of moving waters.[11]

In the seventeenth century a Japanese painter extended the scope of the subject matter of Yamato painting and made a series of pictures illustrating the everyday life of the people in the streets, trade-houses, theaters, and countryside, which from their subject matter were called *Ukiyo-yé*, "pictures of this fleeting world." They became very popular with the people, especially when, a little later, the perfection and application of wood-block printing brought these pictures within the reach of the masses. Japanese prints are not representations of the great art of Japan, and are not comparable to the work of its great masters; yet they possess a winsome charm that is very appealing, and in them, as in the other crafts so skillfully pursued in this country, we recognize the sound artistic sense and good taste of a really esthetic people. For in the best of the prints — those of Hokusai (1760–1849 A.D.) or Hiroshige (1797–1858 A.D.) — we always find keen observation of nature and of people, imagination, a lively sense of exquisite color harmony, easy, accomplished drawing, and subtle balance, often asymmetrical. In addition to these artistic qualities is great technical skill in wood-block printing.

[11] P. 441.

MINOR ARTS

The superb craftsmanship and also the fine taste of the Japanese are well illustrated by the minor arts, especially the metal work and lacquer. The bronze workers of Japan have always been skillful to an unusual degree. It was an inherited craft, and the most famous families traced their ancestry back to mythical times. The casting was done by the *cire perdue* process, and the finishing by a considerable use of the chisel. Evidences of this skill we have already seen in the Buddhas and Bodhisattvas that compose the Trinity groups; and also in the *Tachibana Fujin Screen*, so exquisite in its conception, design, and execution.

Important among these metal workers were the armorers, for the powerful samurai created a demand for the finest sword blades and sword furniture. A thorough knowledge of the properties of metals and alloys enabled the swordsmith to obtain various colors and textures; while for decorations he employed a variety of metal processes in casting, chasing, stamping, and damascening. The blade was made of many layers, each forged and tempered with all the expert skill of generations.[12] It is this multiplicity of layers that causes the watered effect seen in fine blades.

Another medium in which Japan has excelled is lacquer (PL. 173 A), which was derived from China. Lacquer is a natural varnish of exceptional hardness derived from the sap of the lac tree. The object to be lacquered is usually made of wood carefully prepared and covered with paper, hempen cloth, or silk and lacquer, and polished with a whetstone to give a firm, marblelike surface for the lacquering. The process reminds one of the preparation of a panel for tempera painting. On the finished surface, layer after layer of lacquer is laid, dried, and polished to obtain a deep lustrous surface. Gold is applied in a variety of ways, and its rich glow is a decoration in itself. When painting or modeling is added, it is applied to the ground and then covered with a final coat of translucent lacquer as a finish.

SUMMARY

While much of the art of Japan has been derived from China and has followed much the same course of evolution, still there are certain characteristics that differentiate Japanese art quite strongly from Chinese. One is the greater adaptability of the

---

[12] For a detailed account of this forging of a sword see Dick, *Arts and Crafts of Old Japan*, p. 85.

Japanese. There is a mobility and a plasticity in his temperament that contrasts with the immobility and stolidity of the Chinese. He is by nature more susceptible to change and less insistent upon following the past. For this reason his originality is more obvious and more daring. In architecture, in his roof composition he evolves exquisite designs of harmonious curves. In painting, he delights in the most exquisite ink monochromes; while at times, as in Korin and others, he revels in sumptuous color and gold, though never at the loss of decorative fitness. His careful craftsmanship in all things, large and small, is due to a considerable extent to his willingness to perfect his detail, perhaps one detail only, even to hidden parts like the inside of a lacquer box. That this is characteristic, the following story shows.

. . . In the sixteenth century the morning-glory was as yet a rare plant with us. Rikiu had an entire garden planted with it, which he cultivated with assiduous care. The fame of his convolvuli reached the ear of the Taiko, and he expressed a desire to see them, in consequence of which Rikiu invited him to a morning tea at his house. On the appointed day Taiko walked through the garden, but nowhere could he see any vestige of the convolvulus. The ground had been leveled and strewn with fine pebbles and sand. With sullen anger the despot entered the tea-room, but a sight waited him there which completely restored his humour. On the tokonoma, in a rare bronze of Sung workmanship, lay a single morning-glory — the queen of the whole garden! [13]

BIBLIOGRAPHY

ANESAKI, MASAHARU, Buddhist Art in Its Relation to Buddhist Ideals. Boston, Houghton, 1915.

BINYON, LAURENCE, Painting in the Far East. London, Arnold, 1923.

BOSTON MUSEUM OF FINE ARTS, Synopsis of History. Boston, 1922.

BOWIE, H. P., On the Laws of Japanese Painting. San Francisco, Elder, 1911.

BRITISH MUSEUM, Pictorial postcards: Set VI, Japanese Drawings of Hokusai; IX, LIII, Japanese Paintings; C6, Japanese Colour Prints.

CRAM, R. A., Impressions of Japanese Architecture. N.Y., Baker, 1905.

DAWSON, E. B., Enamels. London, Methuen, 1906.

DICK, STEWART, Arts and Crafts of Old Japan. Chicago, McClurg, 1905.

DILLON, EDWARD, Arts of Japan. Chicago, McClurg, 1914.

HOLMES, C. J., Hokusai. London, Longmans, n.d.

KUEMMELL, OTTO, Kunst Ostasiens. Berlin, Cassirer, 1922.

OKAKURA-KAKUZO, Awakening of Japan. N.Y., Century, 1905.

—— ——, Book of Tea. N.Y., Duffield, 1912.

—— ——, Ideals of the East. London, Murray, 1920.

SEIDLITZ, WOLDEMAR VON, History of Japanese Colour Prints. Philadelphia, Lippincott, 1920.

TAKI, SEI-ICHI, Three Essays on Oriental Painting. London, Quaritch, 1910.

WARNER, LANGDON, Japanese Sculpture of the Suiko Period. New Haven, Yale University Press, 1923.

WITH, KARL, Buddhistische Plastik in Japan. Vienna, Schroll, 1922.

[13] Okakura, *Book of Tea*, p. 145.

CHAPTER XXX
CONTEMPORARY ART IN EUROPE AND AMERICA
1900–1925 A.D.

Any evaluation of the art of the last two decades must be only tentative. The best we can do is to estimate the general trend of the present, and consider to what extent contemporary art is an expression of contemporary life.

The world situation today is the logical outgrowth of the nineteenth century. This was a century of investigation, revolution, and destruction: the critical investigation of the facts of nature (Darwin's *Origin of Species* was published in 1859); the industrial revolution with its tremendous influence upon social and economic conditions; the revolt from authority, and the attempted destruction of the forces against which the revolt took place.

What has been the result of this activity? (1) Critical investigation has brought about the greatest scientific age with the most marvelous discoveries that the world has ever known; and, as these discoveries have been applied chiefly to industry, it has brought also the greatest industrial era of the world. (2) Industry has compelled people to congregate into great cities. Science has tremendously influenced living conditions, bringing ease, comfort, and even luxury within the reach of a far greater number of people than ever before. One aspect alone of modern civilization well illustrates this fact — the sanitation and the conquest of disease in the modern city as compared with the unsanitary, plague-besieged cities of Europe up to a century ago. (3) Politically, the nineteenth century saw the revolt of the people from authority. One by one the representatives of the doctrine of the divine right of kings have been dethroned or converted into figureheads; the franchise has been widely extended; and active participation in the government, if not actual control of it, by the masses has taken the place of the rule of kings or of privileged classes. Political experimentation is going on under forms varying from mild democracy to Bolshevism. (4) Ease of intercommunication has brought the world together into an inextricable economic unity, and sincere attempts are being made toward closer political unity. Especially broadening is the more sympathetic recognition of the great cultures of the Orient, of which the Occident is just becoming aware. (5) Through the printing press and democratic institutions, illiteracy is disappearing; though this is not the same as saying that culture is proportionately increasing. (6) In religion, psychology and critical research have brought about a conflict in the realm of belief and observance that is one of the outstanding features of contemporary life.

These are but a few of the great movements of the day that are making life more complex than ever before. The break from authority and tradition has emphasized the importance of the individual together with the freedom of the individual to follow his own impulses, rather than the importance of the community. Phenomenal success in business, with the massing of great fortunes, has placed an overwhelming emphasis upon the material things of life, and has brought lack of faith, with indifference to the ethical, the spiritual, and the cultural. For the easy liver, life is easy and free, superficial, and conscienceless; for the real thinker, it is difficult and perplexing. In an age thus characterized by experimentation, emancipation, transition, and revolution, it is but natural that there should be many manifestations of restlessness, impatience, capriciousness, lack of restraint, and the sense of freedom in general. It is also not surprising that art, too, has been affected by the disturbances of life at large.

Like religion, art has become segregated from the affairs of life as something to be treated with indifference, or disregarded, or as a luxury, something to be indulged in, upon occasions, or as a means of ostentation. It is the age of the museum and the exhibition — both unnatural. That impulse of the people as a whole which impelled the craftsman to use time and patience to make the church vessel or the everyday utensil expressive and beautiful, which recognized good taste and sound craftsmanship, and which rose in certain individuals to a degree that enabled them to create masterpieces — that impulse finds no expression today, because machinery has taken away the opportunity for self-expression, and because taste has been dulled by our being compelled to accept the uniform and standardized products of a commercial world that frankly looks to profit first. Thus the minor arts have been practically eliminated. The builder's art, it is true, shows logical constructive thinking and, especially in America, appears to be one of the saner of the arts. It is in the fields of painting and sculpture that we find the fiercest contentions. Opposing groups of conservatives and of radicals contain exponents of all varieties and shades of conservatism and radicalism. The conservatives believe in the fundamental traditions of the past, though many even of them see the value of revolting from abject slavery to tradition. The radicals, in general, would break with authority and tradition, and leave the individual impulse free and unrestricted for experimentation and expression.

These contentions of conservatives and radicals are only a repetition of history; for in every transitional age has arisen a similar situation. Recalling Florence early in the fifteenth century, for example, we remember how Fra Angelico, the conservative, continued working in the traditions of the monastery, that is of the Middle Ages, though he was not entirely uninfluenced by the new ideas of his contemporaries. Masaccio and Donatello, on the other hand, represent the radical element who, stimulated by the new attitude toward life in general, were experimenting and struggling with a new type of expression. And among these, as among us, were extremists.

Today, more or less excellent work is being produced by the conservatives in Europe and America. It is, however, so similar in principle to what we have seen in the preceding chapters that here we shall speak chiefly of that of the radicals.

It is in painting that we see the trend of contemporary art most clearly; and as Paris has been the center of these movements, the work produced in France is typical. We have already seen something of the revolution of the nineteenth century in France, both in subject matter and in technique; and of its culmination in Cézanne. In his elemental simplicity, in his vision of nature in terms of geometric form and of color, in his distortion, though slight, of natural form for the purpose of a forceful expression, and in his sense of design that was naturally a corollary of these principles — in all this he took issue with the Impressionists on the one hand and laid the foundations of contemporary art on the other. His own statement, "I have not 'realized' — I shall always remain the primitive of the way I have opened," has proved true.

The chief movements that have grown out of the nineteenth century, beginning with Cézanne, may be loosely called Post Impressionism, or, as the artists themselves prefer, Expressionism. Certain groups have given rise to more restricted terms,

PLATE 175

(*A*) Woolworth Building. New York. Cass Gilbert, arch. 1911–13 A.D. (Copyright by Detroit Publishing Co.)

(*B*) Meštrović. My Mother. Marble. 1908 A.D. Property of the Jugoslav Government.

(*C*) Picasso. Woman with a Mandolin.

(*D*) Gauguin. Maternity.

PLATE 176

(*A*) Arthur B. Davies. Unicorns.

(*B*) Paul Manship. Memorial Tablet Erected to John Pierpont Morgan.
Detail. Metropolitan Museum of Art, New York. (Metropolitan Museum)

such as Cubism, Futurism, Synchromism. Closely associated with Cézanne as strong influences toward a new art expression were Vincent Van Gogh (1853–1890 A.D.) and Paul Gauguin (1848–1903 A.D.). In Van Gogh we see an intensely individual expression; whether of an overwrought mind or not is a moot point. One feels the strained emotions and the passionate confidence he placed in pigment as a medium of expression; so that in his *Sunflowers*, for example, or his *Landscape near Arles* we have not only a simple elemental revelation of the life of the plant itself and of the scene, but a vibrating surface of great decorative beauty. Decorative pattern is a characteristic of Gauguin also, but of a very different kind. For here it depends upon rhythmic line, pure, brilliant color laid on in flat masses and selected arbitrarily as far as natural appearance is concerned, in the manner of the twelfth century glassworkers; beautiful drawing of essentials only; and elimination of detail. In this accomplished use of essential line and also in a certain quietude that pervades the work of Gauguin, one is made to think of Giotto. It was in the South Sea Islands that Gauguin found types of people and of life that suited his mode of expression (PL. 175 D). This desire for a more elemental kind of life has led to the present enthusiasm for archaic and primitive art, for exotic savage art, and for negro sculpture. In Gauguin we see a more reasonable fusion of primitive life and European tradition than in most of the followers of "primitivism." For many forget that primitive or archaic art is the honest manifestation of a certain period of man's experience or development; that its outward form is determined by that experience; and that to copy the outward form without being impelled by the inner experience is destined to lead into emptiness and artificiality.

The innovations of Cézanne, Van Gogh, and Gauguin [1] became accentuated in Henri Matisse (1869–) and Pablo Picasso (1881–). This we note in their spirit of experimentation, in their definite tendency toward design, in their recognition of the mathematical principle in nature, in their distortions, and in their manifestation of intensely individual emotional expression. Matisse carries simplification of drawing — and his draughtsmanship is highly accomplished — to the point of distortion and unintelligibility, declaring that he is attempting to give not a complete visual impression, but an emotional experience. This is the creed of Picasso also, who, incited by Cézanne's

---

[1] Another tendency of the day is the unusual amount of writing on the part of the artists themselves about their art: by Whistler, Rodin, Gauguin, Seurat, Matisse, to mention a few.

remark that "everything in nature is modeled on the lines of the sphere, the cone, and the cylinder," began to experiment in carrying this theory to its logical conclusion, by reducing nature to geometrical form and, furthermore, by combining simultaneously in one figure several aspects, that is, by representing what the mind knows and remembers rather than what the eye sees. Thus Cubism came into existence. Picasso's *Woman with a Mandolin* (PL. 175 c) is a typical example in which recognizable form is not entirely lost. In extreme Cubism color is disregarded, for the painting is usually in monochrome, and curved lines are eliminated. Though Picasso founded Cubism, he has not continued to paint in this style, but now and again returns to a close approximation of the visual appearance of nature. Great versatility — one wonders how often the purpose is merely to cause surprise and notoriety — is characteristic not only of Picasso but of many contemporary artists.

Futurism had its rise in Italy. The name derives from one aspect only of the movement, that is, entire separation from the past. Its doctrines are based upon the modern scientific theory that the ultimate reality of all nature is energy. Therefore the purpose of the artist is to suggest the energy, not to represent the outward appearance, to picture "not the engine, but the go." Therefore line and color are used arbitrarily to produce this sensation. The *Bal Tabarin* of Gino Severini (1883–) and the *Dynamics of an Automobile* by Luigi Russolo are typical examples. Before these apparently unintelligible compositions we are expected to experience the movement of the dance and the passing of the automobile.

One more ism perhaps needs mention: Synchromism, which, as its name implies, means that "with color" the expression is made. As the representational element is practically eliminated and everything is pure abstraction, color alone is left as an emotional stimulant. Probably, as Mr. Wright suggests,[2] this art is not the art of painting, but an art whose purpose is to stimulate the imagination by one means — color.

In the United States there appears to be more conservatism than in Europe and less tendency to be carried away by the radical movements above described. Three painters may be mentioned as representative of the best work — George Wesley Bellows (1882–1925), Arthur B. Davies (1862–), and Rockwell Kent (1882–). The highly accomplished draughtsmanship of George Bellows is evident in his lithographs. Not only

[2] In *The Future of Painting.*

in lithography but in painting, one basic principle that has contributed to his success is a sound craftsmanship. He had a clear vision, an artist's vision of the everyday life about him, and with his strong vigorous brush work he gave this vision strong, honest expression, entirely free from virtuosity. His sane attitude toward the past and toward tradition, and his persistent refusal to be enslaved by "periods," strengthened the sincerity of his work.

Arthur B. Davies represents an altogether different type. In his work we enter a dream world filled with the mood of poetic fancy (PL. 176 A). Across a long panel filled with a spacious, majestic landscape, slender figures that are imaginative and almost dematerialized weave a rhythmic pattern. One cares not about the subject; it is only the lyrical mood, the suggestion of music, that matters. The freedom of the composition, of its rhythm and balance, the elongation of the figure, the glowing color, and the imaginative and emotional appeal that characterize much of Mr. Davies' work, bring him closer to the contemporary European movements than the majority of American painters.

In Rockwell Kent we find a man who is interested not in the everyday life about him, nor in the realm of poetic fancy, but in the most elemental aspects of nature. This instinct has taken him to the distant quiet places of the earth, to Alaska and the far southern regions; and his work is an artist's record of first-hand experiences with the simple, profound truths that are revealed by an austere aspect of nature. Thus all his work has rugged vigor and monumentality. In it one discerns bare truth revealed by a vision that has scorned and cast aside everything that was trivial or inessential.

The sculpture of the last two decades shows much the same tendency as the painting. In the nineteenth century the naturalism of Rodin arose as a protest against the sleek surfaces, structureless bodies, and restricted subject matter sanctioned by the Academy. Other traits also appeared in this sculptor that correspond to those of the Impressionists: the momentary expression, the fading off of the figure into the block of stone, the pictorial effect of light and shade. The reaction of sculpture to these traits of Impressionism is seen in the French sculptors Aristide Maillol (1861–) and Émile Antoine Bourdelle (1861–), and the Jugoslav, Ivan Meštrović (1883–). In Maillol and Meštrović we see the primitive tendency, high simplification, large structural planes, conventional drapery, a robust monumentality and, in Bourdelle especially, an emphasis upon decorative design. In Meštrović, pattern, strongly reminiscent of that of the Byzantines, is used for the purpose of enhancing spiritual significance. *My Mother* (PL. 175 B), for example, is impregnated with great intensity of life together with great calm and restraint. In the sober, downcast face and tightly clasped hands, and in the whole pose, there is a generalized expression, noble and poignant, of patience and resignation. These qualities are tremendously enhanced by the rhythmic flow of repeated curves in the conventional treatment of the drapery and by the suppression of realism in all parts of the figure for the purpose of concentration upon inner meaning rather than outward appearance.

The general tendency of sculpture has been away from naturalistic appearance toward a more abstract and emotional expression. An extreme result is the work of the Lithuanian, Alexander Archipenko (1887–). Archipenko, like Picasso, is versatile, and with a knowledge of the fundamentals of figure sculpture is capable of masterly naturalistic representation when in the mood of it. But his most characteristic works are his elongated figures, swung into marvelously beautiful curves, in which form has been reduced to a mere suggestion of the human figure, or even mere part of it, for the head, arms, or legs are frequently omitted. The sculptor's purpose seems to be to express his emotions abstractly by means of the beautiful lines and masses that the human figure suggests. In some of his work where the distortions are not too distracting there is a living quality, an almost disembodied and highly concentrated essence of aliveness that an unprejudiced spectator can feel for the very reason that realism has been so uncompromisingly subordinated. Such work as that of Picasso and Archipenko is based upon the principles used by many great artists of all ages. It is only a matter of the extreme degree to which these principles have been carried in recent times. In this lack of restraint these artists are highly characteristic of their age.

Among American sculptors these movements have not influenced the more conservative, traditional work as vitally as they have that of Europe. The sculptor whose work probably gives the greatest promise of real power is Paul Manship (1885–). With a masterly technique, he has combined great knowledge and appreciation of the art of various ages, now of the Italian Renaissance, now Archaic Greece, now India, and now Egypt. These archaisms, frequently to be found in details only, as in the drapery and hair, have not been entirely imitations. In the well-known *Dancer and Gazelles*, for example, one feels both India and Greece. The spontaneity, the exquisite beauty of rhythm and balance in the composition, are the manifestation of a feeling that is sensitive to lyric grace. A later work which shows Mr. Manship's archaistic tendency more subordinated and which also reveals his fine taste, with his successful combining of monumentality and ease, is the *Memorial Tablet to J. P. Morgan* erected in the Metropolitan Museum (PL. 176 B).

A very vigorous source of art production in literature, music, drama, painting, and sculpture that is both arresting in its power and strong in its influence is Russia. Here is one of the few places where there is an elemental vigor that is not savage, but quietly profound. Russian art is a fusion of the Byzantine tradition and the Slavic racial character. About 1000 A.D. Russia accepted Christianity from Constantinople in the form of the Greek Church, and it has always maintained a close relationship between the Church and the State. The Russian peasant is a man of simple faith, of quiet fervor and aspiration, of great vigor and great capacity for patient endurance. He has lived a life of repression filled with enmity toward the government. The early art of Russia was ecclesiastical. The churches of Kiev, Novgorod, Moscow, and Leningrad were modeled more or less closely after Santa Sophia. Mural paintings and ikons were decorative, hieratic, of solemn color, and filled with a feeling of mysticism and ecstasy. In the nineteenth century a realistic illustrative school of painting arose, represented by Vassili Verestchagin (1842–1904 A.D.) and Ilya Repin (1844–1918 A.D.), which served as propaganda against the officialdom that was crushing the mass of the Russian people. The result was dull and unconvincing. It served its purpose, however, in that the reaction from it, beginning about 1890, turned artistic expression back into native channels and gave it the impetus toward a genuinely Slavic expression based upon inherited traditions. For subject matter the artists turned to the primeval, mythical days of their race, to the world of imagination and fantasy; and for means of expression, to their native traditions inherited from the ikon-painters who had secured so much emotional intensity through their powerful color and decorative design. The result has been a tremendous manifestation of the esthetic power of the Russian people, an expression that is more racial than individual. We realized it first, perhaps, in the Russian ballet, that quintessence of fancy, color, and movement; then in the Russian drama, the stage designs of Leon Bakst (1866–1925 A.D.), the painting of Boris Anisfeld (1879–) and Nicolas Roerich (1874–) and the music of Igor Stravinsky (1882–), to mention but a few. Probably no modern people have correlated the fine arts as have the Russians. Through them all run creative fancy, powerful elemental rhythm, strong, brilliant color, highly sensitive decorative fitness, and an intense fervor that is the sign of an unspoiled latent power seeking expression. And at the base of all the varying manifestations of Russian art lies an accomplished technique.

In architecture we can see clearly the influence of contemporary life. The growth of large cities, the phenomenal development of industry, and the consequent complexity of life, have demanded a great variety of buildings, especially those devoted to civic, industrial, and educational work, and to transportation. Some of the architects are still under the influence of the historic styles, especially in ecclesiastical architecture, as one sees in such churches as *Saint John the Divine* in New York, and the *Cathedral* overlooking Washington, both in process of construction. More and more, however, the modern architect is designing a building that is frankly expressive both of its purpose and of its material and construction. The outstanding example of this tendency is the skyscraper, the fundamental principles of whose structure we have already noted (PL. 153 B). The development of those principles one sees in many of the recent skyscrapers of New York and Chicago. A typical example is the *Woolworth Building* (PL. 175 A) with its sixty-story tower reaching a height of nearly eight hundred feet. Even here there is a lingering echo of Gothic decoration, carried out, however, with great adaptability and effectiveness.

One conspicuous lack in the art of the last two decades, as we have noted, is the absence of the minor arts as an art expression. This condition is due, particularly in Europe and America, to the industrial revolution, that is, to the supplanting of the work of the craftsman by the machine-made article. The attempt has been made to carry on with machinery, that is with a new method, the traditions of the handmade article, just as the early printed book attempted to reproduce both in its type and decoration the appearance of the manuscript. The world is still readjusting itself to this situation. Machinery has come to stay and no one would desire to eliminate it. Yet there is a growing realization of the fact that machinery is not the *summum bonum;* and one of the most hopeful features of the present is the recognition, on the part of industry, of the economic value of the skilled designer and craftsman; and the necessity of training public taste, by placing before the people articles that are good in color, line, and pattern. This elevation of taste on the part of a larger number of people is resulting in the creation of the demand for the beautiful which is necessary as a stimulation for a really great art expression.

What shall we venture to presage? We seem to have found that contemporary art is quite expressive of this transitional age, an age in which destructive and constructive forces are still working side by side. An inevitable tendency has been to go to extremes, to exalt the individual, to run into unintelligible abstractions lacking in real significance, to be content with the sensational, fantastic, or superficial.

A great art will come again into the world [says Mr. Mather] only on condition that the artist is willing to live greatly and generously in acknowledgment of all his social bonds. Art is not a subtle algebra to be comprehended only through higher mathematics, but the common property of proud, wise, and sensitive communities. The artist must be a great human being, a thoroughly representative man before he can aspire to be a great artist. And no art can thrive where the individual is deified and nature is scorned. . . . It is because the latest art has overrated the individual and underrated nature and tradition that I believe that it cannot stand. When it vanishes like a bad dream, it may at least have served the purpose of a conclusive demonstration of a false theory. The way will then be open for a better adjustment, so that the artist may once more find his place in a society that gives him generous stimulus and support. To that end all who think with sanity and humanely about art may contribute.[3]

The artists of today are breaking ground for the future, for that great art expression which optimistic thinkers see not far away. In our life today there is abundance of vitality, initiative, and technical skill. The great need is a noble passion that will dominate life with artistic impulse. Then from this solid foundation will rise truly significant expressions of the human mind and spirit.

BIBLIOGRAPHY

Many important articles on contemporary art are to be found in the current art periodicals, especially the *Architectural Record*, *Architectural Review*, *Art in America*, *The Arts*, *Arts and Decoration*, and the *Burlington*.

AMERICAN INSTITUTE OF ARCHITECTS, Significance of the Fine Arts. Boston, Marshall Jones, 1923.

BALDERSTON, J. C., "Dusk of the Gods: A Conversation on Art with George Moore." *Atlantic Monthly*, v. 118 (1916), p. 165. See the reply by Caffin, "Cheating the Coroner," *International Studio*, v. 62 (1917), p. III.

[3] "Newest Movements in Painting," in "Art Studies, Medieval, Renaissance and Modern." *American Journal of Archaeology*, 1923, extra number.

BELL, CLIVE, Pot-Boilers. London, Chatto, 1918.

—— ——, Since Cézanne. N.Y., Harcourt, 1922.

BENOIS, A. N., Russian School of Painting (tr. Yarmolinsky). N.Y., Knopf, 1916.

CHASE, G. H., AND POST, C. R., History of Sculpture. N.Y., Harper, 1924.

CHENEY, SHELDON, Primer of Modern Art. N.Y., Boni, 1924.

CLARK, ELIOT, "Considerations on Modernistic Aesthetics." In *Art in America*, v. 9 (1921), p. 210.

CLUTTON-BROCK, ARTHUR, AND OTHERS, Necessity of Art. London, Student Christian Movement, 1924.

CONSTABLE, W. G., "Painting." *Encyclopædia Britannica* (12th ed.), v. 32, p. 3.

CORTISSOZ, ROYAL, American Artists. N.Y., Scribner, 1923.

CRAM, R. A., "Limits of Modernism in Art." In *Arts and Decoration*, v. 20 (1924), p. 11.

CURČIN, M. (COMPILER), Ivan Meštrović, a Monograph. London, Williams, 1919.

EDDY, A. J., Cubists and Post-Impressionists. Chicago, McClurg, 1919.

FAURE, ELIE, History of Art: v. 4, Modern Art (tr. Pach). N.Y., Harper, 1924.

FLETCHER, SIR BANISTER, History of Architecture on the Comparative Method. N.Y., Scribner, 1924.

FRY, ROGER, Vision and Design. London, Chatto, 1920.

GORDON, JAN, Modern French Painters. London, Lane, 1923.

HIND, C. L., Art and I. N.Y., Lane, 1921.

—— ——, Post Impressionists. London, Methuen, 1911.

HOLMES, C. J., Notes on Post Impressionist Painting. London, Chatto, 1909.

KENT, ROCKWELL, Wilderness: A Journal of Quiet Adventure in Alaska. N.Y., Putnam, 1920.

KIMBALL, FISKE, AND EDGELL, G. H., History of Architecture. N.Y., Harper, 1918.

LAURVIK, J. N., Is It Art? Post Impressionism, Futurism, Cubism. N.Y., International Press, 1913.

LETHABY, W. R., Form in Civilization. London, Oxford University Press, 1922.

MARRIOTT, CHARLES, Modern Movements in Painting. London, Chapman, 1920.

MATHER, F. J., JR., "Newest Movements in Painting (1890–1910)." In "Art Studies, Medieval, Renaissance and Modern," *American Journal of Archaeology*, 1923, extra number.

MEIER-GRAEFE, JULIUS, Modern Art (tr. Simmonds and Chrystal). N.Y., Putnam, 1908.

MOORE, GEORGE, Modern Painting. N.Y., Scribner, 1898.

MUMFORD, LEWIS, Sticks and Stones: A Study of American Architecture and Civilization. N.Y., Boni, 1924.

NATIONAL SCULPTURE SOCIETY OF NEW YORK, Exhibition of American Sculpture, 1923.

NEWMARCH, R. H., Russian Arts. N.Y., Dutton, 1916.

PACH, WALTER, Masters of Modern Art. N.Y., Huebsch, 1924.

PARKES, KINETON, Sculpture of To-day. 2v. London, Chapman, 1921.

PHILLIPS PUBLICATIONS, No. 3, Arthur B. Davies; Essays on the Man and His Art. Cambridge, Mass., Riverside Press, 1924.

POST, C. R., History of European and American Sculpture. 2v. Cambridge, Harvard University Press, 1921.

RICHARDS, C. R., Art in Industry. N.Y., Macmillan, 1922.

SPEED, HAROLD, Science and Practice of Oil Painting. London, Chapman, 1924.

TAFT, LORADO, History of American Sculpture. N.Y., Macmillan, 1924.

—— ——, Modern Tendencies in Sculpture. Chicago, University of Chicago Press, 1921.

WRIGHT, W. H., Future of Painting. N.Y., Huebsch, 1923.

—— ——, Modern Painting: Its Tendency and Meaning. N.Y., Lane, 1915.

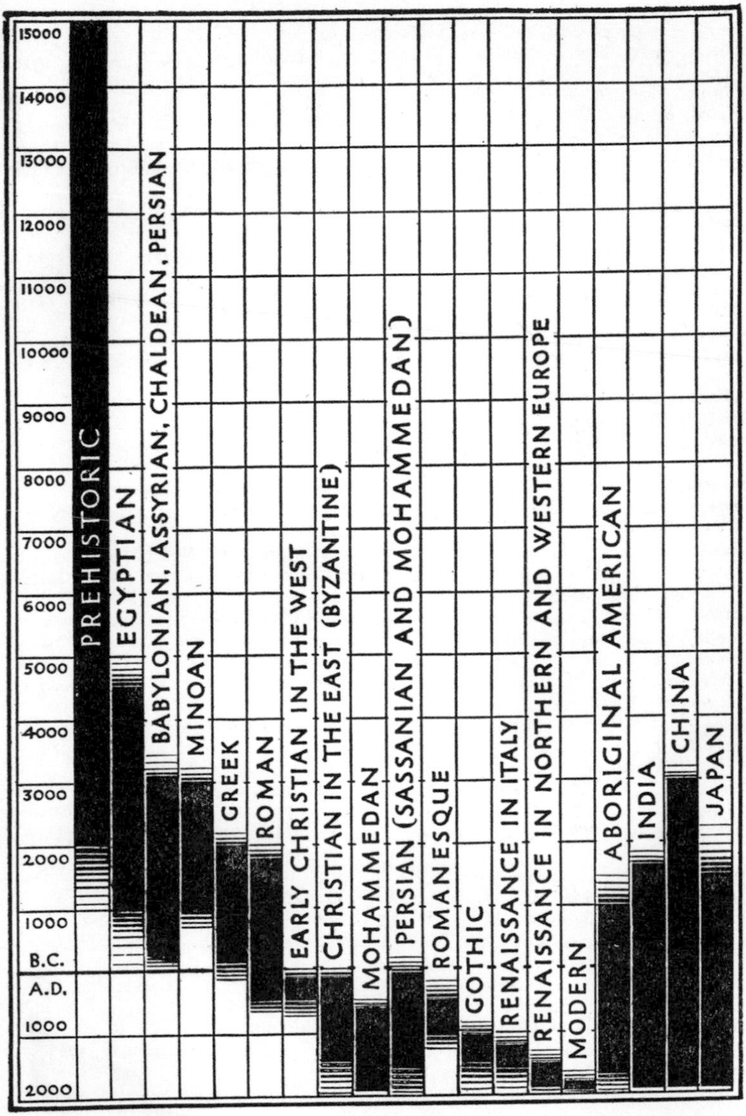

Fig. 132. A Chart to Illustrate the Comparative Chronology of the Great Periods of Art Production.

APPENDIX

SELECTED BIBLIOGRAPHY ON ESTHETICS, THEORY, AND PRACTICE

(For books dealing with special countries, periods, and artists, see the Bibliography at the end of each chapter.)

ALLEN, GRANT, Physiological Aesthetics. N.Y., Appleton, 1877.

ANSTRUTHER-THOMSON, CLEMENTINA, Art and Man: Essays and Fragments. Introduction by Vernon Lee. N.Y., Lane, 1924.

BABBITT, IRVING, The New Laokoon. Boston, Houghton, 1910.

BATCHELDER, E. A., Design in Theory and Practice. N.Y., Macmillan, 1910.

BELL, CLIVE, Art. N.Y., Stokes, 1913.

BINYON, LAURENCE, Flight of the Dragon. London, Murray, 1922.

BOSANQUET, BERNARD, History of Aesthetic. N.Y., Macmillan, 1904.

—— ——, Three Lectures on the Aesthetic. N.Y., Macmillan, 1915.

BROWN, G. B., Fine Arts. London, Murray, 1920.

CARRITT, E. F., Theory of Beauty. N.Y., Macmillan, 1914.

COOMARASWAMY, A. K., Dance of Siva. N.Y., Sunwise Turn, 1918.

CROCE, BENEDETTO, Aesthetic as a Science of Expression and General Linguistic (tr. Ainslee). N.Y., Macmillan, 1909.

—— ——, Essence of Aesthetic (tr. Ainslee). London, Heinemann, 1921.

DOW, A. W., Composition. Garden City, N.Y., Doubleday, 1913.

GORDON, KATE, Esthetics. N.Y., Holt, 1922.

HIRN, YRJÖ, Origins of Art. N.Y., Macmillan, 1900.

HOLMES, C. J., Notes on the Science of Picture-Making. London, Chatto, 1920.

JACKSON, T. G., Reason in Architecture. London, Murray, 1906.

KNIGHT, W. A., Philosophy of the Beautiful. 2 v. N.Y., Scribner, 1891-92.

LANGFELD, H. S., The Aesthetic Attitude. N.Y., Harcourt, 1920.

LAURIE, A. P., Materials of the Painter's Craft. Philadelphia, Lippincott, 1911.

LEE, VERNON (PAGET, VIOLET), The Beautiful. N.Y., Putnam, 1913.

—— ——, AND ANSTRUTHER-THOMSON, C., Beauty and Ugliness. N.Y., Lane, 1912.

LESSING, G. E., Laocoön (tr. Frothingham). Boston, Roberts, 1874.

MARSHALL, H. R., Aesthetic Principles. N.Y., Macmillan, 1901.

MORRIS, WILLIAM, Hopes and Fears for Art. Boston, Roberts, 1898.

MUNSELL, A. H., A Color Notation. Boston, Ellis and Co., 1905.

NEUHAUS, EUGEN, Appreciation of Art. Boston, Ginn, 1924.

NOYES, CARLETON, Enjoyment of Art. Boston, Houghton, 1904.

—— ——, Gate of Appreciation. Boston, Houghton, 1907.

PARKER, D. H., Principles of Aesthetics. Boston, Silver, Burdett, 1920.

PUFFER, E. D., Psychology of Beauty. Boston, Houghton, 1905.

RAYMOND, G. L., Essentials of Aesthetics. N.Y., Putnam, 1906.

RODIN, AUGUSTE, Art (tr. Fedden). Boston, Small, Maynard, 1912.

ROSS, D. W., On Drawing and Painting. Boston, Houghton, 1912.

—— ——, Theory of Pure Design. Boston, Houghton, 1907.

SANTAYANA, GEORGE, Life of Reason. N.Y., Scribner, 1905-06.

—— ——, Sense of Beauty. N.Y., Scribner, 1910.

SARGENT, WALTER, Enjoyment and Use of Color. N.Y., Scribner, 1923.
SCOTT, GEOFFREY, Architecture of Humanism. N.Y., Scribner, 1924.
TAINE, H. A., Lectures on Art (tr. Durand). 2 v. N.Y., Holt, 1875–77.
TOLSTOY, COUNT LEO, What Is Art? (tr. Johnston). Philadelphia, Altemus, 1898.
WHISTLER, J. A. M., Ten O'Clock. Boston, Houghton, 1888.
WILDE, OSCAR, Intentions. N.Y., Brentano, 1912.

SELECTED LIST OF ART PERIODICALS

American Architect. 243 W. 39th St., New York.
American Journal of Archaeology. New York University, University Heights, New York.
American Magazine of Art. 1741 New York Ave., Washington, D.C.
Apollo. 6 Robert St., Adelphi, London, W.C. 2.
Architectural Record. 115–119 W. 40th St., New York.
Architectural Review. 9 Queen Anne's Gate, Westminster, London, S.W. 1.
Architecture. Scribner, New York.
Art and Archaeology. 521 18th St., Washington, D.C.
Art in America. 28 E. 58th St., New York.
Art News. 49 W. 45th St., New York.
Arts, The. 19 E. 59th St., New York.
Arts and Decoration. 45 W. 45th St., New York.
Bulletin of the Art Institute of Chicago. Chicago.
Bulletin of the Metropolitan Museum of Art. New York.
Burlington Magazine. 17 Old Burlington St., London, W. 1.
Colour. Blackfriars Road, London, S.E. 1.
International Studio. 49 W. 45th St., New York.
Museum of Fine Arts Bulletin. Boston.

SOURCES FOR PROCURING REPRODUCTIONS

PHOTOGRAPHS

Photographs of objects in American museums can usually be obtained directly from the museum.
Alinari Bros. 8 Via Nazionale, Florence, Italy. Italy, Greece, Louvre, Dresden. Catalogue.
American Museum of Natural History. 77th St. and Central Park West, New York. Aboriginal American.
Anderson, D. Via Salaria 7a, Rome, Italy. Italy, Prado, National Gallery. Catalogue.
Les Archives Photographiques d'Art et d'Histoire. Palais-Royal 1 bis, Rue de Valois, Paris. Invaluable classified catalogue, *Catalogue Illustré des Clichés Photographiques des Archives de la Commission des Monuments Historiques*. French subjects.
Braun, A., et Cie. Dornach, Alsace, France; or 26 E. 55th St., New York. Paintings, drawings, and sculpture particularly. Exceptional quality in large framing-size photographs. Catalogue.
British Museum, London. Photographs, photogravures, and collotype reproductions of objects in the museum. Pamphlet of reproductions.
Bruckmann, Friedrich. Munich. Galleries of central and northern Europe; classical sculpture.
County Studio. 3 Priory Street, Monmouth, England. English architecture.
Curtis and Cameron. 12 Harcourt St., Boston. American painting and sculpture. Copley Prints, both small and framing size. Catalogue.

Detroit Publishing Company. Detroit, Michigan. American painting and architecture.

Druet, E. 20 Rue Royale, Paris. Modern painting and sculpture.

Essex Institute. Salem, Mass. American colonial architecture and furniture, details, gardens. Catalogue.

Frith and Company. Reigate, Surrey, England. English architecture.

Gaddis and Seif. Winter Palace Building, Luxor, Egypt. Egyptian subjects.

Giraudon, A. 9 Rue des Beaux-Arts, Paris. General subjects, especially those in French galleries.

Grantz, Else. Templehofer Ufer 32, Berlin. Objects in the Berlin museums.

Hanfstaengl, Franz. Herzog Rudolfstrasse 1, Munich. Galleries of central and northern Europe.

Johnson and Hoffmann. Chowringhee, Calcutta. Indian subjects.

Kennedy, Clarence. Smith College, Northampton, Mass. Unexcelled photographs of sculpture, artistically mounted; both for study and for framing.

Kodak (Egypt). Cairo, Egypt. Ancient Egyptian and Mohammedan subjects.

Mansell, W. F. Teddington, England. Subjects in the British Museum and National Gallery; English cathedrals. Catalogue.

Roig, Casa. Calle de San Agustin 13, Madrid. Spanish subjects.

Romaides, D. B. 3 Place de la Constitution, Athens. Greek subjects.

Smith, Sam. Minster Shop, 36 Steep Hill, Lincoln, England. English architecture; especially fine details.

Victoria and Albert Museum. South Kensington, London. Especially the minor arts of all periods and countries; Mohammedan and East Indian subjects.

COLOR PRINTS

Braun, A., et Cie. Dornach, Alsace, France; or 26 E. 55th St., New York. Framing size.

British Museum. London. Post card, 8 x 10 in., and framing sizes. Catalogue of reproductions.

Brown-Robertson Company. 415 Madison Ave., New York. 8 x 10 in. size.

Detroit Publishing Company. Detroit, Michigan. Framing size.

Institute Prints. Art Institute of Chicago. Of subjects in the Art Institute only. Pamphlet of reproductions.

Medici Society of America. 755 Boylston St., Boston. Large framing size and miniatures. Catalogue.

Metropolitan Museum. New York. Vermeer Prints. Framing size. Pamphlet of reproductions.

Seemann, E. A. Leipzig, Germany. Seemann Prints. Large collection of old and modern masters. 8 x 10 in. size. Can be obtained from Rudolph Lesch, 225 Fifth Ave., New York.

POST CARDS

Among many excellent post cards that can be procured at most museums, of particular value are the British Museum post-card sets with descriptive material, which have been listed in many of the bibliographies. Catalogue.

INEXPENSIVE HALF-TONE PRINTS

University Prints. Newton, Mass. Catalogue.

CASTS AND MISCELLANEOUS REPRODUCTIONS

British Museum. London. Electrotypes of Greek coins.

Caproni, P. P., and Bro. 1914 Washington St., Boston. Casts of architecture and sculpture. Catalogue.

Gilliéron, E., and Fils. 43 Rue Skoufa, Athens. Reproductions of the Vaphio Cups, inlaid daggers, and other Minoan metal work; of Minoan painting; and of Minoan and Greek polychrome sculpture.

Lisio, G. Via dei Fossi 17, Florence, Italy. Antique Italian brocades in sample lengths.

Metropolitan Museum. New York. Casts of Arretine bowls, Egyptian sculpture, ivory carvings. Pamphlet of reproductions.

Miller, F. W. 121 Angell St., Providence, R.I. Casts of Byzantine and medieval ivories.

Roman Bronze Works. 275 Greene St., Brooklyn, New York. Statuary and architecture.

LANTERN SLIDES

As the subject matter of available lantern slides is limited, particularly as regards the minor arts, plans, sections, details of all kinds, it is often more satisfactory and often necessary to have lantern slides made from one's own copy. Negatives should be made from originals whenever possible; otherwise only the best photographs, photogravure or collotype plates, or clear line drawings should be used as copy.

Braun, A., et Cie. Dornach, Alsace, France; or 26 E. 55th St., New York.

Chicago Slide Company. 6 E. Lake St., Chicago.

Detroit Publishing Company. Detroit, Michigan.

Hawks, Joseph. 108 Fulton St., New York.

Keystone View Company, Inc. 97 Seventh Ave., New York.

McAllister-Keller Company. 176 Fulton St., New York.

Mansell, W. F. Teddington, England.

National Geographic Society. Hubbard Memorial Hall, Washington, D.C.

Radiguet and Massiot. 15 Blvd. des Filles-du-Calvaire, Paris.

Stoedtner, Franz. Universitätstrasse 3b, Berlin.

LENDING COLLECTIONS

Art Institute of Chicago, Ryerson Library. Photographs, color prints, post cards, lantern slides. Material sent to all parts of the United States. Pamphlet of the lending collection.

Metropolitan Museum, New York. Cinema films, lantern slides, photographs, color prints, casts, textiles, maps, electrotypes of ancient coins. Some of this material is restricted to New York and vicinity. Pamphlet of the lending collections.

GLOSSARY OF TECHNICAL TERMS

(The references to Plate and Figure numbers are not exhaustive.)

ABACUS. A flat block forming the upper member of the capital of a column, on which the architrave rests. Fig. 68.

AMBULATORY. The passageway around the apse. Fig. 93.

AMPHORA. A jar with two handles for general storage purposes. Fig. 56, Pl. 30 c.

APSE. The recess, usually semicircular, at the end of a Roman basilica, or of a Christian church. Figs. 74 B, 77, 88. In the Gothic cathedral, the semicircular end of the choir. Fig. 93, Pl. 83 B.

ARABESQUE. Literally, like the Arabian, referring to the intricate interweaving of lines, and geometric and floral motifs so characteristic of Mohammedan ornament. Pls. 66–69. Used also of any kind of fanciful ornament with flowing lines, foliage, fruit, flowers, or figures variously combined or interwoven. Pls. 93 and 123.

ARCADE. A series of arches supported on piers or columns. Pls. 51 B, 74 B.

Arch. A structural member to span an opening; curved in shape, made of wedge-shaped blocks (voussoirs) in such a way that it holds stable if supported at the sides. Fig. 73, Pls. 22 A, 51 B, 80c.

Architrave. The lintel or lowest division of the entablature. Fig. 68.

Atrium. The chief room in a Roman house, near the entrance and partly open to the sky. Fig. 75. The open court in front of an early Christian basilica, probably derived from the Roman atrium. Fig. 77, Pl. 73 B.

Aureole. A frame or halo around the figure of a sacred personage. Pl. 75 c.

Baroque. Literally, odd, bizarre, irregular in form. A term applied to a style of decoration, in the late Renaissance, characterized by over-ornamentation, broken lines, fantastic and picturesque effects. Pl. 95 A.

Basilica. In Roman architecture, a public building for assemblies, especially tribunals, oblong in shape, with a central nave terminating in an apse, and carrying a clerestory, and with side aisles separated from the nave by pillars. Figs. 71 and 74. In Christian architecture, an early church somewhat resembling the Roman basilica; usually entered through an atrium. Figs. 77, 78, Pl. 57 E and F.

Bay. A vertical compartment that serves as a unit of division in a building. In a Gothic cathedral the transverse arches and adjacent piers of the arcade divide the building into bays, the design of which is an architectural unit repeated in each bay. Figs. 88, 93, Pl. 81 A.

Blind Arcade (Wall Arcade). An arcade, applied to a wall surface, with no actual openings, to serve as a decoration. Pl. 74 B, 76 B.

Bottega. A shop. The studio-shop of an Italian artist.

Buttress. A masonry support to counterbalance the thrust of an arch or vault. A pier buttress is a solid mass of masonry. A flying buttress is an arch or series of arches that carry the thrust over the aisles to the solid buttresses. Figs. 91, 95, 97, Pls. 81 B, 83 B.

Capital. The upper member of a column, usually decorated, that serves as a transition from the shaft to the lintel. Fig. 68.

Cartoon. A preliminary drawing for a painting.

Caryatid. A draped female figure that serves, like a column, to support an entablature.

Cassone. A large chest. An important piece of Italian furniture. Pl. 121 A.

Cella. The enclosed chamber, the essential feature of a classical temple, in which usually stood the cult statue. Figs. 66, 67, Pl. 50 B.

Centering. A wooden framework to hold an arch, or vault, during its construction until, when complete, it becomes self-supporting.

Ceramics (Keramics). A general term for the art of pottery.

Chamfer. To cut off a square angle; to bevel.

Champlevé Enamel. A process of enameling in which the design is cut out of a metal plate, leaving thin raised lines that correspond to the cloisons in the cloisonné process, to hold the enamel. P. 228. Pl. 89 B.

Chevet. The term applied to the apse of a cathedral, together with its ambulatories and apsidal chapels. Fig. 93.

Chiaroscuro. Literally clear-obscure. The treatment of lights and darks in a picture.

Chiton. A Greek tunic, the essential and often only garment of both men and women, the other being a mantle. See Himation. There were two kinds of tunics, the Doric and Ionic. The Doric was a rectangular piece of woolen stuff usually folded over at the top, wrapped about the body and left open at the left side, sleeveless, fastened on the shoulders with buckles, and girdled. Pl. 39 B.

The Ionic was longer, more voluminous, of soft goods such as cotton or linen, and often caught at intervals by fastenings to form sleeves. Pl. 40 c. The outstanding characteristic of Greek dress, apart from its practicability, was the possibility that it afforded for obtaining the most artistic effects by simple means, that is, by the graceful or majestic fall of stuff and by the effective contrasts of various stuffs. Pls. 39 B, 40 C, 42 B.

CHOIR. The space separated from the rest of the church by a screen and reserved for the clergy and choir. In the Gothic cathedral it occupies the central part of the church east of the crossing. Fig. 93, Pl. 88 A.

CHOIR STALLS. Seats for the clergy and choristers, usually ranged along the sides of the choir. Pl. 88 A.

CIRE PERDUE PROCESS. Literally the wax-lost process. A method of bronze casting by which the wax in which the figure is modeled is melted away and the space thus left filled with molten bronze. P. 115, note 6.

CLERESTORY. That part of a building which rises above the roofs of the other parts and whose walls contain openings for lighting. Figs. 25, 74 A, 78, 95, Pls. 11 A, 57 E, 81 A, 83 B.

CLOISON. Literally, a partition. A metal wire or narrow strip, usually gold, soldered to a metal base to form cells for holding enamel. Pls. 24 D, 62 C.

CLOISONNÉ ENAMEL. A process of enameling in which strips of metal (cloisons) are soldered to a base forming cells into which the enamel is poured and fused. P. 164. Pls. 63 C and D, 64 A, 79 C.

CODEX. A manuscript in the form of a volume with pages bound together instead of a roll. P. 159, note 3.

COFFER. A sunken, ornamental panel in a soffit, vault, or ceiling. Pl. 51 A.

COIN-TYPE. The pattern or design used to decorate a coin.

COLONNADE. A series or range of columns. Pls. 9 B, 35 B, 50 B, 143 C.

COLOR. See COOL, WARM, HUE, INTENSITY, VALUE.

COLUMN. A circular supporting member, consisting of a base (sometimes omitted), a shaft, and a capital. Fig. 68.

COMPOUND OR CLUSTERED PIER. A pier composed of a group of supporting members from each of which springs one or more ribs of the vaulting. Especially characteristic of Gothic architecture. Pls. 74 A, 80 C, 81 A.

CONSOLE. A scroll bracket, usually S-shape.

COOL COLOR. Blue and the hues that approach blue, blue-green, and blue-violet, are cool. Color Pl. III.

CORBEL. A projecting stone used as a support. Fig. 106.

CORBEL TABLE. A projecting course of masonry supported by corbels, frequently connected by arches. Pl. 73 B.

CORBELED ARCH. An arch built up of horizontal layers, each projecting over the one below until the space is covered. Fig. 47, Pl. 25 B.

CORNICE. The projecting, crowning member of the entablature. Also used for any crowning projection. Fig. 68, Pls. 36, 50–52, 90–91, 139 B, 140 A, etc.

CRATER (KRATER). A large bowl for mixing the wine and the water, the usual beverage of the Greek. Fig. 58, Pls. 30 A, 43 A.

CROCKET. A projecting foliate ornament that decorates a pinnacle, gable, or spire. Its purpose is to break a long line against the sky. Fig. 97, Pl. 84.

CROSSING. The space in a cruciform church where the nave and transepts intersect. Fig. 93, Pl. 81 A.

CROWN OF AN ARCH OR VAULT. The highest point of the external surface of the arch or vault.

CUNEIFORM. Literally wedge-shaped. A system of writing, used in Babylonia-Assyria, in which the characters are wedge-shaped. Pls. 19 A and 21 A.

CUSTODIA. An elaborate tabernacle, usually architectural in design, for the host. Fine examples are found in the Spanish cathedrals. Pl. 128 A.

CYLIX (KYLIX). A Greek drinking cup. Fig. 59, Pl. 31 A.

DAMASCENE. To inlay metal with another kind of metal or other material for decorative purposes. Figs. 54, 85, Pls. 71 D, 165 A.

DENTILS. Small toothlike projecting blocks in the bed-molding, or supporting molding, of a cornice. Pl. 52 C.

DIPTYCH. Consisting of two leaves. A Roman two-hinged writing tablet. Used also for commemorative purposes by the Christian church. Pl. 63 A.

DIVISION OF COLOR. The method of juxtaposing small strokes of pure color directly upon the canvas for the eye to mix at a distance rather than mixing the colors first upon the palette. A method practiced by Constable, Turner, and Delacroix, and perfected by the French Impressionists. The principle was used also by the twelfth century glassworkers.

DOWEL. A wooden or metallic pin to hold together two pieces of stone or other material. Fig. 69.

DRUM. The circular wall which supports a dome. Pl. 50 C. The circular stones of which a built shaft is made. Fig. 69.

ECHINUS. Literally a sea urchin. The convex member of a capital, somewhat resembling a sea urchin, that supports the abacus. Fig. 68, Pl. 36 C and D.

ENGAGED COLUMN. A columnlike member forming part of the wall and projecting more or less from it. Pl. 50 B.

ENGRAVING. The process of incising a design upon a substance with a sharp instrument. Fig. 40, Pl. 17 B. The process of incising a design upon a copper plate from which a printed impression can be made. Also the impression made from such a plate. Pls. 51 A, 136 B.

ENTABLATURE. The upper part of a building of lintel construction that rests upon the columns and supports the roof and pediment. Fig. 68, Pl. 36 C and D.

ENTASIS. A slight swelling in a column, greatest about one-third way up and gradually diminishing. In the best architecture it is almost invisible.

ETCHING. The process of engraving a design upon a copper plate, by means of an acid or mordant, from which a printed impression can be taken. Also the impression from a plate so made. P. 336. Pl. 134 C.

FAÏENCE. From Faenza, in Italy, a center for the manufacture of majolica; and restricted in meaning by some authors to tin-glazed pottery. By others the meaning has been extended to include any kind of glazed pottery except porcelain; and by others it is a general term for all kinds of glazed earthenware.

FAN VAULTING. A development of lierne vaulting, found in English Perpendicular Gothic, in which the ribs radiate from the impost in such a way that they form an inverted cone. The cloister of Gloucester Cathedral is an excellent example.

FINIAL. A knoblike ornament, usually with a foliate design, in which a pinnacle terminates. Fig. 97.

FLAMBOYANT. Meaning flamelike, applied to the late Gothic style in which the restless type of decoration is based upon wavy lines and the ogee arch. Pls. 86 A, 88 A.

FLUTE (FLUTING). Vertical channeling usually semicircular. Used principally on columns and pilasters. Pls. 36, 50 B, 118 C.

FRESCO. Painting on freshly spread moist plaster. The pigments are mixed with water and become chemically incorporated with the plaster. Also a painting so executed.

GESSO. Prepared plaster mixed with a binding material used as a ground for painting or for relief work.

GLAZE. A vitreous coating applied to the surface of pottery to make it impervious and for decorative purposes.

GOPURAM. In Hindu architecture, the high elaborate gateway of the southern Indian temples. Fig. 122.

GROIN. The edge formed by the intersection of two vaults. Fig. 73.

HAMMERBEAM ROOF. A late Gothic, open timber roof in which pairs of hammer-beams — that is, short beams projecting from the walls at the base of the main rafters and supported by curved brackets rising from corbels — support in turn large brackets that rise to the collar-beam (a short beam between the rafters in the upper narrow part). The hammer-beam acts as a lever and dispenses with the tie-beam. It often terminates in a winged angel. The space above is frequently filled with tracery. Fig. 106, Pl. 138 c.

HAUNCH. That part of an arch about one-third the distance between the springing and the crown.

HIEROGLYPHS (HIEROGLYPHICS). A system of writing, derived from picture-writing, but also phonetic, used by the ancient Egyptians. By extension, to other peoples also, as the Maya. Figs. 29, 114, Pls. 14 A, 157 D.

HIMATION. A Greek mantle worn by men and women over the tunic and draped in various ways. Pls. 40 C, 42 B, 46 A, 48 D. See CHITON.

HISTORIATED. Ornamented with figures that have a representational or narrative element, such as plants, animals, or human figures, in distinction from purely decorative elements. Historiated initial letters were a popular form of manuscript decoration in the Middle Ages. Pl. 121 B.

HUE. The hue is the name of the color. The primary hues are blue, red, and yellow, which, together with green, orange, and violet, form the chief colors of the spectrum. Between these lie the intermediates, which partake of the qualifications of both adjacent hues: red-orange, yellow-orange, yellow-green, blue-green, blue-violet, and red-violet. In determining a hue use some commercial chart. The *University Colors* (Milton Bradley Co.) is convenient.

HYPOSTYLE HALL. A hall whose roof is supported by columns. Applied to the colonnaded hall of the Egyptian pylon temple. Pl. 11.

IKON. Literally a portrait or image. Used especially in the Greek church for the small Byzantine plaques containing representations of sacred personages and greatly venerated by the Greek Christians.

IMPOST. The architectural member from which an arch springs.

INTAGLIO. A design sunk below the surface so that an impression made from it is in relief. Used especially on gems, seals, and dies for coins. Also applied to an object so decorated. Pls. 20 B and C, 34 E and F, 44 C–F.

INTENSITY OF COLOR. Strength of a color in comparison with gray. Often expressed as more or less brilliant, or rich.

INTERCOLUMNIATION. The space between the columns in a colonnade.

ISOCEPHALY. Literally, heads equal or on a level. A principle by which natural proportion is distorted so as to bring all the objects in a composition to an equal height for the purpose of design. Pls. 30–31, 42 A, 162 C.

KAKEMONO. A Chinese or Japanese painting in the form of a hanging, not framed, but usually mounted on a piece of brocade.

KEYSTONE. The uppermost voussoir in an arch. See VOUSSOIR.

LACQUER. A varnish containing lac; or a hard varnish obtained from the sap of the lacquer tree, *Rhus Vernicifera*, by making incisions in the bark. The latter is the Chinese and Japanese lacquer. Pl. 173 A.

LANTERN. A small structure that crowns a dome, turret, or roof with openings for lighting, though frequently the purpose of the lantern is design only. Pls. 90 A, 142 B.

LIERNE. A short cross rib inserted between the main ribs of a vaulting. Pl. 86 B.

LINTEL. A horizontal beam of any material that spans an opening and supports any superstructure. Pls. 3 B, 25 B, 35 B, etc.

LOGGIA. A gallery that has an open arcade or colonnade on one side.

LUNETTE. Literally, little or half moon. Having the shape of a crescent or half-moon; especially a wall space over an arched door or window. PL. 61 A.

LUSTER. A metallic film sometimes found on pottery, especially Persian pottery, and Spanish and Italian majolica, that produces wonderfully rich color, often iridescent, when it catches the light.

MAJOLICA. Specifically, a kind of Italian pottery coated with a whitish tin-enamel, brilliantly painted and often lustered. It reached its climax in the sixteenth century. Pl. 122 C.

MAKIMONO. A Chinese or Japanese painting in the form of a long scroll. Pl. 168 A.

MANDAPAM. In Hindu architecture, an assembly hall attached to a temple. Fig. 121, Pl. 159 B.

MASTABA. Literally, a bench. A bench-shaped Egyptian tomb. Figs. 22, 23.

MEDIUM. The vehicle or liquid with which pigment is mixed, such as water, egg, oil, wax. In a more general sense, the substance, material, or agency through which an artist expresses his idea, such as stone, pigment, metal, wood, enamel, words, tones, movements.

METOPE. The space between two triglyphs in a Doric frieze. Fig. 68, Pl. 36 A and C.

MINARET. A tall slender tower belonging to a mosque with one or more balconies from which the summons to prayer is chanted. Pl. 66 C.

MOLDING. An architectural term for a continuous narrow surface, either projecting or recessed, plain or ornamented, whose purpose is to break up a surface, to accent, or to decorate by means of the light and shade that it produces.

MOSAIC. A surface or decoration made of small squares of stone or glass (tesserae) set in cement. Pls. 61, 158 C.

MULLION. A slender vertical bar that separates a window into more than one light. Pls. 81 A, 84, 86 B, 92 B.

NARTHEX. A porch, generally colonnaded or arcaded, forming the vestibule of a church. Fig. 77, Pls. 57 E, 73 B.

NAVE. From navis, ship, an early symbol of the Church. The main part of a church, between the chief entrance and the chancel, and separated from the aisles, if present, by piers. Figs. 77, 93, Pl. 80 C.

OBVERSE OF A COIN OR MEDAL. The side of a coin or medal that bears the principal type or inscription. The opposite side is the reverse.

OGEE. A molding having a double or S-shape curve. An arch of this form. Pls. 86 A, 88 A.

ORDER. A system of design of the column and entablature. Fig. 68, Pl. 36 A and B.

ORIEL. A window projecting from the face of the wall. Pl. 138 C.

PATINA. An incrustation that forms on bronze through chemical action. The term is also applied to incrustation on other materials. P. 448, note 17.

PEDIMENT. The triangular gable at the end of a building formed by the sloping roof. Pl. 50 B. Also an ornamental feature of this character. Pl. 91 B.

PENDENTIVE. A term applied to the triangular curved masonry that assists in supporting a dome over a rectangular area. Fig. 80, Pl. 59 A.

PERIPTERAL. Surrounded by a colonnade. Pl. 35 B.

PERISTYLE. A continuous range of columns surrounding a building or a court. Pls. 35 B, 51 C.

PIER. A vertical masonry support for a superstructure.

PILASTER. A flat rectangular member projecting from the wall of which it forms a part. It usually carries a base and a capital and is often fluted. Pls. 90 B, 91 A, 94 B, 142 A, 151 A, etc.

PILLAR. A general inclusive term used for a supporting member of any kind. It may be a pier or a column. Also an isolated structure used for a commemorative purpose.

PORCELAIN. Strictly speaking, pottery, made on a base of kaolin, that is translucent, impervious, and resonant. P. 451, note 20. Color Pl. IV, Pl. 170 B. By extension the term is sometimes applied to pottery that is transparent, whether made of kaolin or not.

POTTERY. Objects of any kind that are made of clay and hardened by firing.

PREDELLA. Literally, a footstool. In Italian art the narrow panel, at the back of the altar, on which the altarpiece rests. P. 280, note 12.

PUTTO. A young boy. A favorite subject in Italian painting and sculpture. Pls. 114 A, 115 C, 118 C.

PYLON. The monumental entrance of an Egyptian temple. Pls. 10 A, 12 B.

QUOINS. Large, slightly projecting stones at the angle of a building, sometimes rusticated. Pl. 91 B.

RAMP. An inclined plane that takes the place of steps in the ascent of a structure. Fig. 39, Pls. 3 A, 21 C.

REINFORCED CONCRETE (FERRO-CONCRETE). Concrete strengthened by iron or steel network or bars imbedded before the concrete hardens.

REJA. A wrought-iron grille, usually gilded, to enclose a shrine or chapel. The finest are found in the Spanish churches. Pls. 127 D, 128 B.

RELIQUARY. A small receptacle for holding a sacred relic. Usually of precious material richly decorated. Pl. 89 B.

REPOUSSÉ. The process of decorating metal by beating it into relief from the back, leaving the impression on the face. The metal plate is hammered into a hollow mold of wood or some pliable material with hammer and punch and finished with the graver. Pls. 17 B, 22 C, 29 A and B, 44 A, 57 A.

RETABLE. Shortened form of *retrotabulum*, behind the altar. An architectural screen or wall-facing set up behind an altar usually containing painting, sculpture, carving, or other decorations. Especially elaborate is the Spanish retable that sometimes occupies an entire bay and rises to the vaulting. Pl. 127 C and D.

REVERSE OF A COIN OR MEDAL. The side opposite the obverse. *See* OBVERSE.

RIB. A masonry arch, usually projecting from the surface and molded. In Gothic architecture the ribs form an important part of the skeleton framework of the building. The transverse ribs spring across the nave or aisle at right angles to it, separating the structure into bays; the longitudinal ribs spring from pier to pier parallel to the nave and aisle, forming the arcade; the diagonal ribs spring from pier to pier diagonally across the bay, intersecting at the crown. Fig. 94, Pls. 74 A, 80 C, 81 A.

ROCOCO. A style of ornament particularly popular about the time of Louis XV. It consists of a profusion of rock-work, wheels, scrolls, and the like. P. 362, note 1.

ROOF-CREST. A pierced wall rising above the roof. Found in Mayan architecture. Fig. 109.

ROSE *or* WHEEL WINDOW. The round window with tracery frequently found on the façade and transepts of Romanesque and Gothic churches. In early examples the tracery is likely to be plate; in the middle and later periods, bar. Pls. 80 B, 84. *See* TRACERY.

RUSTICATED STONE. Stone masonry with beveled joints and roughened surface. Pls. 90 c, 91 b, 139 b.

SHAFT. The part of a column between the capital and base. Fig. 68.

SHIKARA. In Hindu architecture, the high tower that rises over the shrine of the temples of Vishnu. Fig. 121, Pl. 159 b.

SOFFIT. The underside of a subordinate architectural member, such as an arch, cornice, or stairway.

SPANDREL. The triangular space between the curve of an arch and the rectangle formed by enclosing moldings. It is usually decorated. Pl. 59 b.

SPLAYED OPENINGS. A splay (a shortened form of "display") is a large chamfer. In splayed openings the wall is cut away diagonally so that the outer opening is wider than the inner. Pls. 76 b and c, 84.

STELE. A stone slab or pillar used commemoratively, as a gravestone, or to mark a site. Pls. 42 c, 167 c.

STILTED ARCH OR DOME. An arch or dome having its springing higher than the level of the impost. Pl. 66 c.

STONE MOSAIC. A kind of decoration made with small pieces of cut stone embedded in cement. Used most effectively by the Maya. Fig. 111, Pl. 156 b and c.

STRINGCOURSE. A horizontal molding to indicate a division in the architectural design. Pls. 36, 73 b, 80 b.

STUCCO. Fine plaster or cement used as a coating for walls or for decorations. Pls. 53 a, 157 a.

STUPA. In the Buddhist architecture of India, a domelike structure which marks a sacred site. Fig. 119.

STYLOBATE. The upper member of the base of a building that serves as a continuous base of the columns. Fig. 68, Pl. 36 a.

SUPERPOSED ORDER. The placing of one order of architecture above another in an arcaded or colonnaded building; usually Doric on the first story, Ionic on the second, and Corinthian on the third. Found in the Greek stoas, used widely by the Romans, and thence, by the Renaissance builders. Pls. 51 b, 91 c, 94 c.

TEMPERA. A technical method of painting upon an especially prepared panel with pigment mixed with egg. P. 252. Pls. 97 a, 98.

TESSERAE. Small squares of glass or stone used in making mosaics.

THRUST. The outward force exerted by an arch or vault that must be counter-balanced by abutments. Most skillfully worked out in the Gothic cathedrals.

TRACERY. Stone ornament that decorates a window and holds the glass; particularly characteristic of Gothic. In plate tracery, the stone is pierced with geometric designs. In bar tracery the design is built up of stone bars or moldings fitted together on the principle of the arch. Bar tracery has greater possibilities for design than plate, and soon replaced the latter. Most of the great rose, lancet, and perpendicular windows are bar tracery. The western rose of Chartres (Pl. 80 b) is plate; those at Amiens and Reims (Pl. 84), bar. Tracery is also used in woodwork. Fig. 106, Pls. 86 b, 88 a, 92 b. In India entire windows were filled with elaborate marble tracery. Pl. 160 c.

TRANSEPT. The arm of a cruciform church at right angles with the nave. Fig. 93.

TRIFORIUM. In a Gothic cathedral, the space between the vault of the aisle and the sloping roof over it; it is represented in the nave wall by the story that lies between the ground-story arcade and the clerestory. Pl. 81 a, Fig. 95.

TRIGLYPH. The projecting grooved member of the Doric frieze separating the metopes. Fig. 68, Pl. 36 a and c.

TYMPANUM. The space over a doorway, enclosed by the lintel and the arch. Pl. 75 c.

URÆUS. The serpent used as a symbol of royalty in Egyptian art. Color Pl. I, Fig. 30, Pl. 16 c.

VALUE OF A COLOR. The amount of light and dark in a color. The greater the amount of light, the higher its value; the greater amount of dark, the lower its value.

VAULT. A stone, brick, or concrete roof constructed on the arch principle. A barrel vault is semicylindrical in shape; a groin vault consists of two barrel vaults intersecting at right angles. Fig. 73, Pl. 52 B. A ribbed vault is one in which a framework of ribs supports light masonry. Pls. 80 c, 81 A, 86 B. See RIB. A dome is a hemispherical vault. See PENDENTIVE.

VOLUTE. A spiral scroll, especially characteristic of the Ionic Greek capital. Pl. 36 B and D.

VOUSSOIR. A wedge-shaped block used in the construction of a true arch. The central voussoir, that sets the arch, is called the keystone. See ARCH.

WAINSCOT. A wooden facing for an interior wall, usually paneled. Pl. 139 A.

WARM COLOR. Red and the hues that approach red, orange, yellow, and possibly yellow-green, are warm. Color Pl. III.

WOODCUT. A design engraved upon a block of wood in such a way that all the wood is cut away to a slight depth except the lines forming the design. Also the printed impression made from the woodblock. Figs. 99, 102, 104, Pl. 137 c.

ZIGGURAT. In Babylonia-Assyria, a staged tower with ramps for ascent. Fig. 39.

INDEX

491

I. QUEEN NOFRETETE

Limestone, Painted, with Eyes of Rock Crystal. Life Size.
Egyptian, 1375–1358 B.C. Staatliche Museum, Berlin.